PICKED-UP PIECES

John Updike

PICKED-UP PIECES

New York · Alfred · A · Knopf

1976

THIS IS A BORZOI BOOK

PUBLISHED BY ALFRED A. KNOPF, INC.

Library of Congress Cataloging in Publication Data
Updike, John.   Picked-up pieces.
Includes index.   I.   Title.
PS3571.P4P48   813'.5'4   75–8252
ISBN 0–394–49849–6

Manufactured in the United States of America

Published November 26, 1975
Second Printing, January 1976

by John Updike

POETRY

THE CARPENTERED HEN (*1958*)

TELEPHONE POLES (*1963*)

MIDPOINT (*1969*)

NOVELS

THE POORHOUSE FAIR (*1959*)

RABBIT, RUN (*1960*)

THE CENTAUR (*1963*)

OF THE FARM (*1965*)

COUPLES (*1968*)

RABBIT REDUX (*1971*)

A MONTH OF SUNDAYS (*1975*)

SHORT STORIES

THE SAME DOOR (*1959*)

PIGEON FEATHERS (*1962*)

OLINGER STORIES: *A Selection* (*1964*)

THE MUSIC SCHOOL (*1966*)

BECH: A BOOK (*1970*)

MUSEUMS AND WOMEN (*1972*)

ESSAYS

ASSORTED PROSE (*1965*)

PICKED-UP PIECES (*1975*)

PLAY

BUCHANAN DYING (*1974*)

FOR CHILDREN

THE MAGIC FLUTE (*1962*)

THE RING (*1964*)

A CHILD'S CALENDAR (*1965*)

BOTTOM'S DREAM (*1969*)

Acknowledgments

Grateful acknowledgment is made to the following magazines and publishers, who first printed the pieces specified, sometimes under other titles:

THE NEW YORKER: "Amor Vincit Omnia Ad Nauseam," "The First Lunar Invitational," "Letter from Anguilla," "Voznesensky Met," and fifty of the book reviews, including seven published as "Briefly Noted."

THE NEW YORK TIMES: "On Meeting Writers," "Bech Meets Me," "Tips on a Trip," "His Own Horn," and "Coffee-Table Books for High Coffee Tables."

THE NEW REPUBLIC: "The Mastery of Miss Warner" and the poem in "P. S."

THE NEW STATESMAN: "Papa's Sad Testament" and "Notes to a Poem."

THE LISTENER: "Notes of a Temporary Resident."

THE SUNDAY TIMES (London): "And Yet Again Wonderful."

TRANSATLANTIC REVIEW: "Cemeteries."

THE ATLANTIC MONTHLY: "Black Suicide" and "Talk of a Sad Town."

HORIZON: "Remembrance of Things Past Remembered."

MOTIVE: "Auden Fecit."

LIFE: "Mnemosyne Chastened" and "A Raw Something."

PLAYBOY: Comment on creativity.

MADEMOISELLE: Comment on female sexuality.

BOOKS AND BOOKMEN: "The Future of the Novel."

THE AMERICAN PEN (Vol. 2, No. 3): "Humor in Fiction."

SOUTHERN REVIEW (South Australia): "Why Write?"

GAMBIT, INC.: Introduction to *Pens and Needles*, drawings by David Levine.

HOUGHTON MIFFLIN CO.: Introduction to *The Harvard Lampoon Centennial Celebration 1876–1973.*

SHEED AND WARD, INC.: Introduction to *Soundings in Satanism.*

DELACORTE PRESS AND PENGUIN BOOKS, LTD., LONDON: Three translations of Borges poems from *Jorge Luis Borges: Selected Poems 1924–1967,* edited by Norman Thomas di Giovanni, Copyright © 1972 by Delacorte Press.

SUNTORY LTD. (Tokyo, Japan): "Farewell to the Middle Class" reprinted from *Suntory Fiction and Essays.*

TRIQUARTERLY BOOKS (Northwestern University Press): "A Tribute" from *Nabokov,* edited by Alfred Appel, Jr., and Charles Newman (1970).

UNITED STATES INFORMATION SERVICE: Excerpts from "Reality and the Novel in Africa and America," a symposium (Lagos, 1972).

TO ROGERS WHITAKER

Contents

FOREWORD

SINCE THE PUBLICATION, ten years ago, of *Assorted Prose*, most of my pieces of non-fictional prose have been book reviews. And these were written mostly for *The New Yorker*. It has not been easy, I dare say, for the editors of "the kindest magazine in the world" (as Nabokov describes its pseudonym *The Beau and the Butterfly*) to locate books that might fall within my nebulous competence. When, *circa* 1960, I gratuitously volunteered to be a critic, humorous verse and theology were the only areas where a data-density map of my brain would have shown even a faint darkening. In this latter area my information appeared out-of-the-ordinary primarily because the ordinary, in those bad old materialist days, before the Beatles spiritualized us all, was nil. Out of deference to my curious hobby, Christianity, I was permitted to treat, at suitably anxious length, of Karl Barth (in the earlier collection) and (in this) of Kierkegaard. For a time, indeed, there was some danger of my becoming a kind of *ad hominem* Religious Department; those slim, worthy-looking volumes by Tillich and Heidegger that keep cluttering a book editor's desk—what better disposal than to send them off to Updike for a "note"? The section "Religious Notes" remembers this epoch, a time of faith on all sides.

An aspiring American writer myself, I clearly could not be trusted to clip the tender new shoots of my competitors. The esoteric fiction of Europe, however, was an ocean removed from envy's blight, and my practitioner's technical side was glad to investigate imported gadgetry. Borges, Queneau, Pinget, van Ostaijen, Cortázar—I am happy thus to have made their acquaintance, and made note of their lessons. Sure enough, when an American (Kosinski, Piercy) or an Englishman (Ayrton, Collier) got mixed into my periodic dose of the avant garde, a brusquer assurance and a chummy impatience did creep into my tone, which when dealing with translated works assumed the even omnivorous rumble of a grist mill.

More lately, the Fates that spin *The New Yorker*'s "Books" Department have taken to testing my iron digestion with books about Brazilian Indians and body cells. Evidently I can read anything in English and muster up an opinion about it. I am not sure, however, the stunt is good for me. Among these reviews I am proudest of—though what I feel for my utmost favorites is still a step-emotion to the parent's pride taken in the feeblest tyke of a story or poem—those most voluntary: essays of celebration and promulgation moved by a prior enthusiasm (Kierkegaard, Borges, Proust, Fuchs) or assignments that provoked me to read more, or think deeper, than was strictly called for (the pieces on Camus, Hamsun, Hemingway, Joyce, and Africans seem such). Apologies, if any, would be tendered to those authors, like Grass and Gombrowicz, who came to me coated with a muffling murk of missed nuances—dusty plaster replicas of statues whose pure marble glowed in an inaccessible museum. But even when the visibility was poorest I tried to give each book the benefit of a code of reviewing drawn up inwardly when I embarked on this craft, or ("a man should have a trade," my father used to insist) trade.

My rules, shaped intaglio-fashion by youthful traumas at the receiving end of critical opinion, were and are:

1. Try to understand what the author wished to do, and do not blame him for not achieving what he did not attempt.

2. Give enough direct quotation—at least one extended passage—of the book's prose so the review's reader can form his own impression, can get his own taste.

3. Confirm your description of the book with quotation from the book, if only phrase-long, rather than proceeding by fuzzy *précis*.

4. Go easy on plot summary, and do not give away the ending. (How astounded and indignant was I, when innocent, to find reviewers blabbing, and with the sublime inaccuracy of drunken lords reporting on a peasants' revolt, all the turns of my suspenseful and surpriseful narrative! Most ironically, the only readers who approach a book as the author intends, unpolluted by pre-knowledge of the plot, are the detested reviewers themselves. And then, years later, the blessed fool who picks the volume at random from a library shelf.)

5. If the book is judged deficient, cite a successful example along the same lines, from the author's *oeuvre* or elsewhere. Try to understand the failure. Sure it's his and not yours?

To these concrete five might be added a vaguer sixth, having to do with maintaining a chemical purity in the reaction between product and appraiser. Do not accept for review a book you are predisposed to dislike, or committed by friendship to like. Do not imagine yourself a caretaker of any tradition, an enforcer of any party standards, a warrior in any ideological battle, a corrections officer of any kind. Never, never (John Aldridge, Norman Podhoretz) try to put the author "in his place," making of him a pawn in a contest with other reviewers. Review the book, not the reputation. Submit to whatever spell, weak or strong, is being cast. Better to praise and share than blame and ban. The communion between reviewer and his public is based upon the presumption of certain possible joys of reading, and all our discriminations should curve toward that end.

Easier said than done, of course. Here and there filial affection for an older writer has pulled my punch. Fear of reprisal may have forced a grin or two. In a few reprehensible cases I may have dreamed of sleeping with the authoress. In other cases irritations of the moment added their personal pepper. A reviewer, unlike an ideal reader, is committed to finish the book; I read slower than I write, and sheer exasperation over time expended may have shortened my patience with the Cozzens novel and, even, *Ada*. The little Dostoevsky review was done for *Life* during a mysterious attack of tendonitis; I could not sleep, and sat up all one night, watching dawn infiltrate Menemsha Bight, my throbbing left

ove my head while my right hand confidently advised
᎑ keep trying. "The Crunch of Happiness" was com-
after my leg had been broken, making me perhaps
᎑ve to the hugs and crunches in Nabokov's *Glory.*
᎑ne of the oldest pieces here, on Sylvia Townsend Warner (who
deserves, ten years later, an extended tribute to her vigorously continuing production), was hilariously fractured and mis-assembled
when printed in *The New Republic;* this collection holds for me
no greater satisfaction than that of getting its hexed text at last
correct.

The fabled care *The New Yorker* takes with the texts it prints
presides like Providence over most of these reviews. Many the
untruth quietly curbed, the misspelling invisibly mended. My habit
of ample quotation compels the "checkers" virtually to read the
book through, a scrupulousness that amounts to sanctity. My editor for the "Books" pieces has been Mr. Rogers Whitaker (telephone operators, take note of the *s*). Gruff wise bear of a man, he
has given most of these contents a lick and a spank, and in gratitude for his collaboration I dedicate this book to him. May he edit
ad infinitum.

The "Views" section (which ends with a review) salvages some
of the debris of a writer's life. One is invited to do this and that,
and one doesn't always refuse. My year in London (1968–1969)
was especially prolific of accepted invitations. Also while there I
composed my decade's one precious parody, and a necrotic meditation ("Cemeteries") that didn't quite make it into fiction. My
four speeches, delivered on as many continents, serve as index of
the itinerary that even a reluctantly public man can find himself
undergoing. I have restrained myself from including a talk in
Venezuela comparing *Doña Barbara* with movie Westerns, and
a weighty speech on the American writer's cultural situation that
I kept giving as I moved across central Africa, shedding large
chunks of it as I went. If there's one thing the Third World does
not want to hear about, it's parallelisms with the United States.
Henry Bech should write a story.

And I, no doubt, should write, in the decades left to me, in the
highest forms I can reach, matter of my own devising. There was

an educational value, for a man with lazy eyes, in accepting some review assignments; but my laziness is now such that I can scarcely read a book without a pencil in my hand, and without the expectation of being paid for a verdict. Innocence deserts one's tryst with a printed page when a review has been promised and begins writing itself in the margin. Meanwhile, the classics languish, and even blank pages begin to look suspect. Let us hope, for the sakes of artistic purity and paper conservation, that ten years from now the pieces to be picked up will make a smaller heap.

There could have been a third section, "Interviews." They are a form to be loathed, a half-form like maggots, but in some cases (notably my *Paris Review* travail with Charles Samuels) have benefitted from written revisions; and one is forced to say things sometimes true and not always said elsewhere. The only topic upon which my offhand opinions carry authority is, of course, my own works; so I have excerpted a few self-centered quotations from the six or so interviews I have saved, and closeted them in an appendix, where none but the morbidly curious, or academically compelled, need peek.

And, speaking of half-forms: hard-pressed magazine editors perpetually bombard a writer's tenuous vicinity with questions, questionnaires, and quizzes. Most of these meteors from outer space burn up in the ionosphere of unanswered mail, but a few get through, coinciding with a moment of euphoria or efficiency in the inscrutable authorial rhythms, and receive an answer. Here are two Answers to Hard Questions that turned up in my files, which are hereby, as of October 25, 1974, exhausted.

MADEMOISELLE: *What is female sexuality?*

You ask me about this most wordless of subjects. I know nothing; but the "nothing" stirs, breathes, takes on a vague and vaguely inviting form. To begin, I would understand "sexuality" to be the subject and "male" and "female" to be adjectives, not polar opposites. In infancy both sexes enjoy an identical introduction to erotic sensation, so that fondling, sucking, teasing, cradling, crooning, tickling, rocking, stroking, and murmuring form a common base of amorous vocabulary. Somewhere before adolescence the male, that little hunter, tips his sexual curiosity with an optical point, whereas the female remains a blind snuggler, impervious to photopornography, dependent to some extent upon brute *duration* of contact. When the sexual functions ripen, the male assignment becomes penetration and distribution, the female duty acceptance and retention. Yet our insatiable minds, with their unique gift for empathy, seek to broaden sexual experience into the domain of the opposite (*en face* rather than inimical) number; the rapacious female and passive male are delightful variations. Harmlessly, insofar as any human transaction is harmless, they seek to appropriate sensations biology has only diffidently made possible for them. Again, our aspiring spirits drive erotic sensitivity outward from the monstrous and gummy organs of sex, which look like wounds, to the ethereal fringes of the body; the hands, the skull, the soles of the feet, the backs of the knees are where perhaps you, *mademoiselle*, begin to quicken. There is a poetry in sexual convolution that would bring the scattered centers of our being—the brain, the heart, the genitals—into a unity of juxtaposition. The sexual unpredictability of females must be, in part, an attempt to subordinate to the angelic prerogatives of choice and will the sexual function still bewilderingly mired in the ancient ooze of the involuntary. Perversion, like continence, would reclaim from our animal ore the gold of the purely human. In females, if anatomy is an adequate metaphor, sexuality is more central and more buried than in males. Love, then, becomes an exploration toward a muffled center, a quest whose terrain is the woman and the grail her deep self. The man who advances this exploration bestows a totality meagerly paid for with anything less than enslavement. The man who does not fails disastrously. Hence the extremes of fastidiousness and wantonness that perennially astound men, and the strange sharp note of bitter disappointment we hear whenever women offer to throw light into these warm shadows.

PLAYBOY: *What is creativity?*

For one thing, creativity is merely a plus name for regular activity; the ditchdigger, dentist, and artist go about their tasks in much the same way, and any activity becomes creative when the doer cares about doing it right, or better. Out of my own slim experience, I would venture the opinion that the artistic impulse is a mix, in varying proportions, of childhood habits of fantasizing brought on by not necessarily unhappy periods of solitude; a certain hard wish to perpetuate and propagate the self; a craftsmanly affection for the materials and process; a perhaps superstitious receptivity to moods of wonder; and a not-often-enough-mentioned ability, within the microcosm of the art, to organize, predict, and persevere.

PICKED-UP PIECES

Views

THE LITERARY LIFE

On Meeting Writers

THE LUST to meet authors ranks low, I think, on the roll of holy appetites; but it is an authentic pang. The county where I and my literary ambitions were conceived held only one writer, whose pen name, Mildred Jordan, masked her true identity as an unmeetably rich industrialist's wife. At Harvard I stood with crowds of other students to hear, and to glimpse in the mysterious flesh, anthology presences like Eliot, Sandburg, Frost, and Wilder. After his lecture in Sanders Theater, Eliot, a gem of composure within a crater of applause, inserted his feet into his rubbers, first the right, then the left, as we poured down upon him a grateful tumult that had less to do with his rather sleepy-making discourse on poetic drama than with the fabulous descent of his vast name into an actual, visible, and mortal body. Whereas Sandburg, playing ballads in New Lecture Hall, rambled on into our dinner hour; as the audience noisily diminished he told us, his white bangs glowing in the gloom, that it was all right, that often in his life he had sat in hotel rooms with only his guitar for company.

The first author I met socially was Joyce Cary. It was in England's Oxford. Someone kindly had us to tea, and into the stiff little party bounced a well-knit sandy man with light quick eyes and an intensely handsome chin; unhesitatingly he assumed his right to dominate the conversation. He was full of a tender excitement, the excitement of those certain they are loved, and anxious to share, before it spills over and is wasted, the bubbling treasure of themselves. He described to us his sitting in Paris writing at an outdoor table while around him in the Tuileries little boys were going pee-

pee; he read us, with an excessive Irish accent, the opening and then the closing words of *Finnegans Wake*, to show that they interlocked.

Now I had never read Cary, but had myself recently tasted the emboldening black blood of print. When he stated that Joyce's influence was enormous, I churlishly grunted disagreement; he cited e. e. cummings, and I absurdly shook my head No. His eyebrows lifted, and for a second I lived within the curiosity of those very quick eyes. They flicked away, and somewhat later I began to read him, and found him to be—above all in his two African novels—a splendid writer, peculiarly alive to nuances of power and competition such as my jealous rudeness that afternoon. For years the incident embarrassed me in memory, and in 1957 Cary heroically suffered his prolonged death, and I lost forever my chance to apologize.

Quite different was my preparation for meeting James Thurber, in London later that year. As a boy I had hoarded pennies to buy Thurber's books, and owned them all; he was for me the brightest star in that galaxy of New York wits I yearned to emulate, however dimly. A college acquaintance who knew of my adoration arranged the meeting: into her flat Thurber was led by his wife Helen. He was taller than I had expected, not Walter Mitty but a big-boned blind giant, and his upstanding hair was snowier than photographs had led me to expect, and there could have been no anticipating the alarming way his eyes caromed around under the refracting magnification of his glasses.

He sat, talking and drinking tea until I wondered why his bladder didn't burst. We listened, I raptly at first and finally becoming, to my own amazement, bored. Though Thurber cocked his head alertly at my poor fawning attempts to make conversation, these attempts did not appreciably distract him from the anecdotes of Columbus, Ohio, he had told a thousand times before, and that I had read ten years before, in their definitive, printed versions. Pages of *The Thurber Album* and *My Life and Hard Times* issued from his lips virtually intact.

His performance, though remarkable, was, alas, a performance; I had been privileged to join an auditory audience slightly less anonymous than readership, and there was no question of living for even a second in his curiosity. Fifteen years later, with another adored writer, Jorge Luis Borges, I was to reëxperience the disappointing revelation that blindness and fame and years do island a man, do isolate him within a monologue that, if he is a literary man, he had delivered to you already, in finer and grander form— "grander" because literary obsessions appear to have been selected from an infinite field, whereas personal obsessions seem to betray a mere narrowness. Sad to say, my love of Thurber's works was slightly stunted ever after his generous teatime monologue.

All the writers I have met—and they have not been many; I must be one of the few Americans with a bachelor-of-arts degree who has never met either Robert Lowell or Norman Mailer *— carry around with them a field force that compels objects in the vicinity to conform to their literary style. Standing next to E. B. White, one is imbued with something of the man's fierce modesty, and one's sentences haltingly seek to approximate the wonderful way his own never say more than he means. Whereas Thurber's humor bore a trace of the tyrannical, a wish to impose confusion from above, White's seems to stem from an extreme of attentiveness that would grant to things the graceful completion they lack in reality. Once I barged through a door in *The New Yorker* offices, and powerfully struck an obstacle on the other side; White had been hurrying down the hall, and stood there dazed. Reading in my face my horror, my fear that I had injured this sacred and fragile person, this living embodiment of the magazine's legend, he obligingly fell down as if dead.

A room containing Philip Roth, I have noticed, begins hilariously to whirl and pulse with a mix of rebelliousness and constriction that I take to be Oedipal. And I have seen John Cheever, for ten days we shared in Russia, turn the dour world of Soviet literary officials

---

* True in 1968 but no longer. Lowell, who seemed to be leaning above me like a raked mast, later described me to a mutual friend as "elusive and shy." I think I was afraid he would fall on me from his height of eminence. Mailer, as much shorter than I had expected as Lowell was taller, danced about me on a darkened street corner (44th and Second Avenue, if memory serves), taunting me with my supposed handsomeness, with being the handsomest guy he had ever seen. I took it to be Maileresque hyperbole, absurd yet nevertheless with something profound in it—perhaps my secret wish to *be* handsome, which only he, and that by dim streetlight, at a drunken hour, has ever perceived.

into a bright scuttle of somehow suburban characters, invented with marvellous speed and arranged in sudden tableaux expressive, amid wistful neo-Czarist trappings, of the lyric desperation associated with affluence. As if transported to the moon, people in Cheever's neighborhood lose half their bodily weight. My most traumatic experience of gravitational attraction came with John O'Hara. I had consented to read at a White House entertainment for the National Honor Students; crossing the lobby of the Hay-Adams, I spied brooding on a chair a broad-shouldered presence strongly reminiscent of the back of a book jacket. Deferentially I moved closer. "Mr. O'Hara?" said I.

O'Hara held out his hand. "Pull," he said. I hesitated. "My back," O'Hara explained. I pulled. He grunted in pain and did not budge. "Again," said O'Hara.

This time he made it, wincing, to his feet. Our laconic but characteristic dialogue continued. He, too, was attending the White House function. I offered him a ride in the limousine that had been sent for me, since I was one of the entertainers. I explained to the suspicious driver that this gentleman was John O'Hara, a very great writer and a guest of the President. The driver with maximum grudgingness made space for him in the front seat, while my wife and I settled regally in the back.

Within the few seconds of this encounter I had been plunged into a cruel complex of stoic pain and social irony—a Negro chauffeur and a stammering light-verse writer had transformed a millionaire author into a front-seat hitchhiker. Mortified by the situation, feeling all its edges grating on O'Hara's acute nerves, I fled conversationally to the state of Pennsylvania, which we had in common. O'Hara moved us to a plane both higher and more concrete—the number of Updikes in Princeton, New Jersey. At the White House he showed a distinct preference for the company of Marianne Moore, bending his big ear to her tiny precise voice like a schoolboy listening to a transistor radio he has smuggled into class.

These not entirely fanciful reminiscences (which have omitted how I met Bernard Malamud in a museum lavatory, or how James Dickey entertained me one hungover 6 a.m. with a concert of country guitar music that fetched tears to my hillbilly eyes) mean to suggest that writers, like everyone else, see a world their personalities to some extent create. Denis de Rougemont claims that Chateaubriand could never have written Stendhal's essays on seduction because seduction was simply no problem for Chateaubriand. The cosmos of delay and obfuscation rendered in *The Castle* surely in part reflects the special environment Kafka's neurotic mannerisms spun around him. And we all recall how Hemingway scouted the world for those marginal places where violence might feed his style.

Also, as one who in a small way is himself now and then "met," I suggest that forces within the writer-reader personal encounter foment unreality. The reader comes equipped with a vivid, fresh, outside impression of works the writer remembers wearily from the inside, as a blur of intention, a stretch of doubting drudgery, a tangle of memories and fabrications, a batch of nonsensical reviews, and a disappointed sigh from the publisher. The reader knows the writer better than he knows himself; but the writer's physical presence is light from a star that has moved on.

Evasive temperaments are drawn to the practice of fiction. Their work is done far behind the heat-shield of face and voice that advances against a room of strangers. The performance can be a shambling and ingratiating one as much as a cocksure and intimidating one, but performance it is: a pity, for these anonymous devoted readers who press affectionately toward a blind man are his lovers, who have accepted into themselves his most intimate and earnest thrusts. I would like to meet, I suppose, Vladimir Nabokov and Henry Green, but recognize the urge as superstitious, a seeking of a physical ritual to formalize the fact that we already are (I write as a reader) so well met.

Voznesensky Met

(*A* New Yorker *Notes and Comment: August 1967*)

SEVERAL TIMES, a few years ago, we dined with Andrei Voznesensky in the dining hall of the Writers' Union in Moscow. The Union's building, on Vorovsky Street, was Tolstoy's Moscow mansion, and the model for the home of the Rostovs in *War and Peace*. One drives in through the gates through which the Rostovs and a wagonload of possessions fled Napoleon's approaching armies; straight ahead, past a bust of Tolstoy, are the yellow doors to the long, parqueted ballroom. The dining hall—to the right, in a wing of the building—is still pleasantly redolent of Czarist days. Walnut panelling reaches to the ceiling; a carved staircase leads up to a balcony. Here, in the same smoky atmosphere of clashing silver and prolonged table talk that one finds in any New York club for the privileged, come and go the local members of the immense Soviet literary Establishment. We met a few of them: the perky young *Yunost* editor, full of chaffing and "routines"; the cheerful translatoress, spouting the latest names in beatnik poetry; the tough yet comradely gray-haired lady who sat on the editorial board that had declined to publish *Doctor Zhivago*; the war novelist who after three vodkas began to look through us toward something desolating he had once seen; the round-faced art critic whose subtlest thoughts had to be couched, protectively, in French; the Union official, all a-twinkle—gold teeth, gold spectacles—a volley in his laugh and an executioner's chop in his hands. In this company, Voznesensky was a pet, a shy, shrugging pet, with a cold sore on his lower lip, politely sipping water at each toast offered in vodka, but nevertheless, amid so many literary foremen and mechanics, the real thing, a poet—a poet whose voice had already broken through to Russian youth and was on the verge of being heard in the West. Now his breakthrough has been made, and has led him to a perhaps disastrous defiance of the Writers' Union, which tried, as far as its fundamentally anti-artistic function permitted, to cherish him.

We worry that our side might do him in. Introducing him at a poetry reading in this country last May, Robert Lowell confided to the audience that he thought both he and Voznesensky had "really terrible governments." Such a remark could not hurt Lowell but would certainly arrest the attention of the Russian Embassy watchdog who invariably attends displays of Russo-American cultural exchange. Now the *Times* has zealously and, we suppose, rightly, published the outraged letter from Voznesensky denouncing the Writers' Union's clumsy and mendacious cancellation of his scheduled reading at Lincoln Center in June—a letter that *Pravda* declined to print. Perhaps the time is ripe for open opposition to the "atmosphere of blackmail, confusion, and provocation"—as Voznesensky put it—in which the heirs of Tolstoy and Chekhov and Pushkin do their work. The Writers' Union's control over publication is absolute. Yet a poet of Voznesensky's fame and genius is not defenseless; the Soviet system, unlike ours, admits that it needs artists, as blazoners of the ideals of the state. Hence, along with the censorship, there are the summer dachas and assured incomes and pleasant dining halls and erratic indulgences. Stalin sheltered the maverick Mayakovsky; Khrushchev let Yevtushenko keep writing. The Sinyavsky-Daniel trial was carried to its foregone conclusion, but a petition of dissent was signed by Russia's best writers. Thaw cannot be imported from the West. If Voznesensky carries his point, it will not be thanks to indignant editorials in this country or petitions signed by writers smug in their pre-bought freedom. If he cannot carry his point, let him at least survive. His mere survival, like Pasternak's, would be a victory.

Studying his photograph in the *Times* (our own delicate experts in propaganda have selected one that looks especially worried), we remember him across the table trying, in his then fragmentary English, to communicate. His pale face appeared faintly bloated, like a nun's squeezed in her wimple. His manner was both boyish and elderly, his thinning hair studiously licked down, his nose an innocent ski jump. Only a certain steadiness in his heavy blue eyes betrayed awareness that to be Pasternak's spiritual son, the hope of poetry in a nation hungry for poetry, was a mighty thing. One does not advance in post-Stalin Russia without some steel. Voznesensky, the gentlest of men until he stands to recite, becomes then a prophet, clangorous and stern; the reunion of Russian and modern poetry demands an ambitious campaign. To speak and write honestly in the Soviet Union is still a more difficult enterprise than an American can imagine.

Bech Meets Me

(The New York Times Book Review *Persuades Henry Bech,*
Literary Man for All Thin Seasons,
to Conduct an Interview: November 1971)

UPDIKE'S OFFICE is concealed in a kind of false-bottomed drawer
in the heart of downtown Ipswich (Mass.), but the drowsy locals,
for a mere 30 pieces of silver, can be conned into betraying its
location. A stuck-looking door is pulled open; an endless flight of
stairs, lit by a team of dusty fireflies, is climbed. Within the sanctum, squalor reigns unchallenged. A lugubrious army-green metal
desk rests in the center of a threadbare Oriental rug reticulate
with mouse-paths; the walls are camouflaged in the kind of cardboard walnut panelling used in newly graduated lawyers' offices
or in those Los Angeles motels favored by the hand-held camera-
men and quick-tongued *directeurs* of blue movies. On these sad
walls hang pictures, mostly souvenirs of his childhood, artistic or
otherwise. On the bookshelves, evidently stained by a leopard in
the process of shedding his spots, rest repellent books—garish
schoolboy anthologies secreting some decaying Updikean morsel,
seven feet of James Buchanan's bound works adumbrating the next
opus, some daffodil-yellow building-trade manuals penumbrating
Couples; and, most repellent of all, a jacketless row of the total
oeuvre, spines naked as the chorus of *Hair,* revealing what only the
more morbid have hitherto suspected, that since 1959 (*The Poorhouse Fair,* surely his masterpiece) Updike with Alfred A. Knopf's
connivance has been perpetrating a uniform edition of himself.
Beclouding all, the stink of nickel cigarillos, which the shifty,
tremulous, asthmatic author puffs to sting the muse's eyes into
watering ever since, at the Surgeon General's behest, he excised
cigarettes from his armory of crutches.

Updike, at first sight, seems bigger than he is, perhaps because
the dainty stitchwork of his prose style readies one for an apparition of elfin dimensions. An instant layer of cordial humorousness
veneers a tough thickness of total opacity, which may in turn coat

a center of heartfelt semi-liquid. Shamefacedly I confessed my errand—to fabricate an "interview" for one of those desperate publications that seek to make weekly "news" of remorselessly accumulating Gutenbergian silt. Shamefacedly, Updike submitted. Yet, throughout the interview that limped in the van of this consent, as the pumpkin-orange New England sun lowered above the chimney pots of a dry-cleaning establishment seen darkly through an unwashed window, Updike gave the impression of (and who wouldn't?) wanting to be elsewhere. He kept interjecting his desire to go "home" and "shingle" his "barn"; it occurred to this interviewer (the Interviewer, as Mailer would say), that the uniform books, varied in tint and size as subtly as cedar shakes, were themselves shingles, with the which this shivering poor fellow hopes to keep his own skin dry in the soaking downpour of mortality.

I observed, feinting for an opening, that he has stopped writing about Jews. He replied that the book about me had not so much been about a Jew as about a writer, who was a Jew with the same inevitability that a fictional rug-salesman would be an American. I riposted that *he* was a writer, though a Wasp. With the languid shrug of the chronically pained, he bitterly inveighed against the term Wasp, which implies, he said, wealth where he had been poor, Calvinism where he had been Lutheran, and ethnic consciousness where he had had none. That his entire professional life had been spent among Jews and women, that his paternal grandmother had been partly Irish, that he had disliked James Gould Cozzens' last novel, that false loyalties were the plague of a divided Republic, that racism as an aesthetic category was one thing but as an incitement to massacre another, etc.

With the chinks in his armor gaping before me like marigolds at the height of noon, I lunged deftly as a hummingbird. Didn't I detect, I asked, in his later work, an almost blunt determination to, as it were, sing America? Would he describe himself, I asked, switching the tape recorder up to fortissimo, as (a) pro-American, (b) a conservative? His turtleish green eyes blinked, recognizing that his shell was being tickled, and that there was no way out but forward. He said he was pro-American in the sense that he was married to America and did not wish a divorce. That the American style and landscape and impetus were, by predetermination, his meat; though he had also keenly felt love of fatherland in England, in Russia, in Egypt. That nations were like people, lovable and wonderful in their simple existence. That, in answer to the second prong of my probe, there were some things he thought worth conserving, such as the electoral college and the Great Lakes; but that by registration he was a Democrat and by disposition an apologist for the spirit of anarchy—our animal or divine margin of resistance to the social contract. That, given the need for a contract, he preferred the American Constitution, with its 18th-century bow to the pursuit of individual happiness, to any of the totalisms presently running around rabid. That the decisions of any establishment, though properly suspect and frightfully hedged by self-interest and the myopia power brings, must be understood as choices among imperfect alternatives; power participates in the weight and guilt of the world and shrill impotence never has to cash in its chips.

I inkled that this diatribe was meant to lead up to some discussion of his new novel, with its jacket of red, gray, and blue stripes, but, having neglected to read more than the first pages, which concern a middle-aged ex-athlete enjoying a beer with his elderly father, I was compelled to cast my interrogation in rather general terms. Viz.:

Q: Are you happy?

A: Yes, this is a happy limbo for me, this time. I haven't got the first finished copies yet, and haven't spotted the first typo. I haven't had to read any reviews.

Q: How do you find reviews?

A: Humiliating. It isn't merely that the reviewers are so much cleverer than I, and could write such superior fictions if they deigned to; it's that even the on-cheering ones have read a different book than the one you wrote. All the little congruences and arabesques you prepared with such delicate anticipatory pleasure are gobbled up as if by pigs at a pastry cart. Still, the ideal reader must —by the ontological argument—exist, and his invisibility therefore be a demonic illusion sustained to tempt us to despair.

Q: Do you envision novels as pills, broadcasts, tapestries, explosions of self, cantilevered constructs, or what?

A: For me, they are crystallizations of visceral hopefulness extruded as a slow paste which in the glitter of print regains something of the original, absolute gaiety. I try to do my best and then walk away rapidly, so as not to be incriminated. Right now, I am going over old short stories, arranging them in little wreaths, trimming away a strikingly infelicitous sentence here, adding a paper ribbon there. Describing it like this makes me sound more Nabokovian than I feel. Chiefly, I feel fatigued by my previous vitality.

Q: I'd like to talk about the new book, but the truth is I can't hold bound galley pages, my thumbs keep going to sleep, so I didn't get too far into this, what? *Rabbit Rerun?*

A (*eagerly, pluggingly*): *Redux.* Latin for led back. You know Latin: *Apologia Pro Vita Sua.* The next installment, ten years from now, I expect to call *Rural Rabbit*—you'll notice at the end of this book Janice talks about them getting a farm. The fourth and last, to come out in 1991 if we all live, is tentatively titled *Rabbit Is Rich.* Nice, huh?

Q (*turning tape recorder down to pianissimo*): Not bad. *Pas mal.* Not bad.

A (*gratefully, his shingling hand itching*): Thanks. Thanks a lot.

Farewell to the Middle Class

*(Hitherto Published Only, Strange to Say, in Japanese,
as One of a Series of Ads for Suntory Whisky,
on the Strength of its having been Written
under the Influence of Alcohol)*

TODAY I WAS TOLD I had made half a million dollars. My wife calls me a half-ass millionaire. The man on the other end of the phone seemed a little disappointed that I couldn't react. He had swung the deal and felt closer to it than I did. I expressed a doubt, just to make conversation, and that produced a series of phone calls on his part that produced another hundred thousand dollars. The second time he called, my wife kept shouting "Give it away!"

from the other room, and I could hardly hear him, and explained that he had given my wife a headache, and he laughed, thinking I was making a joke. I wasn't.

Sad, yes. I couldn't think of how to keep the government from taking the major share. The contract wasn't even signed, and I was a tax dodger. I couldn't think where to put the money. Our savings accounts were full to the insurable maximum. My wife had a new electric dishwasher, and I had a new pair of Fiberglas skis. We lived in an old house in the middle of an old neighborhood, making a little more than our neighbors but too lazy to spend it and taking a (if you examine it closely) snobbish pride in our worn-out sneakers, our dented cars, our threadbare backyard full of broken toys and unharvested dog dung.

Tonight I am a rich man. Tomorrow my wife is thirty-eight. I went out in a blizzard and bought her, rapidly, at the five and ten and then the local electric shop, a Joan Baez record, an electric waffle iron, and a four-slice toaster. In the old days, I would have bought her either the toaster or the waffle iron, but not both. I also bought some four-ninety wine. I said to the liquor-store proprietor, with whom I have grown intimate over the years, that people who paid five bucks for a bottle of wine must be nuts. Then I bought some. It was all a routine, half-planned on my part. He laughed, though. And the strange thing is, the wine was terrific, really distinctly better than three-dollar Bordeaux, or two-dollar Almadén. Fuller, smokier, with more grape, more landscape, more sorrow in it. We drank it all and, drunk, horsed around with the kids, who were feeling sorry for the old toaster and old waffle iron. The smaller girl took these appliances up to her bed and tucked them in. The snow kept coming. I had to cancel a church meeting that was going to be held at my house—too many old people on the committee to make it up the slippery curb.

Now I stand here, frugging to the Joan Baez record, looking out my window at my neighbor's television screen through the snow-storm. He is a train conductor and watches television every night from six to midnight. His endurance is fabulous. It is beautiful. His bluish set, more familiar to my wife and myself than the moon, is beautiful. We have watched it from our bedroom window often, before making love, after making love, before fights, after them.

Its electric shadows twitch. Its blue is smeared, glorified, made abstract by the snow, the falling flurrying flying snow, falling in clumps, bunched; only God could make so much snow. Five hundred thousand flakes. My neighbor's wife's head, silhouetted by the set, turns, and I guess I am visible, and she is watching. I turn off the light and keep frugging. Go, Joan. Good-bye, good-bye. She is doing "Where Have All the Flowers Gone?" in German. *Sagt mir wo die Blumen sind.* Good-bye, dear neighborhood of smoking chimneys and speckled roofs. My children yearn to be put to bed. One of the boys had a bath and is running around the house naked, flipping his penis; somehow he knows already we are rich and anything goes. The smaller girl comes to me and cries; she wants me to protect her in our storm of good fortune. My wife is out getting gas for the car. It didn't need gas but she loves snowstorms, whirlwinds, births, menstrual periods, and other such inexpensive excitements. Maybe she is saying good-bye to thirty-seven, hello to middle age. She sees money as a curse, that is why I love her. Who else would have lived here so long, on this noisy nondescript corner, amid widows and semi-shaven men who mutter off to mysterious jobs before the sun is up? Lord, I have loved them. I love you too, Joan. And you, old house, and you, Old Toaster. And you, you blue-smeared snow. Let's fuck once more. Good-bye, good-bye.

FOUR SPEECHES

Accuracy

I THANK the donors of the prize and the judges of the award for this honor. Its receipt makes me both glad and uneasy—uneasy perhaps because the writing of fiction is so rewarding in itself, so intimately necessary, that public bonuses seem bestowed under some misapprehension, to somebody else, to that fantastical and totally remote person whose picture very occasionally appears in the Sunday book supplements and whose opinions of art, life, and technology are so hopefully solicited by the editors of undergraduate magazines. On his behalf, as it were, I gratefully accept; and since he has been asked to say a few words, I will mention, in the manner of writing fiction, a virtue seldom extolled these days, that of *accuracy*, or *lifelikeness*.

It may seem too daring of me to touch on this when my book appeared, to many, a bewildering, arbitrary, and forced mixture of uncongenial elements, of mythology and remembrance, of the drably natural and the bookishly supernatural. I can only plead that the shape of the book formally approximates, for me, the mixed and somewhat antic experience it was trying to convey. The book as well as the hero is a centaur. Anyone dignified with the name of "writer" should strive, surely, to discover or invent the verbal texture that most closely corresponds to the tone of life as it arrives on his nerves. This tone, whose imitation induces style, will vary from soul to soul. Glancing upward, one is struck by the dispersion of recent constellations, by how far apart the prose masters of the century—say, Proust and Joyce, Kafka and Hem-

Given in New York City, in March 1964, in acceptance of the 1963 National Book Awards fiction prize, awarded to *The Centaur*.

ingway—are from one another. It may be partly an optical illusion, but modern fiction does seem, more than its antecedents, the work of eccentrics. The writer now makes his marks on paper blanker than it has ever been. Our common store of assumptions has dwindled, and with it the stock of viable artistic conventions. Each generation—and readers and writers are brothers in this—inherits a vast attic of machinery that once worked and decorative dodads whose silhouettes no longer sing. We must each of us clear enough space in this attic so that we in turn can unpack. Does plot, for example, as commonly understood and expected, mirror Providential notions of retribution and ultimate balance that our hearts doubt? Is the syntactical sentence plastic enough to render the flux, the blurring, the endless innuendo of experience as we feel it? No aesthetic theory will cover the case; what is needed is a habit of honesty on the part of the writer. He must, rather athletically, instill his wrists with the refusal to write whatever is lazily assumed, or hastily perceived, or piously hoped. Fiction is a tissue of literal lies that refreshes and informs our sense of actuality. Reality is—chemically, atomically, biologically—a fabric of microscopic accuracies. Language approximates phenomena through a series of hesitations and qualifications; I miss, in much contemporary writing, this sense of self-qualification, the kind of timid reverence toward what exists that Cézanne shows when he grapples for the shape and shade of a fruit through a mist of delicate stabs. The intensity of the grapple is the surest pleasure a writer receives. Though our first and final impression of Creation is not that it was achieved by taking pains, perhaps we should proceed in the humble faith that, by taking pains, word by word, to be accurate, we put ourselves on the way toward making something useful and beautiful and, in a word, good.

The Future of the Novel

FIRST, let us ask, to what extent is The Future of the Novel a non-question, a non-issue repeatedly raised by literary journalists about a non-thing, the Novel? Do we worry ourselves with the future of

---

Given in Bristol, England, in February 1969, after a dinner arranged by the Bristol Literary Society.

the Poem? Surprisingly, not. Yet verse, compared to narrative prose, would seem to be the more fragile device, far more vulnerable to the clamorous counterclaims of television, the cinema, and traffic noise, far less likely to survive into an age of McLuhanism, Computerization, and whatever other polysyllables would dull our sensibilities and eclipse our humanistic heritage. In fact, poetry has survived. Great poets appear, do their work, and die. Waves of excitement and revolution occur, and are followed by lulls of consolidation and repose. An Ezra Pound or an Allen Ginsberg issues proclamations and generates apostles; relatively isolated and soft-spoken figures such as our Wallace Stevens and your Philip Larkin also meditate, and create. No doubt some decades are more fruitful of enduring verse than others; but each generation seems to supply its quota of poets and, odder still, of poetry readers. A certain slender ardent audience for poetry persists, and indeed in the United States seems to be widening; and if we include as "poets" (and why not?) the ubiquitous pop lyricists in the style of Bob Dylan and the Beatles, the audience is very wide indeed. The appetite for song—for things singingly said—would seem to be so fundamental to human nature that no foreseeable turn of technology or history could soon root it out.

Now, might we not assume the same of prose narrative? Perhaps; but the impression does linger that the Novel is not quite a category of human expression as eternal as Poetry, or the Dance, or the Joke, but is instead, like the Verse Epic, like the dramatic form called Tragedy, a genre with a life cycle and a death—a death, indeed, that may have already occurred.

Dr. Johnson, in his Dictionary, defined the word "novel" as "a small tale, generally of love." What he had in mind, of course, were the Italian *novelle*, written in great quantity from the 14th century to the 17th, of which Boccaccio's were the most famous, and from which Shakespeare derived the plots of, among other plays, *Romeo and Juliet* and *Othello*. The novel form in England was greatly enriched and broadened: Richardson brought to it the imitation of the epistle and Defoe the imitation of the journal; with Fielding and Jane Austen it becomes an inhabitable microcosm of society; and with Dickens the many-chambered Novel is expanded to include a courtroom for the indictment of social abuse. In the 19th century, length—physical bulk, the rendering of the sonorous music of passing time—becomes so intrinsic to the idea of the once-modest *novella* that Tennyson speaks of the ideal novel as one that will just "go on and on and never end." Throughout, however, and right down to the classics of modernism, love is a pervasive, perhaps obsessive, thread. The French say, "Without adultery, there is no novel," and while this may be more true of *their* novels than yours, it is indeed difficult to imagine a novel, even one by Lord Snow, without its—as the phrase goes—"romantic interest."

I would suggest that this is a *genre* trait of the Novel rather than an undistorted reflection of our lives. There *are* areas of concern in our lives apart from love; yet as a literary practitioner, and as a sometimes compulsory reader of unsuccessful novels, I have observed that it is difficult to make them interesting in a novel. Disease and pain, for instance, are of consuming concern to the person suffering from them, but while we will follow for eight hundred pages the course of a romance, and suffer with each love pang, the course of a physical disease, and the description of pain and discomfort, however sympathetic the character afflicted, weary us within a few paragraphs. Similarly, the amassment of sums of money, fascinating in reality, acquires interest in a novel only if the acquisition of wealth advances the hero or heroine toward that eventual copulation that seems to be every reader's insatiable and exclusive desire. Indeed, it is part of the peculiar democracy of fiction, and one way in which the air of its world is fresher than our own, that although in real life we *do* find wealthy and famous men more interesting than poor and obscure ones, in novels we do not. Even intelligence does not recommend a fictional character to us. No, in the strange egalitarian world of the Novel a man must earn our interest by virtue of his—how shall I say?—his *authentic sentiments*.

So we arrive at the not very spectacular inkling that the Novel is by nature sentimental. I use the word without pejorative intent, but merely as descriptive of the kind of coinage with which we transact our business in one literary realm. This coinage is not legal tender, I think, in the New Testament, or in *Beowulf*, or in *Prometheus Bound*, or to any predominant degree in the *Odyssey* or *Para-*

dise Lost. It is current, though not the only currency, in *The Divine Comedy*, and it would seem to have been introduced in Italy, with the breakup of the Middle Ages, and to be concurrent with the rise of capitalism. That is, when human worth began to be measured in terms of capital, and men became counters upon a board of productivity, the uneconomic emotions went underground, into literature. We can scarcely imagine it: but with the massive cosmic drama of Fall and Redemption always before him, and the momentous potentialities of sin and repentance always alive within him, medieval man may well have needed less reassurance than we that his emotions were substantial and significant, that his inner life and outward status were integrated. Even today, religious fundamentalists are not notable novel-readers.

This scale of generalization is uncomfortable for a novelist, concerned as he properly is with the strict small circumstance, the quizzical but verifiable fact. I wish to describe, merely, the Novel as a product of private enterprise, for which a market is created when the state, or tribe, or church, withdraws itself from the emotional sector of the individual's life. Erotic love then becomes a symbol, a kind of code for all the nebulous, perishable sensations which we persist in thinking of as *living*. Living and loving: the titles of two novels by the splendid Henry Green, and an equation, but for one transposed vowel, to which all novel readers consent— the housewife reading away the dull afternoon, the schoolboy concentrating amid the stupid family din, the banker sitting prim in the homeward commuting train. All are members of a conspiracy to preserve the secret that people *feel*. Please do not suppose that I am describing only penny fiction, trash. The most elegant and respectable of modern novels, from *Remembrance of Things Past* to *Lolita*, enlist in this conspiracy with all the boldness of their virtuosity. Even as all-including and unyielding a masterwork as *Ulysses* is finally about lovers; Leopold and Molly Bloom are great lovers, great in compassion and fidelity, fidelity to each other and to their inner sensations, their authentic sentiments. Perhaps the reason Stephen Dedalus is slightly tedious in this novel is that he is not in love. Not to be in love, the capital N Novel whispers to capital W Western Man, is to be dying.

*

So much for the past; what of the future? The Novel's Victorian heyday has passed. If my impression is correct, that capitalism put sex in a treasure chest, the chest, after so many raids upon it, is battered to the point of collapse. The set of tensions and surprises we call *plot* to a great extent depends upon the assumption that bourgeois society discourages and obstructs free-ranging sex. In the 19th-century novels and the 20th-century movies, the punishment for adultery is death. Yet even in *Madame Bovary*, one feels, reading it, that the heroine in swallowing arsenic is being hysterical, that there is nothing in her situation a sudden inheritance of money wouldn't solve. In the novels, say, of Evelyn Waugh, adultery has become a dangerous pleasantry, and by now I think even the aura of danger is fading. As Denis de Rougemont has pointed out, the conventional obstructions to love no longer impress us; a somewhat extravagant situation, such as in *Lolita*, alone can bestow dignity upon a romantic passion. Freud, misunderstood or not, has given sex the right to be free, and the new methods of contraception have minimized the bail. Remove the genuine prohibitions and difficulty, and the three-dimensional interweave of the Novel collapses, becomes slack and linear. The novels of Henry Miller are not novels, they are acts of intercourse strung alternately with segments of personal harangue. They are closer to the *Arabian Nights* than to Tolstoy; they are not novels but *tales*.

Dr. Johnson defined "novel" as a type of tale; and, though the classic Novel, the sentimental underground of bourgeois Europe, may belong to a moment of history that is passing, the appetite for tales is probably not less fundamental to the human species than the appetite for songs. Books of prose about imaginary events will continue to appear, and they will be called, out of semantic inertia, novels.

What will be the shape of these books? Some will continue the direction of Miller, and be more or less angry personal accounts of coitus and conversation among bohemians. The tradition is not dishonorable—Dostoevsky's *Notes from the Underground* is such a book—and will veer very close to pornography, which itself has a tradition that is, at the least, venerable. The subversive burden will shift, I fear, from sex to violence, and the threat of society, and the problem for censorship, lies not, in my opinion, with the description of sexual acts but with fantasies of violence and torture. Books like *Last Exit to Brooklyn* and *The Painted Bird*, with their unrelieved brutality, and the relish that seethes beneath their creditable surface pretensions, augur an unhappy direction. Cruel events do occur in reality, of course; but the obligation of the artist, when dealing with them, as with sex, is to be, not inexplicit, but accurately alive to their complicated human context. Today's bohemia, or hippiedom, seems to aspire toward a political effectiveness that precludes much compass of sympathy or subtlety of craft. Rather, a fanatic and dazed narrowing of comprehension seems to be in progress. The sour riots of the Sixties are not likely to call forth the ebullient rapture of a Kerouac, let alone the refined anguish of a Huysmans.

Other books of fiction will, I think, try to employ the inherited machinery of the romantic novel for drier purposes than the dramatization of erotic vicissitudes. The novels of Vladimir Nabokov already ingeniously toy with romantic triangles to produce more intricate patterns. His novels approach the condition of puzzles— *Pale Fire* was rigged on the scheme of an annotated poem and the introduction playfully invited us to buy two copies to read it properly. Novels by other men play hopscotch with us, or invite us to shuffle the pages and make our own plots. Robbe-Grillet gives us an overlapping sequence of repetitions of actions; all such inventions have a somewhat capricious air, but I think the two directions, of novel as philosophy, of novel as object, will be fruitfully pursued. Heightened intellectual demands should compress the conventional size of the novel; hundreds of thousands of words in Dickens' time, it may settle at around two hundred pages, the length of a mystery story, of *Candide*, or of a novel by Samuel Beckett.

The surface of the page, now a generally dead rectangle of gray, a transparent window into the action, could be a lively plane of typographic invention, as it was for Apollinaire—a surface that says "This is printing" much as Impressionism forsook the licked illusionistic surface and announced, "This is painting." The comic strip offers a blend of picture and word that, though it has not attained the status of high art, has, in strips like the old "Krazy Kat" and the contemporary "Peanuts," climbed rather high. I see no intrinsic reason why a doubly talented artist might not arise and create a comic-strip novel masterpiece. Artistically, this century has belonged to the eye; concrete poetry, medieval manuscripts, and Egyptian hieroglyphs all hint at paths of accommodation in an ecumenical movement among eye-oriented media.

If these suggestions sound frivolous, let me say that tale-telling *is* a kind of toying, and that something of primitive magic does linger about the manipulation of verbal dolls. When the speaker was an undergraduate student of "creative writing," a guest writer, John Hawkes, told our class—amazingly, I thought— "When I want a character to fly, I just say, 'He flew.'" We are, all of us novelists, like neoclassic playwrights captive to the three unities, prisoners of conventions we cannot imagine our way around; a wonderful freedom awaits us, and extraordinary opportunities. Let me admit to the hopeful fancy that some book such as I have imagined—a short novel, approaching the compact, riddling condition of an object—may serve as the vehicle of a philosophic revolution. That a new Rousseau or a new Marx or a new Kierkegaard may choose to speak to us through the Novel. That the Novel, relieved of some of its old duties as an emotional masseur, may prove to be a light and nimble messenger. That, though at the moment the Novel roosts a little heavily in the bookshops, to fly it only needs him to come along who will say, "It flies."

From *Humor in Fiction*

THE TITLE of this talk has been assigned to me; and, though I confess I find it congenial, I confess also that I can hardly imagine a language *less* international than that of written humor. For humor, written or otherwise, operates in the nuancé margins of experience and communication; not only is a pun lost in translation from one language to another, but also lost are rhythm, slang, and the many fine halftones of verbal allusion. The Argentine writer Jorge Luis Borges, in parenthetically discussing the failure of Shake-

Given in Seoul, South Korea, in June 1970, at a conference of the International P.E.N.; the general conference theme was "Humor."

speare's humor to amuse him, ventures the surprising thought that "humor . . . is an oral genre, a sudden spark in conversation, not a written thing." And, if we reflect upon those occasions when we laugh, we perceive how delicate and complex are the forces giving rise to our reaction, how close to pathos or banality these forces verge, and how difficult it is to describe, later, what, in the heat of conversation or, it may be, in the forward surge of reading, seemed so funny.

The phenomenon of humor, or laughter, has not failed to attract theorists. Henri Bergson locates the comic essence in an "encrustation of the mechanical upon the organic." Twins, for example, are humorous because duplication of individuals hints at a mechanical intervention in the species; a man slipping upon a banana peel is comic in that he behaves like a machine, rigidly perpetuating his motion without the foresight and allowances proper to vitality. By Bergson's theory, the comic incident is a misapplication of momentum and the comic character is a monomaniac, which well enough describes the heroes of French farce but does not encompass such a nimble and many-faced comic hero as Shakespeare's Falstaff.

Confusingly, just as weeping can express joy as well as sorrow, laughter arises from states of mind that appear not merely various but even opposite: laughter can announce scorn and contempt, but may also be applause. Our laughter at Falstaff, for instance, has much applause and admiration in it, as well as feelings of superiority, and in literary humor especially, we find an ingredient of the genial. Within a comic work we are relaxed in a world of essential safety, where the dangers of death and destruction have been exchanged for mock penalties, for semblances of defeat and punishment that are erased by the next comic scene. The comic character, whether a cat in an animated cartoon or the hero of a classic like Don Quixote, is rubbery; he bounces back, and suffers no scars. Contrast the brittle, stony characters of Greek tragedy, who, under the unforgiving pressure of fate's engines, irrevocably shatter.

Sigmund Freud attempted to extend the methods of his dream analysis into the analysis of jokes. His book *Wit and Its Relation to the Unconscious* explains jokes and examples of verbal wit and, by extension, all instances of the comic in terms of a difference in psychical expenditures; the characteristic joke sets up an instant of bewilderment, and laughter follows in the recognition that a kind of sense has been made, but different from what we expected. As Kant said, the comic is "an expectation that has turned to nothing." Certainly jokes, like dreams, do function in a realm liberated from the laws of logic and logical consequence; and there is melancholy profundity in Freud's tentative suggestion that humor, the art of the comic, is an intellectual adult attempt to recover "the lost laughter of childhood."

And what might be this original laughter, the laughter of childhood? A recent, popular, but not uninformative book called, a little provocatively, *The Naked Ape,* discusses, from a zoologist's point of view, the origin of laughter. Desmond Morris first notes that crying is present from birth but laughter does not appear until the third or fourth month of life. It arises in circumstances like these: the mother, holding the child in her lap, pretends to let him drop, or does something else startling. The infant's instinctive crying reaction is cancelled by his recognition that he is safe, that the mother is with him, and his cry merges with the parental-recognition gurgle that by this time is part of his vocabulary. In this manner, laughter is born. How many of the games parents instinctively play with infants, for instance, the tossing and clutching, the chasing and tickling, are in fact a systematic daring and scaring, a systematic widening of the circle of safety in which the children may feel privileged to laugh? A hundred and fifty years ago, William Hazlitt wrote this on the theory of laughter:

> If we hold a mask before our face, and approach a child with this disguise on, it will at first, from the oddity and incongruity of the appearance, be inclined to laugh; if we go nearer to it, steadily, and without saying a word, it will begin to be alarmed, and be half inclined to cry; if we suddenly take off the mask, it will recover from its fears, and burst out a-laughing; but if, instead of presenting the old well-known countenance, we have concealed a satyr's head or some frightful caricature behind the first mask, the suddenness of the change will not in this case be a source of merriment to it, but will convert its surprise into an agony of consternation, and will make it scream out for help, even though it may be convinced that the whole thing is a trick at bottom.
>
> The alternation of tears and laughter, in this little episode in common life, depends almost entirely on the greater or less degree of

interest attached to the different changes of appearance. The mere suddenness of the transition, the mere baulking our expectations, and turning them abruptly into another channel, seems to give additional liveliness and gaiety to the animal spirits; but the instant the change is not only sudden, but threatens serious consequences, or calls up the shape of danger, terror supersedes our disposition to mirth, and laughter gives place to tears.

Laughter, then, can be construed as a signal of danger past or dismissed. It occurs within an arena, whether the arms of a mother or the covers of a novel, where the customary threats of life have been suspended. Dreams, jokes, play, and aesthetic pleasure alike mark a truce with the destructive forces of life. The oldest laugh may be the crow of triumph a warrior emits when his enemy is at his feet. We giggle when we are nervous; we scream hilariously when, in the old silent pictures, the comedian totters on the parapet of the skyscraper. The margin of glee in our scream is the knowledge that, being a comedian, he will not fall. The clown, the fool, is traditionally exempt from laws and taboos. Yet his activities, and our laughter, take their point from the backdrop of gravity, of necessary prohibition and actual danger. In literature, comic adventure is woven from the same threads as tragedy and pathos; we laugh within the remittance from seriousness that the artist has momentarily won for us. . . .

The episode, in *Don Quixote*, of the windmills contains many of the elements that our theorists of the comic would have us look for. Don Quixote's monomania, his determination to see romantic adventures in mundane happenstance, is comic in its rigidity, and admirable in its ingenuity. At first he seems to see the windmills through a cloud, so that sails of wood and canvas take on the appearance of giant human arms; he charges forward despite the shouted warnings of his clear-sighted squire. Then, rebuffed by a whack one sail gives him, and perhaps his vision clarified by his physical closeness to these supposed giants, he reconstructs his delusion upon a new, and invulnerable, ground: his enemy the magician Freston has turned real giants into apparent windmills. All of Sancho's realism is overthrown by sublime assertions: "Thou art but little acquainted with adventures" and "There is nothing so subject to the Inconstancy of Fortune as War." Like some modern statesmen, Don Quixote has constructed from much real information and one wildly false premise an impregnable castle of self-justification; awkward realities are made to argue against themselves, and to reconfirm the malice of the enemy and the nobility of the unreal quest.

His dream does not shatter under reality because the author and Sancho Panza protect him; the author by conferring upon this lean old man a magical rubbery toughness, and Sancho Panza—with a loving and wondering fidelity that is one of the book's masterstrokes—by always rushing forward and picking up the pieces. Don Quixote suffers no ill effects from this adventure; it is Rozinante, his horse, who limps, his shoulder half dislocated by their fall. It is the horse, who cannot reason or go mad but who can suffer, who absorbs and mutely carries off this adventure's residue of pain.

Even this early in the novel, Cervantes seems indifferent to his stated objective—of burlesquing the pseudo-medieval adventures of Tasso and Ariosto. A cruder author would have hurt his hero severely, or had him spin delusions less plausibly, or accompanied him with a mocking and sardonic squire. Our laughter would have been quicker and sharper, but thin, and quickly automatic. Satire, as an attack upon an idea or set of ideas, quickly bores us, since the author, manipulating his puppets, makes the same statement over and over. Here, with Cervantes—himself as often battered and disappointed as his hero—our laughter is deepened by a certain ambiguous poetry in the narrative; the windmills are not merely mistaken for giants but somehow loom *as* giants. The wind, springing up opportunely to turn their giant arms, seems to join the fun; and the knight's unshakable dignity in some sense argues for his delusions, and gives him that air of triumph which is, we noted above, an ancient tributary of laughter. . . .

Dr. Pangloss, like Don Quixote, irrepressibly applies the mechanism of his *idée fixe* to the incongruous material of life. But here there is no mistaking the satiric edge, and the author performs his comedy on the edge of pain. We are anesthetized, and allowed therefore to laugh, by the flitting quickness and neatness of the narrative style. When the Lisbon earthquake occurs in *Candide*, we are told, as if the statistic had been gathered in an instant, that "Thirty thousand men, women and children were crushed to death." The characters with mechanical promptness react in character: the pious and innocent Candide exclaims that the Day of Judgment is near, Dr. Pangloss poses himself a philosophical riddle amid the toppling ruins, and the sailor, cheerfully heartless, seizes the opportunity for theft and lechery. Such stylization preserves the earthquake as an item in an abstract argument and heightens our sense of play. In a sentence, we are told Candide is injured and half-buried, but are not asked to dwell upon his condition—Rozinante's limp is more sensuously present. The central figure remains Dr. Pangloss, whose musing in such circumstances approaches heroic detachment and whose lack of pity for Candide is partially redeemed by his equal lack of self-pity. Pangloss' preposterous conclusion of a vein of sulphur running halfway around the world, defended with the stoutness of a Quixote, makes us laugh; and if we look into our laughter we detect there:

1. a sense of superiority to the scientific speculation of the 18th century;

2. a certain pleasure in the image, gaudy and simple as a child's crayon stroke;

3. applause at the good doctor's unfailing intellectual curiosity;

4. a kind of hysteria at the frightful facts of calamity and heavenly indifference that Voltaire sets before us;

5. a confession of pleasurable warmth, which the farcical tempo of the narrative has created in us, and which disposes us to laugh reflexively.

Laughter, as we know from its social instances, is infectious and carries a curious momentum; an image, mixed of such incongruities as a man's call for the oil and wine of the last rites mixed with another man's meditations upon sulphur, trips the trigger of laughter and, recurring (as it does when Pangloss insists, "I maintain it's proved!"), trips it again, harder. Here we touch upon the mystery, in presentation of the comic, of *timing;* in personal presentation, of timing and facial expression. A wrong twist of the face, betraying over-eagerness, like an excessive adjective in a sentence, will with mysterious thoroughness defuse a joke and frustrate a laugh. The moment of blank bewilderment that Freud describes has been

sullied. There must be a headlong, clean, economical something, a swift and careless music perhaps descended from the
rhythm of ticklings in infancy. No purer example of this comic
music exists than *Candide*. Indeed, its example leads us to wonder
if any efficient display of energy—an elegant mathematical proof,
a well-made young woman briskly walking by—doesn't dispose us
to jubilation, to a smile or laugh that is a salute, a shout of greeting
to the angels of health and life. . . .

Why Write?

MY TITLE offers me an opportunity to set a record of brevity at this
Festival of Arts; for an adequate treatment would be made were I
to ask, in turn, "Why not?" and sit down.

But instead I hope to explore, for not too many minutes, the
question from the inside of a man who, rather mysteriously to himself, has earned a livelihood for close to twenty years by engaging
in the rather selfish and gratuitous activity called "writing." I do
not propose to examine the rather different question of what use is
writing to the society that surrounds and, if he is fortunate, supports the writer. The ancients said the purpose of poetry, of writing, was to entertain and to instruct; Aristotle put forward the still
fascinating notion that a dramatic action, however terrible and
piteous, carries off at the end, in catharsis, the morbid, personal,
subjective impurities of our emotions. The enlargement of sympathy, through identification with the lives of fictional others, is
frequently presented as an aim of narrative; D. H. Lawrence, with
characteristic fervor, wrote, "And here lies the vast importance of
the novel, properly handled. It can inform and lead into new places
the flow of our sympathetic consciousness, and can lead our sympathy away in recoil from things that are dead." Kafka wrote that
a book is an ax to break the frozen sea within us. The frozen sea
within himself, he must have meant; though the ax of Kafka's own
art (which, but for Max Brod's posthumous disobedience, Kafka

Given in Adelaide, South Australia, in March 1974.

would have taken with him into the grave), has served an analogous purpose for others. This note of pain, of saintly suffering, is a modern one, far removed from the serene and harmonious bards and poets of the courts of olden time. Listen to Flaubert, in one of his letters to Louise Colet:

> I love my work with a love that is frenzied and perverted, as an ascetic loves the hair shirt that scratches his belly. Sometimes, when I am empty, when words don't come, when I find I haven't written a single sentence after scribbling whole pages, I collapse on my couch and lie there dazed, bogged in a swamp of despair, hating myself and blaming myself for this demented pride which makes me pant after a chimera. A quarter of an hour later everything changes; my heart is pounding with joy. Last Wednesday I had to get up and fetch my handkerchief; tears were streaming down my face. I had been moved by my own writing; the emotion I had conceived, the phrase that rendered it, and satisfaction of having found the phrase—all were causing me to experience the most exquisite pleasure.

Well, if such is the writer at work, one wonders why he doesn't find a pleasanter job; and one also wonders why he appears himself to be the chief market for his own product.

Most people sensibly assume that writing is propaganda. Of course, they admit, there is bad propaganda, like the boy-meets-tractor novels of socialist realism, and old-fashioned propaganda, like Christian melodrama and the capitalist success stories of Horatio Alger or Samuel Smiles. But that some message is intended, wrapped in the story like a piece of crystal carefully mailed in cardboard and excelsior, is not doubted. Scarcely a day passes in my native land that I don't receive some letter from a student or teacher asking me *what I meant to say* in such a book, asking me to elaborate more fully on some sentence I deliberately whittled into minimal shape, or inviting me to speak on some topic, usually theological or sexual, on which it is pleasantly assumed I am an expert. The writer as hero, as Hemingway or Saint-Exupéry or D'Annunzio, a tradition of which Camus was perhaps the last example, has been replaced in America by the writer as educationist. Most writers teach, a great many teach writing; writing is furiously taught in the colleges even as the death knell of the book and the written word is monotonously tolled; any writer, it is assumed, can give a lecture, and the purer products of his academic mind, the "writings" themselves, are sifted and, if found of sufficient quality, installed in their places on the assembly belt of study, as objects of educational contemplation.

How dare one confess, to the politely but firmly inquiring letter-writer who takes for granted that as a remote but functioning element of his education you are duty-bound to provide the information and elucidating essay that will enable him to complete his term paper, or his Ph.D. thesis, or his critical *opus*—how dare one confess that the absence of a swiftly expressible message is, often, *the* message; that reticence is as important a tool to the writer as expression; that the hasty filling out of a questionnaire is not merely irrelevant but *inimical* to the writer's proper activity; that this activity is rather curiously private and finicking, a matter of exorcism and manufacture rather than of toplofty proclamation; that what he makes is ideally as ambiguous and opaque as life itself; that, to be blunt, the social usefulness of writing matters to him primarily in that it somehow creates a few job opportunities—in Australia, a few government grants—a few opportunities to live as a writer.

Not counting journalists and suppliers of scripts to the media, hardly a hundred American men and women earn their living by writing, in a wealthy nation of two hundred million. Does not then, you ask, such a tiny band of privileged spokesmen owe its country, if not the trophy of a Nobel Prize,* at least the benign services of a spiritual aristocracy? Is not the writer's role, indeed, to speak for humanity, as conscience and prophet and servant of the billions not able to speak for themselves? The conception is attractive, and there are some authors, mostly Russian, who have aspired to such grandeur without entirely compromising their gifts. But in general, when a writer such as Sartre or Faulkner becomes a great man, a well-intentioned garrulity replaces the specific witness that has been theirs to give.

The last time I dared appear on a platform in a foreign land, it was in Kenya, where I had to confess, under some vigorous questioning from a large white man in the audience, that the general

---

* That year awarded to Australia's Patrick White.

betterment of mankind, and even the improvement of social conditions within my own violently imperfect nation, were *not* my basic motivation as a writer. To be sure, *as a citizen* one votes, attends meetings, subscribes to liberal pieties, pays or withholds taxes, and contributes to charities even more generously than—it turns out—one's own President. But as a writer, for me to attempt to extend my artistic scope into all the areas of my human concern, to substitute nobility of purpose for accuracy of execution, would certainly be to forfeit whatever social usefulness I *do* have. It has befallen a Solzhenitsyn to have experienced the Soviet labor camps; it has befallen Miss Gordimer and Mr. Mtshali * to suffer the tensions and paradoxes and outrages of a racist police state; social protest, and a hope of reform, is in the very fiber of their witness. But a writer's witness, surely, is of value in its circumstantiality. Solzhenitsyn's visible and brave defiance of the Soviet state is magnificent; but a novel like *The First Circle* affords us more than a blind flash of conditioned and—let's face it—chauvinistic indignation; it affords us entry into an unknown world, it offers a complex and only implicitly indignant portrait of how human beings live under a certain sort of political system. When I think of the claustrophobic and seething gray world of *The First Circle*, I am reminded in texture of Henry Miller's infamous Paris novels. Here, too, we have truth, and an undeniable passion to proclaim the truth—a seedy and repellent yet vital truth—though the human conditions Miller describes are far removed from any hope of political cure. And Miller, in his way, was also a martyr: as with Solzhenitsyn, his works could not be published in his native land.

We must write where we stand; wherever we do stand, there is life; and an imitation of the life we know, however narrow, is our only ground. As I sat on that stage in Kenya, a symbolic American in a corner of that immense range of peoples symbolically called The Third World, I felt guilty and bewildered that I could not hear in my formidable accuser's orotund phrases anything that had to do with my practice of the writer's profession; I was discomfited that my concerns—to survive, to improve, to make my microcosms amusing to me and then to others, to fail, if fail I must, through

---

* Oswald Mtshali, Zulu poet. Both he and Nadine Gordimer were present at the Adelaide Festival.

neither artistic cowardice nor laziness, to catch all the typographical errors in my proofs, to see that my books appear in jackets
both striking and fairly representative of the contents, to arrange
words and spaces and imagined realities in patterns never exactly
achieved before, to be able to defend any sentence I publish—I was
embarrassed that my concerns were so ignoble, compared to his.
But, once off the stage (where a writer should rarely be), I tend to
be less apologetic, and even to believe that my well-intentioned
questioner, and the silent faces in the same audience looking to me
to atone for America's sins real and supposed, and the touching
schoolchildren begging me by letter to get them through the sev-
enth grade—that none of these people have any felt comprehension
of my vocation.

Why write? As soon ask, why rivet? Because a number of personal accidents drift us toward the occupation of riveter, which
pre-exists, and, most importantly, the riveting-gun exists, and we
love it.

Think of a pencil. What a quiet, nimble, slender and then stubby
wonder-worker he is! At his touch, worlds leap into being; a tiger
with no danger, a steam-roller with no weight, a palace at no cost.
All children are alive to the spell of pencil and crayons, of making something, as it were, from nothing; a few children never
move out from under this spell, and try to become artists. I
was once a rapturous child drawing at the dining-room table,
under a stained-glass chandelier that sat like a hat on the swollen
orb of my excitement. What is exciting that child, so distant from
us in time and space? He appears, from the vantage of this lectern
unimaginable to him, to be in the grip of two philosophical perceptions.

One, mimesis demands no displacement; the cat I drew did not
have to fight for food or love with the real cat that came to the
back porch. I was in drawing *adding* to the world rather than rearranging the finite amount of goods within it. We were a family
struggling on the poverty edge of the middle class during the Depression; I was keen to avoid my father's noisy plight within the
plague of competition; pencil and paper were cheap, unlike most
other toys.

And, Two, the world called into being on the pencilled paper admitted of connections. An early exercise, whose pleasure returns to me whenever I assemble a collection of prose or poetry or whenever, indeed, I work several disparate incidents or impressions into the shape of a single story, was this: I would draw on one sheet of paper an assortment of objects—flowers, animals, stars, toaster, chairs, comic-strip creatures, ghosts, noses—and connect them with lines, a path of two lines, so that they all became the fruit of a single impossible tree. The exact age when this creative act so powerfully pleased me I cannot recall; the wish to make collections, to assemble sets, is surely a deep urge of the human mind in its playful, artistic aspect. As deep, it may be, as the urge to hear a story from beginning to end, or the little ecstacy of extracting resemblances from different things. Proust, of course, made simile the cornerstone of his theory of aesthetic bliss, and Plato, if I understand him right, felt that that which a set of like objects have in common *must* have a separate existence in itself, as the *idea* which delivers us, in our perception of the world, from the nightmare of nominalism. At any rate, to make a man of pencil and paper is as much a magical act as painting a bison with blood on the wall of a cave; a child, frail and overshadowed, and groping for his fate, herein *captures* something and, further, brings down praise from on high.

I have described the artistic transaction as being between the awakening ego and the world of matter to which it awakes; but no doubt the wish to please one's parents enters early, and remains with the artist all his life, as a desire to please the world, however displeasing his behavior may seem, and however self-satisfying the work pretends to be. We are surprised to discover, for instance, that Henry James hoped to make lots of money, and that James Joyce read all of his reviews. The artist's personality has an awkward ambivalence: he is a cave dweller who yet hopes to be pursued into his cave. The need for privacy, the need for recognition: a child's vulnerability speaks in both needs, and in my own reaction to, say, the beseeching mail just described, I detect the live ambiguity—one is avid to receive the letters, and loath to answer them. Or (to make some reference to the literary scene I know best) consider the striking contrast between the eager, even breathless warmth of Saul Bellow's fiction, inviting our love and closeness with every phrase, and Bellow's own faintly haughty, distinctly edgy personal surface. Again, J. D. Salinger wrote a masterpiece, *The Catcher in the Rye*, recommending that readers who enjoy a book call up the author; then he spent his next twenty years avoiding the telephone. A writer, I would say, out of no doubt deficiencies of character, has constructed a cave-shaped organ, hollow more like a mouth than like an ear, through which he communicates with the world at one remove. Somewhat, perhaps, as his own subconscious communicates with him through dreams. Because the opportunities for feedback have been reduced to letters that need not be answered and telephones that can be unlisted, to an annual gauntlet of reviews and non-bestowal of prizes, the communication can be more honest than is any but the most trusting personal exchange; yet also great opportunities for distortion exist unchecked. For one more of these rather sub-terranean and reprehensible satisfactions of writing that I am here confessing is that the world, so balky and resistant and humiliating, can in the act of mimesis be rectified, adjusted, chastened, purified. Fantasies defeated in reality can be fully indulged; tendencies de-flected by the cramp of circumstance can be followed to an end. In my own case I have noticed, so often it has ceased to surprise me, a prophetic quality of my fictions, even to the subsequent appearance in my life of originally fictional characters. We write, that is, out of latency as much as memory; and years later our laggard lives in reality act out, often with eerie fidelity, the pat-terns projected in our imaginings.

But we have come too far, too fast, from that ambitious child making his pencil move beneath the stained-glass chandelier. In my adolescence I discovered one could write with a pencil as well as draw, without the annoying need to consult reality so frequently. Also, the cave beneath the written page holds many more kinds of space than the one beneath the drawing pad. My writing tends, I think, to be pictorial, not only in its groping for visual precision but in the way the books are conceived, as objects in space, with events and persons composed within them like shapes on a canvas. I do not recommend this approach; it is perhaps a perversion of the primal narrative urge. Storytelling, for all its powers of depiction, shares with music the medium of time, and perhaps its genius, its most central transformation, has to do with time, with rhythm and echo and the sense of time not frozen as in a painting but channelled and harnessed as in a symphony.

But one can give no more than what one has received, and we try to create for others, in our writings, aesthetic sensations we have experienced. In my case, some of these would be: the graphic precision of a Dürer or a Vermeer, the offhand-and-backwards-feeling verbal and psychological accuracy of a Henry Green, the wonderful embowering metaphors of Proust, the enigmatic concreteness of Kafka and Joyce, the collapse into components of a solved mathematical problem, the unriddling of a scrupulous mystery story, the earth-scorning scope of science fiction, the tear-producing results of a truly humorous piece of writing. Writing, really, can make us do rather few substantial things: it can make us laugh, it can make us weep, and if it is pornography and we are rather young, it can make us come. It can also, of course, make us sleep; and though in the frequent discussion of the writer's social purpose this soporific effect is unfailingly ignored, I suspect it is the most widespread practical effect of writing—a book is less often a flaming sword or a beam of light than a bedtime toddy. Whatever the use, we hope that some members of society will find our product useful enough to purchase; but I think it would be a hypocrisy to pretend that these other people's welfare, or communication with them, or desire to ennoble or radicalize or terrify or lull them, is the primary reason why one writes.

No, what a writer wants, as every aspiring writer can tell you, is to *get into print*. To transform the changing shadows of one's dimly and fitfully lived life into print—into metal or, with the advent of offset printing, into rather mysteriously electrified rubber —to lift through the doubled magic of language and mechanical reproduction our own impressions and dreams and playful constructions into another realm of existence, a multiplied and far-flung existence, into a space far wider than that which we occupy, into a time theoretically eternal: *that* is the siren song that holds us to our desks, our dismal revisions, our insomnia panics, our dictionaries and encyclopedias, our lonely and, the odds long are, superfluous labor. "Of making many books there is no end; and much study is a weariness of the flesh." A weariness one can certainly feel entering even a modestly well-stocked bookstore. Yet it is just this involvement in the world of commerce and industry, this imposition of one's otherwise evanescent fancies upon the machinery of manufacture and distribution, that excites the writer's ego, and gives an illusion of triumph over his finitude.

Although, as a child, I lived what was to become my material and message, my wish to write did not begin with that material and message; rather, it was a wish to escape from it, into an altogether better world. When I was thirteen, a magazine came into the house, *The New Yorker* by name, and I loved that magazine so much I concentrated all my wishing into an effort to make myself small and inky and intense enough to be received into its pages. Once there, I imagined, some transfigured mode of being, called a "writer's life," would begin for me. My fantasy was not entirely fantastic, as my domineering position on this platform and the first-class airplane tickets that brought me halfway around the world testify. But what I would not altogether insincerely ask you to accept is something shabby, precarious, and even craven about a writer's life.

Among artists, a writer's equipment is least out-of-reach—the language we all more or less use, a little patience at grammar and spelling, the common adventures of blundering mortals. A painter must learn to paint; his studio is redolent of alchemic substances and physical force. The musician's arcanum of specialized knowledge and personal dexterity is even more intimidating, less accessible to the untrained, and therefore somehow less corruptible than the writer's craft. Though some painters and musicians go bad in the prime of their lives, far fewer do, and few so drastically, as writers. Our trick is treacherously thin; our art is so incorrigibly amateur that novices constantly set the world of letters on its ear, and the very phrase "professional writer" has a grimy sound. Hilaire Belloc said that the trouble with writing was that it was never meant to be a profession, it was meant to be a hobby. An act of willful play, as I have described it.

So I have not spoken up to now of language, of the joys of using it well, of the role of the writer as a keeper of the keys of language, a guardian of usage and enforcer of precision. This does not seem to me a very real notion, however often it is put forward.* Language goes on evolving in the street and in the spoken media, and well-written books are the last places it looks for direction. The writer follows after the spoken language, usually timidly. I see myself described in reviews as a doter upon words. It is true, I am grateful to have been born into English, with its polyglot flexibility and the happy accident, in the wake of two empires, of its worldwide currency. But what I am conscious of doting on is not English *per se*, its pliable grammar and abundant synonyms, but its potential, for the space of some phrases or paragraphs, of becoming reality, of engendering out of imitation another reality, infinitely lesser but thoroughly possessed, thoroughly human.

Pascal says, "When a natural discourse paints a passion or an effect, one feels within oneself the truth of what one reads, which was there before, although one did not know it. Hence one is inclined to love him who makes us feel it, for he has not shown us his own riches, but ours." The writer's strength is not his own; he is a conduit who so positions himself that the world at his back flows through to the readers on the other side of the page. To keep this conduit scoured is his laborious task; to be, in the act of writing, anonymous, the end of his quest for fame.

Beginning, then, with cunning private ambitions and a childish fascination with the implements of graphic representation, I find myself arrived, in this audible search for self-justification, at an embarrassed altruism. Beginning with the wish to make an impression, one ends wishing to erase the impression, to make of it a perfect transparency, to make of oneself a point of focus purely, as selfless as a lens. One begins by seeking celebrity and ends by feeling a terrible impatience with everything—every flattering attention, every invitation to speak and to impersonate a wise man, every hunger of the ego and of the body—an impatience with everything that clouds and clots our rapt witness to the world that surrounds and transcends us. A writer begins with his personal truth, with that obscure but vulnerable and, once lost, precious life that he lived before becoming a writer; but, those first impressions dis-

---

* As, say, by Iris Murdoch, in the 1972 Blashfield Address.

charged—a process of years—he finds himself, though empty, still posed in the role of a writer, with it may be an expectant audience of sorts and certainly a habit of communion. It is then that he dies as a writer, and becomes an inert cultural object merely, or is born again, by re-submitting his ego, as it were, to fresh drafts of experience and refined operations of his mind. *To remain interested* —of American novelists, only Henry James continued in old age to advance his art; most, indeed, wrote their best novels first, or virtually first. Energy ebbs as we live; success breeds disillusion as surely as failure; the power of hope to generate action and vision lessens. Almost alone the writer can reap profit from this loss. An opportunity to sing louder from within the slackening ego is his. For his song has never been all his own: he has been its excuse as much as its source. The little tyrant's delight in wielding a pencil always carried with it an empathy into the condition of *being* a pencil; more and more the writer thinks of himself as an instrument, a means whereby a time and a place make their mark. To become less and transmit more, to replenish energy with wisdom— some such hope, at this more than mid-point of my life, is the reason why I write.

LONDON LIFE

Notes of a Temporary Resident
(for *The Listener*)

January 1969

AN AMERICAN IN LONDON, whether he has come here to work for Esso or to escape the draft, cannot but be impressed and charmed by the city. The monumentality of Washington, the thriving busyness of New York, the antique intimacy of Boston, plus a certain spacious and open feeling reminiscent of Denver and San Francisco —all these he finds combined for his pleasure. If he is on foot, considerately designed buses and taxis offer to lift him along a maze of streets; if he has a car, the roadways, however intimidating to a pedestrian instinctively looking in the wrong direction, reveal themselves as paragons of clear marking and disciplined flow. This, surely, is a city, a *civitas* in the root sense, a collection of citizens whose collective life and conscience is bespoken by the wealth of parks and museums, the gracious abundance of public services. Food, for example, which in France must be won by slightly daring forays into restaurants and *épiceries* that have the shuttered air of brothel-fronts, is here everywhere—fresh fruit heaped for sale in the most densely trafficked streets, candy machines on trees, counters of meat in clothing stores. If the telephone booths are scarcer than an American is used to, at least the ones he finds have not been vandalized. He moves through London with no fear, as in Rome, of being cheated and with no fear, as in Paris, of being willfully misunderstood. It is not merely the English language that makes this ease, it is a language of social expectation and response that in his own country is a rather harsh dialect. He finds, in London, tickets to concerts and plays easy to come by; yet when he arrives the hall is full, or nearly. The balance between supply and demand is maintained with a reasonableness as mysterious as the opaque imbalances of Moscow. Its central institution is, I suppose, the docile, ubiquitous queue.

In the house that I rent hangs a large map of London and environs in 1741. City blocks stop at Marylebone: the eye travels north across stippled fields to Hampstead. Paddington, St. Pancras, and Kentish Towns are villages; St. John's Wood a matter of two or three houses. Elsewhere on the map, Brompton and Chelsea, Camberwell, Peckham, and Stepney are all distinct and full of delicately etched orchards. Why should this seem special to me? All cities grow by swallowing their satellite towns. But these have kept their names and, somehow beneath the asphalt, a sense of locality, of neighborhood. If, as everyone (or at least every American) says, London is a city one can live in, credit the variety of demi-cities within it, few of them hopelessly unfashionable or ugly, all of them with some possibilities and style. London's genius is conglomerate; how restricted, relatively, is New York, four of its five boroughs more or less unheard-of and the Manhattanites with pretensions to respectability penned into a few dozen blocks east of lower Central Park, or clinging to several side-streets in the increasingly decadent Village, or to the once solidly middle-class West Side. And these are sizable enclaves, compared to the "good" neighborhoods of inner-core Philadelphia or Cleveland. No doubt the contrast can be overdrawn. The square miles of chimney pots and sullen slate one sees from a southbound train window match for dreariness any American ghetto. Yet some of the factors blighting American cities (their ruthless grid-plan expansion, our centuries of racial discrimination and the bitter harvest of impoverishment, the rural nostalgia that foments the flight to the suburbs) do seem to have been absent or mitigated here, and London's long primacy has made possible a kind of civic self-confidence absent or ambiguously ironical in America, except in small towns. I have moved here from a small American town, and find familiar virtues: some things are free, some are cheap, one walks among strangers without feeling menaced, the institutions of communal existence feel accessible.

A city, then, of sections rather than layers, where latitude mitigates pressure. The latitude of costume, for instance: it is impossible to dress too oddly for the streets. The clothes along Piccadilly are a spree for the eyes, as shameless as the underwear ads that flow past the startled standee on the Underground escalator, as hard to believe, at first sight, as the Post Office Tower. On a sunny day along Regent Street it is as if England has costumed itself for one more Gilbert and Sullivan operetta, bobbies in their helmets and bankers in their bowlers and a chorus of clowns in bell-bottomed pants and slouch hats, with powdered faces and painted doll's eyes. The miniskirts, too (unlike the ones on Fifth Avenue, perhaps because they are shorter) have a dolly look of unassailable innocence. The spirit of comedy lurks beneath the jubilantly erotic surfaces —and after all isn't English literature, from the Wife of Bath and Rosalind to Moll Flanders and Sara Monday, peculiarly rich in comic heroines? Women parade in everything from yak hides to cellophane—everything except the stern little uniform of black cocktail dress and single pearl strand in which the sleek matron of Park Avenue or Paris sallies forth, sweet soldier, to do battle with her lover, broker, or furrier.

The hip young men seem sad. The uncut hair, which in America does hark back to a native wildness, to Davy Crockett and the redmen, here evokes some sickly Prince Valiant—a squad of pallid, faithless Christs. The faces of the American young reflect excitement: their struggle is for the center of the world stage, and there is an impressive largeness in their dreams of revolutionizing Western morality. I do not feel that excitement here; *Private Eye* is an updated *Tidbits*, the young socialists on television have the rabid punctilio of Dracula turned commissar, and the music is all sung in an American accent. What does Dusty Springfield know about a "preacher man"? Insofar as the popular music here is not derivative, it is Elizabethan balladeering beamed back after centuries of fermentation in the Appalachians, by way of Elvis Presley. It is white man's music, grown in the package. Beyond the luxuriance of London (all those Rolls-Royces!) and the bustling bravura of its shopping streets, there is an England a foreigner glimpses mostly on television—a soggy little island huffing and puffing to keep up with Western Europe, John Bull counting his change as he runs for the bus. An American has difficulty understanding the technical headlines promulgated by your government of glum economists.* But even your Queen looks somehow thrifty. The television news can seem desperately local —for a fortnight this fall, one besieged man in Shropshire eclipsed Asia, Africa, and our elections. Asia, indeed, appears as remote as the moon—let the Yanks and the Reds fight over it. As to Africa, and ex-colonies elsewhere—"our commonwealth friends," as Mr. Wilson a shade wryly terms them—they are like people with whom one was very intimate once, on a long lovely cruise, but who now are, well, *embarrassing*. Embarrassing, too, are all these darkish immigrants that make Mr. Powell's eyebrows lift so high, and those marching Catholics in Londonderry (what *do* they want?), and the crazy Welsh (not Tom Jones and Burton, but the ones that blew up the reservoir), and those impossible French (we'd let them into *our* club, if we had one) and rude Herr Hochhuth . . . really, if we'd known the world was going to be such a nagging bore, we wouldn't have bothered to beat the Spanish Armada.

Marcus Cunliffe, in his biography of Washington, says of the American outlook: "In comparison with the dense, shrewd, worldly British texture from which it is derived, it is surprisingly thin, diffuse, and romantic." True; yet, like an Andean Indian, one born to this thin air learns to breathe it and feels a slight heaviness on the chest elsewhere. There come moments when the "dense, shrewd" texture seems stifling. Two enjoyable American experiences are mailing letters and going to the movies; post offices and movie houses are central in most towns, yet rarely crowded and briskly managed. In England I have learned to dread the moment in the cinema, so stuffy with smoke, when after the short subjects the lights shockingly leap on and weary-looking girls in white insist that we purchase from them yet more sweets before being allowed, freighted with pap, to plunge back into dreamland. And in the post office, after floundering to the stamp counter past the long queues waiting to purchase licenses, receive pensions, and whatever else their life-long wrangle with the Welfare State involves, it is maddening to watch the clerk (whose clerkliness is of Gogolian intensity, the product of generations of breeding carried

---

* No sentence in this set of aging impressions seems farther away than this one now, when all Western governments are of glum economists.

on with dip pens and inkwells) as he tries to balance your letter against a number of brass weights, fiddling to find the right combination, having the letter slip from its tray, replacing it, and at last like blind Justice locating a state approximating balance and then mincing out your postage to you in a series of oddly denominated stamps whose sum he frequently botches, thanks to the intrinsic awkwardness of non-decimal addition. And the way one can get a bank statement only by writing for it to the manager! And those ponderous three-prong electric plugs! Clumsiness, I suspect, is cherished as a British resource, like muddle and heroism. It forms a code, a lock, to which one needs a key. In the end, there are recesses of England that exist only for initiates. The alien moves through pleasant green hallways and anterooms, always conscious of spike fences and polished locks. Some Duchess, if memory serves, said at the funeral of our greatest Anglophile, Henry James: "Poor Mr. James. He never quite met the right people."

June 1969

THE AMERICAN (ME) who last winter thrust upon the readers of *The Listener* his impressions of London left so much still to say that, with his homeward flight number announced for the second time and all suitcases excitedly popping their catches, he feels compelled to add a ragged postscript.

The English National Character. Such a thing must exist, yet residing in England has not brought me closer to it. Quintessential Englishmen here, with their combed tweeds and calibrated drawls, turn out to come from Hungary or Buffalo. In conjuring up for myself the essence of Britishness, I remember men encountered far from Albion. For example, I remember A.B., with his leather-patched elbows and hideously sensible shoes, who walked miles of Manhattan, unmarried, alone, unafraid, cheerful. The bookcases of his West Side room, amid the siren-loud night and the scuttle of Puerto Rican heroin pushers, breathed of Oxford—dear little blue classics, Waugh and Powell in their pastel British jackets, and poetry volumes as thin as shingles. Over a decade has rolled by; he lives in Connecticut, has four daughters, sails boats, wears the same shoes, and takes a tolerant anthropological interest in local rites like P.-T.A. meetings and three-hour cocktail hours. America amuses him. Or I think of C.D., met in Cairo, with the same bony pink forehead and strategic, disarming stammer. He had been a professor of moral philosophy; abruptly, on some road to Damascus, he had switched to Islamic architecture and mastered Turkish, Arabic, and Russian. That morning when he took me on a tour of mosques, he brushed away begging children as one would brush away the summer midges that come between you and the page of a book. Dazed by his torrent of precise information about a succession of indistinguishably murky and friable buildings, I asked him, with an American's naïve faith that the universe is a collection of Freudian symbols, the significance of the dome. I shall not soon forget the quality of his blue gaze as his tongue shifted gears. I had become a begging child. "The dome?" he at last said. "It has no significance. It is a *dome*."

Only in England would Donne's assertion that no man is an island have seemed a paradox and not a commonplace. Son of an island, each man is himself an island, secure in the certainty of his own boundaries. Things foreign break upon him like waves. He is the world's toughest traveller. What an incredible diaspora of amateur explorers, footloose second sons, dissatisfied colonels, and inquisitive ladies in hoop skirts creates and fills an Empire between Drake's accidental circumnavigation of the globe and Scott's doomed saunter toward the South Pole! The Africans called Mungo Park "the one who travels alone," and the same term would apply to Livingstone, Lawrence, Doughty, Burton. The attraction between the British and the Arabs must rest in part on a common austerity, an ability to travel light.

When did this character differentiate itself from the German character, from the Germans who cannot go anywhere except as a gang? Geographical insularity, relatively early consolidation as a nation, an underlying Celtic pawkishness, a dash of French bitters via the Normans—whatever its cause, its enforcer is the public school system that tears a lad from his mother's still-foaming breast and plunges him into ice water. To those prophets distressed by the possibility of test-tube conception and mechanized rearing, the

British national character should be a great reassurance. After the shock of his education, nothing can shake an Englishman. True, he might emerge a little woozy, and mistake a sports car for a woman, or a birch rod for a mother's kiss. But in this kingdom of bachelors, hobbyists, and pet-lovers, a little amiable confusion is wisely allowed. Recently I took my innocent children to a British movie about a man who fell in love with an otter. Our hero is first seen morosely strolling London's streets with one of those Nero haircuts that signify a queer as surely as a dangling handbag used to signify a prostitute. He spies an otter in a pet-shop window, buys it, and more or less marries it. For their honeymoon they go to remotest, most picturesque Scotland, where the otter (chummily dubbed "Mitch") eats eels in the cove. To make the abnormality of these arrangements unignorable, the plot provides a Scots lass who, though pretty as a picture and loyal to a fault, is not only denied physical satisfaction by the hero but is degradingly compelled to feign fondness for his hirsute, quadruped, amphibian little consort. Providence is not entirely a-doze, however; a burly Scots ditch-digger dispatches "Mitch" with a shovel. The man with the Nero hairdo never stops mooning, and the fade-out shows him penning the first lines of a kind of *In Memoriam* for Mitch, just like Tennyson for Hallam. Now, I suppose such a bestial film might be made in other countries, but only in England would it be given a U rating.

English Women. They are wonderful. They remind me of, in America, those tall, precocious boys of education-oriented households who are given rooms of their own and plenty of time for model airplanes. Only ample neglect brings such dreamy, disdainful poise. They are masterful flirts and have the miraculously steady hands of rhinoceros hunters and of women who apply eye make-up first thing in the morning. Shaw doubted that England deserved its great men; I wonder if it deserves its women. But what land does? "You Americans," said Lady Pynchme, "you are so romantic. You all think your little dolly is Helen of Troy." "You mean," said I, startled, "she's not? What, then, is she?" "Simply a jolly good lay," was the answer. Two things shocked me here: the dog-food ads on television and the language of the upper classes.

*

Great Men. The British seem to prefer, in leaders, rogues or men with a streak of the rogue. Henry VIII, Charles II, Nelson, Disraeli, Lloyd George, Churchill. If a rogue is unattainable, the next best thing is a nonentity. An earnest, clever man like Harold Wilson is universally distrusted.

Class Warfare. The only phenomenon in the United States comparable to the catting, at an English party, between an *arriviste* working-class intellectual and a swinging duchess is the banter, at a Manhattan conclave, between a liberated Negro and a liberalized lady of Southern birth. The hostile tension of sexual attraction. Maxim of human behavior: we want to fuck what we fear. The primordial drive toward cross-fertilization.

All those "pleases" and "thank you's," which the fresh visitor mistakes for elaborate courtesy, in fact prove, like the chirps of birds, to be warnings establishing territoriality. Those fierce fences and high brick walls, sometimes enclosing scarcely a square yard of cement. The passion for separation and class distinction leads to absurdities: a fourpenny post it costs money to delay, an A classification at the cinema that compels parents to accompany their children to puerile films.

The Englishman is under no constitutional obligation to believe that all men are created equal. The American agony is therefore scarcely intelligible, like a saint's self-flagellation viewed by an atheist.

The beheading of Charles I, the repeal of the Corn Laws: the only times an *idea* has entered English politics. A king easier to restore than foreign markets.

America is a land whose center is nowhere; England one whose center is everywhere. In America every town has its Chamber of Commerce; here every shire has been the site of a poem.

Christianity has been disposed of by giving the clergy a social status, a part in the pageant. After Trollope's novels, there can be no apocalypse. An odd number of steeples with their tips cut off, like daggers made safe for children to play with.

Americans love England. For every tulip that comes up in Hyde Park, a tourist lands at Heathrow. I have not spoken to one American resident in London, not counting my eight-year-old daughter, who wouldn't like to stay. And there are thousands, thousands of those mysterious men "in oil," with their haircuts transparently cleaving to their skulls, with their expensively dressed wives, whose very good legs and taut figures are disappointingly capped by tan, hard, rather cross faces. (What do we *do* to our women, I ask myself, that is so brutalizing? What happens to our magnificent teen-age girls, with their clothes allowances, their fuzzy sweaters, their convertibles and batons and "steadies," to give them as adults such a bitter, pushy narrowness and voices from which all melody has been squeezed?) America is uncomfortable now. On the continent fascism or anarchy reigns. Here things are civilized, cheap, pretty, educational, clean, green. Here the police and the poor are polite. The bully of the seven seas is in danger of becoming a nation of gigolos and tour guides. In the newspapers, imbalance of trade and impending bankruptcy; in the restaurants, girls dressed like houris and men with nugget cuff-links.

Living in Regent's Park. During a candle-lit dinner there comes a moment when one does not know whether a lion in the zoo, or the stomach of one's table partner, has just growled.

Notes to a Poem
(for *The New Statesman*)

My beloved land,	1
here I sit in London	2
overlooking Regent's Park	3
overlooking my new Citroën } both green,	4
exiled by success of sorts.	5
I listen to Mozart	6
in my English suit and weep,	7
remembering a Swedish film.	8
But it is you,	9
really you I think of:	10
your nothing streetcorners	11
your ugly eateries	12
your dear barbarities	13
and vacant lots	14
(Br'er Rabbit demonstrated:	15
freedom is made of brambles).	16
They say over here you are choking	17
to death on your cities and slaves,	18
but they have never smelled dry grass,	19
smoked Kools in a drugstore,	20
or pronounced a flat "a," an honest "r."	21
Don't read your reviews,	22
A☆M☆E☆R☆I☆C☆A:	23
you are the only land.	24

Line 2. At 59, Cumberland Terrace, N.W.1, where I can no longer be found. In a sense I never was found there. For nine months in England I felt like a balloon on too long a tether.

*

Lines 6–8. The Mozart would be Piano Concerto No. 21, in C Major, and the Swedish film, of course, *Elvira Madigan.* The English suit is by Cyril A. Castle, 42 Conduit Street.

Line 12. Is this fair? Many are ugly from the outside (see Nabokov, V., *Lolita,* on roadside restaurants) but inside have a certain appropriateness and comfort. Though America's "better" restaurants are stuffy and pappy compared to those you can find on almost any side-street on the Continent, our casual food—the hurried hamburger, the presto pastrami—is unsurpassed. At a formative stage of my life, at the age when young Frenchmen are being seduced by their governesses and young Englishmen by their headmasters, I was compelled to spend hours of every day in a homely luncheonette next to a small post office. There was nothing ugly about it except the griddle and the politics, possibly, of the proprietor. But then being economically dependent upon a crowd of teen-agers would bring out the reactionary in anyone. I have never been happier than in those idle hours mixed of cigarette smoke, pinball clatter, schoolgirl odors, hot dogs, and the recorded voices of Doris Day and Frankie Laine. Come to think of it, there was one period, many months long, when Petrillo had called all the musicians out on strike and the jukebox was supplied with strange recordings of humming voices and scab oddball instruments like the banjo and the sweet potato. But I ramble.

Line 14. Common in the land of my childhood. There was one beside our house, and others dotted all over the town. They were not parks, of course; they lacked daffodil beds and small mumbling men with turf edgers, but they made their own gift of space and freedom. Nobody owned them. Not even the Queen. Those vacant lots where the thistles waxed tall and we played fungo and kick-the-can were scraps of surviving Indian land, nowhereland. Compare parks: Hyde Park is a piece of royal domain graciously released to the commonweal, Central Park a wilderness of rape, torture, drug-induced trance, and savage whoops.

Lines 15–16. Br'er Rabbit is a native folk hero like Till Eulenspiegel in Scandinavia and Ra in Egypt. The reference is to his escape from Br'er Fox and other enemies; he said, Do anything you want to me, but don't, please *don't*, throw me into the briar patch. So they did. It was where he wanted to be. He had immigrated.

Line 17. "over here"—in fact the English press seemed to me to be sufficiently fair and wise in scrutinizing its alarming trans-Atlantic offspring. The poet, perhaps, is expressing an irritation with the new style of American self-criticism, a kind of Calvinism that assumes all those who hold power are damned, that nothing is relative, that rhetoric is truth, that destruction is action, and that a holiday has been declared wherein we are all excused from learning our lessons. Goodness, effectiveness, and love live among particulars; hate feeds on sweeping categories.

Line 21. Doesn't really do justice to the American accent. It is something, that accent, that happens between the throat and the heart, and has to do with bourbon, or heat, or talking to farm animals, or Jacobean pronunciation. Hearing across a London hotel lobby a silver-haired Texas businessman growl "My friend" to the fastidiously recoiling desk clerk, or eavesdropping on a bus while a pair of elderly female compatriots cackle and giggle together in their strange bubbling twang, or listening to a young American talk in that soft, rather cautious drawl (a drawl just as the American walk is, compared to the British strut, a prowl), I see those breezy big kitchens, and the lawns burnt brown by August, and the twirling sprinklers and fainting skies, and wonder at the cracked tender terrible confident emptiness of it all, and wonder how it happened so quickly, in two or three centuries, and think that we are the last new race, and that we are all inside the bus now, and there is nothing to do but ride out together the billion or so years before the sun swamps the planet.

Line 22. Advice I have often given myself.

AMOR VINCIT OMNIA
AD NAUSEAM

(After Awakening from Bruno's Dream, *by Iris Murdoch, and Falling into the Nursery)*

"Hey diddle—?"

"Diddle."

"You're thinking about God again."

It was true. She had been. The cat had been thinking about the fiddle. She had been looking at him. He had a long stringy neck and a plump brown resinous hollow body. His voice had vibrato. She had been his mistress for four years. It had been ecstatic but not extremely. She was a small-boned calico with high tender ears and a broad subdivided brow and a moist nose and an abrasive triangular tongue the color of faded drapes. She had been attracted by his voice. They had met at a benefit concert being given for churchmice. A bow had scraped him and he had sung. The cat had gone up afterwards and had rubbed herself against him and in her whiskers, so decisively parallel, he had recognized something kindred. He had sung to her of Viennese woods and she had related to him tales of her previous lovers. There had been a succession of toms behind the Bromley gasworks. They had had terrible voices. They had clawed her. They had bitten. As the palms of a religious come to be indented by stigmata so the image slowly formed itself upon her mind of a hairless toothless lover, fragile and lean. He would have resonance. He would be powerless to pounce. Her telling the fiddle all this in those days had pleased and flattered them both. That had been in those days. These were these days. All day she took a small abrasive pleasure in licking the calico fur of her chest with her triangular tongue while he failed to sing but instead leaned in the corner and almost hummed. She looked at him, his shape, his texture, his state of tension. One of her toms had been made into a tennis racquet. Perhaps that had been the attraction. She thought, I need a larger fate, warmer, kinder, yet more perilous in its dimensions, coarsely infinite yet mottled like me. Her vertically slit eyes, hoarding depths of amber, dilated at a shadow from her barnyard days as a kitten in the straw in Surrey. Something large had often been above her. Something smelling of milk. It had mooed.

The cow was in love with the moon. Throughout the first three quarters she had wept solidly, streams and streams. The moon had become full. Tears poured down her muzzle in an invincible tide.

"You are seeking," said the full moon, "to purify yourself by giving rein to impossibility."

"Oh, God—I can't—I don't—"

"Go on."

"When I first saw you, you were new—a sort of weak bent splinter of a sort of nibbled thing. How loathsome, thought I. I think even then I was protecting myself from the truth. I believe even then I deeply knew you were cheese. You began to grow. Mare Serenitatis showed, and one bluish blind mad eye, and the side of your lopsided leprous smile. At first I loved you in spite of your leprosity. Then I loved it because it was part of *you*. Then I loved the leprosity itself, and you because you were the vehicle whereby it was boldly imposed upon the cold night sky. I have never known pain so ungainsayable. I beg you, What—?"

"Jump."

"Jump?"

"*Jump*."

"Jump—"

"JUMP!"

"Imagine the moon," advised a little dog who had been eaves-dropping, "as only slightly higher than the Albert Memorial. Or consider the Albert Hall. It is round and deep and vast and many-entranced, like a woman's love. Oppositely, the Memorial is phallic. Between them there is only the Kensington Road."

The cow was jumping. Splendidly. Galaxies concentrically countervaulted. Sphere upon diamantine sphere chimed the diatonic music that mesmerized Jerusalem the Golden. Time and space were fooled at their own game. *Ab ovo*, lactogalactic. He was near, Him, ashy, awful, barren, lunar, luminous, Him. *He was Him.* They grazed. The hint of a ghost of a breath of a touch. The cow was descending. The cow was reëntering Earth's orbit. The atmosphere sizzled. The cat's eyes dilated as the shadow gathered. She felt the ponderous loved thing close and warm above her.

"Is it to be—?"

"Can't stop. Gravity."

"Oh—how *right!*" Black ecstasy flattened the cat. Her ego was, if not eliminated, expanded beyond the bounds of dissatisfaction. She was ever so utterly content. The little dog laughed to see such sport.

The fiddle cleared his long narrow throat. "Er—when you laughed like that—I, er, *twanged.* Strange to say, I love you insanely."

"Too bad," said the little dog. "I love the cow. This fact was asleep in me until I saw her jump. Christ, what an august uncanny leap that was!" He was a beagleish dog. A history of bitches had lengthened his ears and bloodied his eyes. His forepaws however had an engaging outward twist. He yapped amorously at the cow. She stepped backward into the fiddle. Her glossy hoof fragmented the ruddy wood.

"Thank you—thank you—" sobbed the fiddle. He had been excessively pampered heretofore. It was bliss to be hurt. "Of course I love *you.*" He of course meant the cow. She became haughty. Her high hot sides made a mist like fog off the Greenwich Reach. She indicated distinctly that she had consecrated herself to the memory of the cat. Or rather the cat had become the angel of death whose abiding iron presence it is the destiny of all life to worship. What else is love? Nothing else.

The little dog yowled. "I discover I was confused. It is the moon

I adore, for having permitted itself to be so splendidly jumped."
He yowled and yowled.

The moon beamed. "I love everyone. I shine on just and unjust
alike. I give to all the gift of madness. That is my charm. That is my
truth."

The fiddle lived with his wound for a fortnight, as one would
live with the shifting shades and fluorescent evanescences of an
unduly prolonged sunset. Then he found he could sing. He had
once sung. He was again singing. He sang,

> "*A questo seno, deh! vieni, idolo mio,*
> *Quanti timori, quante lacrime . . .*"

And the dish ran away with the spoon.

CEMETERIES

"PERSONAL RELATIONSHIPS must have been very strange," the tall young State Department man said to me. We were speaking of Russia in the 1930's; we had just turned from the tomb of Stalin's wife, a square stone column the height of a woman, capped by a sculptured female head with something touchingly vivid about the nape of the marble neck. Along tight paths we walked among the heavy tombstones of generals, scientists, commissars, engineers. Many bore inset photographs of the departed; a miniature iron tank adorned the tomb of a tank commander famous in World War II. A ballerina's slippers had been carved on a stone block as if casually set there, creased and warm from use. It was a sunny October Sunday years before Svetlana's memoirs had clarified the mysterious death of her mother; my escort had been describing to me the rumors of poisoning, of murderous Kremlin concubinage, of intricate betrayals.

"Even more than usual," I agreed, and tried to picture men and women rearing children, honoring parents, and seeking each other's love in a decade like a low-ceilinged subway tunnel where the lights are flickering off and the air is suffocatingly stale. I couldn't picture it, life continuing, but here was proof, here were the survivors, Soviet citizens honored in death, standing erect, in close order, in the open, enjoying the pale sunshine and late flowers of the day and season. Life-sized, with faces and trinkets, the tombs conveyed a cheerful substantial impression, as if this atheist state, like ancient Egypt, considered death a short and eminently practical voyage. I felt happy here; I am usually happy in cemeteries.

*

In Highgate Cemetery—the old, neglected section above the famous monument to Karl Marx—the English journalist asked me about oral love. He was short and middle-aged and had cleverly sensed I would like a cemetery. It was again a warm October day. Intensely green overgrowth narrowed the paths and all but smothered the tombs. Some vaults had been burst open by flourishing saplings; there was a kind of mews of tombs, an arcade of green vault doors so rusted and silted shut no Judgment Day, one felt, could ever crack them open, though there were keyholes and doorknobs and numbers and knockers, as on any genteel, if shady, street.

I discovered I had no opinion on oral love. I ventured that, all other things being equal, I was as much for it as not. In irritation the journalist tucked his notebook away and began to rail at the dead. Their pretensions to immortality enraged him. He rattled at the door of a grenadiers colonel interred in 1903 and invited me, where vandals had smashed a grating, to peer in and see how a burrowing creature, a rat or badger, had penetrated the coffin, adding sawdust to the rubble of bricks and powdered mortar. The pious mottoes—"From strength to strength in the everlasting," "Love shines yet more brightly above"—abraded against my escort like supercilious assertions at a party where he was socially insecure. And indeed he came, with his cleverness, from a Midlands working-class family, and the tombs represented Victorian gentry. "The fools!" he shouted. "'Honor perisheth never.' Well, Mr. Nevil Cunninghame-Wright Esq., O.M., M.B.E., it bloody well has!" He kicked at the black drift of rustflakes and leafmold clogging the Cunninghame-Wright portal, and read the next motto. "'Earth's shadows testify to radiance eternal.' Oh, my buggering God! Oh, my dear old Eustace Pickering, you poor old sodden mouse-nest of agglutinated bones, how do you like your radiance eternal now?"

He was most affronted by the immense mausoleum of a man called Julius Beer. Chinks in its cupola had admitted generations of pigeons; their excrement, feathers, and corpses covered the marble floor. The mosaic murals of pre-Raphaelite angels were clouded with lime. The journalist, when I had satisfied his desire that I look in, put his mouth against the crusty grating and shouted,

"*Hooh!*" Nothing happened. He bellowed louder, "HOOH!" Evidently, the pigeons were supposed to fly out. He squinted into the depths of the befouled and forgotten memorial. "Damn," he said. "I think they've cleaned it up a bit." He backed off, and his face brightened. "But can you catch that smell, that evil stench? It's a pigeon Dachau. You ass, Julius, you absolutely silly puffed-up old capitalist ass, you were so full of yourself we don't even know what you *did!*" It was true; no identification, not even dates, qualified the high carved name of Julius Beer, the emperor of doveshit.

The cemetery had been private and fashionable. An outward-spreading cypress, now obscured by deciduous trees that had grown up, was to have been the center of a symmetrical system of vault lanes and individual tombs. One tomb, of a "menagerist," had a smiling lion carved upon it. Deep in the woods—elm and oak and ailanthus that had taken root, perhaps, at the outset of World War II—a stone angel lifted her weather-blurred face, vague as Anglican theology, toward green leaves. We were far from the urban compactness of Novodyevichi Cemetery. I was impressed by England's tropical luxuriance; the force so decisively tamed in the parks was here, untended, shattering marble and swallowing crypts whole. Yet I felt that these genteel 19th-century dead, who to judge from the novels about them had loved a country wildness, were not as overthrown as my escort believed. They were merely immersed, much as the living are immersed. A wild sapling grafts onto the spirit no less snugly than a toy tank.

Both of my escorts—the State Department man tacitly, obliquely; the journalist boisterously, indignantly—disapproved of the dead, implying that they were still alive. A cemetery, which like a golf course bestows the gift of space, also touches us with the excitement, the generalized friction, of a party.

The Chemin du Puy steeply climbed the hill from Antibes and on the long gradual downslope, before the farmhouse with the sign MÉCHANTS CHIENS, passed a cemetery of bright plaster, where things twirled to discourage birds. Though lonesome, I never dared enter; the dead were speaking French.

In Mayrhofen, at Christmas, candles glowed and guttered in the snow, before strict upright stones of black marble. The faces of

Tyrolean burghers alternated with that of an anguished Jesus. *Hier ruhen in Gott*, the stones said.

And in Peredelkino, in the village graveyard where Pasternak is buried, scrolling iron crosses spoke of an Orthodox Russia where burial took place in springtime, and metal echoed the burgeoning shape of the flowers.

In Prague, the tombstones of the Jewish cemetery were squeezed together like cards, conjuring up a jumble of bodies underneath. Visitors left pebbles on them instead of flowers. Was it an ancient custom, or something forced upon the Jews by Hitler? A kind of chapel here had walls gray with the names, six hundred thousand of them, of Jews whose death-dates were 1943, 1944, 1945. Years whose smoke permanently stained the ceiling of Heaven.

And the mass graves of the Siege dead near Leningrad, acres of hummocks, like giant bulb beds in winter, marked with stone tablets 1941, 1942, 1943.

And the Pyramids, and the gaily painted corridors leading into the robbed chambers of Ramses, and the even gayer cells of the nobles, into which light is shuttled by a set of mirrors held by silent brown guides. In Cairo, the necropolis is inhabited by children and beggars, and is a slum.

The Long Island necropolis seen from an airplane: a pegboard that abruptly yields to the equally regular avenues of the living, each gray rooftop companioned by a green backyard pool, like a wide-awake eye.

Also from the air, descending I think into Cleveland, I saw a little triangular family cemetery, precious soil spared from the corner of a field, like the book page whose corner I had turned down to mark my place.

And the stingy clusters of markers, too many of them children, in rocky abandoned places once farmed, like Star Island off Portsmouth, or the mountainsides of Vermont north of Montpelier.

In Marigot, on St. Martin's, one noon, my wife and I walked a mile to a restaurant that was closed, along the shimmering white road, and came back along the beach to cool our feet, and came to a cemetery that was being nibbled away by the sea. There were no signs of an attempt to halt the gentle erosion; one tombstone was teetering, another had fallen upside down, and fragments of a third were being washed and ground into sand. We went up into the cemetery, and there, amid the French *colons* and the tessellated patterns suggestive of voodoo and the conch-shell borders and the paper flowers and the real flowers that looked like paper, my wife, starved and weary, sat on a crypt and dried her feet with her bandana and put on her shoes. I took her picture; I have the slide.

Years before, when we were at college, a girl whose major was biology and whose hobby was fungi used to make me bicycle with her to ancient burying-grounds in Cambridge and Concord. There, on the tipping old Puritan slate tombstones half sunk in the earth and sometimes wearing artfully shaped weatherproof hats of lead, she would show me lichen, in a surprising variety of colors, each round specimen, scarcely thicker than a stain, somehow an individual creature or, rather, two creatures—a fungus living symbiotically with an alga. Whitish, brownish, bluish, the lichens enforced their circles upon the incised, uniquely graceful Puritan lettering and the winged skulls which, as the 17th century softened into the 19th, became mere angels, with human faces. She was, perhaps because she majored in biology, wonderful at sex—talk of oral love!—and the lichen, the winged skulls, the sweaty ache in my calves from bicycling, and her plump cleavage as she bent low for a determined inspection and scraping all merged in a confused lazy anticipation of our return and my reward, her round mouth. Cemeteries, where women make themselves at home, are in one sense dormitories, rows of beds.

"But the *view* is so lovely," my mother said to me. We were standing on the family burial plot, in Pennsylvania. Around us, and sloping down the hill, were the red sandstone markers of planted farmers, named and dated in the innocent rectangular lettering that used to be on patent-medicine labels. My grandfather's stone, rough-hewn granite with the family name carved in the form of bent branches, did not seem very much like him. My grandmother's Christian name, cut below his, was longer and, characteristically, dominated while taking the subservient position. Elsewhere on the plot were his parents, and great-aunts and uncles I had met only at spicy-smelling funerals in my remotest childhood.

My mother paced off two yards, saying, "Here's Daddy and me. See how much room is left?"

"But she"—I didn't have to name my wife—"has never *lived* here." I was again a child at one of those dreaded family gatherings on dark holiday afternoons—awkward and stuffed and suffocating under the constant need for tact. Only in Pennsylvania, among my kin, am I pressured into such difficult dance-steps of evasion and placation. Every buried coffin was a potential hurt feeling. I tried a perky sideways jig, hopefully humorous, and added, "And the children would feel crowded and keep everybody awake."

She turned her face and gazed downward at the view—a lush valley, a whitewashed farmhouse, a straggling orchard, and curved sections of the highway leading to the city whose glistening tip, a television relay, could just be glimpsed five ridges in the distance. She had expected my evasion—she could hardly have expected me to pace off my six feet greedily and plant stakes—but had needed to bring me to it, to breast my refusal and the consequence that, upon receiving her and my father, the plot would be closed, would cease to be a working piece of land. Why is it that nothing that happens to me is as real as these dramas that my mother arranges around herself, like Titania calling Peaseblossom and Mustardseed from the air? Why is it that everyone else lacks the sanguine, corporeal, anguished reality of these farmers, these people of red sandstone? When was Pennsylvania an ocean, to lay down all this gritty rock, that stains your palms pink when you lift it?

Placatory, I agreed, "The view *is* lovely."

"Think of poor Daddy," she said, turning away, Mustardseed dismissed. "He has no sense of landscape. He says he wants to be buried under a sidewalk."

The cemetery of the town where I live, like many, has climbed a hill, and the newest graves are on the top, arranged along ample smooth roadways of asphalt. Some friends of ours have buried children here. But I had stayed away until it was time to teach my son to ride a bicycle. It is safe; on weekdays few cars visit the fresh graves, with their plastic-potted morning glories and exotic metal badges from veterans' organizations. The stones are marble, modernly glossy and simple, though I suppose that time will eventually reveal them as another fashion, dated and quaint. Now, the sod is still raw, the sutures of turf are unhealed, the earth still humped, the wreaths scarcely withered. Sometimes we see, my son and I, the strained murmurous breakup of a ceremony, or a woman in mourning emerge from an automobile and kneel, or stand nonplussed, as in a social gap. I remember my grandfather's funeral, the hurried cross of sand the minister drew on the coffin lid, the whine of the lowering straps, the lengthening, cleanly cut sides of clay, the thought of air, the lack of air forever in the close dark space lined with pink satin, the foreverness, the towering foreverness—it does not bear thinking about, it is too heavy, like my son's body as he wobbles away from me on his bicycle. "Keep moving," I shout, the words turning chalky in my mouth, as they tend to do when I seek to give instruction—"the essence of the process is to keep moving!"

LETTER FROM ANGUILLA

February 1968

UNTIL ITS REVOLUTION last summer, Anguilla was one of the most obscure islands in the Caribbean. A long, low coral formation of thirty-four square miles, it seems from the air a cloud shadow, or a shadow image of St. Martin, which lies twelve miles to the south and whose green mountains loom dramatically in the view from Anguilla. Whereas from St. Martin, Anguilla, at its highest elevation scarcely two hundred feet above sea level, can easily be overlooked. It is even obscure who named it "Eel"—the Spaniards, who may have cruised close enough under Columbus to call it *Anguila*, or the French, who, under Captain René Laudonnière in

1564, definitely called there, en route to Florida from Dominica, and may have bestowed the appellation *L'Anguille*. Both nations left this modest island to the British to colonize. In 1609, a Captain Harcourt, after touching at Nevis, "disembogued" on the north side of Anguilla, where "I think never Englishmen disembogued before us." Southey's history of the West Indies records under the year 1650, "The island of Anguilla, so called from its snake-like form, is said to have been discovered and colonized by the English this year; it was filled with alligators and other noxious animals, but the soil was good for raising tobacco and corn, and the cattle imported multiplied very fast. It was not colonized under any public encouragement; each planter laboured for himself, and the island was frequently plundered by marauders."

The lack of external encouragement sounds a constant note in Anguilla's history. In 1707, Captain Thomas Bolton and nine other survivors of a sunken ship, after thirty-one days adrift in a small boat, were cast up at Long Bay. His journal acknowledges that "the People were very kind to us"—"The Islanders very much bewail'd our Condition, and were ready to fight among themselves, in shewing their Eagerness to welcome us to their Houses"—but complains of their stay that "the worst was, we could not have any News from other Islands; this being an Island of little Trade, and no Shipping." J. Oldmixon's *The British Empire in America* (second edition, 1741) states that in Anguilla people lived "without Government or Religion, having no Minister nor Governor, no Magistrates, no Law, and no Property worth keeping," and adds that they "live poorly, and we might say miserably, if they were not contented." In 1825, when Henry Nelson Coleridge visited Anguilla, the people seemed "a good sort of folks, though they have been living for a long time in a curious state of suspended civilization. They acknowledge the English laws, but the climate is said to induce fits of drowsiness on them, during which Justice sleepeth, and Execution tarrieth." In 1920, Mrs. Katharine Janet Burdon, in *A Handbook of St. Kitts-Nevis*, wrote, "Strangers are so rarely seen that the last one who visited Anguilla, in 1917, an enterprising and eminent official from a neighbouring British Colony, was taken for a German spy, and greatly to his amusement was followed by the whole police force of the Island until he had presented his credentials to the Magistrate." And in 1960, when my wife, three children, and I lived for five weeks in Sandy Ground, we had the pleasure of being, for intervals, the entire tourist population of the island. I will not forget an evening spent with Mr. Vincent Lake —one of Anguilla's leading citizens, the scion of a family whose holdings in island land and cargo-carrying sloops amounted to a fortune—in which I found myself describing to him, as if to a latter-day Miranda, such commonplace wonders of the Western world as four-lane highways and skyscrapers and neon lights. He had never seen them even in a movie. In those days, when Anguilla was a British colony, a lonely generator supplied power to a telephone line serving fourteen users, most of them island officials. There was also a Social Center at the East End, with electric lights and a jukebox. Later that year, in September, the eye of Hurricane Donna passed directly over Anguilla. Miss Selma Buchanan wrote my wife, "Mrs you can only imagin what a time we had that night. . . . The Carty's house half is gone and the Cocial Centre at the east end is gone there are only two school standing on island church to flew off every boat sink in the harbour so many big trees fell what a sight to see little Anguilla." In 1968, returning, we find that the homes destroyed by Donna have been replaced, but the telephone line has not been reactivated.

Henry Nelson Coleridge's 1825 description still serves:

> Anguilla presents a very singular appearance for a West Indian island. A little wall of cliff of some forty feet in height generally rises from the beach, and when you have mounted this, the whole country lies before you, gently sloping inwards in a concave form, and sliding away, as it were, to the south where the land is only just above the level of the sea. . . . Seven-tenths of the country are entirely uncultivated; in some parts a few coppices, but more commonly a pretty species of myrtle called by the negros maiden-berry, seems to cover the whole soil: the roads are level grassy tracks over which it is most delightful to ride, and the houses and huts of the inhabitants are scattered about in so picturesque a manner that I was put in mind of many similar scenes in Kent and Devonshire. Indeed there were scarcely any of the usual features of West Indian landscape visible; neither of those prominent ones, the lively wind-

mill or the columnar palm, was to be seen, and there was a rusticity, a pastoral character on the face of the land, its roads and its vegetation, which is the exact antipode of large plantations of sugar.

The roads, at least to the driver of a rented jeep, are now quite undelightful puddings of potholes and coral protrusions, and the scanty crops of cotton and yams and sisal seem to occupy rather less than three-tenths of the soil, and a certain pastel Los Angeles look is creeping into Kent and Devonshire, but the dominant impression, of scattered homes and no windmills, remains to tell the tale: Anguilla was but lightly involved in the sugar economy. Captain Bolton in 1707, over sixty years after cultivation of sugarcane had been introduced into Barbados and the shift from tobacco to sugar had swept the Leeward Islands, found on Anguilla "2 or 300 English" engaged in the planting of tobacco, "which is highly esteem'd." Anguilla was too rocky and dry for the great mechanized plantations the sugar industry required, and hence was exempted from the full force of the social transformation whereby communities of white planter-proprietors gave way to feudal estates supporting vast slave populations. Anguilla has no equivalent of the slums of St. John's on Antigua or Basseterre on St. Kitts. As drought, piratical raids, and the abolition of slavery (in 1834) thinned the ranks of the white settlers, the ungrateful land fell by default to the Negro inhabitants. By 1847, of about twenty sugar estates once under cultivation, only three or four survived. Mrs. Burdon states that as of 1911 the population consisted "almost exclusively of peasant proprietors." She goes on, "Anguillans are a particularly sturdy, independent, intelligent type, their high character being developed by the hard school of nature in which they live, and by the system of proprietorship which has existed for generations." The island, she notes, is free of tropical diseases to a unique degree, in part because "the people of Anguilla, differing from the usual habits of the West Indian negro, build their houses some distance apart."

So nature, in neglecting Anguilla, has not been entirely unkind; nor has the neglect been total. There is good fishing. There are pockets of fertile soil, and ample pasturage for goats and sheep. Ancient wells supposedly dug by the Caribs provide fresh water for those who do not have private cisterns. The harvest of salt from the large, diked saltponds behind Sandy Ground, a peculiar industry established in the early 1800's, still goes on, generating an annual burst of employment, mostly for women. The export of Sea Island cotton, a silky, long-fiber variety used in underwear, produced for a time thousands of pounds in annual revenue and financed the construction of the island's own ginnery—now defunct. And there exists a native tradition of shipbuilding; elegant all-wood hulls, the keel timbers shaped from branched tree trunks, dot the beaches, though work on them proceeds imperceptibly, at about the speed of coral formation. Fundamentally the economy runs by remittance. Anguillan men emigrate to work in the cane fields of Jamaica, or the oil refineries of Curaçao and Aruba, or the hotels and construction crews of St. Thomas. Though the men are gone for years, money returns regularly, and across the island pleasant and sturdy houses of imported cement block slowly rise. There are few tarpaper shacks; there is no begging. Literacy is a relatively high 70 per cent. A young American resident on Anguilla in recent months analyzes last summer's upheaval as a middle-class revolution—Anguilla's refusal to join the Socialist revolution being perpetrated in Basseterre by the Labor government of Robert Bradshaw. Bradshaw is the walrus-mustachioed, dictatorial premier of the St. Kitts–Nevis–Anguilla state to which Britain granted local self-government on February 27, 1967. St. Kitts and Nevis have long been one-crop sugar islands, and the sugar depression has created problems unknown in perennially depressed Anguilla, including a drastic split between the white proprietorial class and the black laborers, and the start of political terrorism. Last August, an unnamed Anguillan was quoted in the *Times* as saying, "St. Kitts is a millstone around our necks."

Anguilla's association with St. Kitts (St. Christopher) has always been tenuous. St. Kitts is the nearest British island, but lies seventy miles to the south, beyond St. Martin/Sint Maarten (French and Dutch), St. Bart's (French), and Saba and Sint Eustatius (both Dutch). When, in 1796, a French force invaded Anguilla under orders to exterminate the English inhabitants (legend says the fishermen of Anguilla loaded their cannon with lead seine weights), help arrived not from St. Kitts but from more distant Antigua, in the form of the man-of-war *Lapwing;* the St. Kittians,

to be fair, did address to the *Lapwing* commander a letter of thanks
for his rescue of a "sister colony." In Anguilla, the laws lay dor-
mant for want of a magistrate, and not until after 1800 did the
Anguillans send a representative to the St. Kitts legislature. In lieu
of anarchy, the Anglican vestry ruled the island, headed by the
parson and the warden; until very recently, the manager of the
island's rather minimal affairs has borne the proud title of Warden.
The West Indian archives contain more than one instance of a
colonial official's shirking and bemoaning his assignment to Anguilla. "Indeed such an assignment," one penned in 1842, "is but
poor reward for a life devoted to the Service of the Crown." In
1871, when the Federal Colony of the Leeward Islands, with its
capital in Antigua, was created by Parliament, Anguilla expressed
a desire not to be lumped with St. Kitts, but Governor Benjamin
Pine, already sufficiently harassed by a plethora of presidencies
under his government, ignored the request. During the Second
World War, when St. Martin was a Vichy fuelling station for
German submarines, American soldiers built an airstrip on Anguilla
and impressed the Anguillans so favorably that as late as 1960
wistful hopes of an American takeover were still alive. One rumor
claimed that the United States had offered to forgive Great Britain
her entire lend-lease debt in exchange for Anguilla, and had been
refused. Anguilla's poor-sister status within the Leewards worsened
after the St. Kitts–Nevis–Anguilla state was granted home rule.
Anecdotes of the short shrift that Anguilla thereafter received
from the Bradshaw government have the orotund ring of legend.
For instance, when Great Britain requisitioned money for a much-
needed pier on Anguilla, where anything bigger than a sack of
wheat must be tediously rafted in, the St. Kitts government took the
money and built the pier on its own island, christening it, deadpan,
Anguilla Pier. School supplies and salaries for Anguillans were held
up. Anguillan public-works projects—such as the planting of
hundreds of unwired telephone poles along the roads—were carried forward with labor brought from St. Kitts. "Anguilla men go
all over the islands looking for work," our taxi-driver said, gestur-
ing toward these poles. "Anguilla men know enough to build big
boats and plant a sixty-foot mast when the boats sit in the water,
but Anguilla men don't know enough to dig a hole." The St.

Kittian policemen on Anguilla were not beloved. In March of 1967, their precipitate use of tear gas turned into a riot an intended demonstration at a potentially benign gathering—the contest to choose a Miss Anguilla to compete for the title of Miss Statehood. It is a parable of the slenderness of St. Kitts–Anguilla ties that when the revolution came, on May 30th last year, it consisted simply of rounding up the seventeen St. Kitts policemen, putting them into a boat, and pushing them out to sea.

Though everyone, including the Anguillans themselves, emphasizes the revolution's comic-opera episodes, bloodshed was threatened, and there was no going back. On June 11th, gunmen attacked police headquarters in Basseterre; earlier that spring, fifty shots had been fired into the lodgings of a Warden sent from St. Kitts. On June 16th, Peter Adams, who had been Anguilla's representative in the state legislature, proposed that the United States make Anguilla an American territory. His proposal was ignored in Washington. On July 11th, a popular referendum showed 1,813 to 5 for independence; Peter Adams was chosen president and asked for talks with President Johnson. Our President's response, if any, did not make the newspapers. On August 1st, under the supervision of a Caribbean Commonwealth Conference in Barbados, a reconciliation was worked out whereby Anguilla ended its secession and Bradshaw promised greatly increased financial aid. On August 4th, Anguilla deposed Peter Adams and installed as president Mr. Ronald Webster, a member of the Seventh-Day Adventist Church, one of the wealthiest men on the island, and Adams' Minister of Interior. Two days later, Jeremiah Gumbs went to the United Nations and told reporters, "The people are very aware about not losing control of their land. . . . We want to keep the island the way God made it." By the middle of August, the frigate *Lynx*, with a contingent of British Marines, moored off Blowing Point but was warned by Webster that blood would flow if a landing was attempted. (One strange tale from this period of crisis is that some Marines did land, distributed candy to the children who had gathered, and were seen off by a band playing "God Save the Queen.") By the end of August, Jamaica had refused to condone an expeditionary force from various islands that would put down the rebellion, and it became clear that Bradshaw lacked the military muscle to impose his will. On August 29th, the U.N. hearing ended, with no action advised, and a nebulous, nervous peace prevailed. Even now, an incoming tourist is sternly questioned as to what his "mission" might be, and one can see on the dirt runway of the airfield barrels and rolls of barbed wire to obstruct the landing of any planes other than the two-engine Aztecs that run daily shuttles to St. Martin and St. Thomas. Our first evening here, a British pleasure craft lowered a few female swimmers into Rendezvous Bay, and a carload of Anguillan militia rushed to investigate the invasion. Without doubt, Anguilla is under economic siege; the Bradshaw government has cut off even the island doctor's salary, and the schools and public services are kept going by infusions of private money, including tens of thousands of dollars from the pocket of Ronald Webster himself. A young man held on suspicion of murder languishes in the island's jail; not only is there no magistrate to hear his case but St. Kitts, which has the facilities to test the murder weapon for fingerprints, both refuses to do so and refuses to let the gun be examined on another island. The suspect's story is typically bizarre for these bewitched times: he was walking with one hand on a girl and the other on his bicycle when suddenly she fell down dead, a bullet in her heart.

Anguilla is currently run by a seven-man council, headed by Webster, that was elected on October 17th. The island's international status is suspended for a year under the so-called Interim Agreement forged in December by a delegation of two British Members of Parliament; under the agreement, the Anguillan government supposedly accepts the advice and counsel of a Parliamentary mission headed by Mr. Tony Lee, a distinguished veteran of the British Colonial Service and a graduate of the hard schools of Kenya and Aden. Mr. Lee, an intelligent, tall, faintly corpulent Englishman of the breed whose diffident persistence once imposed British order on a quarter of the globe, is possibly the most popular man on Anguilla. "NO COMMUNISM—NO GANGSTERISM!" proclaims a legend painted on a building next to the old Methodist church on Road Hill. "WE WANT BRITISH RULE AND DEMOCRACY. GIVE US BRITAIN!" After its initial appeal to the United States, Anguilla has placed its hopes for stability and protection upon the power that elsewhere in the world is liquidating the last scraps of its empire.

Lee's task is not easy, nor is his role clear. Even if Great Britain wished to grant Anguilla perfect independence, it is powerless to do so, for by the terms of the creation of the St. Kitts–Nevis–Anguilla state it abdicated all control over the state's internal affairs, which include secession. Lee is present on Bradshaw's sufferance as well as on Webster's, and his principal leverage in local affairs seems to be the threat to leave. As he drives about the island in his Morris Mini, the quality of the salutes he receives suggests that, in the eyes at least of the older Anguillans, who have lived most of their lives under the scarcely palpable rule of an appointed white Warden, Lee is the new Warden. But in fact Anguilla's destiny rests in the hands of Anguillans, and Lee's task may be to persuade them to take their destiny seriously.

A population of six thousand is the size of a small American town. Like small-town politics everywhere, Anguillan politics appears to an outsider an inscrutable tangle of personalities, old grudges, and bad habits. The island, for instance, is geographically divided into the East End and the West End, and white and mulatto East Enders dominated the drive for independence. Is this resented? Anguilla surely is one of the most color-blind places left in an increasingly racist world, but an egalitarian tolerance bred by centuries of colonial obscurity may well be strained by the opportunities and adversities of independence. And what of nepotism, where every third person is named Rey, Richardson, or Gumbs? We attended a political rally on the cricket field and heard a young man called Atlin Harrigan try to defend, under some vicious badgering, his newspaper, the *Beacon*, which had asked for new elections and an expanded council, and had implied graft and log-rolling in the present council. "I am in a fearful bind," he said into the microphone, "for if I print half of what I know, I fear Bradshaw will use it to prove that Anguillans cannot govern themselves." In turn, a council member, Mr. Wallace Rey, rose up and claimed that it was highly improper for the *Beacon* to be printed on the Anglican Church's duplicator. This demand for separation of church and state strikes a rather new note on an island governed for generations as an adjunct of the Anglican Church, and may not be unrelated to the whiteness of the present rector. Although the crowd of several hundred acted much like any bored and amused small-town rally, two old ladies came to blows beneath a mahogany tree, and some of the speakers, including an urbane refugee from one of Bradshaw's jails, seemed all too expertly demagogic. When the council secretary spoke suavely of the council's right to secret discussion and of its wisdom of choice as to what "the people" should know, I myself, as children scampered around the mustered trucks in the tropic twilight, felt chilled by a whisper of Fascism. The crowd seemed puzzled and somewhat cynical, and voiced unity only at the mention of the hated name of Bradshaw, a bogey whose usefulness cannot be infinite.

The Anguillan national flag, designed by an American firm, shows three orange dolphins in a circle on a white field above a stripe of sea blue. The dolphins seem to be chasing each other

around and around. If one of them is Tony Lee, the representative of empire, of Britain's desire to salvage a colony she shaped, and another is Ronald Webster, the representative of independence, of Anguilla's honorable heritage of self-reliance, the third might be Jeremiah Gumbs, the representative of enterprise, which can eat up the other two. Mr. Gumbs, an energetic, bearish man who had visited the island shortly before we arrived, was enterprising enough to leave Anguilla as a youth (he was born in 1913) and become a successful fuel-oil dealer in Edison, New Jersey. It was Jere Gumbs who hired as advocate and adviser the Harvard Law School professor Roger Fisher and, with him, took Anguilla's case to the U.N. Assembly's Special Committee on Colonialism. He owns the island's only passably modern hotel, the Rendezvous Bay, which his sister Beatrice runs in a breezy American style. Jere

Gumbs has also recently bought from the Lake family Dog Island, an uninhabited but sizable satellite island, where, rumor goes, he would like to construct a convalescent home. It was Jere Gumbs who, on his flying visit, restored to workability two of the five St. Kittian bulldozers confiscated in the revolution; it was also Jere Gumbs who arranged to rent these same bulldozers, at a price thought by some to be nominal, from the public-works department for the purpose of excavating a large cistern at his own hotel.

Anguilla needs but distrusts enterprise. A new resident in the community of nations is apparently subjected to a Welcome Wagon of international opportunists: after the American flag designers and the Swiss stamp printers, come the offers to float in a gambling casino, to set up a quickie-divorce and/or abortion haven, intermixed with a trickle of utopian anarchists and political scientists preparing studies of the mini-state. Foremost among the latter has been Dr. Leopold Kohr, of the University of Puerto Rico; an admirer of the Pennsylvania Amish, Dr. Kohr advocates a world of self-sufficient agricultural villages. A San Francisco group interested in copping out of the 20th-century nexus of *Realpolitik* was actively fascinated by Anguilla last summer; they placed in *The New York Times* a slick full-page ad written by one of their number, Mr. Howard Gossage, an advertising man, asserting that Anguilla "does not want to become a nation of busboys" and impetuously offering honorary citizenships at a hundred dollars a head. More recently, a young hippie couple, penniless but equipped with a shotgun and several cameras, set up a tent on the beach near Shaddick Point and begged food from a wealthy American woman who has built a home there; after several weeks of this idyll, they were expelled back to St. Martin. Anguilla has thus far defended herself from these crude assaults, but any defense of virginity runs the risk of altogether succeeding. "ANGUILLA has been DELIBERATELY RETARDED," reads a sign nailed up on a cement-block shed near Rendezvous Bay, and the question that hovers over the island's scruffy pastures and empty beaches and minuscule taverns named Amity and Sea View and Lonely Valley and United Nation is how to bring Anguilla into the present without destroying the charm and virtue of its tardiness.

Tony Lee, in the interim year of grace, would like to see the roads improved and telephone service inaugurated, and has called in a United Nations planner to survey the island. He described to me the Christmas holidays, when over two thousand Anguillan men returned from St. Thomas and other unretarded islands, and dances were held all over Anguilla; "It's their place, you see; there aren't any big hotels they aren't allowed into. I don't know, it may be airy-fairy of me, but I think it would be nice somehow, if one could, to keep it, you know, their place." Ronald Webster, a tea-colored man with the trim, stiff carriage of a self-taught school-teacher, speaks of ten or more small hotels, one at each beach, and of Anguilla's supporting a population larger than that of St. Thomas. He gives native industry priority over the tourist trade, but though there is a young furniture factory, and an American has set up a tiny shop for the manufacture of trinket jewelry, and two indigenous airlines are operating (despite a mysterious case of arson that grounded one plane), it is difficult to imagine any appreciable industry that would not have to import all its raw materials—to an island without a pier. Nor is the limbo status of the present government, while Bradshaw in Basseterre waits for Anguilla to prove unviable, likely to attract much investment capital. Americans hoping to acquire a cheap spot in the sun will be discouraged by the high value that the "peasant proprietors" place on their land. "This is paradise," Ronald Webster said to me, with a quick, wicked smile, "and paradise is not cheap." What Jeremiah Gumbs thought was expressed by the roaring and growling of the bulldozers as they slowly scraped a long hole in the coral earth beside our room at the Rendezvous Bay Hotel. By the end of a week, one bulldozer had sprung a tread and, after futile attempts to lift it with an automobile jack, stood mired in the pit it had dug. On the other bulldozer, one of the two cables supporting the front blade had snapped. Ronald Webster thought that the first dozer had merely lost a pin; so the concern of the Anguilla Department of Public Works, and of a displeased Tony Lee, and, behind him, of the British government (two British radio operators were daily exchanging messages with Whitehall), and, behind *that*, of the brooding American hemispherical over-presence on guard against a mini-Cuba, all danced for the moment on a pin lost in the dust.

And meanwhile the patient goats are tethered to the bushes of maiden-berry, and the sun beats down, and the Methodist churches thrive, and any tourist willing to jet from the mainland to St. Martin and stay overnight in Marigot or Philipsburg and take the next morning's more-or-less-ten-o'clock, ten-minute, five-dollar flight to Anguilla's dollhouse airport can experience, as did I and my wife, the aboriginal luxury of walking barefoot along miles of soft white coral sand and encountering no footprint but one's own of the day before. It will not last forever. Transistor radios are creeping into Anguilla, conveying the Top Forty hits in the U.S.A. by way of Radio Antilles in Montserrat, and a few Americans and an Irish airline pilot have built permanent vacation homes, and Anguillans who travel, like Mr. Émile Gumbs, say that now strangers nod knowingly when told you are from Anguilla: they have heard of it. Progress will come—these are the finest undeveloped beaches in the Caribbean—but slowly, resisted, one feels, by the instincts of the Anguillans themselves. The crowd at the political rally make a happy, erect impression in their Sunday suits and chiffon dresses, with an occasional miniskirt and a few motorcyclists—the impression of a colored population free, for this interim, of anger and shame. In the West Indies as a whole, these "islands in the sun" whose history is so scored with slaughter (the first modern genocide was committed by the Spaniards on the Arawaks), with the oppression of slaves and the rebellions of slaves, with piracy and massacre and cruelty—with the rage, in short, that seems to afflict Europeans whenever they leave their own ugly climate—one now feels a benevolent remove from world conflicts and a precious possibility: the possibility that blacks, torn as slaves from their African tribes and roughly implanted with Western languages and traditions, can now construct a fresh society. One goes to the Caribbean not only for the sun but for a tone—the tone of a culture based upon negritude but as different from that of the American Negro as the blues and the desperate joy of jazz are from calypso wit and the translucent pealing of the steel band. The large number of slave revolts in the islands, as opposed to their remarkable rareness on the North American continent, is an index of how much more demoralizing our subjugation was, and how much more durable its bad effects will be. Integration in the United States must be primarily an act of the white majority; in the Caribbean, where the majority is black, integration feels closer. A backwater like Anguilla, where black and white settlers were bound together in a fraternity of poverty, seems to offer a chance of skipping several nightmare chapters of race relations and of moving rather promptly into the polyracial future.

Various quotations occur to me as I wonder about Anguilla's chances for independent survival. One of the Englishmen attached to the Parliamentary mission referred to the Anguillans as "the poor dears," and another, as we lay on the beach, in answer to my question as to what St. Kitts was like, answered, with a wave that included the immaculate beach and the turqoise sea, " 'Bout like this. A bloody 'ole." Then there is a quote from Postlethwayt's 18th-century *Dictionary of Commerce* that says, "Every man being a kind of sovereign in his own family . . . no other government there is in Anguilla." And a sentence by Aldous Huxley: "The worst enemy of life, freedom, and the common decencies is total anarchy; their second worst enemy is total efficiency." Our taxi-driver, whose name is Charlie Gumbs and who has sent his two sons to college, again gestures at the telephone poles as he drives us back to the airport. "We're waiting for them to grow branches to hang the wires from." We pass the three other earthmovers, bright yellow and motionless, that were lengthening the airstrip before the revolution. "Men from St. Kitts bring them in, have to run them themselves; Anguilla men put sixty-foot masts on boats in the water, but they don't know how to run bulldozers." He turns and grins, apparently oblivious of the fact that these machines are derelict and that the two back at the hotel are out of repair again. "Well, now we show them Anguilla men know how to run bull-dozers."

P.S.

September 1974

A YEAR AND A MONTH after the visit to Anguilla that prompted my letter, banner headlines announced to me in London that Great Britain had invaded little Anguilla: early in the morning of March

19, 1969, two frigates landed three hundred fifteen Red Devil paratroopers, forty Marines, and forty-nine London policemen, in response to a supposed insult delivered to William Whitlock, Parliamentary Under-Secretary of State for Foreign and Commonwealth Affairs, by an unruly Anguillan mob six days before. This Lilliputian exercise of gunboat diplomacy (the Anguillans, foreseeing the invasion, had buried all their guns, and not one person was injured) attracted derisive world attention and terminated Anguilla's claim to being "one of the most obscure islands in the Caribbean." Also terminated were whatever proprietary feelings I had had for her. The full Anguilla story is told, thoroughly but all too facetiously, by Donald E. Westlake, in his *Under an English Heaven* (Doubleday, 1972). The uneasy interim condition prevailing in early 1968 persisted through the year, while various raffish Americans infiltrated advice into Ronald Webster's ear and the young Anguillans of the "Defence Force" that had replaced the St. Kittian policemen grew to resemble licensed hoodlums. Our friend Tony Lee, Mr. Westlake feels, proved too airy-fairy for his responsibilities as Our Man on Anguilla, and failed as the Commissioner installed by the invasion forces. Certainly he looked very tired the last time we saw him, on page 13 of the March 23, 1969, London Sunday *Times*, beside the wrap-up headline, "BRUTE FARCE AND IGNORANCE." The British press, generally anti-Vietnam, was stridently unsympathetic with their own government's interventionism. "This 'wag the flag and flog the wog' farce," the *Evening News* termed it, and the *Times* drew the conclusion that "a British Government is still capable of replaying Suez not as tragedy but as farce."

Farce or no, reinstatement to the status of an English colony was just what the Anguillans wanted, and under subsequent Commissioners the Royal Engineers busied themselves, according to Westlake, "building schools, paving roads, starting an electrification program, studying the water table, and generally tidying up the effects of the previous three hundred years of neglect." The last of them left, to kudos from the *Beacon*, on September 14, 1971, leaving a better island than they found, a *de facto* colony still technically part of the paper federation of St. Kitts–Nevis–Anguilla. Anguilla has dropped from the news these last years, nor have we

returned to compare her with the lost world of 1960 remembered
in this poem:

> The boy who came at night
> to light the Tilly lamps
> (they hissed, too bright;
> he always looked frightened)
> in the morning dragged his bait pail
> through the beryl seawater
> sauntering barelegged
> without once looking down.
>
> The night Rebecca's—
> she lived beneath us—
> sailor lover returned from sea
> and beat her for hours,
> it was as hard to sleep as the time
> she tied a rooster
> inside an oil drum.
>
> The woman across the road,
> pregnant by an annual visit,
> cursed ungratefully, tossing rocks
> at her weeping children.
> The radio on her windowsill
> played hymns from Antigua all day.
>
> And the black children in blue
> trotted down the white-dust road
> to learn cricket and Victorian history,
> and the princesses
> balancing water drawn
> from the faucet by our porch
> held their heads at an insolent angle.
>
> The constellations
> that evaded our naming.
> The blind man. The drunk.

The albino,
his fat lips blistered by the sun.
The beaches empty of any hotel.
Dear island of such poor beauty,
meekly waiting to rebel.

FOUR INTRODUCTIONS

To Pens and Needles, *a collection of literary
caricatures by David Levine* (Gambit, *1969*)

IN 1963, when the newly founded *New York Review of Books*
began to publish the drawings of David Levine, the art of caricature in America was quiescent; the theatrical cartoons of Al
Frueh in *The New Yorker* had ceased, Al Hirschfeld had become
primarily a decorator of advertisements, and William Auerbach-
Levy, the most artful of them all, had rounded off his career with
an elegant album entitled—a question he had too often heard—
Is That Me? These men had followed the linear tradition of Ralph
Barton and Max Beerbohm; economy was the soul of their wit,
and their mood, as they reduced the features of this or that celebrity to a cunning black-and-white design, partook of the genial
mood of showbiz.

Levine, instead, flung himself in a fury of crosshatching upon his
subjects. His style looked past Beerbohm to the three-dimensional
grotesques of Daumier and Tenniel. No weary pucker or complacent bulge of physiognomy could slip through the supple net
of his penstrokes, and every corner of the face—that vulnerable
patch between the eyebrows, the unseemly area behind the chin,
the mute folds of the ears—was brought into a focus whose keenness transcended the mild demands of "humor." On the gray ex-
panses of the *NYRB* pages his etched homunculi seemed astound-
ingly *there;* one wanted to pick them up and put them on the shelf.
Now, in the form of this book, one can.

Our selection concentrates upon literary figures. Drawn in fort-
nightly installments to illustrate topical book reviews, the gallery

of modern authors approaches completeness. Mann and Borges are missing, and one wonders what Levine would do with Salinger's sad handsomeness or Kierkegaard's bent beauty. But how good it is to know that Gide has no top to his head, and that Truman Capote has no chin, resting, like Baudelaire, within his bow tie like an egg in an egg cup. Levine is not so much an observer as a visionary. Working principally from photographs, he evolves a concept, a monstrous breathing idea. His grasp of this idea deepens with time; of the two versions of Malraux in this volume, the one is a caricature and the other is a caricature of a caricature. Of the three Becketts, the smallest and earliest has the innocence of wit; it puns the man and buzzard. This simile is absorbed and heightened in the alarming metaphor of the profile, with its drastically eroded cheek, its delirious pinpoint eye, its incredible chopping-knife of an ear. And the lava contours and volcanic turtle-neck of the third drawing seem gouged from chaos and quite intimidate any thought of satire. Levine's evolving style reinvents the gargoyle, that antidote to the angel and necessary adjunct to a complete humanism. All we humans, beneath the faces that would proclaim for each a separate individuality, share the worse-than-simian weirdness of thinking reeds. Mankind is a riddle it takes the Gothic style to pose.

Since Levine, as clairvoyant, has liberated himself from the physical presence of the subject, the living and the dead are the same to him, and with uncanny authority he conveys, out of fudged old portraits and stylized prints, the essence of the immortals. Take Browning's wonderfully astute, plump, and conceited left hand; or Ben Franklin's cherry-nosed, finger-snapping display of pragmatic pep; or Casanova's evidently numbing virility. The artist discovers a surprising dandyish sneer on the time-softened face of John Milton, and elicits from the noseless bust of Catullus, at the farthest rim of Caricature's reach, the agonized satyr's howl that resounds through imperial Rome. One looks forward to, yet rather dreads, Levine's inevitable cartoon of Jesus.

Our artist was born in 1926 in Brooklyn, where he still lives. He has been quoted as describing himself as "a painter supported by a hobby—satirical drawings." As a painter he is representational and has been described, by John Canaday, as "a legitimate anachronism." In his comic art also he displays somewhat anachronistic qualities. Besides offering us the delight of recognition, his drawings comfort us, in an exacerbated and potentially desperate age, with the sense of a watching presence, an eye informed by an intelligence that has not panicked, a pen ready to encapsulate the latest apparitions of publicity (Twiggy inspires a drawing too lovely to omit) as well as those historical devils who haunt our unease.

To the Czech edition of Of the Farm, *translated by Igor Hájek in 1968 and left unpublished in post-Dubček Czechoslovakia*

As I REMEMBER, I wrote *Of the Farm* (the title originally was simply *The Farm*, but this had a monumentality that seemed bogus to me, which the preposition "Of" suitably reduced; I intended to mean that the book was *about* the farm, and that the people in it belonged *to* the farm, were of the earth, earthy, mortal, fallen, and imperfect) in the late summer and early autumn of 1964, in pencilled longhand. Then I embarked on a trip through the Soviet Union and Eastern Europe that lasted six weeks; the last night of this tour, and perhaps the most pleasant and unconstrained, was spent in Prague, in the apartment of Mr. Igor Hájek, the brilliant and engaging young man then involved in translating my previous novel *The Centaur*. Upon returning to the United States, I rewrote and typed *Of the Farm*, and in due course it was published, enjoying the mild sale and mixed reviews that usually greet my productions. Now, when Eastern Europe presents an aspect more troubled yet more hopeful than four years ago, Mr. Hájek and I both find ourselves in London, and he is translating my novella. And it has amused him to point out to me that I, like Joey Robinson, now possess, if not a new wife, a Citroën station wagon. Of such circling strands are past and present, fact and fiction, woven.

Of the Farm was my first attempt at book-length fiction after the writing of *The Centaur;* it was undertaken after a long hesitant interval fruitful of short stories. Like a short story, it has a continuous action, a narrow setting, a small cast. I thought of it as chamber music, containing only four voices—the various ghosts in it do not speak, and the minister's sermon, you will notice, is delivered in close paraphrase, without the benefit of quotation marks. The voices, like musical instruments, echo each other's phrases and themes, take turns dominating, embark on brief narrative solos, and recombine in argument or harmony. The underlying thematic transaction, as I conceived it, was the mutual forgiveness of mother and son, the acceptance each of the other's guilt in taking what they had wanted, to the discomfort, respectively, of the dead father and the divorced wife.

Threads connect it to *The Centaur:* the farm is the same, and the father, even to his name, George, seems much the same in both books. Mr. Hájek has directed my attention to a strange phrase, "his humorous prancing whine," in which the prancing is purely a remnant, like a badly erased pencil line, of the half-horse half-man. In a sense this novella is *The Centaur* after the centaur has died; the mythical has fled the ethical, and a quartet of scattered survivors grope with their voices toward cohesion. And seek to give each other the stern blessing of freedom mentioned in the epigraph from Sartre.* Let us hope that all nations will in their varying languages seek to bestow this stern blessing upon one another. I am honored at this moment [that is, when the cultural liberalization under Dubček had just been crushed by Russian tanks] to be translated into Czech.

---

* "Consequently, when, in all honesty, I've recognized that man is a being in whom existence precedes essence, that he is a free being who, in various circumstances, can want only his freedom, I have at the same time recognized that I can want only the freedom of others." [*En conséquence, lorsque sur le plan d'authenticité totale, j'ai reconnu que l'homme est un être chez qui l'essence est précédée par l'existence, qu'il est un être libre qui ne peut, dans des circonstances diverses, que vouloir sa liberté, j'ai reconnu en même temps que je ne peux vouloir que la liberté des autres.*]

To
The Harvard Lampoon Centennial Celebration 1876–1973
a collection of cartoons, verse, parodies, and humor
edited by Martin Kaplan (Atlantic Monthly Press, 1937)

THERE IT STANDS, in the shadow of Adams House, where Mt. Auburn Street unaccountably branches into Bow, an unaccountable little flatiron building with Amsterdam gables and a face—two round windows that look crosseyed, a red lantern for a nose, and, above the bright bowtie of its door, an exclamatory mouth of which the upper lip is so complex it might be a mustache. A copper hardhat tassled with a cage completes the apparition. This is the Lampoon Building. One's first impression is of an extravagance, and even in the 1950's, before the national-parody money shored up the subsiding foundations and restored lustre to the furnishings, this impression was confirmed by entering the tiled, worn, odorous, festooned interior. The gorgeous playful thing was put up, as a civilized prank, by American wealth when it was untaxed and un-conscience-stricken; it is a folly and a toy and a bastion, an out-cropping, like the brick mass of Harvard itself, of that awful seismic force which has displaced nine-tenths of the world: Wasp Power. The Lampoon is a club and, as do all clubs, feeds on the delicious immensity of the excluded. Robert Lampoon, born Robert Stew-art, lucidly advances the doctrine usually left unspoken: college men are the "highest type in the world," Harvard men are "the best of all," and Poonsters are "the cream of Harvard men." And with him we travel to an enchanted realm where young Lord Byrons, garbed as monks and nuns, are served roast pigs on platters and sit each "with a bottle of imported sherry between his knees." In 1973, sipping our bitter domestic sherry, we feel, even without John Reed and Granville Hicks to remind us, that there is a shadow side to this "Harvard of the chosen few," the underworld of callow snobbishness and automatic jokes about "Kikeland House," of arrest-exempt lawlessness and an inherited consensus of the "dull and sated and blind." To be fair, the same page which reprints this last phrase from John Reed's reminiscences also shows a Lampoon window dedicated to Reed's memory; The Lampoon, though a flower of the Establishment, is a twisted flower, stemmed from the Establishment's wise instinct to grant itself license—license to be idle and (hence) open, license to mock and hence (symbolically) to destroy. Of my uneasy year as President, I remember fondly certain moments of ecstatic, probably revolutionary confusion. Trying to deliver stern speeches about impending deadlines, I was pelted with buttered rolls. A born follower, I found myself leading a bellowed medley of preposterously obscene songs, waving my potent baton, the Presidential jester's stick donated, as I remember, by the beneficent Sadri Khan. Where is it now? Not stolen, I hope, as was my engraved mug, and my youth.

The Lampoon is saved from mere sociable fatuity by being also *The Lampoon*, a magazine. Month after month, through thin seasons and thick, it insists on coming out, even though it contain naught but hastily hustled ads and snippets of past issues scrambled together through a haze of beer and boisterous kibitzing. Along with the anarchic camaraderie of Thursday nights, I cherish those groggy Monday-morning subway rides down to the South Station stop and thence to the emporium (up several flights in a quivering elevator of Art Nouveau tracery) of Best Print, Inc., where a mild, mustached, and unblinking craftsman called Harold (Harold o' Bestprint, he was invariably called in the Common Books) relieved me of my raggedy pasted-up dummy and, unless his lawyer advised him otherwise, turned it into 1,200 (more or less) shiny magazines, with real staples, on real paper—or "stock," as we learned to term it, lisping resonant professional terms such as "pica" and "ital" and "halftone" and "mortise" and "bleed." An undergraduate magazine loses its maturest contributors every June, a fact which, combined with the distracted condition of the average collegiate head, creates a wonderfully ongoing vacuum for those few who want to fill it. Fop though it pretends to be, *The Lampoon* has apprenticed a sturdy number of professional writers and artists. It was the editorial aspect, presumably, that weighed so heavily on the young Robert Benchley as he wrote to his mother of his election as President, "It will mean a lot of work and a lot of worry and responsibility, for it is a responsible position." George Santayana, a half-century earlier, even more solemnly felt the invisible pressure of the "forthnightly edition" conjured up in "an atmosphere of respect for holy things," by young men with "literary tastes, leaning toward the sentimental and nobly moral." The vocabulary surprises but the reverent tone is right. Raising a smile is a delicate piece of artistic engineering that may well prepare one for higher things. "It's all in the execution," we used to say of some particularly lame cartoon idea hatched in a Sanctum gag session. That is to say, there *was* such a thing as execution; no humor is so broad it cannot be relayed badly or ably. The suppressed *Pontoon*, for instance (police-confiscated for reprinting Midwestern cartoons of which my favorite showed an ovum surrounded by long-tailed sperm one of whom was saying, "Joe sent me"—a dramatization that would not raise an eyebrow in a high-school contraception class now), contained much wit, where little was needed; Bink Young's editorial, "Easy, Breezy, You'll Slide a Mile," seemed an especial gem, and I was glad to find it in this anthology.

Martin Kaplan '71, between earning his *summa* in molecular biology and serving as head of every undergraduate organization but the YAF, has done a brave deed; he has descended into the dank abyss of the archives and clambered back with a staggering amount of Pooniana. Not only did he cull the back issues, he spelunked past slippery stalagmites of compacted Common Books into unthinkable caves of ancient correspondence, and even panned the memoirs of old grads for germane nuggets. The result is a beautiful and scholarly labor of love. Mr. Kaplan has drawn heavily on the parodies, which makes for something of a social history as well as a private album. He has given generous helpings of the cartoons and light verse, wherein the jejune can shine, and skimped mercifully on the prose. Here is nostalgia enough for anyone who has ever gone dizzy down the Narthex stairs, and laughter enough for any general reader. May the next ninety-seven years yield as happy a century's harvest.

To Soundings in Satanism, *a collection of essays assembled by F. J. Sheed (Sheed and Ward, 1972)*

MOST OF THE CONTRIBUTORS to this volume are Catholic or European or both; an American Protestant feels an understandable diffidence at leading such a parade, as it confidently marches from the mustering ground of Biblical exegesis into the weird marshes of possession, exorcism, and witchcraft and onward to the familiar firm terrain of psychopathology and literary criticism. To be honest, most of us Americans who out of reasons quixotic and sentimental and inertial persist in playing disciple to Calvin and Luther and Henry VIII have trouble enough conceiving of a deity, without dabbling at diabolism. Can evil be a personal, dynamic principle? The suggestion seems clownish; instinctively we reject it. If we must have a supernatural, at the price of intellectual scandal, at least let it be a minimal supernatural, clean, monotonous, hygienic, featureless— just a *little* supernatural, as the unwed mother said of her baby. There is no doubt a primitive resonance in the notion of God battling, across the surface of the universe, with a malevolent near-equal. But can we morally tolerate the God who would permit such an opponent to arise, who would arm him with death and pain, who would allow suffering Mankind to become one huge Job, teased and tested in heavenly play? Alas, we have become, in our Protestantism, more virtuous than the myths that taught us virtue; we judge them barbaric. We resist the bloody legalities of the Redemption; we face Judgment Day, in our hearts, much as young radicals face the mundane courts—convinced that acquittal is the one just verdict. We judge our Judge; and we magnanimously grant our Creator His existence by a "leap" of our own wills, incidentally reducing His "ancient foe" to the dimensions of a bad comic strip.

Yet these grand ghosts did not arise from a vacuum; they grow (and if pruned back will sprout again) from the deep exigencies and paradoxes of the human condition. We know that we live, and know that we will die. We love the creation that upholds us and sense that it is good, yet pain and plague and destruction are everywhere. It is not my province to discuss the shadowy Old Testament Satan so well evoked by Father Valensin; nor the demons swarming through all cultures, touched upon by M. Bazin in his essay on art; nor the disturbing boundary area where sexual hysteria and Christ's ministry of healing and the (to a Protestant) incredible rite of exorcism intertwine. I would, timidly, in my capacity as feeble believer and worse scholar, open the question of the devil as metaphysical possibility, if not necessity. For the assertion "God exists" is a drastic one that imposes upon the universe a structure; given this main beam, subordinate beams and joists, if reason and logic are anything, must follow. But let a true theologian speak. Karl Barth somewhere, coping with the massive—nay, central—theological problem of evil, speaks of God "turning His back" upon a section of the cosmos. Unable to locate this frightening metaphor, I found instead, in *Church Dogmatics*, a systematic portrait of "nothingness," which I here abridge:

> Only God and His creature really and properly are. But nothingness is neither God nor His creature. . . . But it would be foolhardy to rush to the conclusion that it is therefore nothing, i.e., that it does not exist. God takes it into account. He is concerned with it. He strives against it, resists and overcomes it. . . . Nothingness is that which God does not will. It lives only by the fact that it is that which God does not will. But it does live by this fact. For not only what God wills, but what He does not will, is potent, and must have a real correspondence. . . . The character of nothingness derives from its ontic peculiarity. It is evil. What God positively wills and performs in the *opus proprium* of His election, of His creation, of His preservation and overruling rule of the creature revealed in the history of His covenant with man, is His grace. . . . What God does not will and therefore negates and rejects, what can thus be only the object of His *opus alienum*, of His jealousy, wrath and judgment, is a being that refuses and resists and therefore lacks His grace. This being which is alien and adverse to grace and therefore without it, is that of nothingness. This negation of His grace is chaos, the world which He did not choose or will, which He could not and did not create, but which, as He created the actual world, He passed over and set aside, marking and excluding it. . . . And this is evil in the Christian sense, namely, what is alien and adverse to grace, and therefore without it. In this sense nothingness is really privation, the attempt to defraud God of His honour and right and

at the same time to rob the creature of its salvation and right. For it is God's honour and right to be gracious, and this is what nothingness contests. . . . In this capacity it does not confront either God or the creature neutrally. It is not merely a third factor. It opposes both as an enemy, offending God and threatening His creature. From above as well as below, it is the impossible and intolerable. By reason of this character, whether in the form of sin, evil, or death, it is inexplicable as a natural process or condition. . . . It "is" only as the disorder at which this counter-offensive is aimed, only as the non-essence which it judges, only as the enemy of God and His creation. We thus affirm that it is necessary to dismiss as non-Christian all those conceptions in which its character as evil is openly or secretly, directly or indirectly, conjured away, and its reality is in some way regarded or grouped with that of God and His creature.

(*Church Dogmatics*, 3, 3)

Pantheism on one side, Manichaeanism on the other, clutch at the theologian's skirts. A potent "nothingness" was unavoidably conjured up by God's creating *something*. The existence of something demands the existence of *something else*. And this same ontic inevitability serves Barth to explain man's strange capacity, under God, to choose evil.

Without this possibility of defection or of evil, creation would not be distinct from God and therefore not really His creation. The fact that the creature can fall away from God and perish does not imply any imperfection on the part of creation or the Creator. . . . A creature freed from the possibility of falling away would not really be living as a creature. It could only be a second God—and as no second God exists, it could only be God Himself.

Are there not tendencies in our private psychologies that would give these cosmic propositions credence? Is not destructiveness within us as a positive lust, an active hatred? Who does not exult in fires, collapses, the ruin and death of friends? Who has seen a baby sleeping in a crib and not wanted, for an instant of wrath that rises in the throat like vomit, to puncture such innocence? What child is not fascinated by torture and monstrosity? What man can exempt, from his purest sexual passion and most chivalrous love, the itch to defile? What man or woman does not carry within, as tempter and last resort, the thought of suicide? After satisfaction, revulsion. Into the most ample contentment rushes, not an impulse to sing gratitude, but a frightful impatience that would, like Lucifer, overthrow the tyranny of order, however benign. Indeed, the more fortunate our condition, the stronger the lure of negation, of perversity, of refusal. For the more completely order would enclose us, the greater the threat to our precious creaturely freedom, which finds self-assertion in defiance and existence in sin and dreads beyond hell a heaven of automatons forever "freed from the possibility of falling away." Thus the devil—to give "nothingness" his name—thrives in proportion, never falls hopelessly behind, is always ready to enrich the rich man with ruin, the wise man with folly, the beautiful woman with degradation, the kind average man with debauches of savagery. The world always topples. A century of progressivism bears the fruit of Hitler; our own supertechnology breeds witches and warlocks from the loins of engineers.

We resist what is good for us; humanity cannot be imagined doing otherwise and remaining human. Barth's formulas fit: man is a battlefield, and Satan at best is "behind" one. But what of creation in general? Does a black-and-white *opus proprium* and *opus alienum* really satisfy our perception of the universe as a curious explosion, a chaos wherein mathematical balances achieve momentary islands of calm? Man as organism is beset not by "nothingness" but by predators and parasites themselves obeying the Creator's command to survive and propagate. Disease is a clash of competing vitalities. And what of those shrugs, those earthquakes and floods and mudslides, whereby the Earth demonstrates her utter indifference to her little scum of life? Nature—Nature, whom we love more than our own bodies, from whose face we have extracted a thousand metaphors and affectionate messages—cares nothing for us. Is this the Satanic nothingness? In fact, it has been taken as such; the Christian West, with its myth of the devil, has taken the fight to Nature with a vengeance, has sought out the microbe and dammed the river and poisoned the mosquito in his marsh and gouged the mineral from its hidden vein and invented the machines that now threaten to scrape Nature into the infernal abyss as Lucifer's angels were scraped from Heaven. Oriental fatalism, which would see death and nothingness as limbs of God, could not have done this. Yet we wonder, as now our human species like some giant strand of bacteria fills every vacuum and re-creates chaos artificially, if this was intended. Or if the essence of our creature-hood is coöperation, with even the devil.

I do not know. I call myself Christian by defining "a Christian" as "a person willing to profess the Apostles' Creed." I am willing, unlike most of my friends—many more moral than myself—to profess it (which does not mean understand it, or fill its every syllable with the breath of sainthood), because I know of no other combination of words that gives such life, that so seeks the *crux*. The Creed asks us to believe not in Satan but only in the "Hell" into which Christ descends. That Hell, in the sense at least of a profound and desolating absence, exists I do not doubt; the news-papers give us its daily bulletins. And my sense of things, senti-mental I fear, is that wherever a church spire is raised, though dismal slums surround it and a single dazed widow kneels under it, this Hell is opposed by a rumor of good news, by an irrational confirmation of the plenitude we feel is our birthright. The instinct that life is good is where natural theology begins. The realization that life is flawed admits the possibility of a Fall, of a cause behind the Fall, of Satan. How seriously we must take this possibility, and under what forms we might imagine it, these "soundings" will elucidate.

GOLF

The First Lunar Invitational

FIVE SHORT YEARS after Alan Shepard, swinging an improvised 6-iron, took a one-handed poke at a golf ball on the moon, space suits were developed which permitted a nice full shoulder turn and the Vardon overlapping grip. The next year, 1977, the first Semi-Invitational Tournament was scheduled, under the joint sponsorship of NASA, ALCOA, M.I.T., and Bob Hope. An elimination tournament was held under simulated conditions in the Mojave Desert, and the refined field of thirty pros, plus twenty invited celebrities, was lifted from Cape Kennedy on the Monday following the Azalea Open. A maximum of three woods per bag was allowed, mallet-head putters were forbidden, and caddies were expected to double. Two modules, of the "bus" type developed by Lockheed to transport the football teams matched in the previous January's Crater Classic, cast off from the mother ship Thursday morning, for a tee-off time of 9 a.m. Players grumbled of sleeplessness and the failure of officials to provide for a practice round, but praised the dry, open fairways and evidently relished the absence of wind and water hazards. "We'll tear this sucker apart," Lee Trevino's voice crackled confidently across the vastness of space.

Robert Trent Jones, working from detailed relief maps of the lunar surface, had designed with the aid of computers in Lacus Somniorum a 42,000-yard layout, threaded among the natural outcroppings and effluvia and the debris left by previous expeditions. The cups were cut and the eighteen cores thus taken shipped back to the Manned Spacecraft Center in Houston for pulverization, analysis, and adoration. The rules committee pondered the inch or so of ubiquitous dust and suspended the law against grounding your club in a sand trap. But preferred lies were banned. One of the invited amateurs, a Texas oilman playing snugly to a handicap of 23, had brought along a piece of Astroturf to make his own lies preferable. American flags of titanium foil, battery-powered to simulate rippling, vividly signalled the pin placements. The tee markers were pineapples rocketed fresh each day from the private Dole launching pad in Oahu, at not a penny's cost to the taxpayer.

The pros quickly adjusted to the extraterrestrial conditions. The dust, for instance, was "fluffy" rather than "gritty" and the ball could be "struck" rather than "stung," as if from a lie of bedded dandelion polls; though it was hard to put enough "stop" on the ball for the rock-hard "greens" of smooth lunar gneiss. "It's a chipper's game up here," big-hitting George Archer confided to the three hundred million televiewers of the tournament. "It's like playing in a flour bin," Miller Barber observed from behind his accustomed sunglasses, and the Earthbound gallery could verify, despite the ragged television transmission, that owing to the tendency of the divots to hang cloudlike in the air the players slowly accumulated bulk, like snowmen.

Moon play had other peculiarities. Without an atmosphere, balls could not hook or slice, which licensed lashers like Arnold Palmer to overswing with impunity. Drives one mile long became standard by the second day of play. Smartly struck wedge shots, however, had a worrisome tendency to float into orbit; Jack Nicklaus lost two successive approaches to the fourth green this way, taking a humiliating eight on the hole. "It's a puncher's game," said Nicklaus. "Keep the ball low, and don't gulp oxygen." A ball lying in shadow, even a mere few inches from the razor-sharp sunlight, had to be played promptly, lest it freeze and shatter when struck. And unexplained concentrations of basalt beneath the crust played magnetic havoc on some fairways; the shortest hole on the course, a 1,000-yard cutie nestled between a lava flow and a three-billion-year-old impact crater—for most pros an easy 8-iron—was birdied only four times the first two days of play.

Toward the end of the second afternoon, as the frigid lunar dusk was tracing long shadows across the course, Spiro Agnew,* playing in a foursome with Bobby Nichols, Bob Lunn, and Robert McNamara, shanked a difficult spoon shot with such penetrating puissance that, from 900 yards away, it punctured the fuel tank of one lunar module and rendered it inoperable. The P.G.A. ruled from Palm Beach that those who failed to make the 36-hole cut should not only receive no prize money but should be the ones to stay on the moon and perish. Since this included most of the participating amateurs, several government officials demanded another ruling from the C.I.A., which refused, however, to identify itself over public networks. So the P.G.A. ruling appeared to stand. The next day, however, while the active field was playing the eleventh through fourteenth holes deep in the Taurian Highlands, the disqualified golfers commandeered the operable module and rejoined the mother ship.

"Easy as sinking a six-inch putt," comedian Jerry Lewis later confided to newsmen.

The tournament, interestingly, was played to a conclusion, though the backpack radios did not send sufficiently powerful signals to announce to Earth the winner. The Dole Company continued to rocket pineapples moonward, and the Mount Palomar Observatory reported sighting on Sunday afternoon a crisp hit to the left of the pin by a player who, judging from his restricted backswing, must have been Doug Sanders.

The participants who returned to Earth found that their ardor for the game had permanently cooled. As singer Andy Williams put it, "I don't know, it just feels down here like you're swinging underwater at lumps of putty." Plans were projected for the next year's competition, with an enlarged purse and solar-powered golf carts contributed by the Russians; but that autumn the major powers, honoring their commitments to the contending factions in the Ethiopian civil war, staged a prolonged nuclear exchange, and in the subsequent regression of technology not only was the secret of solid-fuel rockets lost but of tapered tempered-steel golf shafts as well.

---

* Still a real person as of February 1971, when this jape was composed.

Tips on a Trip

I HAVE BEEN ASKED * to write about golf as a hobby. But of course golf is not a hobby. Hobbies take place in the cellar and smell of airplane glue. Nor is golf, though some men turn it into such, meant to be a profession or a pleasure. Indeed, few sights are more odious on the golf course than a sauntering, beered-up foursome obviously having a good time. Some golfers, we are told, enjoy the landscape; but properly the landscape shrivels and compresses into the grim, surrealistically vivid patch of grass directly under the golfer's eyes as he morosely walks toward where he thinks his ball might be. We should be conscious of no more grass, the old Scots adage goes, than will cover our own graves. If neither work nor play, if more pain than pleasure but not essentially either, what, then, can golf be? Luckily, a word newly coined rings on the blank Formica of the conundrum. Golf is a *trip*.

A non-chemical hallucinogen, golf breaks the human body into components so strangely elongated and so tenuously linked, yet with anxious little bunches of hyper-consciousness and undue effort bulging here and there, along with rotating blind patches and a sort of cartilaginous euphoria—golf so transforms one's somatic sense, in short, that truth itself seems about to break through the exacerbated and as it were debunked fabric of mundane reality.

An exceedingly small ball is placed a large distance from one's face, and a silver wand curiously warped at one end is placed in one's hands. Additionally, one's head is set a-flitting with a swarm of dimly remembered "tips." Tommy Armour says to hit the ball with the right hand. Ben Hogan says to push off with the right foot. Arnold Palmer says keep your head still. Arnold Palmer has painted hands in his golf book. Gary Player says *don't* lift the left heel. There is a white circle around his heel. Dick Aultman says keep everything square, even your right foot to the line of flight. His book is full of beautiful pictures of straight lines lying along wrists like carpenter's rules on planed wood. Mindy Blake, in *his* golf book, says "square-to-square" is an evolutionary half-step on

* By *The New York Times Book Review*, in the summer of 1973.

the way to a stance in which both feet are skewed toward the hole and at the extremity of the backswing the angle between the left arm and the line to the target is a mere 14 degrees. Not 15 degrees. Not 13 degrees. Fourteen degrees. Jack Nicklaus, who is a big man, says you should stand up to the ball the way you'd stand around doing nothing in particular. Hogan and Player, who are small men, show a lot of strenuous arrows generating terrific torque at the hips. Player says pass the right shoulder under the chin. Somebody else says count two knuckles on the left hand at address. Somebody else says *no* knuckle should show. Which is to say nothing about knees, open or closed clubface at top of backswing, passive right side, "sitting down" to the ball, looking at the ball with the right eye—all of which are crucial.

This unpleasant paragraph above, strange to say, got me so excited I had to rush out into the yard and hit a few shots, even though it was pitch dark, and only the daffodils showed. Golf converts oddly well into words. Wodehouse's golf stories delighted me years before I touched a club. The story of Jones's Grand Slam, and Vardon's triumph over J. H. Taylor at Muirfield in 1896, and Palmer's catching Mike Souchak at Cherry Hills in 1960, are always enthralling—as is, indeed, the anecdote of the most abject duffer. For example:

Once, my head buzzing with a mess of anatomical and aeronautical information that was not relating to the golf balls I was hitting, I went to a pro and had a lesson. Put your weight on the right foot, the man told me, and then the left. "That's all?" I asked. "That's all," he said. "What about the wrists pronating?" I asked. "What about the angle of shoulder-plane vis-à-vis that of hip-plane?" "Forget them," he said. Ironically, then, in order to demonstrate to him the folly of his command (much as the Six Hundred rode into the valley of Death), I obeyed. The ball clicked into the air, soared straight as a string, and fell in a distant ecstasy of backspin. For some weeks, harboring this absurd instruction, I went around golf courses like a giant, pounding out pars, humiliating my friends. But I never could identify with my new prowess; I couldn't *internalize* it. There was an immense semi-circular area, transparent, mysterious, anesthetized, above the monotonous weight-shift of my feet. All richness had fled the game. So gradually I went back on my lessons, ignored my feet, made a number of other studied adjustments, and restored my swing to its original, fascinating *terribilità*.

Like that golf story of mine? Let me tell you another: the greatest shot of my life. It was years ago, on a little dog-leg left, downhill. Apple trees were in blossom. Or the maples were turning; I forget which. My drive was badly smothered, and after some painful wounded bounces found rest in the deep rough at the crook of the dog-leg. My second shot, a 9-iron too tensely gripped, moved a great deal of grass. The third shot, a smoother swing with the knees nicely flexed, nudged the ball a good six feet out onto the fairway. The lie was downhill. The distance to the green was perhaps 230 yards at this point. I chose (of course) a 3-wood. The lie was not only downhill but sidehill. I tried to remember some tip about sidehill lies; it was either (1) play the ball farther forward from the center of the stance, with the stance more open, or (2) play the ball farther back, off a closed stance, or (3) some combination. I compromised by swinging with locked elbows and looking up quickly, to see how it turned out. A divot the size of an undershirt was taken some 18 inches behind the ball. The ball moved a few puzzled inches. *Now here comes my great shot.* Perfectly demented by frustration, I swung as if the club were an ax with which I was reducing an orange crate to kindling wood. Emitting a sucking, oval sound, the astounded ball, smitten, soared far up the fairway, curling toward the fat part of the green with just the daintiest trace of a fade, hit once on the fringe, kicked smartly toward the flagstick, and stopped two feet from the cup. I sank the putt for what my partner justly termed a "remarkable six."

In this mystical experience, some deep golf revelation was doubtless offered me, but I have never been able to grasp it, or to duplicate the shot. In fact, the only two golf tips I have found consistently useful are these. One (from Jack Nicklaus): on long putts, think of yourself putting the ball half the distance and having it roll the rest of the way. Two (from I forget—Mac Divot?): on chip shots, to keep from underhitting, imagine yourself *throwing* the ball to the green with the right hand.

Otherwise, though once in a while a 7-iron rips off the clubface with that pleasant tearing sound, as if pulling a zipper in space, and falls toward the hole like a raindrop down a well; or a drive draws sweetly with the bend of the fairway and disappears, still rolling, far beyond the applauding sprinkler, these things happen in spite of me, and not because of me. On the golf course as nowhere else, the tyranny of causality is suspended, and men are free.

Is There Life After Golf?

GOLF IN THE KINGDOM, by Michael Murphy, 205 pp. Viking, 1972.

Like a religion, a game seeks to codify and lighten life. Played earnestly enough (spectatorship being merely a degenerate form of playing), a game can gather to itself awesome dimensions of subtlety and transcendental significance. Consult George Steiner's hymn to the fathomless wonder of chess, or Roger Angell's startlingly intense meditations upon the time-stopping, mathematical beauty of baseball. Some sports, surely, are more religious than others; ice hockey, fervent though its devotees be, retains a dross of brutal messiness, and handball, though undoubtedly it has its fine points, has not generated many holy books. Golf, on the other hand, inspires as much verbiage as astrology. In the television era, the sport has added to its antiquity and air of privilege the aura of sudden fame and fortune earned by broad-backed boys from Latrobe, Pennsylvania, and El Paso, Texas; millions now trudge out to the dawn starting lines inwardly clutching a tip from the Saturday sports page or the driving-range pro; an esoteric cult has become a mass cult while remaining esoteric. In Palmer's disastrous lapses, in Casper's persistent slump, golf reasserts its essential enigma. It is of games the most mysterious, the least earthbound, the one wherein the wall between us and the supernatural is rubbed thinnest. The exaltation of its great spaces; the eerie effortlessness of a good shot; the hellish effortfulness of a bad round; the grotesque disparity between a drive that eats up two-thirds of the fairway and the ten-yard dribble hit with an almost identical swing; the unpredictable warps and turns of fortune in the game; its tranced silences; its altering perspectives; its psychosomatic sensitivity to our interior

monologue and the sway of our moods; the sullen, menacing sheen
the monotonous grass can suddenly assume; the quirks of visibility;
the dread of lostness; the ritual interment and resurrection of the
ball at each green—such are the ingredients that make golf seem a
magic mirror, an outward projection of an inner self. Even the
most mechanical-minded books about golf evoke, for initiates, the
game's intoxicating mysteries; Michael Murphy, in his curious and
benign *Golf in the Kingdom*, takes these mysteries as his major
topic.

Mr. Murphy, a Californian, is a co-founder of the Esalen Institute, described as "a research and development center established
to explore those trends in the behavioral sciences, religion, and
philosophy which emphasize the potentialities and values of human
existence." On the back of the jacket of his book he is grinning
with perfect teeth, and but for a faraway, faintly metaphysical
gleam in his eyes he might be one of the interchangeable square-
jawed young pros who clutter the tournament circuit with their
competence. His book appears to be as open as his visage—he talks
about himself as harried executive and student truth seeker; he
names friends and gives dates, he describes rounds of golf we do
not doubt he has played. Yet the basic autobiographical episode,
involving a Scots guru/pro named Shivas Irons, is, like the name
itself, frankly fantastic. The book liltingly begins:

> In Scotland, between the Firth of Forth and the Firth of Tay, lies
> the Kingdom of Fife—known to certain lovers of that land simply
> as "The Kingdom." There, on the shore of the North Sea, lies a
> golfing links that shimmers in my memory—an innocent stretch of
> heather and grassy dunes that cradled the unlikely events which grew
> into this book. . . . There I met Shivas Irons, introduced to me
> simply as a golf professional, by accident one day in June 1956. I
> played a round of golf with him then, joined him in a gathering of
> friends that evening, followed him into a ravine at midnight looking
> for his mysterious teacher, watched him go into ecstatic trance as the
> sun came up, and left for London the following afternoon—just
> twenty-four hours after we had met—shaken, exalted, my percep-
> tion of things permanently altered.

Mr. Murphy was on his way to India, to study philosophy and
practice meditation with the seer Aurobindo, and it may be that

he retrospectively assigned much of what he learned there to this mythical golf instructor, who plays supernaturally well, keeps a library of the occult in his digs, and, in the dead of the night, scores a hole-in-one with a feather-stuffed ball and an antique shillelagh belonging to an immortal hermit named Seamus MacDuff. Yet the course, called Burningbush, is by its location and layout recognizably St. Andrews—golf's holy place. The book never totally strays from its base subject of golf, and it even contains some practical tips: Don't strain after a good score, play it as it lies, don't try too hard. "Let the nothingness into yer shots," Shivas tells Murphy— a memorable admonition to all of us who, not trusting the unconscious mechanics of the swing, smother the ball with too much hand-and-arm action. When Murphy tenses up on the first tee, Shivas makes a gesture that eases him "into a feeling of stomach and hips, making a center there for my swing." The well-worn advice "Hit from the inside" is metaphysicalized to "Ken the world from the inside." Warming to his theme of "true gravity," Shivas bids his pupil "feel yer inner body." Murphy, evidently a natural athlete, travels, club in hand, through a number of yoga-like states (he feels like an hourglass, then enormously tall), and sees turquoise "auras" expand and contract, and experiences other vivid intimations of "energy-dimensions" that might more distract than settle your average 20-handicapper. Unity and harmony are the goals of Shivas' instruction; imagine the ball and the "sweet spot" on the club as one, he says. Further, see and feel "the club and ball as one unbroken field." Further still, "sometimes a path appears in your mind's eye for the ball to follow: let it blend with your body." Murphy recalls a moment on Burningbush when all his senses joined: "For the moment . . . the world was a single field of music, joy, and light." Shivas has the ultimate word: "Aye ane fiedle [always one field] afore ye e're swung."

This religious bias, which would break down the opposition between game and player, between striker and thing struck, between man and landscape, comes as alien to the Occidental followers of aggressive Jahweh and tragic Jesus. This Occidental, for one, remains suspicious of a cosmic philosophy that so easily devolves into golf instruction. Murphy, drawing upon Shivas' supposed journals, has little trouble expanding the first part of his book, the golf part, into the comprehensive mysteries of the second. Because of the lightness of the golf ball (one and a half ounces), Shivas is led to conclude that the world, too, is feather-light, "an earthy nothingness." It is also "an icon of Man the Multiple Amphibian, a smaller, waffled version of the crystal ball, a mirror for the inner body; it is a lodestone, an old stone to polarize your psyche with." Its whiteness suggests (hello, Melville) the terror of the hueless void; its flight serves as "reminder of our hunting history and our future powers of astral flight." The hole is another mystery, linked to nostrils and other significant bodily apertures; Jean-Paul Sartre is called in to testify (from *Being and Nothingness*): "A good part of our life is passed in plugging up holes, in filling empty places, in realizing and symbolically establishing a plenitude." Not all such symbol-spinning is vapid, but it does border on the facile and the fanciful—less mysticism than mystchief. And it reduces, in practice, all this talk about luminous bodies and manifesting planes, about *hamartia* and *darshan*, about Agni the Primal Fire and the Net of Jewels, to something like witchcraft. The victory of Jack Fleck over Ben Hogan in the 1955 Open, for instance, is explained to have been Fleck's appropriation of Hogan's "inner body," and Murphy relates that while watching a baseball game he and his neighbors in the stands set up a "psychic fire-storm" that permanently injured the opposing pitcher's arm. Even if it works, is black magic what we need now? " 'Tis a thin line," Shivas himself says, " 'tween the madness of God and the madness of the Devil."

The Western spirit longs for a peaceable creed that would flatter the flesh instead of mortifying it, that would blur away the painful mind-body split and ease the agonies of egoism. But these wisdoms imported from the Orient have a disturbing way of melting into physical therapy—of a harmless, deep-breathing, sweet-swinging sort—and trivial spookiness. In regard to traditional Christian problems like the existence of evil and the paradoxes of ethical action, *Golf in the Kingdom* says little. During the raucous symposium that follows his round of golf with Shivas, Murphy claims, there was a "lively discussion of shanking and the problem of evil," but we never hear it. Murphy/Shivas does offer, for the length of a page, ethical distinctions between "Mind-at-Large" and "Higher Self"; it is good to know the latter before you drown in the former.

LSD is distinguished from disciplined contemplation, moral entropy from nirvana. "Ye need a solid place to swing from," Shivas says, which is half of the truth; you also need a spot to aim at. Shivas would be a complete prophet if the world were a golf course and life a game. In a game, purposes and means are indisputably ordained; in golf, rules regulate the most minute points of etiquette and equipment. A golf wherein some players were using tennis rackets and hockey pucks, some were teeing off backward from the green to the tee, and some thought the object of the game was to spear other players with the flagsticks—such a contest might produce a philosophy we could carry everywhere. As it is, analogies should be very tenderly extended outward from an island that, like golf, has been created as an artificial haven from real problems. Even within the analogy, Murphy is limited by his natural happiness at the game; for a description of the infernal misery possible *within* golf, read George Plimpton's *The Bogey Man*, especially the hideous chapter wherein Plimpton practices with four golf balls on a tinselly, night-lit par-3 course in the desert, each ball diabolically possessed of individual bad habits.

Yet there is much wit and good will in *Golf in the Kingdom*. "We are spread wide as we play, then brought to a tiny place" beautifully describes both golf and life. And why *not* make the world more of a golf course, where our acts would take validity from within, and we would replace our divots in apology for each blow, and joy would attach to the leisurely walking, the in-between times? There is a goodness in the experience of golf that may well be, as Mr. Murphy would have it, a *pitha*, "a place where something breaks into our workaday world and bothers us forevermore with the hints it gives."

Golf in the Kingdom put me in mind of another curious devotional work, William Price Fox's *Doctor Golf*, published in 1963 and long out of print. Doctor Golf, a fanatic even quainter and keener than Shivas Irons, runs a thirty-nine-member golf sanctuary in Arkansas called Eagle-Ho, refers to "young Hagen," advocates caddy-flogging, sells by mail order a clanking, cumbersome line of golf paraphernalia, and conducts a large correspondence. When one correspondent writes, "I am in my 65th year and I have been seized by golf like a mouse in the claws of a golden eagle," Doctor Golf congratulates him:

> Only after the fetters of youth have been flung aside can golf enter. Only then can the man know the folly of his adolescent belief of the swing answering to the man and perceive the joy and the truth of the complete man answering to the swing.
>
> And, as the years and the eagles cascade by, the even greater joy is realized when he stands in the bright sunlight of complete fulfillment and comes to realize that the *swing is the man.*

The swing is the man. The Dance of Shiva, Michael Murphy concludes, is at the heart of everything. Doctor Golf is more mystical still:

> The swing by its very nature transcends the human form. The swing is there when you pass on. . . . The swing, sir . . . is like the blue in the sky, immutable, eternal, indeed transcendental.

Reviews

THE FORK

THE LAST YEARS: JOURNALS 1853–1855, by Søren Kierkegaard, edited and translated by Ronald Gregor Smith. 384 pp. Harper & Row, 1965.

It is not certain that the United States needs still more translations of Kierkegaard. The Kierkegaard bibliography in this country is already amply confusing; led by the dauntless Walter Lowrie,* a campaign of translation coincident with the Second World War endowed the English-speaking world with almost all of the torrential *oeuvre* that the Danish thinker had created a century before. Eight books, including the immense *Concluding Unscientific Postscript*, were published here in 1941 alone. The current index of

---

* The reviewer, in his versifying youth, once indicted, for a threnody never finished, these lines "On the Death of Dr. Lowrie":

The Reverend Doctor Walter Lowrie, 91, is dead.
The *Times* of August 12th contains a picture of his head.
I never knew the man but his translations often read.

I never read his forty books, I never sought him whole;
I had to pass right through him when, returning from a stroll,
I flung myself on Kierkegaard to save my flagging soul.

For Walter Lowrie had no peer at Englishing the Dane:
Of twenty-six translated works, thirteen are his domain,
And in those dreadful castles his kind heart will always reign.

His prefaces relate the tale with modest balladry,
Of how a tiny band—scarce more than Swensen, Dru, and he—
Subdued a hostile continent of dark theology.

He led them; old, a clergyman, he led. Retired, old,
He started; goaded Swensen; wrestled *Angst*, battled *Forehold*,
Bestemelse, and *Aufgehoben;* strove. The presses rolled

At Princeton and at Oxford; the pastor's blue eyes bled
On the thorns of an ugly language; *The Concept of Dread*
He wept through in a month's long sitting; *inspirator*, he led.

books in print lists twenty-two Kierkegaard titles, not counting duplications and anthologies. Distributed among a number of commercial, university, and religious presses (notably Harper, Princeton, and Augsburg) and bedevilled by overlappings and omissions (*Stages on Life's Way* seems to be out of print, whereas some of the *Discourses* crop up repeatedly), the list is nevertheless the fullest outside of Germany and Denmark itself. We lack in English only some topical and humorous trifles and the very voluminous total of the journals and stray papers.

The Last Years: Journals 1853–1855 draws upon the papers from 1853 onward and the journals from their resumption on March 1, 1854, after a four-month gap. This material, which represents Kierkegaard in his most haranguing and repetitious phase, is not unknown to previous translation. The final fifty-five pages of Alexander Dru's selection derive from the same portion of the journals. Professor Smith, though he compiles three hundred and forty pages, omits half of what Dru includes. Absent in Smith are some of the most pungent entries in Dru:

> Oh, Luther, Luther; your responsibility is great indeed, for the closer I look the more clearly do I see that you overthrew the Pope—and set the public on the throne.

> Hypocrisy is quite as inseparable from being a man as sliminess is from being a fish.

> What could be more ridiculous than to use a jack to pick up a pin— or to make use of the eternal punishment of hell in order to make men into that half-demoralized, half-honest bagatelle which is roughly what it means to be a man.

Professor Smith prefers the extensive to the epigrammatic, and he might claim that his selection emphasizes Kierkegaard's religious thought—the ideas that were projected outward in his pamphleteering attack upon the established Christianity of Denmark. But the pamphlets (ten in all, called *The Instant*) and the open letters that Kierkegaard issued have been already rendered into English by Lowrie, under the title *Attack Upon "Christendom."* This book relates to *The Last Years* much as the outside of a sock relates to the inside; the pattern is not identical, but the threads are the same.

After minimizing the considerable duplication, the editor of *The Last Years* justifies its publication by saying, "The last years of Kierkegaard's life saw a remarkable concentration of the motifs which controlled his whole authorship. This comes vividly to life in the present selection from the journals and papers of that time, and casts light on all that went before it." True, if "concentration" is taken to mean a narrowing. The prolix philosophizing of the "aesthetic works" and the fervent exhortation of the "religious works" have been succeeded by a third stage—an apostolic or pathological vehemence. *The Last Years* shows Kierkegaard's mind narrowed to a very hard point. More precisely, it shows his mind and life, those antagonistic twins, both narrowed to a very hard point, the point of attack, which becomes the point of vanishing.

Søren Aabye Kierkegaard (the name means "churchyard," and is pronounced "Kĕrkĕgōr") was born in Copenhagen in 1813—"the year," he was to say, "when so many worthless notes were put in circulation." His father, Michael, was a man of great force and complexity. A shepherd lad from the desolate West Jutland heath, he had become a prosperous cloth merchant and grocer in the city, only to retire at the age of forty, perhaps to devote himself to religious brooding. Within a year of his first wife's death, Michael married a household servant, Ane Lund, who bore him a child four months after their wedding. This marriage was to produce seven children, of whom Søren Aabye (as distinguished from his older brother, Søren Michael) was the last. His father was fifty-six, his mother forty-five; the advanced age of his parents accounts in part for Kierkegaard's physical frailty, and his position as the family Benjamin for his pertness and conceit. His nickname within the family was Fork—bestowed when, rebuked for shovelling food greedily at the table, he announced, "I *am* a fork, and I will stick you." Descriptions of his childhood abound in his journals:

> I was already an old man when I was born. . . . Delicate, slender, and weak, deprived of almost every condition for holding my own with other boys, or even for passing as a complete human being in comparison with others; melancholy, sick in soul, in many ways profoundly unfortunate, one thing I had: an eminently shrewd wit, given me presumably in order that I might not be defenseless.

But many weak boys with sharp tongues are born into the world, and Kierkegaard's heightened sense of himself reaches for more:

> I am in the deepest sense an unfortunate individual who has from the earliest age been nailed fast to one suffering or another, to the very verge of insanity, which may have its deeper ground in a disproportion between my soul and my body.

And in *The Last Years*, in the last entry, within a few weeks of his death, this sense of initial misfortune attains a frightening pitch:

> Through a crime I came into existence, I came into existence against God's will. The fault, which in one sense is not mine, even if it makes me a criminal in God's eyes, is to give life. The punishment fits the fault: it is to be deprived of all joy of life, to be brought to the supreme degree of disgust with life.

His adult life consisted of a series of quixotic, or expiatory, gestures. His father wanted him to study for the ministry, so he spent his youth in frivolity, drunkenness, and dandyism. His father died, so he settled down to pass the theological examination. He fell in love with and successfully courted Regine Olsen; then he broke off the engagement and buried himself in a frenetic literary activity dedicated to her. He became, under his own name and under the open secret of his pseudonyms, the most remarkable writer in Denmark, the only author above attack by the scurrilous magazine the *Corsair;* so he incited the *Corsair,* though its editor, Meïr Goldschmidt, revered him, to attack, which it did with such success that Kierkegaard's personal life was made a torment. Lastly, he who had long been on the verge of becoming a country parson mounted a savage attack upon organized Christianity, exhorting true Christians to abstain from the sin of church worship. He refused the Eucharist, since it could not be administered by a layman, on his deathbed.

Kierkegaard's American reputation was long deferred and is still esoteric, but in Denmark he was a celebrity. Indeed, he seems to have been the Benjamin of Copenhagen, the marketplace capital of a small and homogeneous country. His break with Regine was surrounded by so much gossip that it amounted to a public event. His pseudonyms, with their interlocking prefaces and compliments, must have been private jokes to a considerable group. His books, surprisingly, sold well enough to make money. During the *Corsair* persecution, his twisted back and uneven trouser legs were caricatured every week for a year, and the students at the university produced a comedy whose ridiculous hero was called Søren Kirk. Children taunted him on the streets. In his journals, he lamented, "To let oneself be trampled by geese is a slow way of dying," and complained that "when . . . I have sought recreation by driving ten or twelve miles, and my body has gradually become somewhat weak . . . when I alight from the carriage . . . there is sure to be someone at hand who is jolly enough to call me names." Astonishingly, the very name Søren, up to then the most common male baptismal name, became a byword for the ridiculous, and Danish parents, according to Lowrie, took to admonishing their children, "Don't be a Søren." Though helpless under such assault, Kierkegaard was not without power. A staunch monarchist, he was on conversational terms with King Christian VIII, and Lowrie asserts that in the relationship it was Kierkegaard who "held himself a little aloof." (In his journals, Kierkegaard dryly noted, "On the whole, Christian VIII has enriched me with many psychological observations. Perhaps psychologists ought to pay particular attention to kings, and especially to absolute monarchs; for the freer a man is, the better he can be known.") Kierkegaard's satirical pen was a feared weapon. He undoubtedly ruined the life of a former friend, P. S. Møller, with a personal attack published in the newspaper *Fatherland*. So his assault upon the ecclesiastical establishment was delivered from the strength of notoriety, and, far from being the private fulminations of an obscure aesthete and mystic, was a demagogic assault, a well-publicized uproar reverberating throughout Scandinavia. (*The Instant* was immediately translated into Swedish and, not needing translation in Norway, aroused the interest of young Ibsen, to become the basis of *Brand*.) Kierkegaard's expectation of arrest and imprisonment was not fulfilled, but at his funeral a crowd of students gathered to protest the church's appropriation of the body, and a riot was barely averted. W. H. Auden, in introducing his own Kierkegaard anthology, regards *The Attack Upon "Christendom"* as not a book but an act: "What for the author was the most important book of his life is for us, as readers, the least, for to us the important point is not what it contains, but the fact that Kierkegaard wrote it."

Certainly, the journals of *The Last Years* are difficult to enjoy. How different are, say, the *Last Diaries* of Tolstoy, wherein the old man, honored all over the world, a sacred figure to his countrymen, struggles with the naïveté of a child to become good! Kierkegaard never had Tolstoy's candid willingness to learn and grow. He was endowed from birth with a somewhat elderly mind. Though he read voraciously and could be gregarious and charming, only five people seem to have really interested him: Jesus, Socrates, Hegel, Regine Olsen, and his father. Though his ability to vary and extend his voice is marvellous, a single field of ideas appears to have been in his possession since the beginning. It remained only for him to explore it and to arrive at the ultimate conclusion. One does not find in *The Last Years* those categories— "the absurd," "the leap," "dread"—that modern Existentialism has made fashionable; they were expounded in the earlier "aesthetic works." What one does find, theologically, is a wholehearted insistence upon the inhumanity of God. Through the bitter clamor of these journals—the outrageous but telling satires on bourgeois Christianity, the complaints about priests and professors and Bishop Mynster, the searching diagnoses of Luther and Schopenhauer, the not always tender deprecations of women, the copious self-dramatization, the tedious extollation of "the individual," the slashing dismissals of "knavish religiosity," "scoundrelly posterity," and the "increasing mass of drivel which is called science"—there sounds a note that attains a crescendo in the last pages: Christianity is torture, and God a torturer:

> In Christianity God is spirit—and therefore so immensely severe, from love: for he longs for spirit from man. . . . God is never so severe with those he loves in the Old Testament as he is with the apostles, for example, whose life was sheer suffering and then a martyr's death. . . . In the Old Testament, when the prophet is in need, God always finds a way out—but as for the apostle . . . there is no talk of unexpected help which shall bring him his strictest necessities; no, God just leaves him in the lurch, leaves him to die of hunger and thirst—it can be as severe as that.

If I were a pagan and had to speak Greek, I should say that God has arranged everything for his own entertainment; he amuses himself like a man who puts a piece of bacon in a mousetrap and watches all the tricks of the mice to get the bacon out without being gripped —so God amuses himself at the leaps and springs and contortions of these millions of men to get hold of the truth without suffering.

. . . What torture! If a man is really to be the instrument of God, for the infinite will that God is, then God must first take all his will from him. What a fearful operation! And it is natural that no one knows how to examine so painfully as one who is omniscient and omnipotent. Certainly with other forms of torture there are doctors present to estimate how long the tortured man can hold out without losing his life. Yet mistakes can happen, and the tortured man can die before their eyes. This never happens with one who is omniscient.

To be a Christian is the most terrible of all torments, it is—and it must be—to have one's hell here on earth. . . . One shudders to read what an animal must suffer which is used for vivisection; yet this is only a fugitive image of the suffering involved in being a Christian—in being kept alive in the state of death.

The vision is so terrible that Kierkegaard almost relents; "What I write is from a Christian standpoint so true, so true, and from a Christian standpoint this is how I must write. And yet I can say that what I write here tortures me to produce . . . it is repugnant to me." Again: "Ah, it is with sorrow that I write this. In melancholy sympathy, though myself unhappy, I loved men and the mass of men. Their bestial conduct toward me compelled me, in order to endure it, to have more and more to do with God."

And what is the essence of God's nature, that makes "having to do" with Him so painful? Majesty:

Suffering, that there must be suffering, is connected with the majesty of God. His majesty is so infinite that it can be characterized or expressed only by a paradox; it is the paradox of the majesty which is bound to make the beloved unhappy. . . . Suffering depends on the fact that God and man are qualitatively different, and that the clash of time and eternity in time is bound to cause suffering.

A little later, the formula is given a personal turn:

O infinite majesty, even if you were not love, even if you were cold in your infinite majesty I could not cease to love you, I need something majestic to love. . . . There was and there is a need of majesty in my soul, of a majesty I can never tire of worshipping.

Yet elsewhere this majesty acquires human attributes, even weaknesses. God knows sorrow. "Alas, the more I think about it the more I come to imagine God as sitting in sorrow, for he most of all knows what sorrow is." God loves, out of need. "It is God's passion to love and to be loved, almost—infinite love!—as though he himself were bound in this passion, so that he cannot cease to love, almost as though it were a weakness. . . ." And: "I know that in love you suffer with me, more than I, infinite Love—even if you cannot change."

The paragraph preceding this last quotation is revealing:

If my contemporaries could understand how I suffer, how Providence, if I may dare to say so, maltreats me, I am certain that they would be so profoundly moved that in human sympathy they would make an attempt (as sometimes happens with a child which is being maltreated by its parents) to wrest me free from Providence.

The hypothetical cruel parents return in another metaphor:

As the child of a tight-rope walker is from his earliest years made supple in his back and in every muscle so that, after daily practice, he is sheer suppleness and can carry out every movement, absolutely every movement, in the most excruciating positions, yet always easily and smiling: so with prayer to the absolute majesty.

And in a third image, world history is likened to "the uproar and hubbub which children make in their playroom, instead of sitting still and reading their books (as their parents would like)." With these similes, we touch a central nerve of Kierkegaard's thought— the identification of God with his father, whom he both loved and hated, who treated him cruelly and who loved him.

Much is known of Kierkegaard's relation with his father, but more is mysterious. Kierkegaard wrote in his journals: "Perhaps I could recount the tragedy of my childhood, the fearful secret explanation of religion, suggesting an apprehensive presentiment which my imagination elaborated, my offence at religion—I could recount it in a novel entitled *The Enigmatical Family*." And another entry reads:

It is terrible whenever for a single instant I come to think of the dark background of my life, from the very earliest time. The anxious dread with which my father filled my soul, his own frightful melancholy, the many things which I cannot record—I got such a dread of Christianity, and yet I felt myself so strongly drawn to it.

A childhood classmate later wrote, "To the rest of us who led a genuinely boyish life S.K. was a stranger and an object of compassion, especially on account of his dress. . . . This [his costume, which resembled the costume of charity schools] procured him the nickname of Choirboy, which alternated with Søren Sock, in allusion to his father's previous business as hosier. S.K. was regarded by us all as one whose home was wrapped in a mysterious half-darkness of severity and oddity." And in his autobiographical *The Point of View for My Work as an Author*, Kierkegaard wrote, "As a child I was strictly and austerely brought up in Christianity; humanly speaking, crazily brought up. A child crazily travestied as a melancholy old man. Terrible!"

Yet the boy's relation to his father was also intimate and admiring. One of Kierkegaard's pseudonyms, Johannes Climacus, reminisces:

His father was a very severe man, apparently dry and prosaic, but under this rough coat he concealed a glowing imagination which even old age could not quench. When Johannes occasionally asked of him permission to go out, he generally refused to give it, though once in a while he proposed instead that Johannes should take his hand and walk back and forth in the room. . . . While they went back and forth in the room the father described all that they saw; they greeted passersby, carriages rattled past them and drowned the father's voice; the cake-woman's goodies were more enticing than ever. He described so accurately, so vividly, so explicitly even to the least details, everything that was known to Johannes and so fully and perspicuously what was unknown to him, that after half an hour of such a walk with his father he was as much overwhelmed and fatigued as if he had been a whole day out of doors. . . . To Johannes it seemed as if the world were coming into existence during the conversation, *as if the father were our Lord and he were his favorite*, who was allowed to interpose his foolish conceits as merrily as he would; for he was never repulsed, the father was never put out, he agreed to everything.

I have abbreviated this often quoted passage and italicized a signal clause. By the same light, Kierkegaard did not expect to live past the age of thirty-three (the age of Christ) and *did* expect his father, though fifty-seven years older, to outlive him (to be immortal). In fact, his father lived to the patriarchal age of eighty-two and Kierkegaard died when he was only forty-two, so the premonition was in spirit correct. There is no doubt that his father fearfully dominated the household. Incredibly, in all of Kierkegaard's writings there is not one mention of his mother. And an age that has been able to peruse Kafka's diaries need not be reminded that, severity aside, the *competence*, the very wonderfulness of a father can be felt as a crushing tyranny. "It is a fearful thing," Kierkegaard wrote, "to fall into the hands of the living God."

To all this add a precocious compassion. In his journals Kierkegaard writes of the perils of religious education:

> The most dangerous case is not when the father is a free thinker, and not even when he is a hypocrite. No, the danger is when he is a pious and God-fearing man, when the child is inwardly and deeply convinced of it, and yet in spite of all this observes that a profound unrest is deeply hidden in his soul, so that not even piety and the fear of God can bestow peace. The danger lies just here, that the child in this relationship is almost compelled to draw a conclusion about God, that after all God is not infinite love.

It does not seem to me contradictory to posit a father who appears as both God and a victim of God. Such a paradox, after all, is fundamental to Christian theology, and Kierkegaard's imagination often returns to the forsaken Christ's outcry on the Cross. Duplicity was the very engine of Kierkegaard's thought, a habit he elevated to a metaphysical principle—the principle of "indirect communication," which he found both in Socrates' intellectual midwifery and in God's decision to embody Himself in a scorned and mocked sufferer. In all Kierkegaard's production, nothing is more powerful, more beautiful and typical, than the sweeping Prelude to *Fear and Trembling*, wherein the story of Abraham and Isaac is pursued through a sequence of differing versions. All portray, in similar language, Abraham and Isaac rising in the morning, leaving Sarah, and travelling to Mount Moriah, where God has told Abraham he must sacrifice his son. In the first version, Abra-

ham, whose face has shown sorrow and "fatherliness," turns away
a moment,

> and when Isaac again saw Abraham's face it was changed, his glance
> was wild, his form was horror. He seized Isaac by the throat, threw
> him to the ground, and said, "Stupid boy, dost thou then suppose
> that I am thy father? I am an idolater. Dost thou suppose that this
> is God's bidding? No, it is my desire." Then, Isaac trembled and
> cried out in his terror. "O God in heaven; have compassion upon
> me. God of Abraham, have compassion upon me. If I have no
> father upon earth, be Thou my father!" But Abraham in a low
> voice said to himself, "O Lord in heaven, I thank Thee. After all it
> is better for him to believe that I am a monster, rather than that
> he should lose faith in Thee."

Here, in this shocking twist of a myth, that nerve is bared. Here,
in this play of ironies and deceits carried out under the highest
pressure of dread, we feel close to Kierkegaard's mysterious and
searing experience of his father.

A specific revelation about his father troubled Kierkegaard's
young manhood and was transmuted, or absorbed, into a gnawing
guilt or uneasiness that he refers to in his journals as "the thorn
in my flesh," which in turn seems to be synonymous with his
singularity, his fate, as "the individual," to suffer a martyrdom not
incomparable with Christ's. Some crucial confidence was imparted
on his twenty-second birthday: "Then it was that the great earthquake occurred, the frightful upheaval which suddenly forced
upon me a new infallible rule for interpreting the phenomena one
and all. Then I surmised that my father's great age was not a
divine blessing, but rather a curse. . . . Guilt must rest upon the
whole family, a divine punishment must be impending over it."
The exact nature of the "earthquake" is forever buried in the por-
tentous secrecy Kierkegaard assigned it. Possibly the old man's
confession had to do with sex. On the mere statistical records,
Michael Kierkegaard seduced his housekeeper in the year of mourning his first wife, married the woman when she was five months
pregnant, and fathered upon her a total of seven children, the last,
Søren Aabye, being born when the parents, if not as ancient as
Abraham and Sarah, were of an age when, in Lowrie's delicate
phrase, "no such blessing was expected." Kierkegaard frequently

speaks of his own existence as a "mistake," and in the journals of *The Last Years* this sense of himself has spread to include all humanity: "This whole human existence, dating from the Fall, and which we men are so puffed up about as a devilish *tour de force* . . . is merely the consequence of a false step." Of a hypothetical son he writes:

> Concerning himself he learns that he was conceived in sin, born in transgression—that his existence is therefore a crime, that therefore his father, in giving him life, has done something which is as far as possible from being well-pleasing to God.

His vivid, even sensual awareness of Original Sin, of life itself as a crime, may be traceable to an embarrassment he felt about being himself living proof of an elderly couple's concupiscence. He ranged from the heights of conceit to abysmal depths of shame; near the end of his life, he suffered a stroke while visiting friends and, falling helpless to the floor, rejected the attempts to lift him up by saying, "Oh, leave it [his body] until the maid clears it away in the morning." In the last journals, he thanks God "that no living being owes existence to me," urges celibacy upon all Christians, faces cheerfully the consequence that the race would die out, and asserts that "human egoism is concentrated in the sexual relation, the propagation of the species, the giving of life."

Or the "earthquake" may have been learning that his father, as a eleven-year-old boy, had cursed God. An entry in the journals of 1846 reads:

> How terrible about the man who once as a little boy, while herding the flocks on the heaths of Jutland, suffering greatly, in hunger and in want, stood upon a hill and cursed God—and the man was unable to forget it even when he was eighty-two years old.

The first editor of Kierkegaard's papers, Barfod, showed this passage to Bishop Peter Kierkegaard, the one surviving sibling, who confirmed that this was indeed his father, and that, since shortly thereafter the shepherd boy was adopted by an uncle and set on the road to prosperity, he regarded this prosperity as an inverted curse, as God's vengeance for, to quote Peter, "the sin against the

Holy Ghost which never can be forgiven." It seems likely that this, and not a sexual confession, is the matter of the "earthquake." And it seems to me, furthermore, that Kierkegaard's attack upon Christendom is a repetition of his father's curse—an attack, ostensibly directed against the Danish Protestant Church, upon God Himself, on behalf of the father who had suffered, and yet also against this same father, who had made his son suffer and bound him to Christian belief.

In 1849, Kierkegaard wrote in his journals, under the heading *Something about myself which must always be remembered:* "If, with my imagination, and with my passions, etc., I had been in any ordinary human sense a man, then I should certainly have forgotten Christianity entirely. But I am bound in agonizing misery, like a bird whose wings have been clipped, yet retaining the power of my mind undiminished, and its undoubtedly exceptional powers." And the pamphlets comprising *The Attack* have been, in every language except English, the first things by Kierkegaard to be translated, as anti-clerical, anti-Christian literature. The "Christendom" Kierkegaard denounced was popularly taken to be synonymous with Christianity, and perhaps it was. It is hard to account otherwise for the strange qualities of the attack as found in *The Instant* and in these journals. Are specific abuses, as in Luther's attack upon the Papal church, named? No: "Luther nailed up niney-five theses on the church door; that was a fight about doctrine. Nowadays one might publish one single thesis in the papers: 'Christianity does not exist;' and offer to dispute with all parsons and dons." This is from a journal of 1851; by 1854, Kierkegaard had developed a piercing critique of Luther, stated wittily as:

> Luther suffered extremely from an anxious conscience, he needed treatment. Very well: but is that a reason for completely transforming Christianity into a matter of calming anxious consciences?

Kierkegaard does not want consciences to be calmed, he wants them to be exacerbated by the truth about Christianity. "My task is to put a halt to a lying diffusion of Christianity, and to help it to shake off a mass of nominal Christians." And what is the truth about Christianity?

The ideal means hatred of man. What man naturally loves is finitude. To face him with the ideal is the most dreadful torture . . . it kills in him, in the most painful way, everything in which he really finds his life, in the most painful way it shows him his own wretchedness, it keeps him in sleepless unrest, whereas finitude lulls him into enjoyment. That is why Christianity is called, and is, hatred of man.

Now, is such advocacy not a hidden prosecution? It may be argued that harsh words were a needed corrective to an existing complacency and that the New Testament itself is sternly world-denying. But I notice that, just as liberal apologists are troubled to explain away the "hard" sayings of Jesus, Kierkegaard is embarrassed by the Gospels' softer moments—the genial miracle at the wedding of Cana, the sufferance of little children, the promise to the thief on the cross. Kierkegaard says, "Men live their life in the strength of the assurance that of such as children is the kingdom of God, and in death they look for consolation to the image of the thief. That is the whole of their Christianity, and, characteristically enough, it is a mixture of childishness and crime." Surely here he is attacking something essential to Biblical teaching—the forgivingness that balances majesty. He seems impatient with divine mercy, much as a true revolutionary despises the philanthropies whereby misery is abated and revolution delayed. The "Christendom" he attacks has strangely little substance, apart from the person of Bishop Mynster, his father's pastor, who is criticized only for his urbanity and eloquence and his refusal to confess that "what he represented was not really Christianity but a milder form of it." Indeed, the whole attack is an invitation to the Church to commit suicide: "Yes, truly, suicide, and yet an action well-pleasing to God." Any specific reform—a revival of monasteries, an abolition of "livings"—he explicitly disavows. The one concrete result he expects from his attack is his own imprisonment and death. Though the Church's functionaries barely troubled to respond even in writing, he did die. He suffered his fatal stroke while returning from the bank with the last scrap of his fortune. He had nowhere further to go, and his death, whose causes eluded diagnosis, seems willed.

In the hospital, he told his only intimate friend, the pastor Emil Boesen, "The doctors do not understand my illness; it is psychic, and they want to treat it in the ordinary medical way." His conversations with Boesen, a kind of continuation of the journals (printed as such by Dru), have a relaxed sweetness; his terrible "task" is done, and he is happy that so much in his life has "come out right" and is melancholy that he cannot share his happiness with everyone. He refuses to put flowers sent him into water: "it is the fate of flowers to blossom, smell, and die." Of *The Instant*, whose tenth number lay unpublished on his desk, he said, "You must remember that I have seen everything from the inmost center of Christianity, it is all very poor and clumsy. . . . I only said it to be rid of evil, and so to reach an Alleluia! Alleluia! Alleluia!" This "Alleluia," it may be, could be reached only through a scandal in which, alone like a shepherd boy on the Jutland heath, Kierkegaard execrated God. At any rate, with Kierkegaard, as with Proust, we feel writing as a demon—the one way to set a bent life straight.

Kierkegaard would hardly be pleased to know that more than any other thinker of the 19th century—not excluding Newman and Dostoevsky—he has made Christianity intellectually possible for the 20th. Not that the "millions of men falling away from Christianity" that he foresaw and desired has not occurred. But, by giving metaphysical dignity to "the subjective," by showing faith to be not an intellectual development but a movement of the will, by holding out for existential duality against the tide of all the monisms, materialist or mystical or political, that would absorb the individual consciousness, Kierkegaard has given Christianity new life, a handhold, the "Archimedean point." From Jaspers and Barth, Unamuno and Marcel, Heidegger and Sartre, his thought has filtered down through the seminaries to the laity. He has become, as he angrily predicted, the property of those men "more abominable and gruesome than the cannibals," professors and clergymen, and he is used, in the form of a few phrases or a bolder style, to prop up the feeble, always tottering faith of contemporary "Christians." He has become an instrument in the conspiracy to "make a fool of God." Those who read him eat the aesthetic coating and leave the religious pill, and "neo-Orthodox" Protestantism, his direct beneficiary, has accepted the antinomianism and ignored the savage austerity, the scornful authoritarianism. Yet Kierkegaard himself, this two-tined Fork with his trouser legs of unequal length, this man in love with duplicity and irony and all double-edged things, lived luxuriously to the last and is nowhere quite free of sophism and vanity. (His sermons, for example, so symphonic and ardent, somehow belong with the memorable sermons of fiction, like those of Father Mapple in *Moby Dick* and of Père Paneloux in *The Plague*.) In the journal of 1849 he reminded himself, "It must never be forgotten that Christ also succored temporal and worldly needs. One can also, untruly, make Christ so spiritual that he becomes sheer cruelty." If this is what Kierkegaard seemed to do in the end, he also remembered that infinite majesty infinitely relents. Late in *The Last Years* we find this surprising entry: "For with such clarity as I have, I must say I am not a Christian. For the situation as I see it is that in spite of the abyss of nonsense in which we are caught, we shall all alike be saved."

RELIGIOUS NOTES

On the Boundary, by Paul Tillich. 104 pp. Scribners, 1966.
The Future of Religions, by Paul Tillich. 94 pp. Harper & Row, 1966.

These two small posthumous volumes cast a sympathetic backward light upon a somewhat puzzling figure. Tillich, though possessed of a personal radiance that penetrated even the speckled fog
of a television interview, seemed in his writing pervasively ambiguous and tortuously euphemistic. In *On the Boundary*, a terse autobiographical sketch, he declares that for all of his long life he
considered his proper place to be on both sides of the fence.
Theologian and philosopher, conservative and socialist, German
and American, he felt himself a mediator in a world of fragmentation, and entertained atheism in the church parlor. It took an
exceptional serenity to do this: "The man who stands on many
boundaries experiences the unrest, insecurity, and inner limitation
of existence in many forms." His tolerance of uncertainty and of
contradiction was perhaps specifically Lutheran, and Tillich may
have been the first Lutheran voice in American intellectual history. Lutheranism (existing throughout the United States in geographical enclaves whose atmosphere, oppressive and stagnant and
idyllic, can be felt in the novels of Conrad Richter) is itemized by
Tillich as "a consciousness of the 'corruption' of existence, a re-
pudiation of every kind of social Utopia (including the metaphysics of progressivism), an awareness of the irrational and
demonic nature of existence, an appreciation of the mystical element in religion, and a rejection of Puritanical legalism in private
and corporal life." In *The Future of Religions*, which contains,
amid much eulogistic padding, four short addresses, he more spe-

cifically relates Utopianism and the concept of progress to the Calvinism that has informed American ideals. On the other hand, Lutheranism, with Greek Orthodoxy, is a church of "withdrawal from history." One wonders, considering the exhaustion of the frontier, where Puritanism had point, whether the future of Christianity in America does not lie with some such withdrawal. History is proving to elude apotheosis, and Tillich's remarkable rapport with young students appears prophetic of the mystical, latitudinarian, and rather Asiatic new wave of American religious expression.

MY TRAVEL DIARY: 1936, by Paul Tillich, edited and with an introduction by Jerald C. Brauer, translated from the German by Maria Pelikan. 192 pp. Harper & Row, 1970.

The late Professor Tillich, having fled Nazi Germany in 1933, returned to Europe three years later for a round of lectures and conferences, and he mailed his wife installments of the diary he kept from April to September. Now this affectionate record has been published, and while it is neither very amusing nor very enlightening, it is something of both. Tillich's own generous and receptive nature shines through his notation of countless conversations, audiences, bottles of wine, beautiful vistas, nights of good or less good sleep. In Paris he visits night clubs featuring "very nude" girls; in Switzerland he climbs glaciers. In Scotland he is "seated at the Dean's right, next to Patterson, an old systematic theologian"; in Holland he marvels at the Rembrandts. At all stops he counsels and consoles friends he may never see again—expatriated and polarized citizens of a Europe that was on the edge of the abyss and knew it, yet was still the immemorial Europe of good food, mountain views, well-mannered prostitutes, hikes, ideas, and rain showers that enliven rather than ruin an afternoon. Though Tillich visits Barth and gossips about Heidegger, he rarely reads a book or goes to church. In a way, this is everybody's summer abroad, right down to the well-evoked days at sea, except that Hitler's handwriting is now no longer a topic of analysis, and trips to Russia are not the latest thing among the intelligentsia. This charming memento of a vanished man and era has been indifferently served by its publishers: typographical errors abound, and where contemporary photographs of the scenery would have helped, there are quite superfluous pen-and-ink scribbles (by Alfonso Ossorio) of nothing in particular.

DELIVERANCE TO THE CAPTIVES, by Karl Barth, translated from the German by Marguerite Wieser. 160 pp. Harper, 1961.

This collection of recent sermons displays the grave, generous, and—often—genial humanity of "anti-humanist" theology's living Olympian. Seekers of novelty and subtlety in philosophical accommodation should seek elsewhere; it has been Barth's work to turn the Christian field with a resharpened plow, rather than to look for new pastures or draw new boundaries. The force of these sermons lies in that—minus a few topical references and with a few adjustments of emphasis—they might have been preached any time in the last two millennia, and, but for their exceptional compactness and pertinence of expression, by a conservative clergyman anywhere. Perhaps because they were for the most part delivered to inmates of the prison in Basel, their dominant note—an unusual one in contemporary Christian literature—is of hope, of joy in the Lord, of an ardor that can assert, concerning faith, that "no human being has ever prayed for this in vain."

HOW I CHANGED MY MIND, by Karl Barth, with an introduction and epilogue by John D. Godsey. 96 pp. John Knox Press, 1966.

A bracing demi-autobiography, essentially composed of three self-descriptive articles Barth wrote for the *Christian Century* in 1938, 1948, and 1958 under the heading "How I Changed My

Mind." Actually, in the three decades considered, Barth changed his mind rather little, holding fast to his central vision of God's otherness through all political and theological storms. The dominant impression these pages leave is of Barth's heroic stubbornness, the reasoned yet pugnacious refusal to let others think for him: when political relativism was fashionable, he implacably opposed Hitler, and when political absolutism prevailed, he took a mediating attitude toward Communism. Though his theology, a virtual reinvention of Christian orthodoxy, must be described as conservative, it has been viewed by himself as a "restless" activity, a "process" in which he has been concerned "not to forfeit my freedom." What also emerges from these essays, amplified by the editor's description of a visit to Barth in 1965 and the theologian's concluding letter, is an account of the aging process as it has been experienced, with rare good grace, by a man of firm health, normal worldliness, and enviable sense of vocation.

DISCOURSE ON THINKING, by Martin Heidegger, translated from the German by John M. Anderson and E. Hans Freund. 93 pp. Harper & Row, 1966.

A small book, of which nearly half is occupied by a not very helpful introduction. The other half consists of a "Memorial Address" delivered by Heidegger in honor of the German composer Conradin Kreutzer, and a trialogue between a scientist, a scholar, and a teacher entitled "Conversation on a Country Path About Thinking." The address, with a certain donnish orotundity, lucidly sets forth the propositions that there are two kinds of thinking—calculative and meditative—and that amid the technological triumphs of calculative thinking man must survive as a meditative being. This he can do by saying both yes and no to technology, the yes being a "releasement toward things" and the no a continuing "openness to the mystery." These concepts are developed into total obscurity by the "Conversation," whose English version abounds in possibly precise but gritty equivalents like "re-present," "autochthonic," and "that-which-regions." Meditative thinking is explained as "the coming-into-the-nearness of distance," and our human position as a kind of holy "waiting"— "The relation to that-which-regions is waiting." And "That-which-regions [*die Gegnet* in German] is an abiding expanse which, gathering all, opens itself, so that in it openness is halted and held, letting everything merge in its own resting." What emerges is a humanism tied to a mysticism shorn of theology; the final coalescence of meaning is a metaphor of the night that, without seam or thread, binds the distant stars together in apparent nearness. The rarefied poetry of the discourse is made eerie by our knowledge that it was based on a conversation that really occurred, within Germany, in 1944–1945, when the anvils of Hitler's hell were beating loudest.

THE HEART PREPARED: GRACE AND CONVERSION IN PURITAN SPIRITUAL LIFE, by Norman Pettit. 252 pp. Yale, 1966.

This finely written and beautifully printed study of post-Reformation theological niceties doubles as an analysis of the infant American psyche. Zwingli and Calvin held that man in his utter depravity "could neither anticipate salvation nor look to the inner self for signs of regeneration." The English founders of Puritanism tentatively qualified the severity of predestinarian doctrine with suggestions that the heart, however unworthy, might predispose or prepare itself for the invasion of saving grace. In the theocratic communities of New England, a proclaimed inner experience of conversion became a criterion for church membership, and the "grappling with the heart" developed, notably in the discourses of Thomas Hooker, of Hartford, into a veritable poetics of introspection. Preparationism, never without its opponents, eventually succumbed to a reasserted Calvinism and to the practical problems of church enrollment, but its experiential emphasis remains a feature of American religious revivals and perhaps accounts for a Pelagian bias in our spiritual heritage. Dr. Pettit, though he traces the image of the prepared heart down to its final diffusion in Emerson, leaves to implication the present relevance of his thesis. His approach is strikingly concrete and, dealing with quibbles that might seem quaint, convincingly serious. In a prose whose clarity belies the volumes of cobwebbed tracts he has suffered through, he renders penumbral nuances of theology distinct, gives personality to a dozen divines, and somewhat sweetens our impression of the Puritan tenets.

DOSTOEVSKY

A Raw Something

THE ADOLESCENT, by Fyodor Dostoevsky, translated by Andrew R. MacAndrew. 585 pp. Doubleday, 1971.

Why a new translation? And, if a new translation, why of this novel? Written between *The Possessed* and *The Brothers Karamazov*, *The Adolescent* (entitled *A Raw Youth* in the 1916 translation by Constance Garnett) possesses the greatness of neither. The novel, though it bears many marks of Dostoevsky's devotion, and definitively enunciates some of the themes dearest to him, has that penetrating badness that casts doubt over even the peaks of an author's accomplishment—as, say, *Across the River and into the Trees* drained magic from *all* of Hemingway's head-waiters and undermined forever the consolations of café stoicism. In *The Adolescent* the frequent feverishness of Dostoevsky's characters appears compulsory and their willful, self-careless perversity seems merely automatic, an author's trick he employs in scene after scene. For once, the elements of Dostoevsky's fictional universe—the fantastically compressed action, the stunning tirades, the melodramatic welter of coincidences and encounters and incriminating documents and postponed revelations—fail to fuse into a fiery whole. Rather, a string of firecrackers goes off, some louder than others, and some so damply we turn back the pages to catch what we missed. Four novels, Dostoevsky once told his wife, fight for attention within the covers of this one; his original instinct, Mr. MacAndrew tells us in his lengthy and gossipy introduction, was to entitle the book "Disorder."

The hero is a young bastard, Arkady Dolgoruky. Unlike some of Dostoevsky's first-person narrators, Arkady does not conveniently vanish when the action becomes heated, but wears out several pairs of boots rushing around St. Petersburg to keep eavesdropping appointments and wears out our ears with expostulations over the difficulties of maintaining a narrative so tangled. His voice and psyche, however, are the strongest thing in the novel: a "raw youth's" passion for exploration and posturing and humiliation have rarely been more indulgently dramatized. Arkady aside, the characters seem inferior copies of characters met in the other novels—Versilov a more trivial Stavrogin, Katarina a feeble sister of *The Idiot's* Nastasia, Makar a preliminary study for Father Zosima. The plot, on a circumstantial level, absurdly revolves around a slightly embarrassing letter that rides out six hundred pages in Arkady's coat pocket; on a thematic level, it gropes toward secrets of parenthood and kinship that are firmly seized in the next novel, *The Brothers Karamazov*.

Why this novel? Perhaps, though Mr. MacAndrew does not say so, he felt it to be especially appropriate to America's present condition of self-doubt and generational estrangement. Here is the Russia of the 1870's:

> All the better people are crazy . . . only the mediocrities, the unimaginative bystanders, are having a great time. . . . Selfishness displaces the old unifying principle, and the whole system breaks up into a multitude of individuals, each with a full set of civil rights. . . . whole batches of our best people are tearing themselves away from it and lightheartedly joining the roving packs of the disorderly and the envious.

Sound familiar? Yes, but I doubt that a majority of Americans will embrace Dostoevsky's solution: "any order as long as it is our native one."

And why a new translation? Presumably because the old one, by the tireless Mrs. Garnett, was judged to be improvable. I have compared passages of Garnett vs. MacAndrew, and read the last third of the novel in alternate chapters from each; and my impression is that more has been lost than has been gained. Mr. MacAndrew's modern idiom does very well with the jerks and halts of interior monologue, and occasionally captures a precision where Mrs. Garnett either flunked the Russian or held to a Victorian middle style—"as though pouring his words through a funnel" betters "dropping out his words one by one"; "crush him until there's only a wet spot left behind" outcruels "pound him to a jelly." But more often the precision is on Garnett's side: "worldwide compassion for all" pales to "universal concern"; "she was now evil" simpers as "she was not a nice person." MacAndrew drops the patronymics, which may save some confusion but sacrifices a peculiar warmth of Russian novels, and when terms of endearment are employed he is almost helpless. Where Garnett's phrasing is moving, his is often blank tin: "They rejoiced, like birds, did not feel their ruin, and their voices were like little bells" becomes in MacAndrew's version, "They're happy like little birds and their voices sound like jingle bells." And surprisingly, the modern translator shows less feel for the philosophic checkpoints of the novel: the key concept that Garnett imaginatively renders as "seemliness" is blandly presented by MacAndrew as "beauty," in quotation marks. The most famous sentence in *A Raw Youth*—

> It always has been a mystery, and I have marvelled a thousand times at that faculty in man (and in the Russian, I believe, more especially) of cherishing in his soul his loftiest ideal side by side with the most abject baseness, and all quite sincerely—

comes out all muddled and adverbial in MacAndrew's version—

> Yes, it has always been a mystery to me and thousands of times I've stopped and marveled at man's capacity (especially a Russian's, I believe) to cherish in himself some infinitely lofty ideal alongside something unspeakably base, and all this quite openly.

Even the title feels wrong. MacAndrew has Arkady as nineteen, Garnett as twenty years old: either way, he is too old to be an "adolescent." In general, two translators being more or less competent, the one closer in time to the original is apt to be better, more instinctively sharing the author's universe. Manners and moral concerns become distant and take language with them. The characters in the Garnett translation behave bizarrely, but as foreigners do. In MacAndrew's translation they are bizarre like figures in a dream.

Polina and Aleksei and Anna and Losnitsky

THE GAMBLER, by Fyodor Dostoevski, with Polina Suslova's Dairy, translated by Victor Terras. 366 pp. University of Chicago Press, 1972.

The University of Chicago Press, which has issued, under the editorship of Edward Wasiolek, Dostoevsky's notebooks for his five major novels, has extended this valuable series with a new, complexly augmented translation of the short novel *The Gambler*. The augmentations include: letters from Dostoevsky during the hectic period of his life when he was obsessed by gambling, debts, his dying wife, his dying brother, and Polina Suslova; the diary of this same Polina Suslova, who is described by the normally unemphatic *Encyclopaedia Britannica* as a "young woman of sensual, proud, and 'demoniac' character" and who is often cited by critics as a prototype for the perverse and taunting Dostoevsky heroines; and a short story by her about a love affair between "Losnitsky" and "Anna." This bundle of interrelated materials is intelligently edited and fluently translated, though I blinked at the exclamation "Wow!!!"—the Garnett translation has "What!!!"— and regretted that the proofreaders allowed one doubled slug to slip through. And I would have been grateful for a little factual background to Polina's diary, "published here in English for the first time." Why does it begin and end so conveniently and abruptly, August 19, 1863, to November 6, 1865, in effect bracketing the European phase of her affair with Dostoevsky? Did she keep a diary only then? And the chronology of this affair is not set forward as clearly as it is in, say, Avrahm Yarmolinsky's biography.

Polina and Dostoevsky probably met, in Petersburg, before September of 1861, when a story of hers appeared in *Vremya* (*Time*), which he edited. He was forty; she was little more than half his age. They became friends and, by the time she was twenty-three, lovers. He kept the secret from his wife and made no offer to divorce her, which may have offended Polina. However, she went to Paris in the spring of 1863 with the understanding that Dostoevsky would join her there and that they would travel together in Italy. A tangle of business generated by the government's suppression of his magazine held him in Petersburg until mid-August, and en route to his mistress he stopped off at Wiesbaden and Baden-Baden to gamble—first winning, then losing. By the time he arrived in Paris, Polina had been captivated, seduced, and abandoned by Salvador, a young South American medical student, who did not love her. Dostoevsky quickly adjusted to this new embarrassment and proposed that he and Polina travel to Italy anyway, not as lovers but "remaining like brother and sister." Thus uneasily attached, they toured for two months; then Dostoevsky returned to Petersburg, to write *Notes from the Underground* and most of *Crime and Punishment*. He did not see Polina until nearly two years later, in the summer of 1865, in Wiesbaden. Though his wife (Maria Dmitrievna Isaeva, a she-devil in her own right) had died in the interim, the affair did not prosper. In the few days he and Polina were together, Dostoevsky lost his last kopeck at roulette, and proved no luckier at love. The reunion didn't rate a line in her diary, though it did elicit from him two frantic but amiable letters to her, postage due, begging for a hundred and fifty gulden. Their final encounters occurred that fall and winter, in Petersburg, to which Polina returned in November; "he has been offering me his hand and his heart," Polina wrote, "and he only makes me angry doing so." She departed three months later. He finished *Crime and Punishment* and in October of 1866 dictated *The Gambler* to a competent, patient, and smitten young stenographer, Anna Snitkina. Dostoevsky married Anna in February of 1867, and that spring, in response to a letter from Polina, informed her of his marriage and added, *"Au revoir,* my good friend forever!" He and Polina did not—if one discounts a romantic story Dostoevsky's daughter tells of a "woman in black" who called on her father in the late seventies—meet again.

Reading through *The Gambler* and its attendant documents produces several unexpected impressions—chief among them that the lovers did not much like one another. Indeed, through the mist of egoistical preoccupations they hardly *saw* each other. Polina's story "The Stranger and Her Lover" betrays no awareness that she is representing, in fictional guise, one of the century's most fascinating spirits: "He started telling her various anecdotes and stories from his own life. These tales might have been, perhaps, of some interest to other people, but Anna saw little wit, and even less refinement, about them." Once Dostoevsky returns to Russia, he drops out of her diary with scarcely a thud, to be replaced by a titillating series of (at the least) flirtations. Mr. Wasiolek, in his introduction, protests: "one is dismayed to find that it is only our interest that lifts the image of Dostoevsky in her diary from the mesh of her prosaisms." The literary scholar, necessarily in love with greatness, cannot help scolding this mediocre little blue-stocking who, awarded the living Dostoevsky's love, betrayed him with a—Wasiolek's phrase—"trivial and insensitive medi-cal student." Worse yet, in her fictional representation Dostoevsky appears "petty, boastful, and vulgar; his only redeeming features consist in his appreciation of her majestic character and beauty, in his astonishment at having possessed her, and in his contrition at having lost her." It is true that Polina's "The Stranger and Her Lover" is pitiably inept and self-promoting; the persistently "ma-jestic" heroine obtusely refuses to perceive that her one ticket to significance, from the standpoint of posterity, lies with this re-pulsive, repelled lover, whose immortal genius is never for an instant permitted to wink through the vapors of her narcissism.

But does Polina fare better in Dostoevsky's version of their affair, in the minor masterpiece *The Gambler*? Not much. The pages dealing with "Polina Aleksandrovna" and her willful abuse of the infatuated "Aleksei Ivanovich" seem rather perfunctory, as though the author were blocking out an idea instead of giving flesh to inspiration. "I simply don't understand what I find in her. All right, she is beautiful, that she is; or it seems that she is. She drives other men out of their minds, too. She is tall and slender, though very slim. It seems as if one could tie her in a knot or bend her double. Her foot is long and narrow: tormenting. Exactly so: tormenting." The focus is on the torment, not on the woman. When she dares Aleksei to insult a passing baron, the vivacity of the incident depends on his zealous willingness to play the fool; he overreacts to her, as he overreacts to the seductive spin of the roulette wheel. Her moods, indeed, have for Aleksei the blind chanciness of roulette, and they offer him the same opportunity to humiliate and impoverish himself and thereby to demonstrate his exalted Russian disregard of material consequence. Aleksei, and the author, do not attempt to discover an inner logic of Polina's behavior, because a cruel arbitrariness is what satisfies them. So Polina remains too volatile to be grasped by our imaginations; "one could tie her in a knot or bend her double." In contrast, a secondary female character, the French adventuress Blanche, is quite solid:

> She is tall, with broad, strong shoulders. Her neck and bosom are magnificent. Her complexion is a swarthy yellow, her hair raven black, and she's got a great deal of it, enough for two coiffures. Her eyes are black with yellowish whites, her look insolent, her teeth very white, and her lips always painted. Her perfume smells of musk.

This musky creature develops amusingly when Aleksei, in a feverish trance of gambling clairvoyance, wins a hundred thousand gulden; Polina, though she is deeply in debt, in good Slavic style disdains the money ("The bankroll hit me painfully in the face and scattered all over the floor"), whereupon Blanche delightedly pounces upon the fortune: "First of all, *je veux cinquante mille francs*. You will give them to me in Frankfort. *Nous allons à Paris.* We'll be living together there *et je te ferai voir des étoiles en plein jour.*" In Paris, however, instead of making him see stars in daytime, Blanche deigns to tie his necktie for him every morning and shrewdly uses his money to set herself up as a respectable person: "So now I have established myself in decent style once and for all, and nobody is going to put me out, not for a long time, at least that's the way I've got it planned." To crown her new status, she weds a useless but ornamental general, a Russian aristocrat whose mother's fortune has been disastrously depreciated at the voracious tables of "Roulettenburg." Nevertheless, Blanche will make the best of the bargain: "To begin with, he's got his pension, and second, he'll live in a back room, where he'll be perfectly happy. I shall be *'madame la Générale.'* I'll belong to a nice social set. . . . Later I'll be a Russian landowner; *j'aurai un château, des moujiks, et puis j'aurai toujours mon million.*" In this interplay between brisk French avarice and the mystical wastefulness of the Russian character, *The Gambler* finds its best

comedy and its serious point, anticipating the magnificent if deluded Slavophilism of the great novels to follow. Seen, carica-
turally, as a hard-headed, hard-hearted European, with her mainspring plainly diagrammed, Blanche succeeds as a character and
as a lovable woman. "Blanche, it ought to be said, was indeed a
very nice, good-natured girl—in her own way, of course; I did
not appreciate her enough in the beginning." Whereas Polina remains mysterious, and rather unlikable, to the end.

Polina Suslova's diary explains her more sympathetically than
does either work of fiction. The grandiose, ill-coordinated self-
assertiveness that her own story expresses and that Dostoevsky's
portrays is here muted and disclosed as fruit of a central plight:
she is a woman.

> Now I feel and see clearly that I cannot live, that I cannot find hap-
> piness in the enjoyment of love, because the caresses of men will
> remind me of my humiliations and my sufferings.

Clinically she observes herself in love with the indifferent Salvador, transcribing each of her pleading, unanswered letters; mor-
dantly noting the fluctuations of her disease. "Any mention of
S[alvador] gives me a terrifying, painful, and sweet feeling. However, what rubbish that whole thing was, everything that happened between me and Salv[ador]." Coolly, with her nearest
approaches to irony, she admires her beloved's stratagems of withdrawal while she records her own maneuvers with Dostoevsky,
moderated "so that he could neither cherish hope nor be quite
without it." Out of her pain, she rises to chilling heights of detachment: "Today I have been thinking a great deal, and I almost
felt glad that Salvador loves me so little; it makes me freer." Freedom is what she wants and cannot attain:

> I am now thinking about my return to Russia. Where shall I go, to
> whom? To my brother, to my father? I will never be as free as I
> would like to, and to what end should I suffer this dependency?
> What have I in common with these people? Carry out my ideas!
> Stupid.

She distrusts her ideas as she distrusts her loves. In the midst of a
discussion with one of her intellectual, revolutionary boy friends,
she flashes out, "Why go to see a woman? There isn't much in-

teresting about me, is there? If you are looking for intellect and erudition, you won't come here to find them." In a shocking passage, she is abruptly, without anesthesia or psychological preparation, operated upon by a doctor:

> He said, as he was putting away his instruments, that after this operation I could have children if I got married. I said that I found no comfort in this. "Why so?" he asked; "all women want to have children." "Because I don't know how to bring them up," I said. The thoughts which occurred to me in connection with this conversation made me sad and caused me to shed tears, which I did not hold back.

Polina's feminism turns her diary outward from the stifling self-concern of her fiction; her jottings abound in sharp vignettes of the life about her as she moves from Baden-Baden to Turin and Genoa and Rome, and then to Paris and Zurich and back to Petersburg. She is unself-consciously sensitive, as the pain of Salvador ebbs, to other women: waitresses, flower girls, kept women, landladies, lady novelists, countesses. Only with another woman can she relax and spill her grief: "I could not restrain myself, but dropped on my knees before her [the Countess Salias] and began to sob aloud. She was frightened and wanted to get me a glass of water. 'No, no,' I said, 'forget it; I feel good this way.' " As she receives compassion from women, so she gives it; she offers to find work for a young woman who begs for two sous on the street, and she takes note of the inequities between a young student and his mistress:

> The relationship between the student and the lady is a touching one. At table, she lets him have the choice morsels; when she pours herself some wine, she always lets him have some first.

With the same eye, she observes her feelings, in the course of her entanglements, of humiliation, disgust, and uncertainty, and the contradictory behavior these feelings engender. As she tussles with an admirer called Robescourt:

> Then there began an incoherent conversation, interrupted by kisses. He was trembling all over, and he had such a happy, smiling face. I was also feeling happy, but kept breaking off our ardent embraces, with my pleas to be left alone. I kept pushing him away, then again passionately stretched out my arms to him.

Her awareness of her own ambivalence gives some episodes the sentence-by-sentence surprisingness of the best fiction:

> I stroked his hair and kissed his forehead. We talked all kinds of light-hearted nonsense, no worries or doubts of any sort entered my mind. Then I drove over to the C[ountess's]. He accompanied me. As we were sitting in the carriage hand in hand, I felt that his love was not a good one, if this can be called love. We got up. We parted in the park. Having walked a considerable distance I turned around and saw him standing there, following me with his eyes, but it was a farce, and an awkward one, in fact. He came the next night. There was no limit to his rapture and passion, and I surrendered to these moments without any anxiety or doubt.
>
> He wanted more than that, but I wouldn't let it happen, and he saw his mistake. I said that I was leaving.

Such a passage, in which the subtle female heart begs dignity and verity of a world that offers her only motherhood and "love," illuminates from within the self-punishing, lover-punishing perversity that Dostoevsky was content to represent as an inscrutable delirium.

Yet these two people, who saw into each other so imperfectly, so carelessly, were useful to one another. Dostoevsky's "turbulent and destructive affair with Polina Suslova," as Wasiolek calls it, coincides, he admits, with the writer's final awakening, the production of two works—*Notes from the Underground* in 1864, *Crime and Punishment* in 1866—that lift him into the empyrean of Western literature, into that small circle of writers who have appreciably enlarged Man's self-knowledge. In her story, Polina has Dostoevsky's surrogate say, "You have meant a lot to me. Your love descended upon me like a gift from God, against all hope and expectation, when I was weary and desperate. This young life at my side promised me so much and has already given me so much. It has resurrected my faith and what remained of my former strength." Was this a real speech, or her own sentimental fantasy? At any rate, the heroine responds with a startlingly dry inner observation: " 'You've really put it to good use,' thought Anna, but she said nothing." This mirrors a passage in *The Gambler*, as Aleksei meditates:

She doesn't bother to hide her aversion to me at all, this I can see. But she also does not conceal from me either the fact that she needs me for some purpose and that she is saving me for some future use.

What were these uses? In Dostoevsky's case, Polina—apart from her sexual benefactions in the short period before she shut them off—helped him debase himself toward that ground of suffering nullity from which he drew creative strength. Self-humiliation is one of the writer's most useful aids; it puts him in touch with the basal humanity that dignity, honors, flattery, and prosperity would estrange him from. It frees the artist of a respectable man's baggage. Biting the dirt, he recovers the taste of comedy and dread. Among contemporary practitioners, Norman Mailer most diligently, or at least most publicly, humiliates himself, but any serious writer needs keep some access to shame and abasement. Dostoevsky's need was acute; that Polina taunted him with her lovers, banished him from her bed, ignored his immense gifts, and urged him to play the fool should not be counted against her. In her unhappiness, she had an instinct for the necessary plunge. With odd generosity, she lent Dostoevsky money for his gambling, which became to his temperament a religious trance, a frightful prostration to the divine *nihil*, a kind of induced epilepsy, a giddy descent into himself, a defiance of worldly wisdom. In his begging letters to Polina he exults in his pennilessness, in the contempt expressed by his German servants, for "there is no greater crime in the eyes of a German than to have no money." But there *is*, he announces in the next letter, food beyond bread: "I continue to go without dinner, subsisting on my morning and evening tea for the third day now, and strangely enough, I am not very hungry at all." Eventually, such a regimen kills; Dostoevsky turns from Polina and takes shelter in marriage to a kind woman.

What of Polina, though; what was Dostoevsky's use to her? Not, I suspect, as an intellectual companion. In her diary, though she mentions a healing talk with him about "the emancipation of women," it is the feline Frenchman Jean-Baptiste Gaut who manages to speak her heart's language.

> Yesterday Gaut was here and I had a sentimental discussion with him: on love, marriage, etc. . . . "And love," he said, "passion, what

are they? Just a needless scandal. Surround yourself with sensible people, that's all."

I agreed with him.

Her soul finds flattery, too, in the company of her revolutionary countrymen—Herzen, Bakunin, Luginin. Dostoevsky by this time is not even a liberal. And before she begins this diary, she has committed herself to younger lovers. Dostoevsky tells her, "You fell in love with me by mistake." But there is evidence in her diary that he did, once, perform for her the lover's essential service: he shook her up. "I hear about F[yodor] M[ikhailovich]. I simply hate him. He made me suffer so much, when it was possible not to suffer." And "As I remember what happened two years ago, I begin to hate D[ostoevsky]. He was the first to kill my faith." Yet a proud otherworldliness is perhaps what they shared. Though he accuses her, when she first refuses to sleep with him, of a "utilitarian attitude," in the end, in the last entry in the diary, all passion useless, she talks teasingly, in a vein dear to his heart: "I said that I was going to become a holy woman, that I would walk through the Kremlin gardens in Moscow in my bare feet, telling people that I was having conversations with angels."

In fact, she married, in her middle years, a much younger man who was, strangely, an ardent devotee of Dostoevsky—the critic and *littérateur* V. V. Rozanov. He grew to hate her. Her later life has the flavor of *The Possessed*. After parting with Dostoevsky, she opened a village school that the authorities closed on the grounds that she bobbed her hair, never went to church, and had consorted abroad with revolutionaries. Six years after marrying Rozanov, she fled with a young lover; when this neo-Salvador spurned her, she denounced him to the police as a revolutionary. Her husband, whom she refused to divorce, likened her to Catherine de Medici and claimed to have found a perfect description of her in Dostoevsky's *The Insulted and Injured:* a woman who "looked upon everyone with impartial severity, like the abbess of a medieval convent," yet whose "sensuality was such that even the Marquis de Sade might have taken lessons from her. . . . In the very heat of voluptuousness she would suddenly laugh like one possessed." Dostoevsky wrote the description first; then he met Polina.

KNUT HAMSUN

"*My Mind Was Without a Shadow*"

HUNGER, by Knut Hamsun, translated from the Norwegian by Robert Bly. 232 pp. Farrar, Straus & Giroux, 1967.

ON OVERGROWN PATHS, by Knut Hamsun, translated from the Norwegian by Carl L. Anderson. 176 pp. Paul S. Eriksson, 1967.

Coincidence, of the rather amiable kind it amused Knut Hamsun to record, marks the simultaneous publication in the United States of his first novel, *Hunger*, and his last book, a memoir entitled *On Overgrown Paths*. *Hunger* was written by a starving young man in the late 1880's and finally published, after serialization, in 1890, when Hamsun was thirty-one; *On Overgrown Paths* was written by a disgraced old man, held accused of treason, in the late 1940's and was published in 1949, when Hamsun was ninety. Sixty years and a career that included a Nobel Prize lie between them, yet the books are similar, and are beautiful in the same way. They are laconic, brutal, joyous, and not quite formless. Their literary freshness flows from a positive human quality of, to give it a negative name, *defenselessness*. The "I" of both accounts has scorned all systems, has formed no alliances, not even with a woman; Hamsun's wife, though she shared his ordeal of ostracism and harassment after the war, is virtually absent from the pages of *On Overgrown Paths*. The ratty boarding houses of *Hunger* and the various institutions of Hamsun's internment and, for that matter, the hunter's hut occupied by the hero of his novel *Pan* are all temporary shelters unregretfully shed by a spirit intent upon the inner play of mood, a rapt yet detached spirit to whom pain is merely one of the many winds that tug and shift the soul. Such lucidity approaches madness; in the absence of all other armor, a carapace of willful eccentricity must be grown. As a young transient in this country, Hamsun began to spit blood, and countered the diagnosis of terminal tuberculosis by riding on top of a locomotive from Minneapolis to New York, gulping fresh air all the way. The cure worked; but the same headlong stubbornness also led him to support the Nazis to the end, writing, upon Hitler's death, "He was a warrior, a warrior for mankind and a prophet of the gospel of justice for all nations." At the very outset of his career, the young Hamsun undertook a lecture tour attacking the living great writers of Norway, culminating in a verbal assault upon Ibsen while Ibsen sat glowering in the front row. Hamsun was always more enthusiastically admired in Germany and Slavic Europe than in Norway itself. Of American writers, he resembles Hemingway in his estrangement from the cultural establishment, in his proud follies, in his cauterization of prose style, in the impression of lightness and transparency his pessimism produces. By this analogy, *On Overgrown Paths* is like *A Moveable Feast*—a return, after troubled middle years spent pursuing "depth" with a puerile ideology, to an instinctive youthful allegiance to surfaces and moments.

Hunger, first published in English in 1899, is flattered by its new translation and by its two introductions. In one, the Yiddish writer I. B. Singer describes, with an emphatic generosity that may surprise younger literary generations, Hamsun's importance to his own: "European writers know that he is the father of the modern school of literature in his every aspect—his subjectiveness, his fragmentariness, his use of flashbacks, his lyricism. The whole modern school of fiction in the twentieth century stems from Hamsun, just as Russian literature in the nineteenth century 'came out of Gogol's greatcoat.' . . . Hamsun belonged to that select group of writers who not only interested a reader but virtually hypnotized him." The other introduction, by the translator, Robert Bly, sensitively points up the novel's paradoxical affirmation: "The hero of *Hunger* obeys the unconscious, and remains in hunger, despite suffering, until he has lived through what he must, or learned what he had to. What seems to us catastrophe, his spirit experiences as secret victory. His anarchic inability to support himself is experienced by his spirit as obedience." This first-person narration compresses into a few months the ten years (1879–1888) Hamsun spent in extreme poverty—sporadically relieved by laborers' jobs and immigrations to the United States—in Oslo, then called Kristiania. The nameless hero seeks to make his living by writing grandiose newspaper articles that, on the rare occasions when one is accepted, each earn him about three and a half dollars. The action moves from one five-kroner windfall to the next—an article is bought, a waistcoat is pawned, a grocery clerk errs in making change, an editor or acquaintance unexpectedly proffers a loan. Between these financial peaks are long, not unhappy troughs of emptiness:

> I kept on going through streets, rambling on with no purpose in mind at all. I stopped at a corner without needing to, turned and went up small alleys without having anything to do there. I just drifted on, floating in the joyful morning, rolling along without a care among other happy people. The air was clear and bright and my mind was without a shadow.

He is unable to organize his thoughts into any plan of enterprise or escape:

> I could not sit on a park bench by myself or put my foot down anywhere without being besieged by tiny and pointless events, absurd nonsense, which forced itself into my brain and scattered my powers to the four winds. A dog that shot past me, a yellow rose in someone's lapel, could set my thoughts in motion and obsess me for hours.

His external actions, his contacts with human society appear ludicrously antic and whimsical; he spouts frenzied nonsense to strangers on the street, he attracts and then rejects a prostitute called Ylayali, he prays to and then curses God, he refuses to beg from those who might succor him. When he is miraculously granted money, he squanders it on a rich meal he instantly vomits, or gives it away to an uncomprehending old cake peddler, or hurls a ten-kroner note in the face of a landlady who has ceased to expect anything. Though the physical humiliations of starvation are fascinatingly, grindingly detailed and the hero ostensibly yearns for a respectable, normal existence ("What a marvellous sensation to be sitting in a human house again and to hear a clock tick, and to talk with a spirited young girl instead of with myself!"), his self-realization lies with "the joyful insanity hunger was."

> My hair lay on my forehead wet and cold; I sat up on my elbow and looked down at the pillow: wet hair was also lying there in small tufts. My feet had swollen during the night inside my shoes; there was no pain, but I could barely move my toes.
>
> Toward late afternoon, when it was already beginning to be dusk, I got up and started puttering about the room. I tried walking with short, deliberate steps, careful to keep my balance and spare my feet as much as I could. I was not really suffering, and I didn't cry; on the whole I wasn't even sad; I was on the contrary wonderfully at peace—the thought that anything could be any different than it was never once crossed my mind.
>
> Finally I went out.

Finally he accepts, without premeditation, employment on a Russian freighter bound for Cadiz, and *Hunger* ends.

On Overgrown Paths—a journal Hamsun kept from his arrest, on May 26th of 1945, for treasonous activities during the German occupation, to his conviction and sentencing, on Midsummer Day of 1948—shows that his willingness to embrace isolation and deprivation had survived a life of success. The prose is still swift, fitful, immediate, innocently quick to feed on trifles: "These are trifles I write about, and trifles that I write. . . . All prisoners can only write about the eternally everyday occurrences and wait for their doom." But we are all prisoners. "We are all guilty. We are legion in our guilt." We are all doomed. "Now and then there is also some one of us who dies; it cannot be avoided, but it does not make much impression on us who remain. We follow the white coffin with our eyes, but when the hearse has driven away, we turn back to ourselves again." Hamsun is apathetic, tranquil. "I am weary of myself, have no wishes, no interests, no pleasures. Four or five senses in torpor and the sixth sense [he is deaf] snatched away. . . . I have attained the condition of certain Orientals: the necessary silence. I do not even talk to myself any more, having got out of that bad habit. . . . It is three years today since I was arrested.

And here I sit. It has not mattered to me, not bothered me. It has gone by as though merely one more event."

Of the several hospitals and nursing homes where he is incarcerated, only a psychiatric clinic shatters his calm of resignation. He is unable, in this memoir, to describe his months there except by allusive fragments: "Domination over a living being, regulations lacking mercy and tact, a psychology of blank spaces and labels, a whole science bristling defiance. Others can endure that sort of torture; that is no concern of mine. For my part, I could not. Which the psychiatrist ought perhaps to have understood. I was in good health; I was turned into jelly." Only in his letter to the attorney general about this experience does Hamsun rant, and seem to deserve the official judgment of him as a person with "permanently impaired faculties." His defense, when he presents it in the form of a courtroom statement, is coherent and almost adequate: his crimes were confined to a few newspaper articles urging Norwegians not to waste their lives in futile resistance; he constantly interceded with the Germans, even with Hitler himself, for the lives of Norwegian resistance fighters; he never belonged to the Nazi Party; he scorned fleeing his native land to Sweden or England; he was captivated by the promise that Norway would occupy a high place in Hitler's Germanic empire. In short, he stands defenseless, having based his actions upon the premise that Norway was defenseless. One reads this section of the book, and the prefatory description of Hamsun's trial, with some sympathy for the predicament of governments confronted with politically aberrant great writers, and with a feeling that the Norwegian government exacted less suffering from Hamsun than the United States government did from Ezra Pound, though both eventually settled upon a factitious mental incompetence.

As Bly points out, Hamsun, the son of a farmer, unschooled and for years indigent, was alienated from the bourgeois Europe that believed in progress and social reform. His years of hunger had left him with few expectations of human society; even his lovers, such as Glahn and Edvarda in *Pan*, are whimsical and cruel. He responds only, and is ever alert, to nature—the torrential, unanswerable nature within and beyond man. "Here are only cropped hills without a flower bed. The weather is biting, the wind almost always blows; but nearby are trees and woods with songbirds aloft and all sorts of creeping things on the ground. Oh, the world is beautiful here too, and we are to be very grateful for being in it. How rich the colors are here in the very rocks and the heather, how incomparable the forms in the bracken! And the taste of a piece of wall fern that I found is still good on the tongue." We find him unaged, in these valedictory pages, his appetites still undisciplined ("But completely contrary to my good intentions to ration my reading, I fell voraciously on Topsøe's book and devoured it in one gulp"), his conversations still quixotic—talking with a lady at a bus stop, the elderly Hamsun rips off his jacket and lays it in the snow for her to sit upon. He is still fond of outcasts and still able, in the depths, to attract women who wish to minister to him and with whom he grows impatient. Irascibility remains the sign of his independent genius. Of his poetry, he admits it lacks tenderness: "And it was not only tenderness that was lacking but all too many other things as well, the whole kit and caboodle." Lacking the kit and caboodle of civilized prejudice, he was able to confront experience direct, and to convey it magically. Toward the end of this book of therapeutic jottings, his thoughts revert to his confirmation and first communion:

> The pastor put something in my mouth, and afterwards let me sip from a cup. There were many people around who watched, but they restrained themselves and did not smile.
> Why remember that now? I have no earthly use for it and there is no wisdom in it. It uplifts me merely because I am happy and am teeming.

His memory wanders on, to his "first time in America," and the sails of his artistry fill, and he embarks upon a fine funny story without a moral—"merely a series of simple experiences from day to day on foreign soil and in a little arid prairie town." On the last page he remembers a woman's hands: "Those hands astonished me; they were yellow in complexion, but very soft and fine, never having been used to do anything with, never especially clean, but so beautiful to look at." The last two phrases tell the tale—"never especially clean, but so beautiful to look at." Hamsun speaks, still freshly, to us out of the human creatureliness that knows no accountability, no ideal systems. He has not dated; his prose remains tonic. Though convicted of collaboration with a tyrant, he is in literature a democrat, in the spirit of Proust's prescription:

> The great quality of true art is that it rediscovers, grasps, and reveals to us that reality far from which we live, from which we get farther and farther away as the conventional knowledge we substitute for it becomes thicker and more impermeable, the reality that we might die without having known and which is simply our life, real life, life finally discovered and clarified, consequently the only life that has been really lived—that life which in one sense is to be found at any time in all men as well as in artists.

Half-Mad and Maddening

MYSTERIES, by Knut Hamsun, translated from the Norwegian by Gerry Bothmer. 340 pp. Farrar, Straus & Giroux, 1971.

Perhaps too furiously, *Mysteries* struggles to express most of the themes that obsessed the young Hamsun. Like *Hunger*, it has a half-mad and maddening hero; as in *Pan*, the hero kills the dog his beloved cherishes; as in *Victoria*, he saves someone from drowning and regrets it. First published in Norway in 1892, two years later than *Hunger*, this novel lacks the weird jubilation of the masterpiece, and denies us empathy with the principal figure, Nagel, who, neither impoverished nor a writer, seems in his perversity merely a prankster. He arrives abruptly in a small Norwegian coastal town, creates an air of capricious wealth, defends the town scapegoat against the town bully, falls in love with the town beauty, proposes marriage to the local spinster, astounds and affronts several gatherings of the local bourgeoisie, sheds money, spouts words, and attempts suicide, not always unsuccessfully. The laconic formal control that usually imposes crystalline dignity on Hamsun's brutal vision here slackens; the plot abounds in false hares, unsolved mysteries, and editorial digressions. The atmosphere is heavy with emotional energy that expends itself, lightning-like, in mere display. The trolls of the subconscious infest not only the characters but the narration. Nevertheless, there are some remarkably harrowing moments, frequent streaks of brilliant fancy, and always a presiding vitality. Not many books published in 1892 could make us as uncomfortable as this one.

Love as a Standoff

VICTORIA, by Knut Hamsun, translated from the Norwegian by Oliver Stallybrass. 170 pp. Farrar, Straus & Giroux, 1969.

This short novel dates from 1898, when Hamsun, though no longer young as a man, was still rather young as a writer. Perhaps Hamsun always wrote a young man's books. He was one of modern literature's great fresheners; his loyalty to the elemental, his impatience with Ibsenian social moralizing, and his expressed determination to "grant the individual soul its due" contributed to the great liberation of artistic energy in the generation succeeding his and elicited gratitude from writers as different as H.G. Wells and Thomas Mann. To mention Mann, however, and to think of Mann's own naïveté, his disarmingly material curiosity and his blunt little inventories of furniture and weather, is to remind ourselves of a certain broad, balanced, *educated* humanism that cannot be included in the considerable list of Hamsun's virtues.

Victoria seems young in its proximity to the fabulous, in the magical edge of its quick imagery—"over by the sluice the water fell sheer, like a brightly colored fabric hung out to dry." Or "Again the weeks and the months went by, and spring returned. The snow had gone: the distant roar of liberated waters gave the illusion of coming from the sun and the moon." The novel also seems young in its air of disconnectedness, of being partly hidden from the author as well as from us, of being the residue of an emotional experience more than a re-creation of one. The hero, Johannes Møller, is a miller's son (Møllerens Sønn). We meet him walking and thinking, "bursting with ideas"—"When he grew up he would work in a match factory. It would be pleasantly dangerous, and he could get sulfur on his fingers so that nobody would dare to shake hands with him." He dreams of the future, has for friends the trees and the birds and the stones in the granite quarry, and is, of course, in love with Victoria, the daughter of the Castle, the manor house near the mill. As children, they play and flirt, but as social unequals. Well, Johannes leaves home and becomes, guess what, a writer. His frenzied habits of work—every night from the evening church bells to dawn, despite the complaints of the insomniac next door—sound very like those of the hero of *Hunger*. Except that Johannes is a success, critical and commercial, from the start. He returns home educated, famous, and a man. Meanwhile, Victoria, to save the sagging Castle fortunes, has had her troth plighted for her to a caddish toff called Otto. Victoria and Johannes hold several hot-and-cold conversations establishing their love on a firmly star-crossed basis. As a consolation prize, she offers him, at her engagement party, their mutual friend little Camilla, whom our hero once saved from drowning (as a nature expert, he is amphibian; "I know the shoals," the dripping boy modestly avers), and to whom he now (and this is an honest Hamsun touch) takes enough of a shine, true love notwithstanding, to plight *his* troth. *But*, just then, what should happen but that Otto should go hunting, and—you know how sloppy caddish toffs are with guns; please don't let me spoil the story for you. Suffice to say that the lovers stay star-crossed and tuberculosis intervenes to keep the book brief.

If the plot sounds quaint and somewhat mechanically Tristan-and-Iseultish, it may be that Hamsun was masking a personal experience still puzzling to himself. Like Edvarda in *Pan*, Victoria compulsively humiliates her rustic admirer at parties. Party scenes seem to operate for Hamsun as a point of painful reference, in contrast to nature walks: love is made outdoors and destroyed indoors. Behind the vivid, cruel, hectically flushed women of his parties stands some bitter recollection. In *Victoria*, Hamsun suddenly digresses: "Watch any woman in profile when she drinks. Let her drink from a cup, a glass, anything you care to mention, but watch her in profile. It's a terrifying sight, the act she puts on. She purses up her mouth, dips only the extreme edge in the drink, and gets desperate if during the performance anybody notices her hand."

Though mutilated, as it were, by the jerky action of the puppet-theatre plot and by the pained reticences of Hamsun's memory, Victoria lives in each fragmentary glimpse of her, from the flighty but gracious child to the dying woman, still mostly a child, who writes Johannes a magnificently pathetic letter of farewell. *Victoria* adds a small portrait to literature's gallery of 19th-century women, those hapless creatures denied all rights but the right to be adored, those poor properties assigned an exclusively sexual value and given only a black market to trade it on—those scapegoats of romanticism, those saints of intrigue and dreaming who lived only in books, those oppressed innocents whose one method of protest was self-destruction.

The pride of these women, their defiant perversity and desperate gaiety, Hamsun can depict. But he is dealing here with an attenuated case. Whereas Madame Bovary, borrowing some iron from her bourgeois captors, did jimmy her way out and become for a moment that dark, sensual apparition who alarms Léon in Rouen, Victoria stands helpless and stares. The obstacles between the lovers drop away: Otto and Camilla vanish; the debt-ridden Castle and its paternalistic proprietor go up in smoke. Still, Johannes and Victoria do not move toward each other but preserve a silence one is tempted to call stubborn. They are Romeo and Juliet without the Nurse, without the night of love. The action of the book is their few conversations—they have none, except as children, that we do not overhear—and when she breaks silence for the last time, most fully, the book ends.

Stubborn silence was dear to Hamsun; he fled from publicity, played no games but solitaire, and kept silent during his trial. His laconic style feels engraved upon silence. Speech, and events in general, have a peculiar, exceptional air in his work. It is not merely that the characters do odd things—the hero of *Pan*, asked by the heroine, whom he loves, for the gift of his pet dog, shoots the dog and sends her the body; in *Victoria*, Johannes, needing a pipe cleaner, wrenches a hand from the face of a clock—but that very simple objects hop onto the page with an enigmatic, trollish wink. Victoria halts at a shopwindow and moves away; Johannes spies her and stops at the same window:

Why was she standing there? The window was a mean one, a small shop window displaying for sale a few bars of red soap, grain barley in a glass jar, a handful of cancelled postage stamps.

How oddly charged and sharp and potent is this little inventory of the inconsequential! Of Johannes' fiction we are told, "Often, his imagination played crazy tricks on him, obtruding into his book irrelevant conceits which he afterward had to strike out and throw away." For example, he imagines, "A man is at the point of death, he writes to a friend, a note, a little request. The man dies, leaving this note. It is dated and signed, it has capital letters and small letters, though the writer would die within the hour. Very strange." Later, when he receives Victoria's note, he sees that "there were capital letters and small letters, the lines were straight, and she who had written them was dead!" This interest in not merely peculiar circumstances but the *peculiarity of circumstance* deflects his prose from the path of high seriousness and rounded intention but does give it a continuous quirky life and stabs of unexpected power. In *Victoria*, a long dream is recounted to no immediate purpose but with a concrete wildness given to few dreams in fiction:

> He wades out into the ocean and dives down. He finds himself standing in front of a great doorway where he meets a huge barking fish. It has a mane on its back and barks at him like a dog. Behind the fish stands Victoria. He reaches out his hands toward her, she has no clothes on, she laughs at him and a gale blows through her hair.

Dreamlike also is Victoria's explanation of why, at the party, she rudely interrupted Johannes' speech: "All I heard was your voice. It was like an organ, and the power it had over me made me frantic." In Doris Lessing's *The Golden Notebook*, the heroine relates how as soon as she heard a certain man's voice she knew she would sleep with him. What is mere confession in a female writer amounts to intuitive genius in Hamsun.

Just as dreams and passionate impulses erupt into our conscious lives, so the flow of this novel is interrupted, at the end, by a gratuitous spate of anecdotes on the topic of love. One of them describes a cuckolded husband who knowingly returns when his wife is entertaining her lover. He knocks, the lover sneaks away, the husband enters, and a strange conversation ensues—a groping amid mutual compassion and deceit. Then:

> But suddenly he threw his arms around her, in an ironlike grip of terrifying strength, and whispered in her ear, "What do you say, shall we put horns on him . . . on the fellow who left. . . . Shall we put horns on him?"

She screams for the maid, and in the morning describes his proposal as "a very strange attack." He answers, "Yes, it's a strain being witty at my age. I'm giving it up." The entire encounter, in its comic knottiness, in the depths and turns of uxoriousness it reveals, is quite startling, and shows the degree of psychological complexity Hamsun's strange simplicity could conjure with. Strindberg and Nietzsche were his tutors, but he drew upon the Nordic cultural tradition that underlies the realism of the sagas, the anti-philosophy of Kierkegaard,* and the films of Ingmar Bergman. Like Hamsun, Bergman loves plain textures and tangled minds, renders details with surreal clarity, indulges a savage streak of fantasy, and sometimes depends ingenuously upon fable and a mysticism of brooks and saplings. Scandinavia, untouched by Hellenism and only lately and lightly submissive to Christianity, sees things in its own slant of sunlight. Platonic precedences do not obtain; the riddle and not the Idea lurks behind phenomena. The wish to "grant the individual soul its due" has roots in an ancient Germanic individualism: the 6th-century *Strategicon* says of German warriors, "Headstrong, despising strategy, precaution, or foresight, they show contempt for every tactical command." The Viking god of battle, Odin, was the god of inspiration, whether as battle frenzy, intoxication, or supernatural wisdom; Hamsun is a literary Viking whose reliance upon inspiration is his strength and his weakness. Born in a rural valley, by predilection a recluse and a farmer, he belongs in the company of those tanned, clear-eyed truants (the Basque Unamuno, the Algerian Camus, the Egyptian Cavafy, the Russian Tolstoy) who jeer into the classroom of European civilization. A heathen visionary, he sees peculiar particulars that resist being smoothed

---

* "I am anything but a devilish good fellow at philosophy . . . I am a poor, individual existing man. . . ." "[Philosophy] is disinterested; but the difficulty inherent in existence constitutes the interest of the existing individual, who is infinitely interested in existing."—*Concluding Unscientific Postscript.*

into plots, exemplary characters, or slogans to live by. The moral of *Victoria* is profferred as "There's always a catch somewhere," or "God has fashioned [love] of many kinds and seen it endure or perish." Such an inconclusive conclusion, a standoff, well caps this intensely static love story, whose characters, though immersed in bookish circumstances, proudly reject the dynamism of characters.

JOYCE AND PROUST

Questions Concerning Giacomo

WHAT IS "GIACOMO JOYCE"?

It is (a) a tiny prose work of some twenty-six hundred words, whose first sentence is interrogative—"Who?"—and whose substance is so evanescent with tentativity and mysteriousness that the reviewer, like the heroine, finds it handy to don "quizzing glasses." Variously described as a "short story" and "the notebook" and "a love poem which is never recited" and "this most delicate of novels," *Giacomo Joyce* was probably copied out, in his best schoolbook hand, by James Joyce (1882–1941) in 1914 in Trieste.

(b) It is also an elegantly produced, boxed, ten-dollar object of veneration published by Viking Press on January 1, 1968—a saint's bone whose marrow is (a) and whose surrounding calcium consists of nine pages of introduction by the foremost of American Joyce scholars, Mr. Richard Ellmann; four and a fraction pages of notes amplifying and exemplifying correspondences and echoes already noted in the introduction; and, most delightfully and luxuriantly, a photographic facsimile of the manuscript pages, two of them full size (13¼ inches by 10¼ inches) and folded quarto, the six others reduced by half but still legible.

DOES THE SUMPTUOUS FORMAT OF (B) ENTIRELY SUIT THE MODEST TEXT OF (A)?

It is a pleasure to handle, in an age when the crafts languish, so fine a piece of book production. Mr. Ellmann, as master of scholarly ceremonies, writes gracefully, employing his matchless intimacy with the Joycean universe to demonstrate how phrases from this slender text were dispersed, with surprising transmutations, through *A Portrait of the Artist as a Young Man, Exiles, Pomes Penyeach*, and *Ulysses*. The decision to print, however, this text line for line as it appears in the manuscript, with all the spaces, not only compels a rather stingy size of type but somehow weakens the voice of the prose; the sections of this notebook quoted in Ellmann's massive biography of Joyce (Oxford, 1959) and set in orthodox justified lines, read more vividly, with more of the narrative energy whose lack is the most puzzling aesthetic quality of *Giacomo Joyce*. Departing from normal typographic procedures seems chichi, since the facsimile manuscript is also bound into the volume.

The facsimile is doubly welcome, as a specimen of Joyce's fluent, lucid hand and as light upon the central riddle—of what the work wishes to *do;* we seem to draw a little closer to Joyce's intention in examining the graphic texture of these paragraphs and phrases spaced and scattered upon large sheets of art paper. There is no crossing-out or emendation, though there is some trouble with "websoft" on page 7. This indicates a fair copy from preëxistent notes, yet on some pages the tone of ink (page 10), or the size of the writing (page 15), or the speed of the penmanship (page 13) changes between paragraphs. Mr. Ellman's suggestion is that, "perhaps with Mallarmé in mind," Joyce was indicating "pauses of varying duration measured by spaces of varying length." If that is so, this pictographic intention is indifferently carried out; the amount of waste space—the lower third of the sheets is frequently blank, and some of the space gaps, as on pages 5 and 8, are huge— seems inartistic and its distribution rather random. More likely that this enterprise, whether of copying or composition, was executed at several sittings, with a mixture of purposes, among them crystallization and formal ordering for the author's own benefit, as a way of pinning these images to a surface from which they could be later plucked and employed in published works. I doubt that *Giacomo Joyce* was ever intended for print. It is too personal, too unformed and febrile; it would scarcely be published now were its author not a classic. Publication in a very private sense, however, may have been intended: these pages, one's impression grows, were copied out to be shown or given to someone, like the parchment

sheets upon which Joyce five years earlier copied out the poems of
Chamber Music as a gift for his wife.

SHOWN OR GIVEN TO WHOM?

One possibility is Italo Svevo, Joyce's fellow-author and fellow-
Triestine of the time, who contributed so much information and
temperament to the character of Leopold Bloom, and who had
written and shown to Joyce a novel called *Senilità* (the English
title, at Joyce's suggestion, became *As a Man Grows Older*), concerning a middle-aged man's love for a young woman, and who had
asked Joyce, in a letter dated June 26, 1914, "When will you write
an Italian work about our town? Why not?" Joyce had recently
shown Svevo a typescript of the first three chapters of *Portrait of
the Artist*, and *Giacomo Joyce* could be his response to Svevo's
challenge. The story's complex tone, literary and personal and
polyglot and arch, and its distinct Triestine locality are congenial
with this thesis; any clear-cut echo of *Senilità* would be virtually
clinching. But Mr. Ellmann offers none, and Svevo's elegiac and
wry psychologizing belongs to a different literary era from Joyce's
compacted personal imagery. The friendship between Svevo and
Joyce was a curious one. The letter of June 26th, read in full, is
stilted even beyond the stiltedness of Svevo's English; his inquiry
in context seems more polite than spirited. Svevo was in his fifties,
a prosperous and amiable businessman who had diffidently abandoned writing after two early, neglected novels; Joyce was in his
early thirties, an impoverished and unamiable Berlitz instructor,
full of faith in his own genius and, as his brother Stanislaus put it,
"that inflexibility firmly rooted in failure." Joyce's fierce enthusiasm for Svevo's novels—tinged, perhaps, by the generosity authors
feel toward non-competitors and by Svevo's usefulness to him as
a hoard of Jewish lore—seems to have rather baffled the older man.
They came together as student and teacher, since Svevo wanted
to improve his English. His letters retain a student's shyness and
tact.

A more piquant possibility is that the intended readership of one
was the work's subject herself. *Giacomo Joyce* tells us that she had
been shown some of *A Portrait*, including the third chapter,
wherein Stephen's erotic sins are described, for "She says that, had

The Portrait of the Artist been frank only for frankness' sake, she would have asked why I had given it to her to read." On the next page the author broods, "Those quiet cold fingers have touched the pages, foul and fair, on which my shame shall glow for ever." It can be objected that within *Giacomo Joyce* its heroine is sometimes mocked and sometimes hymned in physical terms she could only have found embarrassing. But Joyce was peculiarly fond of this mode of wooing—courtship by shamelessness. He detailed to Nora Barnacle his sexual life before he met her. In the long letter of August 29, 1904, he refers to another letter, in which he dwelt on the details of their first liaison: "You have misunderstood, I think, some passages in a letter I wrote you and I have noticed a certain shyness in your manner as if the recollection of that night troubled you." And, amid that extraordinary torrent of letters he directed toward her from Dublin in 1909, while she remained in Trieste, he beseeches her, "Now, my darling Nora, I want you to read over and over all I have written to you. Some of it is ugly, obscene, and bestial, some of it is pure and holy and spiritual: all of it is myself." He dotes on the "something obscene and lecherous in the very look" of certain words, and hopes that "you too will write me letters even madder and dirtier than mine to you." It was always one of his marital sorrows that she would not read his books. Voyeurism and exhibitionism both were exercised by his perform- ance of writing. In 1918, Joyce, seeing Martha Fleischmann on a Zurich street, sent her four ardent and presumptuous letters in French and German. In the first, he tells this unknown lady she is "*un joli* animal," likens himself to Dante espying Beatrice, and concludes by saying, in French, "I believe you are good at ——." The word, evidently obscene, was torn from the corner by the recipient. He also sent her a copy of *Chamber Music*, and Ell- mann's biography describes how Joyce "from his vantage point on the street had watched her take it from the letter box and sit down with it in her front room." Among Stephen Dedalus' sins are "the foul long letters he had written in the joy of guilty confession and carried secretly for days and days only to throw them under cover of night among the grass in the corner of a field or beneath some hingeless door or in some niche in the hedges where a girl might come upon them as she walked by and read them secretly." When, in *Exiles*, Robert Hand rebukes Joyce's alter ego Richard Rowan for waking his wife from sleep and confessing the night's infidelity, Rowan answers, "She must know me as I am." But one suspects that in Joyce's case candor was an act not merely of integrity but of concupiscence. It would not have been out of character for him to display this delineation of passion to its young but intelligent and nubile object.

One is forced into these conjectures by the definite omissions of Ellmann's introduction. He tells us at the outset of the manuscript that "The present owner . . . wishes to remain anonymous." He goes on to discuss the "title" of these pages, which are "loosely held within the nondescript gray-paper covers of a school notebook. . . . On the upper left-hand corner of the front cover, the name 'Giacomo Joyce' is inscribed in another hand." Well, *whose* hand? Can no comparison be made of the handwritings of Joyce's intimates at this time? Is it a matter of indifference who was permitted to bestow this ironical title? It looks to me, assuming that the label on the Viking volume is an accurate reproduction, as if the word "Joyce" were written in the center, with a spidery "Giacomo" added above it, perhaps in the "cobweb handwriting" of the little book's heroine. Ellmann declines to speculate. And he withholds two points of information given in his biography of Joyce. "Giacomo" was Casanova's first name and "a familiar epithet in Italy for a great lover" and the lady, the young student with whom Joyce fell in love and who inspired this work, also had a name. She was Amalia Popper, the daughter of a Jewish businessman called not quite Leopold Bloom but Leopoldo Popper.

How much—er—actual contact did Joyce make with Signorina Popper?

A good question. Ellmann assumes that the affair is "of eyes rather than of bodies" and that the sexual episodes of the manuscript represent "morose delectation—diet of writers." This is not hard to believe of overheated passages like

> Soft sucking lips kiss my left armpit: a coiling kiss on myriad veins. I burn! I crumple like a burning leaf! From my right armpit a fang of flame leaps out. A starry snake has kissed me: a cold nightsnake. I am lost!

But there are quieter passages with an air of reality:

> Whirling wreaths of grey vapour upon the heath. Her face, how grey and grave! Dank matted hair. Her lips press softly, her sighing breath comes through. Kissed.

Joyce observes that "her body has no smell: an odourless flower" and describes a seduction with a soft clarity of detail that belongs either to reality or to an imagination of genius:

> I hold the websoft edges of her gown and drawing them out to hook them I see through the opening of the black veil her lithe body sheathed in an orange shift. It slips its ribbons of moorings at her shoulders and falls slowly: a lithe smooth naked body shimmering with silvery scales. It slips slowly over the slender buttocks of smooth tarnished silver and over their furrow, a tarnished silver shadow. . . .

True, Joyce was an imaginative genius. True, his adventures with women, Nora Barnacle excepted, appear to have tended toward either plain whoring or timid, voyeuristic adoration. But his attentions to Martha Fleischmann, of which only the correspondence remains, caused her lover and *Vormund*, Rudolph Hiltpold, to write Joyce (all this is confided in a note to Frank Budgen) "a threatening violent letter" leading to a "long interview" in Hiltpold's apartment with "violent gestures" on Hiltpold's part and "that timidity which yet is courage" on Joyce's, ending in a return of Martha's letters and a "*Waffenstillstand.*" The photographs of these years * show a somewhat rakish dandy; in 1915, the Joyce strumming a guitar is positively handsome. Richard Rowan of *Exiles* says he has betrayed his wife "grossly and many times." The one moment of psychological tension in *Giacomo Joyce* occurs when the heroine's father tells Joyce in Italian that "My daughter has the greatest admiration for her English teacher." This assertion, whose manner purportedly combines "suspicion, naturalness, helplessness of age, confidence, frankness, urbanity, sincerity, warning," is inwardly greeted by Joyce with the exclamation "Ignatius Loyola, make haste to help me!" The girl's susceptibility is as moot

---

* Ellmann's two volumes of Joyce's letters contain many, and Viking published in 1968 a fascinatingly illustrated study, *James Joyce and His World*, by Chester G. Anderson.

as the strength of his advances. Concerning the percentage of wealthy middle-class Jewish girls seduced by their instructors in prewar Austria-Hungary, there was no Kinsey to gather statistics. The elliptical, fraught allusiveness of *Giacomo Joyce* and the powerful resonance with which the experience reverberates through Joyce's work (Signorina Popper not only is credited with being Beatrice Justice of *Exiles* and the Irish girl of the last chapter of the *Portrait* but is supposed to have contributed the something Mediterranean in the character of Molly Bloom) do seem insufficiently explained by a one-sided infatuation. The relationship, at any rate, made an impression upon Signorina Popper. Nineteen years later, in 1933, now Signora Risola of Florence, she wrote Joyce asking for permission to translate *Dubliners* into Italian. Permission was granted, and a book entitled *Araby* did appear in Italian, but the standard Italian translation was done by other hands. She died not much longer than a year ago, and perhaps her death (again we must resort to speculation) released *Giacomo Joyce* to posterity.

Is "GIACOMO JOYCE" GOOD OR BAD ART?

Difficult to answer, even discounting the extent to which it is not art at all but personal therapy and private communication. Parts of it sing with the familiar voice: "She follows her mother with ungainly grace, the mare leading her filly foal." Some images bring the heroine into good focus: "A pale face surrounded by heavy odorous furs. . . . The long eyelids beat and lift: a burning needleprick stings and quivers in the velvet iris." Other images float oddly, unattached: "Long lewdly leering lips: dark-blooded molluscs." Some of the writing is Joyce at his most palely swooning: "Her eyes have drunk my thoughts: and into the moist warm yielding welcoming darkness of her womanhood my soul, itself dissolving, has poured and flooded a liquid and abundant seed." Some of it is mere noise: "Weep not for me, O daughter of Jerusalem!" And some downright trite: "This heart is sore and sad. Crossed in love?" These many glimpses, exclamations, and parodic spurts, though anticipating, in Ellmann's happy phrase, the "clashing of dictions" that becomes the method of *Ulysses*, do not quite hang together, perhaps because they are engraved upon a personal incident that remains obscure rather than upon the mundane, mappable events of Bloomsday. *Giacomo Joyce* does point up the lack of psychological presence Joyce's characters, even in the masterworks, often have. His dialogue, for example, where it is not comic or telegraphic (and largely excepting *Dubliners*), more suggests worked-up notes than the living exchange of speech. The key utterance in *Giacomo Joyce* is Amalia's saying, "Because otherwise I could not see you," a remark which meant so much to Joyce that he gives it twice to Beatrice Justice in *Exiles;* neither here nor there does it make much sense. In both places the statement, like many things said in *Ulysses*, arrives unprepared-for, devoid of context, and without weight. Compared to Tolstoy's protagonists or those of Henry James, Joyce's characters do not take each other seriously; they seem detached, for all the formal significance arrayed behind them, from concern with their own fate, and move sluggishly beneath the semi-opaque thickness of their artistic rendering. They are the creations of an artist-God who is himself "refined out of existence, indifferent, paring his fingernails." Indeed, *Giacomo Joyce* is most interesting for its illustration of a stage of the aesthetic sequence that Stephen Dedalus expounds to Lynch in Chapter Five of *A Portrait*, which was completed later in 1914, and abounds in echoes of *Giacomo;* Stephen might well have this tiny work in mind as marking the exact point where the lyrical form—"the simplest verbal vesture of an instant of emotion"—becomes the simplest epical form, "when the artist prolongs and broods upon himself as the centre of an epical event. . . . The personality of the artist passes into the narration itself, flowing round and round the persons and the action like a vital sea." *Giacomo* anticipates not only the triumph but the limits of *Ulysses*. We do not see as well in water as in air, and the chief character Joyce's books glorify is himself, the writer as God and oceanic mind, the frail and arrogant sponger/saint with the black eye patch, holding all literature and languages inside his head, mixed with "pebbles and rubbish and broken matches and lots of glass." It is this monstrous and marvellous self-dramatization whose adventures we follow in his books, whose fanaticism transfigures gritty old photographs of Dublin and Paris, and whose relics we revere.

Remembrance of Things Past Remembered

"ONLY THREE OR FOUR BOOKS IN A LIFETIME," Swann says in *Remembrance of Things Past*, "give us anything that is of real importance." For a book to be great in a reader's life it is not enough for the book to be great; the reader must be ready. I began to read Proust the first months I lived in Manhattan, on Riverside Drive. I was twenty-three, newly a father, newly employed. Since boyhood I had wanted to live in New York. I had wanted to work for the magazine that now I did work for. I had wanted to be a writer and now a few poems and short stories were filtering into print. In this atmosphere, then, of dreams come true, I opened my wife's tattered college copy of *Swann's Way;* she used to read under a sun lamp, and the cover was stained by a spot of oil. While our baby cooed in her white, screened crib, and the evening traffic swished north on the West Side Highway, and Manhattan at my back cooled like a stone, and my young wife fussed softly in our triangular kitchen at one of the meals that, by the undeservable grace of marriage, regularly appeared, I would read:

> . . . if my aunt were feeling "upset," she would ask instead for her "tisane," and it would be my duty to shake out of the chemist's little package on to a plate the amount of lime-blossom required for infusion in boiling water. The drying of the stems had twisted them into a fantastic trellis, in whose intervals the pale flowers opened, as though a painter had arranged them there, grouping them in the most decorative poses. The leaves, which had lost or altered their own appearance, assumed those instead of the most incongruous things imaginable, as though the transparent wings of flies or the blank sides of labels or the petals of roses had been collected and pounded, or interwoven as birds weave the material for their nests. A thousand trifling little details—the charming prodigality of the chemist—details which would have been eliminated from an artificial preparation, gave me, like a book in which one is astonished to read the name of a person whom one knows, the pleasure of finding that these were indeed real lime-blossoms, like those I had seen, when coming from the train, in the Avenue de la Gare, altered, but only because they were not imitations but the very same blossoms, which had grown old. And as each new character is merely a metamorpho-

sis from something older, in these little grey balls I recognised green buds plucked before their time; but beyond all else the rosy, moony, tender glow which lit up the blossoms among the frail forest of stems from which they hung like little golden roses—marking, as the radiance upon an old wall still marks the place of a vanished fresco, the difference between those parts of the tree which had and those which had not been "in bloom"—shewed me that these were petals which, before their flowering-time, the chemist's package had embalmed on warm evenings of spring. That rosy candlelight was still their colour, but half-extinguished and deadened in the diminished life which was now theirs, and which may be called the twilight of a flower. Presently my aunt was able to dip in the boiling infusion, in which she would relish the savour of dead or faded blossom, a little madeleine, of which she would hold out a piece to me when it was sufficiently soft.*

A thousand other passages equally wonderful could be quoted from the four thousand pages of Proust's novel. Everyone knows of the madeleine from whose long-forgotten taste the whole of Combray sprang into renewed being; the paragraph I have quoted gives us the tea direct, as it was fed by Aunt Léonie to little "Marcel." Hemingway would have rendered this action in twenty words; Balzac, in a hundred and made us feel the chemist's shop, and hear the ring of francs on the counter. Proust's tendrilous sentences seek out an essence so fine the search itself is an act of faith. It was a revelation to me that words could entwine and curl so, yet keep a live crispness and the breath of utterance. I was dazzled by the witty similes—the vanished fresco, the book holding the known name—that wove art and nature into a single luminous fabric. This was not "better" writing, it was writing with a whole new nervous system.

The passage manifests the work's great theme: the metamorphoses wrought by Time. This sense of metamorphosis—tied to Proust's neurasthenically keen sense of the organic, especially of

---

* As rendered in C. K. Scott Moncrieff's very fluent and ornate translation. Looking, since, at Proust in French, I am struck by how often Proust is terse —less Proustian, indeed, than he is in English. The few proof sheets in the Harvard collection show his alterations to be often (unlike those of Joyce, who usually added) shortenings and simplifications. Yet, that Moncrieff caught the essential power and perfume I do not doubt.

botany—carries into the tragic, temporal dimension Proust's peculiar sensitivity to *changing perspectives*. Perspectives change in space (the steeples at Martinville), in the heart (Swann's views of Odette), in society (Mme. Verdurin's rise; Swann as seen in Combray and in Paris). External reality is but a cluster of moments no two of which subtend the same angle. This is impressionism, but impressionism on the move, whether the moving object is the narrator's life or the "little train" to Balbec:

> . . . but, the course of the line altering, the train turned, the morning scene gave place in the frame of the window to a nocturnal village, its roofs still blue with moonlight, its pond encrusted with the opalescent nacre of night, beneath a firmament still powdered with all its stars, and I was lamenting the loss of my strip of pink sky when I caught sight of it afresh, but red this time, in the opposite window which it left at a second bend in the line, so that I spent my time running from one window to the other to reassemble, to collect on a single canvas the intermittent, antipodean fragments of my fine, scarlet, ever-changing morning, and to obtain a comprehensive view of it and a continuous picture.

Einstein used moving trains to illustrate the special theory of relativity, propounded in 1905. Also in 1905, Proust's mother died, releasing him to final loneliness and earnest search for entrée into his own endowment, his precocious powers of evocation. In his relativity Proust is a modern, though the modern most lavish with old-fashioned virtues—characterization, ambitious scale, idealistic rapture, stylistic confidence. *Remembrance of Things Past* is to 19th-century novels as a magic lantern is to little landscape models with plaster hills, matchstick houses, and trees of green sponge. Proust abolished the nagging contradiction between the author as God and the author as nebulous character, as reader's confidant. In Proust's cosmos, Marcel (so called only once, in an elaborately hedged aside) is both the most supine of witnesses and the mightiest of creators. There is no "outside" to the firmament of his skull. His perceptions are not derived from substance; they *are* substance. And the plot is not what connects the images and gestures and masks; their enclosure within one field of perception *is* the plot, the drama. Our excitement as we traverse these immensities of prose has to do with their Providential coherence: microcosmically, with the dissecting delicacy of each sentence and the ecology of mutual assistance the tender images extend toward one another; and macrocosmically, with the thrilling leaps of far-flung continuations (Vinteuil's manifestations, for example, or De Forcheville's reappearance after three thousand pages, to marry Odette) and a grand architectural completeness (the Swann side, in Gilberte, unites with the Guermantes side, in Saint-Loup, to produce a daughter who, we are told casually, "later on married an obscure man of letters"). As in a cathedral, organic profusion is subdued to a design. It might be said that by deviating from his original design (*circa* 1909) of two Testamental volumes—the way of innocence and the way of experience—to insert the immense dirge to Agostinelli (d. 1914) that comprises the Albertine books, Proust created a Flamboyant rather than a Romanesque cathedral. Yet, without those sometimes monotonous stretches of misty Albertine, how much would be diminished the culminating effect of vastness, of dizzying height? *Time Regained* ends with acrophobia. Like Marcel, the reader turns "giddy at seeing so many years below and in me as though I were leagues high." Among other writers only Dante lifts us to such an altitude.

Like Dante, Proust lives in one work. There is a great dropping off elsewhere. We read *Jean Santeuil* or *Contre Sainte-Beuve*, or try to, much as we read Proust's nattering letters, or criticism of him—for the lover's pleasure of being with Proust and being reminded of the raptures he has given us. No other 20th-century writer has inspired such a bulk of appreciation and analysis; the shelves at Widener Library include the bound bulletins of *La Societé des Amis de Marcel Proust et des Amis de Combray*. In English the Proust chapters by Edmund Wilson in *Axel's Castle* and by Harry Levin in *The Gates of Horn* show omnivorous critics sagaciously digesting; the small books by Howard Moss and Roger Shattuck with special affection polish and refocus some of the lenses of Proust's panopticon; and the brilliant two-volume biography by George Painter in one sense offers more adventure than *À la Recherche du Temps Perdu* itself, since in Painter's account we see Proust journeying toward the mastery that the novel possesses from the very first page. There are also Samuel Beckett's rather acerb essay and, in translation by Elsie Prell, a memoir by François Mauriac that combines a young writer's awe at the "sudden occupation of the literary heaven by the Proustain constellation," a generous appraisal from a Catholic viewpoint of the corrosion and stagnation felt to overtake the latter half of the masterpiece, and a vivid personal recollection of "that gloomy room on the rue Hamlin, that black den, that bed where an overcoat served as a blanket, that waxy mask through which it could have been said our host watched us eat, and whose hair alone seemed living." Proust is not only the greatest modern creator of characters; he is among modern authors the most amusing character, the most self-dramatizing (see his letters) and bizarre, whose cork-lined room has become the very symbol of hypertrophied aestheticism. In 1971 the hundredth anniversary of his birth was observed in the American literary press with tributes, by such writers as Melvin Maddocks and William Gass, surprisingly grudging and irritated in tone, even jeering—as if in these distributors of contemporary relevance had been reborn those *fin-de-siècle* smarts, the Comte de Montesquiou and his peers, who could not believe that "little Proust," that sickly parasite and queer half-Jew, had vaulted over them into immortality.

American readers in general, I suspect, have been put off by the unwieldy, intimidating twin-elephant Random House edition of *Remembrance of Things Past.* Better to read it in the seven Modern Library volumes, now reprinted in a Vintage paperback edition, and better still to obtain the charming twelve volumes of the English edition by Chatto & Windus (this edition has recently been disfigured by the insertion of totally insipid pencil illustrations by Philippe Jullian, but they can be excised with a razor blade). The pagination of the Chatto & Windus edition (and, but for *Swann's Way*, the Modern Library edition, which was a photograph of it) fits the extremely useful index-guide compiled by P. S. Spalding, which serves not only as a memory freshener as one reads along but as a way to extract all the references to, say, Hawthorn, Heredity, or Victor Hugo from their vast matrix.*

---

* I have been told, since writing this Proust advisory for the readers of *Horizon*, that the Spalding index is out of print. Too bad, if true.

Americans also, perhaps in their zeal for practical instruction, tend to expect too much of Proust as a social critic. Satire of snobs and anatomizing of society occur, of course, and Proust was a climber in his day; but a personal obsession should not be confused with an artistic one. He writes about aristocrats, in their banality and glamour, their vanity and gallantry, because they are there: *were* there, in the life he has ceased to live, the life that lostness has bathed in paradisiacal colors. As soon call Proust an anti-snob as a gargoyle-carver anti-devil; hatred is swallowed in an art of homage. Proust would take the entire living population of France as a *trésor trouvé*, a paleontological imprint left by the past, a clue to the central mystery of France herself, with her cathedrals, her blossoms, her place names. As the hero, aging, discovers deceit everywhere and absurdity everywhere, only two things remain worth loving: Marcel and France, which are everything. The book is not a tract but a religious travail.

In those August and September Manhattan days, themselves now paradisiacal, when I first read Proust, I also began to read Kierkegaard. College had left them out of my education; now I embraced them. I was not only a would-be writer but a would-be Christian. I was happy, but happiness, as Harold Brodkey observed in a short story from those same 1950's, makes us afraid. And Proust and Kierkegaard seemed (though both had been petite men) two giant brothers, whose bullying and showing-off I forgave because between them I could walk safely down the street, the street of my life. The remorseless pessimism of Proust's disquisitions on the heart, the abyss he makes of human motives, the finality of all our little deaths, did not appall me; morbid myself, I only trusted morbidity. In the interminable rain of his prose, I felt goodness. Proust was one of those men—increasingly rare, as faith further ebbs—who lost the consolations of belief but retained the attitudes and ambitions of a worshipper. For all his biochemistry, Proust emphasizes the medieval duality of body/spirit: "the body imprisons the spirit in a fortress." For all the disillusion and cruelty it depicts, *Remembrance of Things Past* is, like the Bible, a work of consolation. Einstein's relativity developed its formulas from the recognition of an absolute, the speed of light. Marcel, having experienced—in the madeleine, in the uneven paving stones—"a sense of eternity," vows to "leave this behind me to enrich others with my treasure." The next sentence goes on to uncover in his momentary "sense of eternity" a strangely modest secret, a kind of Godless Golden Rule and the germinating principle of art:

> My experience in the library which I wanted to preserve was that of pleasure, but not an egotistical pleasure, or at all events it was a form of egoism which is useful to others—for all the fruitful altruisms of Nature develop in an egotistical mode.

BORGES

The Author as Librarian

OTHER INQUISITIONS, 1937–1952, by Jorge Luis Borges, translated from the Spanish by Ruth L. C. Simms. 205 pp. University of Texas Press, 1964.

DREAMTIGERS, by Jorge Luis Borges, translated from the Spanish by Mildred Boyer and Harold Morland. 95 pp. University of Texas Press, 1964.

BORGES THE LABYRINTH MAKER, by Ana María Barrenechea, edited and translated from the Spanish by Robert Lima. 175 pp. New York University Press, 1965.

The belated North American acknowledgment of the genius of Jorge Luis Borges proceeds apace. The University of Texas Press last year published two volumes by this Argentine fantasist, critic, poet, and librarian. These translations, together with Grove Press's *Ficciones*, bring to three the number of complete books by Borges available in English. There is also New Directions' *Labyrinths*, a selection. And now the New York University Press has published a book *about* him.*

Four years ago, when Borges shared with Samuel Beckett the Prix International des Éditeurs, he was known here to few but Hispanic specialists. A handful of poems and short stories had appeared in scattered anthologies and magazines. I myself had read only "The Garden of the Forking Paths," originally published in

---

* In the decade since this rather pioneering piece of homage was framed, the Borges bibliography in English, with the forceful midwifery of Norman Thomas di Giovanni, has added an offspring a year, including a Personal Anthology and, that ultimate elegance, some Conversations With.

Ellery Queen's Mystery Magazine and subsequently a favorite of detective-story anthologies. Though vivid and intellectual beyond the requirements of its genre, the story can be read without awareness that its creator is a giant of world literature. I was prompted to read Borges seriously by a remark made—internationally enough—in Rumania, where, after a blanket disparagement of contemporary French and German fiction, Borges was praised by a young critic in a tone he had previously reserved for Kafka. An analogy with Kafka is inevitable, but I wonder if Borges' abrupt projection, by the university and avant-garde presses, into the bookstores will prove as momentous as Kafka's publication, by the commercial firm of Knopf, in the thirties. It is not a question of Borges' excellence. His driest paragraph is somehow compelling. His fables are written from a height of intelligence less rare in philosophy and physics than in fiction. Furthermore, he is, at least for anyone whose taste runs to puzzles or pure speculation, delightfully entertaining. The question is, I think, whether or not Borges' lifework, arriving in a lump now (he was born in 1899 and since his youth has been an active and honored figure in Argentine literature), can serve, in its gravely considered oddity, as any kind of clue to the way out of the dead-end narcissism and downright trashiness of present American fiction.

Borges' narrative innovations spring from a clear sense of technical crisis. For all his modesty and reasonableness of tone, he proposes some sort of essential revision in literature itself. The concision of his style and the comprehensiveness of his career (in addition to writing poems, essays, and stories, he has collaborated on detective novels, translated from many tongues, edited, taught, and even executed film scripts) produce a strangely terminal impression: he seems to be the man for whom literature has no future. I am haunted by knowing that this insatiable reader is now virtually blind.

A constant bookishness gives Borges' varied production an unusual consistency. His stories have the close texture of argument; his critical articles have the suspense and tension of fiction. The criticism collected in *Other Inquisitions, 1937–1952* almost all takes the form of detection, of uncovering what was secret. He looks for, and locates, the hidden pivots of history: the moment (in Iceland in 1225) when a chronicler first pays tribute to an enemy, the very line (in Chaucer in 1382) when allegory yields to naturalism. His interest gravitates toward the obscure, the forgotten: John Wilkins, the 17th-century inventor *ab nihilo* of an analytical language; J. W. Dunne, the 20th-century proponent of a grotesque theory of time; Layamon, the 13th-century poet isolated between the death of Saxon culture and the birth of the English language. Where an arcane quality does not already exist, Borges injects it. His appreciation of the classic Spanish satirist and stylist Francisco de Quevedo begins, "Like the history of the world, the history of literature abounds in enigmas. I found, and continue to find, none so disconcerting as the strange partial glory that has been accorded to Quevedo." His essay on Layamon concludes, " '*No one knows who he is,*' said Léon Bloy. Of that intimate ignorance no symbol is better than this forgotten man, who abhorred his Saxon heritage with Saxon vigor, and who was the last Saxon poet and never knew it."

Implacably, Borges reduces everything to a condition of mystery. His gnomic style and encyclopedic supply of allusions generate a kind of inverse illumination, a Gothic atmosphere in which the most lucid and famous authors loom somewhat menacingly. His essay on Bernard Shaw begins, "At the end of the thirteenth century Raymond Lully (Ramón Lull) attempted to solve all the mysteries by means of a frame with unequal, revolving, concentric disks, subdivided into sectors with Latin words." It ends on an equally ominous and surprising note: "[Existentialists] may play at desperation and anguish, but at bottom they flatter the vanity; in that sense, they are immoral. Shaw's work, on the other hand, leaves an aftertaste of liberation. The taste of the doctrines of Zeno's Porch and the taste of the sagas."

Borges' harsh conjunctions and plausible paradoxes are not confined to literary matters. In "A Comment on August 23, 1944," Borges meditates on the ambivalent reaction of his Fascist friends to the Allied occupation of Paris and ends with this daring paragraph:

> I do not know whether the facts I have related require elucidation. I believe I can interpret them like this: for Europeans and

Americans, one order—and only one—is possible: it used to be called Rome and now it is called Western Culture. To be a Nazi (to play the game of energetic barbarism, to play at being a Viking, a Tartar, a sixteenth-century conquistador, a Gaucho, a redskin) is, after all, a mental and moral impossibility. Nazism suffers from unreality, like Erigena's hells. It is uninhabitable; men can only die for it, lie for it, kill and wound for it. No one, in the intimate depths of his being, can wish it to triumph. I shall hazard this conjecture: *Hitler wants to be defeated*. Hitler is collaborating blindly with the inevitable armies that will annihilate him, as the metal vultures and the dragon (which must not have been unaware that they were monsters) collaborated, mysteriously, with Hercules.

The tracing of hidden resemblances, of philosophical genealogies, is Borges' favorite mental exercise. Out of his vast reading he distills a few related images, whose parallelism, tersely presented, has the force of a fresh thought. "Perhaps universal history is the history of a few metaphors. I should like to sketch one chapter of that history," he writes in "Pascal's Sphere," and goes on to compile, in less than four pages, twenty-odd instances of the image of a sphere "whose center is everywhere and whose circumference nowhere." These references are arranged like a plot, beginning with Xenophanes, who joyously substituted for the anthropomorphic gods of Greece a divine and eternal Sphere, and ending with Pascal, who, in describing nature as "an infinite sphere" had first written and then rejected the word *"effroyable"*—"a frightful sphere." Many of Borges' genealogies trace a degeneration: he detects a similar "magnification to nothingness" in the evolutions of theology and of Shakespeare's reputation; he watches an Indian legend succumb, through its successive versions, to the bloating of unreality. He follows in the works of Léon Bloy the increasingly desperate interpretations of a single phrase in St. Paul—*"per speculum in aenigmate"* ("through a glass darkly"). Borges himself recurrently considers Zeno's second paradox—the never-completed race between Achilles and the tortoise, the formal argument of *regressus in infinitum*—and comes to a conclusion that is, to use his favorite adjective, monstrous: "One concept corrupts and confuses the others. . . . I am speaking of the infinite. . . . We (the undivided divinity that operates within us) have dreamed the world. We have dreamed it strong, mysterious, visible, ubiquitous in space and secure in time; but we have allowed tenuous, eternal interstices of injustice in its structure so we may know that it is false."

Borges is not an antiseptic pathologist of the irrational; he is himself susceptible to infection. His connoisseurship has in it a touch of madness. In his "Kafka and His Precursors," he discovers, in certain parables and anecdotes by Zeno, Han Yü, Kierkegaard, Browning, Bloy, and Lord Dunsany, a prefiguration of Kafka's tone. He concludes that each writer creates his own precursors: "His work modifies our conception of the past, as it will modify the future." This is sensible enough, and, indeed, has been pointed out by T. S. Eliot, whom Borges cites in a footnote. But Borges goes on: "In this correlation the identity or plurality of men matters not at all." This sentence, I believe, expresses not a thought but a *sensation* that Borges has; he describes it—a mixture of deathlike detachment and ecstatic timelessness—in his most ambitious essay, "New Refutation of Time." It is this sensation that encourages his peculiar view of human thought as the product of a single mind, and of human history as a vast magic book that can be read cabalistically. His highest praise, bestowed upon the fantastic narratives of the early H. G. Wells, is to claim that "they will be incorporated, like the fables of Theseus of Ahasuerus, into the general memory of the species and even transcend the fame of their creator or the extinction of the language in which they were written."

As a literary critic, Borges demonstrates much sensitivity and sense. The American reader of these essays will be gratified by the generous amount of space devoted to writers of the English language. Borges, from within the Spanish literary tradition of "dictionaries and rhetoric," is attracted by the oneiric and hallucinatory quality he finds in North American, German, and English writing. He values Hawthorne and Whitman for their intense unreality, and bestows special fondness upon the English writers he read in his boyhood. The *fin-de-siècle* and Edwardian giants, whose reputations are generally etiolated, excite Borges afresh each time he rereads them:

> Reading and rereading Wilde through the years, I notice something that his panegyrists do not seem to have even suspected: the provable and elementary fact that Wilde is almost always right. . . .

he was a man of the eighteenth century who sometimes condescended to play the game of symbolism. Like Gibbon, like Johnson, like Voltaire, he was an ingenious man who was also right.

Borges' tributes to Shaw and Wells have been quoted above. In connection with Wells and Henry James, it is a salutary shock to find the terms of the usual invidious comparison reversed: "the sad and labyrinthine Henry James . . . a much more complex writer than Wells, although he was less gifted with those pleasant virtues that are usually called classical." But of this generation none is dearer to Borges than Chesterton, in whom he finds, beneath the surface of dogmatic optimism, a disposition like Kafka's: "Chesterton restrained himself from being Edgar Allan Poe or Franz Kafka, but something in the makeup of his personality leaned toward the nightmarish, something secret, and blind, and central . . . the powerful work of Chesterton, the prototype of physical and moral sanity, is always on the verge of becoming a nightmare . . . he tends inevitably to revert to atrocious observations." Much in Borges' fiction that suggests Kafka in fact derives from Chesterton. As critic and artist both, Borges mediates between the post-modern present and the colorful, prolific, and neglected pre-moderns.

Of the moderns themselves, of Yeats, Eliot, and Rilke, of Proust and Joyce, he has, at least in *Other Inquisitions*, little to say. Pound and Eliot, he asserts in passing, practice "the deliberate manipulation of anachronisms to produce an appearance of eternity" (which seems, if true at all, rather incidentally so), and he admires Valéry less for his work than for his personality, "the symbol of a man who is infinitely sensitive to every fact." The essays abound in insights delivered parenthetically—"God must not theologize"; "to fall in love is to create a religion that has a fallible god"—but their texts as a whole do not open outward into enlightenment. Whereas, say, Eliot's relatively tentative considerations offer to renew a continuing tradition of literary criticism, Borges' tight arrangements seem a bizarre specialization of the tradition. His essays have a quality I can only call *sealed*. They are structured like mazes and, like mirrors, they reflect back and forth on one another. There is frequent repetition of the adjectives and phrases that denote Borges' favorite notions of mystery, of secrecy, of "intimate ignorance." From his immense reading he has distilled a fervent narrowness. The same parables, the same quotations recur; one lengthy passage from Chesterton is reproduced three times.

Here and there appear sentences ("One literature differs from another, either before or after it, not so much because of the text as for the manner in which it is read") that elsewhere have been developed into "fictions"; in "Pierre Menard, Author of Don Quixote," a modern writer as his masterwork reconstructs passages from *Don Quixote* that, though verbally identical, are read very differently. This story, in fact, was, according to an interview given in Buenos Aires in 1960, the first Borges ever wrote. Long a respected poet and critic, he turned to fiction with a grim diffidence. In his words:

> I know that the least perishable part of my literary production is the narrative, yet for many years I did not dare to write stories. I thought that the paradise of the tale was forbidden to me. One day, I suffered an accident. I was in a sanitarium where I was operated upon. . . . a time I cannot recall without horror, a period of fever, insomnia, and extreme insecurity. . . . If after the operation and the extremely long convalescence I tried to write a poem or an essay and failed, I would know that I had lost . . . intellectual integrity. Thus, I decided upon another approach. I said to myself: "I am going to write a story and if I cannot do so it does not matter because I have not written one before. In any case, it will be a first attempt." Then, I began to write a story . . . which turned out rather well; this was followed by others . . . and I discovered that I had not lost my intellectual integrity and that I could now write stories. I have written many since.

Turning from Borges' criticism to his fiction, one senses the liberation he must have felt upon entering "the paradise of the tale." For there is something disturbing as well as fascinating, something distorted and strained about his literary essays. His ideas border on delusions; the dark hints—of a cult of books, of a cabalistic unity hidden in history—that he so studiously develops are special to the corrupt light of libraries and might vanish outdoors. It is uncertain how seriously he intends his textual diagrams, which seem ciphers for concealed emotions. Borges crowds into the margins of others' books passion enough to fill blank pages;

his essays all tend to open inward, disclosing an obsessed imagination and a proud, Stoic, almost cruelly masculine personality.

Dreamtigers, a collection of paragraphs, sketches, poems, and apocryphal quotations titled in Spanish *El Hacedor* (*The Maker*), succeeds in time the creative period of narrative fiction his essays foreshadow. It is frankly the miscellany of an aging man, fondly dedicated to a dead enemy—the Modernist poet Leopoldo Lugones, like Borges the director of a national library.

> Leaving behind the babble of the plaza, I enter the Library. I feel, almost physically, the gravitation of the books, the enveloping serenity of order, time magically desiccated and preserved. . . . These reflections bring me to the door of your office. I go in; we exchange a few words, conventional and cordial, and I give you this book. . . . My vanity and nostalgia have set up an impossible scene. Perhaps so (I tell myself), but tomorrow I too will have died, and our times will intermingle and chronology will be lost in a sphere of symbols. And then in some way it will be right to claim that I have brought you this book, and that you have accepted it.

The epilogue repeats this prediction of his own death:

> Few things have happened to me, and I have read a great many. Or rather, few things have happened to me more worth remembering than Schopenhauer's thought or the music of England's words.
>
> A man sets himself the task of portraying the world. Through the years he peoples a space with images of provinces, kingdoms, mountains, bays, ships, islands, fishes, rooms, instruments, stars, horses, and people. Shortly before his death, he discovers that that patient labyrinth of lines traces the image of his face.

The book is in two parts. The first, translated by Mildred Boyer, consists of those short prose sketches, musical and firm, that Borges, unable to see to write, composes in his head. The first of these describes Homer: "Gradually now the beautiful universe was slipping away from him. A stubborn mist erased the outline of his hand, the night was no longer peopled by stars, the earth beneath his feet was unsure." In a critical essay, Borges had traced the evolution of God and Shakespeare, as reputations, from something to nothing; now this nothingness is discovered in Shakespeare himself, intimately: "There was no one in him; behind his face (which even in the poor paintings of the period is unlike any other) and his words, which were copious, imaginative, and emotional, there was nothing but a little chill, a dream not dreamed by anyone." Dante is imagined dying in Ravenna, "as unjustified and as alone as any other man." God in a dream declares to him the secret purpose of his life and his work, which is like that of the leopard who endured a caged existence so that Dante might see him and place him in the first canto of the *Inferno*. "You suffer captivity, but you will have given a word to the poem," God told the leopard, "but when he awoke, there was only a dark resignation in him; a valiant ignorance. . . ." And the illustrious Italian Giambattista Marino—"proclaimed as the new Homer and the new Dante"— dying, perceives that "the tall, proud volumes casting a golden shadow in a corner were not—as his vanity had dreamed—a mirror of the world, but rather one thing more added to the world." It is as if, in his blindness and age, the oneness of all men that Borges had so often entertained as a theory and premonition has become a fact; he *is* Homer, Shakespeare, Dante, and tastes fully the bitter emptiness of creative splendor. The usurpation of a writer's private identity by his literary one has not been more sadly, or wittily, expressed than in "Borges and I":

> It's the other one, it's Borges, that things happen to. I stroll about Buenos Aires and stop, perhaps mechanically now, to look at the arch of an entrance or an iron gate. News of Borges reaches me through the mail and I see his name on an academic ballot or in a biographical dictionary. I like hourglasses, maps, eighteenth-century typography, the taste of coffee, and Stevenson's prose. The other one shares these preferences with me, but in a vain way that converts them into the attributes of an actor.

Borges tempts one to quote him at too great length. These brief paragraphs composed in his head have an infrangible aptness. His ability to crystallize vague ideas and vaguer emotions into specific images has grown. The image of Layamon, the last Saxon poet, returns in the form of an anonymous old man, dying, unaware that he is the last man to have witnessed the worship of Woden. He lies in a stable: "Outside are the plowed fields and a deep ditch clogged with dead leaves and an occasional wolf track in the black earth at the edge of the forest." This stark sentence, with its unexpectedly vivid ditch, has in it the whole of a primitive England, and pierces us with a confused sense of elapsed time. These sketches see a diminishing of those adjectives—"mysterious," "secret," "atrocious"—with which the younger Borges insisted on his sense of strangeness. Instead, there is a delicate manipulation of the concrete—lists and catalogues in which one or two of the series seem anomalous (". . . islands, fishes, rooms, instruments, stars, horses . . .") and the application now and then of a surprising color adjective (the volumes' "golden shadow" above, "red Adam in Paradise," and, apropos of Homer, "black vessels searching the sea for a beloved isle"). Immensity is reified in terms of color: "Every hundred paces a tower cleft the air; to the eye their color was identical, yet the first of all was yellow, and the last, scarlet, so delicate were the gradations and so long the series." In this image the concept of the infinite—the concept that "corrupts and con-fuses the others"—is tamed into something lyrical and even pretty. One feels in *Dreamtigers* a calm, an intimation of truce, a tranquil fragility. Like so many last or near-last works—like *The Tempest*, *The Millionairess*, or "Investigations of a Dog"—*Dreamtigers* pre-serves the author's life-long concerns, but drained of urgency; horror has yielded to a resigned humorousness. These sketches can be read for their grace and wit but scarcely for narrative excite-ment; the most exciting of them, "Ragnarök," embodies Borges' most terrible vision, of an imbecilic God or body of gods. But it occurs within a dream, and ends easily: "We drew our heavy re-volvers—all at once there were revolvers in the dream—and joyously put the Gods to death."

The second half of this slim volume consists of poems, late and early. Poetry was where Borges' ramifying literary career origi-nally took root. The translations, by Harold Morland, into roughly four-beat and intermittently rhymed lines, seem sturdy and clear, and occasional stanzas must approximate very closely the felicity of the original:

> In their grave corner, the players
> Deploy the slow pieces. And the chessboard
> Detains them until dawn in its severe
> Compass in which two colors hate each other.

As a poet, Borges has some of the qualities—a meditative circularity, a heavy-lidded elegance—of Wallace Stevens:

> With slow love she looked at the scattered
> Colors of afternoon. It pleased her
> to lose herself in intricate melody
> or in the curious life of verses.

And

> We shall seek a third tiger. This
> Will be like those others a shape
> Of my dreaming, a system of words
> A man makes and not the vertebrate tiger
> That, beyond the mythologies,
> Is treading the earth.

But in English the poems are chiefly interesting for their content; they are more autobiographical and emotionally direct than Borges' prose. The first one, "Poem About Gifts," movingly portrays himself in his blindness:

> Slow in my darkness, I explore
> The hollow gloom with my hesitant stick,
> I, that used to figure Paradise
> In such a library's guise.

Thoughts anonymously cached in the maze of his fictions are enunciated in his own voice. In a fabricated encyclopedia article he describes the "philosophers of Uqbar" as believing that "Copulation and mirrors are abominable. . . . For one of those gnostics, the visible universe was an illusion or, more precisely, a sophism. Mirrors and fatherhood are abominable because they multiply it and extend it." In a poem, "Mirrors," the belief turns out to be Borges' own:

> I see them as infinite, elemental
> Executors of an ancient pact,
> To multiply the world like the act
> Of begetting. Sleepless. Bringing doom.

The profound sense of timelessness that in the prose activates so much textual apparatus becomes in verse an elementary nostalgia:

> Rain is something happening in the past. . . .
> And the drenched afternoon brings back the sound
> How longed for, of my father's voice, not dead.

And his long poem about his childhood home at Adrogué culminates:

> The ancient amazement of the elegy
> Loads me down when I think of that house
> And I do not understand how time goes by,
> I, who am time and blood and agony.

Together, the prose and poetry of *Dreamtigers* afford some glimpses into Borges' major obscurities—his religious concerns and his affective life. Physical love, when it appears at all in his work, figures as something remote, like an ancient religion. "[Shakespeare] thought that in the exercise of an elemental human rite he might well find what he sought, and he let himself be initiated by Anne Hathaway one long June afternoon." And Homer remembers when "a woman, the first the gods set aside for him, had waited for him in the shadow of a hypogeum, and he had searched for her through corridors that were like stone nets, along slopes that sank into the shadow." Though *Dreamtigers* contains two fine poems addressed to women—Susana Soca and Elvira de Alvear—they are eulogies couched in a tone of heroic affection not different from the affection with which he writes elsewhere of male friends like Alfonso Reyes and Macedonio Fernández. This is at the opposite pole from homosexuality; femaleness, far from being identified with, is felt as a local estrangement that blends with man's cosmic estrangement. There are two prose sketches that, by another writer, might have shown some erotic warmth, some surrender to femininity. In one, he writes of Julia, a "sombre girl" with "an unbending body," in whom he sensed "an intensity that was altogether foreign to the erotic." In their walks together, he must have talked about mirrors, for now (in 1931) he has learned that she is insane and has draped her mirrors because she imagines that his reflection has replaced her own. In the other, he writes of Delia Elena San Marco, from whom he parted one day beside "a river of vehicles and people." They did not meet again, and in a year she was dead. From the casualness of their unwitting farewell, he concludes, tentatively, that we are immortal. "For if souls do not die, it is right that we should not make much of saying goodbye."

It would be wrong to think that Borges dogmatically writes as an atheist. God is often invoked by him, not always in an ironical or pantheistic way.

> God has created nighttime, which he arms
> With dreams, and mirrors, to make clear
> To man he is a reflection and a mere
> Vanity.

He hopes seriously for immortality. Death is "the mirror/In which I shall see no-one or I shall see another." One of the many riddles that interest him is Christ's aspect, and he is moved by the possibility that "the profile of a Jew in the subway is perhaps the profile of Christ; perhaps the hands that give us our change at a ticket window duplicate the ones some soldiers nailed one day to the cross." But we feel that he *entertains* these possibilities, almost blasphemously; they are isolated, for him, from the corpus of ethics and argument which is historical Christianity. He dismisses the orthodox afterlife: "We distrust his intelligence, as we would distrust the intelligence of a God who maintained heavens and hells." He ransacks Christian apologetics for oddities of forced reasoning. He writes, "Those who automatically reject the supernatural (I try, always, to belong to this group). . . ." While Christianity is not dead in Borges, it *sleeps* in him, and its dreams are fitful. His ethical allegiance is to pre-Christian heroism, to Stoicism, to "the doctrines of Zeno's Porch and . . . the sagas," to the harsh gaucho ethos celebrated in the Argentine folk poem of Martín Fierro. Borges is a pre-Christian whom the memory of Christianity suffuses with premonitions and dread. He is European in everything except the detachment with which he views European civilization, as something intrinsically strange—a heap of relics, a universe of books without a central clue. This detachment must be, in part, geographical; by many devious routes he returns to the home in space and time that he finds

> in the tumbledown
> Decadence of the widespread suburbs,
> And in the thistledown that the pampas wind

Blows into the entrance hall . . .
And in a flag sort of blue and white
Over a barracks, and in unappetizing stories
Of street-corner knifings, and in the sameness
Of afternoons that are wiped out and leave us . . .

Perhaps Latin America, which has already given us the absolute skepticism of Machado de Assis, is destined to reënact the intellectual patterns of ancient Greece. Borges' voracious and vaguely idle learning, his ecumenic and problematical and unconsoling theology, his willingness to reconsider the most primitive philosophical questions, his tolerance of superstition in both himself and others, his gingerly and regretful acknowledgment of women and his disinterest in the psychological and social worlds that women dominate, his almost Oriental modesty, his final solitude, his serene pride—this constellation of Stoic attributes, mirrored in the southern hemisphere, appears inverted and frightful.

Borges the Labyrinth Maker, by Ana María Barrenechea, has for its jacket design a labyrinth from which there is no exit. I do not know whether this is intentional or a mistake in drawing. The book is a methodical and efficient arrangement of quotations from Borges in abstract categories—The Infinite, Chaos and the Cosmos, Pantheism and Personality, Time and Eternity, Idealism and Other Forms of Unreality. In a foreword, Borges says that the book "has unearthed many secret links and affinities in my own literary output of which I had been quite unaware. I thank her for those revelations of an unconscious process." Professor Barrenechea's collations, however—including many sentences and paragraphs of Borges not elsewhere translated—seem to me an admirable explication of his conscious philosophical concerns as they shape, adjective by adjective, his fiction. What is truly unconscious—the sense of life that drives him from unequivocal philosophical and critical assertion to the essential ambiguity of fiction—she scarcely touches. The labyrinth of his thought-forms is drawn without an indication of how his concrete and vigorous art has emerged. She admits this: "Only one aspect of the writer's work—the expression of irreality—has been treated; but Borges' creativity is characterized by the richness and complexity of his art."

The great achievement of his art is his short stories. To round off this review of accessory volumes, I will describe two of my favorites.

"The Waiting" is from his second major collection, *El Aleph*, and is found, translated by James E. Irby, in *Labyrinths*. It is a rarity in Borges' *oeuvre*—a story in which nothing incredible occurs. A gangster fleeing from the vengeance of another gangster seeks anonymity in a northwest part of Buenos Aires. After some weeks of solitary existence, he is discovered and killed. These events are assigned a detailed and mundane setting. The very number of the boarding house where he lives is given (4004: a Borgian formula for immensity), and the neighborhood is flatly described: "The man noted with approval the spotted plane trees, the square plot of earth at the foot of each, the respectable houses with their little balconies, the pharmacy alongside, the dull lozenges of the paint and hardware store. A long windowless hospital wall backed the sidewalk on the other side of the street; the sun reverberated, farther down, from some greenhouses." Yet much information is withheld. "The man" mistakenly gives a cabdriver a Uruguayan coin, which "had been in his pocket since that night in the hotel at Melo." What had happened that night in Melo and the nature of his offense against his enemy are not disclosed. And when the landlady—herself unnamed, and specified as having "a distracted or tired air"—asks the man his name he gives the name, Villari, of the man hunting him! He does this, Borges explains, "not as a secret challenge, not to mitigate the humiliation which actually he did not feel, but because that name troubled him, because it was impossible for him to think of any other. Certainly he was not seduced by the literary error of thinking that assumption of the enemy's name might be an astute maneuver."

Villari—Villari the hunted—is consistently prosaic, even stupid. He ventures out to the movies and, though he sees stories of the underworld that contain images of his old life, takes no notice of them, "because the idea of a coincidence between art and reality was alien to him." Reading of another underworld in Dante, "he did not judge the punishments of hell to be unbelievable or excessive." He has a toothache and is compelled to have the tooth pulled. "In this ordeal he was neither more cowardly nor more

tranquil than other people." His very will to live is couched nega-
tively: "It only wanted to endure, not to come to an end." The
next sentence, grounding the abhorrence of death upon the simplest
and mildest things, recalls Unamuno. "The taste of the maté, the
taste of black tobacco, the growing line of shadows gradually
covering the patio—these were sufficient incentives."

Unobtrusively, the reader comes to love Villari, to respect his
dull humility and to share his animal fear. Each brush with the
outer world is a touch of terror. The toothache—"an intimate dis-
charge of pain in the back of his mouth"—has the force of a
"horrible miracle." Returning from the movies, he feels pushed,
and, turning "with anger, with indignation, with secret relief,"
he spits out "a coarse insult." The passerby and the reader are alike
startled by this glimpse into the savage criminal that Villari has
been. Each night, at dawn, he dreams of Villari—Villari the
hunter—and his accomplices overtaking him, and of shooting them
with the revolver he keeps in the drawer of the bedside table. At
last—whether betrayed by the trip to the dentist, the visits to the
movie house, or the assumption of the other's name we do not
know—he is awakened one July dawn by his pursuers:

> Tall in the shadows of the room, curiously simplified by those
> shadows (in the fearful dreams they had always been clearer), vigi-
> lant, motionless and patient, their eyes lowered as if weighted down
> by the heaviness of their weapons, Alejandro Villari and a stranger
> had overtaken him at last. With a gesture, he asked them to wait
> and turned his face to the wall, as if to resume his sleep. Did he do
> it to arouse the pity of those who killed him, or because it is less
> difficult to endure a frightful happening than to imagine it and
> endlessly await it, or—and this is perhaps most likely—so that the
> murderers would be a dream, as they had already been so many
> times, in the same place, at the same hour?

So the inner action of the narrative has been to turn the utterly
unimaginative hero into a magician. In retrospect, this conversion
has been scrupulously foreshadowed. The story, indeed, is a beautiful cinematic succession of shadows; the most beautiful are those
above, which simplify the assassins—"(in the fearful dreams they
had always been clearer)." The parenthesis of course makes a
philosophic point: it opposes the ambiguity of reality to the rela-

tive clarity and simplicity of what our minds conceive. It functions as well in the realistic level of the story, bodying forth all at once the climate, the moment of dawn, the atmosphere of the room, the sleeper's state of vision, the menace and matter-of-factness of the men, "their eyes lowered as if weighted down by the heaviness of their weapons." Working from the artificial reality of films and gangster novels, and imposing his hyper-subtle sensations of un-reality on the underworld of his plot, Borges has created an episode of criminal brutality in some ways more convincing than those in Hemingway. One remembers that in "The Killers" Ole Andreson also turns his face to the wall. It is barely possible that Borges had in mind a kind of gloss of Hemingway's classic. If that is so, with superior compassion and keener attention to peripheral phenomena he has enriched the theme. In his essay on Hawthorne, Borges speaks of the Argentine literary aptitude for realism; his own florid fantasy is grafted onto that native stock.

"The Library of Babel," which appears in *Ficciones*, is wholly fantastic, yet refers to the librarian's experience of books. Anyone who has been in the stacks of a great library will recognize the emotional aura, the wearying impression of an inexhaustible and mechanically ordered chaos, that suffuses Borges' mythical universe, "composed of an indefinite, perhaps an infinite, number of hexagonal galleries, with enormous ventilation shafts in the middle, encircled by very low railings." Each hexagon contains twenty shelves, each shelf thirty-two books, each book four hundred and ten pages, each page forty lines, each line eighty letters. The arrangement of these letters is almost uniformly chaotic and form-less. The nameless narrator of "The Library of Babel" sets forward, pedantically, the history of philosophical speculation by the human beings who inhabit this inflexible and inscrutable cosmos, which is equipped, apparently for their convenience, with spiral stairs, mirrors, toilets, and lamps ("The light they emit is insufficient, incessant").

This monstrous and comic model of the universe contains a full range of philosophical schools—idealism, mysticism, nihilism:

> The idealists argue that the hexagonal halls are a necessary form of absolute space, or, at least, of our intuition of space. They contend that a triangular or pentagonal hall is inconceivable.

The mystics claim that to them ecstasy reveals a round chamber containing a great book with a continuous back circling the walls of the room. . . . That cyclical book is God.

I know of a wild region whose librarians repudiate the vain superstitious custom of seeking any sense in books and compare it to looking for meaning in dreams or in the chaotic lines of one's hands. . . . They speak (I know) of "the febrile Library, whose hazardous volumes run the constant risk of being changed into others and in which everything is affirmed, denied, and confused as by a divinity in delirium."

Though the Library appears to be eternal, the men within it are not, and they have a history punctuated by certain discoveries and certain deductions now considered axiomatic. Five hundred years ago, in an upper hexagon, two pages of homogeneous lines were discovered that within a century were identified as "a Samoyed-Lithuanian dialect of Guaraní, with classical Arabic inflections" and translated. The contents of these two pages—"notions of combinational analysis"—led to the deduction that the Library is total; that is, its shelves contain all possible combinations of the orthographic symbols:

Everything is there: the minute history of the future, the autobiographies of the archangels, the faithful catalogue of the Library, thousands and thousands of false catalogues, a demonstration of the fallacy of these catalogues, a demonstration of the fallacy of the true catalogue, the Gnostic gospel of Basilides, the commentary on this gospel, the commentary on the commentary on this gospel, the veridical account of your death, a version of each book in all languages, the interpolations of every book in all books.

Men greeted this revelation with joy; "the universe suddenly expanded to the limitless dimensions of hope." They surged onto the stairs, searching for Vindications—books that would vindicate and explain his life to each man. Sects sprang up. One used dice and metal letters in an attempt to "mimic the divine disorder" and compose by chance the canonical volumes. Another, the Purifiers, destroyed millions of books, hurling them down the air shafts. They believed in "the Crimson Hexagon: books of a smaller than ordinary format, omnipotent, illustrated, magical." A third sect worshipped the Man of the Book—a hypothetical librarian who, in some remote hexagon, must have perused a book "which is the cipher and perfect compendium of *all the rest*." This librarian is a god. "Many pilgrimages have sought Him out."

The analogies with Christianity are pursued inventively and without the tedium of satire. The narrator himself confides, "To me, it does not seem unlikely that on some shelf of the universe there lies a total book. I pray the unknown gods that some man— even if only one man, and though it have been thousands of years ago!—may have examined and read it." But in his own person he has only the "elegant hope" that the Library, if traversed far enough, would repeat itself in the same disorder, which then would constitute an order. At hand, in the illegible chaos, are only tiny rays of momentary sense, conglomerations of letters spelling *O Time your pyramids*, *Combed Clap of Thunder*, or *The Plaster Cramp*.

This kind of comedy and desperation, these themes of vindication and unattainability, suggest Kafka. But *The Castle* is a more human work, more personal and neurotic; the fantastic realities of Kafka's fiction are projections of the narrator-hero's anxieties, and have no communion, no interlocking structure, without him. The Library of Babel instead has an adamant solidity. Built of mathematics and science, it will certainly survive the weary voice describing it, and outlast all its librarians, already decimated, we learn in a footnote, by "suicide and pulmonary diseases." We move, with Borges, beyond psychology, beyond the human, and confront, in his work, the world atomized and vacant. Perhaps not since Lucretius has a poet so definitely felt men as incidents in space.

What are we to make of him? The economy of his prose, the tact of his imagery, the courage of his thought are there to be admired and emulated. In resounding the note of the marvellous last struck in English by Wells and Chesterton, in permitting infinity to enter and distort his imagination, he has lifted fiction away from the flat earth where most of our novels and short stories still take place. Yet discouragingly large areas of truth seem excluded from his vision. Though the population of the Library somehow replenishes itself, and "fecal necessities" are provided for, neither food nor fornication is mentioned—and in truth they are not generally seen in libraries. I feel in Borges a curious implication: the unrealities of physical science and the senseless repetitions of history have made the world outside the library an uninhabitable vacuum. Literature—that European empire augmented with translations from remote kingdoms—is now the only world capable of housing and sustaining new literature. Is this too curious? Did not Eliot recommend forty years ago, in reviewing *Ulysses*, that new novels be retellings of old myths? Is not the greatest of modern novels, *Remembrance of Things Past*, about its own inspiration? Have not many books already been written from within Homer and the Bible? Did not Cervantes write from within Ariosto and Shakespeare from within Holinshed? Borges, by predilection and by program, carries these inklings toward a logical extreme: the view of books as, in sum, an alternate creation, vast, accessible, highly colored, rich in arcana, possibly sacred. Just as physical man, in his cities, has manufactured an environment whose scope and challenge and hostility eclipse that of the natural world, so literate man has heaped up a counterfeit universe capable of supporting life. Certainly the traditional novel as a transparent imitation of human circumstance has "a distracted or tired air." Ironic and blasphemous as Borges' hidden message may seem, the texture and method of his creations, though strictly inimitable, answer to a deep need in contemporary fiction—the need to confess the fact of artifice.

Three Translations
(*with Norman Thomas di Giovanni*)

THE SEA

Before our human dream (or terror) wove
Mythologies, cosmogonies, and love,
Before time coined its substance into days,
The sea, the always sea, existed: was.
Who is the sea? Who is that violent being,
Violent and ancient, who gnaws the foundations

Of earth? He is both one and many oceans;
He is abyss and splendor, chance and wind.
Who looks on the sea sees it the first time,
Every time, with the wonder distilled
From elementary things—from beautiful
Evenings, the moon, the leap of a bonfire.
Who is the sea, and who am I? The day
That follows my last agony shall say.

THE ENIGMAS

I who am singing these lines today
Will be tomorrow the enigmatic corpse
Who dwells in a realm, magical and barren,
Without a before or a when.
So say the mystics. I say I believe
Myself undeserving of Heaven or Hell,
But make no predictions. Each man's tale
Shifts like the forms of Proteus.
What errant labyrinth, what blinding flash
Of splendor and glory shall become my fate
When the end of this adventure presents me with
The curious experience of death?
I want to drink its crystal-pure oblivion,
To be forever; but never to have been.

THE LABYRINTH

Zeus himself could not undo these nets
Of stone encircling me. My mind forgets
The persons I have been along the way,
The hated way of monotonous walls
That is my fate. The galleries seem straight
But curve furtively, forming secret circles
At the terminus of years; and the parapets
Have been worn smooth by the passage of the days.

In the tepid alabaster dust I discern
Tracks that frighten me. The hollow air
Of evening sometimes brings a bellowing,
Or the echo, desolate, of bellowing.
I know that hidden in the shadows lurks
Another, whose task it is to exhaust
The loneliness that weaves this unravelling Hell,
To crave my blood, to fatten on my death.
We seek each other. O if only this
Were the last day of our antithesis!

NABOKOV

Mnemosyne Chastened

SPEAK, MEMORY, *An Autobiography Revisited*, by Vladimir Nabokov.
316 pp. G. P. Putnam's Sons, 1966.

Alas, Nabokov doesn't want to be an American writer after all.
He has moved to Switzerland and, instead of composing the delightful, devilish, and unimaginable successor to *Pale Fire*, fusses
with backward-looking projects such as ushering his minor Russian works (*Despair, The Eye, The Waltz Invention*) into English,
defending in *Encounter* his sumptuous but ungratefully received
version of *Eugene Onegin*, and translating *Lolita* into Russian, a
virtually posthumous maneuver not likely to win much gratitude
either.

The pity is, his greatness waits here. To my taste his American
novels are his best, with a fiercer frivolity and a cruelty more
humane than in the fiction of his European decades. In America
his almost impossible style encountered, after twenty years of
hermetic exile, a subject as impossible as itself, ungainly with the
same affluence. He rediscovered our monstrosity. His fascinatingly
astigmatic stereopticon projected not only the landscape—the eerie
arboreal suburbs, the grand emptinesses, the exotic and touchingly
temporary junk of roadside America—but the wistful citizens of
a violent society desperately oversold, in the absence of other connectives, on love. If the perceiver of John Shade and Charlotte Haze
and Clare Quilty and the Waindell College that impinged on poor
Pnin devotes the rest of his days to fond rummaging in the Russian attic of his mind, the loss is national, and sadder than Sputnik.

The latest memento confided to the care of Nabokov's American public is a revision of *Speak, Memory*, whose chapters were published one by one in (mostly) *The New Yorker* from 1948 to 1950 and assembled as *Conclusive Evidence* in 1951. As readers then already know, twelve of the fifteen chapters portray an aspect of the writer's happy boyhood as the eldest son of a St. Petersburg aristocrat, and the last three, more briefly but as enchantingly, sketch his rootless years in Cambridge, Berlin, and Paris. Nabokov has never written English better than in these reminiscences; never since has he written so sweetly. With tender precision and copious wit, exploiting a vocabulary and a sensibility enriched by the methodical pursuit of lepidoptera, inspired by an atheist's faith in the magic of simile and the sacredness of lost time, Nabokov makes of his past a brilliant icon—bejewelled, perspectiveless, untouchable. While there are frequent passages of Joycean trickiness, Proust presides in the metaphorical arabesques, the floral rhythms, and the immobilized surrender to memory. Proust, however, by fictionalizing Illiers into Combray, threw his childhood open to everyone; whereas the Nabokov memoir is narrowed by its implication that only an expatriate Russian, a well-born and intellectual Russian at that, can know nostalgia so exquisite.

The revisions, which a laborious collation with the 1951 edition has bared to my scrutiny, tend to narrow the memoir further. The author, back in Europe, has consulted with his sisters and cousins, who have chastened his imperfect recollections. Much new information about the Nabokov tribe, bristling with parenthetic dates and hyphenated alliances with the Prussian nobility, has been foisted off on Chapter Three; a tidy dry biography of his father now inaugurates Chapter Nine. (Compare, invidiously, the fabulous epic of filial admiration worked into his novel *The Gift*.) Elsewhere gardeners and dachshunds have been named, tutors sorted out, and apologies delivered to his previously suppressed brother Sergey. Some of the interpolations are welcome (the family tennis game in Chapter Two, the wooing of Tamara in Chapter Twelve, the differentiated drawing masters in Chapter Four); but sentences at times limp under their new load of accuracy and the ending of one vignette, "Mademoiselle O" (Chapter Five), is quite dulled by the gratuitous postscript of some recent personal history. The additions, and the addition of pleasant but imagination-cramping photographs, make the book more of a family album and slightly less of a miracle of impressionistic recall.

Very few changes are stylistic. The grand evocations of the Nord-Express and the blending parks and gardens of exile are not improved—how could they be? On page 19, "sensitive youth" becomes "young chronophobiac," and on page 284, "Dostoevskian emotion" becomes the more scornful "Dostoevskian drisk." On page 100, a rather conventional image of "that great heavenly O shining above the Russian wilderness" has very wonderfully become "the moon, fancy's rear-vision mirror." And on page 48, a burned bridge has been unkindled; Nabokov has smoothly stricken an irreverent reference to a dachshund descended from a dog of Anton Chekhov's as being "one of my few connections with the main current of Russian literature." Alas, that now seems his hope —to rejoin, by some sparkling future rivulet beyond the grim hydroelectric dam of Sovietism, that remote Zemblan current.

Mary Unrevamped

MARY, by Vladimir Nabokov, translated from the Russian by Michael Glenny in collaboration with the author. 114 pp. McGraw-Hill, 1970.

His first novel, written in 1925. Faithful Nabokovians have met Mary before; she sat for her portrait as Tamara in *Speak, Memory*, lurks near the heart of *Lolita*, and was deified in *Ada*. Here, artistically as well as chronologically young, she is the first love of the autobiographical hero, Ganin, for whom her wanton yet delicate Tartar beauty condenses into pure perfume the idyll of rural Russia and the enchantment of privileged youth. But Ganin remembers her from afar, when he is in a Berlin boarding house surrounded by other émigrés, comic and pathetic types of exile from reality—a race as of film extras, "flickering, shadowy doppelgangers, the casual Russian film extras, sold for ten marks apiece and still flitting, God knows where, across the white gleam of a screen." Ganin wakes from the shadows, from dreaming of Mary, at the end, and slopes off to his future as, it may be, an internationally renowned poet/scholar/novelist. *Mary* not only adumbrates the future of a master, it shines by its own light. From the start, Nabokov had his sharp peripheral vision, an intent deftness at netting the gaudy phrase, and the knack (crucial to novelists and chess players) of setting up combinations. Though his materials are tender, his treatment shows the good-natured toughness that gives an artist long life. Wisely, and nicely, he has spared this venerable text the—he admits—"high-handed revampments" to which his elder self is prone, and has supervised an exact, deferential translation.

The Crunch of Happiness

GLORY, by Vladimir Nabokov, translated from the Russian by Dmitri Nabokov in collaboration with the author. 205 pp. McGraw-Hill, 1971.

Here is a book that deserves not a review but a party. Let us all rejoice with Vladimir Nabokov. Before he was twenty, revolution deprived him of his Mother Russia and of an estate worth millions. When he was forty, Hitler deprived him of his second home, Europe, and of another fortune—the accumulated treasure of fiction and poetry that his pseudonym V. Sirin had composed in the Russian language, a precious *oeuvre* unpublishable in the Soviet Union and destined, it seemed, to fade into oblivion as the sub-nation of Russian émigrés was scattered and absorbed by the passage of time. When Nabokov landed here, in 1940, his genius had neither a visible past nor an imaginable future. However, he had known English since his boyhood, and in this second language he recast his aloofly original inspirations, reignited his singular verbal fire, and bestowed upon America a literary master it had done nothing to raise. This second career, crowned by the notorious and re-munerative and splendid *Lolita*, has in its strength reached down and redeemed from limbo the substance of the first career—the novels composed by "Sirin" in Berlin between 1925 and 1937. Now, with Nabokov sailing nicely into his eighth decade, the last of these Russian novels to reach the safe haven of definitive English

translation, *Glory*, has been published. The rainbow of romances
(nine Russian, six American) now arches complete, from *Mary*
to *Ada*, and though, along with some short stories and poems and
feuilletons, a few fine vibrations have no doubt been left behind
in the Russian—a fuzz of nuance and euphony as untransferable
as the dust on a butterfly's wing—Nabokov's diligence and self-
respect have essentially defied a cruel century's blind attempt to
silence his sensibility and disarray his shelf of work.

Why *Glory* (up to now translated on bibliographical lists as
The Exploit) waited until last must be guessed at. It was written
in 1930, immediately after *The Eye;* if *The Eye* is discounted as
a novella, *Glory* falls between two masterly novels—*The Defense*
and *Laughter in the Dark*. By comparison, it is weak; the ending
baffles, and what happens on the way to the ending occurs with a
curious, rather ingratiating casualness. *Glory* never really awakens
to its condition as a novel, its obligation to generate suspense. Its
secondary characters—Darwin, the sanguine and gentlemanly Englishman, and Sonia, the sulky little émigrée—come into view el-
liptically, as if they were revolving around some other sun. The
youthful hero, Martin Edelweiss, is a center of anti-gravity; we
feel that things flee him. Though he is Russian, his name is Swiss,
cluing some atomic split within. In one of those landlordly prefaces
that slam shut the doors of unsightly closets, inveigh against the
Freudian in the hall, and roughly nudge the prospective tenant
toward the one window with a view, Nabokov likens the design
of *Glory* to a chess problem whose crux is the impotence of the
customarily high-powered Queen. The hint is helpful. In the
backward look, the book's two faults, if faults they be (sleepy
development, stark conclusion), do combine into a single, intended
quality—a weak strength, or sad joy.

Martin is led along some of the paths of Nabokov's autobiography—the country house with its sandy *allées*, the numinous shadowy albums and tinted porch glass, the English biscuits and toothpaste imported from afar, the idyllic days in the warm Crimea
while civil war rages, the improvised departure on a Black Sea
freighter, the arrival in a Europe that will never shed the postcard
brightness and carved-clock quaintness of a place visited, of a place
that is not Russia and therefore not quite real. We have been here

before, in Luzhin's boyhood and in Van Veen's private mythology and, above all, in *Speak, Memory*. Nabokov, in his role of over-solicitous proprietor, warns us away from seeking out "duplicate items or kindred scenery" in *Speak, Memory*, but who could miss the marvellous newspaper-phoenix, the sheet of the London *Times* held across the fireplace to make it draw?

> The taut sheet would grow warm and transparent, and the lines of print, mingling with the lines showing through from the reverse side, looked like the bizarre lettering of some mumbo-jumbo language. Then, as the hum and tumult of the fire increased, a fox-red, darkening spot would appear on the paper and suddenly burst through. The whole sheet, now aflame, would be instantly sucked in and sent flying up. And a belated passerby, a gowned don, could observe, through the gloom of the gothic night, a fiery-haired witch emerge from the chimney into the starry sky. Next day Martin would pay a fine.

When, a quarter of a century later, Nabokov set down in English his memories of Cambridge, this imagery returned, almost sentence by sentence: "Then the flaming sheet, with the whirr of a liberated phoenix, would fly up the chimney to join the stars. It cost one a fine of twelve shillings if that firebird was observed." In that same Chapter Thirteen of *Speak, Memory*, Nabokov states, "The story of my college years in England is really the story of my trying to become a Russian writer." Martin Edelweiss is an alter ego gutted of Nabokov's artistic vocation; this deliberate lobotomy leaves an oddly hollow protagonist, a "travelling playboy" with dreams but no ambitions, graduating from college into tennis and vagabondage and, at the end, a suicidal return to Russia. But Martin has always, come to think of it, been close to death:

> Lying in the next room and feigning to snore so his mother would not think he was awake, Martin also recalled harrowing things, also tried to comprehend his father's death and to catch a wisp of posthumous tenderness in the dark of the room.

Not only his father but friends die—contemporaries fighting with the White armies—and in the Crimea, on a dark road, he is challenged by a drunk with a gun, and in the Alps he challenges himself to venture out onto a dizzying ledge. If in retrospect the reader finds that he has failed to take these dark hints seriously enough, the reason may be that Martin is Nabokov's healthiest hero and *Glory* his sunniest book.

Page after page brims with glistening physical description:

> With the onset of summer the cross-marked sheep were herded higher into the mountains. A babbling metallic tinkling, of unknown origin and from an unknown direction, would gradually become audible. Floating nearer, it enveloped the listener, giving him an odd tickling sensation in the mouth. Then, in a cloud of dust, came flowing a gray, curly, tightly packed mass of sheep rubbing against each other, and the moist, hollow tinkle of the bells, which delighted all of one's senses, mounted, swelled so mysteriously that the dust itself seemed to be ringing as it billowed above the moving backs of the sheep.

By denying Martin any artistic or political passion while not denying him his own full complement of senses, Nabokov has released a genie rare in fiction—a robust sense of physical well-being. The sensations of vigorous tennis, of goal tending at soccer, of a bareknuckled fistfight are in *Glory* given their due by an artist and meditator who was also an athlete; so, too, are the subtler but not less physical sensations of train travel, of pipe smoke and male companionship over tea, of "the fresh rough smell of earth and melting snow," of agriculture—"the hollowed earth would fill with bubbling brown water and, feeling in it with a spade, he mercifully softened the soil, until something gave delightfully, and the percolating water sank away, washing the roots. He felt happy he knew how to satisfy a plant's thirst." Happiness, as with an earlier Russian author, is the fragile, somehow terrible theme. Martin's sexual encounters tend to be felt in terms of the woman's fragility:

> He thought with rapt nostalgia about that amiable woman, with the touchingly hollow chest and the clear eyes, and about the way her fragile frame crunched in his embrace, causing her to say softly, "Ouch, you'll break me."

Similarly rapt, the sentences seek to embrace, with the crunch of a superb adjective, the full and fainting body of a moment.

> A wave would swell, boil with foam, and topple rotundly, spreading and running up on the shingle. Then, unable to hold fast, it would slip back to the grumbling of *awakened* pebbles.

. . . the country coolness of the rooms, so keenly perceptible after the outdoor heat; a fat bumblebee knocking against the ceiling with a *chagrined* droning; the paws of the fir trees against the blue of the sky. . . .

From that year on Martin developed a passion for trains, travels, distant lights, the heartrending wails of locomotives in the dark of night, and the *waxworks* vividness of local stations flashing by.

The author's efforts to fix the sensations, the gestures—"he would compress his thin lips, take off his pince-nez as carefully as if it were a dragonfly"—so freshly and precisely become a means whereby the third-person hero accrues moral credit, or at least a certain scrupulous stubbornness. An old man dies, and "Martin felt sorry for the originality of the deceased, who was truly ir-replaceable—his gestures, his beard, his sculpturesque wrinkles, the sudden shy smile, the jacket button that hung by a thread, and his way of licking a stamp with his entire tongue before sticking it on the envelope and banging it with his fist. In a certain sense this was all of greater value than the social merits for which there existed such easy little clichés." Martin is credited with a "medita-tive *joie de vivre*" and a search for "scintilla," but is declared untormented "by a writer's covetousness (so akin to the fear of death), by that constant state of anxiety compelling one to fix indelibly this or that evanescent trifle"; the declaration is rather formal and does have about it the cruelty of some dissecting ex-periment that permits a creature to twitch without benefit of a head. Yet it is true, as our decade has again borne witness, that youth, in the sensitivity of its animal health, tends to be artistic, and that without the task of art before it the artistic temper wastes itself in symbolic actions, in "trips" that are meaningless self-tests and whose secret destination is death. This point is contained in *Glory*, but it is not the point of the book. The point, surely, lies in its rapturous evocations and the *frissons* they give us—what Martin terms "the unexpected, sunlit clearings, where you can stretch until your joints crunch, and remain entranced," what Nabokov in his afterword to *Lolita* announces he "shall bluntly call aesthetic bliss." In its residue of bliss experienced, and in its charge of bliss conveyed, *Glory* measures up as, though the last to arrive, far from the least of this happy man's Russian novels.

Van Loves Ada, Ada Loves Van

ADA, by Vladimir Nabokov. 589 pp. McGraw-Hill, 1969.

When a book fails to agree with a reader, it is either because the author has failed to realize his intentions or because his intentions are disagreeable. Since Vladimir Nabokov is, all in all, the best-equipped writer in the English-speaking world (of which he inhabits a personal promontory by the side of Lake Geneva), the opening chapters of his giant new novel, *Ada*, must be taken as intentionally repellent. His prose has never—not even in his haughty prefaces to works resurrected from the Russian, not even in Humbert Humbert's maddest flights—menaced a cowering reader with more bristling erudition, garlicky puns, bearish parentheses, and ogreish winks. For example:

> "I can add," said the girl [Ada], "that the petal belongs to the common Butterfly Orchis; that my mother was even crazier than her sister; and that the paper flower so cavalierly dismissed is a perfectly recognizable reproduction of an early-spring sanicle that I saw in profusion on hills in coastal California last February. Dr. Krolik, our local naturalist, to whom you, Van, have referred, as Jane Austen might have phrased it, for the sake of rapid narrative information (you recall Brown, don't you, Smith?), has determined the example I brought back from Sacramento to Ardis, as the Bear-Foot, B,E,A,R, my love, not my foot or yours, or the Stabian flower girl's—an allusion, which your father, who, according to Blanche, is also mine, would understand like this (American fingersnap)."

Nor is the matter being thus roughly intruded into our consciousness of a compensating solidity or persuasive immediacy. *Ada* is subtitled "Or Ardor: A Family Chronicle," and the central family matter, not easily grasped, concerns the marriage of the two Durmanov sisters, Marina and Aqua, to two men each called Walter D. Veen, first cousins differentiated by the nicknames Red (or Dan) and Demon. Demon has an extensive love affair with Marina but marries Aqua, who readily goes insane; this unhappy marriage has one apparent offspring, Ivan, who is not to be confused with Uncle Ivan, the Durmanov sisters' short-lived brother. "Apparent," I say, because young "Van's" real mother is Marina, who, fertile as well as obliging, is also the mother of Demon's other illegitimate child, Ada, and—by her own husband, Red Veen, the well-known art dealer—another daughter, Lucette. The very incestuous ("very" because besides being ostensible first cousins and actual siblings they are also third cousins, descended from Prince Vseslav Zemski) love affair between Van and Ada preoccupies nearly six hundred rollicking pages.

The genealogical maze rests upon the unquiet geography of the planet Demonia, or Antiterra, where our homely Terra is a disconnected rumor, pieced together from the visions of madmen and "believed in," or not, like Heaven. On Antiterra, Canady and Estoty contain large French and Russian territories (much as Nabokov's memory must) and surprising sights, like "the peasant-bare footprint of Tolstoy preserved in the clay of a motor court in Utah where he had written the tale of Murat, the Navajo chieftain, a French general's bastard." Most of *Ada* occurs in the second half of Antiterra's 19th century, after the "L disaster" has caused electricity to be banned, leaving people to communicate with "dorophones," which ring by making all the toilets in the house gurgle; one answers by saying "*A l'eau!*" The atmosphere of this "distortive glass of our distorted glebe" is dreamy with the stale air of classic novels and swarms with swattable little midges like "Mr. Eliot, a Jewish businessman," "Dr. Froit of Signy-Mondieu-Mondieu," "*Les Amours du Docteur Mertvago,*" "*Collected Works of Falknermann,*" "that dislikable Norbert von Miller," and "James Jones, a formula whose complete lack of connotation made an ideal pseudonym despite its happening to be his real name."

Now, why should an author not create a "nulliverse" to represent "oneirologically" the contents of his own mind? The "L disaster," "which had the singular effect of both causing and cursing the notion of 'Terra,'" is surely the Russian Revolution, which caused such a great dislocation in Nabokov's life. The confusion of America (Estotiland) and Russia (Tartary) into one idyllic nation where everyone speaks French is, more than a joke upon Canada, a metaphor of personal history. Vain, venereal Van Veen verges on V.N.; Nabokov = Van + book. Ada (rhymes with Nevada) is ardor and art—but not, I think, the Americans for Democratic Action. She is also, in a dimension or two, Nabokov's wife Véra, his constant collaboratrice and the invariable dedicatee of his works. Ada's marginal comments on Van's manuscript, reproduced in print, are among the liveliest bits in the book, and offer an occasional check upon the author's rampaging genius. I suspect that many of the details in this novel double as personal communication between husband and wife; some of the bothersomely exact dates, for instance, must be, to use a favorite word of our author, "fatadic." I am certain that trilingual puns crowd and crawl (*"Je raffole de tout ce qui rampe"*—"I'm crazy about everything that crawls"—Ada says) beneath the surface of this novel like wood lice under the bark of an old stump. Their patient explication, and the formal arrangement of the parallels and contraries that geometricize "our rambling romance," the hurried reviewer may confidently leave to the graduate student who, between puffs of pot, while his wife strums the baby or dandles the guitar—by Log, this deadly style is infectious!—can spend many a pleasant and blameless hour unstitching the sequinned embroidery of Nabokov's five years' labor of love. He might begin with the prominently displayed anagram of "insect" ("incest," nicest," "scient"), move on to the orchid-imitating butterflies and butterfly-imitating orchids, get his feet wet in the water imagery (Aqua, Marina, *"A l'eau!"* yourself), and then do something with "cruciform," which crops up in several surprising connections, such as mounted moths, the hero's feces, and the arrangement of a mature woman's four patches of hair. Indeed, this book is Nabokov's most religious—his Testament as well as his *Tempest*—and manages several oblique squints at the Christian religion, a previous sketch of a structured supernature. *Ada* is the feminine form of the Russian "Ad," for Hades or Hell, and there is a Van in Nirvana and Heaven, for instance.

But, to answer the question posed above, one reason that an author should not create a nulliverse is that it is difficult to generate on an Antiterra the gravity that even the feeblest terrestrial tale appropriates. The details, the sometimes comical and sometimes waspish extensions of the author's prejudices and fancy, distract us from the angels and demons, who are, it turns out, meant to be human. Specifically, Ada and Van adventure amid obstacles so automatic, so confessedly retrieved from the attics of Mme. de La Fayette and Count Tolstoy, that it is hard to care about their intermittences of copulation as much as they and their creator do. In a landscape of "Ladore, Ladoga, Laguna, Lugano, and Luga," everything melts into foolery. I confess to a prejudice: fiction is earthbound, and while in decency the names of small towns and middling cities must be faked, metropolises and nations are unique and should be given their own names or none. I did not even like it when Nabokov, in *Pale Fire*, gave New York State the preëmpted appellation of Appalachia. He is, among other titles to our love, the foremost poet of Earth's geography, who in his remarkable story "Lance" saw long before the actual astronauts "the praying woman of the Baltic, and . . . the elegant Americas caught in their trapeze act, and Australia like a baby Africa lying on its side." His vision and flair are themselves so supermundane that to apply them to a fairyland is to put icing on icing. There is nothing in the landscapes of *Ada* to rank with the Russian scenery of *Speak, Memory* or the trans-American hegira of Lolita and Humbert Humbert.

As with place names, so with face names; we never get over the playful twinning of Aqua and Marina, Demon and Dan, and though Aqua's madness spins a few beautiful pages and Demon makes some noises approximating those of a flesh-and-blood father, the four remain animated anagrams, symmetrical appendages that want to be characters. To be sure, we are in a world of chrysalis and metamorphosis; as in *Invitation to a Beheading* and *Bend Sinister,* the cardboard flats and gauze trappings collapse, and the author/hero, heavy with death, lumbers toward the lip of the stage. This does happen, and the last pages of *Ada* are the best, and rank with Nabokov's best, but to get to them we traverse too wide a waste of facetious, airy, side-slipped semi-reality.

Define reality.

That which exists.

Don't you mean merely that which is perceived? Can we divide the universe, of which you seem so wholly fond, from our perception of it? And can we, more to the point, divide the reality of a book from what the author says it is? Does a "dorophone" exist

less on the paper than a "telephone" because a hundred million
"real" telephones echo in coarse Bakelite the latter, while the
former is a unique coinage of the writer's imperious imagination?
And isn't an author entitled to applause and gratitude for daring
to work not in dreary Zolaesque dredging of a swampy "external
world" as hallucinatory as the next but along the living rainbow
edge where writer's mind meets reader's in the mist of the retreat-
ing thunderstorms of "traditional" novels, a retreat most prettily
signalled by the jovial iridescence of parody? Don't you think that
your plebeian cavils were anticipated and scornfully dismissed in
advance by this towering, snorting wizard?

To be sure, the risks have been calculated. Some offenses are intentional. On the second page, Van disarmingly confesses his
"ancestral strain of whimsical, and not seldom deplorable, taste."
And defensive jabs at "cretinic critics" abound. But is it intentional
that the conversations between the two lovers so stiflingly reek of
mutual congratulation, that the dialogue everywhere defuses itself
with quibbles and pranks, and that the hero is such a brute? When
the girl who relieves him of his virginity, courteously described
as "a fubsy pig-pink whorlet," tries to kiss him, Van "elbow[s] her
face away." When Lucette, Ada's younger sister, falls in love with
him, he drives her to suicide. When Kim, a servant boy at Ardis
Hall, photographs Van and Ada making love and tries to blackmail them, Van arranges to have him blinded—"carried out of his
cottage with one eye hanging on a red thread and the other
drowned in its blood." Ada, bless her, now and then rebukes him
for his hard-heartedness, explaining that "not everybody is as
happy as we are," but Van holds aloof from "silly pity—a sentiment
I rarely experience" and continues to nourish at the expense of
others an ego "richer and prouder than anything those two poor
worms could imagine," the two worms being two lovers of Ada
whom the author dispatches before duel-crazy Van can get to
them. As to Kim: " 'Amends have been made,' replied fat Van
with a fat man's chuckle. 'I'm keeping Kim safe and snug in a
nice Home for Disabled Professional People, where he gets from
me loads of nicely brailled books on new processes in chromo-
photography.' " This useful therapy is cousin, presumably, to
"those helpful hobbies which polio patients, lunatics, and convicts

are taught by generous institutions, by enlightened administrators, by ingenious psychiatrists—such as bookbinding, or putting blue beads into the orbits of dolls made by other criminals, cripples, and madmen."

It is not always easy, but it is necessary, to distinguish between the hero's callousness and the author's zest for describing deformity and pain. Gentle Professor Pnin, we remember, was going to give someday a course on "The History of Pain." Throughout Nabokov's work, pain appears as the twin, in the physical world, of madness in the psychical. *Ada* contains a cruel vision of the afterlife: "The only consciousness that persists in the hereafter is the consciousness of pain." Little sensitive particles, a web of toothaches here, a bundle of nightmares there, cling to each other "like tiny groups of obsure refugees from some obliterated country huddling together for a little smelly warmth, for dingy charities or shared recollections of nameless tortures in Tartar camps." The fragmentation of Lucette's consciousness as she drowns ("she thought it proper to inform a series of receding Lucettes . . . that what death amounted to was only a more complete assortment of the infinite fractions of solitude") is monstrously well felt. Such sharp focus on pain, death, and madness incriminates not Van but the world. After Lucette's death, he longs in a letter for "more deeply moral worlds than this pellet of muck." Yet the phrase "pellet of muck" is a dandy's dismissal, and as Van goes about the world swaddled in his millions, exposing himself to chambermaids, feasting off of adolescent prostitutes, squashing literary critics, despising his lecture audiences, and fiercely repelling all who would trespass upon his inviolate ego and his adoration of Ada, he bares, perhaps unintentionally, a moral deformity comparable to the physical deformities that fascinate him.

Nabokov was born and reared as an aristocrat. Rich, healthy, brilliant, physically successful, he lacks the neurasthenic infirmities that gave the modernism of Proust, Joyce, Kafka, and Mann its tender underside. Asked, in a recent Japanese magazine (*The Umi*, Volume 1, No. 1), the question "What authors or works have influenced you most?" Nabokov answered serenely, "None." In truth, it is hard, in the ranks of literary genius, recruited as they are from the shabby-genteel and the bedridden, to find his aristocratic, vigorous peers. There is Tolstoy, and there is Chateaubriand. Tolstoy is much on Nabokov's mind. *Ada* begins by inverting the opening sentence of *Anna Karenina* and closes by likening itself, "in pure joyousness, and Arcadian innocence," to Tolstoy's reminiscences. It contains a Vronsky, a Kitty, a Dolly; Levin's code-word courtship of Kitty is parodied by Scrabble games between Van and Ada. The country-house atmosphere of Ardis Hall mimics yet partakes of the Tolstoyan idyll. Van's father accuses him of belonging to "the Decadent School of writing, in company of naughty old Leo and consumptive Anton," and Ada does a "clever pastiche . . . mimicking Tolstoy's paragraph rhythm and chapter closings." The list of concealed allusions and twittings could doubtless be lengthened. (Graduate student, go do it!)

But Chateaubriand, to whom the author tips his hat at half a dozen intersections, looms more fondly, as grandfathers will over fathers—and boorish, booted, crypto-Communist fathers at that. *Ada* shares with *Atala* its heroine's vowels and the setting of a fantasized America, with *René* the theme of incest, and with *Mémoires d'Outre-Tombe* its posthumous posture and an affinity of tone. Even through the brown varnish of translation, certain colors and twists in Chateaubriand's prose suggest Nabokov. In *Atala*, the Mississippi (which Chateaubriand probably never saw) is described in flood:

> But in the scenes of nature grace and magnificence always go together: while the main current drags the corpses of pines and oaks to the sea, floating islands of lotus and water-lily, their yellow blooms raised like standards, are borne upstream along either bank. Green snakes, blue herons, red flamingoes, and young crocodiles travel as passengers on these flowering boats, and each colony, spreading its golden sails to the wind, will come to rest in its own quiet backwater.

The observation of the *counter*-current, the magical precision applied to a vision, the detection of an idyll at the heart of a tumult, have a kinship with the prose flights of our Russian; Chateaubriand, too, was a survivor of revolution and a naturalist:

The scene is no less picturesque in broad daylight; for a crowd of butterflies, dragonflies, humming-birds, green parakeets, blue jays, attach themselves to these mosses, which are then like a tapestry in white wool, upon which the European craftsman has worked insects and dazzling birds.

The habit of viewing nature as an artifact blends with a trick of seeing human personality as a mechanism, wherein certain rather sad inevitabilities produce jerky effects:

Apolline de Bedée [Chateaubriand's mother] had large features and was dark, dainty, and ugly; her elegant manners and lively temperament contrasted with my father's stiffness and equanimity. As fond of society as he was of solitude, and as high-spirited and cheerful as he was cold and unemotional, she did not have a single taste which was not at variance with those of her husband. . . . Obliged to keep silent when she would have liked to speak, she found consolation in a kind of noisy sadness broken by sighs which formed the only interruption to the mute sadness of my father. In matters of piety, my mother was an angel.

Later in the *Mémoires*, Chateaubriand evokes the imaginary woman that his solitude in the château at Combourg created:

A young queen would come to me, decked in diamonds and flowers (it was my sylph). She sought me out at midnight, through gardens of orange trees . . . beneath a sky of love bathed in the light of Endymion's star; she moved forward, a living statue by Praxiteles, in the midst of motionless statues, pale pictures, and silent frescoes whitened by the moonlight . . . the silken tresses from her loosened diadem fell caressingly on my brow as she bent her sixteen-year-old head over my face, and her hands rested on my breast, throbbing with respect and desire.

This is Ada, to the diamonds and flowers, the *respect* and desire. Our sensation is confirmed that Ada is Van; that the duo is a single "A" of refracted solitude; that she is too ardent and intelligent, too *respectful*, to be external. She tells him, "All my thoughts, oh, my darling, are mimotypes of yours."

Rape is the sexual sin of the mob, adultery of the bourgeoisie, and incest of the aristocracy. Romanticism, which made of every ego an aristocrat, spawned Wordsworth and Dorothy, Byron and Augusta, and Chateaubriand and Lucile, the sister who shared his

Combourg solitude, who took on the moonlit lineaments of his "sylph," and who fled into a nunnery. "When we spoke of the world," Chateaubriand recalls, "it was of that which we carried within ourselves, a world which bore little resemblance to the real world." "Van," Ada writes in the margin of *Ada*, "I trust your taste and your talent but are we *quite sure* we should keep reverting so *zestfully* to that wicked world which after all may have existed only oneirologically, Van?" The idyll of Ardis Hall has its roots in the childhood fictionalized in the early pages of *The Gift* and *The Defense*. The idyll concerns self-discovery, the discovery of poetry, of chess, of lepidoptery (Ada's passion, not Van's), of one's own genius. *Ada* allegorizes self-love, self-respect; its spirituality (and it is a spiritual book) generates itself along the circular lines that to love one's self under the guise of a sister is to feminize one's soul, to make it other than the masculine ego, to externalize it—to give oneself, then, a soul.

The outward process is less pleasing, incestuous self-sufficiency plunging rapidly through world denigration into despair. Though Van sleeps with harlots and Ada with fools, only Lucette, their half sister, has enough precious substance to come between them; when she is drowned (as movingly as possible, from Van's rather aerial point of view), the union of Ada and Van is only a matter of time, which we are told is a motionless "grayish gauze." In a world without substance, the twinned genius-ego risks acrophobia.

CHATEAUBRIAND: I made progress in the study of languages; I became strong in mathematics, for which I have always had a pronounced leaning: I would have made a good naval officer or sapper. . . . I was good at chess, billiards, shooting, and fencing; I drew tolerably well; I would have sung well, too, if my voice had been trained.

VAN: He was ten. His father had lingered in the West where the many-colored mountains acted upon Van as they had on all young Russians of genius. He could solve an Euler-type problem or learn by heart Pushkin's "Headless Horseman" poem in less than twenty minutes.

CHATEAUBRIAND: My imagination, kindled into flame and spreading in all directions, failed to find adequate nourishment anywhere and could have devoured heaven and earth.

VAN: He had to do it his own way, but the cognac was frightful, and the history of thought bristled with clichés, and it was that history he had to surmount.

CHATEAUBRIAND: In life weighed by its light weight, measured by its short measure, and stripped of all deception, there are only two things of real value: religion married with intelligence and love married with youth . . . the rest is not worth while.

VAN: . . . this pellet of muck. . . .

CHATEAUBRIAND: Finally, one thing completed my misery: the groundless despair which I carried in the depths of my heart.

VAN: He wondered what really kept him alive on terrible Antiterra, with Terra a myth and all art a game. . . .

Is art a game? Nabokov stakes his career on it, and there exist enterprising young critics who, in replacing Proust, Joyce, and Mann with the alliterative new trinity of Beckett, Borges, and naBokov,* imply that these wonderful old fellows make fine airtight boxes, like five-foot plastic cubes in a Minimal Art show, all inner reflection and shimmer, perfectly self-contained, detached from even the language of their composition. I think not. Art is part game, part grim erotic tussle with Things As They Are; the boxes must have holes where reality can look out and readers can look in. Beckett shows us the depraved rudiments of our mortal existence; Borges opens a window on the desolation of history's maze and the tang of heroism that blows off the Argentine plain. And *Ada*, though aspiring to "an art now become pure and abstract, and therefore genuine," is full of holes, stretches and pages and phrases whose life derives from life.

Oh? Such as? Your praise-space is cramped.

(1) Ada herself. Witty and convolute *and* kind in her marginal addenda, wanly feminine in her lapses and evasions, quite lovable as a pornographic heroine progressively engaged in fancier pranks. The frontier of sexual explicitness, where *Lolita* was once an outpost, has been rolled way back; Nabokov adds a charming page

---

* "Oh, I am well aware of those commentators: slow minds, hasty typewriters! They would do better to link Beckett with Maeterlinck and Borges with Anatole France."—N., interviewed by Allene Talmey, of *Vogue*, on June 26, 1969.

(page 141) to the rapidly expanding American anthology of fellatio, and the inventory of Ada's charms beginning on page 215 is of Sapphic purity and Homeric grandeur.

(2) The essays, toward the end, on time and memory. Though his rebuttals of Freud and Einstein suggest the efforts of a very impressively costumed witch doctor to analyze an internal combustion engine in terms of mana and sympathetic magic, it is fun to watch; and his attempt, in droll lecturese, to pry open the innermost secrets of existence has the uncanny dignity of high blasphemy. Science fiction in the best sense.

(3) A thousand images and verbal moments where intelligence winks and wonder gleams. At random: the moment when Demon dorophones Marina from "a roadside booth of pure crystal still tear-stained after a tremendous thunderstorm" to beg her to come see "the daze of desert flowers that the rain had brought out."

(4) All of Part V, which is "not meant as an epilogue; it is the true introduction of my ninety-seven percent true and three percent likely, *Ada or Ardor, a family chronicle.*" The author, "a crotchety gray old wordman on the edge of a hotel bed," confides to us from the height of his ninety-seven years what it is like to be old, famous, impotent, and content. He describes his medicines, including "the delightful effect of a spoonful of sodium bicarbonate dissolved in water that was sure to release three or four belches as big as the speech balloons in the 'funnies' of his boyhood." He faces death, and its preliminary pain: "A giant, with an effort-contorted face, clamping and twisting an engine of agony." He reveals that Terra and Antiterra, rather casually, have merged. Ada and Van together translate into Russian some lines of John Shade, casting the last of many backward looks into Nabokov's *oeuvre.* Then they die, "into Eden or Hades, into the prose of the book or the poetry of its blurb." The blurb ends the book. It is strange but solid; sensations close to the edge of experience have been given equivalence in print. Would that such a marriage of lovely mind and surly matter had occurred earlier in *Ada!*

Wait a minute, une petite minute, pazhalsta—*what sort of loose, not to say queasily quasi-mystical, talk is "sensations close to the edge of experience"?*

Well, a man's religious life is the last province of privacy these days, but it is clear from *Ada* and other evidences that Nabokov is a mystic. "You believe," Ada asks Van, "you believe in the existence of Terra? Oh, you do!" And Nabokov, when asked by his *Playboy* interviewer if he believed in God, answered, "I know more than I can express in words, and the little I can express would not have been expressed had I not known more." In the same interview, he describes his preparations for a novel, which consist of random jottings at the behest of a "force" like that which makes a bird collect bits of straw and fluff in preparation for a nest. Just as Chateaubriand found accommodation for his massive egotism and morbidity within Catholic orthodoxy, Nabokov has made a church for himself out of fanatic pedantry; the thousand pages of his *Onegin* footnotes are a cathedralic structure where even the capitals that face the wall are painstakingly carved. Chateaubriand's morose and windy communion with nature at Combourg has its counterpart in Nabokov's happier intimations at Vyra of natural intricacy, particularly that of mimetic patterns in lepidoptera, a mimicry whose extravagant ingenuity seems unaccountable in a mechanical scheme of evolution. His fiction, from its punning prose and its twinning of characters to the elegance of each tale's deceptive design, re-presents his boyhood's revelation of art-for-art's-sake within Nature. If Nature is an artifact, however, there must be, if not an Artist, at least a kind of raw reality beneath or behind it, and the most daring and distressing quality of his novels is their attempt to rub themselves bare, to display their own vestments of artifice and then to remove them. Hence the recurrent device of the uncompleted, imperfect manuscript; this text embodies not only Ada's marginal notes but various false paragraph starts and editor's bracketed notes of the type frequent in proof sheets. Van says of a moment of semi-recognition, "It was a queer feeling—as of something replayed by mistake, part of a sentence misplaced on the proof sheet, a scene run prematurely, a repeated blemish, a wrong turn of time." This "queer feeling" is the sensation "close to the edge of experience" that Nabokov seeks to embody in *Ada;* this "queer feeling" is the heart of his artistic rapture and devotion, and also of his not always delicious mystification, his not invariably enlightening pursuit of nuancé inklings. In *Pale Fire,* John Shade showed a surprisingly literal interest in the afterlife; in *Ada*, Nabokov has sought to construct, with his Hades and Nirvana, an Otherlife. Art begins with magic. Though Nabokov operates, it seems to me, without the sanctions, the charity and humility, that make a priest, he lays claim to the more ancient title of magician.

The Translucing of Hugh Person

TRANSPARENT THINGS, by Vladimir Nabokov. 104 pp. McGraw-Hill, 1972.

Confessions: I have never understood how they saw the woman in half. Any willful child can dumbfound me with card tricks learned from the back of a comic book. Mystery novelists find in me their ideal gull, obligingly misled by the fishiest red herring. In calculus, I never grasped the infinitesimal but utile distinction between dt and Δt. And I do not understand Vladimir Nabokov's new novel, *Transparent Things*. This is a confession, not a complaint; the world abounds in excellent apparatuses, from automobile engines to digestive tracts, resistant to my understanding. So be it. I am grateful. I am grateful that Nabokov, at an age when most writers are content to rearrange their medals and bank their anthology royalties, rides his old hobby-horses with such tenacious mount and such jubilant tallyhos. A new book by him, any new book by him, serves as reminder that art is a holiday, however grim workdays grow in the sweatshops of reality. His exuberance is catching, as readers of this hyperbole-pocked paragraph can at a glance diagnose. Well, to work.

If the critic attempts to consider *Transparent Things* as itself transparent, he can perceive several impulses pressing their faces against the glass. One is an impulse to make the most of language: a hearty impulse, even jolly, by no means above the coarse buffoonery of pun ("Giulia . . . wore a Doppler shift over her luminous body," "An electric sign, DOPPLER, shifted to Violet") and alliteration ("ruts, rocks, and roots," "cracked that crooked cricoid"). The language bubbles, chortles, and in its abundance of simmering exactitude boils over into mad exhortation:

> The tap expostulated, letting forth a strong squirt of rusty water before settling down to produce the meek normal stuff—which you do not appreciate sufficiently, which is a flowing mystery, and, yes, yes, which deserves monuments to be erected to it, cool shrines!

Transparent Things's hero, Hugh Person, is an editor of, among other authors, one "R." (a mirroring of the Russian я, *ya*, meaning "I"), who, though more corpulent and less uxorious than Nabokov himself, does live in Switzerland, composes "surrealistic novels of the poetic sort," and regards the rest of the world as a grotesquely clumsy siege upon his artistic integrity. "Our Person, our reader, was not sure he entirely approved of R.'s luxuriant and bastard style; yet, at its best ('the gray rainbow of a fog-dogged moon'), it was diabolically evocative." Nabokov's is really an amorous style—foreplay in the guise of horseplay. It yearns to clasp diaphanous exactitude into its hairy arms. To convey a child's nocturnal unease, it can toss off the looming metaphor "Night is always a giant"; or with tender euphonic trippings it can limn a woman's facial expression during intercourse as "the never deceived expectancy of the dazed ecstasy that gradually idiotized her dear features." Such a yen to evoke, to use the full spectrum latent in the dictionary, would teach us how to read again. If not always a comfortable, it is surely a commendable impulse.

Less so, perhaps, the murderous impulse visible through the workings of *Transparent Things*. Since the book is something of a thriller, its plot should be left its secrets; but, needless to say, almost no character, major or minor, survives its last turn. Strangulation, conflagration, embolism, cancer—these are some of the methods employed. Characters who barely appear onstage have their offstage demises dutifully reported: a detective who researched an incidental infidelity is "at present dying in a hot dirty hospital on Formosa," a momentary lover of the heroine is smartly crushed under an avalanche in "Chute, Colorado." A worse than Calvinist sense of rigor constricts the poor bright creatures into the narrowness of the killing bottle. When Muriel Spark, another deft dealer in fatality, conjures up a hotel fire, a building's collapse, or a multiple murder, an implacable God is prefigured and the crime transcends the writer's will. Not so with Nabokov. He proposes, he disposes. A design must be completed. The sometimes touchingly vivid characters exist as spots of color bounded on all sides by a shimmering nothingness; their deaths come as a rubbing out. And the reader, too, is put in his place, exterminated by the announcement that this is all an invention—*poof!* This announcement surfaces explicitly * in *Transparent Things*, as it does in *Invitation to a Beheading* and *Bend Sinister,* but the gesture of withdrawal, of Prospero's retirement, of termination and disavowal, closes even such relatively straight fiction as *Pnin* and *Laughter in the Dark.* Here, in a book that freely uses the second person and that calls its central figure (a professional reader) Hugh, the wish to personify in order to destroy carries well out into the reader's lap. You (Hugh) person, whoever you are, are nobody (*personne*): vanish, die.

A third impulse is to formulate, at the highest level of intelligence and subtlety, some statement about space/time, death, and being. R., dying, writes to his publisher:

> I believed that treasured memories in a dying man's mind dwindled to rainbow wisps; but now I feel just the contrary: my most trivial sentiments and those of all men have acquired gigantic proportions. The entire solar system is but a reflection in the crystal of my (or your) wrist watch. . . . Total rejection of all religions ever dreamt up by man and total composure in the face of total death! If I could explain this triple totality in one big book, that would become no doubt a new bible and its author the founder of a new creed.

And Vladimir Nabokov writes, on the last page, "This is, I believe, *it*: not the crude anguish of physical death but the incomparable pangs of the mysterious mental maneuver needed to pass from one state of being to another." This at least helps explain this artificer's compulsive revelations of artifice; in the moment of a fictional world's collapse, one state of being yields to another. But are we to take this as an analogy for death? If death

* Though not quite so explicitly in the finished book as in the bound galley proofs, wherein the last sentence, "Easy, you know, does it, son," indented like the valediction of a letter, is followed by "Vladimir Nabokov" flush right and, flush left, "*Montreaux*/April 1, 1972." The novel as published omits these prankish proofs or spoor bestowed by the author's passing.

is total, is it a "state of being" at all? And—to examine the last sentence quoted—aren't adjectives like "incomparable" and "mysterious" the refuge of an incommunicable mysticism?

The central impulse behind the novel remains obscure. At first, it seems that the "transparency" of things refers to their dimension in time—an ordinary pencil found in a drawer is taken back to its birth as a rod of agglutinated graphite and a splinter buried in the heart of a pine tree. Then it seems that the transparency has to do with an artful overlapping of beds, bureaus, carpets catching a slant of sunshine, shuttlecocks, dogs, and so on, as Hugh Person returns several times, between the ages of eight and forty, to the Swiss village of Trux. Other things are transparent, such as book titles "that shone through the book like a watermark," and a loved one "whose image was stamped on the eye of his mind and shone through the show at various levels." But the culminating image of transparency ("the incandescence of a book or a box grown completely transparent and hollow"), though the author presents it as if it were the crown of his life's thought and passion, arrives as the answer to a conundrum that has not been posed. Alas, what we remember of *Transparent Things* are its agreeable opacities: the busy clots of choice adjectives ("frail, lax, merry America"), the erotic peculiarities of Person's charming and difficult wife, Armande (she likes to make love as fully dressed as possible, while maintaining a flow of cocktail chatter), the delicious, glacial scene of a ski resort particularized by "the glaze of the upper runs, the blue herringbones lower down, the varicolored little figures outlined by the brush of chance against the brilliant white as if by a Flemish master's hand." We close the book guiltily, having licked the sugar coating but avoided, somehow, swallowing the pill.

If an artistic life so variously productive, so self-assured, so hermetically satisfactory to its perpetrator could be said to have a failing, Nabokov has failed to get himself taken seriously enough. A sad shadow of modesty touches this narrative. "This part of our translucing is pretty boring." "Mr. R., though perhaps not a master of the very first rank. . . ." Only "some of the less demanding reviewers in his adopted country" call R. a "master stylist." The book abounds, indeed, in wry self-portraits. The heroine's perverse sexual charades, in which her excitement derives "from the contrast between the fictitious and the factual," parody Nabokov's "*it*"—the "pangs" of the "maneuver" needed to pass from one state to another. A further "maneuver" with "pangs": Armande's Russian mother sits trapped by her own bulk in a chair, waiting for the "one precise little wiggle" that will "fool gravity" and, like "the miracle of a sneeze," lift her. Nabokov's own tricky legerity discourages solemn praise; he makes his acolytes and exegetes seem ridiculous as they compile their check lists of puns and chase his butterfly allusions. His aesthetic of gravity-fooling confronts us with a fiction that purposely undervalues its own humanistic content, that openly scorns the psychology and sociology that might bring with them an unfoolable gravity. Joyce also loved puns, and Proust was as lopsided an emotional monster as Humbert Humbert. But these older writers did submit their logomachy and their maimed private lives to a kind of historical commonalty; the Europe of the epics and the cathedrals spoke through them. The impression created by Nabokov's works in Russian, I am told, differs from that given by his spectacular works in English; he can be compared to Dostoevsky and Tolstoy in a way in which he cannot be compared with Thoreau and Twain. In his post-*Lolita* novels, especially, he seems more illusionist than seer. Though he offers us sensations never before verbally induced, and performs stunts that lift him right off the page, we are more amused than convinced. The failing may be ours; we are not ready, we are too dull of ear, too slow of eye, too much in love with the stubborn muteness of the earth to read the meaning behind his magic. He mutters from his sky, this comical comet, and hints, through his masks, of "a new bible." His measure is that we hope for nothing less from him.

Motley But True

Look at the Harlequins!, by Vladimir Nabokov. 253 pp. McGraw-Hill, 1974.

Nabokov's last three novels form, in the squinting retrospect of at least this surveyor, a trilogy of sorts: one, *Ada*, is remarkably long; another, *Transparent Things*, is remarkably short; and the third, the newly published *Look at the Harlequins!*, is, like Mama Bear's bed, comfortably middle-sized. All three books feature on the jacket back (in three different tonalities, if you line them up) the same frontal, staring, intimidatingly cranial photograph of the author; and all three, composed in the sparkling and salubrious vacuum of Switzerland, are—in the nicest possible sense—narcissistic to a degree unprecedented in his other English-language fiction, where a distinct madness differentiates the narrator (Humbert Humbert, Charles Kinbote) from the author, or where at the end Nabokov himself breaks in, as if to establish that these unfortunate heroes (Krug, Pnin) are somebody else entirely. But no such disclaimer attaches to Van Veen of *Ada* or to R. of *Transparent Things*—creations that flagrantly flirt with our knowledge of their creator. And the main movement of *Look at the Harlequins!*, the core of its "combinational delight" (to quote *Pale Fire*), is the reduction to zero of the difference between the author and the apparently contrasting Russian émigré author, Vadim, whose last name we never learn, though he is nicknamed "MacNab" and receives by mistake the press clippings of a British politician called Nabarro.

Much of the fun of *Look at the Harlequins!* arises from Nabokov's apparent invention of a contemporary and peer who is nevertheless conspicuously unlike him—oft-married where Nabokov's monogamy is declared in every book's dedication to his wife, anti-athletic where Nabokov was a soccer player and a tennis instructor, dipsomaniacal where wholesome, outdoorsy ("My own life is fresh bread with country butter and Alpine honey"—interview with James Mossman of the BBC) Nabokov is satisfied with "an occasional cup of wine or a triangular gulp of canned beer" (interview with Kurt Hoffman for the *Bayerischer Rundfunk*). Nabokov provides this alter ego with a list of works—but even at first glance the master's *oeuvre* peeps through its mimotype: *Tamara* (1925) is surely *Mary* (1926); *Camera Lucida* (*Slaughter in the Sun*) replicates *Laughter in the Dark* (*Camera Obscura*); *The Dare* mistranslates *The Gift* [*Dar*]; *See under Real* and *Dr. Olga Repnin* openly conceal *The Real Life of Sebastian Knight* and *Pnin*; and *Ardis* (1970) is scarcely even a pseudonym for *Ada, or Ardor* (1969). The persona of Vadim, too, is thin to translucence, and rubs thinner as the book goes on. Though he advertises himself as "a complete non-athlete," he lapses into athletic imagery —"a crack player's brio and chalk-biting serve"—and likens his literary prowess in two languages to being "World Champion of Lawn Tennis *and* Ski." Vadim's novels as he describes them are oneiric distortions of Nabokov's own; he signs himself as "Dumbert Dumbert" in one nightmare episode of nymphetolatry, and his central psychological problem, an inability to imagine certain permutations of Space, transposes *Ada*'s elaborate speculations on Time. Rightly Vadim is haunted by "a dream feeling that my life was the non-identical twin, a parody, an inferior variant of another man's life, somewhere on this or another earth." When he comes to describe himself, his face is line for line the face on the back of the jacket. Even his three wives, so lovingly limned and so various—Iris, Annette, Louise—finally seem metamorphic phases of the nameless fourth mate, the "you" to whom this "autobiography" is addressed and who, when she enters Vadim's hospital room, is saluted as "Reality"—"I emitted a bellow of joy, and Reality entered."

Nabokov's long joust and lovefeast with reality seems notably good-humored in this novel, the best, in *my* book, of his last three. If *Transparent Things* is a splintered hand-mirror, and *Ada* cotton-candy spun to the size of sunset cumulus, *Look at the Harlequins!* is a brown briefcase, as full of compartments as a magician's sleeve and lovingly thumbed to a scuff-colored limpness. It holds, in sometimes crumpled form, all the Nabokovian themes, from ardor to Zembla, and shares with us more frankly than any book since *The Gift* his writer's bliss, "the endless re-creation of my fluid self":

> . . . I regarded Paris, with it gray-toned days and charcoal nights, merely as the chance setting for the most authentic and faithful joys of my life: the colored phrase in my mind under the drizzle, the white page under the desk lamp awaiting me in my humble home.

Describing his three wives gives Vadim a quite contagious pleasure. First, there is Iris, a petite brunette, "a suntanned beauty with a black bob and eyes like clear honey":

The moldings of her brown back, with a patch-size beauty spot below the left shoulder blade and a long spinal hollow, which redeemed all the errors of animal evolution, distracted me painfully. . . . A few aquamarines of water still glistened on the underside of her brown thighs and on her strong brown calves, and a few grains of wet gravel had stuck to her rose-brown ankles.

Then there is Annette, a Russian blonde, "with very attractive though not exceptionally pretty features":

> . . . her graceful neck seemed even longer and thinner. An expression of mild melancholy lent a new, unwelcome, beauty to her Botticellian face: its hollowed outline below the zygoma was accentuated by her increasing habit of sucking in her cheeks when hesitant or pensive.

And thirdly Louise, an American, "porcelain-pretty and very fast":

> She . . . pulled off her wet sweater over her tumbled chestnut-brown, violet-brown curls and naked clavicles. Artistically, strictly artistically, I daresay she was the best-looking of my three major loves. She had upward-directed thin eyebrows, sapphire eyes registering (and that's the right word) constant amazement at earth's paradise (the only one she would ever know, I'm afraid), pink-flushed cheekbones, a rosebud mouth, and a lovely concave abdomen.

The manner in which these three wives (Nabokov's three languages?) travel in fictional space, enlarging from first glimpses into love objects and marriage partners and then diminishing through disenchantment into death or abandonment, is no mean feat of projection. And the hero describes other women as well—Lolita-like creatures such as the whorish little Dolly and his own elusive daughter Bel and the schoolmate of Bel's who turns out to be "you," repulsive creatures such as the adoring but sub-brachially pungent Lyuba and the stocky, whiskery, pro-Soviet Ninella. But then Nabokov has always loved to describe women, and the landscapes of childhood, and the student chill of Cambridge, and twins, and butterflies, and insomnia, and all the gaudy mirages of "a happy expatriation that began practically on the day of my birth" (to quote a letter to *The New York Times*). But toward the end of *Look at the Harlequins!* Vadim does two things never, to our imperfect knowledge, experienced by Vladimir Nabokov: he travels to the Soviet Union, and he has a stroke.

Both episodes show an exercising of the imaginative powers that one rather wishes had not had so strenuously to vie, over Nabokov's career, with his passion for trickery and annihilation. For a rabid Soviet-hater, the imagined return is surprisingly mild and calm in tone—and, to this one-time guest of the Soviet state, surprisingly accurate, from the smells on the Aeroflot turboprop to the insolence of the hotel lift-operators and the slowness of the restaurant service to the "morose, drab, oddly old-fashioned aspect that Soviet kids have." The thrilleresque details of intrigue that get Vadim there are funny, and his conversation afterwards, in the Paris airport, with a Soviet spy who has shadowed him all the way, is hilarious:

> "*Ekh!*" he explained, "*Ekh*, Vadim Vadimovich *dorogoy* (dear), aren't you ashamed of deceiving our great warm-hearted country, our benevolent, credulous government, our overworked Intourist staff, in this nasty infantile manner! A Russian writer! Snooping! Incognito!"

The agent (himself an old émigré, turned Communist) confuses, as the conversation goes on in this bumptious style, Vadim with Nabokov, and when the elderly author (whoever he is) knocks him down, exclaims, with timeless Russian stoicism, "*Nu, dali v mordu. Nu, tak chtozh?*" ("Well, you've given me one in the mug. Well, what does it matter?"). Somehow, absurd and sketchy as it is, this episode contains a warmth, a humor and suspense, that only unguarded feeling bestows, and that are too much missing from the professedly ardent filigree of Nabokov's later fiction. The stroke, a moment of near-fatal paralysis that overtakes Vadim at the turning-point of a preprandial walk, is amazing in its authentication, in the near-mystical swoops of its inner detail:

> Speed! If I could have given my definition of death to . . . the black horses gaping at me like people with trick dentures all through my strange skimming progress, I would have cried one word: Speed! . . . Imagine me, an old gentleman, a distinguished author, gliding rapidly on my back, in the wake of my outstretched dead feet, first through that gap in the granite, then over a pinewood, then along misty water meadows, and then simply between marges of mist, on and on, imagine that sight!

Or imagine any other writer since the beginning of time providing such a blend of sensation, metaphysics, and comedy.

Oh, yes, the title. Vadim's great-aunt, when he is an impressionable seven or eight, cries out to him, "Stop moping! . . . Look at the harlequins!"

> "What harlequins? Where?"
> "Oh, everywhere, all around you. Trees are harlequins, words are harlequins. So are situations and sums. Put two things together—jokes, images—and you get a triple harlequin. Come on! Play! Invent the world! Invent reality!"

Throughout the invented reality of this novel, harlequins recur, as a butterfly glimpsed with Annette and as an Iranian circus troupe that boards a Soviet plane, as the "motley of madness" the hero wears and as a cunning multiplicity of lozenge-shapes, some as small as a "sequence of suspension dots in diamond type." As the jacket design reminds us, a harlequin's traditional lozenge-pattern is a chessboard made oblique. Beside him on the hospital bedside table, as Vadim/Vladimir, "paralyzed in symmetrical patches," slowly reassembles the world, he notices "a pair of harlequin sunglasses, which for some reason suggested not protection from a harsh light but the masking of tear-swollen lids." Which hint of masked grief suggests, more strongly than is his wont, why our author has so insistently harlequinized the world and tweaked the chessboard of reality awry.

A Tribute

Contributed to the Triquarterly, Winter 1970, Issue, Celebrating Nabokov's Seventieth Birthday

YOUR INVITATION to Vladimir Nabokov's birthday party reaches me in England, and it was in England, nearly fifteen years ago, in Oxford, that I first read this great man: in *The New Yorker*, the Pnin story where the pencil sharpener says *ticonderoga, ticonderoga* and Pnin bursts into tears during a flickering Russian film. It was another fictional universe, or at least a stunning intensification of the ordinary one, and it has been one of the steadier pleasures of the fifteen years since to catch up on the considerable amount of Nabokov then in English and to keep up with the ample installments of reincarnated Russian and newly spawned American that have been issued through an untidy assortment of publishers, ranging from the elegant Bollingen Press to a miserable little bindery called, I think, Phaedra.* Though I may have nodded here and there among the two volumes of notes to *Onegin*, I have not knowingly missed any of the rest; for Nabokov is never lazy, never ungenerous with his jewels and flourishes, and his *oeuvre* is of sufficient majesty to afford interesting perspectives even from the closets and back hallways. I have expressed in print my opinion that he is now an American writer and the best living; I have also expressed my doubt that his aesthetic models—chess puzzles and protective colorations in lepidoptera—can be very helpful ideals for the rest of us. His importance for me as a writer has been his holding high, in an age when the phrase "artistic integrity" has a somewhat paradoxical if not reactionary ring, the stony image of his self-sufficiency: perverse he can be, but not abject; prankish but not hasty; sterile but not impotent. Even the least warming aspects of his image—the implacable hatreds, the reflexive contempt —testify, like fortress walls, to the reality of the siege this strange century lays against our privacy and pride.

As a reader, I want to register my impression that Nabokov does not (as Philip Toynbee, and other critics, have claimed) lack heart. *Speak, Memory* and *Lolita* fairly bulge with heart, and even the less ingratiating works, such as *King, Queen, Knave*, show, in the interstices of their rigorous designs, a plenitude of human understanding. The ability to animate into memorability minor, disagreeable characters bespeaks a kind of love. The little prostitute that Humbert Humbert recalls undressing herself so quickly, the fatally homely daughter of John Shade, the intolerably pretentious

---

* The great man, in his peppery supplement to *Triquarterly*'s fat (371 pp.) bundle of paeans, bridled at this "harsh and contemptuous reference to a small publishing house, which brought out excellent editions of four books of mine." I have seen only three of these volumes, but they *are* miserably bound, in the sleazy pseudo-cloth of high-school yearbooks; the signature on the covers has Nabokov dotting his *i*'s with circles like Walt Disney. Of course, *nichyvo*, if the text is right. But I wish for him and his works the best of everything, from the integument in.

and sloppy-minded woman whom Pnin undyingly loves, the German street figures in *The Gift*, the extras momentarily on-screen in the American novels—all make a nick in the mind. Even characters Nabokov himself was plainly prejudiced against, like the toadlike heroine of *King, Queen, Knave*, linger vividly, with the outlines of the case they must plead on Judgment Day etched in the air; how fully we feel, for example, her descent into fever at the end. And only an artist full of emotion could make us hate the way we hate Axel Rex in *Laughter in the Dark*. If we feel that Nabokov is keeping, for all his expenditure of verbal small coin, some treasure in reserve, it is because of the riches he has revealed. Far from cold, he has access to European vaults of sentiment sealed to Americans; if he feasts the mind like a prodigal son, it is because the heart's patrimony is assured.

ENGLISH LIVES

A Short Life

A VOICE THROUGH A CLOUD, by Denton Welch. 254 pp. University of Texas Press, 1966.

"Promising" is a pale term of praise reviewers customarily employ to excuse themselves from reading closely the work at hand. But the term applies with some force to Denton Welch, an Englishman born in 1917, severely injured in a highway accident at the age of eighteen, and dead by 1948. In his thirteen years of pain and invalidism, Welch composed three novels, of which the last, entitled *A Voice Through a Cloud*, was left uncompleted at his death. While not quite a masterpiece (not only does it not end, it gives no sign of knowing how to end), the book is, especially in its first half, masterly: a fine intelligence, a brave candor, a voracious eye, and a sweet, fresh prose are exercised. Possibly these gifts, liberated to wider use by a healthy life, would have proved equal to many subjects. It is also possible that Welch's gifts were best realized by the one subject he had—the effects of his absurd and savage accident—and that nothing else would have burnt away so much of his dilettantism or turned his somewhat sinister detachment to such good artistic account. Again, it could be argued that save for his accident he would have outgrown the distrustful and diffident brilliance of a schoolboy. But in the end a man is what happens to him plus what he does. In a world aswarm with might-have-beens, Welch took his shortened life, his remittances of pain and fever, and delivered a unique account of shattered flesh and refracted spirit.

This "novel," in which Welch rechristened himself Maurice

: 223 :

and presumably used the convenience of fiction to change some names and fake a few details, begins with the hero, a London art student, setting out on his bicycle for his uncle's vicarage in Surrey. The landscape and a tea shoppe are rather adjectivally evoked; the hero resumes his pleasant ride; then

> I heard a voice through a great cloud of agony and sickness. The voice was asking questions. It seemed to be opening and closing like a concertina. The words were loud, as the swelling notes of an organ, then they melted to the tiniest wiry tinkle of water in a glass.
> I knew that I was lying on my back on the grass; I could feel the shiny blades on my neck. I was staring at the sky and I could not move. Everything about me seemed to be reeling and breaking up. My whole body was screaming with pain, filling my head with its roaring, and my eyes were swimming in a sort of gum mucilage. . . . Bright little points glittered all down the front of the liquid man kneeling beside me. I knew at once that he was a policeman, and I thought that, in his official capacity, he was performing some ritual operation on me. There was a confusion in my mind between being brought to life—forceps, navel-cords, midwives—and being put to death—ropes, axes, and black masks; but whatever it was that was happening, I felt that all men came to this at last.

In spite of certain lazy, boyish locutions ("the tiniest," "screaming with pain," "swimming in a sort of"), a private apocalypse is rendered with icy exactness, and throughout the succeeding pages of hospital ordeal Welch does not funk his essential task—the portrayal of "the savage change from fair to dark":

> In the middle of the furnace inside me there was a clear thought like a text in cross-stitch. I wanted to warn the nurses, to tell them that nothing was real but torture. Nobody seemed to realize that this was the only thing on earth.

It is strange to realize how incidentally narrative fiction treats the physical base of human existence; food is an occasion for conversation, sleep an interval of action, elimination a joke. Bodies are felt as mobile scaffoldings for conversing sensibilities, and pain, that sensation of ultimate priority, is almost never (Tolstoy and Samuel Beckett are exceptions) rendered solidly. In Welch's nar-

rative, agony precedes psychology; introspection takes place only
as pain's monopoly loosens. The mind worms in the chinks of
suffering.

> I tried to lull myself to sleep. . . . but all the pleasant things
> that only yesterday I liked so much rose up to haunt me. I thought
> of eating delicious food, wearing good clothes, feeling proud and
> gay, going for walks, singing and dancing alone, fencing and
> swimming and painting pictures with other people, reading books.
> And everything seemed horrible and thin and nasty as soiled paper.
> I wondered how I could ever have believed in these things, how I
> could even for a moment have thought they were real. Now I
> knew nothing was real but pain, heat, blood, tingling, loneliness,
> and sweat. I began almost to gloat on the horror of my situation and
> surroundings. I felt paid out, dragged down, punished finally.
> Never again would my own good fortune make me feel guilty. I
> could look any beggars, blind people in the face now. Everything
> I had loved was disgusting; and I was disgusting, too.
>
> As this terrible gloating unhappiness flooded over me, my head
> began to swim; the pain sucked me under and I wanted to die and
> not be tortured any more.

The action of this narrative is the narrator's recovery of the
world, a recovery effected without much assistance from other
people. Welch, though he can do a sketch of a doomed eccentric
as well as the next literate hospital patient, is not a creator of characters. All the persons he meets are depicted flatly, on the inner
walls of a neurasthenia that probably existed before his catastrophe.
At the worst, other people outrage and torture him—most of the
hospital attendants he met struck him as sadists—and at best they
merely disappoint and irritate, like static obstructing a delicate
tuning-in. Welch/Maurice seeks rapport not with any other person but with the world at large, and it is remarkable, considering
that more than ten years had passed since his accident, how fully,
how delicately he can conjure up the sense impressions that make
this search credible:

> The bare walls [of the hospital corridor] seemed to be waiting for
> just another human sight or sound or smell to be swallowed up in
> them. They had sucked in so much hope and fear and boredom;
> but nothing showed. Their blank faces stared back and sinister
> little draughts struck against my face and ears and hair.

As he ventures into the outer world, everything is hungrily snapped up—"the leathery gray spread of the sea," "the faint gunpowdery smell of new stone," "the broad leaves in the gutter, splendid, decaying, rich, like some rare food." Returning from the verge of oblivion, he writes of familiar sights as might a visitor from another planet:

> I had not been in a night street scene for a long time. I watched the people's faces as they pushed through the theatre doors. The faces changed when they passed from the street into the building. Outside they were more hardened, more scoured and flinty, tragic too from all they had withstood. Inside they grew more cushiony and fluid; they lost the vagrant haunted look. The look of anxiety melted into the sparkling monkey, or the soft bear look. And people undid belts and buttons, loosened their hair, patted, polished, breathed out their warm breath, like animals penned together in a farmyard.

In an age quick to label any sufficiently bleak and sententious novel "existential," here is a work, by an author born again out of agony into the world, that seems to reconstitute human existence particle by particle.

Fiction captures and holds our interest with two kinds of suspense: circumstantial suspense—the lowly appetite, aroused by even comic strips, to know the outcome of an unresolved situation—and what might be called gnostic suspense, the expectation that at any moment an illumination will occur. Bald plot caters to the first; style, wit of expression, truth of observation, vivid painterliness, brooding musicality, and all the commendable rest pay court to the second. Gnostic suspense is not negligible—almost alone it moves us through those many volumes of Proust—but it stands to the other rather like charm to sex in a woman. We hope for both, and can even be more durably satisfied by charm than by sex (all animals are sad after coitus and after reading a detective story); but charm remains the ancillary and dispensable quality.

Toward the end of *A Voice Through a Cloud*, the hero acquires some use of his legs, and the plane of concern shifts from the struggle with oblivion to a search for suitable housing. The writing, though more polished than before, begins to feel aimless. Detail becomes obsessive. Maurice walks up an ordinary road of two-family dwellings: "There was something monstrous about the long avenue of coupled pink brick boxes. I felt that I was climbing up between gigantic naked Siamese twins with eyes all over their bodies." Circumstantial suspense is deliberately generated; old characters reappear and are skillfully "used." The book, as the dying author wearies, begins to act like a conventional novel. Though Welch had the abilities of a novelist, misfortune made him a kind of prophet, and it is as a prophetic document, a proclamation of our terrible fragility, that his book possesses value.

Ayrton Fecit

FABRICATIONS, by Michael Ayrton. 224 pp. Holt, Rinehart & Winston, 1972.

In 1967, the English painter and sculptor Michael Ayrton published *The Maze Maker*, one of the best of the many mythological novels written in English since 1955, when Robert Graves offered, in his two-volume Penguin *Greek Myths*, a handy compendium with-it and far-out enough to make the Hellenic legends interesting again. Mr. Ayrton's tale of Daedalus, supposedly written by Daedalus himself, picks its way nimbly among the scattered and conflicting classical references to its hero, ingeniously exploits Graves's jumbled treasure of semantic and anthropological explications, and—though the narrative turns rather mazy amid a welter of mysticism and interlocked symbols—repeatedly draws energy from the author's excitement over the art, business, and mystery of fabrication. The primitive craftsman's careful magic comes to life in a dozen procedural descriptions—how to cast bronze, how to make wings, how to counterfeit a honeycomb in gold, how to construct an artificial cow in which a real woman may enjoy intercourse with a god who has assumed the form of a bull. Daedalus gives us the book's thematic core: "Poets have much in common with heroes. They are neither of them aware of the world, of its true appearance nor its real consequence, its structure nor its marvellous imperfection. They are blind to that, and because my methods of gaining experience have been observation, deduction, and experiment, I have been no worse off and much better instructed than any poets or heroes known to me. . . . I am involved in matters which I do not wish disturbed nor interrupted by eloquent activities, the facile assumption of power, speculation on immeasurable phenomena, nor any apotheosis. What I make exists."

Fittingly, then, Mr. Ayrton's next, and present, volume of fiction is entitled *Fabrications*. Twenty-seven short prose pieces, fashioned in a variety of styles and with a variety of pictographic devices, propose to insert into the packed and stacked reality of documented history various shims of speculation and fantasy. Imaginary pages of actual memoirs are supplied. Gilles de Rais takes his part in a performance of Shaw's *Saint Joan* in wartime Southampton, and enlarges the part with a stirring self-defense. An invented Scots artist, "John Calder of Kelty," is plausibly intertwined with known facts and surviving works of 16th-century Italy. An extant 12th-century manuscript illustration is explained by a fable involving one of Mr. Ayrton's favorite themes, taurophilia. The man whose ear St. Peter sliced off lends the other to the mendacities of Flavius Josephus. And so on. The stories presuppose a reader able to delight in pedantry, with enough sense of history to find enchantment in its odd nooks and corners—Rome in 1001, Jotapata in 67. Embroidery of the archival texts is not, in this eclectic era, an unfamiliar form of art: witness the stories of Borges and Barthelme, the poems of Richard Howard and, a century ago, Robert Browning. As a cherisher of old oddities, Mr. Ayrton shows much erudition, wit, and spirit. He tells us about John Philip Sousa's novels, about the curious cookery (flourishing in the dyspeptic reign of Charles I) that incorporated consenting dwarves into large pies called "surprise pastries," and about the eerie heroic statuary of the Saluvii, a Celtic tribe that dominated the valley of the Rhone in pre-Christian times. He is especially vivid, predictably, when he deals with art. Brunelleschi and Giacometti are seen interfering with the space of their time, and Piero della Francesca and Caravaggio deliver monologues that startle with their intensity—for Mr. Ayrton, not predictably, is an excellent mimic of dead styles.

Yet, though *Fabrications* pulls us willingly along from one con-

ceit to the next, and a number seem perfect, something makes resistance all the way, and we emerge feeling that we have left the
shop not of an artist but of a hobbyist. Why is this? For one, Mr.
Ayrton's voice, when not engaged in a work of impersonation,
gravitates toward an off-putting archness:

> If I suggest that an art dealer, with whom I have for some time been
> acquainted, is exceptional even among his coevals, I might, if I
> named him here, be thought basely to seek to curry favor with him.

In flirting with clichés, he does not always avoid being seduced by
them:

> He is particularly knowledgeable about, and on the best of terms
> with some of those commanding and seminal figures whose names
> hang, in the world of art, upon every lip.

> . . . not without a substratum of truth to which I at least sub-
> scribe.

And, from this same unfortunate pair of pages (the first two in the
book, and we never quite trust him again), a specimen of the clarifying that stupefies:

> His later life was spent in endlessly seeking to penetrate the barrier
> and establish the spatial and human dimensions of those few
> personages whom experience had taught him he could grope truly
> to perceive when face to face with one.

More than a matter of an occasional careless or windy sentence,
it is an error of tone, this trivializing fussiness of diction. In contrast, Borges (whom Mr. Ayrton several times names, as if defying
an invidious comparison), though equally recondite in his matter,
maintains a directness and simplicity of prose that carry us into
the heart of his shadows and bestow upon *his* fabrications—his
Ficciones and *Labyrinths*—the nobility of monoliths.

Nor are Mr. Ayrton's fancies uniformly pretty. It is one thing
to bring Dionysus to modern America in search of devotees ("Cool
it, man" is the greeting he receives) and another to have Kierkegaard watch the progress of Abraham and Isaac up Mount Moriah
in an episode of a television Western. The former impossibility has
a certain pith; given the existence of gods, this is how they might
behave. The latter is merely impossible; given the existence of tele-

vision, it could not have been turned on in 1843. The incongruity seems wantonly—even, with the attendant gibes at the Dane's theology, spitefully—produced. Mr. Ayrton takes too lightly his own dreadful freedom to invent what he pleases. Some of his fabrications—"The Minocorn," "Dr. A. R. Broga"—are feeble japes, if not family jokes; others—"A Gesture of the Hand," "The Vanishing Point"—are so graphic in conception that they are too difficult, even with illustrations, to "picture." The illustrations, some of them indispensable, are not very snugly married to the text, or very sharply engraved. Indeed, and alas, the book as a whole is not very well produced. Unlikely to reach a large audience, it should have been exquisitely aimed, as a fine fabrication, at the few who would relish its dry learning and delicate mirror play. But the American publisher has imported the English edition, with its strong savor of thrift. The pages have slender upper and outside margins, matched with disproportionately wide lower and inside margins; these large margins make it possible to add illustrations here and there without the expensive trouble of resetting type around them, but they look mistaken on the pages (two out of three) that carry no illustrations or footnotes. And I have never seen a book contain, for its size, so many widows. A widow (a short line, especially one ending a paragraph, that turns up at the top of a page, where it looks bereft) can usually be avoided, either by tampering with the text or by adjusting the pagination; it is elementary book-production manners to do so. Of the first thirty-one pages in *Fabrications* that could be possibly headed by widows, seven are; a deliberate widow-maker could scarcely have contrived more. What would Daedalus have said? Daedalan strictures will seem picayune to writers of a Dionysian persuasion; and of course no story or poem is purely constructed, or purely inspired, any more than the event of sailing can be all sail or all wind. This time out, Mr. Ayrton's intricate rigging creaks, in puffs of erratic breeze.

The Mastery of Miss Warner

SWANS ON AN AUTUMN RIVER, by Sylvia Townsend Warner. 200 pp. Viking, 1966.

The stories of Sylvia Townsend Warner stick up from *The New Yorker*'s fluent fiction-stream with a certain stony air of mastery. They are granular and adamant and irregular in shape. The prose has a much-worked yet abrasive texture of minute juxtaposition and compounded accuracies. Candles are lit in an antique shop, and "The polished surfaces reflected the little flames with an intensification of their various colors—amber in satinwood, audit ale in mahogany, dragon's blood in tortoise shell." Two old ladies reminisce: "They talked untiringly about their girlhood—about the winters when they went skating, the summers when they went boating, the period when they were so very pious, the period when they were pious no longer and sent a valentine to the curate: the curate blushed, a crack rang out like a pistol shot and Hector Gillespie went through the ice, the fox terriers fought under old Mrs. Bulliver's chair, the laundry ruined the blue voile, the dentist cut his throat in Century Wood, Claude Hopkins came back from Cambridge with a motorcar and drove it at thirty miles an hour with flames shooting out behind, Addie Carew was married with a wasp under her veil." Though Miss Warner can be trivial in her effects and vague in her intentions, she rarely lacks concreteness. On every page there is something to be seen or smelled or felt.

In *Repetition*, Kierkegaard, who had considerable fabling powers, interrupted his narrative to write: "If I were to pursue in detail the moods of the young man as I learned to know them, not to speak of including in a poetical manner a multitude of irrelevant matters—salons, wearing apparel, beautiful scenery, relatives and friends—this story might be drawn out to yard lengths. That, however, I have no inclination to do. I eat lettuce, it is true, but I eat only the heart; the leaves, in my opinion, are fit for swine." Contrariwise, Miss Warner's appetite for the leaves of circumstance is excellent. One story in this collection ("An Act of Reparation") is basically a recipe for oxtail stew; several others ("Happiness," "The View of Rome") are like architectural drawings of houses with people sketched in for scale. The furniture in her fiction is always vivacious and in her stories about Mr. Edom's antique-shop, not included in this collection, *objets* dominate. The grit of factuality scintillates for her, and she inhales the world's rank melancholy as if it were ambrosial perfume. Churches especially arouse her olfactory relish:

> Candles were burning, some before this image, some before that. They gave a sort of top-dressing of warmth to the building, but basically it was as cold as river mud, and under a glazing of incense it smelt of poverty.

In another church, the preserved corpse of a local saint is wonderingly detailed:

> What extraordinary gloves—so thin that the nails, long and rather dirty, showed through. . . . She looked at the face. It had blue glass eyes, to match the blue dress. One of them projected from the face, squeezed out by the shrivelling socket into which it had been fitted. It seemed to stare at her with alarm. The other eye was still in place, and placid.

The story containing this placid glass eye, "Fenella," and others such as "Healthy Landscape with Dormouse" and "Total Loss" pursue a steadily deepening drabness with a remorseless exhilaration. The septuagenarian Miss Warner's continued health as a writer of fiction is a testimonial to her iron diet. She has the spiritual digestion of a goat, and a ravenous eye for unpleasantness.

Between her firm particulars and the overbrooding Olympian forbearance of tone there is, sometimes, an unexpected vacuum. Her sense of form, of direction, is erratic, which is to say she has no prejudices about her material. Her endings are often weak— abrupt and enigmatic ("A Stranger with a Bag," "Their Quiet Lives"), sentimental ("Happiness"), crowded and vague ("Johnnie Brewer"). Here, where an author normally gathers his matter to a point in a final phrase or word, a dominant that will reverberate backward, Miss Warner wanders off in the middle of the measure, or goes on a measure too long, or comes down hard on a note so wrong we doubt our ears. As I read these bound stories I had the impression that some were better when I first read them in *The New Yorker*. A little research proved it to be so.

"The View of Rome" is a generally charming story about an old engraver recovering from a nearly fatal illness. He is very anxious to return to his home and in order to secure early release from the hospital pretends that his cat, Hattie, is a stepniece coming from the Isle of Wight to nurse him. Though rather lightweight, the story gathers substance from the many sharp small touches ("The clock, with its light hopping gait, like a robin's, ticked on"), the persuasive portrait of a gentle old bachelor (Miss Warner makes herself quite at home in male minds), and its articulation of a kind of joy, the joy of domestic possession, not often dramatized. I enjoyed rereading it until the last sentences, which went: "God is an Oriental potentate, unaffectedly lavish and sumptuous. He would not think it extravagant to heap up all these apples into a cenotaph for a Rural Dean. Here was no need for jam pots. They could stay in the attic." The apples, we know, are lying all about, and making jam of them has preoccupied the hero in the hospital, and we have been told of the Dean who died of a wasp sting incurred at a Harvest Festival. But those last two sentences, besides choppily cutting across the preceding grand strophes about God as an Oriental potentate, bring some unlooked-for words to the fore. Jam pots? Attic? The house's attic has not been previously mentioned, and abruptly occupies the position of a keystone. It is bewildering, and dulling. *The New Yorker* version, in place of these last two sentences, has: "There was no call for jam pots here." Surely this is better: "call" for "need," "here" for "attic," and the simpler phrasing permits the potentate-lavish-extravagant-cenotaph conceit to sound the conclusive chord in this wry fugue of mortality and gratitude.

Miss Warner thought well enough of "Swans on an Autumn River" to name her collection after it. It tells of Norman Repton, overweight and sixty-nine, attending a congress of sanitary engineers in Dublin. He has never been in Ireland, though when he was young it had represented romance to him. He sightsees confusedly, overeats in a restaurant, and, while feeding bread to some swans on

a river and angrily fending off hungry seagulls, dies of a heart attack. Some women waiting for a bus and a *garda* directing traffic
witness his death. The book version ends with the paragraph:

> The *garda*, who had left his place amid the traffic, now came up
> to where Norman Repton lay motionless. After a momentary hesita-
> tion, as though he were hastily summoning up something he had
> learned, he knelt beside him. The women drew closer together,
> and one of them pulled her coat about her, as though she had
> suddenly become conscious of the cold. Presently the *garda* looked
> up. "Will one of you ladies go across to the hotel," he said, "and
> ask them to telephone for the ambulance?" Two women detached
> themselves from the group and hurried across the road, arguing
> in whispers.

The New Yorker version is the same, until:

> Presently, the *garda* got up from his knees. Looking gravely down
> at the figure on the pavement, he pulled off his cap and crossed
> himself. The action unloosed a flutter of hands, a murmur of sound,
> among those waiting for the bus, as though it had stirred a
> dovecote.

Now, this at least gives us a vivid image in which Ireland, an exotic
Catholic land, and birds, whose aloof beauty and sordid hunger
have lured the hero to his death, intersect. The ending Miss Warner
has chosen to preserve in her book is totally centrifugal, a burst of
irrelevancies. Of what significance is the mechanical request for
an ambulance? Who are the two women who go to telephone, and
what if they argue "in whispers"? Whispers have nothing to do
with Norman Repton, and though neither ending is quite satisfactory, it is Miss Warner's that confirms our suspicion that this story
is aimless. It is an insistently ugly story whose ugliness has not been
shaped to any purpose. We do not know enough about Repton to
feel his terminal fight with the seagulls as anything more than the
irritable fit of a choleric man. The editorial process that brought
two endings into being is not at issue; either *The New Yorker* version is the original one, later revised, or it is a revision prompted
by the magazine and finally discarded. In either case, Miss Warner
has expressed her old-fashioned preference for events over gestures. The two women walking across the road to the telephone,
however flat and irrelevant as an image, are, as an event, more

world-engaging and, as it were, negotiable. In an artistic age of credit manipulation, Miss Warner deals in quaintly hard cash.

Her stories tend to convince us in process and baffle us in conclusion; they are not rounded with meaning but lift jaggedly toward new, unseen, developments. "Healthy Landscape with Dormouse" presents with unblinking clairvoyance a miserably married and (therefore) unrepentantly mischievous young woman, Belinda. The story's locale is Belinda's consciousness, but instead of ending there the story leaps out of her head and concludes on a village street. Some suddenly introduced bus passengers have seen Belinda and her husband fight and jump into a car: "They ran to the car, leaped in, drove away. Several quick-witted voices exclaimed, 'Take the number! Take the number!' But the car went so fast, there wasn't time." It suggests a Mack Sennett comedy; it suggests furthermore an almost compulsive need, in Miss Warner's work, for witnesses. Her world is thoroughly social, like those rings of Hades where the sinners, frozen into eternal postures, must stare at each other. "A Stranger with a Bag" and "A Long Night" make the act of onlooking centrally dramatic; and the excellent "A Jump Ahead" ends with the narrator understanding what he has seen: his ex-wife preparing to die of leukemia.

The very best story in the book, thirty pages that feel as spacious as a novel, is "A Love Match." It too is a story of witnessing: a brother and sister, Justin and Celia, live incestuously in a small English town and finally, killed by a stray bomb while in bed together, are discovered. The witnesses, the men who find their bodies, agree upon a fiction:

> Then young Foe spoke out. "He must have come in to comfort her. That's my opinion." The others concurred.

This tale, with its congenial mixture of the Gothic and the pedestrian, excites the author's prose to a fine vividness:

> The rescue workers . . . followed the trail of bricks and rubble upstairs and into a bedroom whose door slanted from its hinges. A cold air met them; looking up, they saw the sky. The floor was deep in rubble; bits of broken masonry, clots of brickwork, stood up from it like rocks on a beach. A dark bulk crouched on the hearth, and was part of the chimney stack, and a torrent of slates had fallen on the bed, crushing the two bodies that lay there.

The first act of love, the initial violation of this most sacred taboo, is beautifully described and justified as an incident within the horror and fatalism and hysteria of the First World War. Their quiet life and smoldering secret allegorize England between the wars. Twenty years of truce pass in terms of private social strategies and public social movements. Justin arranges the dusty items of a dead eccentric's military collection; Celia interests herself in the poor, in Communism. They make a few friends and sometimes attend church.

> There was a nice, stuffy pitch-pine St. Cuthbert's near by, and at judicious intervals they went there for evensong—thereby renewing another bond of childhood: the pleasure of hurrying home on a cold evening to eat baked potatoes hot from the oven.

The odors and occupations of *inter-bella* England, evoking Miss Warner's full vocabulary of flowers and foods and architectures, are suffused with the blameless decadence of the central situation. The cozy sibling idyll of Victorian mythology has gone mad. Incest has become the civilized person's ultimate recourse:

> Loving each other criminally and sincerely, they took pains to live together happily and to safeguard their happiness from injuries of their own inflicton or from outside.

Of course, no touch of implied condemnation, or of undue compassion, intrudes upon the perfect sympathy with which this scandalous marriage is chronicled. Miss Warner's genius is an uncannily equable openness to human data, and beneath her refined witchery lies a strange freshness one can only call, in praise, primitive.

A Sere Life; or, Sprigge's Ivy

THE LIFE OF IVY COMPTON-BURNETT, by Elizabeth Sprigge. 191 pp. Braziller, 1973.

In a time of outsize literary biographies, Elizabeth Sprigge has written a pleasantly compact and understated life of Ivy Compton-Burnett, called just that. Miss Sprigge writes, her foreword tells us, "as a friend," and her book enjoys the privileged insights of close acquaintanceship, and suffers just slightly from the tactful reticence that friendship imposes. How nice it would be if, of Shakespeare, we knew details such as these of Miss Compton-Burnett: that she kept her work-in-progress stacked on one end of her living-room sofa; that when she acquired a refrigerator she "played with the new possession like a little girl with a doll's house, delighted that each time she opened it a light came on"; that she loved fires, flowers, and fruit; that the walls of her flat held almost no pictures and all the floors were covered in linoleum; that when, in the Second World War, oranges became scarce and other adults let children have their share, she kept on eating hers, saying, "My need is greater than theirs. They have that nasty yellow bottled stuff at school." Miss Sprigge shows something of her subject's mastery of indirection, for, without ever dropping her affectionate tone, she manages to let us know that Ivy Compton-Burnett was a curiously hardened specimen of humanity: forbidding in manner, fascinated by money, blind to painting, deaf to music, fierce on etiquette, and, like so many of her characters, tyrannical. Miss Sprigge sketches unendearing traits as if they were endearing:

> If a conversation took a turn alien to her, Ivy would bring it to heel. For example, one day at a friend's tea-party a number of people began discussing a Russian icon hanging on the wall. Ivy listened for a few moments abstractedly, then observed decisively, "I do like a laburnum."

This author's life was not, to use her own word, "deedy." Ivy Compton-Burnett was born on June 5, 1884, the first child of the marriage of Dr. James Compton Burnett, a homeopathic physician large in size and formidable in intellect (philology was his private passion), and Katharine Rees, a young woman of distinguished family and striking beauty—her mane of bright gold was so wonderful that even now a nephew in his eighties remembers "the glory of Aunt Katie's hair." It was not the Doctor's first marriage; fifteen years older than Miss Rees, he had had five children by his first wife, a chemist's daughter, who died when the youngest was an infant. The new bride brought a hyphen to the family name ("to make the name sound grander"; the Doctor and her stepchildren

never used it) and added to the household seven children, of whom
Ivy was the first. Four sisters and two brothers followed. (A remarkable fact, which Miss Sprigge declines to emphasize, is that *not
one* of Dr. Compton Burnett's eight daughters ever married.) Ivy
—"a small child . . . with grey-blue eyes and long fair hair which,
although lacking her mother's brilliance of colour, was very pretty"
—grew up, then, amid siblings and step-siblings, servants and tutors,
in a comfortable hubbub of charades and family prayers, of incestuous cross-currents and precocious inklings, all presided over
by a "splendid, great, bearded" father and a mother haloed by her
glorious hair. The Doctor's office was at 86, Wigmore Street, and
his immense household finally settled at 20, The Drive, an ornate
red brick mansion in Hove. Throughout her long creative life Ivy's
imagination never left that crowded, prosperous household and its
late-Victorian ambience. "I do not feel," she told an interviewer,
"that I have any real or organic knowledge of life later than about
1910. I should not write of later times with enough grasp or confidence." As with Nabokov's Russia, disaster sealed shut an enchanted cave. Both her parents died rather younger than demigods
should: her father, suddenly, at the age of sixty-one, in 1901, and
her mother, after "last sad days" that became "a sore trial to her
family," in 1911, at the age of fifty-six. Ivy, in 1902, had gone to
Royal Holloway College, founded by the manufacturer of Holloway's pills and ointments in order "to give women of the middle
and upper middle classes the educational advantages afforded by
universities to young men." She read Classics and won a scholarship. Back home at Hove, while tutoring her younger sisters, she
began to write, and in 1911 she published, to enthusiastic reviews,
her first novel, *Dolores*. Later that year, upon her mother's death,
"Ivy at the age of twenty-seven became the undisputed head of the
household." Miss Sprigge's discreet phrasing can only hint at the
ominous quality of the next years: "She enjoyed this power and
became something of a tyrant, which was difficult both for Minnie
[their old nurse] and for Ivy's sisters, particularly for Topsy and
'Baby,' who were still in their teens and far from happy." So far
from happy, indeed, that in 1916 Topsy and Baby, the younger
pair of sisters, committed suicide together, in the house to which
all four sisters, led by the older pair, Vera and Judy, had fled Ivy's

tyranny a year earlier. Vera and Judy later found a cottage in Hertfordshire, and still live there. After her sisters had revolted against her rule, there was little for Ivy to do but sell the family home and, alone in the world (her brother Guy had died, in 1904, of pneumonia, and her other brother, Noël, was killed in battle in 1916), to make herself one of a pair. Her first companion, Dorothy Beresford, was something of a tyrant herself—a vivacious, argumentative woman "determined that Ivy should not 'come the bluestocking over her.' " However, Miss Sprigge tells us, "Ivy does not appear to have resented Dorothy's tyranny," and the two shared a flat in Bayswater until Dorothy married, in 1919. That same year, Ivy began living with Margaret Jourdain, a woman of letters and furniture expert, who, like Dorothy, appeared to outsiders to be the dominant of the two. Their happy relationship continued until Miss Jourdain's death, in 1951; Ivy "could not forgive Margaret for having left her," and lived, uncompanioned, until her own death, in 1969. She had resumed writing fiction at about the time Margaret Jourdain came into her life, at the end of a decade that, if not "deedy," had seen more than its share of family tragedy. In 1925, fourteen years after the publication of *Dolores*, she began, with *Pastors and Masters*, in her mature style of scarcely adorned conversation, the succession of more or less biennial novels that were to win her her little iron niche in English literature.

This efficient and seemly book reminded me of another biography recently read—Chris Albertson's life of Bessie Smith. The two women, so unlike, were both born late in the 19th century, into large families, and after obscure, unhurried apprenticeships emerged with an artistic power so confident and pure that their lives could not trouble it. Bessie Smith was cheerfully bisexual, while Ivy Compton-Burnett dryly described herself as "neuter," and the one's alcoholic binges and Pullman-car road tours are a far cry from the other's four-o'clock teas and weekends in Dorset; but in either case a social calendar quite fails to penetrate the mystery of a consummate talent. The biography of an artist is hollow because, unlike that of a general or a billionaire, an artist's life is not the sum of its incidents. As we read about Bessie Smith, we can at least put on her records, and let her bottomless, winsome voice override the

clutter of dates and liaisons and anecdotes. With a writer, there is
no such way to apprehend simultaneously the life and the oddly
disparate thing that was made of it. Though Miss Sprigge quotes
reviews (in wise moderation) and gives us her own acute though
never critical appraisal of each novel as it comes out, only in one
place do we get Ivy, as it were, hot. That is in the interview she
concocted with Margaret Jourdain in 1944, when they were living
in the country to escape the London bombing. If Margaret Jourdain's questions were actual, she talked remarkably like a character
in a novel by I. Compton-Burnett:

> I should like to ask you one or two questions; partly my own and
> partly what several friends have asked. There is time enough and
> to spare in Lyme Regis, which is a town well-known to novelists.
> Jane Austen was here, and Miss Mitford.

The answer knits itself into place:

> And now we are here, though our presence does not seem to be
> equally felt. No notice marks our lodging. And we also differ from
> Jane Austen and Miss Mitford in being birds of passage, fleeing
> from the bombs. I have a feeling that they would both have fled,
> and felt it proper to do so, and wish that we could feel it equally
> proper.

With the same absolutely firm diffidence, the novelist turns aside a
number of common objections to her work: "I think that my writing does not seem to me as 'stylised' as it apparently is, though I do
not attempt to make my characters use the words of actual life. I
cannot tell you why I write as I do, as I do not know. I have even
tried not to do it, but find myself falling back into my own way."
To the complaint that her books contain almost no description she
replies, "However detailed such description is, I am sure that everyone forms his own conceptions, that are different from everyone
else's, including the author's." Both these responses appear to emphasize the artist's modesty, but by the end of the interview an
astonishing subordination of life to art has been proposed. To the
question of how closely she derives her characters from real people,
Ivy Compton-Burnett responds that "people in life hardly seem to
be definite enough to appear in print. They are not good or bad
enough, or clever or stupid enough or comic or pitiful enough."
Further,

As regards plots I find real life no help at all. Real life seems to have no plots. And as I think a plot desirable and almost necessary, I have this extra grudge against life.

Astonishing! Almost every other novelist in this century, noticing that life has somehow ceased to coagulate into plots, has sought to bring art into adjustment, by making novels plotless or by relocating plot among the shifts and nuances of virtually formless daily existence. Only a superb tyrant like Miss Compton-Burnett could assert that life, not art, is at fault, and could then in exercise of her grudge thereat manufacture twenty plots whose pivot points of murder, retribution, proposal, inheritance, and deception are not softened by the slightest padding of plausibility or gradualness. As a demonstration of *character*—her own—her work is grand. The perfect, relentless appositeness of her dialogue is but another way of her insisting, in the tea parlor of her *oeuvre*, that manners be observed—manners derived not from the slovenly example of reality but from the precedent of other books and the capabilities of language itself.

But, as a character in *Mother and Son* states, "we must use words as they are used, or stand aside from life." That Ivy Compton-Burnett did stand aside from life, unapologetically, was a great gesture—of greater artistic value, it may be, than the novels themselves. The most deeply felt praise of her has come from Nathalie Sarraute, at the end of the essay "Conversation and Sub-Conversation"; the writer, striving with the seriousness peculiar to the French of the fifties to analyze and solve by decree the formal crisis in fiction, takes the English spinster's shameless, hyper-articulate dialogue to be a step in the direction of her own (Sarraute's) verbal staccato of "little movements" within experience, "somewhere on the fluctuating frontier that separates conversation from sub-conversation." The tribute is strong but a shade theoretical. Reading several Compton-Burnett volumes recently, I myself was reminded of two other critical remarks, on two other writers. (1) Dr. Johnson on Shakespeare: "A quibble, poor and barren as it is, gave him such delight, that he was content to purchase it by the sacrifice of reason, propriety, and truth." (2) Clifton Fadiman on Gertrude Stein: "My notion is that Miss Stein has set herself to solve, and has succeeded in solving, the most difficult problem in prose composition—to write something that will not arrest the attention in any way, manner, shape, or form." Miss Sprigge's book quotes Pamela Hansford Johnson's opinion that Ivy Compton-Burnett's novels "have an extraordinarily good effect upon the critic, because they enforce his entire attention. It is absolutely essential to read every line . . . because to miss a single one turns the whole book gibberish." Which is a nice way of saying that the books demand a fearful effort from the reader, whose attention keeps slipping. Whole pages of malicious banter about ham fat or some microscopic impropriety slide by while the eyes mechanically shuttle. I reread the entirety of one novel without realizing, as handwritten notes in the back of the book proved, that I had read it before. Such tenuity, like life's plotlessness, may be not the artist's fault; it sometimes feels, as we read Ivy Compton-Burnett, that she is trying to force our brain to operate along entirely novel circuits, like those grammar-school penmanship teachers who wanted us to write with our forearms instead of our fingers. The last of the Victorian novelists, she makes the 19th century seem another planet—adamant, mischievous, claustrophobic, cruel— from which her messages emanate with an arresting, exasperating semi-intelligibility. Her planet is so much her own we are pleasantly surprised to read, in this biography, that for a time she inhabited ours.

Milton Adapts Genesis; Collier Adapts Milton

MILTON'S PARADISE LOST, *Screenplay for Cinema of the Mind*, by John Collier. 144 pp. Knopf, 1973.

No clue is offered, on the jacket flap or in the author's rather testy "Apology," as to what possessed John Collier to turn John Milton's *Paradise Lost* into a screenplay. Was this a commercial, practical project—after all, Cecil B. De Mille mined Exodus and Judges for a pretty penny—from whose shipwreck the writer salvaged his script? Or was it always to be a curiosity purely literary —a "Screenplay for Cinema of the Mind," as the title page advertises? Sumptuously produced by Knopf in a kind of Loew's Orpheum Art Deco, it begins as space opera, *2001*-plus: "We are moving upward into a region where the blue is lighter and clearer"; a distant star becomes a comet; the comet's tail becomes a torrent, a waterfall whose mist is bubbles, and each bubble "is made of six or eight living creatures. These are gigantic and glorious beings with beautiful, stricken faces and flying hair. They wear minimal golden armour, such as we are accustomed to associate with demigods or angels." They *are* angels, dressed like Barbarella, millions of them, and then we see them charred and writhing in a lake of lava, and Satan himself, "burned to incandescence, like a log that is red all the way through, ready to fall to pieces." But he does not fall to pieces; instead, inventing magic on the spot (one of Collier's anthropological updatings of Milton's version), he pulls himself together and then invents oratory, announcing to the lake of the tormented, "All is not lost. The unconquerable will, and study of revenge, immortal hate, and courage never to submit nor yield." These three lines from Milton are the only ones Collier quotes entire; elsewhere he resists the delicious thunder of Milton's pentameters and for cinematic speed substitutes his own tinny *vers libre*. Satan's rhetorical question in Milton

> ". . . But first whom shall we send
> In search of this new world, whom shall we find
> Sufficient? who shall tempt with wand'ring feet
> The dark unbottom'd infinite Abyss
> And through the palpable obscure find out
> His uncouth way, or spread his aery flight
> Upborne with indefatigable wings
> Over the vast abrupt, ere he arrive . . ."

becomes in Collier's script

> "Who'll fly through the night, and
> chaos and the endless void?
> And find this race called Man?
> Who'll dare?
> Who'll go?"

The loss in magnificence is well-nigh total, but Milton is already on record, and Collier is attempting a new thing.

His description of the Burning Lake and charred angels evokes Dresden, Hiroshima, and napalming; the conclave of the damned in Pandemonium draws imagery from Fascist rallies, even to a clenched-fist salute. Space flight—the fact and technics of it—infuses the heavy epic with easy momentum. In Milton, Satan's passage from Hell to earth is a sloggy business, a piece of Renaissance exploration: "the fiend / O'er bog or steep, through strait, rough, dense, or rare / With head, hands, wings, or feet pursues his way, / And swims or sinks, or wades, or creeps, or flies. . . ." In Collier, he generates speed as smoothly as an equation, and travels as a "dark ripple in space." We ride "that wave of darkness, which is Satan in flight," and, as under the eyes of our astronauts, the huge, curved horizons of earth and sun float into view. Milton, after Gabriel confronts Satan in Paradise, has Satan hide by circling the earth on the side of darkness; though the possibility fits with Newtonian astronomy, it seems farfetched and uncomfortable in the verse, mixed with antique imagery:

> . . . thrice the Equinoctial Line
> He circl'd, four times cross'd the Car of Night
> From Pole to Pole, traversing each Colure. . . .

For Collier, such an orbiting is a familiar stunt; Satan hangs in darkness "like a surfer awaiting the wave" and exultantly teases both sunset and sunrise in the course of his confident free fall. "Free Fall," for that matter, would be a pretty good title for this movie, were it ever made.

When Satan arrives in Paradise, we arrive at hackneyed territory. Mr. Collier refreshes the fable with a lot of delightfully precise botany, some clever lighting, and an attentiveness to Eve's dreams worthy of a psychoanalyst. But his retelling founders where most modern retellings do: he does not believe in God, and God is the most interesting character in the story. God has a plan and a hope; He experiences love and regret. Satan is just a successful saboteur by comparison, and Adam and Eve are a pair of gullible yokels. The God of Genesis brims with surprises; his question of Adam, "Who told you that you were naked?" has all the cunning of do-your-own-guilt paternalism since the world began. How affably, without a blink, the blame having passed from Adam to Eve to the serpent, does He curse the serpent first, and how obligingly, having delivered the curses to all three, does He squat down like a tailor and make for His two errant children, grown out of nudity, "garments of skins." Adam and Eve are banished from Paradise not spitefully, as punishment for what cannot be undone, but as a simple Self-protective measure, to prevent the created pair, who have already eaten from the tree of the knowledge of good and evil and become "like one of us," from eating now also from the tree of life and living forever; the cherubim and the flaming sword guard not the gates of Paradise but the path to the tree of life—not the way back but the way out. This pleasant plantation owner, safeguarding His prerogatives against a slave uprising, is a remote rustic ancestor of Milton's God, a defensive monarch always ready to argue the legalities of His own decisions. To "justify the ways of God to men" was Milton's announced purpose, and the thorny conundrums of Justice and Mercy, Free Will and Divine Foresight, Liberty and Order, frame the Biblical events in a continual dialetic of serious political argument. Foreseeing Man's Fall, God sends Raphael to Adam to

> ". . . advise him of his happy state,
> Happiness in his power left free to will,
> Left to his own free Will, his Will though free,
> Yet mutable; whence warn him to beware
> He swerve not too secure: tell him withal
> His danger. . . ."

Milton then assures us, "So spake th' Eternal Father, and fulfill'd / All Justice." And Adam, when Eve complains that his failure to command "absolutely" permitted her to sin, answers in echo of God:

> "I warn'd thee, I admonish'd thee, foretold
> The danger, and the lurking Enemy
> That lay in wait; beyond this had been force,
> And force upon free Will hath here no place."

Mr. Collier is a modern atheist, and will have none of this. The long middle of Milton's poem—Raphael's exposition to Adam of the Christocentric universe—he almost entirely omits. The theological reasoning that Satan was permitted to perpetrate evil "but to bring forth / Infinite goodness, grace, and mercy" elicits from Collier the scornful paraphrase "In other words, the prisoner was paroled in order that he might commit fresh crimes and incur a yet heavier sentence. Man, at the cost of death to all and damnation to many, was to serve as bait in this outrageous trap." Mr. Collier then goes on to praise Satan as morally superior to God (". . . he is the rebel against the Establishment, the defeated, the exile, the endungeoned, the resurgent, and the guerrilla. . . . We watch in vain for some example of his wickedness. . . . He inflicts no tortures"). Mr. Collier is of course entitled to his humanist pieties and left-wing wrath, but he has no artistic right to pump the Voice of God into the end of his scenario. The Voice has been labelled hollow. The plot that turns on the strictures of such a moral nonentity as Mr. Collier's God falls to nonsense. You can have a sentimental Satan, and an adorable Jungian Adam and Eve, and an apple that is all vitamins and eroticism, but you cannot have these and Jahweh too. By the time this script reaches its last shot (Satan smiling out of the screen at us, just like Walter Huston in that old Hollywood make of "The Devil and Daniel Webster"), the corniness betrays an inner chaos. The God of Genesis walking in His garden in the cool of the day had a blunt corporeal reality. The God of Milton derives actuality from the believer's tortured strenuousness. Collier's God is just a black hole in a funny old story that must ("*Must!* That's the word now," Adam says) have something profound about it.

What did attract this excellent British fantasist to *Paradise Lost*? Possibly its superficial shimmer of the fantastic, of the hallucinatory. The conceit of making it into cinema recalls an image Santayana uses, of Dante, in *Three Philosophical Poets*: after pages of praise for the medieval poet, Santayana adds the devastating demur ". . . he has no true idea either of the path to happiness or of its real conditions. His notion of nature is an inverted image of the moral world, cast like a gigantic shadow upon the sky. It is a mirage." Some such mirage-sense of Milton's poem may be at the root of the curious metamorphosis Collier has wrought. Of the assembly in Pandemonium his scenario says, "Perhaps this vast, dark sphere is Satan's brain, and the luminous seraphs are the brain cells, glowing or flashing or dimming according to the electrical impulses that pass through them." A frequent (and, I would think, technically implausible) feature of his script is the specification of elaborate trompe-l'oeil effects:

> . . . a reddish flush emanating from the maddened seraphs hangs like a luminous cloud in the centre of the vast, dark sphere. Soon it coalesces into a tangle of fuzzy, incandescent lines which form a fiery tracery, semi-abstract, showing an imagined assault on the battlements of Heaven.

Satan ruffles a tree of dark leaves with light undersides so that from a hundred yards it exactly resembles Eve; Mulciber's body goes transparent and becomes his palace; a vast horde of devils so disperses itself as to shadow forth the forms of Adam and Eve, like a marching band at halftime. What does Collier intend by such illusions except to transfer the entire cosmic epic to the realm of dream and subjective psychology? A movie screen has no substance; it exists only for our eyes, which in turn—physiologists tell us—are specialized segments of the brain, the only ones that have surfaced and protrude through our skins.

But would these grandiose tricks—mist into angels, angels into "semi-abstract" tracery—work? Much is possible to the movie camera; but it remains a camera, a mirror of the external world's texture and accidents. Though there is immense visual ambition in Mr. Collier's directives to his hypothetical technicians, there is little that is effortlessly concrete. Phantasmagoria eclipses the luminously mundane. The human protagonists, for instance, are presumably naked until the fig leaves descend, but the script never brings Eve's body to our awareness like these lines of Milton:

> . . . but Eve
> Undeckt, save with herself more lovely fair
> Than Wood-Nymph, or the fairest Goddess feign'd
> Of three that in Mount Ida naked strove,
> Stood to entertain her guest from Heav'n . . .

Collier's "Apology" announces that his hero is Eve, yet she seems more the subject of speculation than an object of vivifying love. This kind of love Milton shows her when he has Adam say:

> "Neither her out-side form'd so fair, nor aught
> In procreation common to all kinds . . .
> So much delights me, as those graceful acts,

> Those thousand decencies that daily flow
> From all her words and actions. . . ."

Collier's Adam says:

> ". . . she grew so lovely that
> all she does and says seems
> wisest and most virtuous and best."

Which is indeed bleak praise, if not blank verse. Milton has not been generally prized for the virtues of psychological tenderness or lively sensuality; Mr. Collier's script leads us to realize how much of those virtues Milton possessed. And it leads us to suspect that in a fictional universe there is no borrowed gravity; unless an author is writing for his life, images become mere "effects" and fly into space. Precision is a function of attention, and attention is a function of concern. Too diffidently Mr. Collier tells us, of the poem's Christian content, "I do not share these beliefs, and I have substituted other ideas, also not profound in themselves, but which are more in accord with those commonly held today." There are ideas here, but no possessing *idea*. Milton's God may be a tedious old bluffer, but he fascinated Milton, and aligned the poet's inspirations in one magnetic field. A phrase like "those thousand decencies that daily flow" holds a piece of felt reality up to a moral light, and transfigures all women, all wives. Mr. Collier's Eve, on the other hand, is conceived unsteadily: eating the apple on her knees like a drugged porn queen, voting for life like some vociferous Shavian heroine, snivelling like a groupie when the angelic fuzz arrives, jerked through a series of attitudes by the dead strings of Genesis 3. The screenplay ends—for this viewer, at least—as a flicker of unweighted significances and symbols. The projector throws not a beam of light but a tatter of brilliancies.

Auden Fecit

ABOUT THE HOUSE, by W. H. Auden. 84 pp. Random House, 1965.

> There are two atlases: the one
> The public space where acts are done,
> In theory common to us all,

> Where we are needed and feel small . . .
> The other is the inner space
> Of private ownership, the place
> That each of us is forced to own,
> Like his own life from which it's grown,
> The landscape of his will and need
> Where he is sovereign indeed . . .

Thus, in his great *New Year Letter* of 1940, Auden distinguished between the two realms explored by his life-long search for "the City." As a young man, his concern was more with "public space," and he remains *the* poet of the foreboding that preceded World War II, the lucid exhausted voice of "September 1, 1939" and the elegies to Freud and Yeats, both dead in 1939. As an aging post-war man, he has turned more toward the "inner space," the landscape of his will and need and (from the same poem) "the *polis* of our friends." His latest collection, *About the House*, celebrates this intimate city, the microcosm of his privacy, in almost doting detail. But the best of the poems are redeemed from triviality by the seriousness with which Auden considers his own comfort an episode in civilization.

The first, and superior, half of the book is a sequence of twelve poems inspired by the rooms of his recently acquired house in Austria. Each poem carries a personal dedication, and though the anonymous reader may be charmed by intimations of custom-tailored pertinence (a husband and wife get the cellar and attic respectively, and Christopher Isherwood is awarded the toilet), he is more likely to feel merely excluded; what with the Kennedys, the Glasses, the Sinatra Clan, the friends of Norman Podhoretz, and the Pop-Camp-Hip crowd, there seem enough in-groups in the Western world without a formal roll-call of Auden's acquaintanceship. Plato's vision of the Perfect City ruled by philosopher-kings seems somewhat impudently transmuted into genial snobbery:

> The houses of our City
> are real enough but they lie
> haphazardly scattered over the earth,
> and her vagabond forum
> is any space where two of us happen to meet
> who can spot a citizen
> without papers.

Technically, the sequence is marred by the erratic interruption of "Postscripts"—short poems in another meter, often in the irksome form of haiku, tacked on wherever (however vaguely) appropriate. And it must be said that Auden, in developing each room into a cosmic instance and drawing significance from every nook, does not always avoid his besetting sin of, well, silliness. The steamy bath is extolled in an uncharacteristic non-meter which he explains as a "mallarmesque / syllabic fog," and the stanzas to excrement include:

> Freud did not invent the
> Constipated miser:
> Banks have letter boxes
> Built in their facade,
> Marked *For Night Deposits*,
> Stocks are firm or liquid,
> Currencies of nations
> Either soft or hard.

But in sum the twelve poems comprise an impressive essay upon Man the domestic animal; his domesticity is felt as a consecration of his animality.

> city planners are mistaken: a pen
> for a rational animal
> is no fitting habitat for Adam's
> sovereign clone.

Precise biological terms—clone, conurbation, neotene—insist on humanity's living context. The poem on the dining-room with high wit summarizes the full organic history of dining:

> The life of plants
> is one continuous solitary meal,
> and ruminants
> hardly interrupt theirs to sleep or to mate, but most
> predators feel
> ravenous most of the time and competitive
> always, bolting such morsels as they can contrive
> to snatch from the more terrified . . .
> Only man,
> supererogatory beast,
> Dame Kind's thoroughbred lunatic, can

> do the honors of a feast,
> and was doing so
> before the last Glaciation when he offered
> mammoth-marrow
> and, perhaps, Long Pig, will continue till Doomsday
> when at God's board
> the saints chew pickled Leviathan.

The house abounds in remembrances of human prehistory: the cellar "Reminds our warm and windowed quarters upstairs that / Caves water-scooped from limestone were our first dwellings"; the archetype of the poet's workroom is "Weland's Stithy"; like the "prehistoric hearthstone, / round as a birthday-button / and sacred to Granny," the modern kitchen is the center of the dwelling; in conclusion, "every home should be a fortress, / equipped with all the very latest engines / for keeping Nature at bay, / versed in all ancient magic, the arts of quelling / the Dark Lord and his hungry / animivorous chimeras." Nor is history forgotten: the bathroom is seen as a shrunken tepidarium; the dining table is compared with "Christ's cenacle" and "King Arthur's rundle"; and the peace of the living-room is felt against "History's criminal noise." The function of each chamber is searched in such depth that a psychological portrait of man is achieved. Auden finds in defecation the prime Art, an "ur-act of making"; in swallowing "a sign act of reverence"; in sleeping a "switch from personage, / with a state number, a first and family name, / to the naked Adam or Eve." His anatomization is controlled, at times playfully, by religious conceptions:

> then surely those in whose creed
> God is edible may call a fine
> omelette a Christian deed.

Biology tends toward theology; our personal and animal particulars are grounded in the divine ontology. Speech is "a work of re-presenting / the true olamic silence." This sequence of poems, entitled "Thanksgiving for a Habitat," is an essay in architecture, which is to say the creation of a structure enabling the human organism to perform its supernaturally determined functions of praise and service. In a faithless age, there are

> no architects, any more
> than there are heretics or bounders: to take
> umbrage at death, to construct
> a second nature of tomb and temple, lives
> must know the meaning of *If*.

While one regrets that Auden's Christian faith is so iffy, its presence has enabled him to organize his youthfully indiscriminate variety of perceptions and data into a credible humanism.

The second half of *About the House*, "In and Out" (a habitat has been previously defined as "a place / I may go both in and out of"), consists of poems, often about travelling, that are casual in tone and middling in quality. The best is the last, "Whitsunday in Kirchstetten," a kind of annex to the house poems, wherein the poet is discovered temporarily domiciled in church. In the author's favorite late style, the long lines, pedantic terms, and discursive sequiturs evoke what was rather conspicuously absent from the house sequence—a sense of the "public space," the enveloping condition of the world:

> from Loipersbach
> to the Bering Sea not a living stockbroker,
> and church attendance is frowned upon
> like visiting brothels (but the chess and physics
> are still the same). . . .
> Down a Gothic nave
> comes our Pfarrer now, blessing the West with water:
> we may go.

Again, "Hammerfest," a description of Auden's visit to Norway's northernmost township, frames within his baroque sense of lapsed time—"the glum Reptilian Empire / Or the epic journey of the Horse"—the geological innocence of a region whose "only communities . . . / Were cenobite, mosses and lichen, sworn to / Station and reticence." And of the many (too many) poems in haiku-stanzas, I liked best "Et in Arcadia Ego," a rephrasing of his habitual accusatory apostrophe to "Dame Kind"—who "Can imagine the screeching / Virago, the Amazon, / Earth Mother was?"

The poem uses the exigencies of this Japanese form to generate lines of great energy, both polysyllabic ("Her exorbitant monsters abashed") and monosyllabic ("Geese podge home").

Auden is the supreme metrical tinkerer. Haiku, canzoni, ballades, limericks, clerihews, alliterative verse (a whole eclogue's worth) —there is nothing he will not attempt and make, to some extent, pay off. His ability, as in "Tonight at Seven-Thirty," to coin an elaborate stanza-form and effortlessly to repeat it over and over, suggests the 17th-century metaphysicals and Tennyson: the latter more than the former. His technical displays cast doubt upon the urgency of his inspiration. It is one thing to sing in a form, whether it be Homeric hexameters or Popian couplets, until it becomes a natural voice; it is another to challenge your own verbal resources with insatiable experimentation. In any collection by Auden there are hardly two successive poems in the same form, which gives even his most integral sequences, such as the "Horae Canonicae" of *The Shield of Achilles*, a restless and wearing virtuosity. As a poet, his vocation begins in the joy of fabrication rather than in an impulse of celebration: in ways it is strength, enabling him to outlive his youth, to explore, to grow, to continue to think, even—blasphemous suggestion!—to believe, in order to feed the verse-making machine. He is that anachronism, the poet as maker; but he makes expressions rather than, by mimesis, men and deeds. Compared to Eliot, he has no dramatic imagination. Despite an almost desperate metrical juggling, his plays and dialogues are the monologues of one very intellectually imaginative voice. He dramatizes all sides of an issue, but lacks the modesty, the impish and casual self-forgetfulness, that tossed off Prufrock, Cousin Harriet, Sweeney, and the curiously vigorous phantoms of *The Waste Land*. If Eliot was a dramatist, Auden is an essayist, in the root sense: he will try anything, but his adventures never take him beyond the territory of the first-person singular. He is one of the few modern poets whose genius is for the long discursive poem; for all his formal invention, he has written best in two rather accommodating meters—a long, elegiac, unrhymed or loosely rhymed line less regular than pentameter, and the tetrameter quatrains or couplets associated with music hall lyrics and with light verse.

His light vein is very rich. What could be better than, say, this stanza from "On the Circuit"?—

> Since Merit but a dunghill is,
> I mount the rostrum unafraid:
> Indeed, 'twere damnable to ask
> If I am overpaid.

Or this, from "After Reading a Child's Guide to Modern Physics"?—

> Marriage is rarely bliss
> But, surely it would be worse
> As particles to pelt
> At thousands of miles per sec
> About a universe
> In which a lover's kiss
> Would either not be felt
> Or break the loved one's neck.

In his present pleasant house, to which his dream of the City has congenially dwindled, Auden portrays his workroom, "The Cave of Making," with "windows averted from plausible / videnda but admitting a light one / could mend a watch by." By such dry clear light, a dictionary at hand, he is best read—not, as he hopes, as "a minor atlantic Goethe" (the difference in generosity may be less between Goethe and himself than between Goethe's Europe and our America), but as a man who, with a childlike curiosity and a feminine fineness of perception, treats poetry as the exercise of wit. For almost always, in his verse, the oracular and ecstatic flights fail; what we keep are the fractional phrases that could be expressed in prose, but less pointedly. He defined light verse, for his anthology of it, as poetry written in the common language of men. Powerfully attracted by the aristocratic and the arcane, he has worked to preserve his democratic loyalties, his sense of poetry as a mode of discourse between civilized men. *About the House*, though it contains no single poem as fine as "Ode to Gaea" from *The Shield of Achilles*, has nothing in it as tedious as the infatuated concept-chopping of the "Dichtung und Wahrheit" interlude of *Homage to Clio;* and on the whole marks a new frankness and a new relaxation in tone. Auden remains, in the Spirit as well as by the Letter, alive.

A Messed-Up Life

GREAT TOM, *Notes Towards the Definition of T. S. Eliot*, by T. S. Matthews. 219 pp. Harper & Row, 1974.

T. S. Matthews, in *Great Tom*, gives an impressively suave and sprightly demonstration of how to write a book when the book isn't there. You begin by including in your Acknowledgments a gracious mention of "those who did not answer my letters, or who denied me access to various unpublished papers, or who refused to see me." You go on to discuss, with unabashed candor, the New York publisher who approached you to write upon a subject in which you have neither scholarly interest nor personal involvement: Mr. Matthews met Eliot on a few "widely spaced occasions," and, like Eliot, emigrated from America to England, but the publisher seemed bewitched chiefly by the congruence of their first two initials, and his excitement was further whetted by a letter from Eliot's widow and executrix flatly declining to assist in any way; "for reasons which I still fail to understand," Matthews confides, "the publisher found this letter encouraging. I did not; but by this time the idea of writing Eliot's biography had begun to appeal to me strongly. I signed a contract for the book. Was this a mistake? Some people have said so; and if they read this book perhaps they may see no reason to change their minds."

By now, the reader has been roused to a great pitch of suspense as to how the bulk of pages still unread in his hand will be filled. The suspense becomes well-nigh unbearable under a hail of goose-flesh-raising questions:

> Who *was* T. S. Eliot? Why did he want to keep his private life a secret? . . . Is there less, or more, in his poetry than meets the eye? To what extent does his poetry depend on plagiarism and parody? Did he have a "tin ear"? Was he a phony scholar? A phony saint? . . . Was he a homosexual? Did Bertrand Russell seduce Vivienne Eliot?

The Lord only knows; with the same long breath Mr. Matthews admits that, "in the pages that follow," these "awkward questions"

have to be asked, "whether or not they can be satisfactorily answered." This is indeed, as he names the genre, "a biography, of
sorts."

Well, forewarned is disarmed, and only the most impatient seeker
of truth could fail to be beguiled by the succeeding parade of
types of padding. There is the irrelevant catalogue:

> The home remedies, the lotions and standard antiseptics, tonics, and
> germicides of the day were familiar to the Eliot household and
> particularly to little Tom: peroxide, antiphlogistene, *baume anal-*
> *gésique,* Listerine, camphor ice, malt extract, Castoria.

The vacuous speculation:

> Of his interior life we have no record, but we know it existed and
> suspect that it was his home address. Also he was an adolescent,
> and we know, or can partly remember, what that was like.

The impudent assertion:

> Did he masturbate? Of course. And was he ashamed of it? Un-
> speakably.

The water-treading rumination:

> Who can tell what is going on in a small boy's head? The only
> witness, the child himself, is less witness than observer, most of the
> time enthralled, some of the time in flight (either from fear or
> from what he will later call boredom), and never capable of re-
> porting his observations in any form that his elders can understand.

The mystery of Eliot's early sexual attitudes and experience evokes
from Matthews the tone of a hectoring bully:

> But why, surrounded by women as he was, should his feelings about
> them have been so faint-hearted? Because his mother and his
> sisters were ladylike women, terrified of sex and disgusted by it,
> and ashamed of their female bodies. By precept and example, they
> encouraged his own shame.

Out of wholly thin air he constructs an imaginary "facts of life"
interview between Henry Eliot and his thirteen-year-old son:

> Too soon might shock the tender young mind; too late would
> find its petals browned and withering in corruption. (They really
> thought in such terms.) Henry Eliot was a man who knew his
> duty and did it. . . . The boy would have listened with half an
> ear to his father's cautious roundabouts, the customary euphemisms,

about birds and bees. . . . His father's voice overwhelmed him with the weight of Sinai, and he crept from the presence knowing in his heart that all was lost.

The primly liberated biographer unconscionably equates the Eliots' Unitarianism with Calvinism (against which it was a liberal revolt), treats St. Louis as a suburb of a cliché-Puritan Boston, and takes poetic evidence of Eliot's sensuality ("so rank a feline smell") to mean unqualified repugnance. He assures us on no given evidence that the young Eliot was chaste both at Harvard and in Paris, and, more fascinatingly but with little more substantiation, portrays his first marriage as one long sexual rejection by the clever and neurotic Vivienne. Matthews' discussion of this marriage includes the enchanting disclaimer "Here again some significant facts are available, even if we cannot always be quite certain of their significance."

As Eliot's private life moves into the relative light of printed poems and opinion, of worldwide fame and London gossip, Matthews has more material to work with. Yet he handles the *oeuvre* rather brusquely, even dismissively. Of two youthful poems of 1910: "Neither showed the slightest sign of originality or was worth preserving." Of "Mr. Eliot's Sunday Morning Service": "If this isn't showing off with a smirk and a vengeance, what on earth is it?" Of the criticism: "Eliot as critic is also Eliot at his least satisfactory and least likeable—a know-it-all who puts us in our place and keeps us there." Of *The Waste Land*: ". . . the scheme, such as it is, is mostly afterthought." Of the poet's ear: "Examples of Eliot's failure of musical ear abound in his later poems." Matthews elsewhere says generous and shrewd things of Eliot's works, but he rarely seems to examine them with any focussed concern for the life of the mind behind them. Eliot's Christianity, for instance, stimulates a long, fulminating, personal, and rather obtuse essay in which Matthews, himself an Anglo-Catholic, worries the cheap paradox that Christians have made war and inflicted cruelties upon one another. The intellectual atmosphere *de l'entre-deux-guerres*, in which Eliot's profession of faith was a shocking and, to some, an exemplary proclamation, is scanted. Throughout, the tone of the title—crass, jaunty, faintly bellicose—is sustained; one can feel Eliot's fastidious ghost wincing.

Yet the book, in part because of its breezy thinness, is easy to read. Mr. Matthews occasionally strikes off a fine phrase: "Eliot's benign, almost wordless presence seemed to have an encouraging effect on [John Hayward], like the silent flame under a singing tea kettle." He quotes some illuminating remarks: Stravinsky's saying of Eliot, "He is not the most exuberant man I have ever known, but he is one of the purest." And Eliot himself saying, "No honest poet can ever feel quite sure of the permanent value of what he has written: he may have wasted his time and messed up his life for nothing." What a beautiful sadness in this implication that a poet, an artist, "messes up" his life in the hope of producing something immortal. And how startling to know that Eliot composed his poetry standing at a typewriter! "It is a mystery to me how anyone can write poetry except on a typewriter." And how awful to imagine him, in his little office at Lloyds Bank—"a figure stooping," I. A. Richards remembered, "very like a dark bird in a feeder, over a big table covered with all sorts and sizes of foreign correspondence"—working directly under the pavement, with heels hammering on the thick green glass squares above his head all day long. And how touching, after the recent revelation that Eliot diffidently accepted almost all of Ezra Pound's cuts of *The Waste Land*, to read that Pound, shown the manuscript half a century later, was equally diffident about his strokes of editing genius: "He should have ignored me. Why didn't he restore some of the cancelled passages when Liveright wanted more pages?"

And, though an official biography might bring forth an abundance of the correspondence and specificity rather strikingly sparse in these "Notes," Mr. Matthews' silhouette of the life seems unlikely to change: a life disfigured by an unhappy marriage in the middle and distinguished from beginning to end by a proud industry. As a student at Harvard, Eliot compressed four years' work into three; as a graduate student, he added Sanskrit and Italian to his knowledge of French, German, Latin, and Greek; when he worked a full day in Lloyds, he would rise at five to labor at criticism; in the years he was remapping the English literary tradition, he was nursing an ill wife; he lectured; he edited *Criterion* for seventeen years; at both his banking and, later, publishing jobs he not only put in time but won promotions and praise from his

colleagues; after his conversion, he served on many church com-
mittees and even edited an ecclesiastical publication; at an age when
many men retire, he undertook to make himself into a commer-
cially successful playwright. Through all this, the meagre, reluctant, pained trickle of poetry, aiming (in his words) at "the
maximum emotional effect with the minimum verbal decoration."

No doubt the time will never return when, as in the early fifties,
to those of us in college, Eliot's reputation was an encompassing
gray cloud, the very atmosphere of literature. It was a remarkable
looming, a matter of style as well as of content, to a generation that
loved the aloof, the cryptic, the ominous, the wry, the weary. Mr.
Matthews, who offers a variety of verdicts on the worth to posterity of his elusive subject, suggests that when the "emotional
radioactivity" has died away all that will be left of Eliot is "a case
of the dry grins." It is true that Eliot's poetry is, as was his
personality, somehow transuranic, bonded together by a perilous
pressure. The contemporary estimates of its worth ranged as wildly
as a Geiger counter gone crazy—from R. P. Blackmur's reverence
to Van Wyck Brooks's abhorrence—and an archaeologist of literature, exhuming its decayed carbon traces in the far future, may
have trouble identifying it as poetry at all. It is like no other. Its
droning tone underlines a confessed poverty of inspiration and
vitality, yet a steady force of seriousness, of caustic austerity,
engraves it on our minds. The revelation of *The Waste Land* revisions shocked us, of course, because this of all modern poems had
come to seem inevitable; it feels familiar when we read it for the
first time, and by the third time it feels memorized. And when
we reread it after wading through *Great Tom*, we are exhilarated
by its altitude; we are "In the mountains, there you feel free."
Though Eliot's critical phrases ("objective correlative," "dissocia-
tion of sensibility") may no longer serve as signposts for the student, and the plays fade, as most plays do, what lines of poetry
between Yeats's late poems and the verse that Roethke and Sylvia
Plath wrote from within the shadow of death burn deeper, better
remember themselves, than Eliot's? His will asked that no biography of himself be written; we would not be much poorer if his
request had been honored.

FRENCH DEATHS

Death's Heads

THE FIRE WITHIN, by Pierre Drieu La Rochelle, translated from the French by Richard Howard. 183 pp. Knopf, 1965.

SELECTED WORKS OF ALFRED JARRY, edited by Roger Shattuck and Simon Watson Taylor, translated by many hands. 280 pp. Grove Press, 1965.

Pierre Drieu La Rochelle (1893–1945) and Alfred Jarry (1873–1907) were French men of letters whose reputations, inseparable during their lifetimes from personal notoriety, were eclipsed after their suicides (Drieu shot himself, Jarry no less deliberately drank himself to death) but have been revived in contemporary France. Drieu, a Vichy collaborator whose passionate political inconsistency antagonized all parties, has been rehabilitated from disgrace by, an article in *Le Monde* stated in 1964, "a new generation which has chosen *désengagement*, but which is attracted by his outspokenness, his elegant cynicism, his aristocratic aestheticism, and his desperate lucidity." Jarry, an undersized super-bohemian whose play *Ubu Roi* marks the birth of the avant-garde theatre, has been honored not only by continuing editions of his writings but by the founding, in 1949, of the Collège de 'Pataphysique, an eccentric and elusive pseudo-science he invented. In the United States, a book by each author has been recently published.

Drieu's *The Fire Within* is a brief, flickering novel issued in France in 1931 as *Le Feu Follet*—"playful fire," an idiom for "*ignis fatuus*," or "will-o'-the-wisp." The will-o'-the-wisp presumably is the hero himself, Alain, whose weak hold upon life finally yields to the pull of suicide. As Alain moves through his last few days vainly seeking an excuse to live, the author subjects him to a bewildering alternation of acute sympathy and stern lecturing. The sympathy probes emotional nihilism to its last dead end and self-defeating checkmate; the lecturing seems delivered from a standpoint nearly Christian:

> Alain had never looked at the sky or the housefronts or the pavements—palpitating things; he had never looked at a river or a forest; he lived in the empty rooms of this morality: "The world is imperfect, the world is bad. I disapprove, I condemn, I annihilate the world."

Yet although he scolds him as a "fetishist" and a "naïve dandy," Drieu cannot in honesty construct a fictional world that at any point substantially resists Alain's premonitions of futility. So Alain's suicide, instead of afflicting us with the dizzying impression of waste we feel in, say, *Anna Karenina* or *Appointment in Samarra*, arrives serenely, as something appropriate and slightly overdue. It is a kind of happy ending: "A revolver is solid, it's made of steel. It's an object. To touch an object at last."

Alain is much concerned with objects, and part of Drieu's appeal to the modern young must be his flat objectivity, a dispassion that reduces people to a species of object opaque in their psychology and mute even in speech. In Drieu, the tendency has not achieved the doctrinal purity of Robbe-Grillet; his flat narrative texture is bubbled by incongruous outbursts of sermonizing. But his sense of actuality rejects mankind's ancient claims of special importance, the conviction of spiritual destiny that inflames and inflates the living newspapers of Balzac and Dickens. *The Fire Within* ends a moment before death and begins a moment after coitus. The lover and beloved are discovered looking at each other with eyes dreadfully clear of illusions: "All she saw was a hairy chest, no head. It didn't matter: she had felt nothing very violent either, yet the switch had been tripped, and that was the only sensation she had ever known, not permeating but precise." *The switch had been tripped*. Drieu's mordant and entertaining characterizations—and there are many characters; the novel in form is picaresque—work to mechanize humanity, to chisel a series of hard-featured marionettes:

Mademoiselle Farnoux smiled at Alain with meagre lust. . . . She was a little girl between forty and sixty, bald, with a black wig on her bloodless skull.

The doctor was a nervous jailer. His huge round eyes swivelled above cheeks scored by the terror of losing his boarders, and the little beard that substituted for a chin trembled incessantly.

Brancion smiled. He wore his dentures with ostentation; women were not put off by them.

Even the beautiful women are rigid dolls:

[Eva] got up and slid her dress over her head. Then she pulled off her slip, her garter belt, her stockings. She was completely naked, a magnificent, bloodless plaster body.

Maria was Russian. A Russian peasant with a face and a body carved out of wood.

It is natural that Alain, who has some of the instincts of an artist, mocks this de-animated society with ironic collages and random assemblages of objects:

On the mantel, two objects: one a delicate piece of machinery, a perfectly flat platinum chronometer, the other a hideously vulgar painted plaster statuette of a naked woman that he had bought at a fair and took with him everywhere.

In his mirror he has arranged two photographs, a foreshortened man and woman, and between them "a news item pasted on the glass with four stamps reduced the human mind to two dimensions and left it no way out." The third dimension must be the supernatural.

Though *The Fire Within* takes place in Paris, its spiritual locale is the empire of disenchantment whose twin capitals are Paris and New York. The two chief women in Alain's life, his absent wife and his present mistress, are Americans, and his vices and weaknesses seem peculiarly American—drug addiction, sexual inadequacy, fear of losing his youth, a greedy awe of money, an enfeebling dependence upon women. He is described as a Puritan: "a man who saw the vices sprouting from his prejudices, but who was incapable, because of his prejudices, of enjoying his vices." He even has a psychiatrist, who sagely tells him, "A strong, healthy woman like these Americans will make you forget all this." But Americans, as represented in this book, are clearly also "a race exhausted by civilization." The only convinced spokesman for life is a scholar immersed in the study of the gods of ancient Egypt; "he would have liked to recite some of those Egyptian prayers distended with the fullness of being, in which the spiritual life, exploding, pours out all the sap of the earth." Perhaps the reason that the waning of the Christian faith is so peculiarly desolating in France and America is that in these nations the pagan gods, whether Hellenic or Teutonic, were never taken very seriously. The Christian bet was hardly hedged. Pascal and Cotton Mather alike theologize on the basis of a vast gamble, and their heirs feel cheated. "There was, after all, something of the Christian in Alain"—this something, which needs to act righteously and refuses to embrace the mediocre muddle of living, produces, with a purity coolly mathematical, his self-destruction.

The New World to the Old is a hemisphere as disappointingly empty as the heavens. Alain, seeking to save himself, flees to New York and only deepens his plight. Of course, there are differences: Paris is a "lingering, low fever," whereas "New York, at least, was an open atrocity." But the two cities, as spiritual ciphers, are interchangeable. The faddish artistic scene of post-Surrealist Paris strikingly resembles the Camp of contemporary Manhattan:

> Among other delusory projects, Alain had thought of opening a shop in Paris or New York to sell all those dated, ugly, or absurd objects which industry, hovering between the popular and the vulgar, has produced in the last fifty years.

And the lean and sketchy style of the novel itself belongs to the Franco-American world of Hammett/Simenon detective novels and Bogart/Gabin movies and their Existentially fortified *nouvelle-vague* descendants; these things are thin with the thinness that implies a background of immense loss. Drieu La Rochelle is not as cool as his material—hence his erratic imprecations, his disturbing efforts to steer his tale toward an unsighted morality. But this roughness of tone touches the narrative from a source outside itself and recalls a context beyond the mechanical and mocked world Alain haunts, a context in which his extinction can be felt, momentarily, as a waste:

For him, the world was a handful of human beings. He had never thought there could be anything more to it. He had never felt involved with anything larger than himself. He knew nothing of plants, of the stars: he knew only a few faces, and he was dying, far from those faces.

A character in *The Fire Within* is described as "admiring spontaneously only the eccentrics of the past, from Byron to Jarry." In Alfred Jarry we encounter, at the beginning of the century, a personality and an art more radical than the regretful nihilism of Drieu. The art was a copious but incidental emanation of the personality, and Roger Shattuck's chapters on Jarry himself, in *The Banquet Years*, are more readable than the *Selected Works of Alfred Jarry*, which Mr. Shattuck and Simon Watson Taylor have edited. Descriptions of Jarry's bizarre person abound. André Gide remembered him as he was around 1895:

> This plaster-faced Kobold, gotten up like a circus clown and acting a fantastic, strenuously contrived role which showed no human characteristic, exercised a remarkable fascination at the *Mercure*. Almost everyone there attempted, some more successfully than others, to imitate him, to adopt his humor; and above all his bizarre implacable accent—no inflection or nuance and equal stress on every syllable, even the silent ones. A nutcracker, if it could talk, would do no differently.

A schoolmate, C. G. Gens-d'Armes, wrote:

> When he opened the valve of his wit, he seemed to follow after the stream of his words without any control over them. It was no longer a person speaking but a machine driven by some demon. His jerky voice, metallic and nasal, his abrupt puppetlike gestures, his fixed expression, his torrential and incoherent flow of language, his grotesque or brilliant images, this synchronism which today we should compare to the movies or the phonograph—all this astonished me, amused me, irritated me, and ended by upsetting me. . . . His originality was too much like some mental anomaly.

These quotations convey the eerie mechanical quality of Jarry's personality, or, more precisely, its insane immersion in mechanism. Virtually a midget, he insisted that the theatre appropriate the rigid ultra-reality of the marionette theatre, and lived the last years of his life in a half-floor apartment where normal-sized visitors had to crouch. Fascinated by bicycles, hydrology, physical experiments, and machinery of all sorts, he fuelled himself on alcohol and ether and did not so much die as break down; friends knocked on the door of his cupboard and he could not answer because his legs no longer worked. His last request was for a tiny tool, a toothpick. The nickname given him by a hostile critic—"La Tête de Mort"—was earned. Jarry himself had christened his first apartment, a cell at the foot of a dead-end alley, "Dead Man's Calvary."

Certainly there is little life in Jarry's writings. "I imitate nothing," he once said, and his works more resemble graffiti, cartoons, technical treatises, and verbal games than novels and plays seeking to portray human life in action. He achieved fame in 1896 with *Ubu Roi*, which was derived from schoolboy skits perpetrated against an incompetent science teacher in the lycée at Rennes. Its first word is a modified obscenity, and its hurly-burly of schoolboy cruelty and Shakespeare parody (a monstrously simplified Falstaff murderously ascends to the throne of a nonexistent Poland) does not make very good reading now, especially since New Directions has seen fit to publish the play in a scribbly novelty format. *Ubu Roi*—whose first performance occasioned a riot in the audience and left a young spectator from Ireland, William Butler Yeats, to conclude momentously in his journal, "After us the Savage God"— now in its bare text wears the sadness of a faded program, a testament to vanished fireworks. *Selected Works of Alfred Jarry* begins with several sequels to *Ubu Roi*, in which Jarry exercises a more mature wit and allegorizes his instinctive anarchism with scenes such as Ubu flushing his conscience down the toilet. But the outrageousness of such farce does not liberate; rather, one feels suffocated by a stunted sensibility and an arbitrary cruelty. As with the currently admired school of neo-pornography (e.g., *Last Exit to Brooklyn*), the author's participation appears suspiciously enthusiastic. Jarry seems to be having most of the fun in passages like (from *Ubu Cocu*):

> There's nothing to be done with him. We'll have to make do with twisting the nose and nears [*sic*], with removal of the tongue and extraction of the teeth, laceration of the posterior, hacking to pieces

of the spinal marrow and the partial or total spaghettification of the brain through the heels. He shall first be impaled, then beheaded, then finally drawn and quartered. After which the gentleman will be free, through our great clemency, to go and get himself hanged anywhere he chooses.

And this repellent note of inhumanity, of frenzy, runs through Jarry's fiction as uncontrolled hyperbole. The novel *Messalina* is not meant to be absurd, but at the height of applause in a great stadium we are told that "the sound of Messalina smacking her lips dominated the uproar." While she is being impaled on a sword, a bystander behaves most strangely:

> "But it is a sword blade, carrion," slavered the freedman, "it is not a . . ."
> But it was he who then sobbed out aloud and prostrated himself as though struck down by a god; and he buried his face in the ground, biting at the flowers whose perfume throbbed with his cry:
> "But I love her! I love her!"

Purple is too pale a word for such passages. Jarry's non-fiction is better controlled: his remarks on dramaturgical science, calling for a theatre of "man-sized marionettes," are, though irascible in tone, cogent. His scientific and blasphemous essays show demonic ingenuity and humor. After reading H. G. Wells's *The Time Machine*, Jarry, with a relentless wealth of engineering detail, set down plans for one, consisting of an ebony bicycle frame mounted on three gyroscopes aligned with the three planes of Euclidean space. In "The Passion Considered as an Uphill Bicycle Race," the Cross becomes a bicycle "constructed of two tubes soldered together at right angles"—"and it is worth mentioning in this connection that Jesus rode lying flat on his back in order to reduce his air resistance." Jarry's mad hyperbolism veers close to profundity. Refuting the notion that a bicycle rider should pedal slowly to contemplate the view, he argues:

> He should . . . make use of this gear-equipped machine to scoop up forms and colors as rapidly as possible while whizzing along roadway and bicycle track; for fueling one's mind with crushed, confused fragments relieves the memory's secret dungeons of their

destructive work, and after such an assimilation the mind can more readily recreate entirely original forms and colors. We do not know how to create out of nothingness but we are capable of doing so out of chaos.

His faith in unconscious (and therefore natural) processes is serious; he describes what must have resembled his own method of composition:

> Sengle constructed his curiously and precisely equilibrated literary works by sleeping a solid fifteen hours, after eating and drinking, and then ejaculating the result in an odd half hour's scribbling. . . . Some professors of philosophy rhapsodize that this resemblance to natural processes partakes of the ultimate Masterpiece.

Although *Selected Works of Alfred Jarry* contains only a few chapters of what Professor Shattuck elsewhere calls "the best of his novels," *Les Jours et Les Nuits,* and omits entirely "the most difficult and personal of all his texts," *L'Amour Absolu,* it includes *in toto* his exasperating "neo-scientific novel" entitled *Exploits and Opinions of Doctor Faustroll, Pataphysician.* 'Pataphysics, a concept present in Jarry's earliest work, is "the science of that which is superinduced upon metaphysics," or more fully:

> 'Pataphysics is the science of imaginary solutions, which symbolically attributes the properties of objects, described by their virtuality, to their lineaments.

Faustroll grew from Jarry's planned treatise on 'pataphysics, which was modified by a desire to "create a cast of characters to incarnate, practice, and expound the new science." Professor Shattuck's description of the inchoate hybrid that resulted is usefully succinct: "Jarry's good doctor is born full-grown at the age of sixty-three, navigates unendingly across dry land in a sieve, and travels everywhere with a summons server who is trying to collect some hundred thousand francs of back rent from him." In addition to Panmuphle, the summons server, there is Bosse-de-Nage, a dog-faced baboon whose only utterance is an intermittent "Ha ha." Beginning with a replica of the summons and ending with a geometrical discourse on the "surface of God," the book follows the adventurers through several hydrological experiments, visits to many islands, each inhabited by an artistic acquaintance of Jarry's, a banquet ending in a holocaust, a succession of prose poems, Faustroll's death through drowning, and his resurrection, or un-ravelling, into the happy condition of Ethernity. Such a summary makes it sound more entertaining than it is. Though it contains some good metaphors and jokes, the tale is top-heavy with personal allusions and pseudo-science, clotted with obscurities, and darkened by Jarry's infantile cruelty. Here is a specimen:

> The isle of Cyril first appeared to us as the red fire of a volcano, or as the punch bowl full of blood spattered out by the fall of shooting stars. Then we saw that it was mobile, armored, and quadrangular, with a helix at the four corners, shaped like the four demi-diagonals of separate arms able to advance in any direction. We realized that we had approached within gun range when a bullet tore off Bosse-de-Nage's right ear and four of his teeth.
>
> "Ha ha!" stammered the *papio;* but the impact of a steel cylin-drocone against his left zygomatic apophysis made short work of his third word.

How can one judge Jarry? Apollinaire expressed the hope that his weird works "will be the foundation of a new realism which will perhaps not be inferior to that so poetic and learned realism of ancient Greece." Gabriel Brunet explained him by saying, "Every man is capable of showing his contempt for the cruelty and stupidity of the universe by making his own life a poem of in-coherence and absurdity." I think the second estimate more plausi-ble; Jarry's life, as a defiant gesture, matters more than his works, which are largely pranks and propaganda of a rarefied sort. Com-pared to Jarry, most of today's so-called Black Humorists seem merely ex-admen working off their grudges in sloppy travesties of a society whose tame creatures they remain still. Though we can-not grant him the comprehensive sanity and the reverent submis-sion to reality that produce lasting art, we must admire his soldier's courage and his fanatic's will. He made himself into a Death's Head. When Drieu's hero Alain looks into the mirror, he sees evidence of the "terrible emaciations that a year or two before had begun to carve a death mask out of the living substance." Time acts upon him; Jarry assaults time. Alain felt himself sinking in a spiritless and mechanical world, while Jarry, skimming along on his bicycle, turned himself into a machine, with a machine's hectic ferocity and—though, unlike Ubu and Faustroll, he proved destructible—a machine's self-disregard.

Albertine Disparue

THE RUNAWAY, by Albertine Sarrazin, translated from the French by Charles Lam Markmann. 480 pp. Grove Press, 1967.

ASTRAGAL, by Albertine Sarrazin, translated from the French by Patsy Southgate. 172 pp. Grove Press, 1967.

Most men are potential desperadoes; but the concept of the female criminal seems paradoxical. Laws enforce a stability whose ultimate domestic unit is the woman herself; her physiology and psychology turn on the cultivation of inner space, while the man's role calls for the conquest of outer space, for thrust and adventure, for arrowing forms of outward assertion as various as rape and theology, as admirable as scientific exploration and as deplorable as war. The most common form of female criminality—prostitution —is, however masked in toughness, an act of submission, and keeps the peace. True, the insect world (not to mention the world of literary criticism) offers striking instances of female enlargement and predation, but the unhappy history of the male praying mantis confirms that the seminal contribution to the generative process, though not negligible, is momentary and helps account for the primordial willingness of men to undergo risk. Granted that among the highest of the primates sexual instincts androgenously overlap, enough polarity remains so that we approach two autobiographical novels by a repeatedly jailed woman, billed on the dust jackets as "a female Genet," with the expectation of something monstrous, delicious, and revelatory.

Albertine Sarrazin appears in her photograph as a curly-haired, big-eyed street Arab with a wry tuck of intelligence in the corner of her mouth. The bleak jacket notes state that she was born in Algiers in 1937, and that she was an orphan. She ran away from her foster home at the age of fifteen, was placed in reform school, escaped to Paris, "drifted into a life of theft and prostitution," and spent the next nine years either in jail or in hiding. In prison she wrote two novels, *La Cavale* and *L'Astragale*, whose publication in Paris in 1965 made her famous and secured her parole. For two years she "lived quietly with her husband Julien in the south of France," and then died, after a kidney operation, a week before her thirtieth birthday. A female Genet she was not. These two novels, published simultaneously by Grove Press as *The Runaway* and *Astragal*, are not in Genet's class, either as literary creation or as self-proclamation. Though she refers to her prison guards as "angels" and invokes "St. Duty" and "St. Java," Mme. Sarrazin shows none of Genet's myth-making power or the Satanic philosophy that conceives of prison as an inverted Heaven where seraphim swirl in violent rhythms controlled by the Deity-like onanist fantasizing in his cell. This order of originality is well beyond the very young woman who has, she tells us, "only my ball-point to pull me out of the shit and the despair." Whereas Genet celebrates the brutal, homosexual microcosm of prison as his chosen universe, Mme. Sarrazin describes nothing but daily dreariness and dreams only of escape.

The Runaway is a very long piece of scarcely disguised autobiography. Its English title inadequately translates the complex associations of *cavale*, a literary word for "mare," from which has been derived the slang verb *cavaler*, meaning "to run, to decamp, to take a powder." The translator, Mr. Markmann, confronted with a slangy and idiomatic text, has responded with sprinklings of faintly obsolete and off-key terms like "yack" (for "talk") and "mitts" (for "hands") and "nut" and "noodle" (for "head") and with impossible medleys like "What vision froze the guy in his tracks?" and gauche metonymy like "I Colgate the pearly whites," to signify tooth-brushing. In fairness, nothing deteriorates quicker in passage than slang, and there is little to suggest that the original French text is very finely nuanced. The first four hundred pages are really quite dull: the housekeeping details of prison cells, a lot of tape-recorder dialogue, a hope to escape and mount the *cavale* that never comes to anything, a succession of cellmates indistinguishable except that some smell worse than others. There are patches of vivid description:

Sometimes I like to squat on the laundry steps, where the rivulets of soap and dirty water gather in a moldy coldness; motionless, slightly bent over, my head leaning toward my shoulder, I open my mouth a little and feel the breeze vibrating through my cheeks, like a cool breath of air through a harmonica; and, a little higher up, the sun explodes lightly on my eyelids and roots me in the earth, through the rotting stones and the bubbles of laundry water; sudden joy pours out of the sky and swirls round my legs, while without changing position I move forward, with a slight effort, as against a tide.

The details of note-smuggling (in candy, via vagina, from mouth to mouth during kisses) are surprising, and there are some interesting psychological touches, as when Anick, the fastidious and reclusive heroine, takes it upon herself to delouse a senile fellow-inmate. But it all comes upon the reader haphazard, worse organized than even a sociologist would do it—the objectified diary of a precocious girl who detests jail yet is unable to stay out of it, whose self-perception is barely emerged from the chaos of self-pity, whose principal activities are stamp-cadging and daydreaming, whose days ebb by amid conversations like:

"What kind of soap do you think we'll get this week? Cadum? Palmolive?"

"I wonder what view of Paris there'll be in the biscuit boxes."

To be sure, this unstinted dreariness has a mimetic effect of sorts; we become as eager to escape the book as its narrator is to escape prison.

Anick begins her story well after the middle; she is a hardened jailbird when we meet her. The turning point of her life—her falling in love with a man called Zizi during an interval of freedom, and her concomitant conversion from lesbianism—is past, and it figures in the present tense of this novel as a constant pining for him and a futile scheming to rejoin him in the life of burglary they once led. He is in another part of the prison. On his initiative, they get married, winning the privilege of meeting once a week, with glass between them. They can kiss only in the police wagon taking them to and from the interrogations preparatory to their trial. Their final sentence is severe. Zizi is more cautious than Anick, and discourages her hopes of escape. The end of the book, if I understand it, shows her joining him in resignation—"another stroke through the calendar is not so bad. Slowly the mercury is getting down to zero, and from zero you make a fresh start." Her *cavale*, her "runaway mare," has become transformed into the interior escape of imagination. The secret action of this book is the act of its own writing; what Mme. Sarrazin has described, with steadily growing conscious intent, is the process of what we on the outside would call her "rehabilitation." In the last hundred pages, the writing grows cleaner, the imagery more complex, the plot more active. Her lawyer emerges from the shadows and becomes a character. And she herself gains access to the defiant child she once was: "I try to recapture the basic savor that I found in the hole [the isolation cell] during my adolescence. . . . I had my shoulder to the wheel of hardships, I made frightening bets against myself; I fasted, I burned myself, I pricked myself. . . . The hole was a vice, as much a vice as being tattooed or masturbating, a vice that I wanted to savor while I had the chance, and, if possible, to learn to like." She tells her lawyer, "I've been asocial ever since I was born." Earlier in the book she has tersely referred to her "mother," in puzzling variance with the dust jacket's claim that she is an orphan; now she cries out, "I'm a bastard, no one's child." Though at times she prays "Let my fury never abate. Let me always keep intact my wrong, my hurtful ways," an essential perspective has been gained, and an essential peace. "Zi, my love, one day the cycle of days and nights will stop torturing us and turn kind to us again. . . . The hateful blanket in which I roll myself up will vanish like the cold, and I will gorge myself on sun." The monotonous texture of the bulk of the book yields to heartfelt exclamations, glimpses of the past, a poetry of "this golden coma of prison where nothing makes a mark." The process of rehabilitation merges with the process of learning how to write.

The second novel also, femininely, embodies a process—the process of healing. *Astragal* ("anklebone") begins with the drop from the prison wall whereby Anne, a less slangy Anick, escapes and shatters her ankle, and ends with her walking back toward prison, "hardly limping at all." In the months between, she has met Julien (the name of Albertine Sarrazin's actual husband), has been sheltered by him in a series of hideouts, has supported herself by prostitution while he is in jail, and has broken her emotional ties with Rolande, her last female lover. These months of freedom and rescue and healing are, then, the pivotal idyll remembered in *Runaway*. The writing is in every sense happier, and Patsy Southgate's translation, comparatively uncluttered by lingo, keeps pace with the brief scenes, the nice ease of prose:

> An arm went around my shoulders, another slid under my knees, I was lifted up, carried away; the man's face of a moment ago was very close, above mine, moving across the sky and the tree branches. He carried me firmly and gently, I was out of the mud and I was moving, in his arms, between the sky and the earth.

With her new virtuosity, Mme. Sarrazin has no trouble in making the injured foot both a symbolic presence—"I had a new heart in my leg, still irregular, responding inordinately to the other"— and a convincingly painful "stew of shattered bones and flesh." Though not a sensual writer compared to Violette Leduc or to Colette, she can strike off a fresh phrase quick with the life of the moment. When she and Julien are together, "the ground is under our feet like an island"; of her outgrown lesbianism she simply says, "Rolande was the night light, the daylight is here, I turn it off." And she can detect, in the classic manner of French analysis of the sentiments, small motions within herself, such as the "cruel ill will" with which she invites Jean, an unloved protector, to zip up her dress as she goes to meet Julien, so Jean will "sniff at my new skin" and "realize that I was . . . happy; and that he didn't, that he never could, have anything to do with it." True, the depths within herself are still out of reach; her recourse to streetwalking seems screened in the telling, her alcoholism can be deduced from the text but is unacknowledged by it, the will toward self-destruction is never disentangled from her wild will toward freedom, and a certain innocent egotism flattens the other characters, including and especially her hero, Julien.

These two books, for all their developing skill, exist less as literature than as life, as the record of a life that against crippling odds fought through to expression and, in its last two years, success— "she lived quietly with her husband Julien in the south of France." While the novels of Genet insist that the male criminal dwells in a world apart, with a morality and rationale of its own, Albertine Sarrazin's world is not readily distinguishable from that of respectable women: a world of momentary but keenly felt pleasures —a cigarette, a sunbath, a bowl of fruit on a linen tablecloth—in which the chief enemy is boredom rather than (as with men) defeat, in which a prevalent stoicism is qualified by fits of panic, in which a monogamous passion is qualified by phases, almost absent-minded, of wantonness, in which powerful impulses, with a reckless lightness amazing to a male, override conventions. The laws Albertine Sarrazin broke were not, one feels, real to her; only the policemen and warders were real. At the end of *Astragal*, arrest arrives with lyric suddenness, in a courteous flurry:

> I grab my bag, I open the door, I put the key outside; on the landing a man is standing, not very big, looking cheerful and gratified:
> "Hello, Anne," he says to me. "I've been looking for you for a long time, did you know that? Come on, let's get going, I'll follow you. And don't try to run away, O.K.?"
> I smile, Julien will see us go by, he'll understand that I'll be a little late and that it's not my fault.

Now she is gone, her redeemed life cut short, and again it is not her fault.

Saganland and the Back of Beyond

SCARS ON THE SOUL, by Françoise Sagan, translated from the French by Joanna Kilmartin. 141 pp. McGraw-Hill, 1974.

THE BRIDGE OF BEYOND, by Simone Schwarz-Bart, translated from the French by Barbara Bray. 246 pp. Atheneum, 1974.

In the *Herald Tribune* of April 14, 1955, under the headline " 'BONJOUR TRISTESSE' PRODIGY ARRIVES FOR 10 DAYS IN CITY," nineteen-year-old Françoise Sagan, after informing the interviewer that she wrote her sensationally successful novel in one lazy month, confided some thoughts on existentialism and then added, deferentially, "But I am no philosopher. Sometimes I think philosophical thoughts when I have nothing better to do." Well, a generation later, Mlle. Sagan evidently has nothing better to do, for her new (and eighth) novel, *Scars on the Soul*, is full of philosophizing and devoid of almost everything else. A fiction of sorts unfolds between pages of musing and self-display: two gorgeously languid characters from her play, *Castle in Sweden*, the van Milhem siblings Sebastian and Eleanor, are revived ten years later and allowed to drift through a plot whose subsidiary characters keep dropping away (one commits suicide, others are abandoned or forgotten by the author) like petals from a vase of tired roses. The plot is in fact a subplot; the real plot, and the more exciting one, traces the chic, bored, speed-crazy ex-prodigy's attempts, through Normandy vacations and automobile accidents and spells of acedia, to push this little book through to its ending. End it does, with Françoise Sagan, as a character, in the arms of her paper hero, and this bit of origami may be, in her mind, her ticket of admission to the ranks of the New Novelists. Amid her *pensées* are some sentences devoted to these now avuncular experimenters:

> This is what I have against the New Novelists. They play with blank cartridges, defused grenades, leaving their readers to create for themselves characters left undelineated between neutral words, while they, the authors, openly wash their hands of them. God knows, ellipsis is tempting . . . but it's really a little too facile, possibly even unhealthy, to make people puzzle over obscurities when there's nothing to show that they've caused the author himself any real headache.

Whereas readers of *Scars on the Soul* will put down the book convinced, if of nothing else, that it gave the author a headache to write it.

One must be fair. There is a dainty wit, a parody of decadence, in the delineation of the ethereally incestuous and cheerfully parasitical van Milhems. Not all of the author's *aperçus* are banal; she knows her world of night clubs and vacation villas and remorselessly self-conscious love. The book reads easily; it is *company*. The author's cry of personal crisis, which leads to a novel that haltingly invents itself under our eyes, feels sincere; she is honest even in her lameness and limpness of thought, and her self-exposure, as "someone tapping away at her typewriter because she's afraid of herself and the typewriter and the mornings and the evenings and everything else," has its fascination, as do, on this side of the Atlantic, the lurching franknesses of Mailer and Vonnegut. However, there is about *Scars on the Soul* an arrogant flimsiness that invites a quarrel, just as the generous margins and blank interchapter pages invite contentious jotting. "Oh, tush!" and "Ho-hum," I discover myself to have written, respectively, beside these pieces of Mlle. Sagan's wisdom:

> For nothing will alter my conviction that only by pursuing the extremes in one's nature, with all its contradictions, appetites, aversions, rages, can one hope to understand a little—oh, I admit only a very little—of what life is about. At any rate, my life.

> And the women who want equality with men, and the good arguments and the good faith of some and the grotesque obtuseness of others, human just the same and subject to the same god, the only god, whom they try to deny: Time. But who reads Proust?

Françoise Sagan reads Proust, is the answer. But her Proustian meditations have an unstately way of dwindling to nothing, to a flirtatious self-mockery:

> Since, fundamentally, the only idol, the only God I acknowledge is Time, it follows that I cannot experience real pleasure or pain except in relation to Time. I knew that this poplar would outlast me, that this hay, on the contrary, would wither and die before me; I knew I was expected at home and also that I could just as easily spend another hour beneath this tree. I knew that any haste on my part would be as stupid as any delay. And for the rest of my life, I knew everything. Including the fact that such knowledge meant nothing. Nothing but a privileged moment. The only authentic moments, in my view. When I say "authentic," I mean "instructive," which is just as silly.

Proust interweaves his speculations and confessions with the exhaustively evoked details of a world he powerfully loves; Mlle. Sagan has for fabric only the shreds and scraps of a world she has come to despise. She confesses on the first page "the distaste I now feel for a way of life that until now . . . has always attracted me." Later, she rises to the defense of her "Saganland" of the privileged and idle and frivolous; "The majority of critics are appalling hypocrites. . . . What could be more enjoyable than to know that a whiskey on the rocks awaits you at a villa on the other side of this golf course, among people as lively as yourself, and as free from material worries?" But the defense rings hollow. The details are tired. The furniture and chitchat, the spongers and spongees of *Scars on the Soul* are dismissed in the same breath that evokes them; only the aloof weather and landscape of Normandy arouse the writer's respect, that reverence without which description is so much word-trundling. We have indeed come a long, heavy way from *Bonjour Tristesse*, with its sparkling sea and secluding woods, its animal quickness, its academically efficient plot, its heroes and heroines given the perfection of Racine personae by the young author's innocent belief in glamour. The van Milhems, those blond leeches, seem by this retrospect degenerate forms of the incestuous affection between Cecile and her father in *Bonjour Tristesse*. Incest, self-love's first venture outward, feels deliberately burlesqued; Mlle. Sagan—at this juncture in her career, at least—has ceased to love herself, and with love has lost the impetus to create a fictional world.

An abundance of love nearly overburdens *The Bridge of Beyond*, the first novel by Simone Schwarz-Bart. The novelist, a native of Guadeloupe, married to the French author of *The Last of the Just*, describes her intention in an autobiographical note: "For me, the essence of Guadeloupe will always be the most oppressed and proudest Negroes of the island, 'unbroken and unbreakable.' I early dreamed of speaking about them someday so that justice might be done for them." She has written *The Bridge of Beyond* (whose title in French is the very different *Pluie et Vent sur Télumée Miracle*) "in memory of an old peasant woman of my village who was my friend." Telumee tells her story, beginning with her genealogy; she is the daughter of the black woman Victory, who was the daughter of Queen Without a Name, who was the daughter of Minerva, who was "a fortunate woman freed by the abolition of slavery from a master notorious for cruelty and caprice." These matrilineal generations overlap those of Mme. Schwarz-Bart's husband's recent short novel, *A*

Woman Named Solitude, which brings slavery to Guadeloupe in the person of Bayangumay, a girl abducted from an African village of pre-Adamic pleasantness. Schwarz-Bart is a European Jew writing about slavery; his wife is a native Guadeloupean writing about Guadeloupe. Though the two books have a companionable closeness of tone—a kind of tranced lyricism, as if, in her phrase, "dreamed in broad daylight"—her novel is the less surreal and the more substantial, the more convincing as a testament of life. The imagery of rivers flows through it, and its radiant shimmer and feeling of unforced movement are drawn from the center of the stream. "We were steeped in day, the light came in waves through the shifting leaves, and we looked at one another astonished to be there, all three, right in the stream of life." The book takes for its theme nothing less than living: Queen Without a Name "went on doing what God had created her for—living," though she can also ask, "To see so much misery, be spat at so often, become helpless and die—is life on earth really right for man?" Her granddaughter, Telumee, who acquires the title of Miracle, searches for "the thread of [her] life" and pronounces the verdict on her life and on life simultaneously:

> We have no more marks to guide us than the bird in the air or the fish in the water, and in the midst of this uncertainty we live, and some laugh and others sing. I thought I would sleep with one man only and he abused me; I thought Amboise immortal; I believed in a little girl who left me; and yet, without quite knowing why, I don't regard any of all that as a waste of time.

The events of the book are numerous; the author follows three heroines through their lives' adventures—their children, their lovers, their shacks, their occupations on the edge of survival. It is a frontier world, this post-slavery village of Fond-Zombi, where harsh disappointments suddenly wipe out years of tranquil harvesting; the human—or, more particularly, the female—capacity to survive sorrow and reconstitute the work of cultivation is a theme illustrated several times over, always movingly. The "miracle" attached to Telumee's name and present in the French title may be that of the human spirit, with its immortal resilience, its quicksilver moods admirable even when malevolent, its—as the book puts it—*panache*. Another theme is the special shape and tactics forced upon the black spirit in a land ruled by white proprietors. Telumee is advised, "Be a fine little Negress, a real drum with two sides. Let life bang and thump, but keep the underside always intact." The word "Negro" recurs insistently, not as a demoted term of racist distinction but as a metaphor for all men who are oppressed and scant of hope. To be Negro is to be human in a heightened degree: "however beautiful other sounds may be, only Negroes are musicians." Telumee comes to understand "what a Negro is: wind and sail at the same time, at once drummer and dancer, a first-class sham, trying to collect by the basketful the sweetness that falls scattered from above, and inventing sweetness when it doesn't fall on him." We are all, this novel makes us feel, "Negroes at the back of beyond," "flat on our bellies," our main defense "the Negro's ingenuity in forging happiness in spite of everything." "What happiness!" comes as the book's concluding phrase, and if words of wisdom are spoken by too many sibylline Negresses, and a Caribbean brand of black populism pushes some passages into sentimentality, the book's gift of life is so generous, and its imagery so scintillant in the sunlight of love, that we believe every word.

In Praise of the Blind, Black God

A HAPPY DEATH, by Albert Camus, translated from the French by Richard Howard. 192 pp. Alfred A. Knopf, 1972.

Albert Camus' first novel, *A Happy Death*, which he did not allow to be published during his lifetime, has now been issued in a handsome, annotated edition. Read in conjunction with the other writings of the young Camus—the notebooks begun in 1935, the two small collections of essays *The Wrong Side and the Right Side* (1937) and *Nuptials* (1938), the play *Caligula* (composed in 1938 but not performed until 1945), and his second novel, the classic *The Stranger* (completed in 1940 and published in 1942)—his first attempt at extended fiction offers an instructive lesson in the strategies of the imagination. Though shot through with brilliant rays, *A Happy Death* is a chunky, labored work, cumbersome for all its brevity, so cluttered with false starts and halting intentions that it occludes its own themes. In Camus' published *Notebooks*, it first appears as some chapter titles listed in January of 1936, when he was twenty-two; the last relevant notation occurs in March of 1939, when work on *The Stranger* was well advanced. An entry in June of 1938—"Rewrite novel"—implies a finished draft of *A Happy Death* by that time, but a month earlier, in a sketch of a funeral in an old people's home, *The Stranger* had begun to germinate, and some months later the uncanny, chilling first sentences of the masterpiece were written out intact. During the interval when passages for both novels compete in the *Notebooks*, those relating to *A Happy Death* suffer by comparison, seeming febrile and flaccid amid the sharp glimpses of the novel eventually published. Wisely, Camus let the first novel be consumed by the second, reusing a number of descriptions, recasting the main theme (a happy death), and transforming the hero's name by the addition of a *u*—Mersault, the man of sea and sun, darkening to Meursault, with its shadow of *meurtre*, of murder. Technically, the third-person method of *A Happy Death*, frequently an awkward vehicle for alter egos (see, see the sensitive young man light his cigarette; now let's eavesdrop on his thoughts), becomes the hypnotic, unabashed first-person voice of *The Stranger*. Substantively, Camus has located, outside of autobiography, the Archimedean point wherefrom he can acquire leverage upon his world. Often in art less is more, and one must depart to arrive. In the first novel, the author fumbles, trying to pick himself up by too many handles, and growing more handles in the process; in the second, he takes a short but decisive side-step, becomes less himself, and with this achieved narrowness penetrates to the heart of his *raison d'écrire*.

The youthful Camus evidently had many attributes of a normal Algerian working-class lout. He liked soccer, girls, beachbumming, moviegoing, and idleness. He had decided, one feels, to cherish the image of himself as a citizen of the Belcourt slums, a spiritual mate to the proletariat of whom he wrote, in "Summer in Algiers":

> They start work very early, and exhaust the range of human experience in ten short years. A workingman of thirty had already

played all his cards. . . . His delights have been swift and merciless. So has his life. And you understand then that he is born in a
land where everything is given to be taken away. . . . So reflection
or self-improvement are quite irrelevant.

The Camus whose gifts for reflection and self-improvement were
early recognized and nurtured by a grade-school teacher, the
Camus who entered the *lycée* at the age of ten, who studied philosophy at the University of Algiers from 1932 to 1936, who by
the age of twenty-five was a working, travelling, published intellectual and the mastermind of a theatre group—this Camus figures
little in the early essays or in the character of Mersault. Mersault,
though his consciousness is brushed by philosophical speculation,
confesses no ambition for his future and almost never reflects on
his past.

By any standards, Camus' upbringing had been bleak. His father,
an agricultural laborer, was killed in the Battle of the Marne ten
months after Albert was born. His mother, a Spaniard, took the
infant and his older brother Lucien from the village of Mondovi
to the poor district of Algiers, where she became a cleaning
woman. Camus was raised in a ménage that included his mother,
a partially paralyzed uncle, and a domineering grandmother. These
three adults were all illiterate and, in various ways, ill. The grandmother eventually died of cancer of the liver; Camus wrote of her,
"She fainted very easily after family discussions. She also suffered
from painful vomiting caused by a liver complaint. But she showed
not the slightest discretion in the practice of her illness. Far from
shutting herself away, she would vomit noisily into the kitchen
garbage can." His mother, he wrote, "could think only with
difficulty"; deafness, a speech impediment, and a docile temper
combined to enforce a habit of silence. Camus once described his
literary career as the attempt to speak for the "silent mother"—
the inarticulate and disenfranchised of society. An early sketch
portrays a grandmother who persistently asks a child, "Whom do
you like best? Your mother or your grandmother?"

The game was even better when the daughter was present. For the
child would always reply: "My grandmother," with, in his heart, a
great surge of love for his ever silent mother.

Death for a father, silence for a mother: with such a parentage, Camus would never become a fluent or frivolous creator. At the moment of beginning his first novel, what, indeed, was his artistic treasure? A good education, a normal sensuality, a fond ear for working-class dialect, a rapturous sensitivity to nature, a conviction that paganism was being reborn around him in European-ized North Africa. "For twenty centuries, men have strived to impose decency on the insolence and simplicity of the Greeks, to diminish the flesh and elaborate our dress. Today, reaching back over this history, young men sprinting on the Mediterranean beaches are rediscovering the magnificent motions of the athletes of Delos." Two events in his early maturity urged him toward energetic use of his capabilities: in 1930 he nearly died of tuberculosis, and in 1934 he joined the Communist Party. Yet always, in the heart of this young man, coexistent with the desire to celebrate and explicate, lay an unshakable lassitude and a blankness. Caligula (a part Camus wrote for himself to act) says, "There's something deep down in me—an abyss of silence, a pool of stagnant water, rotting weeds." At the age of forty-five, great in fame and accomplishment, Camus wrote of "the profound indifference that haunts me like a natural infirmity." Around this natural infirmity, then, the novice artist must shape his strategies—no, not around it; he must point himself *into* it, for this silence is his message.

The first sketch, in the *Notebooks*, for the novel that is to become *A Happy Death* outlines, with an excessively formal scheme of alternation between past and present tense, what appears to be a story about love and jealousy among students, ending with the hero's death by disease. "Taste of death and of the sun. Love of life," reads a note for the ending, encapsulating the tensions—the sun as life-giving yet cruel, the affirmation of life in the moment of death—that Camus wished to dramatize. Violent death does not figure in this first version, though the hero (called simply Patrice) does tell "his story of the man sentenced to death: 'I can see him, he is inside me. And everything he says pierces my heart. He lives and breathes with me. He is afraid with me.'" This premonition of *The Stranger*, however, remains fallow in the notes; a year and a half later, the novel, still untitled, has become involved with an idea about a gambler and with Camus' European travels. "Theme

of the revolver," however, emerges in one list of chapters, and a
little later a fresh approach to the plot is indicated:

> Novel: the man who realizes that one needs to be rich in order to
> live, who devotes himself completely to the acquisition of money,
> who succeeds, lives and dies *happy*.

The italicization of "happy" signals an arrival; a month later (September of 1937), the title "La Mort Heureuse" appears. That fall,
the character of "an invalid—both legs amputated" begins to talk
in the notes, and before the end of the year he has his curious
name, Zagreus. To this new character adheres the old "theme of
the revolver," elaborated in a remarkable earlier notation about a
man who plays with a loaded revolver before going to sleep: "And,
as he woke up, his mouth filled with an already bitter saliva, he
licked the barrel, poking his tongue into it, and with a death rattle
of infinite happiness said again and again in wonder and astonishment: 'My joy is priceless.' "

The stage is at last prepared, then, for the central action of *A
Happy Death*. Patrice Mersault, a poor young man, makes the
acquaintance, through a mistress, of a legless invalid, Roland
Zagreus, who shows him one day a safe full of money, a loaded
revolver, and an undated suicide note. Some days later (in a
chapter Camus transposed to the beginning of the novel), Mersault
visits Zagreus, takes up the revolver, kills the cripple with it, leaves
the suicide note on a table, and departs with the money. Walking
away from this perfect crime, he sneezes, and the remainder of
the novel traces his wandering, through a variety of countries and
romantic entanglements, toward his own death, of pleurisy, chills,
fever, and weak heart—a somewhat poetic syndrome. Assembled
rather than conceived, the story has too many duplicating parts—
too many women, too many deaths, too many meditative approaches to the lyrical riddle of "happiness." Simple problems of
clarity exist. Has Zagreus deliberately invited Mersault to murder
him? Why, when Mersault holds the gun to his head, doesn't
Zagreus gesture or speak? "When he felt the barrel against his
right temple, he did not turn away. But Patrice, watching him, saw
his eyes fill with tears." These tears are given meaning not by the
context but by an entry in the notebooks: "The man who doesn't

want this easy way out, and who wants to chew over and taste all his fear. He dies without a word, his eyes full of tears." The murder is so abruptly rendered as to seem merely sensational. Nor do its consequences easily flow: after the murder and the theft, Mersault does not live like a rich man; he travels thriftily in Europe and loafs among friends. None of his pleasures are beyond the financial reach of Camus himself at this impoverished stage of his life. Mersault never becomes the proposed hero "who devotes himself completely to the acquisition of money"; money never becomes an embodied theme.

Since *A Happy Death* arrives now with an excellent critical afterword by Jean Sarocchi, and since Camus suppressed the work, why belabor its weaknesses? Only to marvel at how its materials and concerns reëmerge in *The Stranger*, transformed by their new position within a unified action. For instance, chapter two of *A Happy Death* describes for several pages the passage of a Sunday in Algiers as witnessed by Mersault from a window in his room. These pages rank with the youthful essays for poetic power, and, indeed, "Between Yes and No" shows Camus' mother thus sitting and gazing at the street for hours. But the resonance remains private: the Sunday is no particular Sunday; it illustrates Mersault's boredom within a somewhat formless flashback. In *The Stranger*, however, where the passage recurs almost word for word, the Sunday is the Sunday two days after Meursault has buried his mother, and the very day after he has taken a beach pickup, Marie, to a Fernandel movie and begun an affair with her; in this context, the reused description reflects sinisterly upon him and ominously upon life: "It occurred to me that somehow I'd got through another Sunday, that Mother now was buried, and tomorrow I'd be going back to work as usual. Really, nothing in my life had changed." Another instance: the "tough" characters in *A Happy Death*—the customers in Céleste's restaurant and the barrelmaker Cardona, who lives downstairs—provide only background; they exist in the book because Camus, a convinced egalitarian, has invited them in. Whereas, in *The Stranger*, old Salamano and the pimp Raymond Sintès, besides being more vivid, actively lead Meursault into the nexus of violence that dooms him. Further, they testify at his trial, during which Raymond's friendship is cited in proof of Meursault's criminality. All the events of *The Stranger*, indeed, are relevant at the trial; the plot's turns are cast in iron.

No amount of trimming and rearranging can counterfeit the effect of a single concept alertly pursued. How splendidly, at the center of *The Stranger*, event, symbol, and statement fuse! Camus' obsession with that harsh wonder the sun—with the *"Nada* whose birth is possible only at the sight of landscapes crushed by the sun"—creates a furnace in which existential absurdity engenders sensation and action:

> The whole world seemed to have come to a standstill on this little strip of sand between the sunlight and the sea. . . . And just then it crossed my mind that one might fire, or not fire—and it would come to absolutely the same thing. . . . But the heat was so great that it was just as bad staying where I was, under that flood of blinding light falling from the sky. To stay, or to make a move—it came to much the same. . . . The trigger gave, and the smooth underbelly of the butt jogged my palm. And so, with that crisp, whipcrack sound, it all began. I shook off my sweat and the clinging veil of light. I knew I'd shattered the balance of the day, the spacious calm of this beach on which I had been happy. But I fired four shots more into the inert body, on which they left no visible trace.

These four additional shots, fired in dazed indifference, are what condemn him to death. The inner blankness of the Camusian hero, a puzzling sullen driftingness in Mersault, Meursault proclaims as a splendid defiance. "It makes no difference, I am not interested" —such phrases, repeated in the face of society's hatred, reconfirmed in the moment of extinction, become the litany of a new kind of holiness. Before his execution, Meursault opens his heart to the "benign indifference" of the universe. Its indifference and his are akin. "To feel it so like myself, indeed, so brotherly, made me realize that I'd been happy, and that I was happy still." All that is needed to complete his happiness is the howl of execration from the mob around the guillotine. Caligula, under the swords of his assassins, "laughing and choking," cries out, "I'm still alive!" Of himself, Camus wrote, in a youthful essay, "And yet, at the very moment that the world was crumbling, he was alive." A few sentences further: "Every time it seems to me that I've grasped the deep meaning of the world, it is its simplicity that always overwhelms me. My mother, that evening, and its strange indifference." Indifference, life, simplicity, the sun, death: the concepts link up, make a circle. "There is no love of life without despair of life," an essay affirms. Love, despair, silence, mother, nature. A sentence deleted from *A Happy Death* reads, "The sun is the real mirror of the world." Blank, indifferent, merciless, the sun is in each of us, the sun is life. Instead, then, of a soul seeking reunion with God, we contain a stark reflection of "the blind, black god"—another phrase deleted from *A Happy Death*. We serve this god by pretending no more than we feel, though we feel nothing, and by accepting death in a pantheistic ecstasy that Camus called "happiness." Some of Camus' most interesting ethical precepts, as set down in *The Myth of Sisyphus*—written directly after *The Stranger*—are deliberate inversions of Christian suppositions: each man has "his irreparable innocence," "what counts is not the best living but the most living," and the heart the creator needs is "the closed heart."

But *A Happy Death*, with its half-hearted autobiography, too numerous romances, static scenery-painting, and ingenuous melodrama, could not focus this anti-theology. The images that could, however, already lay in Camus' notebook. One of the entries for January of 1936 lists six story ideas; two are "Death of the mother" and "The story of the condemned man." These two preoccupations figure marginally in much of Camus' youthful production; with *The Stranger*, for the first time he *invents* them, in the freedom of fantasy. By proposing a young man who could not shed tears at his mother's funeral and went to the movies instead of mourning, and by rendering her pauper's funeral and his daily life in the full dry light of their absurd inconsequence, Camus placed his hidden theme of blankness where no reader could avoid being challenged by it. Though of course derived from observation (impressions of a funeral occur in the notebooks, and his grandmother's death had already provided matter for an essay), the central circumstance is imagined; Camus' mother, in fact, outlived him. His essays show how deeply he loved her. But by killing her in his mind, he unlocked an essential self, Meursault the essential orphan, in all his "simplicity" and estrangement, this cool monster who is Everyman, with his casual, androgynous voice that would blow down all our castles of Christian decency and conventional delusion. And by making this hero's condemnation to death literal and legal, instead of an attenuated wasting by disease, Camus immensely heightens the pressure. He is forced, observe, by these inventions to conjure up two blank-walled interiors—the old people's home and the jail—that crystallize *Nada* better than the open landscapes he so loved to describe. And the necessary characters of the warden and the chaplain, with their tragicomic eloquence, lead his book into a dimension undeveloped in *A Happy Death*—the dimension of the political. Society acquires spokesmen, and in debate Meursault turns singular, heroic, revolutionary. The fussed-over irrelevancies of *A Happy Death* fall away. The new novel pours smooth and hot from start to finish.

Fiction must hold in healthily tense combination the mimetic and pedagogic impulses. Perhaps because kind teachers had guided his rise from poverty, Camus respected pedagogy, wished always to make things formal and clear, liked stories to have morals. He sometimes reminds us of a schoolteacher standing before us insisting that though there is no headmaster and no grading system and scarcely any blackboard, we must stay at our desks, learning virtue and happiness with the diligence of saints. We must, in short, love our mother—"The earth! . . . that great temple deserted by the gods"—even though she is silent. After *The Stranger* and *The Plague*, Camus' fiction shows more intellectual will than vital, involuntary substance. *The Fall* and the short stories of *Exile and the Kingdom* seem relatively stiff and diagrammatic. The poet stoops in his prophet's robes. *A Happy Death* shows the other extremity of this curve—the beginning, when artistry and philosophy struggled with an abundance of live impressions; the prophet had not yet been robed, the young man stood naked.

EUROPE

Two Points on a Descending Curve

MOUCHETTE, by Georges Bernanos, translated by J. C. Whitehouse. 127 pp. Holt, Rinehart & Winston, 1966.

TWO VIEWS, by Uwe Johnson, translated from the German by Richard and Clara Winston. 183 pp. Harcourt, Brace & World, 1966.

Time passes in America and Asia; in Europe, history occurs. We have this impression, perhaps, because Europe had a Middle Ages, a fusion of faith and action, politics and culture, symbol and reality, after which all things seem to disintegrate and decline. In Georges Bernanos' great sacerdotal novel, *The Diary of a Country Priest*, an old curé tells the hero, "Mind you, it's not that I'm taken in by the usual fairy-tale Middle Ages: people in the thirteenth century didn't pretend to be plaster saints. . . . But we were founding an empire, my boy, an empire that would have made the Caesars' effort look like so much mud." Further on, a soldier indicts the Church for abandoning the Middle Ages: "It was you who first pandered to the lawmakers of the Renaissance, whilst they made short work of Christian rights, and patiently constructed . . . the Pagan State: the state which knows no law but that of its own well-being—the merciless countries full of greed and pride." Medieval nostalgia, bumptiously expressed in English by Chesterton, is not confined to Roman Catholics but pervades secular Europe with a sense of loss, of a historical fall and a progressive demoralization. Modern man is man demoralized. "I'll define you a Christian people by the opposite," the curé says. "The opposite of a Christian people is a people grown sad and old." First went supernatural faith, then faith in kings, then faith in reason, then faith in nature, then faith in science, and, most lately, faith in the subconscious. The texture of prose and the art of narration have changed to fit the case; indeed, since *Don Quixote* fiction has to some extent thrived on disillusion. But in this century the minimal presupposition of human significance, the power of one human to touch another's heart, seems too much to be assumed. Love is, a current epigram* has it, "the friction of two epiderms," and, if Freud is to be believed, we spend our emotional lives vainly seeking, amid a crowd of phantoms, to placate our parent's ghosts. Such solipsism renders obsolete the interconnectedness of action that comprises "plot" and the trust in communication that gives a narration voice and pulse. Formless tales blankly told may be the end result; two recently published novels illustrate the trend.

Mouchette, Bernanos' last novel, has just been brought out. Written in 1937, it seems still older; no automobile violates the muddy roads of its Picard village, and it comes as a surprise to learn that Mouchette, the fourteen-year-old peasant outcast who is its heroine, sometimes sees the "faces of film-stars" in newspapers. The acrid rural poverty, the rain-whipped woods, the nocturnal poaching, the harsh pedantry of her school seem at least as old as Balzac, and of course Bernanos is an old-fashioned writer, Balzacian in his melodrama and in the importance he rather feverishly insists that his characters have. This quality, of feverishness, of inflamed significance, suggests unhealth, and the characters tangent to Mouchette include her bestially alcoholic father and brothers, a mother who suffocates before her eyes, an epileptic and raving poacher, and a gentle old female necrophile. Mouchette lives "on the edge of a stagnant pool," in a countryside whose sandy fields are "swarming with starving rabbits scarcely bigger than rats." The novel itself feels sinisterly underpopulated, as if a plague has passed. Yet these macabre circumstances are set forth in a vivid, even sprightly style constantly alert for telling natural details: "The soil, undermined by rabbits, gave way beneath her feet at almost every step, and if she kept to the edge of the wood, where the interlaced roots made the ground firmer, she was lashed

---

* Current but not recently coined. *"L'amour est l'assouvissement de deux désirs par le contact de deux épidermes"*—Chamfort (1741–1794).

by sodden branches." Or: "Nothing remained but the tall poplar, scarcely visible in the sky, murmuring like a spring." Gallic intelligence plays eagerly across the dismal village, scattering aphorisms on the subject of poverty:

> If the very poor could associate the various images of their poverty they would be overwhelmed by it, but their wretchedness seems to them to consist simply of an endless succession of miseries, a series of unfortunate chances.

> Lying had never seemed wrong to Mouchette, for it was the most precious—probably the only—privilege of the wretched.

> But once they have been induced to despair, the defences of the simple are irretrievably breached and their ignorance knows of no escape save suicide—the suicide of the poor, which is so like that of children.

Bernanos, as he expresses it in his terse foreword, "watched [Mouchette] live and die" with acute tenderness. Her interlude with Arsène, the poacher who shelters her from the rain, confesses to her that he has just committed murder, makes her his accomplice, and finally rapes her, is a superb scene, lit by fire and tempest and the dumb kindling of life within the girl.

> It did not occur to her to find Arsène's face handsome. It was simply that it seemed made for her, and seemed as easy and natural in her gaze as the handle of her old knife in her hand, the old knife which she had found on the road one evening, and had shown to no one, and which was the only thing in the world which she possessed. She would have liked to touch his face, but its golden color, as warm as that of bread, was enough to make her happy.

The idea of bread, beautifully transposed, echoes a few sentences later: "All the pleasure in looking at [his face] came not from him, but from the depths of herself, where it had lain hidden and germinating, like a seed of wheat beneath the snow."

In a 19th-century novel, Mouchette's encounter with Arsène would develop into a prolonged involvement, rich in recurrence and mutual reaction. It is *Mouchette*'s failure, yet also its seal of fidelity to its time, that nothing of the sort happens; the encounter leads nowhere. Arsène disappears, and Mouchette discovers that his crime was imaginary, rendering her pledge of self-sacrifice to him meaningless. Nothing connects. Moved in her extremity of misery to communicate with her mother, Mouchette confides to the deaf ear of a dead woman. The attentions of the villagers— not all of them hard-hearted—repel her exacerbated spirit; she is at last befriended by an old lady who cunningly invites her to die, to find in death the purity that the child naïvely associates with "the physical image of clear water." The image of the poplar "murmuring like a spring" returns as a tiny pool in a sand quarry, where "the water was so clear that no fish would live there." To this place Mouchette comes to terminate her brief story.

Though church bells ring in the distance, as they do in all European novels, God does not break His silence. The squalor is unredeemed. There is small trace of the author's ardent Catholicism (and where, in contemporary France, are the successors to Bernanos and Mauriac, Marcel and Maritain, Claudel and Péguy?) beyond his abrupt assurance that poverty is a "sacred sign." Mouchette's passage into despair yields no more of a moral than the slipping flight of a swallow across the smoky evening sky. Tragedy is dwindled to a mournful pang, a surrender, almost complacent, to universal indifference. Bernanos' Christianity lingers merely as a tone, as the outsize intensity with which he broods upon Mouchette's small lost soul.

This intensity is willfully absent from Uwe Johnson's *Two Views*. While *Mouchette* seems to belong to the past, *Two Views*, which takes place in the Berlin of 1961–1962, has the insubstantial quality of the future. Picardy's sodden fields have yielded to a papery world of maps (the endpapers are maps of the Berlin Wall), newspapers, passports, neon advertisements, airplane and train schedules, flimsy automobiles, and ambiguously worded love letters. The novel's structure is two-dimensional, switching in alternate chapters from the viewpoint of Dietbert, a young West German photographer, to that of Beate, an East Berlin nurse. The views and lives of both are transcribed, if the Winstons' translation is to be believed, in an intelligent but somehow preoccupied prose that hastens past crises to dwell with fond flatness upon daily routines.

Officially First Class was known as the chief's ward so that the patients in Second Class would think of it solely as the head doctor's private preserve, not a place where the patients enjoyed special privileges; unofficially, it was known simply as 1-b, after the traditional corridor whose rooms for a long time after the war had held four or five beds but by and by had been reduced once more to private or semiprivate setup.

That is Beate at work; here is Dietbert:

From a high apartment whose owner rented window places to the photographers he was able to take shots of the slender barrels which from his angle protruded over the border, with the line of battle-equipped soldiers drawn up in front of them, in the distance the conventional Soviet tanks with the white star. And if he happened to arrive when a refugee in the boundary canal had already been shot, another had already plunged to his death from a roof, he photographed the lingering crowd of onlookers, the soldiers in the cutters probing the water or the holes in the roof that the dead man had broken in the course of his fall; was able to sell these, and also the cloud of the teargas bomb that had driven the horde of photographers back from the scene. *Often he felt as if he were living in a movie.*

The pouncing italics are mine. These Iron-curtained lovers move jerkily, as if on celluloid; they seem immersed in "the gray racket of the television set." Their plight has been predigested by the voracious news media that instantly commercialize catastrophe. Furthermore, Dietbert is an indecisive blunderer, who keeps himself tranquillized with alcohol, and Beate a faintly drab prig.

Yet through this crust of inconsequence—indeed, credible because of it—eros breaks, and the perfunctory liaison and nearly accidental reunion of Dietbert and Beate serves, at least for me, as a moving parable of human love and as a sufficient indictment of the political systems that would separate us, "the merciless countries full of greed and pride." Johnson, a native of Pomerania who in 1959 became a West Berliner, does not weight the argument between East and West; Dietbert's need to acquire a fancy sports car beyond his means is as debilitating as Beate's search, in the Communist housing jungle, for a private room. The vulgar scramble of capitalism is balanced against the obstinate bureaucracy of Socialism. Beate does not wish to mingle her friends from the two

Berlins, for "the former would have ridiculed the latter for their faith in the prospects of the East German state, and the latter the former for ignorance of society and the tendency under the influence of alcohol to despair loudly and tearfully of the meaning of life." Partition is made visible as, from a West German airplane, "the transition from the small patches of color on the ground to the large fields that marked East German territory" and, from an East Berlin tram, as "the wet glittering red of neon advertising in West Berlin." If a political emotion is present, it is a Berliner's frustration over the sundering of his city, which becomes, on the human level, a need to have lovers—however mediocre, vague, and ignorant of one another—reunite. Beate's escape, whose methodical details build into a terrific cinematic suspense, is a leap of the heart, a change of angle more than of locus. From where she arrives she can see the platform from which she left. Dietbert, hastening to meet her, misses connections and winds up in a hospital, where he becomes to Beate "a patient like any other." The ending, though not what we expect, seems happy; the author, who in *Mouchette* was a grieving, helpless God, ambles into the last pages as an ordinary Berlin citizen, exuding normal human warmth. The post-apocalyptic irresolution of *Two Views* may well be where European man, after history's extravagant demands, is glad to settle.

The View from the Dental Chair

LOCAL ANAESTHETIC, by Günter Grass, translated from the German by Ralph Manheim. 284 pp. Harcourt, Brace & World, 1970.

"If you're out to buy a pig, talk about the weather." This "old peasant rule" is quoted in Günter Grass's fourth novel, *Local Anaesthetic*, and the book illustrates the tactic. As the author talks, with manic erudition and rather lumpy explicitness, about such weather as dentistry, cement, Seneca, battles, German history, and the aquarium care of guppies, the pig nearly gets away. For the first half of the novel, there are no characters one can visualize, no action one can follow, no reason to persevere, indeed, but the faith that this quirky experiment will begin to add up. And it finally does, into a well-meditated if fliply presented dialogue on the generation gap and the revolutionary urge. "Fliply"—as when one flips the channel knob on a television set. Grass's dominant metaphor and method derive from the medium of television, with its rapid intercuts, its numbing discontinuity, its ectoplasmic freedom from the laws of either truth or art. The framing conceit is this: Eberhard Starusch, a West Berlin schoolteacher, is having his toothache and life-long prognathic bite corrected by capping. His dentist, an omniscient prattler in tennis shoes, distracts his patients with a television screen, where old films and educational panels and lewd commercials and gauzy static flow indiscriminately on. Into this flow, Starusch, his mouth stoppered with cotton and aluminum, mentally hurls scenes supposedly from his life, many of which are mere fantasies. He several times murders, for instance, his ex-fiancée, the goatlike Sieglinde Krings, employing such special weapons as a bicycle chain and a swimming-pool wave-generating machine; the truth seems to be that she is alive and married to an electrician called Schlottau. Or was really named Monica Lindrath and has become a pediatrician. Similarly, Starusch's career as an engineer for the Krings cement works seems a grandiose blow-up of a summer job he had, as a student, with a different company. And what of Krings, the cement-and-pumice magnate returned from prisoner-of-war captivity, the stoic ex-general who spends his dotage reconstructing old battle sites in sandboxes and refighting old defeats into victories? He, too, dissolves into shadow play. Apparitions succeed one another in segments often less than a page long. A sample:

> The soundless picture showed a clerical-looking gentleman who, it being Saturday, wished to say a word about Sunday, although this program is televised after 10 p.m. and never before the Berlin evening news: "Yes, yes, my son, I know, it hurts. But all the pain in the world is powerless to . . ."
> (His finely articulated fingers. When he raised an eyebrow in mockery. Or his delayed head-shaking: Scherbaum calls him Silvertongue.)
> Then the bells rang in Sunday: Bim!—And the pigeons rose up

in fright. Boom!—Ah, and the little tin satellites in my head that knows it all tinkled: Bim! Poom! Pumice!

Grass's shuttle of scenes becomes as fatiguing and irritating as a battery of TVs manipulated by invisible children; verily, one's teeth begin to hurt, sensitized by unsparingly dental doses of short-circuited prose:

> (Eased, tapered off, hardly to be remembered. One more twinge —but that may have been a reflex—then silence.) Outside it was snowing from left to right on Hohenzollerndamm. (Not the .TV, the street side of the office.) The screen was uninhabited. Like my-self: all fuzzy and, I may as well say it, deaf. ("I'm told that anaesthetized tongues have been maimed by the experimental bites of incredulous patients.") His voice was wrapped in tinfoil. ("And now we'll take off the aluminum shells. . . ." And my question— "What do you mean, take off?"—was also muffled as it rose up to fill blubbery balloons. Not until he breathed at me from close, too close, up: "They are removed with tweezers. Kindly open wide," did I surrender and make my big Ah.

Grass's artistic temperament, from *The Tin Drum* on, has been drawn to the gritty and mechanical; even in a nostalgic idyll like *Cat and Mouse*, he devotes a disproportion of words to the me-chanics of getting in and out of a sunken minesweeper and to chemical substances such as flakes of rust and gull droppings. His plots snag on small operational procedures: *The Tin Drum* opens by specifying how a woman rotates five skirts, wearing four and washing one each week. His characterizations ponderously depend on physical deformities—dwarfishness, protuberant ears, a gro-tesque Adam's apple. Whereas Starusch has a prognathic bite, his young antagonist, Scherbaum, turns out to have the opposite de-fect, a distal bite, and is last seen wearing a corrective labial bar. Grass's prose is physically encumbered, chunky, resistant. Even if we allow for the losses of rhythm and penumbral connotation inevitable in any translation, we miss the plastic ease of expression and interconnection that until recently was the common property of even mediocre European writers. The ability, preëminent in Tolstoy, to move exciting spiritual currents through masses of circumstance and sensuous detail is perhaps lost, along with the instinctive belief in the dualism of matter and spirit. Strange to say, materialism in fiction seems to reduce the vitality of physical description, to make it clot into topographic (Robbe-Grillet) or professional (Grass) detail. Compared to relatively recent masters of European humanism like Proust and Mann, Grass is hard to read, hard to "get going" in. His device of aping television, however witty and timely and rigorously exploited, feels superimposed; it is a gesture of the author rather than an outgrowth of the material. Who, we wonder as we read, really retains his life in film-clip form, who but an author at his desk would project these overanimated parables of German guilt and unease?

In an interview given a few weeks ago in New York, Grass spoke of *Mief*, of the stale air that envelops every group and gathering and conversation in the West. His narrative device of a televised, self-cancelling clutter does work as a metaphor for *Mief*, like the cement dust that grayly settles upon every leaf in Krings Park. In his obsessive sense of static, grit, and dust, this author is true to himself; he is true to himself when he moves from romantic triangles that bore him, and from echoes of the Nazi nightmare that are beginning to bore him, into political debates that, though wreathed in *Mief*, interest him. Grass's role as an active campaigner and spokesman for the Social Democratic Party finds a happy correlative in Starusch's role of schoolteacher.

Starusch wants his pupil Scherbaum to take over the school paper and run it, working toward such liberal/reformist objectives as creating a student smokers' corner. Scherbaum instead opts for the radical gesture of burning Max, his pet dachshund, alive, in the heart of cake-eating, dog-loving Berlin, as a protest against the Vietnam war. He is encouraged not only by his Maoist girl friend but by Starusch's female colleague, Irmgard Seifert, who is tormented by the guilt she incurred as a "Hitler bitch" at the age of seventeen. Starusch tries to reason the boy out of it, and, failing, offers to substitute a stray from the dog pound for Max. The boy is tempted, but Starusch then denounces his own plan as "exploitation, rank imperialism." Next, he conceives the idea of poisoning the dog, to "deprive Scherbaum of the object of his demonstration. React radically to a radical project." Throughout all this maneuvering, he confers with his dentist, who speaks suavely from the melioristic center:

"And how do you feel about napalm, Doc?"

"Well, measured against the nuclear weapons known to us, napalm must be termed relatively harmless."

"And what about the living conditions of the Iranian peasants?"

"In the light of conditions in India we can speak, with all due reserve, of a relatively progressive agrarian structure in Iran, though compared to the Sudan India may well strike us as a reformer's paradise."

"Then you see progress!"

"Within limits, my friend, within limits."

In the whirlwind of argument and gesture that surrounds the unwitting dachshund, everybody has something to say. The schoolteacher urges his students "to try to understand the world in all its variety and contradiction." Youth scorns "the daily capitulations characteristic of adults" and prescribes "spontaneous action" as the only way "to make room . . . for new foundations on which to build a pacified existence." The dentist looks toward a day of "worldwide Sickcare" and warns that "with all its display of realism, this younger generation is looking for a new myth. Watch your step!" The terms of the debate are familiar to Americans, but not explicated so many-sidedly, with the charity of humor, and with the specifically German dimension of a disastrous "transvaluation of all values" (Nietzsche's phrase) that did occur. Starusch, though with the dentist's help he seduces his pupil from caninocide, is left with a vision of the violence within himself, a desire to strangle and drown Sieglinde and to bulldoze away all the suffocating junk of industrial affluence. The very tartar on his teeth, the dentist tells him, is "petrified hatred." Seneca is the dentist's favorite philosopher, and the last sentences have a stoic ring: "Nothing lasts. There will always be pain." Grass himself, evidently, has complained that his final phrase in German—"*immer neue Schmerzen*" ("always new pains")—is more active; "new pains are always coming" might be more faithful and faintly more optimistic. Yet the difficulty is inherent; the dentist, like him or not, has the best lines, and the dust jacket, designed by Grass himself, shows a finger over a candle flame—an allusion to the most primitive dental anesthetic, which was to divide the pain by holding the patient's hand over a candle, and a symbol of all our palliations. All anesthetic is local.

Snail on the Stump

FROM THE DIARY OF A SNAIL, by Günter Grass, translated from the German by Ralph Manheim. 310 pp. Harcourt Brace Jovanovich, 1972.

Günter Grass addresses his newest book, *From the Diary of a Snail*, to his four children. The eldest of *my* four children once, under the illusion that she could turn pebbles into jewels, acquired a bright little machine that, loaded with gray sludge and plugged into a socket, revolved and tumbled to a hypothetical lustre whatever bits of the material universe were put inside. That curious device (now defunct) offers the best analogy I can think of to Grass's present authorial method. The gray sludge is *Mief* or "melancholy"—the leaden aura of staleness and inertia possessed by compromised, relative, muddled, hashed-over, snail's-pace reality. The electricity is Grass's phenomenal energy, not only intellectual but personal, soulful, human; however farfetched his fancies, Grass (like the not dissimilarly mustachioed Kurt Vonnegut) convinces us that his heart remains in the right place. The bits of rough matter are whatever obsessions he finds simultaneous within him: in this book, snails, children, hermaphroditism, Dürer's print entitled *Melencolia I*, the fate of the Danzig Jews, the suicide of Manfred Augst (real), the adventures of Hermann Ott (fictional), and the 1969 West German elections, wherein Grass contributed nearly a hundred speeches to Willy Brandt's successful campaign. While functioning, Grass's narrative engine, like the polishing machine, seems inexhaustible and distinctly unmusical, at least in translation. Though my daughter's polisher ran for days and weeks without stopping, the rocks and shards inside never shed, along with their incidental roughnesses, the core of obduracy that makes sea-smoothed stones so dryly disappointing when arranged on the summer cottage mantelpiece. And when *From the Diary of a Snail* stops shuddering and churning, what tumbles out, though of a certain sheen, is not a work of art.

Not that art is overtly aspired to. The snail's diary began as a

Sudelbuch, a scribble book, a book of jottings Grass carried with him on the campaign trail: "My entries come to me on the road. . . . I mean to speak to you by roundabout bypaths: sometimes offended and enraged, often withdrawn and hard to pin down, occasionally brimful of lies, until everything becomes plausible." Some of the notations, then, deal with the incidents of the municipal hall and the hotel room; some are comments on the author's allies in the Social Democratic Party and his enemies in the Christian Democratic Union. A portrait of Germany filters through the jottings—the Germany of the postwar economic miracle (". . . and now after twenty-five years. From rubble and ashes we. From scratch. And today we are once more"), a Germany of glimpses (". . . air shafts, garages, squares, warehouses, building sites, railroad tracks, the city park, the restored Old City: swans and shingled roofs as in the prospectus"), a Germany of little cities Grass particularizes with his nice eye for local industry:

> A small town not far from the Dutch border, which, saturated with history and swan lore, was destroyed shortly before the end of the war, and even today, rebuilt in its original small-checkered pattern, looks as if it were about to fall apart. (Little industry—children's shoes and margarine . . .). . . . Or in Bocholt, where the textile crisis (Erhard calls it a "healthy shrinkage") feeds discussion. . . . I visited a factory where stopwatches are assembled and chatted with the shop committee in a room whose walls were decorated with framed photographs of famous sprinters. . . .

"How beautiful Germany is. So transparently impenetrable. So eerily innocent. So different and the same wherever you go," Grass exclaims as he goes about speechifying, sitting in endless conferences, answering questions, coping with radical youths ("And I discover with what a prodigy of deception hate fosters beauty in youthful faces"), trying "to pull the weeds of German idealism, which spring up again as inexorably as rib grass."

Upon this campaign diary Grass permits to intrude—or has imposed in two years of revision—a number of other concerns, tales, devices, and designs. The primary conceit, which wears out before the book does, is that all this is addressed to his children (Franz, Raoul, Laura, and Bruno) as a justification of their father's long absences in what little Bruno calls the "fight with the whale" (*Walkampf* = *Wahlkampf* = election campaign). Four piping voices break into print, and the paternal author responds with a lecture, an evasion, a piece of self-portraiture, or a digression; his youth in Danzig, for instance, mushrooms into a considerable detailed history of Danzig's ten thousand Jews after the free city was incorporated into Hitler's Germany. Danzig also suggests to Grass a fictional person, a Gentile named Hermann Ott, nick-named Doubt, who teaches in a Jewish school before the war and hides throughout the war in the cellar of a Kashubian bicycle dealer, Anton Stomma; Ott's invented story is the most character-istically Grassian, and most easily followed, thread in this tangle of motifs. An academic thread is the lecture Grass has promised to give on Dürer's dark and symbolically fraught etching *Melen-colia I;* he carries a print with him on the campaign, ruminates in his *Sudelbuch* about it, attempts to see his own efforts of "talk-talktalk" in the light of an abiding opposition between Melencolia and her sister Utopia, and ends the book with the lecture itself, which is excellent and might seem even better had not its major points been several times adumbrated in the preceding pages. An-other theme intrudes when, during the campaign, at an Evangelical Church congress in Stuttgart, a fifty-six-year-old man takes the microphone, delivers a jumbled harangue about fellowship, con-cludes, "Now I've got a provocation for you: I salute my comrades of the S.S.," sits down, drinks something, and dies. His last words are wonderful; turning to the girl student beside him, he says, "That, young lady, was cyanide." The man's name is Manfred Augst, and, though Grass feels he knows his type well—a typical German craving "annihilation and redemption"—he cannot forget the incident, and finally interviews Augst's widow and children. We also witness Grass interviewing Danzig Jews who now live in Israel, and see him taking a vacation with his family in Brittany, and are treated to several recipes and poems of his concoction, and to a rather opaque glorification of Willy Brandt as a kind of recessive Superman—"a man . . . whose loneliness draws large crowds," a man whose "slow, steady ascent" is a "snail's career." Snails, of course, are meant to be the unifying metaphor and theme of this farrago. They peep in everywhere. Hermann Ott collects snails, and a lively abundance of circumstantial snail lore is given, from the "foamy crackling" they emit in even a state of rest to the "calcareous darts (known as love arrows)" that hermaphroditic Roman snails thrust into the soles of one another's feet. The trouble is that the snail symbolizes too many things: Willy Brandt, the vagina, melancholy embodied, the human masses, moderate progressiveness, the author himself. "With my forward, inward drive, with my tendency to dwell, hesitate, and cling, with my restlessness and emotional haste, I am snail-like." Grass is one of the "progressive mobile snails," as opposed to the "conservative clinging snails"—though in the muddle of events and the fug of staleness and "talktalktalk" only an expert could tell the difference. And only a snail-lover could feel that the image is not overworked, overloaded, and harped upon with too much random ingenuity.

What we want from our great imaginers is not fuel but fire, not patterns but an action, not fragmented and interlaced accounts but a story. Amid all this personal and apologetical rubble one story moves, as follows: When Hermann Ott takes refuge in the cellar of Anton Stomma, the household includes Stomma's daughter Lisbeth. She is fair, plump, and stupefied. In the first four days of the war her Polish lover and her small son have been killed; she spends much time visiting cemeteries, and performs all her duties, which come to include sleeping with Ott, in a daze of unfeeling. "She lay mute under his thrusts, which struck the void." Further obliging, she brings him snails from her cemeteries; one day she introduces into Ott's cellar an unidentifiable purple-red slug. By accident, he discovers that when the slug is placed on her skin Lisbeth begins to stammer. Soon she is talking, then laughing; she ceases visiting cemeteries and goes instead to a hairdresser's; she awakens sexually. As her cure progresses, the snail, with each application to her flesh, becomes more discolored and hideous. "It was as though the unidentified slug had sucked up Lisbeth's melancholy, possibly her black bile." The cure is complete; as normal femininity returns to her, she becomes a normal woman—demanding, willful, squeamish. The bloated and black "suction snail" disgusts her. On the first Sunday of Advent in 1944, she steps on it. "It burst with a full-bodied report. On the inside, too, it was black." After the war, she and Ott marry, but he falls prey to melancholia and spends more and more of his time in cemeteries, searching for another of the melancholy-curing snails. Finally, Lisbeth commits him to an asylum. Now, this story is not patently edifying; mysterious and unpleasant and pessimistic, it does not tell us how to vote in the next election. But it draws resonance from an actuality beyond explanation; it objectifies the teller's feelings, sensations, and convictions so that they carry into us more penetratingly than any declarative statement. The snail Grass has from his own substance produced a love arrow. The story takes place in a chilly cellar redolent of the muddy potato lands that are this author's peculiar terrain. Imaginations seem to be as choosy as mollusks about the soil they inhabit; amid a great deal of mental travelogue, this one episode sticks fast and dankly lives.

In fairness to Grass, and with no aspersion on the efforts of Mr. Manheim, who for all I know has done the best of all possible jobs, one feels that exceptionally much has been lost in translation. The poems flung into this diary must be better than they seem. For every piece of wordplay that is explained in a footnote, there must be several too delicate to unravel. Grass's curious trick of unpunctuated word-triplets ("bitter tired finished," "went stood lay") must appear less gratuitous in German. Throughout, the skin of words feels a little raw in English, lacking its epiderm of intelligent verbal nervousness, of voiced sensitivity. And of course the many references to contemporary political figures strike chords muffled here. We do not so much read this book as overhear it: a German is speaking to Germans, intimately and urgently. For Grass, in addition to the universal duties of a writer, has the local duty, with all the German writers of his generation, of guarding and barring the path back into Hell.

Witold Who?

FERDYDURKE, by Witold Gombrowicz, translated from the Polish by Eric Mosbacher. 272 pp. Grove Press, 1967.

PORNOGRAFIA, by Witold Gombrowicz, translated by Alastair Hamilton from the French translation from the Polish by Georges Lisowski. 191 pp. Grove Press, 1967.

Witold Gombrowicz, a Polish writer born in 1904, is being set forward as a master, whose not very copious complete works, mostly composed in the obscurity of Argentine exile, are to be published in America by that zealous exhumer of overlooked classics, Grove Press. The project begins* with two novels—*Ferdydurke* and *Pornografia*. Gombrowicz's claim to be—to quote *L'Express*—"the greatest unknown writer of our time" has reached us via the French, who took him up after his triumphant but short-lived resurrection in Poland itself, during a moment (in 1957) of cultural thaw.

Ferdydurke (the word is Polish schoolboy slang meaning nothing in particular) came out, with considerable success, in 1937 but was suppressed under both the Nazis and the Communists. In Gomulka's Poland of 1957, the novel's burlesque of psychological tyrannies, its premonitions of brainwashing, and its sharp savor of the prewar avant garde must have seemed liberating. The French presumably found congenial Gombrowicz's mixture of intellection and impudence, his familiar air of knowledgeable disillusion. This country may find its own contemporary style reflected in his free-wheeling "black humor" and his avid delineation of interpersonal "games." Myself, I must register my sensation that *Ferdydurke*, a book about the imposition of form, has itself more the form— the assurance, the daring—of greatness than the substance. Beneath the energetic surface there is a static difficulty of event. The recurrent motifs seem merely curious—a strange jealousy of

---

* And evidently ended there: two promised further works, the novel *The Trans-Atlantic* and Gombrowicz's *Diary*, still await, eight years later, publication.

the young, an eccentric trick of seeing human bodies as assemblies of parts. Compared with the ideas (the recovery of time through involuntary memory, the eventual union of the paths of innocence and experience) that give momentum to Proust's masses of description, or with Kafka's intuitions of exclusion and interminability, Gombrowicz's themes are spindly, infertile, too much insisted upon, too little dramatized. There is, at least for a reader deprived of the nuances of the original Polish, not much warmth, of the kind that led Nathalie Sarraute to liken classics to furnaces still giving off the heat of their passion for reality.

In the most up-to-date manner, Gombrowicz disarms criticism by including it in his text, mocking the reader's eagerness "to evaluate and to assess, and to decide whether the work is a novel, or a book of memories, or a parody, or a lampoon, or a variation on imaginative themes, or a psychological study; and to establish its predominant characteristics; whether the whole thing is a joke, or whether its importance lies in its deeper meaning, or whether it is just irony, sarcasm, ridicule, invective, downright stupidity and nonsense, or a piece of pure leg-pulling." *Ferdydurke* is peppered with essays on itself, disarming admissions of its own confusion, invitations to "start dancing with the book instead of asking for meanings." Its author, in the preface to *Pornografia*, writes in an almost liturgical vein, "*Ferdydurke* is undoubtedly my basic work. . . . [It] is intended to reveal the Great Immaturity of humanity. Man, as he is described in this book, is an opaque and neutral being who has to express himself by certain means of behavior and therefore becomes, from outside—for others—far more definite and precise than he is for himself. Hence a tragic disproportion between his secret immaturity and the mask he assumes when he deals with other people. All he can do is to adapt himself internally to his mask, as though he really were what he appears to be." This thesis, however true (and perhaps it seemed truer in the 1930's; might not Fascism be understood as a country's attempt to become "far more definite and precise" than it feels?), is erratically borne out by the narrative, which comes to life in some areas and churns unconvincingly in others.

Ferdydurke begins with a diatribe against literary criticism, and here Gombrowicz is very funny. The narrator (named Johnnie in most places and Anton Swistak in one episode) observes that "the more inept and petty criticism is, the more constricting it is, like a tight shoe." The experience of publishing a book is "like being born in a thousand rather narrow minds." He envies men of letters whose minds move perpetually toward the heights "just as if their backsides had been pricked with a pin!" He inveighs against cultural "aunts," and creates his main comic character, the Cracow philologist Pimko, who enters the room, spots the opening pages of this novel on the desk, and cries, "Well! Well! Well! An author! Let me immediately criticize, encourage, advise!" With "masterly composure" Pimko sits and reads, while Johnnie inwardly writhes: "The minutes lasted for hours and the seconds were unnaturally extended, and I was ill at ease, like a sea that somebody was trying to suck up through a straw." Gombrowicz expresses more vividly than I have seen elsewhere the something intolerable about a literary establishment—any literary establishment. If a harsh Providence were to obliterate, say, Alfred Kazin, Richard Gilman, Stanley Kauffmann, and Irving Howe, tomorrow new critics would arise with the same worthy intelligence, the same complacently agonized humanism, the same inability to read a book except as a disappointing version of one they might have written, the same deadly "auntiness." Gombrowicz's irritation is heartfelt, and the whole style of the book—its fragmentation, its tauntingness, its serene implausibility, its violent catalogues and metaphors—sustains his protest against "being tied to the cultural aunts' apron strings."

Pimko takes the thirty-year-old narrator in hand and unaccountably but irresistibly places him in school, among cruel and obscene boys extolled for their "innocence." Two schoolmates, Mientus and Siphon, engage in a grotesque combat: "The two contestants will stand facing each other and will make a series of faces. Each and every constructive and beautiful face made by Siphon will be answered by an ugly and destructive counter-face made by Mientus. The faces made will be as personal and as wounding as possible, and the contestants will continue to make them until a final decision is reached." Mientus scowls, spits, and dips his finger into a spittoon, but Siphon implacably points at the sky; "his face became diffused with seven colors, like a rainbow after a storm, and lo! there he stood in seven colors, the Boy Scout, Purity Incarnate, the Innocent Adolescent." Defeated, Mientus shouts filth into Siphon's ears, and Siphon dies.

All encounters, for Gombrowicz, are a species of duel by gesture, a clash of impersonations. The opening episode with Pimko and the narrator is such a contest: "He remained seated, so firmly and inexorably seated that the fact of his sitting, though intolerably stupid, was nevertheless all-powerful." Into the main narrative is spliced the anecdote of "Philifor Honeycombed with Childishness," wherein two philosophers—the greatest synthesist of all time and his arch-opponent, the analyst Anti-Philifor—duel by pruning with gunfire the bodies of their wife and mistress, finally killing them both. Johnnie, still a schoolboy, goes to live with a banally "modern" family called the Youthfuls and is caught up in a fierce duel of love with Zutka, the daughter. His maneuvers grow in complexity and ferocity and finally plunge the Youthfuls, plus Pimko, plus a schoolmate, into a lunatic melee, freeing the hero to launch himself into "Asphalt. Emptiness. Dew. Nothing." An antic essay interposes, and a shaggy-dog story symmetrically titled "Philimor Honeycombed with Childishness." The narrative moves to the country estate of Johnnie's rich aunt and Mientus' struggle to fraternize with a stableboy. The consequent duel of class consciousness and physical abuse culminates in yet another, crueller fray. At the end, Johnnie abducts his cousin Isabel, and then flees the blackmail of compliments and kisses ("I writhed under the blows of her admiration as under Satan's whip") that passes, in the Gombrowiczian universe, for heterosexual love.

What is the core of this repetitive whirligig of pretense, bluff, and annihilation? At one point in the country house, four men find themselves in total darkness, standing paralyzed by fear within inches of one another, unable to move, and Johnnie experiences "a sense of becoming enormous, gigantic and simultaneously a sense of growing smaller, shrinking and stiffening, a sense of escape and at the same time a kind of general and particular impoverishment, a sense of paralysing tension and tense paralysis, of being hung by a tense thread, as well as of being converted and changed into something, a sense of transmutation and also of relapse into a kind of accumulating and mounting mechanism." In this frozen moment of overwhelming, contradictory sensation, we seem close to Gombrowicz's central inkling—the duel between consciousness and will. Awareness mocks and clogs and warps action. From our sticky web of apprehension, sporadic and incongruous deeds shake loose. The narrator, "while suspense and repetition still remained ceaselessly at work," abruptly moves: "Suddenly I insolently moved and stepped behind the curtain." In the context of these pages even such a small exercise of volition is intensely dramatic. Perhaps the composition of *Ferdydurke* can be understood as another such act, a random, twitched escape from paralysis. Hence the book's flaws of flimsiness and centrifugality, hence the monotonous mood of wry nervousness. Gombrowicz has made his move, but he is not yet at home behind the curtain.

Pornografia, written twenty years later, is a more conventional and integrated work, perfectly shaped and thoroughly sinister. Set in the Nazi-occupied Poland of 1943 (where Gombrowicz never was), "at the depths of the *fait accompli*," the novel tells of the hyper-subtle corruption worked upon an adolescent boy and girl by a pair of middle-aged Warsaw intellectuals, one of whom is Gombrowicz himself. He narrates the story in accents grimmer and neater than the quirky pellmell of *Ferdydurke*. Compare a landscape from each of these novels:

> Overhead there were fat little reddish, bluish, and whitish clouds, which looked as if they were made of silk paper, sorry and sentimental-looking. Everything was so vague and confused in outline, so silent, so chaste, so full of waiting, so unborn and undefined, that in reality nothing was separate or distinct from anything else; on the contrary, everything was connected with everything else in the bosom of a single, thick, whitish and silent, extinguished mass. Tenuous little brooks murmured, wetted the earth, vaporized or bubbled. And this world dwindled and seemed to shrink, and as it shrank it seemed to tighten, to close round your throat, like a delicate cord strangling you.

> We reached the top of the hill and were confronted with the unaltered view: the earth rising in hills, swollen in a motionless surge in the slanting light which here and there pierced the clouds.

The first is a wordy conjuration of vagueness whose gaiety
tugs strangely against the metaphor of strangulation with which
it is clinched. The second, also vague, needs no specification of
the emotion it is meant to arouse; there is no doubt that we are in
the drab reaches of rural Poland, in a sordid trough of history.
"An oppressive smell of iniquity permeated this landscape," the
author observes, and, in town, on the next page, notices that "something was missing—there were no Jews." Jews are not mentioned
again, and Germans are hardly ever seen. The thematic and meta-
phoric furniture of *Pornografia* is as economically distributed as
the personnel of its plot; the rabid envy of young people, for
instance, which seemed eccentric in the thirtyish author of
Ferdydurke, comes plausibly from a fifty-year-old man "already
poisoned by death." The duels—between a Catholic and an atheist,
between a panicked resistance leader and a household—cluster
tightly around the core struggle of the two adolescents and the
two old men, who are themselves involved in a duel of implication and avoidance. The gratuitous, sudden actions—a boy pulling
up an old woman's skirt, an old woman attacking and biting a
boy—all serve to advance the action by enlarging the possibilities
of depravity, and to enforce the image of man as "an angelic and
demonic abyss, steeper than a mirror!" The notion of "form" has
been reduced to a biting Dostoevskian essence: "There are certain
human deeds which seem totally senseless, but which are necessary
for man because they define him." The notion of "youth" has
succinctly become: "After the age of thirty men lapse into monstrosity." All mutual existence is mutual blackmail. Inexorably the
elements of *Pornografia* combine, in its less than two hundred
pages, to transmute the most delicate and obscurely felt inter-
relations into a climax of multiple murder. The book has the clean
cruelty of *Laughter in the Dark*, without Nabokov's playful pup-
petry; it has the moral pessimism of *Les Liaisons Dangereuses*,
without de Laclos' peremptory restoration of virtue.

In short, Gombrowicz, an apostle of immaturity, has maturely
subdued his formal preoccupations and instinctive obsessions to
the principles of art and created, in his own prefatory words, "a
noble, a classical novel . . . a sensually metaphysical novel." Is
this victory at all Pyrrhic? Have the determined insights and

dramatic thrust of *Pornografia* been obtained at the cost of a certain honesty present in the confusions of *Ferdydurke*? For in penetrating the imaginative curtain separating him from wartime Poland, and in creating behind it a coherent "classical" action, he in a sense hides; a book like *Ferdydurke* exists as a fantastical gloss upon the real world, whereas *Pornografia* is a small world complete in itself and sealed by its own completeness as if in cellophane. Its consummate finish deprives it of osmotic margins; it becomes an object we can turn our backs on, having experienced its catharsis, its systematic arousal and relief of suspense. Does the world require many more such novels? Or does history insist that the writer abolish, by exhortation and trickery, the glaring edge that divides the proscenium novel from its audience of readers? Ask Dr. Pimko, or some other kindly aunt.

Inward and Onward

THE INWARD TURN OF NARRATIVE, by Erich Kahler, translated by Richard and Clara Winston. 216 pp. Princeton, 1973.

Erich Kahler, the late literary philosopher and polymath, published some fifteen years ago, in the *Neue Rundschau*, two long essays on the development of narrative technique and perspective which have now been published in the Bollingen series as *The Inward Turn of Narrative*. Kahler's thesis is more easily stated than grasped. His first sentence proposes "to show the vast changes in the modern novel as the consequence of a process that has been at work throughout the whole history of Western man," and this process seems simply the development of consciousness: "Literary history will be considered here as an aspect of the history of consciousness." The "inward turn" of narrative is in fact an outward envelopment, our mental incorporation of more and more of the outer world: "Man constantly draws outer space into his inner space, into an inner space newly created by consciousness. The world is integrated into the ego, into the illuminated self." This grand one-way process (Kahler speaks of "advancing conscious-

ness" with the confident progressivism of a 19th-century coloni-
alist) finds literary reflection in surprising proportions. Three
brisk sentences, and all of primitive narrative sweeps by:

> Initially, the process of internalization of narrative consists in
> gradually bringing the narrated material down to earth and breath-
> ing into it a human soul. Narrative begins with cosmogonies and
> theogonies. Slowly, then, the themes descend to the level of annals
> and chronicles, to the recording of specific earthly events.

The reader takes this "slowly" on faith, for very rapidly, in
Kahler's exposition, we arrive at Homer and the Old Testament,
narratives of pronounced sophistication and "humanness." Of pre-
Homeric tales, the only example discussed is the fragmentary
Babylonian epic of Gilgamesh, which, though "still entirely within
the primal mythic chaos," does present, in the friendship between
Gilgamesh and Enkidu, an "impulse to attain humanity"; "in it
man is increasingly brought down to earth, is liberated from his
primal link with the elemental powers." More seems meant than
demythicization of experience; as the gods recede into a distinctly
separate realm, feeling arises out of the "internalization of raw
event. By stirring the imagination narration itself—in contradis-
tinction to mere chronicle—provokes feeling." When we arrive,
with Homer, at the threshold of Western literature, the gap between "chronicle" and imaginative "narration" has already been
crossed.

> There can be no doubt that the articulation of human experience
> in the Homeric epic is far beyond that of the Babylonian epic. . . .
> In the Old Testament, finally, complete humanness is revealed.

What remains, humanness revealed, is relatively a matter of detail,
and of increasingly detailed description of masterpieces. With
Virgil's *Aeneid* deliberate artistic construction appears in the epic
form. Early in the Christian era, "novelty itself, the novella," adds
to the telling of acts of heroism and martyrdom "the relation
of curious incidents, preferably spiced with eroticism." Then
"Christian influence [leaves] a new residue in narrative: deliberate,
imposed meaning." With the Renaissance dawns individual psychology; from Boccaccio on, narration becomes "entirely a psychological process." The rise of cities generates a sharp contrast

between town and nature, burgher and knight; from this contrast arises what Kahler calls "the romantic situation": on the one hand, the burgher's illicit impulses and fantasies find embodiment in the obsolete figure of the knight, and, on the other, the "new objectifying awareness of nature" produces sensuous natural description and a complementary realism in the depiction of social classes. Milieu deepens its substance; "perspectivistic narrative" arrives, somewhat later than perspectivistic painting. Of this "baroque" period's masterworks—Cervantes' *Don Quixote*, Grimelshausen's *Simplicissimus*, Rabelais' *Pantagruel* and *Gargantua*—*Don Quixote* is especially momentous, because it supplies the first fully realized instance of "ascending symbolism"; that is, symbolism which proceeds from an individual instance to supra-individual significance entirely within a human world created by the artist, rather than the "descending symbolism" of the Greeks and Dante, wherein the signification descends upon the individual from a higher reality—a divine or mythic entity. From Cervantes on, the writer builds the symbolic structure out of himself, and the reader extracts it *for* himself. This immense "internalization" achieved, little distance remains to modern narrative. Milton, intending to portray the Christian cosmos, unwittingly dramatizes instead the "vast, immeasurable Abyss" opened to view by the new astronomy, and man's dreadful, defiant autonomy within it. First-person narratives such as those of Marivaux, Defoe, and Richardson move the narrator's observation post deeper into the interior of the confessing ego. Eighteenth-century poets, under the influence of deism, for the first time make nature an independent object of observation. As the invention of the microscope opens on the other side of man an infinity as daunting as that revealed through the telescope, Swift, in *Gulliver's Travels*, rings a number of changes on the theme of relativity and arrives at an absolute condemnation of man. And in *Tristram Shandy*—"an end and a beginning, a harvest and a new sowing"—Sterne, making narrative entirely willful and sequence and time dependent upon the narrator's whim, so imbues reality "with the patterns, structures, and techniques of consciousness that the creatively working consciousness finds itself face to face with its own image."

This complex world, which already includes the phenomena of cognition and imagination—this already half-internalized world—becomes the raw material which is handed on to Romanticism as its reality.

There Kahler ends, having surprised us as much with what he dwells upon as with what he skimps. Even in the sparest summary, the book's scope and strength of synthesizing vision must be apparent. Many passing critical felicities adorn the exposition: Milton's Hell, he says, becomes "almost a colony of paradise"; Pope's linguistic wit "is constantly overflowing and leaving no room to breathe." The critic's essential service of *recommending* is enthusiastically performed; I can hardly wait to read *Clarissa* and *Simplicissimus*. The translators append their regret that Kahler did not live to revise his German articles for publication in English, but the translation reads well, and such imbalances toward the German as exist—conspicuously, the lengthy quotation from the poet Barthold Heinrich Brockes—are rather refreshing. Kahler was unaffectedly erudite in at least three European literatures, and the reader of English can only be pleased by the importance assigned Chaucer, Milton, James Thomson, Defoe, Swift, Richardson, Fielding, and Sterne. Amazing how much these Europeans can read into offhand British scribbling!

To Kahler's generosity of spirit and shared learning, reservations must attach apologetically, like limpets to the back of a sleeping walrus. But *The Inward Turn of Narrative* in its sweep describes a bigger circle than it seems to fill. If we are to examine the evolution—the inward turn—of narrative, then we need to grasp primordial narrative at some point deeper than the Gilgamesh epic, which Dr. Albert Lord, in his class in Oral Epic Tradition, used to classify with the "sophisticated" specimens of epic form. Ancient though the Babylonian fragments are, they represent the end of a development whose earlier stages have analogues in the tales collected by anthropology. The world does not (as Kahler implies) age all in one piece; Stone Age cultures survive to this day, and among them the scholar might find clues to the embryology of this mysterious art called narration. Kahler considers a series of forms without searching out the question of *function*.

Why do we harken to stories? What instinct do they arouse and satisfy? What is *happening* between writer and reader? Is the tribal tale-teller in the same relation to his audience as James Joyce to his? Are a medieval allegory, a dirty joke, and a Chekhov short story any more similar *in intent* than an icon, a comic book, and a Cézanne? Kahler does touch upon the issue of audience, provocatively but briefly:

> Early, naïve storytelling proceeded from a rather unsubtle narrator to a ubiquitous and tangible listener. Serious, weightier narrative, which begins in the eighteenth century, involves a personal relationship between a narrator who steps forth in his subjectivity and a virtually individualized specific listener whom the author holds by the lapel, so to speak. The later modern narrator is an impersonally objectified artistic consciousness caught up in the labor of expression. . . . The work requires, demands, and shapes its own ideal recipient.

The progression from "naïve" to "weightier," from "unsubtle" to "ideal," is not so much demonstrated as assumed. Indeed, an almost blithe assumption of progress pervades the book. Repeatedly, Kahler has to explain away some Hellenic anticipation of a post-Renaissance "advance": "The art of classical antiquity often came to the verge of modern achievements—but stopped short at certain limits. Developmental processes do not proceed in a straight line. Rather, they occur in waves, or, if we prefer a three-dimensional image, in ever-widening spirals." But art moves, surely, as often by regression and setting-aside as by any kind of accumulation. Hemingway and Pound said *no* to the elaborate genteel art prevailing around them; Cervantes, Fielding, even Jane Austen began with parody, in a spirit of deflation. Kahler instinctively sees human progress as the dethroning of the gods: "Man has liberated himself from his primordial entanglement with mythic powers." The two-thousand-year episode of Christendom, then, lies rather athwart his synopsis. The narratives of the Middle Ages rate less than a paragraph. Whereas Malraux, in his *Voices of Silence*, persuades us that the portal statuary of Chartres and Rheims expressed something missing from the blank-faced marbles of Greece and Rome, the best Kahler can make of Christian influence on narrative is the "residue" that remains once stories are "freed from their didactic purposes." Milton's conscious purposes (and the overt deism of the nature poets) are brushed aside as transitional illusions: "This wide-ranging epic was inherently contradictory and uncontrolled, a transitional opus expressing the rift that had developed between science and Biblical orthodoxy."

In a footnote, Kahler criticizes Erich Auerbach's *Mimesis* for its "fundamental error in assuming that reality is a stable thing, always the same for all ages and persons," and adds that "different writers have merely approached it in different ways. In fact, the reality of any given period is the product of struggling and advancing consciousness." But Kahler's attempt to formulate his sensation that reality is constantly expanding, and literature with it, produces labored prose:

> In considering the reciprocal creation of consciousness and reality, it is difficult to gauge what share the arts in particular have had in changing reality. The same process of reciprocal effects takes place in several fields: between historical event and historical consciousness (a question which deserves special study); between philosophical, political, and socio-economic theories and the corresponding realities; and of course in the natural sciences, where change in the real environment shows up most distinctly, although these changes are not necessarily the most profound. All these elements coalesce and affect each other.

What does this say but that things are all mixed up? Auerbach's stately and relatively static series of panels, each treating in great detail a lengthy quotation from successive literary epochs, manages not only to register a more sensitive impression of each masterpiece but to convey the feel of evolutionary movement more convincingly than Kahler. For what *is* "advancing consciousness"? Aristotle carried as many pieces of baggage, as many thoughts and facts, in his inner space as any modern savant. True, most of his baggage is now considered nonsense, but so will our baggage be. Does consciousness advance or merely shift its ground? What of the worlds of lore and observation lost to urban civilization? The Eskimos have a hundred words for snow, and the Bedouins as many for camel dung; is not the great poetry of snow and camel dung certainly behind us? How many of the three and a half billion persons living now, on the very frontier of the advance of consciousness, have appropriated more of the real world to their inner space than, say, a Carolingian serf? To most American housewives, electricity is as magical as mana to a Polynesian. The present young generation, steeped in technology, shows an astonishing willingness to live by astrology and diabolism, not to mention hallucinogens and Krishna. Are the fundamentals of human existence amid the wonders and menaces of advanced industrialism much different from the situation of Cro-Magnon man amid the wonders and menaces of untamed nature? All of recorded history has occurred in too brief a span for any evolutionary change; we confront life with the brains of cavemen. A mother suckles us; a joy of the senses crystallizes; alien shapes loom to block our desires; some desires are granted satisfaction; most are not; we age; we die. How has the drama of European cultural history, played on a little forestage of a continent by a cast of characters that was never more than a fraction of the population of the world, affected any of this? More specifically, how does modern narrative, of which *Tristram Shandy* in its self-conscious self-pleasing may be taken as the first instance, change "reality"? Picasso and Pollock turn up on fabric designs, but what happens to the modern masters of narrative? Indeed, the penetration of art into men's lives would seem, by some equation Kahler never suspects, proportional to the strength of its alliance with religion. Compared to the age of the cathedrals, we live remote from our art. Religion and technology are alike at least in that both attempt to cope directly with the pain of our existence: the first by offering us a supernatural consolation, and the second by dealing with our diseases and difficulties piecemeal. In comparison, modern art offers only distraction, sublimation, and a kind of empathy with the mental and spiritual aristocrats who are artists. The "patterns, structures, and techniques of consciousness" are of little profit to the run of men, and as overpopulation and diminishing natural resources reduce the margin of play in the world, refined literary art may be squeezed out even from the colleges.

What *is* "internalization"? There is no doubt that science accumulates, and human life is changed by its expanding discoveries. But culture may "internalize" new knowledge in the sense that the body internalizes the tip of a splinter; that is, cushions and anesthetizes it to make it ignorable. Kahler gives us a lively example of culture at work. The microscope was developed more gradually than the telescope, and the public was slow to grasp its implications. Suddenly, however, late in the 17th century, "observations with the microscope became a fashionable pastime in English society. Amateur experimenters of both sexes ('virtuosos' and 'virtuosas') became curiosity collectors and went about with pocket microscopes as some people do today with Geiger counters, looking for Leeuwenhoek's 'animalcules' in whatever came their way. They found tiny 'water flyes' and 'water lice,' 'eels' and 'worms' in blood and saliva. . . . English literature of the period reacted . . . with satires upon this fad." Are not we, in a world so out of our ken and our control, all "virtuosos" and "virtuosas" running about trying to tame the truth by turning it into group fun, into a fad? What was Pop Art but a way of subduing to fun the frightful raw trashiness of our man-made wilderness? And is the process so different from that whereby the first paintings, of bison and antelope, subdued to an appearance of control the terrible uncertainties of the hunt? Does art, then, operate as a progressive force or as a reactionary one, not to advance consciousness but to lull and muffle it—to make consciousness, indeed, passably bearable?

Some of these questions may be quibbles. Others may be riddles. They arise in response to an elegant and piquing book.

AFRICA

Out of the Glum Continent

BOUND TO VIOLENCE, by Yambo Ouologuem, translated from the French by Ralph Manheim. 182 pp. Harcourt Brace Jovanovich, 1971.

THIS EARTH, MY BROTHER . . . , by Kofi Awoonor. 232 pp. Doubleday, 1971.

THE WANDERERS, by Ezekiel Mphahlele. 351 pp. Macmillan, 1971.

The art of fiction, our beleaguered heroine, glances desperately about for rescue. Perhaps Africa will save her. Has not black music, via jazz and rock, transformed the ears of the world? Did not African masks inspire Cubism and destroy forever the sweet face that had reigned in European art from Giotto to Renoir? More to the point, have not rural societies, such as Russia, Ireland, and the American South, historically poured fresh vernacular energy and heroic simplicity into Europe's tired mainstream of literature? And has not sub-Saharan Africa already figured vividly, in the fiction of Conrad and Greene, Rider Haggard and Joyce Cary, as a skein of exotic color and a "heart" of primal mystery? So might we not expect, as the post-colonial African generations take their place among the world bourgeoisie, a passionate intelligentsia to arise and enunciate native truths, to embody in renewed fictional forms a living reality that has hitherto been seen only through white eyes?

The publication, a dozen years ago, of Chinua Achebe's *Things Fall Apart* gave plausibility to high hopes. Writing with a beautiful economy, Achebe seized the basic African subject—the breakup, under colonialism, of tribal society—so firmly and fairly that the book's tragedy, like Greek tragedy, felt tonic; a space had been cleared, an understanding had been achieved, a new beginning was implied. Now, in an Africa rid of overt European domination, the artist inherits the confusions of anti-climax, of conflicts grounded not in the grand encounter of two cultures but in petty self-interest, leading to tangled catastrophes like the destruction of Mr. Achebe's fellow-Ibos in Biafra. For all their tenderness and brilliance, three recent novels by young Africans —Yambo Ouologuem of Mali, Kofi Awoonor of Ghana, and Ezekiel Mphahlele of South Africa—left this reader in the mood for gloomy generalizations. Myopic lumping being one of the white West's affronts, however, let each book speak.

Yambo Ouologuem's *Bound to Violence*, written in French, interspersed with Arab and Bantu exclamations, conveys, through Ralph Manheim's translation, a startling energy of language. It begins:

> Our eyes drink the brightness of the sun and, overcome, marvel at their tears. *Mashallah! wa bismillah!* . . . To recount the bloody adventure of the niggertrash—shame to the worthless paupers!— there would be no need to go back beyond the present century; but the true history of the Blacks begins much earlier, with the Saifs, in the year 1202 of our era, in the African Empire of Nakem south of Fezzan, long after the conquests of Okba ben Nafi al-Fitri.

Ouologuem writes as a *griot*—"a troubadour, member of a hereditary caste whose function it is to celebrate the great events of history and to uphold the God-given traditions." He tells, or sings, the story of Nakem, an African state much like Mali: bordering the Sahara, watered by the Niger (called here the Yame), ruled since the Middle Ages by a Muslim dynasty called the Saifs. The book's heroic subject, on the public level, is the Saif rule, the cunning and ruthlessness that enable these Berber and Jewish chieftains to subjugate by terror and division the tribes of "niggertrash" and then to outwit the white conquerors when they come, using the colonial officials as a mask for their own continuous, corrupt, and refulgent power. On the private level, the book's hero is Raymond-Spartacus Kassoumi, the son of a slave cook and a serving woman, educated in mission schools and in Paris, and returned to Nakem in hollow triumph as the "man of the hour," the winner of a popular election that is merely Saif rule in yet another guise. The author, however, is often distracted from the relatively domestic events of Kassoumi's progress by gaudy, curiously noisy images of physical violence:

> Saif howled as though wounded and at the same time threw something into Chevalier's eye, which it penetrated with a splashing sound punctuated by a cry.

> His knife whirled, twice he planted it in her left breast, slitted her belly from top to bottom. Suddenly expelled, her pink viscera crackled.

A hyperbolic violence also drives Ouologuem's poetry into absurdity—"I regale the air with the idiotic laugh of my gums undermined by the caries of twenty centuries of history"—and pushes his satire into jubilation. Of Raymond-Spartacus, it is said, "His academic success in the land of the Flencessi [the French] had been bruited among the people, who declared that he was better educated than the best educated of white men—after God, by golly: *o djangui koié!* Wasn't it true that in homage to his science a white woman had savored the ecstatic felicity of marrying Raymond the illustrious builder, for—*tjok!*—he spouted mathematics and physics as easily as his mother had shelled peanuts." Though a Christian missionary is sympathetically presented, Ouologuem mocks mercilessly the pro-African aestheticism of the "Shrobeniusologists," who find in the bloody empires of the African Middle Ages "a society marked by wisdom, beauty, prosperity, order, nonviolence, and humanism." Hoodwinked by fake artifacts hastily planted in the marshes and mud, the Shrobenius family in turn hoodwinks Europe with "a cult of the good nigger," "a philistine Negromania without obligation or sanction." Such romanticism Ouologuem sternly mocks, insisting, "Prehistory in a tailcoat: there stands the African."

The intelligence expressed by this book seems all too withering, all too Gallic. The last chapter is an arch dialogue between the Christian Bishop Henry and the reigning Saif, suddenly as dialectical as Sartre himself: "Destiny never wearies of forgiving, by proxy. How could it weary? If it did, would it not know Tedium,

the empty consciousness of a time without content?" The point
of the debate, and of the novel, seems to be that

> violence, vibrant in its unconditional submission to the will of
> power, becomes a prophetic illumination, a manner of questioning
> and answering, a dialogue, a tension, an oscillation, which from
> murder to murder makes the possibilities respond to each other,
> complete or contradict each other. The outcome is uncertainty.

The Bishop and the Saif fall to playing chess, cozy in the certainty
that rulers like the Saif will be "forever reborn to history beneath
the hot ashes of more than thirty African republics" and that
"such was the earth of men that the balance between air, water,
and fire was no more than a game."

Such refined and utter pessimism may be necessary to surmount
a heritage so despairingly seen. But while Ouologuem senses a
"gigantic hunger for self-destruction" in the world, he also admits
and particularizes "the intoxication of feeling alive"; though no
political solution can be envisioned, the woeful history of Nakem
is indignantly felt. For all the book's incongruities as it leaps from
idiom to idiom, it delivers on its opening promise of intensity; its
furniture is incandescent. Without any note of sentimentality,
apology, or excuse, a fully literate African has opened himself, and
us, to modes of human existence prior to civilization:

> Her head was turned toward Yame and her body in tears was
> covered with watery suns.

> The silence sleeps, dreaming of the sky where the clouds envy the
> moon. Here's the bank of the Yame River, with its black swell,
> its dampness. The river. Southward. Southward. I've got to.
> They're expecting me. Why sleep? Maybe I've arrived. I run to
> catch myself, I follow myself at a gallop. I stop, body erect, arms
> stretched forward. I'm like a lemon without juice. I can't see my-
> self anymore. Neither my hands nor my limbs. Sleep. I'm afraid
> of the snakes. Sleep. Dream. Sleep. I'm afraid of the red ants. I don't
> want to be eaten. I wish I could turn into an animal and survive
> this menacing forest, its mosquitoes, its flies, those black things
> that crawl out of its belly in the darkness. Fire. I want fire. With
> fire I'll fear nothing. The snakes will go away. The rabbits will
> go away. The monkeys will chatter. The animals will think I'm
> armed. I'll be saved. I'll wait till daylight. Only then will I sleep.

*

This Earth, My Brother . . . , by Kofi Awoonor, is a more amiable work, just as Mr. Awoonor's contemplative gaze from his jacket photograph is more amiable than Mr. Ouologuem's flash-lit stare. The jacket and title page insist that the book be called "An Allegorical Tale of Africa," though it seems no more allegorical than any novel is; i.e., its hero represents many men and his plight illustrates an aspect of the human condition. The hero, Amamu, is a young Ghanian lawyer, who, through the alternation of objective and introspective chapters (set, I think too fussily, in different sizes of type), proceeds to nervous break-down and death. The stress he suffers is presumably the inordinate gap (and here the typographic device may have a point) between his primitive, hopeful, partially idyllic past and the mediocre, nag-ging, disappointed present of his life in an African metropolis no better able to cope with corruption and pollution and poverty than any other modern city. While a desert glitter and an im-perial past lend fiendish glamour to Ouologuem's Mali/Nakem, Awoonor's Ghana is familiarly dismal, except that all the faces are black and the problems of overdevelopment experienced in Amer-ica are matched by the not dissimilar embarrassments of under-development. Amamu is a thorough bourgeois male—uneasy in his work, a witness to injustice yet a professional participant in it, a citizen perpetually testifying, inwardly, to his own puzzling incrimination in the venal, weary workings of a mercenary society:

> The Lebanese merchants are bargaining away native lands; even a government that proclaims socialism—a confusion of ideas, beliefs, and magic—cannot provide the answer. So the children turn beg-gars in the market place, as the eminent men play golf on the Achimota course. The best golf course in the country.
> In the Senior Common Room, the scholars of the land are de-bating international communism, and providing new arguments for Fabianism that died in its country of origin. . . .

> The beer is good; there are two excellent breweries and one is soon to be built in the Western Provinces to brew wholesome beer for the people.
> Meanwhile, drinking water is short in the north and in the Ewe country.

On the private level, Amamu's binds are the familiar ones of the bourgeois male: the boyhood/manhood bind, the wife/mistress bind. The mistress, Adisa, a warm and servile whore, merges with boyhood loves and visions—"the woman of the sea, his cousin love of those years long long ago rising from the sea. She rose slowly, head first, adorned with sapphires, corals, and all the ancient beads her mother left for her pubertal rites. She rose slowly from a dream sea." And this vision of Mother Africa merges in the currents of Amamu's nostalgia with the Britannia who ruled the waves. Christian hymns haunt his walks and reveries; he remembers the Empire Days, held on Queen Victoria's birthday—the uniformed dark children singing songs freshly learned, "miniature Union Jacks stuck in their shirt pockets"; the handsome mustached officers; the speeches proclaiming, "To be true imperialists, we must maintain unshaken our faith in God, in the Empire, and in ourselves. God bless you all." With the recession of the Empire, this faith has faded, leaving nothing but empty revolutions. "All revolutions must go astray. That is divine justice." Nkrumah Circle is renamed National Liberation Circle; that is modern Ghanian history.

> It is a land of laughing people, very hospitable people. That's what the tourist posters proclaim. They forgot to add that pussy is cheap here, the liquor is indifferent, and the people suffer from a thousand diseases.

The novel itself struggles against the soggy atmosphere of lassitude. The chapters of interior soliloquy lapse into an unlikely literariness:

> The flash point of creation, birth before birth long tunnels tunnels roads of womb darkness stilled the mind's eye cannot behold, prescience prenativity of total darkness, the foreknowledge of the grave the exhilaration and impatience of the emergence.

Awoonor does not have Ouologuem's access to savagery. Instead of glorying in the sun and the tears it forces upon us, Awoonor's hero says he hates the sun, and finds ease in images of spooky shelter: "Darkness peopled by ghosts in purple velvets shrieks abandoned by fireplaces by the eaves of the thatched hut in rain falling falling falling as the water whitened by cornflour is poured on the sogged earth for the benevolent ones to drink to quench their thirst in the land beyond the field where trees are green and the grove is dark." The interior monologues put us in mind of Eliot's remark (apropos of *Ulysses*) that "this new method of giving the psychology . . . doesn't tell as much as some casual glance from outside often tells." Viewed externally, Amamu is not very impressive or dynamic, and his fate is less tragic than damply sad, a shadow melting back into shadows. Yet the novel's strength is its refusal to be spectacular, to feign anger it doesn't feel, or to present Ghanian life as anything much more than a fumbling, disheartened extension of colonial rule, a blurred carbon. Humanity is not, as it rather is in *Bound to Violence*, locked out; there are pages of faithful, inconsequential dialogue, with a lilt never heard in the West, and perhaps it is this sense of voice and voices that makes *This Earth, My Brother* . . . amiable, despite its allegorical grimace.

Ezekiel Mphahlele's *The Wanderers* is the longest and least sophisticated novel of the three. His English is not always sure. His characters say unsayable things to each other, like "Aren't we happier when our love activates things in people than when it founders on passive ground?" Some sentences are untidy waste-baskets overflowing with words:

> Maybe all these factors checked the downhill thump and roll and leap of the boulder of passion before it could plunge into the placid fountain down there with a horrendous splash before anchoring under its own weight, for good or for bad.

On the other hand, there are some lucky hits a more practiced writer wouldn't have brought off:

> Always for that distance, one's mind seemed to see things in blue and yellow: colors that seemed to have been yoked violently together by some inevitable force that wanted to have fun.

Her figure was the kind that never looked overripe or bitten into. The language adequately moves its freight—an ambitious panoramic story of wandering exiles, black and white, from South Africa. The South African episodes are the most vivid and affectionate; the polychrome peculiarities of this deplorable state, with its "colored" and Indian minorities as well as blacks, are rendered in a sharp sequence of vignettes and accents. Mr. Mphahlele, whose black characters talk a little like stage Englishmen, hears peculiar speech everywhere. Here is an Indian shopkeeper:

> "What you peepel want prom Hindians, eh? Ewery person in dis worl' sweat to eat. . . . It is not enough we Hindians we are removed by gowermint out of town and we looss too much property too much bissness and den you peepel put our shops on pire?"

Here is an Afrikaans woman, at a Promethean extreme of racism:

> "Look at me. You lucky you can see your god like me and Master and Master Van Zyl. I cannot see my god, I cannot reach him he is far, far away. Sometime I t'ink he does not listen. But I only know he is listening and he knows dat the government is doing everyt'ing right to make you heppy, like dey are your fathers and mothers. . . . You heppy, not like ourself, the white people beecoss we have to look after both ourself and you. You know sometime the father and mother must be unheppy so that their children are heppy. I am right, eh? You must keep laughing."

When Timi Tabane, a black schoolteacher exiled for writing newspaper articles about a slave system of penal labor, travels to London, the colony of exiled South Africans there seems to him pathetic; the "South African English accent the whites spoke . . . irritated him as it had never done in his home country." And in Nigeria, after his initial exhilaration at being freed from South Africa's tyranny of passbooks and police, he is irritated by the effeminate way Nigerians slap at each other, and urges them to hit with fists, in good South African style. Prostitution and idleness are also new to him. One of the friends he makes there, in a small circle of intellectuals and mixed marriages, is named Awoonor (another is "an American historian, John Galbraith"), and, whether or not this means Kofi Awoonor, *The Wanderers* moves into the dispirited terrain of *This Earth, My Brother*. . . . Timi's problems become those of the free: a sense of futility, elusive responsibilities, a meagre security. He and his wife agonize over the ethics of hiring a servant. Awoonor lectures them on the duties of mastership. "You see, you have to be a master or none at all, you must be seen to be one. You've got to talk like one. If you're soft, a steward thinks Ah, na he be tenth-rate master. He wants a first-rate master." Morally compromised, unhappy among the post-colonial anti-climaxes of Nigeria and Kenya, they are faced with that ultimate Western luxury, a generation gap. Their son, Felang, after obstinately non-coöperating with the Anglophile school establishment, runs away, joins an African nationalist guerrilla army, and is fed to crocodiles by white farmers.

Where can the Timi Tabanes of the world turn? Tabane rejects the Christianity that enveloped his education. He speaks of "African humanism," but the African wisdom he cites is a Stone Age survival manual: nothing belongs to you but what you have eaten, food is nothing but decayed matter that sticks in the teeth, a woman is like a calabash—do not kick it around. For soul comfort, Tabane turns to his American records, to the music of John Coltrane and Big Bill Broonzy, of Lionel Hampton and Duke Ellington. He asks, "How can I make my children understand we have all wandered away from something—all of us blacks," and gets no answer. He laughs when an elderly white Kenyan says he is going back to Canada: "I've done Africa—eighteen years now—and I must think of my children's future. Africa's no more for us whites." Africa is no more for whites, yet not yet for blacks. Tabane tells himself, "We must move. . . . Where to? Certainly out of Africa, stay out until we can feel needed. . . . I love Africa but . . . I'll serve the country that needs me—more than that, *wants* me." The jacket flap states that Mr. Mphahlele now lives in the United States, an associate professor of English at the University of Denver. Whereas Kofi Awoonor teaches African literature at the Stony Brook campus of the State University of New York. Yambo Ouologuem makes his home in Paris.

Now, the generalizations. Africa is enormous and pluralistic. Muslimized, impoverished Mali is a continent removed from the many-layered, prosperous police state of South Africa. Even between Nigeria and Kenya *The Wanderers* notes significant differences in tone, prospects, and make-up. So expectations of an "African" literary mode are perhaps as fatuous as talk of an "American" literature that would include, along with the United States' classics, the annals of the conquistadors, Hawaiian war chants, and the cosmopolitan avant gardes of Mexico City and Buenos Aires. Indeed, these three African novels show a deficiency not only of continental self-consciousness but of national identification; the governments, white or black, are uniformly deplored, even if Ouologuem does, perversely, seek illumination in the centuries-long bloodbath of Saif rule. Timi Tabane and Amamu feel homesick for narrow scenes—a riverside, a crowded courtyard. Modernism, while it has crushed the tribes, has not produced an emotionally credible substitute.

Of the three novels, only *The Wanderers* demonstrates any pronounced resentment of white colonialism. *Bound to Violence* presents the white colonialists as dupes, along with the "niggertrash," of the demonic Nakem nobility. *This Earth, My Brother* . . . remembers colonial rule with a kind of numb affection. And even *The Wanderers* shows the English-speaking whites (but not the Afrikaners) as people who, like the blacks, are unequally matched against the vast, murderous inertia that is Africa. Steve Cartwright, for instance, Timi's best white friend, is killed, a few pages after Felang himself is killed, in another squalid skirmish. Naledi, Steve's widow, a black woman, announces in the novel's last paragraph her intention to stay in London and study nutrition, supported by her white father-in-law. The book's last word is "sympathy." There is less Fanonesque fury in these novels than one might expect; if their authors are a fair sampling, young Africans do not share their American brothers' sensation of a magical white omnipotence malevolently applied to ring them in. Rather, there is bewilderment at vastness, a sense of ungraspable forces and inutile liberty, reminiscent of New World fiction from Fenimore Cooper to Faulkner.

Un-New World, however, is the dispirited air of these novels. The African bourgeoisie, and the intellectual class within it, seem to have been born discouraged; they have inherited Western consciousness on the downswing. The otherworldly faiths have faded, and the earthly paradises—of Marxism, of industrial capitalism—have been debunked by partially coming true. Modernity's birthday party is over. At the dedication of a new hospital, pagan dancers from the highland make music with tin cans and stones; all Timi Tabane hears is the "grim note of defeat"—"like the doleful song of southern black warriors when they have lost the battle." True, what is there to do but build hospitals, import technology, invent constitutions, mitigate corruption and poverty, take wives and betray them, raise children and lose them—to play the sedulous ape, in short, to the West's aging, diseased Faust? Of course literature can afford to be cynical. It generally is. Our own first masterpiece, *The Scarlet Letter*, is scarcely a paean to the past, and *Moby Dick* shares with *Bound to Violence* a rococo pessimism. Yet one listens in vain in these African works for an echo of Emerson's and Whitman's confident sense of national audience. For whom are these works written, in the languages of departed occupiers? Not for the "niggertrash" still sunk in the tribal dream and the struggle for sustenance. Or for the African whites, ever more anachronistically clinging to their plantations and prerogatives and the 19th-century credos that justified them. At the moment, the black African artist, from his niche in American colleges or continental salons, seems a voice without an auditorium, a sensibility between worlds.

Shades of Black

THE GREAT PONDS, by Elechi Amadi. 217 pp. John Day, 1973.

IN THE FOG OF THE SEASON'S END, by Alex La Guma. 181 pp. The Third Press, 1973.

AGATHA MOUDIO'S SON, by Francis Bebey, translated from the French by Joyce A. Hutchison. 154 pp. Lawrence Hill, 1973.

Three novels from Africa, all now published in the United States, suggest, without being especially long or ambitious, that certain artistic advantages reside with the writers of that continent, in comparison with their overpublicized and overprogrammed counterparts in the West. *The Great Ponds*, by Elechi Amadi, not only gives a Homeric nobility to the tiny war between two Nigerian villages but recovers, in its acceptance of magic as a fact, the power the Greek dramatists had—of making mental acts seem momentous. *In the Fog of the Season's End*, by the exiled South African Alex La Guma, delivers, through its portrait of a few hunted blacks attempting to subvert the brutal regime of apartheid, a social protest reminiscent, in its closely detailed texture and level indignation, of Dreiser and Zola. And *Agatha Moudio's Son*, by the Cameroonian Francis Bebey, gracefully propounds an all but forgotten equation—that between the spirit of comedy and the spirit of forgiveness.

The black African moved to literary expression confronts choices a Westerner need not make. First, he must choose his language—the European language, with its alien tradition and colonial associations, or the tribal language, with its oral tradition and minuscule reading audience. Unless his mother and father came from different tribes and used a European tongue as the lingua franca of the home, his heart first learned to listen in the tribal language, which will forever then be more pungent and nuancé; but English and French command the far broader audience, across Africa and throughout the world. So he must choose his audience: foreigners and the minority of his countrymen educated in white ways, or the majority of his fellow-tribesmen, who can be addressed chiefly through recited poetry and theatrical performance. Television, of course, somewhat widens this latter possibility, and a good deal of the intellectual energy of Ghana goes into it, publication in this impoverished, politically edgy country being practically limited to Nkrumah's bound works. In all of equatorial Africa, only the market towns of Nigeria and Ghana provide enough audience for written English to engender a popular literature—Christian melodramas and self-help fables not much different from the penny dreadfuls consumed by the urban masses of London and New York a century ago. The sales of a classic like Chinua Achebe's *Things Fall Apart* lean preponderantly on the schools, which use it as a text for the teaching of English. And these texts arrive by way of English publishing houses, whose editors and readers can scarcely help prizing an "Africanness" of exotic primitivism and docile quaintness. Hence, in reaction, the aggressive sophistication and anti-"negritude" of such creative black expatriates as Yambo Ouologuem and Wole

Soyinka. The African writer must consciously choose not only his language, audience, and tone but his reality. A village-born, mission-taught, Oxford-anointed African has lived a synopsis of human history. He has outgrown prehistory so quickly that nothing has had time to die; the village gods, the Christian God, and the modern absence of God coexist in him, along with several languages and the madly multiplied number of styles, truths, slants, and stances that the global compression brings tangent to an alert mind. What is truth? At a symposium in Lagos a year ago, I heard a dazzling variety of literary tactics enunciated by a dozen Nigerian writers and critics. Elechi Amadi (addressed as "Captain Amadi," in deference to the Army years of his varied career) put forward with an arresting earnestness the opinion that supernatural reality should play its part in a narrative whose characters believe in magic.* The first question from the audience challenged this notion, or, rather, asked that it be clarified to mean that such belief should be shown to be *subjectively* influencing the characters. Captain Amadi, a slender, gracious, and handsome figure in a white robe, appeared to consent to the modification, there in the juju-proof setting of the university auditorium, amid the steel chairs and the flex-necked microphones and the beaming pink faces of U.S.I.S. officials, with the metropolis of Lagos clattering beyond the windows. But it seemed to me that Captain Amadi did not in fact mean anything quite so reasonable as the proposition that believers believe, but something more supernatural, and his novel confirms my impression.

The Great Ponds tells, in a fine quick style airy with unadorned dialogue, of the contest between two villages, Chiolu and Aliakoro, over fishing rights in the Great Ponds, particularly the very rich Pond of Wagabe. The last of a series of wars evidently settled the ownership in favor of Chiolu, but Aliakoro maintains that it possesses a still older claim, and for years its men have poached unchallenged. Now a party of poachers is ambushed, and several of them are held for ransom. In retaliation, Aliakoro kidnaps several Chiolu women, and the conflict escalates to total predation and terror on both sides:

---

* See "Excerpts from a Symposium," following.

Death lurked behind every bush. At night the pale moonlight cast dubious shadows which none but the brave dared investigate. When there was no moon the curtain of charcoal-black darkness instilled as much fear into people's minds as if it was one vast insubstantial ubiquitous enemy ready to slay any who left the security of the closely guarded houses.

Even animals began to feel the effects of the deadly conflict. No longer was the arena strewn with white drowsy sheep lured by the moonlight. . . . Every path was watched by men whose one desire was to kill. . . . There were no children playing anywhere. Reception halls, the haunts of old men, were deserted; the empty three-legged chairs in them seemed to stare back . . . in protest.

The ceremonious parleys and judicious assemblies whereby this disastrous condition is achieved are related with humorous care and an eye, certainly, on the global wars of the century. Timeless is the mechanism whereby honorable men acting measuredly in what they construe to be self-defense perpetrate ruin. The warfare, performed with arrows and with machetes that behead an enemy at a stroke, is described as in the old chronicles, with a simplicity that leaves the sufferer some dignity without excusing us from fear and pity:

Sparks flew from their knives as they parried each other's blows. Ikechi did not seem to care much for his safety. The possibility of dying did not occur to him. He fought relentlessly with the singleness of purpose of a child. He exhibited the carelessness of inexperience too, now and then leaving openings which might have been fatal if his opponent had been strong enough to exploit them. But he was not. He was a middle-aged man and he weakened under the remorseless attacks of his much younger assailant. His knees began to wobble, his eyes grew dim as he panted. Now there was a plea in his eyes, but he had no breath to translate this plea into words.

Ikechi, unseeing in his mad fury, did not heed this plea as his able hands worked his machete this way and that. Parrying a particularly heavy blow the man sank to his knees. Before he could recover it was all over with him.

There are no bad men in this story, only men. Though the reader is placed nearer in sympathy to the village of Chiolu, Aliakoro is visited, and its *eze* (chief), its *dibia* (medicine man), and its foremost warrior are characterized as interestingly as their opposite numbers in Chiolu. Indeed, Wago "the leopard-killer," the Aliakoro warrior who is fanatical about the ponds, and Igwu the reluctant magic-worker, who is indifferent about the ponds but who is pushed by his villagers into the most demonic kind of sorcery, are rather *more* interesting than their Chiolu counterparts, Olumba and Achichi; Captain Amadi imitates Homer in making the Trojans loom in a way that the Greeks do not. His dozens of characters within the two villages are all distinct. As the war becomes devastating, the book's microcosm expands, and an intercessory force is revealed: the entire Erekwi clan, whose villages are now threatened by the breach of peace. All the *ezes* meet in splendid panoply and put the dispute up to the gods; a representative from one warring village is to "swear." Olumba of Chiolu volunteers, and the elders of Aliakoro nominate the god Ogbunabali, the god of night. The "swearing" is a simple rite; Olumba recites:

> "I swear by Ogbunabali the god of the night that the Pond of Wagaba belongs to Chiolu.
> "If this is not true let me die within six months;
> "If true, let me live and prosper."

The novel then shifts from the social realm to the psychological; Olumba, the strongest man of his village, struggles with the invisible. Though elaborate precautions hem in his activity, he impulsively climbs a palm tree, is stung by wasps, falls, and nearly dies. The event is revealed to be the result of a spell Igwu has cast in Aliakoro; a counter-spell, cast by the consulting *dibia* Anwuanwu, saves his life. But as the weeks of his six months drag by, the impalpable weight of the god Ogbunabali preys on the warrior's mind and wastes him to apathy:

> He was like a man swimming against a strong current. By frantic efforts he could gain short distances, but invariably the current swept him back, draining energy and confidence out of him . . . Olumba was a shadow of his former self. Emaciated and haggard he shuffled about with hunched shoulders. His hollow eye-sockets could hold a cup of water each. Looking at him people feared he would collapse any moment and die.

The suspense of Olumba's struggle not to die is frightful. The motions of his morale feel immense. We see life as pre-scientific man saw it—as a spiritual liquid easily spilled. The invisible forces pressing upon Olumba are totally plausible. The novel treats magic respectfully, as something that usually works. The recipes of witchery are matter-of-factly detailed, as are the fevers and divinations they inarguably produce. But Olumba's heroic battle is against a force deeper than magic—the death wish itself, the urge toward osmotic reabsorption into the encircling ocean of darkness wherein life is a precarious, thin-walled epiphenomenon. Ogbunabali has no shrine in Chiolu; he is "therefore non-directional, distant, menacing, ubiquitous." His silence and neutrality are uncanny and invincible. Ogbunabali is not evil, or even especially concerned; "the gods would rather have fun than run after us." He is simply Ogbunabali.

As Olumba is about to succumb, a second intercession occurs: others in the village begin mysteriously to die. Olumba's fighting spirit returns: "His private fears vanished in the face of the village-wide consternation." *Wonjo*, the coughing sickness, carries off one of his wives and imperils his only son. Nevertheless, as the sixth new moon shines down upon the decimated village, Olumba still lives. And yet, in this defeat, Wago the leopard-killer finds a way to deprive Chiolu of the Pond of Wagaba; the war is carried to a fiendish end, though Aliakoro, too, has been ravaged by *wonjo*. Is *wonjo* the wrath of Ogbunabali, taking vengeance for the impiety of war? The villagers think so, but Captain Amadi tells us, in a last sentence like the lifting of a vast curtain, that

> *Wonjo*, as the villagers called the Great Influenza of 1918, was to claim a grand total of some twenty million lives all over the world.

One world indeed. Until this sentence, the apparent isolation of the Erekwi villages has been total and pure; this novel, so revelatory of the human condition both inward and outward, contains no trace of the world of white men save a few old Portuguese swords worn as adornment.

In Alex La Guma's novel of South Africa, white men are everywhere, "pink and smooth as strawberry jelly." They function as bosses, owners, policemen, and torturers. *In the Fog of the Season's End* has a setting as thoroughly urban as that of *The Great Ponds* is rural:

The suburbs passed quickly and the city skimmed into sight: a
serrated horizon of office blocks with rows of parking meters like
regiments of armless robots in front of them.

There is cosmopolitan glitter for whites:

the clink of glasses; a woman's voice saying nasally, " . . . must
come to Los Angeles some day . . . " soft music from the dim
futuristic cocktail lounge where the Indian stewards moved skillfully among the tables . . .

and ghetto squalor for blacks:

On the narrow, torrid staircase the smell of urine and old cooking
hung on the stale, thick, groping air that touched exposed skin
with a hot caress.

Through this crowded, active, bipartite cityscape (Cape Town,
though not named as such) moves our hero, Beukes, "a brown
man in a brown suit." He works for "the movement," and in the
course of the novel goes about distributing incendiary leaflets,
meeting varieties of coöperation and distrust among his fellow
black Africans, catching odd hours of sleep in borrowed rooms,
reminiscing about his life and his love, Frances, whom we never
meet. At the end, the Security Police surround a tin shack where
he is conferring with Elias Tekwane, an older revolutionary;
Beukes escapes, but Tekwane is captured and tortured to death.
The last scene shows three young blacks being smuggled north
to join the army of freedom fighters while Beukes stands in the
brightening sunlight and thinks, "They have gone to war in the
name of a suffering people. . . . What we see now is only the tip
of an iceberg of resentment against an ignoble regime, the tortured
victims of hatred and humiliation."

Mr. La Guma is not, then, one to let his message slip by un-
noticed, nor is his descriptive prose shy of insistence. Similes pro-
liferate; at their best they quicken their referent:

She was small and fine-boned and pretty as a garden snake.

. . . the dark-skinned children staring out over fences like shabby
glove-puppets . . .

and at their worse smother it beneath a clumsy muchness:

Here and there tiny cafés clung to precarious business with the fingernails of hope, like the foxholes of a last-ditch stand, dust gathering on the stale menu cards.

Faces especially excite the author to a viscous overflow of imagery:

The Sergeant had a flabby, wrinkled face over hard bone, as if a loose, flexible rubber mask had been hastily dropped over a smaller wig-stand.

. . . a woman with tired, bleached hair and the face of a painted waxed doll accidentally left near a fire, then hastily retrieved . . .

. . . a squat man with a face like a badly formed and stale chéese . . .

. . . a small man with bad teeth and a big smile that split his face like a blotched melon.

The writing does, however, convey a jumbled, sweaty sensation not inappropriate to the subject—the human jungle the white man has imposed upon the South African black. And when La Guma's prose connects directly to outrage—as when Tekwane is tortured by two tweedy policemen, or when the maze of permits the police state has created is dramatized—the fuzz of overwriting burns away. As a thriller, *In the Fog of the Season's End* suffers not only from its chosen interweave of flashbacks but from a certain languid futility in its basic mission; the risk Beukes runs distributing the leaflets seems far greater than any possible effect they can have. As political description, the book is less strident than its metaphors. The black population Beukes moves through is represented, in what feel to be fair proportions, as amused, threatened, or inspired by him and his cause. Personal friendship among these oppressed counts for more than political commitment. We are aware how far we have come from the villages of *The Great Ponds* when a character responds, "Strangers? I dunno. I reckon there's always strangers hanging about like. People you don' know." In Chiolu and Aliakoro, there are no people you don't know. In a modern state, strangers are the rule, and Beukes more than once reminds himself of the uncomfortable, comforting fact that he is anonymous while, with his carton of pamphlets addressed to the faceless masses, he dodges from one island of acquaintanceship to another. I have heard it observed that among black Africans South African exiles invariably stand out as the most dynamic. Perhaps "dynamic" should be read as "best able to deal with strangers." The people in La Guma's world are fighting for identity; Amadi's villagers have had theirs bestowed upon them —in their kinship, in their nicknames, in their hierarchical roles. Dragging its captive blacks in the ruck, the South African state has nevertheless dragged them into modernity, into the post-tribal impersonality that makes it necessary for the narrative artist to particularize every face. The need to describe, excessively felt in *In the Fog of the Season's End*, arises when teller and listener no longer share a common reality.

As protest, La Guma's cry from this particular underworld has a value that transcends its artistic faults—a special value, it may be, to Americans. For at this distance it is easy to be complacent or forgetful about South Africa, which sends us only its admirable white athletes and, with less publicity, its pleasant investment dividends. Perhaps one has to visit black Africa to realize how automatically is assumed the complicity of the United States in the continued white rule of that continent's rich southern third. The Portuguese supposedly fight with weapons we supply them through NATO; the Afrikaners buttress their tyranny with our capital; our new Vietnam will (supposedly) come here. *In the Fog of the Season's End* contains only the occasional overheard invitation to Los Angeles, the glimpsed Coca-Cola billboard. But the glistening white world that hangs above the black townships like a forbidden paradise does have a familiar air. We live there.

Agatha Moudio's Son takes place in an agreeable intermediate climate: its Cameroonian fishing village is intact but not untouched. White power has planted a public fountain in the center of the village and run a paved highway through it. A party of hunters comes on Sundays to shoot monkeys in the forest—an intrusion considered "picturesque." They are admired as exotic creatures:

> There were three white men and their two white women. . . .
> The two ladies always wore trousers: what kind of woman was
> this . . . ? One of the men was very rich, at least we thought
> so every time he opened his mouth to speak, for he had replaced

the two rows of ivory that Heaven must surely have given him at birth with two sparkling rows of gold. He was tall and strong and ugly. . . . The children were looking at these men and these women with curiosity and admiration, especially the man with the gold-filled mouth, in spite of his strange ugliness. But why on earth weren't they black, like us?

More admired still, however, is the striding Scotsman on the whiskey bottle—"blessed be thou, oh bottle manufactured by the whites." Another bracing import is law and order, which sends almost all the male villagers to jail for four years. Unlike Beukes, they accept fatalistically these strangers "who rule us, you, me, all the villagers, just as they rule our forest, our stream, our river, and all the animals and fish that live in them." They are puzzled only by how their first set of white masters, the Germans, who drank from mugs, could have been defeated by the French, who drink from "dolls' glasses."

Francis Bebey writes with the lightness and irreverence and affectionate thoughtfulness that the patterns of acculturation have bestowed upon the literature of Francophone Africa. Magic, so deadly in Amadi's Nigerian fastness, is here playful and amorous: a woman throws salt on a fire to bring on a rainstorm that will protect her and her lover from interruption; in the figure of Mother Evil-Eye the witch and midwife merge. The frightful silence of Ogbunabali becomes the kindly silence of the dead, giving assent to the living:

> We waited a few seconds for a possible manifestation. It did not come; nothing moved in the room, neither the door, nor the single window with its scanty light, which was covered by a little rectangular mat of woven raffia; we heard nothing, not even a step on the freshly beaten earth of the floor. Nothing: my father was giving us a free hand.

Even when ritual turns lethal and heaps rocks upon a culprit's head, his neck by a droll miracle refuses to break. The elaborate parleys, which in *The Great Ponds* present a worthy analogue to the discourse of nations, are here portrayed satirically; venerable formulas mask haggling greed as a bride price is agreed upon. Religion has ebbed, leaving a fertile wash of credulity. Little myths sprout into instant being; a stray frog hiding in a sleeve becomes in the telling a devil, and a young wrestler feels himself "in the process of gradually becoming a legend." Darkness, a death-concealing curtain in Chiolu, in this Cameroonian village panders to lovers, covering their comings and goings and even permitting the whispering visits of a white man on a bicycle.

The hero of *The Great Ponds*, Olumba, agonizes between life and death; Mbenda, the hero of *Agatha Moudio's Son*, vacillates between two women and solves his problem, in the way of his ancestors, by marrying them both. Though both present him with illegitimate children, the triangle is essentially amiable— Fanny, the wife whom the village has chosen for him, urges him to marry as well Agatha, the woman his heart has chosen, though she is a white man's tart and with time his desire for her has so cooled that she seems "very little different from any other woman." The novel brims with the village's most precious gift—its bestowal of value upon every life within it. An illegitimate child, far from unwelcome, "prospered and was the sun of our village." Uncle Big-Heart, upon whose head the stones are heaped, is deplored because he "had not acted in a brotherly way" toward his fellow-villagers: "After all, just because Uncle Big-Heart could read and write and talk to foreigners, he had no right to neglect his brothers." And eventually he comes to repentance, appearing at a wedding and announcing, "I was born in this village. I shall stay here all my life, and I don't intend to be ignored at moments as important as this one." All forgive him his cheating them, and he forgives their trying to break his neck, and the men imprisoned because of this escapade forgive him their term in jail.

Mbenda, as he narrates these events in a sidling, unpredictable manner, seems ambiguously situated both within and outside the village. He is a fisherman in love with the fisherman's life, with the "fraternity, solidarity, the sky, the sea, men, men lost in this overwhelming natural setting, simple men living to sea's rhythm" and solidly of the village. Yet he looks back upon it from a mysterious distance: "Happy life, what would I give to return to you again." He alludes to intervening experiences not described within the novel's compass: "Today, time and mixing with people who 'know about life' have given my arguments a certain measure of 'civilization.'" The reader expects, then, a scene of severance from this village recalled through a shimmer of nostalgia. It never comes; Mbenda never leaves. The author, however, the jacket tells us, after being born in Douala, Cameroon, studied at the Sorbonne and has been a "composer, guitarist, broadcaster, and journalist," and has given recitals "throughout Africa, in Paris, and New York." The awkwardly obtrusive narrator consciousness, with its unresolved double focus, is the only stammer in this confidently relaxed novel, and is probably symptomatic of an African unease with the device, so natural to the West, of confession, of the narrator as hero. I recall—to be personal once more—a student in Nairobi explaining her aversion to reading novels by saying they were "too much showing off." Mbenda, in one of his philosophical asides, analyzes his own distrust of books: a book is, "fundamentally, the most indiscreet of friends. . . . In our society, we had preserved the ancestral custom of communicating things only to those we loved, and with the certainty that they would make good use of our information."

Agatha Moudio's Son culminates, as the title foretells, in the birth of a boy. He is born oddly pale, with straight hair. Mbenda tells himself, "Most black children are born white, and only take on . . . local colour a few days after coming into the world." He waits. "You will understand why this child, neither flesh nor fowl, which had just been born, made me so thoughtful, when I tell you the truth: the colour of my own skin is like the deepest shades of ebony. . . . As for Agatha Moudio, very pretty as you know, she too was quite black, from head to foot. . . . I kept on hoping for a whole month after the birth of the little boy, but his milk-chocolate complexion barely changed, or so little as to be barely noticeable." At last, Mother Evil-Eye announces the obvious truth:

> "Perhaps," she said, "perhaps this child will one day have a mouthful of gold, like its father. . . ."
> I rushed to a mirror, on hearing this, and bared my teeth: two rows of ivory, clean and white beyond reproach.

But this, too, is in time forgiven—forgiven Agatha, and forgiven her white son, who as he grows and plays in the village with the other children "looks like a child come from afar." Mbenda, abruptly older, meditates, "When all's said and done, Agatha's son expects from me not the wicked and stupid sneer of a man deceived by fate but the parental advice which will bring him happiness in the strange adventure of life as a man." And he remembers Mother Evil-Eye's predicting to him, of Agatha, "She'll lead you a fine dance till you can't tell black from white." Speed the day.

Addendum: Excerpts from a Symposium

HELD ON January 26, 1973, at the University of Lagos. Text edited by Dr. Theophilus Vincent of the University Department of English and published by the United States Information Service.

"The author is faced with this difficulty. He has to write on a private level, on the social level and on this other level which, for want of a better word, we may call the supernatural. So you may find things happening in the African novel which normally would be quite untenable from the Western point of view. Why should a man die because some gods are angry? It is rubbish, it is childish, it doesn't happen. . . . And yet, down in the village, this is the reality. If someone is sick in the village it is not enough for the medicine man or even for the doctor to give him an injection. It may be a purely organic disease, so he gets this injection. Now if he has not lost his innocence, you will find that he will not recover until he has also satisfied his gods. In other words this emotional aspect of the thing is very much tied up with his illness. Even now in the village you find a relation of yours falls ill and then there is the usual divination. With your sophistication and Western education, you say, 'Look, mommy, this is trash. I will take you to the doctor; you will be all right.' Then you bundle the old lady to the doctor and the doctor does his bit and she does not recover, even with all the drugs. Now she has to go back and, if she believes strongly in this thing, and most of them do, the native doctor is called in, he does his bit and then she recovers.

This is the reality of the African situation. We have not lost all our innocence and if we try to lose it, I think we would be losing a very great deal. So we have to write in three dimensions. . . . One may ask: is this not perpetrating something which really ought to be done away with? Why resurrect all this stuff of the gods and the supernatural and so on? Well, my answer is: we really do not know—I mean, there is so much about nature that we do not know. Nowadays hypnotism is standard practice in psychotherapy. When Mesmer was exploring this art, he was dubbed a quack and he was abused and mesmerism was very much in disrepute. But today, hypnotism is an accepted part of psychotherapy. People are researching in telepathy and gathering evidence every day on this. In other words, we do not really know much about nature and it may well be that the ignorant villagers are right after all."

—CAPTAIN ELECHI AMADI, *novelist*

". . . The old forms, which Capt. Elichi Amadi says we have to bring in, like the fisherman who wants fish and has to go through the gods, are changing. If I want fish I have to go to the water and get the fish and not try to go through some gods. These things are changing. I mean this now and what happens every day. People want fish, they want money from it. They are not going to consult somebody who will get in their nets and make sure it works very well. If they are going to use poison for the fish, they throw it into the water and wait for the fish to die and collect them. The old forms are going to die. The new forms of doing things have not yet taken hold on us, so we are in a society which is in flux and is changing."

—KOLE OMOTOSO, *novelist*

". . . satire has the value of working like an invocation. In traditional society as our fathers have told us, the best way to disarm a baleful influence, an evil spirit, is to call it by its name, that is, evoke it. You can stare this baleful influence in the face and so it becomes powerless. I think this is exactly what satire is doing. . . . Who are the audience of the African writers? I think at this stage of our development the power is not really with the common people. We may deceive ourselves with socialist slogans about power to the masses. The power is in the hands of the few elite who are going to determine the future of the country, and it is among these few that you get the intelligent ones who will read the novels. I do not think it matters very much that the novel is not accessible to the ordinary person. . . ."

—D. S. IZEVBAYE, *critic and scholar*

". . . what our writers are tracing, what they have been charting, is a kind of moral decline due to the shock of the colonizer, the breakdown in values, the incoherence that was sort of an aftermath of our colonial experience which has produced the present situation in which we are living. The writers have always been present to report on this, to tell us about this, to write about this. They have never, it seems to me, abdicated this particular responsibility. So this moral concern may be taken as something that distinguishes the African novel today."

—F. A. IRELE, *critic and scholar*

". . . It should not really matter whether these things get read and understood in America or Europe. I think first our writers should aim at getting their works read locally. This is part of what I see as the failure of works like *The Interpreters*, not only because as some people might say it is faulty in its form, but because it is not really there—it does not belong to the society. That is why works like *Things Fall Apart* get read much more widely; they are directed to a certain simple but literate audience, such as school girls. . . . I think that within the reality of African life and African tradition there is a certain kind of sacredness which even the writer must respect, however iconoclastic he wants to be. There is a certain sacredness bound up with our spirituality. . . . This is the dimension which I would like to add to this discussion."

—IME IKEDDEH, *critic, scholar, editor*

"It seems to me that the suggestion has been made that the African artist lives in a world of his own and that the nature of his own type of reality must necessarily and artistically be different from the nature of European reality. . . . I think we should always look on the African artist or the African writer as belonging to a certain community that speaks generally to humanity. . . . the really solid thing about the good African novel is that it is a novel whose realities have not been so exclusively culturally bound as the topic of this symposium would seem to suggest."

—THEOPHILUS VINCENT, *critic and scholar*

"In this country we have a class of people who are known as poltergeist, medicine men or even rain doctors as they call them—who use incantations, incantations and so forth. That is all oral poetry; and all that the Yoruba praise singers who sing on festive days the praises of chiefs and recall past events and so forth, sing, is poetry. . . . Everybody enjoys and admires these praise singers, these priests; that is everybody in the rural areas. Everybody admires the rain doctor. Why is he so admired? Because his poetry is functional. The poetry tries to change some form of the human condition. If a threatened calamity, say, famine or problem of epidemic rages somewhere, they all crowd to this medicine man. . . . He manipulates words and sounds and appears to change the human condition. . . . He satisfies the demands of the community."

—GABRIEL OKARA, *poet*

". . . if the writer were accepted in African society he would be rather like the bird in the folk-tale that always appears on the wall and pipes a particular tune. When you hear that tune you know that there is tragedy somewhere; someone has died or something quite serious is happening. The bird disappears and within a moment you get the illumination of the bird's visit. The writer is this kind of bird. He pipes the tune which gives the warning."

—CYPRIAN EKWENSI, *novelist, short story writer*

Through a Continent, Darkly

WHICH TRIBE DO YOU BELONG TO?, by Alberto Moravia, translated from the Italian by Angus Davidson. 218 pp. Farrar, Straus and Giroux, 1974.

BY THE EVIDENCE, by L. S. B. Leakey. 276 pp. Harcourt Brace Jovanovich, 1974.

ALPHABETICAL AFRICA, by Walter Abish. 152 pp. New Directions, 1974.

"Africa, that repetitive, bewildering continent in which everything is reiterated until one's ordinary sense of reality reels and one is thrown into stupefied, visionary states of mind"—thus Alberto Moravia describes the geographical enigma that, over nine years' time, beguiled him into making five sub-Saharan journeys, which produced thirty-eight journalistic essays now collected under the too perky title of *Which Tribe Do You Belong To?* The first trip, taking him across Central Africa from Accra to Nairobi in the spring and summer of 1963, produced the most exhilarating impressions and most sweeping theories; the second, during which he was attached to a crew making a film on Tanzania for Italian television, encountered more misadventures (thefts, delays, quarrels with the natives, perilous plane landings) and evoked essays more disgruntled and problematical; the third, fourth, and fifth, touring the hinterlands of black Africa in the early seventies, show considerable traveller's fatigue and exasperation with the monotony, the impoverished sameness, the "oppressive and melancholy" lakes, the "tangled, evil bush country," the "red, obscene cones of anthills," the fleas, the bribes, "the wide prairies enlivened by the despairing gestures of dropsical baobabs." By the book's last incident (Moravia photographs some "truly peculiar women" in Chad and is scolded by "three young men, probably students, reproaching us with nationalist severity"), the impressionable fancy of this highly alert traveller seems defeated by the inexhaustible drabness of what he sees. Moravia, who has composed a fresh, even impudent book about his tour of Red China, is one of the best travel writers in the world; in English only V. S.

Pritchett can match his sharpness of phrase and flair for generalization. Before the muddled, stubborn refusal by everything save the animals to be picturesque gets to him, he says a number of beautiful things about the Dark Continent and its inhabitants:

> The Africans walk; for their long, indefatigable legs space is needed.

> Indeed, all these Africans who were hurrying in small groups toward the market seemed already to be having a foretaste of the moment when they would plunge into the crowd and, mingling with a great number of others in the clouds of dust, in the sweat and the noise, would rid themselves of the unstable, troublesome superfluity of individual difference.

> . . . the African is the only one among the so-called primitives who is capable of fitting happily—in fact actually by dancing—into modern industrial civilization.

> The African, in point of fact, does not know what awaits him in his dance, just as, in general, we do not know what awaits us in life.

> [Of a masked dancer] This mask, in fact, was not intended to arouse fear; it *was* fear. . . . The face, enclosed in the stocking and covered with shells like a reef under the sea, was an allusion to the inability of man to show his face in competition with prolific, overpowering nature.

Anthropologically unprejudiced as only a European confident in his superiority could be, Moravia finds what is specifically African in the thinly populated immensity, in the landscapes that repeat "a single theme or motif [such as the acacia tree] to the point of terror," in the transnational tribalism centering on the market towns, in the "frenzy for trading" that makes Africans "one of the most contriving races in the world," in the African's unique success at "becoming a modern man while still preserving intact his original dancing capacity," and in the fact—apparent, as of 1963, in the shining and incongruous commercial buildings of the African cities—"that, whereas the red star of Communism shines over Asia, it is . . . the white star of neo-capitalism that gleams over Africa."

The crisp first impressions lose some starch in the later travels.

Moravia's initial sense that Africa, "a great natural space, swarming with tribes but devoid of nationality," is destined to become one of "the great continental countries such as India, China, the United States, or the Soviet Union" runs up against the obstinate fact that the Africans cling to the institutions and arbitrary national boundaries created in Europe. The Nigerian civil war of 1967–70 represents for Moravia "a symbolic contest . . . between two different conceptions of nationality, the one previous to colonialism, the other subsequent to it. The defeat of Biafra was the defeat of the tribal conception." And he admits to difficulty, as he moves through the open market of Fort Lamy, in imagining the traders "no longer unoccupied and on the alert but efficient and rational, sitting at European desks in bureaucratic offices." Some of Moravia's perceptions, like the things perceived, repeat to the point of monotony; the image of a red-dirt road as a bloody wound recurs close to a dozen times. But his eye remains basically attentive, his attention basically loving; some of the best pieces (few more than six pages long) are among the last, as he wanders from Timbuktu to the Mountains of the Moon. He combines the passive, even dazed traveller's receptivity to random detail with the thinker's determination to *see through*—to observe, as it were, aggressively. His essays not only describe to us wonders we will never visit, they tell some of us who were there what it is we saw.

Sitting in a posh hotel in Mombasa, Moravia observes across the dining room a tableful of specimens of "homo Victorianus"—a species extinct in Europe but surviving in Kenya:

> The English today rarely have those big, slightly bandy legs, those monumental thighs, those bellies as tight as drums, those muscular chests and massive napes to their necks, those prominent chins and toothbrush moustaches.

To a passing traveller, the late Louis S. B. Leakey might have seemed such—one of those white men whose whiteness, in the Kenyan highlands, had become self-cherishing, muscular, clever, and brutal. His memoir *By the Evidence* savors of the satisfied adventurer, of spacious opportunities ingeniously and unapologetically seized. It was Leakey, of course, who perceived the depth of human prehistory that lay beneath the sunstruck gorges and dried lake beds of East Africa, and who seized the opportunity to verify Darwin's intuition that Africa had been the cradle of humankind. With his discovery, in 1959, of the Zinjanthropus skull, a hominid fragment nearly two million years old, Leakey became the most famous paleoanthropologist of his time. *By the Evidence* is subtitled *Memoirs, 1932–51*, and was meant to be the middle volume of an autobiographical trilogy. The initial installment was *White African*—published in England in 1937, in the United States in 1966. The third volume, because of Leakey's death, of a heart attack the very day after he had completed *By the Evidence*, is now never to be written. The book in hand tells, then, of neither his epochal, career-vindicating discovery nor of his extraordinary African upbringing. *By the Evidence* chronicles his settled middle years, between the ages of thirty and fifty. Too much of it is concerned with the organizational trivia surrounding such promotional triumphs as the 1947 Pan-African Congress of Prehistory; Leakey kept a journal, and our passage through his days sometimes plods. On the other hand, he is intriguingly terse on personal matters; his marriage to Frida Avern, he tells us, literally in parenthesis, "had, regrettably, broken up" while he was roughing it in the bush with Mary Nicol, who becomes Mary Leakey a few pages later. There is more revealed of the man in *White African*—regarded by the author, too lightly, as a "potboiler."

Leakey was born, his first memoir tells us, in 1903 of missionary parents in a mud-and-thatch hut in Kabete, eight miles from Nairobi, then itself "little more than a scattered collection of corrugated-iron bungalows, and offices, gathered for convenience round the railway station." Born prematurely, he was swathed in cotton wool, and had to be kept dry not only from rain leaking through the thatch but from the saliva of Kikuyu visitors, who believed spitting to be an anti-curse courtesy. In the isolated mission outpost, Leakey and his siblings learned Kikuyu along with English, and all his life he dreamed in Kikuyu. He was initiated into the tribe, with full rites, as "Wakaruigi, son of the Sparrowhawk." His playmates, the games they played, the bedtime stories he heard, were all African. Though his family several times made the long trip back to England, the boy found himself, when he entered British public school, in 1919, painfully disadvantaged—unfamiliar with cricket, accustomed to playing football barefooted, incapable of swimming (crocodiles discourage this recreation in Africa), innocent of Greek and of firsthand encounter with the theatre, yet habituated to an independence improper for English schoolboys: at the age of thirteen, in accordance with Kikuyu custom, he had built himself a house and begun to live in it alone; at English boarding school he was required to get permission to go shopping, and to wear a straw hat and dark suit on a Sunday country walk. So his outlook was biased rather differently from the conventional "homo Victorianus," colonial subspecies; on his digs he insisted, to the scandal of Kenyan white settlers, on both digging beside his "boys" and carrying water with them. His imperfect indoctrination into European ways not only made his schooling awkward (at Cambridge he was rebuked for playing tennis in shorts and a sort of bush jacket) but may account for an abrasiveness that rubs through the memoirist's civil manners, for his unseemly delight in academic contests, which he always wins, and for the earthiness and voracity of his scientific approach.

For instance, in *By the Evidence* he heartily advises all would-be zoologists, "Always, as a matter of routine, examine the stomach contents of any dead animal to which you have access," and by way of illustration relates with a zest not quite infectious his own delighted discoveries of "a mass of water beetles" in the stomach of a giant pangolin, of millipedes and centipedes inside a civet, of cucumber seeds and red biting ants in an aardvark, and of "bracelets, beads, necklaces, and many other indisputable indications of the human meals that had been eaten" inside a crocodile he has shot. There is something savage about Leakey's resourcefulness—he tells us how to replace a broken car spring with strips of green hardwood and freshly skinned goat hide—and uncanny about his luck. "Leakey's luck" was a phrase coined by his rival prehistorians. On holiday in England, he was approached by a neighbor about some flakes of flint in one of his fields; though the spot had been snubbed by British archaeologists, Leakey opportunely dug, and uncovered, he tells us, "an example of the earliest known dwelling anywhere in England." The casual skills proclaimed in this volume range from dog judging to handwriting analysis, of both the English and the Gujarati scripts. He displays by his own account authoritative expertness in museum curatorship, ornithology, the care of sick animals, the primitive art of string figures. During the war he functions as spy, broadcaster in African languages, graphologist, even footprint castmaker. Some of his sentences are downright comic in their bustle of enterprise:

> As well as gathering valuable information by chatting with the local people while I watched the Verreaux's eagles, I also located a series of Late Stone Age living sites belonging to the Kenya Wilton culture.

> I could look back on the previous eighteen months as having been very rewarding. I had written three books, *White African*, *Stone Age Africa*, and *Kenya: Contrasts and Problems*. I had also almost completed the research necessary for my first book on Olduvai Gorge and had undertaken some exciting studies of pygmy chimpanzee skulls.

But there was nothing comic, or especially lucky, about the archaeological discoveries that are Leakey's main accomplishment. From the age of twelve, when he began to collect obsidian arrowheads lying about Kabete, he had a passionate, rather patriotic faith in East Africa's richness for the study of Man's prehistory. The Zinjanthropus skull came to light after thirty years, off and on, of "crawling up and down . . . with eyes barely inches from the ground." The spot in the Olduvai Gorge where Zinjanthropus was found is marked by a plaque, and can be reached through a little detour off the main road from the Serengeti Plain to the Ngorongoro Crater; it has become a tourist spot. But even now it seems lonely and barren and strange; a few orange-cloaked Masai herdsmen wander in the middle distance as if the immensities of African space were still untroubled. The great, lovable antagonist of Leakey's memoirs (and the first volume more vividly conveys this than does the second) is African space. The difficulty of getting there, of nursing machines through roadless terrain, of locating water sources in a geologically parching land, of finding a significant bone in an ocean of rubble—against such odds Leakey, no mere scientist, looms as a hero.

*

African space of another kind, and patience of a more literary sort, figure in Walter Abish's remarkable, ludicrously programmatic novel *Alphabetical Africa*. The adventure Mr. Abish has set himself is to compose a novel of twice twenty-six chapters, of which the first employs only words beginning with "A," the second words beginning with "A" and "B," and so on up to "Z," by which time the full lexical possibilities of the English language are available; then, from "Z" to "A," he moves back down the alphabet, subtracting letters one by one until the last chapter, like the first, is composed entirely of words beginning with "A." The hardships of such a journey should not be underestimated; "A" brings with it a handy number of articles and connectives, but not until "H" is reached can the pronoun "he" and the helper verb "have" be used, and for all but the fourteen chapters between "T" and "T" such virtually indispensable formations as "the," "to," "they,' "their," and "this" must be dispensed with. A character called Queen Quat cannot appear until after the middle of the ascending alphabet is reached, and must perish on the downhill side when her letter vanishes. Fortunately, Mr. Abish's style, even when unhampered by artificial constraints, is rather chastened and elliptic, so his fettered progress is steadier than you might imagine. Here is a paragraph from the first chapter:

> Africa again: Antelopes, alligators, ants and attractive Alva, are arousing all angular Africans, also arousing author's analytically aggressive anticipations, again and again. Anyhow author apprehends Alva anatomically, affirmatively, and also accurately.

By the time his verbal safari reaches "G," Abish can make, at length and almost fluently, observations reminiscent of Moravia's:

> Genuine gestures are African gestures, because Africans can by a few gestures demonstrate a deep and abiding affection between altogether different foreign bodies, each clap, each groan, each facial gesture conveying a convincingly eternal dramatic African confusion and also a fusion of bodies, as bodies explore boundaries, generously emitting a fresh African ecstasy . . .

"I" releases the possibility of self-exposition, "M" brings with it the themes of memory and money and murder, and by "S" only an alerted eye and hypersensitive ear would notice that a quarter of the dictionary is still being abjured:

Summarizing Africa: I can speak more freely. I find fewer and fewer impediments. Soon I'll reach my destination. Soon I'll also complete my documentation and my book. Daily Africa is shrinking from extreme heat and fatigue, as rebels in bush battle African armies led by foreigners.

The attainment, long anticipated by the alphabet-battered reader, of "Z"s total freedom brings a disappointingly short chapter, written in the cramped, clicking tone of the others:

Zambia helps fill our zoos, and our doubts, and our extrawide screens as we sit back. Each year we zigzag between the cages, prodding the alligators, the antelopes, the giant ants, just to see them move about a bit, just to make our life more authentic . . .

Each chapter, as it possesses another letter, celebrates its acquisition with a burst of alliteration, so our knowledge of systematic expansion is aurally emphasized; this subtly joyous undertone of organic growth is lost in the book's second half, wherein the subtraction of letters echoes supposed land shrinkage ("Africa's gradual deterioration and Africa's decreasing area"), and some violent events on Zanzibar swallow up Queen Quat (who has painted Tanzania orange to match the maps) and squeeze the novel's protagonists—Alex, Allen, and Alva—into a climax of betrothal. The extremely silly plot begins as a jewel robbery in Antibes and a consequent flight to Angola, Burundi, Chad, etc., and culminates in a kind of people's uprising by the Vietcong-like army ants: "All complain close-by artillery barrage battered beautiful city, battered beautiful avenues, all because ants continue advance, continue creeping along, carving a continent." Though the tale is murky as well as absurd, one is tempted to concede that Mr. Abish has performed as well as anyone could, given such extravagant handicaps. "A masterpiece of its kind" does not seem too strong an accolade for a book apt to be the only one of its kind.

And there is a nice rightness to setting such a work in Africa, where incantations are still potent and national boundaries slice across tribal realities as arbitrarily as the alphabet schematizes language. Teeming yet vacant, mysterious yet monotonous, Africa permits this literary experiment. *Alphabetical Asia* would not have been so funny, *Alphabetical America* would have been cluttered with reality, *Alphabetical Antarctica* would have been blank. "Africa is a favorite topic in literature, it gives license to so much excess," the author explains, and confesses, of his old bush jacket, that it "fed my imagination long before I ever set foot on this continent." Mr. Abish is pictured on the dust jacket wearing this bush jacket, and a romantic black eye patch, in a studio containing African sculptures. For the Western mind, art and fancy and travellers' accounts form Africa's body. Though *Alphabetical Africa* gives some evidence that the author has visited the continent, it was not necessary; his Swahili dictionary and a four-color map took him where he wanted to go. Setting out with his elaborate impedimenta, he chose the mental milieu that offered him the most license and sport. Africa, explored and excavated and neo-capitalized as it now is, remains—for Mr. Abish as for Moravia, as it was for Leakey and Livingstone, for Gide and Hemingway, for Rider Haggard and Edgar Rice Burroughs, for Burton and Speke and Mungo Park and Prince Henry the Navigator—an invitation to the imagination.

THE AVANT GARDE

Grove Is My Press, and Avant My Garde

LA MAISON DE RENDEZ-VOUS, by Alain Robbe-Grillet, translated from the French by Richard Howard. 154 pp. Grove Press, 1966.

MIRACLE OF THE ROSE, by Jean Genet, translated from the French by Bernard Frechtman. 344 pp. Grove Press, 1966.

THE INQUISITORY, by Robert Pinget, translated from the French by Donald Watson. 399 pp. Grove Press, 1966.

Grove Press, that happy caterer to our prurience and our progressivism, continues to nourish the illusion of a literary avant garde by dishing up hitherto obscure modern masters (Borges, Gombrowicz), pornography with a taint of sociological or psychological interest (*My Secret Life, The Story of O*), native scatwriting (LeRoi Jones, William Burroughs), and such imported delicacies as the three French novels about to be savored. The *smörgåsbord* is mixed but not to be sniffed at. On balance, Grove Press has been the one post-war publishing house to show a personality and mission of its own, to serve the fifties and sixties as New Directions served the thirties and forties. Its courage has preceded its commercialism; it pioneered in the territory it now so cheerfully exploits with its black-mass version of the Book-of-the-Month Club, its roguish get-with-the-sexual-revolution ads, its stable of Ph.D.s willing to preface the latest "curious" memoir or "underground" classic with admonitory sermons on the righteousness of fornication. And if Grove Press's best American author remains Eric Berne, its Art Nouveau jackets have enfolded many foreign titles for whose translation the conscientious reader should be grateful.

It is surprising, for instance, that no more orthodox publisher undertook to make the works of Alain Robbe-Grillet available in this country. Robbe-Grillet is the leading theoretician of the *nouveau roman;* he coined the phrase and composed the first example —*The Erasers* (1953). If American writers, and loud worriers like Susan Sontag ("The novel is probably the most rear-guard art form today. . . . Most critically respectable novels . . . are, I think, essentially journalistic in conception. . . . [American novelists] are not essentially concerned with the novel as a work of art in the sense that most other art forms are today . . ."), imagine that progress is being made elsewhere, Robbe-Grillet's astute propagandizing is a prime cause. The tired cry "Make it new" has become new in his essays, and before the consideration of his fifth and most recent novel, his program should be summarized. The first major manifesto, "A Fresh Start for Fiction" (1956), announced:

> The world is neither significant nor absurd. It *is*, quite simply. That, in any case, is the most remarkable thing about it. . . . Around us, defying the mob of our animistic or protective adjectives, the things *are there*. Their surfaces are clear and smooth, *intact*, neither dubiously glittering, nor transparent. All our literature has not yet succeeded in penetrating their smallest corner, in softening their slightest curve.
>
> Instead of . . . "signification" (psychological, social, functional), we must try to construct a world both more solid and more immediate. Let it be first of all by their *presence* that objects and gestures impose themselves, and let this presence continue to make itself felt beyond all explanatory theory that might try to enclose it in some system of reference, whether sentimental, sociological, Freudian, or metaphysical. In this future universe of the novel, gestures and objects will be "there" before being "something," and they will still be there afterward, hard, unalterable, eternally present, mocking their own meaning, which tries in vain to reduce them to the role of precarious tools. . . . Thus objects will little by little lose their inconsistency and their secrets; will renounce their false mystery, that suspect interiority which Roland Barthes has called the "romantic 'heart' of things."

A later essay, "Nature, Humanism, Tragedy" (1958), develops these ideas into a stylistic purge. Metaphor is the villain, weaving a complicity between humanity and the alien world of "things"; metaphor—a concept including all adjectives with moral or anthropocentric coloring—implies a general myth of *depth*, humanizing nature, cheating it of its essential otherness. The categories of the "tragic" and the "absurd" are oblique maneuvers of this persistent humanism, this "bridge of souls thrown between man and things." The task, then, is to "scour" descriptive prose of any "analogical vocabulary" and to restore "things" to "themselves," cleansed of any hint of profundity or preëstablished order. In this scouring, the sense of sight occupies a privileged position, as the sense that measures distances—"our best weapon, especially if it keeps exclusively to outlines." And in a still later essay, "Time and Description in Fiction Today" (1963), Robbe-Grillet adds to the priority of visual precision "the breaks of cutting, the repetitions of scene, the contradictions, the characters suddenly paralyzed as in amateur photographs" that in fact do distinguish his later novels and his films alike. The purpose of these devices is to "afford this perpetual present [of the cinema, of the *nouveau roman*] all its force, all its violence." Temporal and spatial discontinuity, a present that never accumulates, are employed to dissolve "the trap of the anecdote." The thereness of things emerges from their dissolution.

Robbe-Grillet's theories constitute the most ambitious aesthetic program since Surrealism. My summary necessarily has skimped much: his reasoning is close; his remarks upon other writers, including the classics of the bourgeois novel, are reverent and lively. Because of his training as an agronomist, his understanding of science and of how its truths subvert our workaday assumptions exceeds that of most writers. His pronouncements do catch at something—a texture, an austerity—already present in other, often older French novelists, such as Nathalie Sarraute. To an American, however, there is a hollow ring of Thomism. Robbe-Grillet's concept of thereness looks like the medieval *quidditas;* the attempt to treat existence itself as a quality that can be artistically emphasized seems a formal confusion, a scholastic bottling of the wind. Robbe-Grillet's key concept—of "purely external and superficial" things —takes no account of the vast area of mobile and animate phenomena that mediate between *Homo sapiens* and inert matter, or of the difference between raw material and artifacts already imbued with human intention, or of the fact that to one man another is as much a "thing" as a chair or waterfall. In making his cleavage between "humanity" and "things," is he not guilty of a kind of humanism, elevating men into a glorious concept—Man? The real split, surely, is between the single ego and the external world—which would take us back into psychology, where Robbe-Grillet does not want to go. There is a forced naïveté in his vision, and a strange inversion of the pathetic fallacy he detests, for in artistic practice his concern with the inviolable otherness of things charges them, saturates them, with a menace and hostility as distortive of their null inner being as an imagined sympathy. One's reservations about Robbe-Grillet's formulations come down to the discrepancy between his description of what happens in his fiction and what actually happens. Far from striking us with their unsullied thereness, the "things" in his novels are implicated in the pervasive flimsiness and inconsequence.

La Maison de Rendez-Vous could have been translated as The House of Assignation or The Blue Villa or even Up at Lady Ava's. It tells of, or circles around, a night at the elegant brothel run by Lady Ava, or Eva, or Eve, in Hong Kong. There is a police raid, and an American, or Englishman, named Ralph or Sir Ralph Johnson or Jonestone, in love with a prostitute called Lauren, and the murder of a man called Edouard Manneret and of another named Georges Marchat or Marchant or Marchand, and several ferry rides to Kowloon, and a fluctuating penumbra of dope smuggling and white slavery and Cold War intrigue. Above it all is an "old mad king" pounding an iron-tipped cane on the floor and insomniacally rocking in a rocking chair; his name is given as King Boris, but he strongly resembles Manneret. The other presiding presence is a narrator who confesses to being constantly beset by images of female flesh and who sometimes inhabits Johnson's body or partakes of his adventures. Through this fog of events, or anti-events ("What does all that matter? What does it matter?" the book asks itself, answering, "All this comes to the same thing"), rotates a constellation of repeated and refracted images—a broken champagne glass, an envelope containing sand or heroin or documents, a scrap of paper illustrating the evils of drugs or else pushing them, a ubiquitous rickshaw driver, the slit hobble skirt of several interchangeable Eurasian beauties who are also mannequins in shop-windows. True to Robbe-Grillet's credo, the present never accumulates; rather, it unravels. There is a studied false numerical precision. A hand is "about eight or twelve" inches from a serving tray; forty pages later, the distance is given as six inches. Manneret's apartment is on the third floor, or the fifth, or the sixth, or the eighth. Different characters relive the same adventures; a play within the action becomes the action; and twin servant girls have the same name, "pronounced quite similarly, the difference imperceptible except to a Chinese ear." The ingenuity behind all this doubling and shuffling is considerable. The writing is clean and deft and even entertaining, though the reader's interest tends to cling, pathetically, to the excitements of the hackneyed tale of exotic intrigue that is being parodied, fragmented, and systematically frustrated. The popular adventure form underlying the sophisticated *nouveau roman* rises up and revenges itself by imposing upon the book a cliché ending of double-cross and a flat last sentence: "And there is nothing in her eyes." But there has never been anything in her eyes. Upon the basis, I think, of false analogies, Robbe-Grillet has already dissolved, with his "descriptions whose movement destroys all confidence in the things described," the credibility as elemental to the art of narrative as the solidity of stone or metal is to sculpture.

The analogies are with the cinema and modern painting. The 20th-century novelist finds himself in competition with a mode of storytelling—motion pictures—that is astonishing in the directness with which it presents and manipulates imagery and virtually tyrannical in its possession of the viewer's attention and in its power to compel emotion. The novel, rooted in the historical past tense of the histories, legends, journals, and epistles from which it is descended, cannot but envy this constant present that does not tell but simply *is,* dancing and slicing through space, juxtaposing in montage landscapes and faces, swords and roses, violence and stasis—a new poetry, a wordless vocabulary that engulfs us like an environment. *Ulysses* was one of the first attempts, and remains the noblest, to appropriate to prose fiction some of the new medium's properties—the simultaneous intimacy and impersonality, the abrupt shifts from close-up to boom shot, the electric shuttle of scenes. Joyce immerses these effects in an orgy of literariness; Robbe-Grillet's fiction is almost exclusively cinematic. *La Maison de Rendez-Vous* is not so much written as scripted: "The scene which then takes place lacks clarity," "Then the images follow one another very rapidly," "Now we see the young Eurasian girl backed into the corner of a luxurious room, near a lacquer chest whose lines are emphasized by bronze ornaments, all escape cut off by a man in a carefully trimmed gray goatee who is towering over her." The full syntax of splicing, blurring, stop-action, enlargement, panning, and fade-out is employed; the book lacks only camera tracks and a union member operating the dolly. The trouble is that prose does not inherently possess the luminous thereness of a projected image, and all of Robbe-Grillet's montages, visual particularization, careful distinctions between right and left, and so on do not induce the kind of participation imposed by, say, his real movie *Last Year at Marienbad*. A man sitting with a book in his lap is a creature quite different from a man sitting hypnotized in a dark theatre. The mind translates verbal imagery into familiar images innocent of a photograph's staring actuality; it seizes on a single detail and enshrouds it in vague memories from real life. An image, to have more than this hazy recollective vitality, must be weighted with a momentum beyond itself, by that movement of merged relevance that Aristotle called an "action."

For this movement, and the accumulating emotion and concern around the things described, Robbe-Grillet, in his essay "Time and Description in Fiction Today," offers to substitute "the very movement of the description." Here we have the second false analogy—with painting. The practitioners of literature can hardly escape the impression that painting is the century's heroic, dominant art, the art that has won the allegiance of the rich, the art most productive of manifestos, credos, saintliness, and fresh waves of innovation. Above all, it is painting that has purified itself of content; with Cézanne, the canvas ceases to be a window and becomes a flat field whereupon a drama has occurred—the oranges or Mont Sainte-Victoire or Mme. Cézanne serving as a mere excuse. Abstraction eliminates even the excuse. Naturally, novelists seek to attain to this lordly independence of circumstance, this sacerdotal self-sufficiency. As early as 1861, Flaubert was assuring the Goncourt brothers that "The story, the plot of a novel is of no interest to me. When I write a novel I aim at rendering a color, a shade. For instance, in my Carthaginian novel, I want to do something purple. . . . In *Madame Bovary*, all I wanted to do was to render a gray color, the mouldy color of a wood louse's existence. The story of the novel mattered so little to me that a few days before starting on it I still had in mind a very different Madame Bovary from the one I created. . . . she was to have been a chaste and devout old maid." Flaubert's claim seems wistful; he sounds like an Impressionist, and the Impressionists were still short of the final liberation, insofar as their brushwork recalls the beauty of *real* water lilies, sunshine, haystacks. A page of print can never, like a rectangle of paint, lift free of all reference to real objects; it cannot but be some kind of shadow. Further, a painting is from the painter's hand, whereas a book has passed through a mechanical process that erases all the handwriting and crossing-out that would declare the author's presence and effort. Robbe-Grillet's off-center duplications, subtle inaccuracies, and cubistic fragmentation do not convey "the very movement of the description." They instead seem mannered devices intended to give unsubstantial materials an interesting surface.

Compare Kafka's truncated chapters and warps of narrative. They rise, we feel, from within, *in spite of* the author's pained sincerity and conscientious prose; they are neurotic in nature. And a neurosis is a profounder product of a culture than a theory. Robbe-Grillet does have instincts, tropisms toward certain styles of experience; his first novel, *The Erasers*, a coherent detective story, shows the same surveyor's eye, the same fondness for duplication and stalled motion, as does his last. But between the two there has been a buildup of theory, a stylization of intuition. *La Maison de Rendez-Vous* is less a work of art than an objet d'art, shiny with its appliqué of progressive post-Existential thought; it has a fragile air of mere up-to-dateness, of chic.

Whereas *Miracle of the Rose*, by Jean Genet, is as subjective and compulsive as one could wish. This, his second novel, was written in the prisons of La Santé and Tourelles, in 1943, on the pieces of white paper supplied to the convicts for the making of paper bags. Any hope of publication must have been desperate. His first novel, *Our Lady of the Flowers*, written in 1942, proclaims itself, and is acclaimed by Sartre in his introduction, as a jailbird's masturbatory fantasies. *Miracle of the Rose* springs, as it were, from the same aesthetic: "I carried Bulkaen off in the depths of my heart. I went back to my cell, and the abandoned habit of my abandoned childhood took hold of me: the rest of the day and all night long I built an imaginary life of which Bulkaen was the center, and I always gave that life, which was begun over and over and was transformed a dozen times, a violent end: murder, hanging, or beheading." Reality and fantasy are inextricable. *Miracle of the Rose* seems slightly more earthbound than *Our Lady of the Flowers*—a touch less brilliant and soaring, a shade more plausible and didactic. Genet's own person emerges somewhat more solidly; while the earlier novel made the reader marvel that a criminal had become a writer, now it seems stranger that such a writer became a criminal. We are permitted glimpses—in categorical phrases like "a region to which irony has no access," in a critical disquisition on the vulgarity of placing slang words in quotation marks—of a depraved man whose vocation, nevertheless, from boyhood on has been literary. As a thief, he stole books!—"books with heraldic bindings, the Japanese vellum of deluxe editions, the long-grained moroccan copies."

As in *Our Lady*, the story line of *Miracle of the Rose*, obeying no known gravitational laws, flies back and forth among the men Genet loves: Harcamone, the condemned man invisible in the death cell; Bulkaen, the young weakling covered even to his eyelids with tattoos; Villeroy, the big shot whose chicken Genet becomes at the boys' reformatory of Mettray; Divers, Villeroy's successor, who marries Genet in a mock ceremony and reappears fifteen years later, at the state prison of Fontevrault, and again possesses his bride. An occasional physical description or snatch of dialogue reveals the lustreless thugs beneath the extraordinary flowers of metaphor in which they are garlanded, but these pimps and crashers, big shots and chickens, exist primarily as angels and archangels in the inverted heaven of Genet's dreaming. The prison Fontevrault was once a monastery; when Genet arrives, manacled, the doorways are lit up as if for Christmas. Christianity permeates his confinement there. He suffers a series of mystic visions centered upon Harcamone, and indeed the prison world, "the eternal gray season in which I am trapped," does approximate the religious view of the world. Abasement gives rise to transcendent consolations: "And as our life is without external hope, it turns its desires inward. I cannot believe that the Prison is not a mystic community," "Your pride must be able to undergo shame in order to attain glory," "One is a saint by the force of circumstances which is the force of God! . . . I loved Bulkaen for his ignominy." These testimonies, obtained under pressures of deprivation comparable to the oppression in which primitive Christianity thrived, cannot be dismissed as blasphemous any more than the pervasive erotic content can be dismissed as "homosexual." Genet is one of the few writers to make homosexual love credible, both in concrete detail—"Our shaved heads rolled around each other, with our rough cheeks scraping"—and in inner essence, in the tenderness and hysteria it shares with all sex.

Some months ago, the Reverend Tom Driver, writing in the *Saturday Review*, admired *Miracle of the Rose* for showing Genet's transformation from a passive, "female" homosexual, the concubine of Villeroy, into an aggressive "male" one, the assaulter of Bulkaen. The improvement, to Driver, seemed self-evident, but three angry letters responded, one refusing to renew a subscription, another deploring "the literary morass of this decade," and a third likening Genet to the Nazis. Indeed, Genet, whose wartime efforts consisted of weaving, while in prison, camouflage nets for the Germans, does write kindly of the occupation forces: "When it was reported that the Germans were preparing to leave, France realized, in losing the rigidity they had imposed on her, that she had loved them." It must be admitted, especially by those of us admiring of his rhetoric, that Genet, in his submission to rigidity and his quest for the resplendence of emotional extremes, is led into a moral realm where no conventional liberal, or even civilized person, can follow. "War was beautiful in the past because in shedding blood it produced glory. It is even more beautiful now because it creates pain, violence, and despair. . . . I love the war that devoured my handsomest friends. . . . Novels are not humanitarian reports. Indeed, let us be thankful that there remains sufficient cruelty, without which beauty would not be." He worships Harcamone, who gratuitously murders a guard at Fontevrault; at Mettray, he admires Van Roy, who betrays an escape plot and thereby has "dared make a terrible gesture" demonstrating that "the strongest big shots were squealers." He is nostalgic for the superior—compared to mature criminals—ferocity of adolescents and remembers his own cruelty: "My cruelty, when I was sixteen, made me stab the left eye of a child who, frightened by my pitiless stare and realizing that his eye attracted me, tried to save it by putting his fist to it." Consistent with this savagery toward others is a fervent death wish: "My love of beauty (which desired so ardently that my life be crowned with a violent, in fact bloody, death) . . . made me secretly choose decapitation." Genet's outlawry is more thorough than de Sade's, who at least blamed God for the existence of pain; Genet says, "God is good. . . . He strews so many traps along our path." Only the desert saints of early Christianity, perhaps, would so blithely have burned the world to produce visions.

Is *Miracle of the Rose* an avant-garde novel? Genet does not claim it to be: "If I were writing a novel, there might be a point in describing the gestures I made, but the aim of this book is only to relate the experience of freeing myself from a state of painful torpor, from a low, shameful life taken up with prostitution and begging." Certainly it lacks description in the sense of giving persons and objects an appearance of autonomy. The characters, apart from their names, are no more distinguishable than the mosaic figures aligned within a Byzantine dome. The dome is Genet's skull: he is absolute Creator within this universe, not only of persons but of the laws that control their motions. The humanization of nature, which Robbe-Grillet would eliminate from fiction, here operates with a vengeance; everything is transmuted into metaphor, nothing is more than what it means to Genet. The very prison melts so that, at the book's climax, Genet can mystically join Harcamone on his walk to the guillotine. The novel is a loose form, but *Miracle of the Rose* seems to me to fall outside it and to belong rather to that older stream of French literature, contributory to the novel, of essay and *pensée*, memoir and letter, confession and self-revelation. "We belonged to the Middle Ages," Genet says of his fellow-convicts, and when he writes of entering through

Harcamone's gullet a country landscape detailed down to "the remains of a country fair: a spangled jersey, the ashes of a camp-fire, a circus whip," his untrammelled hyperbole belongs—in defiance of intervening centuries of bourgeois empiricism and objectivity—to Rabelais.

Robert Pinget is not as yet well known on this side of the Atlantic. *The Inquisitory* was originally published in 1962; from the jacket copy, and a laudatory review of some earlier novels printed among Robbe-Grillet's essays, I gather that since his first book, a collection of stories entitled *Entre Fantoine et Agapa*, Pinget's fiction has explored an imaginary provincial region between Fantoine and Agapa, a Gallic Yoknapatawpha County—an "absurd suburb of reality," in Robbe-Grillet's phrase. Certainly *The Inquisitory*, which won the Prix des Critiques, abounds with circumstantial information. Thirty pages are devoted to a description, shop by shop, of the main square of the village of Sirancy; the street geography of the town of Agapa is exhaustively examined; eleven pages call the roll of furnishings in the drawing room of a château, which is eventually inventoried from cellar to attic; and an attentive reader with pencil in hand could probably draw, from the various textual indications, a map of the entire region. Now, such feats of particularization demand more patience than passion from writer and reader alike, but the end result is the kind of trustworthiness absent, for different reasons, from both *La Maison de Rendez-Vous* and *Miracle of the Rose*. *The Inquisitory* is of the three by far the best novel, if by novel we understand an imitation of reality rather than a spurning of it.

Not that Pinget is old-fashioned; he has put himself to school with Robbe-Grillet and Beckett. The novel's premise is a Beckettian stripped situation: an infinitely garrulous old château servant is being quizzed by an infinitely curious investigator. Both are nameless. Punctuation marks are abjured. A shadowy secretary is in the room, typing up all three hundred and ninety-nine pages of meandering testimony. The object of the investigation—the disappearance of the château secretary—is never clarified. The dialogue, initially full to bursting of visual measurement and *quidditas*, ebbs into a fatigued exchange, laconic and baffled. All this circumstantiality protests against circumstantiality, both as an adjunct of the novel and as the illusory stuff of life: "Another twenty rooms and then there'll still be more and you'll tell me to describe them, and more and more kitchens servants tell-tale tittle-tattle secrets of the bedchamber families mile upon mile of streets and stairs and lumber-rooms and junk-shops of antique-dealers grocers butchers of skimping and scraping everywhere in our heads how dreary it all is always starting all over again why." The investigator is in a sense the all too ideal reader, asking again and again, "Go on," begging, "Describe the longest route." And the answerer, with his omnivorous memory and solipsistic deafness —the questions put to him must be written on slips of paper—is the aboriginal storyteller, whose enterprise is essentially one of understanding:

> . . . we're bound to understand in the end
> Understand what
> The rest what one's forgotten sometimes I tell myself
> Explain
> Perhaps that's the answer that does the least harm
> What answer
> Understanding what one's forgotten
> What
> It seems so to me unless I'm talking nonsense. . . .

Pinget's very avant-garde novel of the absurd incorporates the full French novelistic tradition. Like Proust, he has a curé who dabbles in the etymology of place names; like Balzac, he avidly traces the fortunes of little provincial shops through all the ups and downs that gossip traces. The number of anecdotes, of minia-ture novels, caught in his nets of description cannot be counted; presumably some are expanded elsewhere in Pinget's *oeuvre*. In this book, the curve of interest moves through the château itself (the two "gentlemen" who own it, their wealth, their homo-sexuality, their fussiness, their decadence, all implied by lengthy humorous descriptions of their house-furnishings), and then out into the social and geographical composition of the region as a whole ("The main resources of the district are in the soil and al-ways will be"), and finally into the character and philosophy of the narrator himself. He has lost a wife and child; he is immensely lonely; he believes in diabolism and locates direct access to Hell in a quarry region called Vaguemort. Heaven's counterpart appears with the revelation that in the medieval section of the château lives a third employer, Monsieur Pierre—"a few intimate friends used to call them the Holy Trinity but to be frank the only holy man is Monsieur Pierre"—who is a hermit and an astronomer. So by the novel's end this district, into which enough historical allusion has been insinuated to render it an analogue of France, serves as a model of the world, with all human possibilities somewhere touched upon. Grove Press will, I hope, publish more of Pinget's work, which seems not only highly accomplished but thoroughly masculine, quite without the eunuchoid air of distress with which too much modern fiction confronts its bride the world.

All praise conceded, it remains to confess that none of these three books was hard to put down and that it is hard to imagine very many Americans, except for reviewers and students of the "art of the novel," reading them. All partake of that resistant modern motionlessness, so different from the lightning speed of Biblical chronicle or the tidal roll of Homeric narrative or the bustling forward march of the 19th-century novel—a motionlessness present in the circular structures of *Finnegans Wake* and *Remembrance of Things Past,* in the unconquerable distances of Kafka and the unconscionable length of Bloom's day, in the final "Let's go" of *Waiting for Godot,* followed by the stage direction "(*They do not move*)." The avant-garde novel itself has been saying "Let's go" for forty years, and has not outdistanced Joyce or left Kafka behind. There is an enfeebling doubt as to *ends:* Do stories end? Do novels have an end, a purpose? To entertain? To educate? To exasperate? To dehumanize literary idiom? To facilitate the author's onanism? The characteristic movement of modern narrative is of prolongation, of postponement. Novels end but do not *have* an end.

Yes or no answer
I'm tired

Thus *The Inquisitory* concludes. It is an honest, inconclusive conclusion. In an age of waiting (of, Christian eschatology would have it, a between-times), we find our loss of teleological sense reflected in books whose intricate energy, like that of barbarian designs, is essentially static.

Infante Terrible

THREE TRAPPED TIGERS, by G. Cabrera Infante, translated from the Spanish by Donald Gardner and Suzanne Jill Levine. 487 pp. Harper & Row, 1971.

Some things are more lost in translation than others; jokes and Racine, for instance, lose more than newspapers and de Maupassant. In its original Spanish, *Tres Tristes Tigres*, by G. Cabrera Infante, won the Biblioteca Breve and contended for the Formentor Prize; in French, it won the Prix du Meilleur Livre Étranger. In English, however, as *Three Trapped Tigers*, the novel comes over as a tedious, verbose, jejune, self-delighting mess, and unless the publisher decides to distribute good-sportsmanship awards to those few readers who persevere to the end it should generate no prizes. One can deduce that the life of *Three Trapped* (though "sad" is what they originally were) *Tigers* lay in its skin of Spanish, and that a creature so ectomorphic, so narrowly vital, was bound to perish away from the nurture of its native climate. Or one might, less kindly, conclude that the novel was derivative, that its excitement derived from the translation of the methods of *Ulysses* into Cuban idiom, and that, restored to Joyce's mother tongue, it shows up as a tired copy.

Three Trapped Tigers offers to do for the Havana of 1958 what *Ulysses* did for the Dublin of 1904: wandering itineraries are mapped street by street, minor characters reappear in a studied interweave, a variety of voices abruptly soliloquize, a kind of "Oxen of the Sun" procession of literary parodies is worked on the theme of Trotsky's assassination, an endless "Nighttown" drunkenness episode picks up the deliberate hungover banality of the Eumaeus sequence, and a female interior monologue closes the book. Unlike Joyce, however, Cabrera Infante packs most of his pyrotechnics and montage into the novel's first half and winds down into a more natural narrative tone. And, instead of attentive, soft-spoken, gradually solidifying Bloom, *Three Trapped Tigers* has for its hero an insubstantial, logomaniacal trio of would-be writers—Arsenio Cué, Bustrófedon (who is dead), and the principal narrator, Silvestre. As these three compile reams of undergraduate gags ("*Crime and Puns*, by Bustrófedor Dostowhiskey," "*Under the Lorry*, by Malcolm Volcano," "*In Caldo Brodo*, by Truman Capone," "*The Company She Peeps*, by Merrimac Arty," etc., etc.) and tootle around Havana in a convertible (Bustrófedon is there in spirit, like the Paraclete, or—as Infante might say—Parakeats), they make little significant contact with the nonverbal world around them. Havana of this era was notoriously full of prostitution and pickups, but the only instance of achieved intercourse throughout four hundred and eighty-seven pages occurs in some *tableaux vivants* staged for tourists. There is a good deal of partial undressing, and the work of one long night of seduction does jimmy a girl loose from her underpants, "*but*, BUT, where old Hitch would have cut to insert and intercut of fireworks, I'll give it to you straight—I didn't get any further than that." Later, Silvestre and Cué pick up two street flowers and proceed to bore them silly with puns and nonsense. One of the girls at last cries out, "Youse weird. You say real strange things. Both of you say the same strange things. Youse like twins, youse somethin' else. Whew! And you talk and talk and talk. Whaddya talk so much for?" To which the reader says, "Amen," and to which the author says, "Could she be a literary critic in disguise?"

A fearful air of congestion, of unconsummation, hangs over this book. Which may be deliberate: Batista's Havana is about to go under to revolution. Cabrera Infante, we are told by the dust jacket, served Castro's government as head of the Council of Culture, as a director of the Film Institute, as editor of a weekly magazine called *Lunes de Revolución*, and as a staff member of the Cuban Embassy in Brussels; in 1965, after returning to Havana, he "decided to leave Cuba," and he now lives in London. So his involvement was not trivial, and his viewpoint cannot be simple. Yet the coming storm impinges on the action of *Three Trapped Tigers* only once, when Cué drunkenly announces his intention to "join

Fffidel." Silvestre argues that he is crazy, it's like joining the Foreign Legion. "Nashional," Cué answers. "The National Leshion." The topic is then dropped, and the two spend another hundred pages driving and drinking and punning and remembering the palindromes of Bustrófedon. An American reader, especially now that Cuba is remoter than China, longs for a more anatomical portrait of this Havana that has vanished. In the first pages, such a portrait—a cross-section of corrupted and dissatisfied lives—seems to be promised. A sharp imitation of a night-club m.c.'s bilingual prattle lifts the curtain on some monologues by a kept woman, a movie-struck child, an underpaid printer. We read a letter written back to her village by a recent emigrant to the city; we eavesdrop on a psychiatric session that reappears throughout the book. Silvestre introduces himself:

> I am a press photographer and my work at that time involved taking shots of singers and people of the *farándula*, which means not only show business but limelights and night life as well. So I spent all my time in cabarets, night clubs, strip joints, bars, *barras*, *boîtes*, dives, saloons, *cantinas, cuevas, caves* or caves. . . . Sometimes, when I had nothing to do after work at three or four in the morning I would make my way to El Sierra or Las Vegas or El Nacional, the night club I mean not the hotel, to talk to a friend who's the emcee there or look at the chorus flesh or listen to the singers, but also to poison my lungs with smoke and stale air and alcohol fumes and be blinded forever by the darkness. That's how I used to live and love that life and there was nobody or nothing that could change me.

O.K., fine; rather lengthily said, but we obediently settle down for a tour of tropical night life. We meet a bongo drummer; we don't quite catch his name, but it doesn't matter, since he talks in Silvestre's voice, though he seems to be hung up on a little gringo chick called Vivian Smith-Corona, whereas Silvestre is hung up on Cuba Venegas, a local singer who looks better than she sings. We go back to Silvestre, who is trying to tell us about a great Negro singer, La Estrella, but the story keeps unravelling on him —maybe because this is "an island of double and triple entendres told by a drunk idiot signifying everything." Our eyes begin to sting in the smoke and stale air. Now an American tourist, a writer called Campbell, writes a funny story about a walking stick he bought fresh off the ferry from Miami, and about taking another off an outraged native because he thinks it's his, and then his wife produces *her* version of what happened, and he rewrites it (or perhaps this is meant to be a translation by somebody called Rine), and the wife does a second version, and then we get pages of the anti-works of the late Bustrófedon, and the above-mentioned parodies of Cuban authors on Trotsky's assassination, which might be the best part of the book if you're Cuban (it seems funny even in English), but by now Arsenio Cué is revving up his convertible, and we blearily realize that, whatever happened in Havana in 1958, this book isn't going to tell us. "Mare Metaphor is loosed upon the world. Rhetoric of the nation?" Cabrera Infante asks, as if hopeful that his stream of literary consciousness will somehow apply to Cuba. He applies it, but it doesn't stick. Though his translators work furiously to shore up the slippage, throwing in anachronisms like space-shot terminology, the slang word "gig," and "Agnewsticism," they can't keep the gobbets of "Esperanglish" and the limp avant gardisms and the liquorish 4 a.m. foolery from pulling loose from any reality we care to recognize or consent to care about.

The eclectic culture of Americanized Havana, Cabrera Infante seems to be saying, deserves an eclectic novel as its nostalgic monument. But eclecticism is itself a borrowed method by now. *Ulysses,* static and claustrophobic enough, is energized throughout by the tactful, evocative prose of a master short-story writer, and it draws for its allusions upon the immense perspective of European culture since Homer. Cabrera Infante writes run-on, like Faulkner but without Faulkner's intensity of self-hypnosis, and his perspective extends little farther than the mass culture of the giant nation to the north; the horizon of felt history for him appears to be Trotsky's murder in 1940. The book crucially lacks tact—the tension and economy that enforce themselves when method and material are in close touch. A mass of memories and a heap of verbal invention have been hopefully tossed toward one another, but confusion isn't fusion.

That Latin America can produce adventurously original novels has been shown many times over, from Machado de Assiz on. A recent striking instance, and an instructive contrast to *Three*

Trapped Tigers, is Gabriel García Márquez's *One Hundred Years of Solitude.* Here an array of fantastic premises (substantial ghosts, everyday miracles, magic that works, a village so isolated only gypsies can find it, a man tattooed on every inch of his skin, a man who fathers seventeen sons by seventeen women, a family of repeating names and insatiable incest) is breezily set forth by topic sentences that seem jokes, and then maintained with an iron consistency and kept rolling until the amusing becomes the magnificent—a magnificent symbolic contraption expressing a family's fate, a continent's experience, and Time's impenetration of humanity. The novel's Olympian ease and its catholic acceptance of horror and splendor as they arise in this our "paradise of misery" could not have been achieved in the United States, and no European novel would contain its joyous emptiness, its awed memory of a world "so recent that many things lacked names, and in order to indicate them it was necessary to point." The book even has a texture all its own: a dense translucence, a flow of long paragraphs that yet do not linger, that feel laconic, like stories the teller and listener already obscurely share and that are being not so much invented as called from the shadows. Such a novel, unlike Infante's sophomoric farrago, has learned from other novels how to become itself.

Satire Without Serifs

PATRIOTISM, INC. *and Other Tales,* by Paul van Ostaijen, edited and translated from the Dutch by E. M. Beekman. 170 pp. University of Massachusetts Press, 1971.

THE ADVENTURES OF MAO ON THE LONG MARCH, by Frederic Tuten. 121 pp. Citadel, 1971.

Sans-serif type belongs to one of those futures that never occurred. Elegantly simple, jauntily functional, it was everything the Bauhaus thought modernity should be, yet except in posters and telephone books it never really caught on. As with so many oddities a revolution would sweep away, serifs exist for a purpose:

they help the eye pick up the shape of the letter. Piquant in little amounts, sans-serif in page-size sheets repels readership as wax paper repels water; it has a sleazy, cloudy look. Yet now we have two works of fiction so printed—the first in a 9-point sans fainter than sandpiper tracks, and the other in a narrow-column boldface sans that fairly stamps itself on the retina. What is being signalled? A defiant chic, a refreshing change.

By printing Paul van Ostaijen's *Patriotism, Inc., and Other Tales*, the University of Massachusetts Press, itself obscure enough, has rescued a poet, proseur, and seer of the twenties from obscurity. E. M. Beekman, the translator, in his rather defensive and fancy introduction, blames van Ostaijen's obscurity on his writing in "Dutch, that poor relation of Northern European languages." He adds, "Van Ostaijen's work is an indictment of the Monroe Doctrine in the world of literature." This false hare (the implication that American foreign policy of some sort has kept the Dutch language down) is but one of several that Mr. Beekman starts; in the high-flown style of easy indignation associated with "black humor" and its apologists, he terms this century "the fool of history." "Never before has there been such an unrelenting succession of absurdities. . . . When a pertinaciously sensitive and sensible mind encounters such a world he is horrified and terror-stricken." Supposedly, however, the century has, in compensation, produced "a flowering of satiric literature" that includes such rich-relation-language types as Mann, Joyce, Gide, Brecht, Beckett, Grass, Nabokov, and Bruce Jay Friedman. Defining satire, Mr. Beekman asserts:

> To expose an ulcerous growth the surgeon must be dextrous with his scalpel. A hatchet job does little to relieve pathology. But control, skill, and a passionate immunity to suffering can chance to alleviate the pains of man. Confronted by an ailing society these authors dissect in order to heal.

This trite opposition between a sick society and a dexterous, antiseptic-handed satirist/doctor does not do justice to the complexity of the humorous impulse. I doubt that many satirists since Voltaire have hoped to change the world even a bit. If a satirist is an entertainer, he is gunning for laughs, in those target areas just to one side of the audience's really sensitive spots; if the satirist is an artist, he is venting a disgust mixed with love, a scorn hard to distinguish from fascination, an indictment that includes himself. Satire less than this is one-dimensional journalism that cannot outlive its object; L. B. J.'s retirement turns *MacBird!* into trash, or, rather, reveals it as the trash it always was. Nineteenth-century America was prolific of vitriolic lampoons, yet the one book with verifiable political repercussions was a sentimental melodrama, *Uncle Tom's Cabin.* Mr. Beekman is wrong to call the satirist "kin to the ideal revolutionary." The ideal revolutionary—Washington, Robespierre, Lenin—is humorless. Illusions are destroyed not by ridicule but by better, more fiercely held illusions. Indeed, insofar as satire fosters the impression of an enemy met and dealt with, it reinforces, like philanthropy, the status quo; an abundance of satire typifies a reactionary and helpless society, such as imperial Rome. In all times, humor is a form of resignation; in modern times, it comes peculiarly charged with self-doubt and moral ambiguity. Kafka can be said to satirize the Austro-Hungarian bureaucracy as something frozen, ornate, inscrutable, and cruel. But his art begins, not ends, there; satire is the mere crust of his real matter—his own confession of incapacity, his heroes' lust for punishment and their pathetic willingness to enlist, if they can find the right official, in the workings of an absurd universe. Society is sick, no doubt, but only the coarsest modern writer would exempt himself as healthy.

Mr. Beekman does, later in his introduction, place satire in the right focus: "Its intention is to cut the reader into awareness." This seems to me excellent, and all that any art should be asked to do. Also excellent, at a guess, is Mr. Beekman's translation from the Dutch; at any rate, van Ostaijen's prose comes over as elliptical and limpid and unlike Mr. Beekman's own overwrought English.

Van Ostaijen is principally renowned in his native Belgium as a poet; his prose pieces, which he called "grotesques," were written after two books of verse had made him a conspicuous presence on the Flemish literary scene, and were not published until after his death, at the age of thirty-two, in 1928. Much of his short life was spent in circumstances of constraint: he began his career in the blockaded port of Antwerp, fled to Berlin in 1919 to escape imprisonment for political offenses against the Walloons, returned to Antwerp only to be drafted and sent back to Germany in the occupation forces, and, after a few years spent struggling with poverty and an addiction to cocaine, died in a Belgian tuberculosis sanitorium. His "grotesques" were mostly written in the Berlin years (1919–1921), and they illumine a bizarre Weimar world of huge inflation and savage political competition, of brothels and cafés, of Dada and jazz, of Dietrich bluebirds singing to Grosz audiences. Van Ostaijen worked for a time in Antwerp's city administration, and the theme of corporate organization runs through his work: "The City of Builders" describes a city where ordinances foster a mad accumulation of buildings; "The Lost House Key" shows a thriving "free city" where syphilis has become the *sine qua non* of citizenship; "Ika Loch's Brothel" and "Hierarchy" are concerned with the organization of whorehouses; "The General" proposes organizing armies by sexual character, in battalions of sadists, masochists, homosexuals, fetishists, and so on; and "Patriotism, Inc." imagines an international conspiracy, among the conservative parties of Teutonia and Fochany, to rig provocative incidents in each other's countries and thereby promote mutual chauvinism. Though politically obsessed and a convicted activist, van Ostaijen did not think of his satire as social therapy; in a Berlin letter he noted, "Wrote a novella in which I try to make monkeys of people. Positive criticism: baloney. . . . People aren't worth criticising. Only material for burlesque novellas."

All these stories are rather schematically developed, with few sensual details and turns of characterization. Though resembling Kafka in his obsession with officialdom, van Ostaijen is incapable of such a passage as this:

> I was not at all certain whether I had any advocates, I could not find out anything definite about it, every face was unfriendly, most people who came toward me and whom I kept meeting in the corridors looked like fat old women; they had huge blue and white striped aprons covering their entire bodies, kept stroking their stomachs and swaying awkwardly to and fro. I could not even find out whether we were in a law court. Some facts spoke for it, others against.

Here are a deep, puzzled humor, vivid particularization, and incalculable, dreamlike turns. Van Ostaijen's mind, at least in his fiction, tends to travel straight to the mark. His pages yield a harvest of acute if dispiriting epigrams:

> For values are only safe when he who is entrusted with their preservation stands above them, when the preserver is not a dupe at the same time.

> Hypochondria is eroticism in atrophied form.

> Do not forget that masculine eroticism has an undertone of melancholy, even when this masculine eroticism is heterosexual. If it is homosexual, however, then the melancholy is both in the object and in the subject.

Expatiating on the subject of war in the persona of "The General," van Ostaijen teems with dark ideas:

> War is the clashing of two parties with the goal of separating the conqueror from the conquered. There is no significant child's game that does not spring from the love of war. Nonsense to believe that we suggest the idea of war to children. A warlike element resides in the sperm.

> The most meaningful and universal trait of humanity, more so than love, is the urge for battle. . . . The essence of every law is to aspire to curb instinct. Instinct wants to kill. Clearly.

> The British psyche . . . has conquered its warlike instinct with a rationally individualistic philosophy of life. They don't know what war is. They only know plunder.

> Actual wars are a cheapening of the ideal war. . . . Actual wars are a test of economic conditions, not of martialism.

With striking contemporaneity, van Ostaijen finds the alternative to war in drugs. "When negotiating for peace," the General tells us, "narcotics are unquestionably important. The so-called primitive peoples have already taught us this. . . . The chieftains gather together and immediately a pipe with opium or Indian hemp is passed from man to man. A peaceful mood cannot be far behind. . . . Next to war, gentle peace is therefore dearest to me. And so I am willing to smoke the opium pipe. And so will all those others who have only waged war to actualize the personality they contemplated."

"To actualize the personality they contemplated"—this is the talk not of a satirist but of a visionary. Van Ostaijen is fascinated by organization because he detests it. Ika Loch, the proprietress of a brothel, is a play on the Dutch *logika* (logic), and her authoritarian mismatching of customer and whore results in the murder of the lovely Promethea, who symbolizes art; the scandal enhances the fame of Ika's establishment. Though in "questions of business management" Ika possesses "a real talent for organization," she cannot perceive that "a head and a neck, as a totality, are still not the same thing as the sum of the two parts."

In the short prose poems, van Ostaijen projects synthesis out of derangement. A cocaine user, he writes out of "that peace of heart and tranquillity of spirit [that] could be his only after his retina became threadbare from the maddest realities of light." He writes sometimes in the texture of a drug trip:

> You must lie on the ground. Thus, across the ground, past much ochre and brown, past much green, your eye gains the bark and again the green, the old and the young and finally this gray, this crazy gray green, which is so exhausting that your eye flees to earth and slowly, only slowly, awakens to the motion of a brown hay wagon in the midst of the yellow-brown bed of needles.

And in "Bankruptcy Jazz," an electric confusion of phrases, placards, scenes, and oddly hydraulic jazz (*The jazz overflows into the street*, one direction reads) sums up an era when wheelbarrowloads of inflated currency were trundled along Europe's cobblestoned squares, between the Gothic cathedrals and the rococo city halls, when Charlie Chaplin might as well have been the government, when jazz tumbled everywhere and Dada took upon itself the slogans of salvation: "DADA is universal reason which the superidiocy of everybody can attain," "DADA is not an artistic Business, but the FORMULA of BANKRUPTCY," "JOIN DADA." The scenario, in its sans-serif spasms, has the fluttering fury of a moth beating against a street lamp. This volume of prose affords glimpses of a poetic genius, and we put it down hoping that soon Mr. Beekman and the University of Massachusetts Press will give us, in a slightly darker and bigger typeface, van Ostaijen's poetry.

*

If Dada was, as "Bankruptcy Jazz" proclaims, Nietzsche Without Nietzsche, a definition of Pop could be Mao Without Mao. *The Adventures of Mao on the Long March,* by Frederic Tuten, wears a nice comic-book jacket by Roy Lichtenstein and is described by Susan Sontag on the inside flap as "soda pop, a cold towel, or a shady spot under a tree for culture-clogged footsoldiers on the American long march." Broken into components, the hundred and twenty-one pages of Mr. Tuten's opus consist of (1) twenty-seven pages of straight history of the Long March (October 1934–October 1935), done in a neutral, factual tone, as by a fellow-travelling *Reader's Digest;* (2) thirty-six and a half pages of quotations in quotation marks, from unidentified sources (such as, diligent research discovers, Hawthorne's *Marble Faun,* Walter Pater's *Marius the Epicurean,* and Engels' *Origin of the Family, Private Property, and the State*); (3) twelve and a half pages of parody, of Faulkner, Hemingway, Kerouac, the Steinbeck/Farrell school, the Malamud/Bellow school, and of modern-art criticism in numerous schools; (4) nineteen pages of a supposed interview with Chairman Mao in 1968, in which the Chairman reveals himself as an avid subscriber to American highbrow periodicals and a keen devotee of Godard films and Minimal Art; (5) twenty-six pages of what might be considered normal novelistic substance —imaginary encounters and conversations. For an example of (5): Chairman Mao is alone in his tent, after the strain of the Tatu campaign. He hears the rumble of a tank :

> A tank, covered with peonies and laurel, advances toward him. Mao thinks the tank will crush him, but it presently clanks to a halt. The turret rises, hesitantly. Greta Garbo, dressed in red sealskin boots, red railway-man's cap, and red satin coveralls, emerges. She speaks: "Mao, I have been bad in Moscow and wicked in Paris, I have been loved in every capital, but I have never met a MAN whom I could love. That man is you Mao, Mao mine."
>
> Mao considers this dialectically. The woman is clearly mad. Yet she is beautiful and the tank seems to work. How did she get through the sentries? Didn't the noise of the clanking tank treads wake the entire camp? Where is everyone?
>
> Mao realizes the camp is empty. He is alone with Garbo. But Mao has always been more attracted to Harlow than to Garbo. What should he do not to break her romantic little heart?

"Madame, I have work to do," says Mao gently.

"It can wait till tomorrow, my love," she answers, unzipping her coveralls.

Mao thinks: "After all, I have worked hard and do deserve a rest." But an internal voice answers him: "Rest only after socialism."

"My Mao, this is no way to treat a woman who has made a long journey to be with you."

"But what of my wife?"

"Ah, that is an old bourgeois ploy, Mao mine."

Mao succumbs, and in the tent recites to her the entirety of the famous conclusion to Pater's *The Renaissance*, wherein we are entreated to "burn always with this hard, gemlike flame."

The whole episode is, like others in the book, charming, and it illustrates how well Mr. Tuten handles deadpan fantasy; except for a rare smirk like "her romantic little heart," a chaste solemnity rules the book. The tone is hard-edged, straight, dry, lyrical—anything but facetious. The tone, and the pamphlet-like type, smooth the different textures of this outrageous collage into an oddly reasonable unity. We never doubt that a lucid intelligence is in control; unlike many experiments of fictional assemblage, *The Adventures of Mao* never sinks into self-display, never becomes the mounted Kleenexes and tangerine peels of an author's private life. Mr. Tuten, in his jacket photograph, is looking not at us but at the flame of a match that is about to light his cigarette; he is wearing long hair and a wristwatch and has no biography. The contents of his book reveal nothing of him but his attitude.

And what is that attitude? What is *The Adventures of Mao* saying? Is it satirical? In general, when confronted with, say, a giant toothpaste tube of sewn canvas or a silkscreen of soup cans, we are predisposed to assume satiric content; our liberal prejudices and romantic aesthetics (in favor of trees, naked women, sunsets, and bowls of fruit) can accept any number of wry putdowns of our comfortably deplorable mass-trash society. But works viewed this way need only a glance. The more rewarding and plausible assumption, I think, is that the artist was obscurely delighted— "turned on"—by toothpaste tubes and soup cans, and that the ancient impulse of mimesis has led him to lift these things from the flow of transient impressions and to cast them into enduring form.

Mr. Tuten *likes* Chairman Mao, is the first message of the novel. The schoolbook account of the Long March inspires admiration on the flat level of propaganda. Sub-heroically (as Homer dimples Hector's heroism with glimpses of the private man), Mr. Tuten portrays Mao as sensitive to criticism of his poetry, as self-doubting and diffident and erotically wistful. In one of the funniest episodes, Mao lies awake coveting Eva Braun and Mussolini's mistress ("Claretta, what was the marvellous creature but the Mediterranean itself") but *not* Mrs. Roosevelt and Señora Franco ("a rosary-kissing midget, as sexy as a decayed turnip"). Mr. Tuten seems to be confessing that his Mao is a figment, a poster personality in a whimsical canon; he likes him as the author of the Gospel of John liked Jesus, but with the difference that he knows the Logos is a myth. Still, this is not satire, and in Mao's spirited championing of the bourgeois avant garde we reach a level of serious statement:

> "Pragmatically speaking, I like the opulent severity of this art, Minimal or ABC, because it both fills the imagination with the baroque by way of dialectical reaction to the absolute starkness of the object, and denudes the false in art and in life. [Such] work is like the Long March, a victory over space and time, a triumph of the necessary over the unnecessary, and, above all, it is like Marxism, or should I say like Heraclitus."

The American interviewer finds this enthusiasm "astonishing" and the Chinese interpreter exclaims, "To be honest, Chairman Mao, hearing all this talk from you confuses and disturbs me." It is, of course, impossible for Mao to be saying these things, but not—and herein the interest, the seriousness—implausible. When, in the same interview, he asserts that

> "youth is never reactionary; youth is progressive in time and hence always in the avant-garde, hence never wrong in spirit, hence *never* to be satirized,"

the statement originates from a profound depth, where the Free World's youth-proud greening merges with the mind that unleashed the Red Guards upon the entrenched Establishment of Communist China. We are confronted, in this elevation of youngness to a moral absolute, in this denial of any possibility of venerable wisdom and selective conservation, with something truly *other* than the reasonable liberalism and sentimental romanticism that have shaped our radically imperfect world.

The ideological fabric of *The Adventures of Mao* is deliciously complicated by Mr. Tuten's heavy reliance, for authority in aesthetic matters, upon fusty old wizards like Hawthorne and Pater —and Pater, it should be said, holds up nobly in this curious context. Another complication is that while the battles of the Long March are presented with the heroic generality of a newspaper recap, vivid and bloody and inglorious episodes of our own Civil War, as described in Whitman's *Specimen Days* and John William De Forest's *Miss Ravenel's Conversion*, are interspersed. The warrior Mao, whose revolution, after all, was bought with millions of lives, is thus displaced, along with the Mao who, on cultural matters, declared (at Yenan in 1942):

> There is in fact no such thing as art for art's sake, art that stands above classes, art that is detached from or independent of politics. Proletarian literature and art are part of the whole proletarian revolutionary cause; they are, as Lenin said, cogs and wheels in the whole revolutionary machine.

For this implacable and dynamic dogmatism Mr. Tuten substitutes a "longing for the great simple primeval things." Mao's interviewer tells him, "All your thoughts have given me the desire to be inert." Tuten's Mao is a suave decadent, whose languor, nevertheless, has a certain appositeness to revolution. The book's last sentence (quoted from Oscar Wilde's *De Profundis*) sounds a call for purification: "I feel sure that in elemental forces there is purification, and I want to go back to them and live in their presence."

So, in part, was Dada a call for purification—a purgation of cant through nonsense. Like Pop, it embraced its age's random materials with a frantic hug that transcended criticism, cynicism, or satire. Such violent gestures seem to ask for revolution in human consciousness; what they achieve is, more modestly, a refreshing of conventional artistic forms. *The Adventures of Mao on the Long March* provides an intelligent, taut, and entertaining change from conventional novels. Its substance is satisfyingly solid and satisfyingly mysterious. Like any work of art, it could not be mindlessly replicated; a sequel might slip into being a mere anthology. Nor would it be easy to locate another symbolic person as fabulous and germane as Mao. As is, Mr. Tuten's studied scrapbook, like van Ostaijen's precipitous scenario, contains the live motion of a novel within a jagged form that does "cut the reader into awareness."

Bombs Made Out of Leftovers

BAD NEWS, by Paul Spike. 152 pp. Holt, Rinehart & Winston, 1971.

BEING THERE, by Jerzy Kosinski. 142 pp. Harcourt Brace Jovanovich, 1971.

THE BARK TREE, by Raymond Queneau, translated from the French by Barbara Wright. 281 pp. New Directions, 1971.

We have with us this week three, ah, experimental works of fiction. In our struggles to understand them, we shall depend heavily on the dust jackets. The jacket of the first, *Bad News*, by Paul Spike (jacket by Push Pin Studios), tells us that the author, "a member of our youngest generation of fiction writers," was born in 1947 and that his work, published mostly in the *Columbia Review*, "could be classified as 'experimental' à la Borges or Pynchon"—though it is not Borges or Pynchon who comes handsomely through with a puff but William Burroughs, to wit: ". . . at once a beautiful and disquieting book, in which seemingly commonplace happenings suddenly open into other planetary perspectives."

Though the jacket is at some pains to avoid creating the (correct) impression that this is a collection of short pieces, it does let slip the word "stories," and stories they are—nine of them. They do, however, contain recurring characters, and they are wired for cross-currents, and some are so episodic that they might have been sliced another way and still be "stories." After O. Henry came the epiphany, the kind of short fiction that an irreverent friend of mine use to call the "so what?" story. Now comes its successor, the "so nothing" story. Mr. Spike owes more to Barthelme than to Borges; the "other planetary" perspectives intrude upon a this-planetary texture of *blague* and *Dreck*, of parody and an unimpeachably deadpan tone, of obscene technology and mechanical sex, of stillborn indignations and friendly puzzlements and, at the end, a curt, fishy-eyed stare, as from a cocktail-party companion upon whom one has, with some sudden warmth of interest or desire, unwittingly presumed. Not that Mr. Spike's cool is perfected yet; there is still something collegiate in his fascination with smelly socks and the word "mess," in his unfeigned delight at cooking up sexual descriptions, in his imperfectly concealed worry that prose fiction ought to amount to more than nervous anti-silence, like the overlapping crackle of a radio tuned between stations. Certain persistent messages want to break through the static. Mr. Spike's generation is one born to riot, and the telegraphy of social concern comes naturally to him:

> "Calcutta has an epidemic and the guerillas won't pump out the Pittsburgh enclave for months, which directly affects all of the East Coast. How about this submarine highway in the Pacific?"
> "You agreed to leave that route for Russia, a token perhaps, they'll go for it. The American government will iron that out."

Certain public events—nothing, naturally, prior to 1947, or even 1957—have sunk into his generation's consciousness, and they surface with symbolic portent; assassination is a recurring trauma. "Okay then I'm paranoid but maybe if the Kennedy family had been a little more paranoid? . . . The DIC is responsible for those assassinations, that's my opinion. . . . In November, 1963, over 400 New Yorkers fell down with 'speck attack' raging in their chests." And our accursed affluence, of course, takes its licks:

> Comfort is a surface, a straight line. The emptiness of comfort astounds man. It is like the world's most powerful ray gun.

Unexpectedly, the "emptiness that comes in the world's biggest ice-cream cone" includes the sexual wealth that the post-Korea generation has created:

> Nikolaus thought how odd it was that now that he could have all the sex he wanted, the world was becoming more and more messy.

The medicine of love unsettlingly merges with the diseases of pollution and aggression:

Man is the dirtiest animal. His pollution is driving him to look for an edge of the world which he can fall off. Yet he loves like no other animal. . . . And his love and beauty, in a sense, are a pollution to the world. They spray emotion into green vegetation.

But these thematic glimpses are mere footsteps in the underbrush of verbal celebration, a young man's luxuriant revenge on the media that have nearly driven him mad. His gifts of mimicry are keen. They range from college-humor jesting ("The Conference Man") to mock letters ("Box 456") and memorabilia ("The Diary of Noel Wells") and computer tapes ("Multi") to a fluid, sprightly Surrealism ("Specks Saga," "A Good Revolution"). The manner of presentation amounts to more than the things presented; the most tactile imagery, apart from the bodies of the young ladies who are handled, comes in the inventory of the hardware store where one of the young heroes works. The language, especially in the takeoffs of detective fiction, drolly bursts with exasperation at saying, after trillions of words of written English, anything at all:

His hands ticked away in his pockets now. A pink rash surfaced lightly across the top of his pectorals.

The sun is beginning to boil the atmosphere into a tight grease.

Her face was reminiscent of a pile of gears softly rounded into one another and covered with dreadful calm.

Bad News is as much a protest against fiction as it is fiction, and since it lacks pitiable characters, a sustained action, and an earnestly felt theme, we do not wish it—as Dr. Johnson said of *Paradise Lost* —longer than it is. Yet it has its poetry and its fidelity to the discontinuous, overpackaged, pre-trivialized way we live now. "The problem is," Spike himself explains, intruding to discourse with one of his characters, "there is a bomb here made out of leftovers." The character responds, "I have nothing to do." "Right" is Spike's answer. "But there is something here," the character insists. Such an affirmation is even weaker than that of Beckett's minimal pilgrims. News is what fiction—nouvelles, novels—once was; Mr. Spike's title implies that since "good" (coherent, morally convinced) stories are impossible, bad news is better than none.

*

The dust jacket of *Being There* tells us that the author, Jerzy Kosinski, was born in Poland in 1933, and that the first of his two earlier novels, *The Painted Bird*, has been translated into thirty-two languages, and the second, *Steps*, into twenty-nine. One wonders what the missing three are—Urdu? Korean? Arawak? *Being There*, simultaneously with its American publication, is being published in England, Holland, Germany, and France, and the flap copy, with its promise of a "modern parable" and a "quintessential anti-hero," seems to be warming up an international audience in easy Esperanto. The description of the book, however, is twelve lines shorter than the description of the author, and, bizarrely, at the end of the novel the typography suggests that Kosinski's biography is the last chapter—two pages' worth of his degrees, his fellowships, his professorships, his awards, his translations. In short, the author, not the novel, is the product being pushed. Which is shrewd, since the novel, like its hero, barely exists.

The hero is called Chance. He is an illiterate foundling kept by a rich old man known, with a simplicity too ominous, as the Old Man. Chance has two activities: he tends the Old Man's garden (Madam, I'm Adam) and watches television. After the Old Man dies, lawyers discover that Chance's existence has generated no external evidence—no driver's license, no credit cards, no tax records, not even dental records. He is cast out of the garden, and instantly encounters (hello, Eve) EE, the wife of another very rich old man, Rand. Everywhere, Chance creates an excellent impression, and he comports himself very well; gardening and television-watching seem to be at least as adequate a preparation for adult life as a college education. Though he doesn't know how to read or make love beyond the preliminaries shown on the idiot box, he can make speeches that win the heart not only of EE but of the President of the United States. As the saga ends, Chance, a total nonentity four days before, has the Vice-Presidential nomination in his pocket. No doubt there is a lot in this, from political satire (Chance = Agnew) to philosophical allegory ("being there" = Heidegger's *Dasein*). Also, there is some kind of joke on McLuhanite coolness; Chance is a walking television screen: people "began to exist, as on TV, when one turned one's eyes on them. . . . The same was true of him." The dust jacket, helpful to a fault, calls Chance "prelapsarian man" and asks, "Is Chance the technocrat of the future? . . . Or is he Rousseauesque, with a touch of natural goodness to which men respond?" Tune in next parable. Myself, I prefer to see him as the blind Chance that rules the universe, into which people touchingly read omniscience and benevolence and anthropomorphic Divinity.

All this symbolic superstructure rests on a realistic base less substantial than sand. Rand has one amusing, almost lifelike speech. Chance's sensations when he appears on television, "the cameras . . . licking up the image of his body," can be felt. There is one sharp image, of "frosty sculptures," in rooms of vague furniture. Otherwise, the texture of events is thin, thin, preposterously thin. The rich and powerful may be stupid, but they would not mistake a comatose illiterate for a financial wizard. A hermit might be innocent, but his body would know how to achieve an erection. Fortune may be arbitrary in bestowing her favors, but she is not totally berserk. When a character in the book expresses incredulity at Chance's abrupt and baseless fame, he is appealing to laws of probability that have been suspended. There is not enough leverage even to spring a laugh. No two things are incongruous, because hardly anything in *Being There* is *there*.

You could say that this is an immigrant's impression of America, an "other planetary perspective." But compare Nabokov; also an immigrant, from the same Slavic hemisphere as Kosinski, he assiduously put himself to school with American particulars and came up with a portrait—not only in *Lolita* but in the background of *Pnin* and the poem "Pale Fire"—of the United States grotesquely and tellingly acute in its details. Mr. Kosinski's portrait expresses little but the portraitist's diffident contempt for his subject—the American financial and political Establishment. He does not enough hate it to look hard at it; the result is not even a cartoon. Stylized also were the nameless villages of the Polish marsh in *The Painted Bird*, but those scenes were in Kosinski's blood, and the plausibility gaps were filled with an experienced terror that redeemed the parade of Grand Guignol episodes from being merely sensational. In *Steps*, an adult man's erotic explorations were interwoven with these same horrific villages, and incriminated in the same sinister cruelty. Perhaps the intention of

Being There was to transfer this sinisterness to an America be-
fogged by media and ruled by stuffed shirts. The result is feebly
pleasant—a dim and truncated television version of those old
Hollywood comedies wherein a handsome bumpkin charms the
swells and makes good. Unlike Kosinski's other novels, *Being
There* is not painful to read, which in his special case is not a
virtue.

Raymond Queneau was born in 1903, in Le Havre; his first novel,
Le Chiendent, published in 1933, has now been translated into
English, by Barbara Wright, as *The Bark Tree*. The dust jacket
tells us that Robbe-Grillet has "hailed" this book as "a new-wave
novel twenty years ahead of its time," and the translator's introduction presents further testimonials, accrediting *The Bark Tree*
as a classic and Queneau as a giant in the generation of modernists
that succeeded Proust and Joyce. The book, we are told, evolved
from Queneau's attempt to translate Descartes' *Discourse on
Method* into French as it is really spoken, dismissing the "conventions of style, spelling, and vocabulary that date from the
grammarians of the sixteenth century and the poets of the seven-
teenth." On the other hand, Queneau, a mathematician and a
pedant, chose to regulate his excursion into demotic philosophy—
which became a novel—with rules as strict as those of a ballade or
rondeau; seven chapters, each of thirteen sections, observe within
themselves the classical unities of place, time, and action. In addition, there are repetitions of image and phrase planted for the
author's personal pleasure, and the reader can subliminally sense
a high degree of coherence and consistency beneath the surface
of this rather sprawling and absurd tale.

The main plot concerns Étienne Marcel, a Parisian bank em-
ployee who lives in the suburb of Obonne, as he is observed by
Pierre Le Grand, a speculative member of the idle rich, while
Étienne makes the transition from flat silhouette to substantial
human existence and back to flat silhouette. Étienne is the Cartesian
man: when he begins to think (he suddenly notices in a store
window two rubber ducks floating in a hat to advertise that the
hat is waterproof), he is. From the window of his commuting
train, he then observes a tiny sign advertising "CHIPS" and de-

termines, as an *acte gratuit,* to visit this place, in the factory slum of Blagny; thereby he puts himself, and his observer, Pierre, and his son, Théo, and his wife, Alberte, and his wife's admirer, Narcense, in touch with a raffish crowd that includes a concierge, an abortionist, a magician, a sailor, an old junk dealer, and a remarkably presumptuous dwarf. This impinging activates a rumor that the junk dealer, Old Taupe, is a rich miser, and a set of frantic schemes to appropriate his fortune, mainly by means of his marriage to a young waitress, Ernestine, who unaccountably dies during a wedding feast that reminded this dazed reader of the Babar books. And there are love affairs and hangings and dreams and dialogues about the meaning of nothing and, for a climax, a war between the French and the Etruscans.

The Bark Tree is full, like *Bad News,* of nonsense and, like *Being There,* of naked contrivance. It is superior to both these books in the rigor of its pattern and in the richness of its matter. A palpable Paris takes shape through a multiplicity of fine strokes:

> Four, five, six drops of water. Some people, anxious about their straw hats, raise their noses. Description of a storm in Paris. In summer. The timid take to their heels; others raise the collars of their jackets, which gives them an air of bravado. It begins to smell of mud. Many people prudently look for shelter, and when the rain is at its height, all that can be seen are blackish groups, clustered around doorways, like mussels around the pile of a pier.

Queneau's wonderful gift for simile tempts one to compile a list:

> His nose has taken on the fiery color of Campari and his eyes are sparkling like lemonade.

> They plunge into their reciprocal destinies, like shrimps into the sand. . . .

> They fill the glasses with wine, which glasses take on the joyous appearance of druggists' display bottles.

> The horizon, that universal castrator . . .

> Bits of vegetables or meat, which had jumped out of the dishes like absurd acrobats, were scattered all over [the table], wilting in little pools of gravy.

And above these odd events, these overanimated souls and artifacts, a real humanity presides; Queneau not only permits each character the dignity of eloquence but rises himself to a fury of sarcasm when he contemplates the chauvinistic farce of the "Etruscan" war: "even the strategists . . . said they'd never seen a simpler, easier, more amusing war."

Queneau's sympathy peculiarly falls upon the banal—upon the empty routines, that is, whereby human ordinariness propels itself along the quotidian. He says of certain conventional greetings that "their apparent complexity concealed a profound simplicity." Pierre, overhearing some clichés about the weather, "notes with some bitterness that these banalities correspond perfectly to reality." Perhaps, since Flaubert, banality is *the* challenge to serious novelists: the gales of romance have died, and the novelist is a sailor on a close reach, trying to use the constant wind of ordinary living to make some kind of headway against it. The melodrama of Queneau's plot is manufactured by the characters, as a vacation from boredom; his own vacation comes in the intervals of metaphysical speculation, and these—though he would not have written the book without them—seem rather mannered and pat. When Pierre talks to the reader about his boredom and his masks, or when Étienne drops the aphorism that "there isn't any gospel, there are only works of fiction," we are aware of an author pressing his claims upon our intelligence; when Ernestine, dying, formulates death as the disappearance of "the little voice that talks in your head when you're by yourself," we are in the presence of human experience and shared terror. Gertrude Stein said it: literature isn't remarks. What we want from fiction, and what fiction is increasingly loath to give us, is vicarious experience. Exiled from the great naïveté that nurtured the 19th-century masterworks of the novel, Queneau yet is old enough—humane enough—to spin, amid a metaphysics of relativity and uncertainty, affectionate images of human life in its curiosity, rapacity, and fragility. Compared to Queneau, our two other authors seem tired; a distance that cannot be exactly measured in generations or wars separates them from an instinctive belief that men are significant and that art must embody enduring principles.

A note on the translation: Barbara Wright did not set herself an easy task, and her version does permit us to glimpse an original whose prose has not only a poetic economy but, in dialogue, a slangy, punning richness. However, either this text was carelessly proofread or some of her renderings are too subtle by half. "Squite" (for "it's quite"), "wz" and "shdve" (for "was" and "should have"), "etxras" (for "extras"), and "sore span" (for "saucepan") are doubtless intentional equivalents of delicate audial distortions in the French; but what about "fairtish," "neved," and "everwhere"? These occur in dialogue, and "aand" appears in expository prose, and "becaues" in a letter in which nothing else is misspelled. Something wrong here?

A note on the price: the dust jacket calmly asks nine dollars and fifty cents for *The Bark Tree*. It is two hundred and eighty-one pages long. The Novel may or may not be dead; soon we won't be able to buy into its casket and see.

Mortal Games

THE FLIGHT OF ICARUS, by Raymond Queneau, translated from the French by Barbara Wright. 192 pp. New Directions, 1973.

ALL FIRES THE FIRE *and Other Stories,* by Julio Cortázar, translated from the Spanish by Suzanne Jill Levine. 152 pp. Pantheon, 1973.

Modernism, we are told, is passé; the Harvard English Department lists a course, "American Modernism," that treats of "American writing from 1900 to 1930," and another, "The Modern Period," that is "an introduction to the poetry, fiction, intellectual prose, and criticism of the period from 1899 to 1939." But what has come after? What now? In the uncertain twilight, where the avant garde has become the rear guard, strange loomings and mistaken perspectives bemuse us. Surely, we suppose, Raymond Queneau, a modern whose masterpiece *The Bark Tree* appeared in 1933, is dead and silent. Not so, for here is a lively new novel, *The Flight of Icarus.* And surely Julio Cortázar, the Brussels-born, Paris-dwelling Argentine expatriate who contrived such frolicsome experiments as *Hopscotch* and *62: A Model Kit,* is, as his handsome jacket photograph attests, a young man. Not so, for from the back flap of his latest book to appear in the United States, *All Fires the*

Fire and Other Stories, we learn that Sr. Cortázar, with his turned-up raincoat collar and his downy cheeks, was born in 1914. So he, scarcely less than Queneau, harks back to the brave first third of this century, when Literature hobnobbed with Life as an equal, when young Dedaluses set forth to forge in their souls' smithies the uncreated consciences of their respective races, when innovations in fictional technique could be dubbed "revolutionary," and when artistic, cerebral excitement carbonated a page of prose so that it tingled in the reader like champagne. The late Pablo Neruda, puffing Cortázar's stories, describes them as "fabrications, myths, contradictions, and mortal games." The final phrase puts well the tension between an earnest sense of reality and a playful sense of active mind that modernism brought to such a fine and precarious pitch—especially precarious in this country, where naturalism tends to breed sprawling verbal slums and, in reaction, anti-naturalists of the most antic, heedless, and dandyish sort.

Queneau, in *The Flight of Icarus,* is something of a dandy himself. The novel, written in the attenuated form of a play containing no fewer than seventy-four short scenes, takes place in Paris in 1895, when absinthe is still drunk, the bicycle and the "automobile carriage" are freshly in motion, Reason rules a feast of gourmet dining, and authors busily function as a superior type of tradesman. Icarus, our hero, escapes from a novel being written by Hubert Lubert, "a novelist by profession, by vocation, even, and . . . of some renown." Lubert, suspecting a character-napping by his rival Surget, hires the farcically inept detective Morcol ("The man who follows adulterous women and finds lost sheep. He has appeared in many novels under different names. A second Vidocq. A second Lecoq"). Morcol makes a number of brilliant deductions but nevertheless lets the escapee remain undetected under his very nose. Icarus has drifted into a low-life café and, having taken his first "flight" on absinthe, is—so appealingly has Lubert designed him—taken in and supported by a prostitute identified as LN. The plot spins faster: other characters escape from other works in progress; their frantic creators fight duels amongst themselves; Icarus buys from a bookstall by the Seine *The Principles of Mechanics* ("the less he understood it the more he enjoyed it") and goes to work for the mechanic M. Berrrier (*sic*), while LN turns from prostitution to the production of bicycle bloomers; Morcol retires, though the lost-character business is booming; most of the fictional escapees creep back into their books, or somebody else's; Icarus and LN attempt flight in a giant kite, and fall. "Everything happened as was anticipated," Lubert assures us at the end, shutting his manuscript complacently.

It is hard to imagine a novel lighter than this that would significantly engage the mind. Yet *The Flight of Icarus*, though it is continuously absurd, never strikes us as silly. The style is chaste and swift, ornamented with inventions translated as "obnubilating," "spondulics," "ostreophagists," "petroliphagious," "cantharodrome." The many threads of the cat's-cradle plot are complicated and regathered with an impressive efficiency. The literary satire is sharp though good-humored; Robbe-Grillet especially seems the butt of such speculations as

> Perhaps that is how it will be for all of us, one day. We won't have any more characters. . . . The novel will perhaps not be dead, but it won't have characters in it anymore. Difficult to imagine, a novel without characters. But isn't all progress, if progress exists, difficult to imagine?

Queneau's own characters are more or less aware that they are caught in a novel. Lubert is preparing for Icarus a "melancholy existence": "I want him to like moonlight, fairy roses, the exotic types of nostalgia, the languors of Spring, fin-de-siècle neuroses— all things that I personally abhor, but which go down well in the present-day novel." Icarus, however, cries, "A fig for the neurasthenias, the neuroses, and the nostalgias of our contemporary writers!" And, escaping the "dismal or disappointing love affairs, with sessions in cosy, dusty apartments" that his author would have arranged for him, he opts for technology: "personally, I'm much more interested in theoretical mechanics, from the fall of heavy bodies to the mechanism of a lock." Not only Icarus acknowledges the matrix of novelistic cliché and melodrama; a waiter, observing him and LN in a cafe, predicts (incorrectly) their fate, assuring himself, "I've read a great many novels and I know what happens next." And while the "fictional" characters are attempting, like bumpkins in from the provinces, to make a go of it in mercantile

Paris, one "real" woman volunteers to become the heroine of a romantic novel. The confusion is slight. Objecting to the plot's basic fantasy, the reader might say that one does not meet fictional characters on the street; the answer would be that one is not on the street but reading a book, where one meets fictional characters all the time. The reader's demand, that is, for reality is turned back upon itself. The characters are uniformly real, "characters" or not. And the milieu is perfectly convincing. We have been there before, in the bicycle-obsessed frenzies of Jarry, in those enchanted pages of Proust where Marcel becomes an Adam among the fresh creations of the telephone, the automobile, the camera. Something in the French spirit embraced with special innocence and energy the inventions—toylike in their first forms—that equip and distinguish the modern age. The same spirit, perhaps traceable to a peculiar delight in Reason and its works, permits the French, uniquely, to produce works of art as intellectual, spare, and impudent as this, as spindly and nakedly theoretical as a primitive machine yet undeniably serious, even majestic.

Julio Cortázar is not so engaging a spirit as Queneau, and the eight pieces in *All Fires the Fire* suffer, in the way of collections, from comparison with one another—the story "Meeting" is less stunning than the title piece, and "Instructions for John Howell" ends less satisfyingly than "The Island at Noon." But in sum these eight "mortal games" correct this reviewer's previous impression (gained by that most thrifty of methods, bookstore perusal) that Cortázar was a decadent avant gardist, a rather desperate innovator snipping autobiography into eye-catching shapes. True, he cannot get started without a gimmick: there is always a fantastic premise or a startling formalistic deviation, and he does not have Borges' power of persuading us that the strangeness flows from the superior vision of a drastically refined sensibility. But, once the trick is established (and no two devices are alike in this set of eight), Cortázar pushes beyond it with surprising powers of realistic development. The first story, "The Southern Thruway," supposes that a traffic jam on the Sunday-night rush back to Paris is truly —as traffic jams often feel—of days and months in duration. The same little locality of cars inches forward together a few yards a day; a community develops. Food is shared, leaders emerge, the girl in the Dauphine sleeps with the engineer in the Peugeot and becomes pregnant by him, the man in the Caravelle behind the engineer commits suicide, a Porsche and a Mercury (the characters take on the names of their cars) peddle black-market provisions through the stalled lines, and so on. The conceit is fleshed out with so many solid details that in the end, when the jam mysteriously breaks and the cars, accelerating, separate, the reader feels as well as comprehends the allegorical meaning—the loss of community in this modern "mad race in the night among unknown cars, where no one knew anything about the others, where everyone looked straight ahead, only ahead."

The next story, "The Health of the Sick," supposes, far from incredibly, that a large family in Buenos Aires, to spare Mama the news that her son Alejandro has been killed in Montevideo, fabricates letters from him, and then invents an attendant string of lies and impostures as his absence lengthens into years, Mama's expected death being slow to arrive. A situation that could be broadly comedic, or politically satirical about the self-delusions of the bourgeoisie, instead deepens in a rather poignant direction: Mama, dying at last, reveals, as the reader has guessed some pages before, that she knows the truth and has been herself protecting the protective perpetrators of the illusion. The survivors then, receiving the last of the forged letters from the phantom Alejandro, find themselves wondering how they can break to him the news that Mama is dead. So something rather tender as well as eerie has been said about the fond and prevalent deceits of family life. Cortázar, though his methods can be jagged, is not mordant. "Nurse Cora," with its initially exasperating device of an interior monologue that shifts from person to person without so much as a paragraph indentation to signal transitions, in the end quite movingly portrays the death, in a hospital, of an adolescent boy as refracted through other minds (his nurse, his mother, his doctor) and reflected in the boy's own subtly traced surrender of pride, desire, and vitality. Another kind of dying concerns "Meeting," wherein the interior soliloquy of Che Guevara is imagined during the rebel invasion of Cuba; all seems lost, and the hopes of the revolution, the music of Mozart's "Hunt" Quartet, and the interweave of tree branches meet in the resigned mind of the exhausted revolutionary: "But it was enough to look at the treetop to feel that the will again put its chaos to order, imposed on it the sketch of the adagio that would someday pass into the final allegro and accede to a reality worthy of that name."

Juxtaposition is Sr. Cortázar's creative habit, and perhaps he is most himself when the juxtaposition is most harsh and least explained; an abyss, narrow as a black knife, gleams in the schizoid split. In "The Other Heaven," a man evidently walks back and forth between his stockbroker's job in Buenos Aires and a sinister arcade district of Paris. In "All Fires the Fire" (and there must be a better way of translating this), without even the rationale of daydream, a Roman gladiatorial fight and the breakup of a modern affair are alternately, accurately described; both events involve a sexual triangle and the cool cruelty of hedonism, and both end in a conflagration, as if a spark had leaped from the striking together of these two flinty worlds. There is also a third world—a far-off voice overheard during the telephone conversation of the modern couple, a "distant, monotonous voice" dictating numbers to "someone who doesn't speak." This little cross-connection reaches our own inner ear with the penetration of a symbolic detail (numbers, minutes, time is the final consuming fire) that is first of all a recognizable, common experience. Cortázar, sparing with his imagery, can achieve masterstrokes of sensation, especially when the sensation involves a gulf. In "Instructions for John Howell," a member of a theatre audience is suddenly enlisted as an actor in the play; a moment before he is pushed onstage, he feels to his left "the great cavern, something like a gigantic contained breath, which, after all, was the real world, where white shirt fronts and perhaps hats or upsweeps were gradually taking shape." And in "The Island at Noon" an airline steward, Marini, every other day at noon on the Rome–Teheran run looks down upon a little Greek island, Xiros, shaped like "a turtle whose paws were barely out of the water." The island becomes an obsession; "everything . . . was blurred and easy and stupid until it was time to lean toward the tail window, to feel the cold crystal like the boundary of an aquarium, where the golden turtle slowly moved in the thick blue." The sensation of looking down from a jet cannot be more beautifully described than that; the serene terror of jet travel—a tubular sample of the cheerful, plasticized mundane floats apparently motionless above an actual *mundus* reduced to the scale of a map and viewed from the top of a towering transparency that is, potentially, death—finds its fable here. And at his most intense Cortázar floods the gaps and mysteries of his tricky structures with a potent negativity—death, that invisible possibility, made electric and palpable, like the atmosphere before lightning. Whereas a curious immortality, the eternal sprightliness of pure mind, fills the airy spaces of Queneau. Both men convince us that surrealism has been elicited from them by the extremity of their ardor for reality—"the reality," Nathalie Sarraute has written, "to which we always return, in spite of our momentary betrayals and deviations, thus proving that, when all is said and done, we . . . prize it above all else." Their games repay our playing.

YOUNG AMERICANS

If at First You Do Succeed, Try, Try Again

Dance the Eagle to Sleep, by Marge Piercy. 232 pp. Doubleday, 1970.

Single File, by Norman Fruchter. 177 pp. Knopf, 1970.

"First Novels" are almost a genre to themselves; *Time* used to refer solemnly to a "First Novelist" with the same capitalization it employed for "First Lady" and "First Baseman." Second novels lack this irksome mystique; they are just supposed to be not as good—scrimped follow-ups of that first furious spending, strained variations on what came naturally. And, true, the two second novels at hand do seem less assured, less exuberantly annunciatory, than the first productions of their gifted young authors. Yet the flaws and deformities show stress *in a direction* and hint at why, in a historical moment when private concerns have lost moral priority to public awareness, it is difficult for an earnest spirit to write novels at all.

Marge Piercy's *Dance the Eagle to Sleep* describes—through the experiences of four major characters—the birth, short and somewhat blissful life, and violent death of a youth movement that one might call a nightmare version of S.D.S. The Piercy group is named the Indians, and early this year Bernardine Dohrn issued from the happy hunting ground of her hiding a proclamation "to express ourselves . . . as tribes at council." Miss Piercy places her history in a futuristic time (there has been a government shelling of Bedford-Stuyvesant, a President called the King of Clubs has been succeeded by one called the White Knight, a compulsory period of national service called the Nineteenth Year of Servitude has ben initiated), but the styles and equipment and brand names are all of our time, and at one point the author specifies that for "twenty-five years" the American people "had been sold a crusader's world of Armed Might Versus the Red Hordes." Twenty-five plus 1945 equals 1970. No matter. The futuristic conceit frees her to work on a large scale, to set her characters in the context of armies and headlines and—crucial to public-spirited agonists—*publicity*. The novel as the saga of private lives, soul journeys invisibly pursued under the heel of power (a tradition that Erich Auerbach's *Mimesis* sees originate in the anecdotes of the Gospels), does not suit our Roman times, when only kings and gods matter. Miss Piercy's heroes would be kings; that attempt failing, she caricatures them as gods. "Shawn felt useless and yet full of energy and light, a turned-on bulb, a ridiculous helium-taut balloon." "The blade hit [Corey] with its dull weight, making him fall. As it rolled over him smashing his bones, his heart burst free like a rising crow, and he fainted."

Shawn has been a member of a screamingly successful rock group. Corey is the part-Indian founder of the Indians; his pilgrimage begins with a vision of a buffalo who tells him (I drastically abridge this bisonian peroration):

> "I was the bread of your people. . . . Your people lived on me as on a mountain. The grass waved and I ate it as far as the clean fresh wind blew. Then I was burnt and left to rot. . . . I became garbage. It had been beautiful, the world made out of my flesh and my bone, my hide and my sinews. The people danced each season on my back. . . . The word was real, and every man had his own poem to connect him to himself. Now what is there? . . . Now there are people in boxes, their heads full of noise, their lungs full of smoke and poison, their bellies full, but their flesh sour. They do what they are told. . . . At the top are a handful of men who buy and sell the mountains and the rivers, who pollute and explode and set aside as preserves all the lands of the earth. The people. . . . are chained together and crippled by shame. They cannot dance. Only the young are alive a little while to dance and feel and touch each other."

The movement thus inspired begins by seizing a high school somewhere in the Midwest and progresses to rioting in Manhattan.

It achieves publicity: "The media discovered them . . . *Esquire*
put Shawn's face on the cover in feathered headdress, and inside
had a snotty article heavily laden with psychoanalytical insights."
These insights, unlike the buffalo's, are not quoted. *Dance the
Eagle to Sleep* fails as a novel of ideas because "the system" is
never allowed to have a cogent, let alone persuasive, spokesman.
The policemen are uniformly faceless and brutal, the schoolteach-
ers are all "frustrated, embittered lumps." The adults in the book
are either venal or oppressed—Brand X and Brand Y of the system,
summarily dismissed in the very tone of presentation. "His father
was a partner in a prestigious Philadelphia law firm. His mother
owned buildings, had studied psychology and been analyzed by
Jung, and was still beautiful in a gaunt silvery way." Or: "His
father was a pale gray drag. Started out as a high-school math
teacher and ended up as a middle-echelon man in a company
specializing in auto insurance." Anything genial in middle-class
life is dismissed as "co-optative softness." Fascinating suggestions
pass unchallenged: research scientists have no alternative to participation in nerve-gas projects, Che and Mao will deliver us from
toilet training, all people over twenty-five hate all people under
twenty-five because television commercials present youthful beauty
as an ideal. The actions of the government, as it blitzkriegs the
movement into smithereens, pretend to no rationale beyond
the author's desire to allegorize the Vietnam war. Comic-book
heroes like Captain Marvel and Plastic Man are frequently invoked,
and the climactic chapters strongly savor of comic-book art; one
can almost see BLAM and RATATATAT in jagged balloons, and (when
Corey is hyper-symbolically crushed by a bulldozer) AEEIIII trailing off into the next panel. The government becomes one of those
almost omnipotent syndicates of evil that Superman did battle
with. No mitigating circumstances are allowed in the Piercy condemnation—no historical causality, no suspicion that the system
is a self-admittedly imperfect patchwork of changeable human
devices, no comparison with other systems, living or dead. The
system is never seen in operation; nobody functioning within it
has any reality. This is not true of Miss Piercy's first novel, *Going
Down Fast*, wherein some of the manipulators of an urban-renewal
boondoggle are substantially, if unsympathetically, realized. It is

even less true of—to cite a masterpiece, as magnanimous as it is devastating, of political disaffection—Solzhenitsyn's *The First Circle;* here the author's compassion moves outward from the jailed to the jailers and does not exclude even the ultimate jailer, Stalin, as he scuttles through his suite of cells beneath the Kremlin, beset by dogma and paranoia.

Yet, in another way, Miss Piercy's second novel does reveal a (let us call it) Christian sense of human fallibility. As an anti-utopian novel, a study of the breakup of a visionary movement into doctrinaire factions, *Dance the Eagle to Sleep* has a credible complexity. It is *Lord of the Flies* with girls on the island. The warrior spirit is here embodied in the Piggy figure, the fat bright boy with glasses, now called Billy Batson. Corey, the Indian chief, remains a mystic theorist. The debates within the councils of the young are vigorous and subtle; Miss Piercy follows the cruel exigencies of the social contract as they arise in the tribe with just the sympathetic understanding she denies the enclosing society. "We were right and wrong," Shawn admits in the end, without surrendering his faith that "the system is all wrong."

Where *did* the Indians go wrong? In a sense, by biting the fruit of the Tree of Knowledge. At first "there were almost no tools available in the tribe to communicate political values, but only to embody them. Which worked, sort of." Then communication becomes all too practiced: "Councils tended to turn into sharp debates now between different sides gathered around leaders who could argue a position and put others down. . . . The louder got louder still. . . . But somehow they were not getting any better at talking to people who were not yet Indians." Marcus, the Negro to whom the mantle of wisdom descends after Corey's death, says, "We thought guns made us real, but it was people, and we didn't have them." (Bernardine Dohrn's statement says, "We became aware that a group of outlaws . . . cannot develop strategies that grow to include large numbers of people.") The delusion that better communication would win "the people" seems shared by the author; her novel leaves us with the impression that the movement's only fault was not being strong enough. In the last chapter, a girl, Ginny, cries out in childbirth, "I thought I was stronger than I am." Marcus' answer comes back: "Human beings aren't

naturally strong enough or nasty enough to live in this world."
So even labor pains seem to be allied with the evils of "the system."
What did the Indians want? For a time they live in a New Jersey
farm commune, and their idyll centers upon a brown hardness of
body, which they gain through the outdoor labor that millions of
their ancestors hastened to escape. Joanna, the heroine, is always
"tough" and "skinny." When she turns traitor and sides with the
system, the first thing Corey notices is that she has put on weight.
She is "a robot that looked a little like Joanna. A plastic doll with
rubbery skin and a smell of plastics about it." In short, the system
—substitute "history" or "technology" or "overpopulation"—has
alienated us from Nature. As in the original myth of Eden, there
is in *Dance the Eagle to Sleep* a suggestion that sex is behind the
Fall. Joanna, once a blithely promiscuous runaway, becomes
Corey's mate, then betrays him with Shawn. Yet this event, though
much discussed, does not offend the sexual code of the tribe or
bear upon its military defeat. Indeed, by this time the reader has
become enough of an Indian himself, having witnessed so much
random and inconsequential copulation, that he cannot give the
incident the emotional significance it would have in a conventional,
bourgeois novel. Shawn himself says it:

> "Don't you think it's strange. We're running for our lives.
> There's a battle going on down below. Maybe it's all over for us.
> Our home is gone. Maybe our tribe is destroyed. And we're analyz-
> ing the subtleties of a love affair."

This confessed awkwardness and the curious failure of Joanna,
though she is the most vividly realized character, to be anything
but a pendant upon the book's essential action finger one crisis in
the novel form. Is sex in the shape of "romantic interest" subject
enough? If sexual "possession" is scorned as part of the hated
private-property bag, fidelity becomes meaningless and betrayal
impossible. Joanna tries to make it possible again; she tells Corey,
"I'm not liberated. . . . I'm your private property." And later,
more wifely still: "I was trying to castrate you." Corey despises
her new psychoanalytical vocabulary as part of her sellout, but
does not answer her questioning of the "freedom" he and his
desperate revolution offer. "I've got a scholarship to a decent

school. I'm going to be a teacher. I'm going to be something on my own"—is the reader meant to scorn, with Corey, her moderate hope? In this ambiguity Miss Piercy uncovers a private feminine theme within the mighty masculine one of social rebirth. Just as the old novels etched the tragedies of private persons within the gray revolution of industry and technology, new ones may trace the personal liabilities of the anti-Establishment Establishment.

Single File, by Norman Fruchter, presents a texture much different from *Dance the Eagle to Sleep*. Whereas Miss Piercy's prose crackles like a comb being hastily pulled through rather tangled hair, Mr. Fruchter's glints like fragments of a mirror. While Miss Piercy, in her haste to get on with it, is not fastidious about clichés, resorts to a hurried sociological tone, makes people talk like press handouts, and declines to linger upon sensual details, Mr. Fruchter deals in the exquisitely concrete:

> Wet white bones, glistening like licked fingernails. Tooth-white. Fleshy hunks that evaded Negrone's knife, clung stubbornly to white bone. Tougher than chicken bone, sharp enough to cut and sting—cross-hatchings of scars creased Negrone's wrist up to his elbow, a foot above the cuff of his rubber gloves. Carp skeletons stacked, moist rattles, in Negrone's brine-soaked buckets.

After Miss Piercy's editorializing, it is a relief to read through the hard news Mr. Fruchter has assembled: mock documents, interior soliloquies, street sayings, descriptions clean as ice chips, dialogue better than tape-recorded, all of it smartly shuffled and laid before our eyes in a fancy typographic dress of ragged-right margins, italics, play format, and an intermittent left-hand hairline. The conceit is that all this heterogeneous material exists in a single file of welfare casework, but my one complaint about this book is that its excessive "interestingness," its continual declaration of itself as a literary object, insulates the reader (whom Miss Piercy does engage in argument, however feverish) from the shocking substance. For this is a novel of the urban humiliated and oppressed, a novel rich far beyond its modest bulk with the sights and smells and processes of present-day city life. In content, indeed, it is more radical than *Dance the Eagle to Sleep*, which deals with middle-class teen-agers and ends with the hoariest of sentimental affirmations—the birth of a baby. Not since Steinbeck and Algren has a writer of Mr. Fruchter's skill demonstrated such unforced love for the proletariat, entered so willingly into their cramped lives, and found so much room for drama and mystery in the cabins of desire, scruple, and frustration that confine their freedom of choice.

Two clusters of days in April and July of 1965 are interwoven to form the plot. In April, Dutch Matto, an illiterate Italian laborer, limps with his mangled, infected knee from a nameless city hospital through the vacantly sociable routines of his utter solitude—pain and memories crowding upon him—to his destiny: at 5:21 a.m., "with the only pure motion of his life," he goes upstairs to where a black woman is pounding on the radiator for heat and "sweeps the pan's handle from her startled fingers and swings it through an arc which, completed, smashes her skull." In July, in the same lower West Side neighborhood, a welfare worker called only "the kid" suffers a rude ending to his affair with Angie, a Puerto Rican woman downstairs: she kicks him out and then piles the sheets he has soiled into the arms of his wife. Matto's memories and "the kid's" casebook amplify this double strand of action outward into a wilderness of other lives, and for each brief scene Mr. Fruchter finds the exact accent, the one poetic yet honest image that might filter through Matto's stupidity or the bleakness of bureaucratic notation. An uptown poolroom, a Chinese man's "bare room that smelled of scalding tea-kettle water dousing already spotless surfaces," a weekend on the water with sunburned call girls, the ins and outs of robbing trailer trucks —no corner of metropolitan existence evades the light of the author's imagining; the many vignettes expand and merge into one large landscape of impoverishment and confusion, individual egos and libidos winking like phosphorescent animalcula in a sea of despair. The "system" is seen functioning in its lowest forms (the neurotic, uncertain, well-intentioned welfare worker; the tired, tough, racist, grudgingly conscientious cop), where it intertwines with the "victims" (the ignorant laborer, the sexy, angry, helpless young hooker and her child). The policeman, Sal, lives with Angie while she is also accommodating "the kid," and he is in on Matto's arrest. Sal and the neighborhood itself are the definite links between the two strands of the novel; the indefinite link, which binds them into a "single file," I take to be a verdict—scarcely audible in its irony—of guilty on the book itself.

That is, "the kid," if not quite the author, is the assembler of these fragments. His interest in Matto's act of murder generates the vivid re-creation of Matto that is set before us; his affair with Angie, his affectionate word-portraits of his welfare cases, his willingness to stretch and overlook regulations for them all stem from a "romantic interest" in the poor. Yet the depth of the poverty he sees swallows and exhausts him. Sal dislikes his type ("I knew the kid was bad news first morning I met him, sipping Angie's coffee. . . . Department was dying for staff, but he hadda pretend he was on a mission!"), and his wife, Laurie, begs him to quit ("You know why you went to work there and it hasn't worked out. . . . It's another one of those private notions you have, nobody's keeping score"). "The kid" pretends to acquiesce, pleasantly envisions returning to college, but then sinks back into his "squalid anemia of the soul." In a world so radically awry, no effort is enough. One man goes upstairs to murder a woman, another man goes downstairs to fornicate with a woman; it equals out, it is the same. A possible response lies outside reality, in art, but his own work of art Mr. Fruchter has enigmatically fractured as if with the blow of a fist.

Both authors offer to tell us about sections of American society —the revolutionary young, the urban poor—more frequently met in the newspapers than in prose fiction. Need it be argued that the novel form accommodates some kinds of people better than others? Lively dialogue, for instance, assumes a degree of articulate self-consciousness beyond the Dutch Mattos of this world. Indoor actions like domestic quarrels are easier to diagram than outdoor actions like the street war of *Dance the Eagle to Sleep.* Secretive sufferers like Matto and Sal, vision-possessed youths like Corey and Billy, behave uncomfortably in the living-rooms of fiction, whereas on the basis of previous acquaintance very marginal figures like "the kid's" wife and Shawn's parents call out heartily to the reader. Good, greedy, guilty, quasi-Christian people: without them, where are the moral tension, the irony, the retribution that give a novel its tug and design? Mr. Fruchter's first novel, *Coat Upon a Stick*, showing the same clairvoyance and the same fascination with the humble and even the same trick of inserted monologue, dealt with an area of urban experience, the Jewish, already under cultivation; while striking his own note firmly, the young author yet based his precocious achievement upon a literary tradition. And the personae of Miss Piercy's first novel were also familiar—young bohemians and small cultural operators, their traditional absorption in sex and art wrenched toward political commitment by a not yet overt streak of demagoguery in the author. These second novels move further from bourgeois conventions.

The bourgeois novel is inherently erotic, just as the basic unit of bourgeois order—the family unit built upon the marriage contract—is erotic. Who loves whom? Once this question seems less than urgent, new kinds of novels must be written, or none at all. If domestic stability and personal salvation are at issue, acts of sexual conquest and surrender are important. If the issue is an economic reordering, and social control of the means of production, then sexual attachments are as they are in Mao's China— irrelevant, and the fewer the better. Vast portions of the world have always lain beyond the boundaries of bourgeois arrangements, and a sizable new population is in conscious revolt against them; the novel, moving into this territory of subject matter, encounters resistance. Sex figures in *Dance the Eagle to Sleep* as a puzzled promiscuity, and in *Single File* as a squalid menace. Yet neither author could quite do without it; indeed, against the grain of their prophetic purposes, it threatens to dominate their narratives, as something inchoate, unchannelled, mysterious. Both second novels —in contrast to the first novels—show people removed from the context of families. In one case, parents have been rejected; in the other, urban pressure has broken families down. Without the multiple perspectives of a family, Miss Piercy's portrait of youth rampant is a lopsided cartoon; writing about city dwellers interconnected with an extreme of tenuousness, Mr. Fruchter has compiled a scrupulous brochure of fragments. Loss of perspective, however, is where vision often begins, and less, in the case of these second novels, may be more.

From Dyna Domes to Turkey-Pressing

DIVINE RIGHT'S TRIP, by Gurney Norman. 302 pp. Dial Press, 1972.

GERONIMO REX, by Barry Hannah. 337 pp. Viking, 1972.

"We *are* as gods and might as well get good at it," announced page 1 of *The Last Whole Earth Catalog*, that mind-blowing, prize-winning compendium of hardware, natural foods, aerial photographs, cosmological tracts, and a thousand and one other handy aids to good-god-making. On the right-hand side of many of the pages, and identified by the device of a dragon, ran a narrative called *Divine Right's Trip*, written by one of the editors, Gurney Norman; this novel has now been published separately, in hard-cover by the Dial Press and as a paperback by Bantam. Though the text is little changed, and has even kept its dragons, it reads very differently out of the *Catalog*'s farraginous, clangorous context; there, competing with advertisements for Synectics and Dyna Domes and Kama Sutra Oil, Norman's episodes appeared slier and more shardlike than they now turn out to be. Within covers of its own, *Divine Right's Trip* shows itself to be a subtly written and morally passionate epic of the counter-culture, a fictional explication of the hopeful new consciousness come to birth—midwifed by hallucinogens—amid the communes and rock concerts of the sixties.

The story is simple: D(ivine) R(ight) (for David Ray) Davenport, stoned crazy, makes his way in a VW bus called Urge, with a girl called Estelle, from the West Coast to his home territory of Appalachian Kentucky, where he finds peace and purpose in soil reclamation by means of rabbit manure. Along the way, he meets a number of more or less allegorical Americans, such as the Lone Outdoorsman, and a garageman who says, "All of you, come back and see us, you hear?" and a Greek who believes the world can be cleansed of mucus by adherence to the walnut diet of the ancient Sumerians, and St. Louis dope dealers, and an Indiana talk-show host, and a Cincinnati housewife who is also Divine Right's sister. D.R.'s favorite accolade is "far out," and all the types he encounters dissolve into harmlessness under his guileless appreciation. Sheer good-heartedness rather saps the saga of tension. The Lone Outdoorsman, for instance, has many ingredients of a villain: an "absurdly handsome" face on a stubby body, a fastidious armor of camping gear, a hard-hatted interior monologue. But, the author reassures us,

> The Lone Outdoorsman is far from your ordinary, everyday one-dimensional heavy: the thing that redeems the Lone Outdoorsman is a refreshing mental complexity of a kind you don't ordinarily run into in folk tales. All mixed in with his gory mental images of bullet-riddled bodies and heroic assaults upon beachheads was a commendable impulse to be nice to these kids, to befriend them and hopefully influence them in some constructive way.

Having spied D.R. and Estelle copulating in the woods, he debates shooting them, and decides instead to feed them steaks. And D.R.'s sister's husband, Doyle, a Cincinnati mechanic, feeds the young tripper at his table, freakiness be damned. "Doyle understood that his brother-in-law was some sort of mild outlaw. But . . . it never occurred to any of them to withdraw their affection just because the kid was in a phase." Doyle himself had been a maverick when he was young, and even today—"Doyle was thirty-four now, but as he bit down on his food the tendons in his big jaw flexed beneath his skin, and for a second the old toughness, and even meanness, of his youth was restored to his face, and for some reason D.R. found that very moving. He loved Doyle." D.R.'s America, indeed, is a web of such benevolent recognitions; nothing is too banal for him to dig, nothing too weird to merit respectful attention. If it is a land despoiled by strip mining and studded with importuning billboards, it is also a land of daily magic, where a credit card fuels a hegira, and collect phone calls bind together a freemasonry of friends, and a West Coast Prospero called the Anaheim Flash foots all bills and mends all missed connections and arrives in backwoods Kentucky in a silver Lotus to conduct a wedding in a silver jumpsuit.

No, the only real dragon our knight errant encounters is himself —one half of himself, when, in an extraordinary episode, he splits, under stress of long drug use, into two persons: D.R. and David.

Surprisingly, D.R., the stoned new-consciousness half, remains our hero, and the dragon is pure, rational David:

> There is David, lurking in the shadows of the ledge. He pulls my flesh around and makes me see his eyes shining in the murky darkness of his lair. My stomach turns, my hair feels wild, but my adoration of the light remains serene. It's only David's eyes, and lower forehead. The rest is monster, the mouth of dragon teeth, the chin and jaws receding to a short, thick neck and back of horns and scales and fur.
>
> Oh, it's true all right.
>
> He's the monster-guardian of the light.

The descriptions throughout *Divine Right's Trip* of drug experience, in its range of revelation and nightmare, its jerkiness, its comically bent perspectives, and its atrocious cumulative fatigue, bear comparison with Malcolm Lowry's descriptions of drunken states in *Under the Volcano*. In both books, an inflamed mind enlarges the universe, dyes it deeper, forces its petals wider. Yet Lowry's Consul is a pathological case, a sick man even in his own judgment, whereas to a young man of D.R.'s cultural conditioning experience normally arrives as a "trip," a "hit," a "flash," a "rush." An image that frequently recurs is of the mind as a movie screen. "As D.R. drove on through the night to Cincinnati he entertained a very complex little drama in his mind, rather like a movie an airline might show its passengers while in flight." Telephoning, he fantasizes that the transparent walls of the booth are "just bad movies projected from somewhere on the other side." The television shows D.R. sees are described as circumstantially as "real" encounters. Reality, the implication is, has lost its objective backbone; inner space is the only space. Living has become continuous spectatorship. This generation was zonked on television before it zonked itself on drugs. What but an ingrained disregard for the workaday, empirical world could breed the swarm of superstitions, such as astrology and the *I Ching*, that distinguish the counter-culture, and that in this novel aid D.R.'s pathetic search for "balance," for harmony with a world drained of substance.

Gurney Norman and Divine Right were born and raised in rural Kentucky, and this regional reality does offer an outer space they can trust. When, midway through, *Divine Right's Trip* hits Kentucky, the book sheds its shimmering snakeskin of fantasy and becomes a stout celebration of the clan, of native soil and hard work and pastoral goodness. Yet it rings less true than in the first, weirder half. Not that the Kentucky voices are not lovingly and amusingly rendered; not that the blasted coal land isn't a cunningly appropriate territory for D.R.'s Dark Passage and Recovery of the Grail. The trouble is the marriage that Mr. Norman wishes to occur, and makes occur, between the rural proletariat of Trace Fork and the young would-be gods of the dome communes. The idyll becomes cute:

> "I think ginseng is the answer to about half of mankind's problems," the freak said.
> "Shoot," said Elmer. "My daddy picked 'sang for a living, when I was a boy. It's as native to these hills as it is to over yonder in China."

The author names all of his friends, hill folk and dome folk, tobacco chewers and cocaine sniffers, and has them all dance round and square to a new sound "dubbed Hillbilly Hindu Rock." And the bride and groom, D.R. and Estelle, take their vows wearing coonskin and gingham, and the Anaheim Flash in his silver jumpsuit pronounces "everybody at this wedding hereby married to one another." Just so, *The Last Whole Earth Catalog* married Buckminster Fuller to L. L. Bean and pronounced the spirits of Buddha and Henry Ford one.

Well, let's not have any dry eyes at the wedding. But a doubt remains whether D.R.'s love affair with rabbit dung and the blisters that come with digging fence-post holes amounts to much more than another "trip." Is Estelle in gingham sufficiently different from Marie Antoinette in the garb of a shepherdess? Can the sated and disgusted offspring of middle-class urban and suburban homes ever do more than condescend, with however good a will, to the remnants of rural America? Agriculture, after all, is not an intrinsically virtuous enterprise. Those who are good at it are capitalists like any other, paying their Chicano fruit pickers no more than they must, manipulating their acreages and machinery and tax loopholes toward the highest profit. Those who are not so good at it hasten (as they have done ever since the first American

communes, the Puritan villages, were broken up by entrepre-
neurism) to the cities, to get the soft desk jobs and the middleman's
cut. The counter-culture's return to the soil is a luxurious gesture,
financed by the Anaheim Flash and other such imps of industrial
affluence.

Divine Right's Trip in book form is subtitled "A Folktale"; its
subtitle in *The Last Whole Earth Catalog* was "Our story thus
far"—more modest and more accurate. A folktale must be made
by the folk, "the gathered people" mentioned in the novel's last
words. But the folk are slow to speak, and in this country, even
as the costumes and mores and prejudices of the once radical young
gain wider acceptance each year, the folk are not yet ready to
yield their suffrage to D.R. and his friends. Mickey Mouse and
Archie Bunker are truer folk heroes, and will probably be re-
elected.* But Divine Right *is* bigger than life, and in giving the
story thus far of a segment of his generation, in prose nicely
threaded between the vernacular and the symbolic, Gurney Norman has shown a noble reach and a healthy grasp.

Although Barry Hannah, the author of *Geronimo Rex*, is several
years younger than Mr. Norman, his novel belongs to an older
tradition—the whining-adolescent novel of the fifties. The action
begins in 1950, when the hero, Harry Monroe, is eight years old,
and ends in the middle sixties, when he is married and a graduate
student of English at the University of Arkansas. America broke
in two in those years, when Johnson committed the half-million
troops to Vietnam, and the new consciousness at the heart of
Divine Right's Trip figures in *Geronimo Rex* as a bleak dawn, an
irony heavily in hock to despair, an accelerating incoherence in
the never very tightly woven events that make up the novel's
action. These events, though they fill three hundred and thirty-
seven large pages, are adequately adumbrated by the author's bio
note on the jacket flap: born down South, educated here and there,

---

* Which they were, by a landslide. Only to resign, separately, in a
devastating self-defeat. Of recent American mysteries, none more need-
fully awaits its sensitive biochemist than, in the years 1972–1974, the simultaneous and evidently symbiotic extermination of all honor in the highest
places and the drying-up of the counter-culture, as if astonished to death
by the super-vindication of its protests.

"plays the trumpet," took detours into "such odd work as a research assistant in pharmacology or trouble-shooter in a turkey-
pressing plant," married, "presently makes his home" someplace,
"where he is at work on his second novel." The major weakness of
a first novel like this is its limp susceptibility to autobiographical
accident; its vitality must lie not in the shaping but in the language
of the telling, and here Mr. Hannah is no mean performer. His
whine is full-throated:

> The old man had a Buick. He liked to wheel it up our brick drive,
> which was bordered by a dense cane patch. He was one of these
> magazine handsomes who was turning gray in the hair at forty-five;
> the gray strands were flames from a hot and ancient mental life,
> or so he thought. His mental life was always the great fake of the
> household. He had three years at L.S.U., makes sixty thousand a
> year, has the name of a bayou poet—Ode Elann Monroe—and has
> read a book or two over above what he was assigned as a sopho-
> more. So he's a snob, and goes about faking an abundant mental
> life. He always had this special kind of bewrenched and evaporated
> tiredness when he came home from the factory.

With the verve of the young Bellow but with little of Bellow's
love, Mr. Hannah can seize a person and hurl him into print:

> Perrino, still sporting his horseshoe beard and instructing trumpets,
> was odd. Eastman had given him license. He came to us wailing;
> he had his hands over his head, and you could see written back in
> his eyes that he had obtained some ruinous Ph.D. from somewhere.
> His tie knot waggled down on his open collar, and his clothes were
> like bandages coming apart over a horrid wound to his chest and
> soul. He wore sandals over black socks, which seemed to represent
> the same anguish at his feet. He was slightly chubby, with bags
> under his eyes like rotting bananas, and behaved as if he were the
> last gasp of Italianism in America.

The author does not shy from pushing an image into absurdity,
and pulling it out on the other side:

> [My father] engaged me in a sort of contest at milk-drinking
> while we waited for the answers to come out. It all ended with
> our drinking so much milk we were ready to puke; the old man
> churning himself into a dull butter of meditation about my life.

Some of the metaphors carry the shock of real poetry:

My youth was an old sick pirate; there was a boy back there lying on the reefs, bleeding. The lad's throat had been cut. I had cut it.

All this energy of expression, however, adorns a listless and ugly tale whose dominant mood is funk. "He wondered . . . if he could get over this period, this hump, which was not a hump really but a whole range of dismal mountains of funk." Harry's father is the third-richest man in Dream of Pines, a Louisiana papermaking town with a pervasive miasma and the cultural scope of a broom closet. Off-hours from the mattress factory he owns, he doodles in his study with the fantasy of being an author; his son flavors boredom with raptures over music. The Dream of Pines Colored High School has funnelled its meagre resources into a crack marching band, "that played Sousa marches and made the sky bang together"; this flare of excellence lights up the sodden mediocrity of all else. Dream of Pines public education is detailed with morbid zest, and the Mississippi college that enrolls Harry seems even more ill-tuned to his inner melody. Nothing links up; Harry keeps dropping things halfway through, including an inspired jazz solo and several instances of sexual intercourse. He tends to see all women as "roaches." The males he knows are possessed of isolating visions: Harley Butte, his mulatto friend, by a passion for John Philip Sousa; Bobby Dove Fleece, his roommate, by a lavishly verbalized obsession with sex; Whitfield Peter Lepoyster, his enemy, by a demented racism; Dr. Lariat, his professor, by a sterile cynicism. And in his own head Harry is Geronimo, the savage Indian rebel, at war with all society.

The youth of the fifties were not, as is sometimes implied, complacent; their contempt for the institutions around them was paralyzingly thorough. Salinger's Holden Caulfield, Keith Waterhouse's Billy Liar saw right through everything, and were too savvy to believe things could ever be otherwise. The vision of becoming as gods, of a neo-primitivist life style alternative to an ironical conformism, of a hot connection between private emotion and public policy, had to wait for a wave of desperation prefigured in *Geronimo Rex* by an unconvincing turn toward violence. This caustic small-town boyhood becomes, finally, a hollow shootout, with real bullets and blood if not real reverberations. Granted, guns seem standard equipment down South, and craziness does sometimes out. But—as in another Louisiana novel with a humid flamboyance, Robert Stone's *A Hall of Mirrors*—the violence feels dreamy, and too much the author's; the plot does not produce the violence as a tree produces fruit, but ends in it as a car ride sometimes ends in an accident. The author loses empathy with the hero. Harry's boyish infatuation with a sluttish millworker is movingly explored, but his later affair with Lepoyster's niece Catherine is nearly inexplicable, and his abrupt marriage to sixteen-year-old Prissy Lombardo totally so. The book ends on a sour note of putdown; Dr. Lariat, the professor of literature, tells Harry Monroe, the budding practitioner of it, that they're in the "wrong field." Music is the one.

Still, after *Divine Right's Trip*, in which America and its general populace form a backdrop for young tourists trailing their roots in some nirvana between here and Mars, it is salutary to read a novel in which the young and the middle-aged are interlocked, albeit in gruesome struggle. To judge by *Geronimo Rex*, young men like Bobby Dove Fleece still writhe and tremble under the old religious taboos; girls like Sylvia Wyche still struggle to save their hymens for their fiancés; instructors like Dr. Perrino still think they have something to teach; and all generations are mired equally in the squalid but substantial provincial ambience. Father and son, in this novel, lust after the same slut and the same muse. Mr. Hannah is nowhere better than he is in showing the complex currents of parent-child sympathy that swirl around acts of overt rebellion. Perhaps the South has a certain retarded solidarity; certainly Gurney Norman's pageant of reconciliation occurs more plausibly in Kentucky than on an Iowa corn farm or in a California orchard. Perhaps, too, the art of fiction is intrinsically mediating and anti-propagandistic; it reduces general issues to the faceted confusion of private lives, with their undoctrinaire mixing of personal quirk, conscious intention, and elementary biology. Of these two novels, Mr. Norman's is winged with surer purpose and Mr. Hannah's has the richer sense of circumstance. One rather skims, the other wallows; both give a fresh angle on the great American subject of Growing Up, and both offer the same American advice: Don't do it until you must.

Jong Love

FEAR OF FLYING, by Erica Jong. 340 pp. Holt, Rinehart & Winston, 1973.

Erica Jong's first novel feels like a winner. It has class and sass, brightness and bite. Containing all the cracked eggs of the feminist litany, her soufflé rises with a poet's afflatus. She sprinkles on the four-letter words as if women had invented them; her cheerful sexual frankness brings a new flavor to female prose. Mrs. Jong's heroine, Isadora Wing, surveying the "shy, shrinking, schizoid" array of women writers in English, asks, "Where was the female Chaucer?" and the Wife of Bath, were she young and gorgeous, neurotic and Jewish, urban and contemporary, might have written like this. *Fear of Flying* not only stands as a notably luxuriant and glowing bloom in the sometimes thistly garden of "raised" femi-nine consciousness but belongs to, and hilariously extends, the tradition of *Catcher in the Rye* and *Portnoy's Complaint*—that of the New York voice on the couch, the smart kid's lament. Though Isadora Wing, as shamelessly and obsessively as Alexander Portnoy, rubs the reader's nose in the fantasies and phobias and family slap-stick of growing up, and masturbates as often, she avoids the solipsism that turns Roth's hero unwittingly cruel; nor does she, like Holden Caulfield, though no less sensitive to phoniness, make of innocence an ideal. She remains alert to this world.

> How little our happiness depends on: an open drugstore, an un-stolen suitcase, a cup of cappuccino! Suddenly I was acutely aware of all the small pleasures of being alive. The superb taste of the coffee, the sunlight streaming down, the people posing on street corners for you to admire them.

Admiring she is even of the impotence, madness, and defective hygiene of her many awful lovers. A feminist since birth (she says), radicalized at the age of thirteen "on the I.R.T. subway when the moronic Horace Mann boy who was my date asked me if I planned to be a secretary," Isadora Wing nevertheless has more kind words for the male body than any author since the penning of *Fanny Hill:*

> He was so beautiful lying there and his body smelled so good. I thought of all those centuries in which men adored women for their bodies while they despised their minds. . . . That was how I so often felt about men. Their minds were hopelessly befuddled, but their bodies were so nice. Their ideas were intolerable, but their penises were silky.

Her account of her travails among these silken creatures, while not exactly a flag of truce in the war between the sexes, does hold out some hope of renewed negotiations.

The second of four daughters of a would-be paintress and a father who designed "ice buckets which looked like beer steins and beer steins which looked like ice buckets," Isadora grew up in a fourteen-room apartment on Central Park West. She heavy-pets (let's call it) at thirteen, remorsefully tries to starve herself at fourteen, embarks upon a series of psychiatrists (the first is Dr. Schrift; he's short, of course, and tells her, "Ackzept being a vohman"), enters Barnard at seventeen, meets the brilliant Brian Stollerman when she is a freshman, seduces him and puts her virginity out of its misery, marries Brian after graduation, endures his swelling madness while she attends graduate school, commits and divorces him at twenty-two, takes up with an unwashed, musical loser called Charlie Fielding, is betrayed by him, embarks upon a swinging tour of Europe with a girl friend at the age of twenty-three, returns to New York, meets a silent thirty-one-year-old Chinese Freudian named Bennett Wing, marries him, and now, five years later, at the age of twenty-nine in 1971, attends with her husband an international congress of psychoanalysts in Vienna, where she meets, loves at first sight, and runs away with an English Laingian psychiatrist called (yes) Adrian Goodlove. This life history is scattered carefreely backward and forward throughout three hundred and forty pages that should be read, one sometimes suspects, in fifty-minute sessions. A pattern and a person emerge, amid the wisecracks, postcards ("Vienna. The very name is like a waltz. But I never could stand the place. It seemed dead to me. Embalmed"), and reflections upon the hard and curious lot of Woman. Intellectual condescension, physical intimidation, deodorant-selling insinuation—women suffer them all. The case for marriage is nailed in a sentence: "Being unmarried in a man's world was such a hassle that *any*thing had to be better." Motherhood is another distrusted institution: "Basically, I think, I was furious with my mother for not teaching me how to be a woman, for not teaching me how to make peace between the raging hunger in my cunt and the hunger in my head." Her mother, a frustrated artist, is full of "misplaced artistic aggression," and Isadora thinks sadly of young wives "making babies out of their loneliness and boredom and not knowing why." The smaller discomforts of femininity are vividly, comically detailed, from the presence of a heavy suitcase to the absence of a needed Tampax; females, we are told, are even at a disadvantage making water by the roadside, tending to piss in their shoes. The one female complaint not registered, surprisingly, is the one most conspicuous in seriously sexy male fiction, such as Mailer's "The Time of Her Time." However adverse her circumstances, Isadora Wing seems to have no trouble attaining orgasm. And maybe this is what makes her saga so uncranky, for all its intelligent pain, and lends its prose a spun-sugar halo of wonder and fun, and gives its conclusion the smug snap of a shopping expedition satisfactorily completed:

> I looked down at my body. The same. The pink V of my thighs, the triangle of curly hair, the Tampax string fishing the water like a Hemingway hero, the white belly, the breasts half floating, the nipples flushed and rosy from the steamy water. A nice body. Mine. I decided to keep it.

The male reviewer, grateful to be served this lovable, delicious novel (each chapter garnished with epigraphs), embarrasses himself with digestive rumblings. While intimacy with Isadora Wing is maintained, the reader accepts the value she puts on her own story: a reconciliation of the hunger at the poles of her being, a triumph, if precarious, over aerophobia and the socially conditioned guilt and slavishness that lie beneath it. At a little remove, however, the story can be viewed as that of a spoiled young woman who after some adventures firmly resolves to keep on spoiling herself. She bounces about on a ubiquitous padding of money: her parents were well-to-do; her first husband's parents were able to pay for private treatment of his madness "fees [of] about $2,000 a month," Charlie Fielding lived on a trust fund, both her present lover and husband are psychiatrists, with the subliminal affluence of that priestly profession. To be sure, the middle class has problems, too, and most novels are written about them, but as an instance of sexist oppression Isadora Wing should be recognized as a privileged case, with no substantial economic barriers between her and liberation, and—by her own choice— no children, either. Edna Pontellier, the heroine of Kate Chopin's elegiac novel of female revolt, *The Awakening*, was a mother as well as a wife, and drowned herself to escape the impasse between her personal, artistic identity and her maternal obligations. Childless, with an American Express card as escort on her pilgrimage, and with a professional forgiver as a husband, Isadora Wing, for all her terrors, is the heroine of a comedy.

On the back jacket flap, Mrs. Jong, with perfect teeth and cascading blond hair, is magnificently laughing, in contrast to the sombre portrait that adorns her two collections of poetry. Rather disconcertingly, not only does Isadora Wing, like Erica Jong, write poetry but she writes Mrs. Jong's poetry, two samples of which are included in this book. And the reader of *Fruits & Vegetables* (1971) and *Half-Lives* (1973) has already encountered Isadora Wing's fractured leg and her burgeoning crow's-feet, her multi-colored notes to herself and the trail of sequins one of her gowns leaves, her mother's avocado tree behind her mother's avocado-colored couch, her mad first husband and her fondness for likening human cheeks to willow tips for softness, her irritated observation of Braque and Utrillo prints in psychiatrists' offices, and her quotation of Sylvia Plath's question "Is there no way out of the mind?" In some of the poems of *Half-Lives*, the husband and the lover of *Fear of Flying* are distinctly silhouetted, and in the earlier collection the sequence entitled "Flying You Home" presents the removal of "Brian Stollerman" to a California hospital in a slightly different light—more moving and ominous than what we find in the corresponding chapter of the novel, where the incident seems one more of the long string of zany mishaps that comprise Isadora Wing's amorous education. *Fear of Flying* wears its gossamer disguise as fiction with a breathtaking impudence; the difference between "The Green Hornet" and the "Blue Wasp series for radio" appears about the thickness of it. Adrian and Isadora playfully discuss how he will be portrayed in the book she will presumably write about their affair, and the sister whose husband later attempts sodomy on Isadora screams at her, "Well, I won't have you putting me and my husband and my children in your filthy writing—do you hear me? I'll kill you if you mention me in any way at all." The disinterested reader, of course, need not tremble, but the flashback sections about romances past do feel more spilled than told, and there is something a shade archetypical about the heroine: for all the times she looks at herself nude, she remains visually misty, and the author's nimble recourse to cultural and psychoanalytical tags verges on nervous patter. As a creator of scenes and characters, Mrs. Jong is at her best in the present—that is, at the Vienna Congress of 1971, with Isadora running back and forth between her husband and her new lover, getting their inexhaustible and incompatible analyses of what is happening. Here, comedy becomes satire and distress becomes drama. The prose flies. Throughout, the poet's verbal keenness rarely snags the flow of breathy vernacular; a few false shifts of tone, an occasional automatism of phrase ("intensely interested," "poring over books," "clutching my baby" within six lines), a few clammy touches of jargon insignificantly mar a joyously extended performance. The novel is so full, indeed, that one wonders whether the author has enough leftover life for another novel. Fearless and fresh, tender and exact, Mrs. Jong has arrived nonstop at the point of being a literary personality; may she now travel on, toward Canterbury.

OLDER AMERICANS

Indifference

MORNING NOON AND NIGHT, by James Gould Cozzens. 408 pp. Harcourt, Brace & World, 1968.

Beginning, forty years ago, with a style of sober purity, James Gould Cozzens has purposefully evolved a prose unique in its mannered ugliness, a monstrous mix of Sir Thomas Browne, legalese, and Best-Remembered Quotations. The opening chapter of his new novel, *Morning Noon and Night,* cloudy as a polluted pond, swarms with verbal organisms of his strange engendering. As Cozzensologists before me have discovered, there is no substitute for the tabulated list. We have the Unresisted Cliché:

Here are clouds of witnesses, faces and forms in serried ranks . . .

I don't intend here any telling in mournful numbers.

Simply, the wood is not to be seen for the trees.

The Lame Echo:

To be sure, in this distraction of the mind, as through a glass darkly . . .

You have not world enough and time. . . .

I feel it leaves man as much as before the glory, jest, and riddle of the world.

The False Precision, the Legal "Or":

. . . to inform yourself of any peculiarities or limitations of his that could have affected his observation or could now be coloring his report.

. . . what they seem in our work or practice. I am not suggesting that I feel we are or ever could be ethically obligated. . . .

. . . by elements of lust whether loving or unloving, a catalog longer or shorter of women . . .

The Vapid Expansion:

What used to be, not just well enough, but often very good indeed, must be left religiously alone.

The Inversion Frightful, Capped by Cute Periphrasis:

In eating employed now are partial dental prosthetic devices.

Be that how it may, Nancy, as friends call her, will not refuse the rites mysterious of connubial love.

The Gratuitous Scientism:

Penetrated, the microscopic cell is fertilized (in accepted language of the process, two gametes fuse to form a zygote).

The Infatuated Sonority:

His course of ripe and ripe is running, and the rot and rot won't fail to follow. . . .

Multitudinous as these remembered works of Nature may be, more multitudinous still, and by far, must be remembered works of man.

What Cozzens has set himself to achieve, and has, as he might say, so regrettably succeeded in achieving, is the literary equivalent for or capture of the all too veritably human quality of *stuffiness*. In tone and tedium, *Morning Noon and Night* is a four-hundred-page-long after-dinner speech.

The speaker is Henry Dodd Worthington; the dinner has been his life. Born at the turn of the century as the son of a small-college English professor, the narrator of this novel, after an acceptable education at an unnamed prep school and Harvard, and after shrugging off both teaching and writing as possible careers, drifted into employment with a Boston collection agency, and from this indifferent beginning rose to found Henry Worthington Associates, a management-consultant firm of prestige so immense that both he and the reader find it implausible. He has been twice married: his first wife, Judith, cuckolded and divorced him; his second, Charlotte, committed suicide. Violence, indeed, has made rather free with his relatives; his parents were asphyxiated in a hotel fire, and his two grandchildren were killed in the crash of a plane. Henry (or "our Hank," as he jocosely calls himself) is of genteel Protestant background, an indirect descendant of President Franklin Pierce; during the Second World War he served as an Air Forces major, mostly in the Pentagon; his present preoccupations are the unhappiness of his daughter Elaine, now on her third divorce, and the composition of this memoir. The events of his life are not related consecutively but emerge as his memory rambles over the past; he ruminates at length upon such diverse matters as his grandfather's feud with the early Freudians, the tricks of management consultation, the technique of running an antiques shop, the sinking of the *Titanic*, the vagaries of chance, the nature of the Puritan heritage, the ups and downs and ins and outs of sexual "appetency," and (an unexpected obsession) the shabbiness of the literary world. Many of these essays, once the muddled sonority of the style is tuned out, possess interest, even a certain surly brilliance, but as a life the book lacks what it must have—life.

Elaine is the only character other than the narrator allowed to have any kind of a say; the novel's keystone scene is an interview between the distressed daughter and the stiff but sorry father, held in the courtyard of H.W. Associates' posh new suburban plant. But when, after seventy solid pages of authorial discourse, quotation marks appear amid the print and Elaine breaks into speech, she talks just like a little Henry, or (since without a doubt our Hank is pretty much our Jim) a little Cozzens. Listen to her:

> "So when Wilfred deflowered me I was pretty much, as the books say, unawakened."

> "You know; lovely Sue makes like softly panting while the geranium tree is planting. And doesn't that show what's up for grabs here is love forever true, and oughtn't he to latch onto it?"

> "You bet! Moving finger writes. Correct. And all my tears, or such as I've let drip, don't wash out a word."

Embarrassed, apparently, by her own wealth of literary tags, she admonishes her father, "Don't forget the expensive liberal-arts education you bought me. When it pays to, I can sound tolerably literate." But it doesn't pay; their conversation is lumpy with false wit and stilted slang and brittle with a supervisory knowingness—not a dramatization of her plight but an awkward exposition of it. So it is with the entire book. Henry's marriage to Judith, by all indications the deepest relationship of his life, is represented by some mocking paragraphs on newlywed lust, a potentially poignant but skimped account of their courtship, an unskimped theory as to how her father's anti-sexual High Anglicanism drove her decades later to promiscuity, a few cursory references to their divorce, a full exposition of Henry's financial advice to the antiques business she sets up in, and a glancing admission that now she is dying. She hardly speaks a sentence; for her one moment onstage, she is seen through her daughter's eyes distantly on a beach, coupling with a lover. Charlotte, the second wife, appears in Henry's account as a suicide note, as a glimpse of her in the shower (heavily misted by panting references to David and Bathsheba), and as an equable compliment to her secretarial ability. All the characters—wives, friends, business associates, service colleagues—are immersed, mute and all but immobile, in the tyrannous flow of Henry Worthington's disquisitional lava.

Now, to what extent does the author stand apart from his persona, as, say, John Marquand does from George Apley? How much of Henry's stuffiness is intentional caricature? Is his sluggish eclipse of the life he has lived a novelistic defect or an ironical comment? Mockery there is in abundance: Henry mocks his youthful ardor, his elderly dignity, his riskless wartime career, the little shams and maneuvers of his trade. His memory seeks out low moments: "mean actions of mine; uglinesses of greed or lust; shameful exhibitions of ignorance; deserved humiliations; mortifying follies and defeats." And the epigraph from Shakespeare's Sonnet 94, describing those who, "moving others, are themselves as stone," suggests that a self-portrait of a type of man and an implicit judgment were intended. But Marquand, even in his later novels, maintained an outsider's perspective on his Brahmins, whereas Worthington's voice and Cozzens' are indistinguishable, and the opinions of author and character merge in a ponderous, pessimistic morass of self-distrust and weary puzzlement.

Having troubled to invent a business profession for his alter ego, and having supplied a convincing amount of data and theory, Cozzens compulsively reverts throughout his narrative to the problems of the literary practitioner, to attacks upon "half-writer pretenders" and "liberal intellectuals." He includes a coy reference to the minor American writer Frederick Cozzens. He gives Henry, the supposed author of a million memos and directives, his own preposterously pedantic style, including the obligatory exotic words—*inappetency, erethism, furibund, condign, innominate, muliebrity, deontology.* Frequently heard is the rumble of hobbyhorses being ridden by that ultra-conservative Cozzens displayed years ago in *Time*—a kind of male Ayn Rand who in this book must dote upon a fictional bank's status "in the best financial circles" as being "better regarded than the latter-day not always prudent House of Morgan," who speaks of Roosevelt's "near-senile megalomania" and the Kremlin's "dupes" and "expert perfidies and duplicities," and who seems pleasurably smitten by the speculation that a typhoon would have wiped out our scheduled invasion of the Japanese home islands had not the war been ended by the atomic bombs, which in passing are viewed as the "means to right a ceaselessly growing imbalance in Nature, to solve quickly and easily theretofore insoluble problems of excess population."

Not that political conservatives should be barred from the halls of fiction; rather, they should be better represented there, to relieve the present rather shrill unanimity on the left. Nor is author/alter-ego closeness an intrinsic handicap; *Herzog*, for example, is an excellent novel. Its superiority to *Morning Noon and Night* lies not only in Bellow's far livelier gift for conjuring up personalities but in his, and Herzog's, belief that a better world somewhere exists, that improvement can be sought and choices can be made. The illusion of free will, illusion or not, is necessary to a novel; excitement and import derive from the reality of human decision. As Henry Dodd Worthington describes himself, he has been always a product, a zygote formed by two fused gametes, in the grip, successively and simultaneously, of biology, heredity, social usage, sexual impulse, chance, and inertia. The turning points of his life—his marriage to Judith, his entry into the world of business, his enlistment in the Army Air Forces, his divorce and remarriage—are all seen as uncaused drift, "little governed by logic or demonstrable cause and effect." Herzog, at the end, can stop writing letters and set the table for a tryst, whereas Henry can only conclude that he knows nothing, that his life has been a "wandering directionless," a game of "blindman's buff—now sightlessly bumping into things, now surprised by sportive unreturnable blows." His memories—in the book's last, best flight of imagery—are seen as ruined fragments and, far off, "a dozen or more aqueduct arches, commencing suddenly, suddenly ending, coming now from nowhere, now going nowhere." There is "thin final sunlight," and then "the child must soon be taken away to bed." A child is someone who lacks responsibility and power of choice; Henry Dodd Worthington, adviser to big business, labels himself as one. This vision of helpless, pointless process is at the heart of the novel's profound inaction, of its analyzed but unrealized events, and even of its reactionary style, seeping backward to include all those tired mottoes and phrases and clichés as if wryly to admit that nothing new can be said. Resigned pessimism is a defensible philosophy, and may be the natural end of American enterprise, but it makes for very dull fiction.

Piqued by this book's curious badness, I turned to Cozzens' first full-length novel, *The Last Adam*. Though a trifle slick, with its climactic town meeting and its magnificent starring role for an aging screen idol (it *was* made into a movie, *Dr. Bull*, starring Will Rogers), it holds up well; the evocation of the Connecticut town of New Winton, the tight knit of weather and geography and people into a plot, the particularity and immediacy of every scene all show a mastery remarkable in a man of thirty. Cozzens then had more grasp of ordinary, middling America—or at least more willingness to transmute his grasp into art—than Hemingway and Fitzgerald ever showed. The hero of the novel, Dr. Bull, is sixty-seven, just about Henry Worthington's age, and he remembers the sentence from the Psalmist with which Henry begins his memoir: "I have been young and now am old." And cosmic nullity is present in both books: "Left to herself [a telephone operator in *The Last Adam*], and to what she could see of the universe, real and ideal were lost together in an indifference so colossal, so utterly indifferent, that there was no defining it." This colossal indifference, this abyss beneath society and conventional success, has always been with Cozzens, but as a threat, as a defining darkness, not as an all-swallowing enemy. From *The Last Adam* to *Morning Noon and Night*, the broad social scene of New Winton, primarily Protestant, has dwindled to one member of the Puritan aristocracy; class consciousness has narrowed to class loyalty. Cozzens has become like a Yale undergraduate in the earlier book: "He knew by now that he and his more intimate friends were right; or, at any rate, he could easily see that people who differed conspicuously in dress or behavior, in ideals or attitudes, were, as far as his college was concerned, wrong. His gray eyes considered all those in error with a level, complete indifference." Arthur Winner, of *By Love Possessed*, gave those not of his sort short shrift. Henry Worthington doesn't see them at all, they are squeezed into the remotest margins of his memoir, and there is nowhere to stand to see *him*, to judge him. Only the bitter vacuity of his conclusions betrays the possibility that somewhere along the way he went wrong.

Papa's Sad Testament

ISLANDS IN THE STREAM, by Ernest Hemingway. 466 pp. Scribner's, 1970.

This book consists of material that the author during his lifetime did not see fit to publish; therefore it should not be held against him. That parts of it are good is entirely to his credit; that other parts are puerile and, in a pained way, aimless testifies to the odds against which Hemingway, in the last two decades of his life, brought anything to completion. It is, I think, to the discredit of his publishers that no introduction * offers to describe from what stage of Hemingway's tormented later career *Islands in the Stream* was salvaged, or to estimate what its completed design might have been, or to confess what editorial choices were exercised in the preparation of this manuscript. Rather, a gallant wreck of a novel is paraded as the real thing, as if the public are such fools as to imagine a great writer's ghost is handing down books intact from Heaven.

So we are left to perform the elementary scholarly decencies ourselves. Carlos Baker's biography speaks of a trilogy about the sea that Hemingway, amid the distractions of Cuba, the cockfights and double Daiquiris and proliferating hangers-on, carried forward with enthusiasm in late 1950 and early 1951. The third item of the trilogy, "The Sea in Being," was separately, and triumphantly, published as *The Old Man and the Sea*. The first part, "The Sea When Young," seems to have been an abridgment of an earlier, disastrously long and gauche novel called *Garden of Eden*. The middle section, "The Sea When Absent," has for its hero an American painter named Thomas Hudson and, in the form that Hemingway announced as "finished" by Christmas of 1950, answers the description of the section entitled "Cuba" in the present book. "The Island and the Stream" (*sic*) had become, by mid-1951, the working title of the first section, presumably the revamped *Garden of Eden*. Baker says: "It contains 'wonderful parts' that he hated to cut out, but he was now clear that it must be reshaped to the style and tempo of the other three sections." Of the "other three," one is the story of Santiago that would soon be a separate novel, one is the "Cuba" mentioned above, and the third is "the sea-chase story," which, in Hemingway's opinion, was "impregnable to criticism" and was almost published in *Cosmopolitan*, in two installments. In the book Scribner's has published, this sea-chase is the third section, "At Sea," and the first section, whose adjusted title now does for the whole, is entitled "Bimini."

What we have, then, is a trio of large fragments crudely unified

---

* Mary Hemingway's 53-word Note scarcely counts; it admits to "some cuts" and correction of spelling and punctuation and that is all.

by a Caribbean setting and the nominal presence of Thomas Hudson. "Bimini" is a collection of episodes that show only a groping acquaintance with one another; "Cuba" is a lively but meandering excursion in local color that, when the painter's first wife materializes, bizarrely veers into a dark and private region; and "At Sea" is an adventure story of ersatz intensity. Hudson, if taken sequentially, does not grow but dwindles, from an affectionate and baffled father and artist into a rather too expertly raffish waterfront character into a bleak manhunter, a comic-book superhuman containing unlooked-for bubbles of stoic meditation and personal sorrow. Some conscious attempt is made to interlock the characterizations—the manhunter remembers that he is a painter, and gives us some hard-edged seascapes to prove it; the bar clown intermittently recalls that he is drowning his grief at the death of a son—but the real congruence of these masks is involuntary: all fit the face of Ernest Hemingway.

Whereas an achieved novel, however autobiographical, dissolves the author and directs our attention beyond him, *Islands in the Stream*, even where most effective, inspires us with a worried concern for the celebrity who wrote it. His famous drinking, his methodical artistic devotions, his dawn awakenings, his women, his cats, even his mail (what painter gets anything like a writer's burdensome, fascinating mail?) are all there, mixed with less easily publicized strains, dark currents that welled into headlines with his last illnesses and shocking suicide. The need to prove himself implacably drives Thomas Hudson toward violence and death. His enemy, pain, has become an object of infatuation. Even in the first, most lyric passages, when he is visited on Bimini by his three sons, what lives for the father-narrator are scenes of savagery— the machine-gunning of a shark and a boy's day-long wrestle with a huge swordfish. The child, bent double, bleeding in hands and feet, is held fast to the fighting chair by the surrounding men, his guardians, so that he can experience "love":

> "Well," David said with his eyes tight shut. "In the worst parts, when I was the tiredest I couldn't tell which was him and which was me."
> "I understand," Roger said.
> "Then I began to love him more than anything on earth."

As if to insulate his fatherhood from his dreadful passion for violence, Hemingway creates in this section (never to reappear) another alter ego, a brawling, brooding writer named Roger Davis, and thrusts upon him a gratuitously brutal fistfight, as well as a number of reckless and self-destructive traits that the placid morning painter Thomas Hudson has supposedly outgrown. But in "Cuba," Hyde has been reunited with Jekyll, and Hudson—always a fond describer of guns, and a lover of blood sports—seems right at home among drinking companions who cheerfully remark, of prostitutes who gave imperfect service, "We ought to have poured gasoline on them and set them on fire." Later, Hudson himself, asked by his wife if their only son is dead, answers with the amazing monosyllable, "Sure." The final episode, "At Sea," sees Hudson's fulfillment as a killer, and Hemingway's as an addict of the casually cruel touch. A large "obscenely white" crab offends Hudson: "the man shot him between his eyes and the crab disintegrated." Removing a bullet from a sun-dried corpse is "like cutting into a pie." A grenade eliminates a wounded German: "How is the Kraut in the bow?" "He's a mess." Truly Hudson tells himself, "The horrors were what you won in the big crap game that they run." Well, the author is helping run this crap game, and it takes a little disintegration to keep him happy; unable to decide which of the hero's three boys to kill, he kills them all, two in one section and the third, with comic rigor, in the next.

Hemingway of course did not invent the world, nor pain, mutilation, and death. In his earlier work his harsh obsessions seem honorable and necessary; an entire generation of American men learned to speak in the accents of Hemingway's stoicism. But here, the tension of art has been snapped and the line between sensitive vision and psychopathy has been crossed. The "sea-chase story" is in many ways excellent, but it has the falsity of the episode in Hemingway's real life upon which it was based. In the early days of World War II, he persuaded his friends in the Havana Embassy to let him equip his private fishing launch the *Pilar* as a Q-boat, with bazookas, grenades, bombs, and machine guns. His dream was to lure a Nazi submarine close enough to toss a bomb down the hatch. He staffed the *Pilar* with cronies and, fruitlessly, but displaying much real courage and stamina, cruised the Cuban coast. Everything in "At Sea" is true, except the encounter with Germans and the imperatives of the mission, which was not demanded from above but invented and propelled from within. Such bravery is not grace under pressure but pressure forced in the hope of inducing Grace.

And even love becomes a species of cruelty, which divides women into whores and bitches on the one hand and on the other a single icy-perfect adored. Some reviewers have complained that the first wife is unreal: to me she has that hard reality of a movie star (which in the book she is), a star on the screen, with "the magic rolling line of the hair that was the same silvery ripe-wheat color as always." But it is an easy transition from the image of this beloved and lost woman, this enforcer of proud loneliness, to the cool gray pistols Hudson sleeps with:

> "How long have you been my girl?" he said to the pistol. "Don't answer," he said to the pistol. "Lie there good and I will see you kill something better than land crabs when the time comes."

Love and death: fused complements in Hemingway's universe. Yet he never formulated the laws that bind them, never dared depart from the knightly code and poser's armor he forged against the towering impressions of suffering received at his father's side in the Michigan woods.

> "Is dying hard, Daddy?"
> "No, I think it's pretty easy, Nick. It all depends."
> . . . In the early morning on the lake sitting in the stern of the boat with his father rowing, he felt quite sure that he would never die.

Sure of certain things, he never achieved the step away from himself, of irony and appraisal. He wanted to; he tried; this book opens in a mood of tonic breadth and humor, and closes with a beatific vision of Hudson dying and beloved:

> "I think I understand, Willie," he said.
> "Oh shit," Willie said. "You never understand anybody that loves you."

The new generations, my impression is, want to abolish both war and love, not love as a physical act but love as a religion, a creed to help us suffer better. The sacred necessity of suffering no longer seems sacred or necessary, and Hemingway speaks across the Sixties as strangely as a medieval saint; I suspect few readers younger than myself could believe, from this sad broken testament, how we *did* love Hemingway and, pity feeling impudent, love him still.

And Yet Again Wonderful

BULLET PARK, by John Cheever. 245 pp. Knopf, 1969.

In the coining of images and incidents, John Cheever has no peer among contemporary American fiction writers. His short stories dance, skid, twirl, and soar on the strength of his abundant invention; his novels tend to fly apart under its impact. His first, *The Wapshot Chronicle*, was unified by a pervading nostalgia and a magnificent old man's journal; his second, *The Wapshot Scandal*, amounted to a debris of brilliant short stories. *Bullet Park*, his third, holds together but just barely, by the thinnest of threads. It begins with an evocation of Bullet Park, a more ominously named version of the suburban essence Cheever used to call Shady Hill:

> The stranger might observe that the place seems very quiet; they seem to have come inland from the sounds of wilderness—gulls, trains, cries of pain and love, creaking things, hammerings, gunfire— not even a child practices the piano in this precinct of disinfected acoustics.

At church one Sunday, Eliot Nailles, our hero, meets Paul Hammer, our other hero. Not unnaturally, they, and we, are roused to foreboding by the coincidence of their names, but for the bulk of the book they merely glimpse one another; their fates intertwine only at the end.

The first half of the novel tells Nailles's story: he is, as male suburbanites go, uxorious and cheerful, but his seventeen-year-old son Tony in a spell of despair takes to his bed, inaccessible to mother, father, and psychiatrist. At last a Negro guru from the town's little ghetto coaxes him, with repetitions of the magic word

"Love," back into the American Way of Life. The second half of
Bullet Park shows Hammer, a wealthy bastard (literally), being
chased from hotel to hotel in both hemispheres by a melancholy-
inducing *cafard;* his temporary occupation of a yellow room where
he feels at peace leads to his marriage to a wood-nymph who, once
wed, becomes a bitch (figuratively). In the end, Hammer goes
mad, decides to crucify Tony, kidnaps the boy, and is overtaken
in that Episcopalian church by Nailles armed with a power saw—
events almost redeemed from implausibility by the bravura speed
of their telling.

The book's broad streak of the fantastic has been deplored by
some critics—the same critics, I suspect, who readily grant emancipation from the probable to younger, overtly "experimental"
novelists like John Hawkes and James Purdy. A more serious
weakness lies in the similarity of the two heroes; though intended,
perhaps, to be contrasting polarities of the American psyche,
Hammer and Nailles are in fact much alike—decent hard-drinking
hommes moyens sensuels oppressed by a shapeless smog of anxiety.
Tony is headed the same way, and the author, in the askew irony
of his upbeat conclusion, with its quartet of "wonderfuls," * seems
to be shrugging off his own *cafard.* The tender, twinkling prose
has an undercurrent of distraction and impatience.

Bullet Park succeeds, I think, as a slowly revolving mobile of
marvellously poeticized moments—the portrait of the hungover
party couple the Wickwires as they struggle to rise on Monday
morning; Hammer's mother's detection of symphonies in the roar
of various airplane motors; Nailles's wife's visit to an off-off-Broad-
way play and her subsequent haunting by a nude actor, "his thick
pubic brush from which hung, like a discouraged and unwatered
flower, his principal member." America's urban hell presses hard
upon the suburbia that was meant to be paradise. Cheever maintains his loyalty to the middling and the decent, but speaks increasingly in the accents of a visionary.

---

* "Tony went back to school on Monday and Nailles—drugged—went off
to work and everything was as wonderful, wonderful, wonderful, wonderful
as it had been." Cf. *As You Like It,* act III, scene ii, Celia saying: "O wonderful, wonderful, and most wonderful wonderful! and yet again wonderful,
and after that, out of all whooping!"

Talk of a Tired Town

THE LONG-WINDED LADY, *Notes from The New Yorker*, by Maeve Brennan. 237 pp. Morrow, 1969.

The New Yorker's "Talk of the Town" department, a space set aside when Ross founded the magazine as a smart-aleck local, survives as a vacuum maintained in case someone has something to say.* When, a dozen years ago, I served on the large team that labored to fill each week this frontal void (a task that White and Thurber had performed with the aid of a few legmen), the problem was to perpetuate a cozy tone about a city that had ceased to seem cozy. We were, we "Talk of the Town" reporters, a sallow crew-cut brigade fresh from Cornell or Harvard, sent forth into the mirthless gray canyons to attend a mechanical promotional exhibit or p.r.-pushed pseudo-event, battering out upon our return six or seven yellow pages of rough copy to be honed into eight hundred gay, excited, factually flawless words by veteran martyrs like John McCarten and Brendan Gill. Some of us did not even live in the city, but had already established families and golf memberships in Bronxville or Rye, and even those who, like myself, did live in Manhattan had their hearts set on the green pastures of Fiction and the absentee ownership of Literary Glory. We were not avid to extract from the Eisenhowered, sullen if not apocalyptic metropolis of those years the enchantment of the Baghdad-on-the-Subway celebrated by O. Henry, by Scott Fitzgerald and Edna Millay, by Dorothy Parker and Benchley and Woollcott—whose chairs were still warm in the Algonquin lobby. It is to Maeve Brennan's credit that she, with the device of her letters from "the long-winded lady," has helped put New York back into *The New Yorker*, and has written about the city of the Sixties with both honesty and affection.

---

* My smart-aleck characterization of course pre-dates the politicization of the magazine's conscience, as expressed in its front columns, by such fiery unsigned editorialists as Jonathan Schell and Richard Harris, who have so much to say the space fairly groans.

Not that the pieces, as collected here, without most of the italics that gave them on first printing a comic breathlessness, entirely escape the "Talk of the Town's" way of making too much of too little and of being complacently, exhaustedly flat. She gives us John D. Rockefeller, Jr.'s entire credo as chiseled into Rockefeller Center, and the menus of a lot of meals she happens to eat, and the names of everyone present at a New Year's party at the Adano Restaurant. And the long-winded lady, read in bulk, reveals certain personal eccentricities. She tends to rise at dawn, to read while she eats, to like street music, to liken real streets to stage sets, to plug her favorite restaurants, to be threatened by large people and animals and loud noises—we deduce that she is small. She walks a lot but her range is curiously restricted; she never strays south of the Village, north of the eighties, and rarely east of Madison Avenue. Her favorite region, dismally enough, is the West Forties, those half-demolished blocks of small hotels and cellar restaurants and old coin shops between Fifth and Eighth Avenue; she most frequently strolls on Sixth, which she never calls the Avenue of the Americas.

Within these limitations she is constantly alert, sharp-eyed as a sparrow for the crumbs of human event, the overheard and the glimpsed and the guessed at, that form the solitary city person's least expensive amusement. A little boy crying, a bigger boy greeting his father, a young man courting over the telephone, a middle-aged couple enacting their estrangement across a restaurant table, an old lady flipping the pages of a letter from her hotel window as she reads—these vignettes are well realized, and need only a touch of padding and bluff to make them short stories. Miss Brennan does not blink when, surveying the cityscape, she sees drunks and crazy men and prostitutes with "the eyes of satisfied furies or unsatisfied prison wardresses," costumed in miniskirts "designed to show even more leg than they had." She is an unfussy but formidable phrase-maker, as in her long poem to the ailanthus (which she never calls the tree of heaven) or in her image of "daylight streaming like cold water" over the curved staircases and papered walls of roofless brownstones. A melancholy picture of New York's streets accumulates:

The night view up Sixth Avenue is eerie now that the blocks on the west side of the avenue are half broken down and half gone.

[Charles] is an attractive street, except that, like all small New York streets, it takes on a dead, menacing air at night, because of the lines and lines of cars that are parked along its sidewalks—cars jammed together, bumper to bumper, stealing all the life and space out of the place.

Broadway is dying, but the big street still looks much as it has looked for some time now—a garish architectural shambles with cheap shop fronts and a few movie houses.

At the moment, the dark shadow in New York is cast not by the past but by the future, and too many streets wear a dull air of "What's the use?"

Our cities, not too long ago the farm boy's dream and the place where every girl with a straight nose was advised to find her fortune, have become the national disgrace, the huge proofs of our native greed and haste. Who wants to live in them? The long-winded lady admits, "New York City is not hospitable. She is very big and she has no heart. She is not charming. She is not sympathetic. She is rushed and noisy and unkempt, a hard, ambitious, irresolute place, not very lively, and never gay." Yet she has lived there, during this slum of a decade, and also testifies, "In fact this is a wonderful city. It is always giving me something to think about."

His Own Horn

THE TRUMPET OF THE SWAN, by E. B. White. 210 pp. Harper & Row, 1970.

E. B. White's third novel for children joins the two others on the shelf for classics. While not quite so sprightly as *Stuart Little*, and less rich in personalities and incident than *Charlotte's Web*— that paean to barnyard life by a city humorist turned farmer—*The Trumpet of the Swan* has superior qualities of its own; it is the most spacious and serene of the three, the one most imbued with the author's sense of the precious instinctual heritage represented by wild nature. Its story persuasively offers itself to children as a parable of growing, yet does not lack the inimitable tone of the two earlier works—the simplicity that never condescends, the straight and earnest telling that happens upon (rather then veers into) comedy, the "grace and humor and praise of life and the good backbone of succinctness" that Eudora Welty noted nearly twenty years ago, reviewing *Charlotte's Web*.

At first glance, one's heart a little falls to see that wash drawings by Edward Frascino have replaced Garth Williams' finely furry pen-and-ink illustrations, which are wedded to White's other children's texts as intimately as Tenniel's to *Alice* and Shepard's to the Pooh books. From the jacket flap we learn that the tale, daring the obvious, tells of a Trumpeter Swan that learns to play the trumpet. More daringly still, he is called Louis. And in the first chapter we meet Sam Beaver, an eleven-year-old boy who, but for the dark touch of Indian about him, is too reminiscent of the many other bland, "interested" boy-heroes of books that bid us crouch behind the tall grass and spy out the wonder in a swan's nest. Yet soon White's love of natural detail lifts the prose into felicity, and the father and mother swan begin to talk to each other with a surprising animation, and the reader settles to a joyride through the rolling terrain of the highly unlikely. Louis discovers himself to be mute, an inconvenience during childhood but downright agony during the mating season. Louis' father, a bombastic old cob, gets him a trumpet, and to pay for it Louis turns professional. How does Louis' father acquire the trumpet? Why, by diving through the display window of a music store in Billings, Montana, and carrying the instrument off through a hail of shards and buckshot. How does Louis pack his trumpet, and the slate upon which he learns to write, and the lifesaving medal he wins, and the purse of money he makes? All are attached by strings around his neck, flapping and clanking together whenever he flies. How does he carve out his career? First, as a bugler in a boys' camp; next, as accompanist, swimming one-footed, to the swan-boats in the Boston Public Garden; last, as a night-club performer in Philadelphia, operating out of a pond in the city zoo.

If the author once winked during this accumulation of pre-posterous particulars, it would all turn flimsy and come tumbling down. But White never forgets that he is telling about serious matters: the overcoming of a handicap, and the joys of music, and the need for creatures to find a mate, and the survival of a beautiful species of swan. When Louis realizes that he must graduate from the bugle to the trumpet with its three finger-operated valves, he unflinchingly asks Sam Beaver to slit the webbing of his right foot. The boy does, not omitting to point out that henceforth the swan will tend to swim in circles. What other writer, in such a work of fancy, would not have contrived to omit this homely, even repellent, bit of surgery?

White's concreteness holds the door open for unpleasantness and also engenders textures of small surprise and delightful rightness. In one chapter Louis spends the night at the Ritz in Boston. He orders a dozen watercress sandwiches for dinner and then puts himself to bed in the bathtub. "Then he turned out the lights, climbed into the tub, curved his long neck around to the right, rested his head on his back, tucked his bill under his wing, and lay there, floating on the water, his head cradled softly in his feathers." The large bird's calm and successful attempt to cope with an unfamiliar environment has a benedictory charm. This is how an intelligent swan of good will behaves in a hotel room; it is also how a child feels, and indeed how we all feel, enchanted out of our ordinary selves by rented solitude.

The world of E. B. White's children's books is eminently a reasonable one. Nature serves as a reservoir of common sense. Nobody panics, and catastrophes are taken in stride. When Mr. Brickle, the director of Camp Kookooskoos, is sprayed by a skunk, he does not do the slow or fast burn a meaner comic spirit would conjure up; he announces that the camp has been given "a delicious dash of wild perfume" and that "A swim will clear the air." Similarly, in *Stuart Little*, when a mouse instead of a baby is born to human parents, they promptly improvise for him a "tiny bed out of four clothespins and a cigarette box." Not birth nor death is meant to dismay us. When, in *Charlotte's Web*, the pig squeals "I don't want to die!" the spider says, "I can't stand hysterics," and eschews hysteria when her own death draws near. Her death-web speech is memorable: "After all, what's a life, anyway? We're born, we live a little while, we die. A spider's life can't help being something of a mess, with all this trapping and eating flies."

Near the end of *The Trumpet of the Swan*, Louis' father faces death with a grandiloquent soliloquy: ". . . Man, in his folly, has given me a mortal wound. The red blood flows in a steady trickle from my veins. My strength fails. . . . Good-bye, life! Good-bye, beautiful world! Good-bye, little lakes in the north! Farewell, springtimes I have known, with their passion and ardor!" The rhetoric is comic, but the tribute is sincere. *The Trumpet of the Swan* glows with the primal ecstasies of space and flight, of night and day, of nurturing and maturing, of courtship and art. On the last page Louis thinks of "how lucky he was to inhabit such a beautiful earth, how lucky he had been to solve his problems with music." How rare that word "lucky" has become! The universe remains chancy, but no one admits to having good luck. We and our children are lucky to have this book.

Remarks

on the Occasion of E. B. White's Receiving the *1971* National Medal for Literature on December 2, *1971*

A GOOD WRITER is hard to talk about, since he has already, directly or by implication, said everything about himself that should be said. In the case of E. B. White, a consummate literary tact and a powerful capacity for reticence further intimidate the would-be eulogist. And indeed where would eulogy begin? E. B. White's *oeuvre*, though not very wide on the shelf, is far-flung in its variety; it is a nation gaily built on scattered islands, and the mind moves retrospectively through it as if sailing in a flirtatious wind. Letters arrive from all points of the compass; peaks glisten in unexpected places; sunny slopes conceal tunnels of anonymity; a graceful giddiness alternates as swiftly as cloud shadows with sombre sense; darkness threatens; and but for the

North Star of the writer's voice, his unflickering tone of truth, we would not know where we are. White's works range from some of the noblest essays of the century to the most famous cartoon caption of the Thirties, the one that goes,

"It's broccoli, dear."
"I say it's spinach and I say to hell with it."

He broke into print as a poet and has most recently triumphed, for the third time, as the author of a novel for children. Along the line he edited and augmented what has become a standard college textbook on English style and usage. He has been associated with *The New Yorker* for almost all of the magazine's life, and indeed he has demonstrated mastery of every kind of thing *The New Yorker* prints, from poetry to fiction to the quips that cap other publications' typographical errors. But also he wrote the grave and graceful essays of *One Man's Meat* for *Harper's Magazine*, and *Holiday* elicited from him his beautiful tribute, *This Is New York*. Daunted, then, by this body of work so polymorphously expressing concern, wit, and love, I will, as writers tend to when confronted with a subject too big for them, take refuge in the more manageable topic of myself. My life and E. B. White.

After reading White's essays in *Harper's* throughout World War II, my mother in 1945 bought a farm and moved her family to it. It is one of the few authenticated cases of literature influencing life. White's adventures in Maine, rather than Thoreau's recourse to the Concord woods or Louis Bromfield's *Malabar Farm* (a book White reviewed in the last verse review I have seen anywhere), gave my mother the necessary courage to buy eighty rundown acres of Pennsylvania loam and turned me overnight into a rural creature, clad in muddy shoes, a cloak of loneliness, and a clinging aura of apples.

Oddly, I sought the antidote for my plight in the poison that had produced it, and devoured the work of White, of Thurber, Benchley, Perelman, Sullivan, and all those other names evocative of the urban romance that not so long ago attached to New York City, the innocent longing for sophistication that focussed here. When, infrequently, my parents brought me to New York, I always imagined I would see E. B. White in Grand Central Station.

I never did, but the wish in its intensity gouged a distinct memory imprint, delicate as a leaf sedimentized in limestone, of White's dapper, crinkled-haired, rather heavy-lidded countenance, that I had studied on book flaps and in caricatures, superimposed upon those caramel-colored walls. I still never enter the station without looking for him. For me, he *was* the city, and I wonder, will anybody ever again love this city, and poeticize it, as he did, when, to quote one of his poems,

In the days of my youth, in the days of my youth,
I lay in West Twelfth Street, writhing with Truth.
I died in Jones Street, dallying with pain,
And flashed up Sixth Avenue, risen again.

I did at last meet White, an ocean away, in Oxford. He and his wife Katharine came through the door of our basement flat on Iffley Road. E. B. White himself! It was an experience that had all the qualities of a nightmare, except that it was not unpleasant. He spoke; he actually uttered words, and they were so appropriate, so neutral and natural yet—in that unique way of his—so *trim*, so well designed to put me at ease, that I have quite forgotten what they were.

A consequence of that awesome visit was employment of sorts; while working on West 43rd Street, I would see White in the halls and what struck me in his walk, in the encouraging memos he once or twice sent me, and in the editorial notes that in lucky weeks headed up the magazine, was how much more fun he had in him than us younger residents of those halls. Not loud or obvious fun, but contained, inturning fun, shaped like a mainspring. I dealt mainly with Mrs. White, I want to add, and what a fine warm mentor she was!—a formidable woman, an editor of the magazine before White was a contributor, gifted with that terrible clear vision some women have—the difference between a good story and a bad one loomed like a canyon in her vision—yet not burdened by it, rather, rejoicing in it, and modest and humorous in her firmness, so that she makes her appearances in White's accounts as a comic heroine, a good sport helping him dispose of their surplus eggs by hurling them against the barn wall.

After I quit my job and the city, my encounters with White became purely those of a reader—a reader to myself, and a reader aloud, to my children. When I asked my ten-year-old girl if I could say today that *Charlotte's Web* was her favorite book, she said, "No, tell them *Stuart Little* is."

Eulogy is disarmed. White has figured in my life the way an author should figure, coming at me from different directions with a nudge, a reminder, a good example. I am not alone in feeling grateful, or he would not be winning this prize. For three generations he has reinforced our hopeful sense that the kingdom of letters is a fiefdom of the kingdom of man. He writes as one among us, not above us, a man pulling his mortal weight while keeping a level head and now and then letting loose with a song.

A Citation

Composed for the Awarding of
the 1968 National Book Award for Fiction
to The Eighth Day, *by Thornton Wilder* *

THROUGH THE LENS of a turn-of-the-century murder mystery, Mr. Wilder surveys a world that is both vanished and coming to birth; in a clean gay prose sharp with aphoristic wit and the sense and scent of Midwestern America and Andean Chile, he takes us on a chase of Providence and delivers us, exhilarated and edified, into the care of an ambiguous conclusion.

An Unpublished Book Note

THE ARMIES OF THE NIGHT, by Norman Mailer. 288 pp. New American Library, 1968.

A fascinating, if hysterically high-flown, account of the October 1967 protest march on the Pentagon, by one of its participants. Mailer's lust for self-display has cast off whatever tenuous tram-

---

* The other judges were Granville Hicks and the late Josephine Herbst. We having made, not too contentiously, our decision, they invited me to write the citation, and I scratched this off. They had no suggestions for its improvement; otherwise I would not thus include it as my work.

mels have hitherto restrained it, and his description of his deplorably drunken speechifying on Friday night, and his headachy jockeying for literary position with Robert Lowell during the next day's march, are fearlessly frank, and funny indeed. Less funny, but the best narrative stretch in the book, is his account of arrest and the twenty-four hours soberingly spent in jail, before being handed an unexpectedly severe sentence. His sociological/ historical analysis of the forces behind the protest goes from the farcical to the brilliant; he proposes no measuring tool but his own hyperbolic sensibility. The Vietnam involvement becomes unremitting Reichian melodrama, where any flash of color will do for an insight, and any aesthetic irritation serves the most sweeping diagnostic purposes. The book's strength—until the vilely written last pages, a post-midnight collapse into bathos—is this finagling author's capacity for awe, for giving his enemies his avid attention, and giving events, in this era of humorless propaganda, a decent, sensual complexity. A good rush job.

An Interesting Emendation

in the Text of Mr. Sammler's Planet, by Saul Bellow

TOWARD THE END of the *Atlantic Monthly*'s two-part serialization of *Mr. Sammler's Planet*, the hero, calling upon his dying nephew, Dr. Elya Gruner, in the hospital, sits in the waiting room next to Gruner's daughter Angela, and thinks,

> There was no odor of Arabian musk, her favorite perfume. Instead her female effluence was very strong today, a salt odor, something from inside the woman. Elya's bitter words had had their effect on Sammler. He could not look at her eyes without thinking of her father's words, imagining her in bed, and—a worse fancy—the white of semen on her mouth. But these were, curiously, images nearly devoid of prejudice. Or very nearly. One must change one's outlook. The past perhaps exaggerated the seriousness of these things.

In the hardcover edition (Viking, 1970), the entire episode has been rewritten, with a freedom and renewed inspiration that speak well for Bellow's venturesome, perfectionistic art—though the changes are not all inarguably for the better. The sentences equivalent for those above read:

> Sitting near her, Sammler could not smell the usual Arabian musk. Instead her female effluence was very strong, a salt odor, similar to tears or tidewater, something from within the woman. Elya's words had taken effect strongly—his "Too much sex." Even the white lipstick suggested perversion. But this was curiously without prejudice. Sammler felt no prejudice about perversion, about sexual matters. Nothing. It was too late in the day for that.

The entire long paragraph containing this passage has been strenuously, anxiously revised; the second version is choppier. Details of Angela's costume (large gold earrings, a miniskirt) have been rearranged, her idol-like immobility has been charged with a certain choked anger, Elya's words are specified. Most interestingly, the vivid "white of semen on her mouth" has been softened to "white lipstick" suggesting "perversion." Why? It is as if Bellow were embarrassed by his own revulsion, and backed away from it, in the same motion as his elderly, fastidious hero moves from being "nearly devoid of prejudice" on the matter to feeling absolutely "no prejudice about perversion, about sexual matters."

Yet what people put into their mouths *does* interest us, as it interested the Biblical Jews. Philip Roth's Alexander Portnoy ragefully marvels at the *goyim*, "these imbecilic eaters of the execrable":

> Let the *goyim* sink *their* teeth into whatever lowly creature crawls and grunts across the face of the dirty earth, we will not contaminate our humanity thus. Let *them* (if you know who I mean) gorge themselves upon anything and everything that moves, no matter how odious and abject the animal, no matter how grotesque or *shmutzig* or dumb the creature in question happens to be. Let them eat eels and frogs and pigs and crabs and lobsters; let them eat vulture, let them eat ape-meat and skunk if they like. . . . They will eat *anything*, anything they can get their big *goy* hands on! And the terrifying corollary, *they will do anything as well*. Deer eat what deer eat, and Jews eat what Jews eat, but not these

goyim. Crawling animals, wallowing animals, leaping and angelic animals—it makes no difference to them— . . .

In the next paragraph, he confesses to sucking on a lobster claw and the same night, an hour later, aiming his erect penis at a *shikse* on a Public Service bus. This at age fifteen; a few years later, Portnoy makes closer but still mostly spiritual contact with one of these legendary "*shikses* Who Will Do Anything," a Catholic Gentile, Bubbles Girardi, who has blown a friend ("And does she suck on it, or does she blow on it, or somehow is it that she does *both*? Oh, God, Ba-ba-lu, did you shoot in her mouth? Oh my God! And did she swallow it right down, or spit it out, or get mad—tell me! what did she do with your hot come!"), and, more than a few years (he is now thirty-two) later, Portnoy finds the real McCoy in the West Virginia hillbilly (the quintessential Protestant Gentile) nicknamed ("let them eat ape-meat") The Monkey—"What a find, I thought, she takes it right down to the root! What a mouth I have fallen into!" Their romance begins with his inspired offer to "eat your pussy, baby" at their first meeting and ends with her complaint that "you care more about the niggers in Harlem that you don't even know, than you do about me, who's been sucking you off for a solid year!" The characters are not unimpressed with their own orality:

> A Jewish man, who cared about the welfare of the poor of the City of New York, was eating her pussy! Someone who had appeared on educational TV was shooting off into her mouth!

Nor does all this delightful uncleanness go unpunished: Portnoy, after a triadic bout with The Monkey and an Italian whore, throws up, and the undiscriminating Bubbles Girardi is killed while consorting with Negroes:

> There's a case of cause and effect that confirms my ideas about human consequence! Bad enough, rotten enough, and you get your cock-sucking head blown off by boogies. Now that's the way the world's supposed to be run!

Bellow is comparatively disingenuous: in the revised paragraph, he quotes Elya as blaming Angela for simply "too much sex," whereas what Elya had really said earlier, which her eyes recall to Sammler, is: "You see a woman who has done it in too many ways with too many men. By now she probably doesn't know the name of the man between her legs. And she looks. . . . Her eyes —she has fucked-out eyes." *Too many ways:* not quantity but the posture is crucial; Elya fears she is around the corner "Frenching an orderly," and her brother Wallace tells Sammler that "she let that twerp in Mexico ball her fore and aft in front of Wharton, with who-knows-what-else thrown in free by her." Sammler's moral dignity at times seems to consist solely of suffering witness to the sexuality of this woman "who was also something good to eat," who nevertheless had once studied Hebrew.

"You were quite studious. I was impressed that you were studying Hebrew."
"Just a front, Uncle. I was a dirty little bitch, really."

How dirty, and why dirty, are the nervous questions that lie behind Bellow's emendation, and much of the novel's moral discussion. Is sex innocent and fulfilling fun in any position, as contemporary culture would teach us, or is it, as the Judaeo-Christian tradition instructs, a fixed and solemn performance devoted to procreation? Specifically, is the eating of semen a natural kiss, caress, and engulfment of the beloved, or a perverse defilement? Recent American fiction traces a swift secularization of this magical act since the days, scarcely more than a decade ago, when the young author of *Rabbit, Run* reverently, reluctantly reduced Ruth to her knees and Nabokov, his flamboyant archness making virtue of the necessity for euphemism, had Lolita pronounce "in all insouciance really, a disgusting slang term which, in a literal French translation, would be *souffler.*"

With what a thrill did one read, in the days when Henry Miller was contraband, such direct and insouciant descriptions as, from *Sexus:*

I awakened gradually, dimly conscious that my prick was in Elsie's mouth.

I stood up and unbuttoned my fly. In a jiffy [Ida] had it out and in her mouth. Gobble, gobble, like a hungry buzzard. I came in her mouth.

Suddenly [a nameless switchboard operator] unclasped her hands and with wet fingers she unbuttoned my fly, took my prick out and made a dive for it with her mouth. She went at it like a professional, teasing it, worrying it, fluting her lips, then choking on it. I came off in her mouth; she swallowed it as if it were nectar and ambrosia.

But, as descriptions of fellatio pass from the literary underground to middle-class fiction, and from the male to the female point of view, the ambrosia takes on another taste. From Lois Gould's lengthy treatment in *Such Good Friends* (1970):

I was down on my knees, struggling with a stuck zipper. Timmy's fly zipper! On my knees trying to take my medicine like a big girl. See? Same old Julie, washing down the nasty stuff with more nasty stuff. I can take it; I'm *supposed* to take it. . . . Okay, but I wasn't dismissed yet. He wanted me to kneel slightly higher for leverage. (When I was eight I'd talked the pediatrician out of using a tongue depressor to examine my sore throat. "Please, the wood makes me gag—see, I can open wide enough. *Ah.*" "Very good, but I still need to insert the stick—just for a minute now. There." "*Ahgh!*" "See, that wasn't so bad." Yes, it was. Yes, it is.) . . . Time for our medicine now—here it comes. Let's see it all go down in one big gulp. No, you can't have water with it; I said you're a big girl now. Don't cry. I said *don't cry,* or we'll hold you down on the bed and paint your throat with Argyrol. Whatever happened to painting your throat with Argyrol?

Wait—he's taking it away. All gone. I called up to him, up over the dreary miles of shirtfront, a sterile snowy field with a neatly planted single row of buttons.

At least the lady protests, if too much. In a novel three years deeper into the Seventies, Erica Jong's *Fear of Flying*, the penis in the mouth has lost its power to stand and make the throat ache with indignation; it is just one wan item in a rather tender catalogue:

His broad neck, which was sunburned. His chest, covered with curly reddish hair. His belly, a bit paunchy—unlike Bennett's brown leanness. His curled pink penis which tasted faintly of urine and refused to stand up in my mouth. His very pink and hairy balls which I took in my mouth one at a time. His muscular thighs. His sunburned knees. His feet.

With the matter-of-factly noted lingering taste of urine, all mystery has fled. Fellatio has become hardly worth describing. Alan Lelchuk, in his novel of the same year, *American Mischief*, seeks, like a pornographic film maker (*cf.* the delicious triadic scene in *The Devil in Miss Jones*), to stir us with visible sperm and lesbian voracity:

> The climax embarrassed me as much as it thrilled me. With moans and shrieks and body English growing more frenzied, I began finally coming into Gwen's mouth. But suddenly she maneuvered away so that I was lathering her face with the white sperm. Whereupon Angie, bellowing like a cow in heat, suddenly dove down upon that face and began lapping it up. Incredible. The denseness of appetites was so thick by then, the flow of juices and secretions and passions so rich, that it was like being at a feast of cannibals. I tell you, those girls would have eaten anything, anything!

But the episode feels exaggerated—more trash than truth, more exploitation than exploration. The frontier has moved on, to buggery, where sex can still touch the forbidden, the religious, the diabolical. Rojak, buggering the German maid in *An American Dream*, sees her as a Nazi, comes to her "cry of rage," and feels he has "come to the Devil a fraction too late." For an age which lusted, as did the late Sixties, for revolution, buggery is the fit deviation; it runs counter to the channels of production, whereas ejaculation into the throat conforms to them, like the liberal variations within the capitalist system. Fellatio feeds; buggery violates.

In these accelerated times, the frontier fills rapidly; Terry Andrews' novel *The Story of Harold* (1974) centers its mystique on "fist-fucking" and the brave new world beyond the anus:

> I described this whole thing to a friend afterwards . . . and he asked . . . "But wasn't it just like sticking your hand in a bowl of spaghetti?" And the answer is no—oh no, not a bit! It's like putting your fingers in fold upon fold of hot, wet velvet, some fabric never felt before, that contains a living pulse within it. For you do feel the life. There are arteries, major blood vessels, along which a human existence trills. And they can be played with and plucked and bowed like the strings of a living violin.

And here, like Mr. Sammler before he was emended, I feel not quite devoid of prejudice. This trans-anal passage tells me more than I want to know; it has the frightful melancholy of the purely physical; I can hardly bear to read it. I flinch, as Bellow (evidently) flinched at his own phrase, as some readers may have flinched at my above oral anthology. Where we draw back varies; but our sexual natures, even in this age of competitive license and Freudian sanction, do ask limits, for their own protection. The angel of disgust guards the seeds of life. Sexual excitement arises from an arcanum; some stimuli must be kept in safe deposit. Just as moral prohibitions have as their end our own safety, some boundary to the exploration of the bodies of others, some economy in knowledge, is asked for, that potency be conserved.

Phantom Life

WEST OF THE ROCKIES, by Daniel Fuchs. 166 pp. Knopf, 1971.

Nobody else writes like Daniel Fuchs:

> All right, then. Munves pressed her tightly to him and shivered. Ooooh, it felt good. Soft, soft. Women were originally built like a jackknife, like a Westchester roll, all one short round lump, he was thinking, and when God opened them up straight, the body protruded in round curved masses. He hugged her tighter and tighter, his skinny arm on her shoulders aching.

That is a young man learning to dance, in *Homage to Blenholt,* the middle novel of the three Fuchs published, quickly and obscurely, in the middle Thirties. When they were reprinted, in 1961, Fuchs wrote, "The books didn't sell—400 copies, 400, 1200. The reviews were scanty, immaterial. The books became odious to me." He goes on to describe his turning to short stories: "I was in the middle of a fourth novel but broke it up and swiftly turned it into three or four short stories. I worked away all spring, one story after the other—perhaps a dozen or fifteen in all. I rested. It was July. Nothing happened." He and his young wife made money by going out to the race track and betting. "I had visions of spending the rest of our lives at the races, travelling from track to track with the seasons. Suddenly I heard from my agent. The editors had simply been away on their summer vacations, that was all. They took the stories, all of them—one afternoon three acceptances in the same mail. I had my racetrack winnings in cash all over me in different pockets; I had checks from the magazines laid away in envelopes." It is a typically happy Fuchs story, and it is how I think of him—as a natural winner, a poet who never had to strain after a poetic effect, a writer so blithely blessed by the gods he never got dug in properly. He gave up short stories in turn and went to Hollywood.

Now, out of Hollywood, after more than three decades in the desert, comes the fourth Fuchs novel: *West of the Rockies*. It is shorter than the others—scenario-length, with odd blank or hurried patches, perhaps for the director to fill in. In his prose of glimmering diffidence, Fuchs tells the story of Adele Hogue, a movie star, and Burt Claris, a handsome nobody who works for her talent agency. The beginning of their romance is tersely sketched indeed: "He had taken up with her, had gotten into her good graces, slept with her. Claris was no better than most. She was accessible." (One of the book's incidental mirages is that Fuchs always refers to the hero as "Claris," which sounds feminine, and often to the heroine as "Hogue," which seems masculine.) The novel centers upon a Palm Springs resort to which Adele Hogue has fled after bolting the set of a movie in production; Burt Claris, on behalf of the agency, has chased her there. The action generally observes the unities of this place in these few days of crisis; as a result, Fuchs spends a high proportion of his pages filling us in—on Adele's old romance with Harry Case, a racketeer whose ex-wife, Fannie, runs the resort; on Adele's recent disastrous fling with the international jet set and an aristocratic English husband who has bankrupted her; on Burt's marriage to an immature young heiress; on the ins and outs of motion-picture financing and the ruin facing the producer, Robert Wigler, who is present, in "the great 117-degree afternoon desert heat," along with Burt's skirt-chasing superior at the talent agency, and the three children the actress has spawned in the course of her marriages, and a hungry host of reporters, and the perennial resort guests, the sun-bathing, well-preserved "second and third wives of men who

made big money in meat, oil, or textiles." Even when the action
is before his eyes, the author's tone is one of reverie:

> She held her shoulders straight, carrying her body with that clear-
> striding, forthright sexual quality they had and which they knew
> they had. It was the way they were put together; it was the bones
> in them. It was a readiness or acquiescence to use the body for all
> the pleasure it could give, a readiness they picked up from their
> mothers, in the Hollywood malt shops, out of the air.

Constructions involving "or" and "way" recur—"either because
she considered him of no account or because she was too care-
worn or because it was her way," "in the ways they had," "whether
it was for this reason or because of some other mental quirk"—as
if Fuchs were groping through a dream that puzzles him, dazzles
him. The blinding California brightness seems pre-smog, and in
the end the reader is told that all this slice of "phantom life" happened "some twelve years ago, when television was comparatively
new and the big picture studios still throbbed, the collapse yet
to come."

What might be faults in another novel feed this one's dreamlike,
movie-like glow. Gentle improbabilities hurry events along. Servants are remarkably obliging: a Filipino hotel steward volunteers
his room as a love nest, and a baby's nurse spontaneously tells
Burt where his wife has hidden her love letters. The imperfectly
guessed motives and sketchily summarized lives give a mysterious
largeness to the world beyond the plot's circumference. Los Angeles becomes a nostalgic presence: "It had been another time, everything closer to the studios in those days, the Los Angeles area still
spread thin and relatively undeveloped, a third of what it was to
become. . . . The wide boulevards with sandy, neglected islands
in the middle of them, the sun pouring down, so still and breath-
takingly brilliant, as it was in those earlier years."

This tone is far from the self-promoting satire and rage usually
offered by "Hollywood novels." Yet the reality to which Fuchs
lends his love is recognizably cruel. A jam halts traffic on the
desert thruway: "Claris looked down and saw the hard, murderous
grain of the pavement concrete, the slits and abrasions, the concrete suddenly stationary and as if magnified." Contracts, erotic
as well as financial, take effect in an arid atmosphere purged of

any Old World notions of honor or noblesse oblige. The dreams of success and love are acted out against a hard awareness of the "they" who control destinies—the bankers, the gangsters, as implacable and irrational as Greek deities. The women who populate Palm Springs form an ominous chorus of Furies. They lie in the sun discussing girdles and beauty operations, they make love with necklaces on, they fly decorators in from New York and Texas, they are not unkind, having "all been in the business at one time or another, as stand-ins or stock girls," but with men their ardor is "overwhelmingly tender and solicitous and at the same time impersonal, a kindness which they could discontinue seemingly without an instant's feeling or trace of remembrance": they are all, Wigler tells Burt Claris, "secret agents." They have all made their "adjustments," and in this they differ from Adele Hogue.

Fuchs's portrait of a star is masterly. He seems to do everything to diminish her. She appears frightened, sick, vulgar, and foolish, callous to her children and destructive wherever she can reach. Even her body is seen sadly: "Claris saw the roundness at the upper arms and shoulders, the weight taking hold there, packing in; he saw the slack, plump roll of the belly, the widening at the waist—that thickening which, it had been surveyed and studied in the business, the young people in the movie houses spotted and resented." And when this Venus does her thing and makes love, the prose plunges into melancholy:

> She opened her arms to him, embraced and clasped him to her, taking him on. . . . Claris responded to the pressure, winding through the ritual, the kisses, the fondling, the contriving of an illusion of love—that knavish, coward's thing people relentlessly do with one another.

The weight of Hogue's mortal envelope is frightful: "Claris wondered . . . at the mauling she had absorbed in her time—the curettages, the operations, the bad operation . . . the brutal intensive reducing regimens, when . . . she installed herself in the hospital and they systematically sloughed the weight off her so that she herself came to view her body with a sick distaste." Since neither beauty nor skill ("She didn't know anything about acting, never had, would be the first to say so") has lifted her up from the high-school malt shops through the petty prostitutions and mismarriages and neurotic ailments into stardom, what has? Fuchs answers, "Fanatic energy." Adele explains it to herself: "Her special effectiveness with the audience was spontaneous, something organic, beyond control. She believed it was the product of the nervous system you were endowed with, and she was convinced her nerves were used up, that you were given just so much." So "star quality" exacts an exceptional toll, and reader and author and lover together come to adore anew this exasperating and worse-than-average woman. Using as his material the shabbiest truths, Fuchs rebuilds the Hollywood myth; a happy ending evolves in an atmosphere of exhausted illusion. When, at the end, Adele Hogue stands with Burt on the edge of a marital partnership per-haps—who knows?—as profitable as that of Doris Day and Marty Melcher, and turns to him in the mass of reporters and mouths "I love you" as if on a sound stage, her sincerity is beyond gaug-ing; we are dazzled by her courage, her real will to go on living her life of unreality.

NON-FICTION

Black Suicide

BLACK SUICIDE, by Herbert Hendin. 176 pp. Basic Books, 1969.

Suicide, that most absolute of acts, is yet relative and can serve as a window into the peculiar stresses of a cultural group. In support of this thesis, Herbert Hendin, a professor at the Columbia University Psychoanalytic Clinic, has produced two books: his well-known, well-applauded study *Suicide and Scandinavia* (1964) and an equally fascinating and surpassingly relevant, though largely ignored, volume, *Black Suicide*. Dr. Hendin proposes, and demonstrates, that suicide is different things in different places. In Denmark, it is commonly an attempt to inflict guilt upon others or to rejoin a loved one in a sentimentally conceived hereafter. In Sweden, suicide tends to be of a "performance" rather than a "dependency" type; the self-hatred of a competitive failure, however, is deepened by a peculiar Swedish coldness that emphasizes emotional control and erects between the sexes a wall of frozen silence. In the black ghettos of America, suicide is one face of a rage that, though ultimately caused by the Negro's frustrating position in the society, originates for almost every individual in maternal rejection.

Not that uniformity prevails in Dr. Hendin's cross section of twenty-five suicide attempts admitted to the Harlem Hospital. Four older men attempted suicide after professional reverses, suggesting the "performance" motive common in Sweden—but with the difference that not so much a rigid achievement standard as an adaptive pattern fragilely based upon outward compliance and contained anger had broken down. These Uncle Toms, after lifetimes spent pushing brooms or hand trucks, found themselves still economically defenseless, and, having been taught docile compliance as a mode of goodness, construed their adaptive failure in moral terms and sought to take their lives in atonement. Again, many of the females included in this study attempted suicide after abandonment by a husband or lover—but there is a radical difference between the Danish matrix of interdependence and the sorry turmoil of abandonment, violence, foster parentage, and neglect that has served black females as models of family life.

The interviews and life histories presented in *Black Suicide* do not bear out the notion that the black female is relatively insulated from the effects of racial discrimination.

> The most disastrous impact of racial institutions seems to be felt so early in life and so overwhelmingly that the plight of the female seems as bad as that of the male. Frustration, rage, and violence already characterize the lives of both sexes when they are teen-agers, and there is little difference between men and women in the degree of despair that is so often present by the time they are young adults.

Given a set of tests called the Buss-Durkee Hostility Inventory, the women in this group of would-be suicides scored higher than the men, and in the "assault category" two females—called "Ina Tracy" and "Agnes Carreth"—obtained perfect scores of ten. Ina Tracy, a tall woman of thirty-one who lived in Alabama until she was twenty, describes one of her frequent fights with friends: "I beat her as long as she moved. As long as she moved I kicked her. Blood both frightens and excites me." Of her childhood, she says, "My mother once told me that she wished I had been born dead or that she had gotten rid of me. The way things worked out, I wished it too. . . . My mother would make me break a branch and she'd beat me with it—hit me wherever it landed. I wanted to take her and choke her to death. Wished that I would die or she would." Yet her mother's desires appear to have controlled her behavior; teased for tallness at school, she was not much of a fighter until, running from another girl one day, she saw her mother, "who she knew would be furious at her running away." Similarly: "At seventeen she told her mother she had never liked boys. When her mother replied that she should, she decided to have sexual relations with the first boy who was willing and soon after became pregnant." Ina left the child with her mother a few years afterward and came to New York alone. Her first suicide attempt came a year later. A recurrent nightmare involves a "very large man who had been dead a long time, so long that one could smell him." This image seems the only peaceful one in the frenzied alternation of her homicidal and suicidal fantasies.

"Louise Greene," an attractive and engagingly childlike woman of twenty-six, scored low on the hostility tests, yet a legacy of maternal rejection also perpetuates itself through her. She was raised by her grandparents in Georgia, and did not meet her mother until the age of twelve, when a woman suddenly appeared and demanded that Louise, her first-born, come live with her and care for the younger children she had had by a variety of men. Though compelled to obey, Louise frequently ran off back to her grandparents, and after one fight was prevented from taking rat poison. She has had two children, by two men, neither of whom she wished to marry; when she did marry, she and her husband quarreled over her refusal to quit her job and stay home with the one child that was, for an interval, living with her. When this man died, under violent circumstances she never investigated, Louise came to New York, where she works as a drugstore waitress. She sends part of her salary south for the care of her children, who live with her aunt and uncle; she insists—even in her suicide note—on her love for her children. Hendin concludes: "Louise feels too keenly her position as a rejected daughter to be able to see herself as a mother. . . . Furious with her mother for abandoning her and for not providing her with a father, Louise is following in her mother's footsteps in having children with various fathers and then rejecting them."

Another type of casualty inflicted by the black home is illustrated by four male homosexuals who turned up among the twelve male suicide attempts—a surprising incidence; among male white suicides fewer than one in twelve is a homosexual. In the homes of these men—and though the statistical sample of homosexuals is small, it has been augmented by six other non-suicidal cases—a father was usually present, but so violent toward mother and son that heterosexuality became intimidating. Also, the boys were disturbed by their mothers' extramarital sexual activities. "Benjamin

Ellis" remembers discovering his mother in bed with a man and says, "It jarred me so much I wept." The violent father and promiscuous mother curiously reverse the typical recessive father and non-sexual mother of white homosexuals. Curious, too, is the usual preference of black homosexuals for white partners: a tragic indication of an unconfessed racial shame. "Andrew Vallen" insists he is proud to be a Negro but wants to have an operation to make his thick lips thinner. "Leroi Nifson," a medium-brown offspring of a black father and a Syrian mother, when asked why he confined his homosexual contacts to whites and Puerto Ricans, answered that he considered himself Arabic, "a white man sympathetic to the Negro cause." Benjamin Ellis, the oldest of the three, and the only one who achieved a high guilt rating in the psychological tests, associates dirt, masculinity, and blackness—"I do things with men, don't with women because men are dirty anyhow. The man was Negro and not as clean as he could be"—but also says, "White men don't care what they do. They'll do anything. Negroes have limitations. If it lowers their pride, they won't do it." His double need to be degraded and to be protected is best served by a white lover.

Black Suicide began as an investigation of the anomaly that, though the overall Negro rate of suicide is lower in this country than the white rate, between the ages of twenty and thirty-five *twice* as many black males as white males kill themselves in New York City. The Negro homicide rate is in all age groups higher than the white rate. The interweave of destructiveness and self-destruction in black ghetto life is everywhere bared by Dr. Hendin's case histories. "Peter Churney," who has been thinking of suicide since the age of twelve, and at nineteen has survived three attempts, was present at his father's violent death.

> [Peter's father's] suspicions that Peter's mother was having affairs led him to jealous rages. One night when he was beating her in a particularly savage way, the police were called. When they arrived, his father began shooting at them. Peter, who was seven at the time, was trapped in the room with his father, who had five guns and, although wounded, continued to fire until he was killed. . . . [Peter] was quite taken aback, however, at the suggestion that his father's death might have been a form of suicide.

Peter, whose IQ is high for this group, admired Hitler as a boy and "says he had the idea of going on a rooftop and shooting people but adds lightly that this was before 'that guy in Dallas' did it." His fantasies of mass murder, however, give him less pleasure now; Peter feels he is on a suicide course and nothing can stop him. "Harrison Eliot," a man of thirty-three, lost his mother, "whose strictness and severe beatings he still recalls," at the age of twelve; his father, a railroad chef, was robbed and beaten to death when Harrison was four. He has a savage temper, and twice has served jail sentences for fighting with policemen. He dreams of murdering his former wife and her boy friend, and drowns his rage in drink. "He mentions that several of his friends drank themselves to death but does not seem to be aware that he is following in their footsteps." "Eddie Marker," a boy of eighteen, is working toward the same goal via drugs; he is a forty-five-dollar-a-day heroin user who must rob to support his habit. A year ago his twenty-two-year-old sister killed his father, who she felt was trying to harm her baby. "Eddie does not believe in death, and thinks his father is alive and that he will meet him someday. . . . He has no plans for the future after he gets out of jail. . . . When Eddie was asked about his getting into so much trouble, he replied, 'No more than most of the people I know. . . .' Eddie uses his Muslim beliefs not simply to deny death but to deny the reality of life as he experiences it."

What, then, the white reader may well ask himself as he gazes into this snake pit of lost lives, is to be done? First he might wonder how accurate a microcosm of Negro life in America these twenty-five failed suicides afford. Certainly this is a disadvantaged group within a disadvantaged group. Seven of the twenty to whom IQ tests were administered scored in the seventies, or on the border line of effective intelligence, and only four (including the wild Ina Tracy) above the standard median of 100. On the other hand, the geographic narrowness of the sample is more apparent than real; many of these Harlemites were born and raised in the South and experienced their formative traumas there. And a look at the graphs in the appendix discovers little change in violence statistics since the 1920's; proportionally as many Negroes were killing themselves and each other in the days of Amos 'n' Andy and the

Cotton Club as in these days of summer riots and the Black Panthers. The birth dates of Hendin's subjects span fifty years; after reading their histories one feels that Negro life in America has changed sadly little except that drugs have replaced drink as the cop-out, and that Islam and paranoid politics now share with Christianity the effort to restrain despair and institutionalize self-respect.

Three conclusions of Hendin's study bear emphasis:

1. The black female, far from being a secondary victim of white racism, bears the brunt of it. As a girl she is exposed equally with her brothers to the psychological injuries inflicted by absentee or distracted parents; from her teens on she is vulnerable to pregnancy; as a woman she is the first and nearest recipient of the black man's anger. And not merely in the form of beatings:

> One senses that for many black men sex serves a double purpose. The children they father serve as living proof of their potency and also as a mark of their anger. Their abandonment of women, often when they are in the most helpless of conditions, may be a way of striking back at their mothers who rejected them or the succession of aunts, grandmothers, or cousins who raised them; of figuratively screwing womankind and lodging a protest against their own lives.

Biology appoints the black woman custodian of order in a subsociety that has no great stake in order. As a mother, then, she transmits to her children her burden of shame, inadequacy, frustration, and fury. Dr. Hendin touches on the thesis, put forward by two black psychiatrists, that "black mothers reject and castrate their sons in order to prepare them better for the life they will encounter in a white world." These same psychiatrists, William H. Grier and Price M. Cobbs (in *Black Rage*) go on to recommend a psychological shift of anger from black mothers to white society. Hendin does not think much either of diagnosis or of remedy. While conceding a limited "useful social purpose" to identifying the institutional sources of black frustration and channelling rage toward corrective action, he insists that black mothers rear their children badly because they were reared badly. "Like all other children, those black children who have experienced the least rejection are best prepared to deal with the world, black or white."

2. Racial discrimination inflicts its worst psychological damage out of sight of the white world, in the heart of the black family.

White people are strangely absent from these narrated lives. The policemen with whom Harrison Eliot battles, and the employer of whom "Jean Wayne" complains, "He didn't care how I am," may be white; but the only white people given any individuality at all are Leroi Nifson's Syrian mother and "Roger," Benjamin Ellis' Jewish lover. Racial self-consciousness seems remarkably faint; of the fifteen patients who executed drawings of human figures, none indicated skin color, and only one determinedly attempted to portray Negroid features—and he, "Owen James," had the special problem of being so pale that all his life other Negroes had picked upon him as a white. But Dr. Hendin does not conclude from the rarity of an overt black self-image—as did an earlier investigator, Charles Prudhomme—that race is not a factor in black suicide.

> The Negro usually needs to repress an awareness that he has so blanketed his entire race with his own self-hatred that he loathes all the characteristics of blackness. Over and over the subjects in this study try to deny racial motivations for their feelings or behavior, though such motives are apparent. Even the man who insisted on having an operation to make his lips thinner denied that he in any way connected the size of his lips with being black. In their most repetitive self-images the patients saw themselves as black bugs or black rats. While these images were often dreamed of as symbols linking sexuality, destructiveness, and blackness, it is no accident that the symbols that come to them originate in the most despised and unwanted living things in the Harlem tenements—the rats and the roaches.

3. Black poverty includes a poverty of motivational fantasy. Along with the low self-esteem goes an inability to imagine successful achievement. One looks almost in vain among the testimony of the young men for instances of heroes. "Luke Dellins," a promising and athletic boy cruelly maimed by hospital maltreatment, has become a bitter black nationalist and admires only Jomo Kenyatta. Peter Churney, whose fascination with Hitler has been noted, wanted to be an archaeologist and now wishes he could make movies like Sergei Eisenstein. And when one tries to imagine how a ghetto child whose father was shot before his eyes is going to become an Eisenstein, or a Hitchcock, or a Mike Nichols, the plausibility of low aspirations sinks in.

In America the rate of white suicide continues to rise after the age of forty-five, and overtakes and exceeds the black rate. Hendin's explanation for this is elegant and eloquent: the white person encounters, in late middle age, the certainty of failure and disappointed hope that his black fellow citizen encountered in the prime of life. Luke Owens, at the age of twenty-nine, has concluded: "There is no place in the world for a fellow like me. I'll always be on the same level; I'll get nowheres."

Little hope can be held for most of the subjects of this study. Yet Dr. Hendin's description of the general black plight in this country is not entirely dispiriting. For one thing, it makes intelligible, as nothing else I have read does, the vehemence of black liberation rhetoric. The roaches and rats that run through these suicides' dreams are close to such images as this one, dictated into a tape recorder by Eldridge Cleaver upon the death of Martin Luther King: "I think that America has already committed suicide and we who now thrash within its dead body are also dead in part and parcel of the corpse. America is truly a disgusting burden upon this planet."

For another, Dr. Hendin's book locates the need for *revolution* within the black psyche. I italicize this alarming and prevalent word because it is a stumbling block. Granted that the unmitigated capitalism special to America has at repeated historical moments— on the large plantations, during the North's post-Reconstruction abandonment of the freedmen, in present-day technology's devaluation of untrained labor—worked to sever the Negro from the general economic evolution, it is difficult to conceive an "overthrow" of the "system" that would not prove counterproductive for all races. Rather, the challenge to the white-dominated system would seem to be merely to make good the numerous statutes and public resolutions that already exist. But there can be no denying that the self-hatred impressed on the black man by three centuries of rope and shackle, low wages, and social insult must be overthrown. And, for all the recalcitrance of private neuroses, psychic revolutions can occur rather quickly, as one generation replaces another. Although it is tempting, as the abysmal statistics from the ghetto mount, to dismiss symbolic triumphs, what value can be given to, say, the disappearance of "conking" or the widespread use of black models in television commercials? Or to the appearance in the streets of African costumes? That whites ape such fashions and commercialize them seems to me the opposite of disheartening: it is one more step toward America's recovery of what it early lost, a sense of itself as a multiracial nation, rather than as a white nation "holding" colored minorities.

The black race presently exists in America as a sunken, underdeveloped other country, exasperated and mocked by the highly developed country that surrounds and permeates it with its imagery of affluence and opportunity. As W. E. B. Du Bois wrote in 1903, "To be a poor man is hard, but to be a poor race in a land of dollars is the very bottom of hardships." No number of damage-mending programs from the white world can lift this black nation as a dead weight. Ambition and righteous pride must be ignited within the black community, and black artists, it seems to me, have an enviable part to play. In an art situation that is generally modish and frivolously nihilistic, the black artist (and the playwright, that natural didact, seems to be foremost) has a work of genuine resurrection before him, of supplying a self-image that though angry is also potent—of generating "motivational fantasies" to which the white world, of course, helps lend substance. As long as young black men cannot "envisage a future in which their situation would improve through work," the black race draws nearer to being the instrument whereby, in Cleaver's metaphor, America commits suicide.

Fool's Gold

THE LOSS OF EL DORADO, by V. S. Naipaul. 335 pp. Knopf, 1970.

Never ask an artist to do the ordinary. Some time ago, an American publisher asked V. S. Naipaul, the Anglo-Indian novelist from Trinidad, to write the Port of Spain volume in a series of historical handbooks on cities of the world. Naipaul produced a masterly anomaly that, under the title *The Loss of El Dorado*, has been brought out, garlanded with British praise, by another American publisher. The book, though minutely researched and presented in a factual prose that verges on the dry, seems less a work of history than a piece of poetry, a rather fevered meditation, a hypnotized concentration upon two focal points in Trinidad's history: the founding of St. Joseph and its port, "which they call of Spain," in 1592 by the "dispossessed conquistador" Antonio de Berrio; and, two hundred years later, the six-year rule of the city and the island by its first British governor, Thomas Picton, a blithe brute who was to die a hero at Waterloo. Both men suggest legendary figures: like Don Quixote, Berrio was old, tough, gallant, and bewitched; while Picton's career seems a shadow of Wellingon's and his final reputation has been "absorbed in Wellington's more complex, nation-building myth." Indeed, it was Wellington who pronounced Picton's epitaph: "A rough foul-mouthed devil as ever lived." Naipaul's portraiture, closely based upon historical records hitherto scarcely tapped, mixes irony and sympathy somewhat enigmatically, yet he does seem to grant Berrio and Picton the stature of founders and a certain tenacity of purpose. In counterpoint stand his portraits of Sir Walter Raleigh and Francisco Miranda, two engaging and intelligent adventurers whom he condemns as—in the end—ineffectual and, oddly, quiescent; both ended in prison, and "prison was perhaps the setting that Miranda, like Raleigh, subconsciously required." Behind these principal actors a host of lesser ones come swarming forward out of the colonial archives: henchmen and buccaneers, Spanish soldiers and French planters and English administrators, lawyers and torturers, agitators, mulattoes, and slaves. The richly detailed episodes of West Indian history hover, however, in a virtual vacuum; the matrix of world circumstances—not only the power struggles on the Continent but even the events on nearby islands—is so lightly indicated that the machinations on Trinidad appear as eerie as the motions of a sleepwalker. This quality would be a fault were it not at the heart of Mr. Naipaul's attempt. He wishes, using his native Trinidad as a microcosm, to uncover the something strange in the entire New World, the something futile and cruel and—to use a word he repeatedly uses, as if recoined with a more sinister meaning—"simple."

There are many surprising facts, fascinating stories, and shrewd epigrammatic thrusts in these pages. Naipaul is very good on the Spaniards—their egoistic "simplicity," the unreality to them of everything but God and gold, their disastrous inability to plant crops, the abstract accounts they left of their marvellous journeys ("The conquistador who found nothing had nothing to report. Believing in wonders, he had no gift of wonder"), their superstitious and murderous abhorrence of the heathen Indian, the mild legalism of their slave code. They experienced the New World as a "medieval adventure." Antonio de Berrio became the last and least of the conquistadors. His wife, whom he married late, was the niece of one of the great ones, Gonzalo Jiménez de Quesada. Quesada had marched into the Colombian plateau, conquered the Chibcha Indians, and founded at Bogotá the kingdom of New Granada—an achievement sufficient to make him rich but not content. He wished to discover another Mexico or Peru and to become, after Cortés and Pizarro, the third marquis of the New World. The rumor of El Dorado—a tale the jungle Indians told, a confusion of the ritual gilding of a Chibchan chieftain with the opulent Inca empire the Spaniards had already seized—drew Quesada into the swamps of the Orinoco River; of the two thousand men in this expedition, twenty-five returned. When, some years later, Quesada died, his nephew-in-law inherited his fortune and his quest. The one consumed the other. Berrio, an old soldier of sixty, came from Spain to the Indies and for fifteen years devoted himself to the search for the gilded man and the city of gold. A collection of straw huts in Trinidad served as the capital of a jungle territory—Trinidad, Guiana, and eastern Venezuela—that for many decades was known in the Spanish colonial records as "these provinces of El Dorado." The tangle of ruinous expeditions and English raids and Indian massacres defies summary; by one of those ironies whereby literature wags history, it was Sir Walter Raleigh —a timid cutthroat, in Naipaul's narrative—who captured the El Dorado legend from its leading devotee, Berrio, by writing a book, *The Discovery of the Large, Rich, and Beautiful Empire of Guiana.* Though "really the story of a defeat and of a nervous six-day journey of exploration," the book "catches part of the New World at that moment between the unseeing brutality of the discovery and conquest and the later brutality of colonization. It was the swiftly passing moment when romance could be apprehended." Berrio's own story has an end worthy not of romance but of an anti-romantic novel. After seizure and release by Raleigh, Berrio, now seventy-five and probably lunatic, was stranded, with a dozen men, on an island in the Orinoco. Meanwhile, Domingo de Vera, his "campmaster for El Dorado," had wangled from the chronically bankrupt Spanish king a support expedition of twenty-eight ships and perhaps two thousand men and women. The New World was not ready to support such a population; unsheltered, unfed, cannibalized by Caribs, the expedition disintegrated and became, in the Spanish Indies, a "folk memory of horror." And Berrio, when Vera got to him on his island, was not grateful. He said (and these are the only spoken words of his that have been recorded), "We are trying to do too much. If we try to do too much we will end by doing nothing at all." So Don Quixote, invited to rise from his deathbed and resume the search for Dulcinea, replied, "No more of that, I beseech you. All the use I shall make of these follies at present is to heighten my repentance." The New World as medieval adventure had ended.

After a brief section on Trinidad's two hundred years as a "ghost province" within the Spanish Empire, and on its sudden, bloodless surrender to the British in 1797, *The Loss of El Dorado* concentrates upon Trinidad as an outpost in the young British Empire and upon the rule, disgrace, and final glory of Thomas Picton. If the collapse of Vera's relief force epitomizes the Spanish quest, the basic symbol of the British establishment is Vallot's jail. Jean-Baptiste Vallot, the conscientious, amiable, tirelessly cruel jailer of Port of Spain, is one of Naipaul's prime catches in the sea of forgotten documents. Vallot, who was paid by fees for each flogging, ear-clipping, and torture by suspension, and Begorrat, the chief magistrate, who prescribed the tortures and punishments, were both French; in Spanish times, Trinidad had suffered an influx of French planters and their slaves from the more turbulent islands of Santo Domingo and Martinique. The planters had brought with them their skill at "the management of Negroes."

> . . . the Negro called Pierre François had been ordered to fall on his knees to hear his sentence. He was then taken to the church. He was not baptized; he was already a Christian. Prayers were read to

him. He was then "heavily ironed" and the soldiers led him to where Bouqui's headless body was tied to the stake. [Bouqui was a previously executed Negro.] Many Negroes watched. Some of Vallot's jail Negroes were waiting with faggots. Pierre François was chained to the stake with the headless body. He was made to put on a shirt. The shirt was filled with sulphur. The jail Negroes built up the faggots. The executioner lit the fire. . . . The smell of sulphur and the two burning bodies drove many people out of their houses and there were some whites who feared a massacre. Begorrat and the French planters had devised the punishment and the ritual. They said afterwards it was what they used to do in Martinique.

Picton brought to his post no aversion to brutality. Instant hangings and fatal lashings were the first order of his new establishment. He signed all of Begorrat's torture orders. The growing agitation of the "radical" English-born artisans and merchants in Port of Spain, and the intervention of Colonel William Fullarton, one of two commissioners appointed to mitigate Picton's one-man rule, succeeded in having him brought to trial in London for a relatively innocent act—signing the order to torture Luisa Calderon, a young free mulatto accused by her lover of theft. Picton's two trials consumed five years. Luisa and the Negro policeman who testified with her had time to learn English between the first and the second. At the first, Picton was technically convicted, on the basis that torture was illegal under the Spanish law that still obtained in Trinidad; at the second, he was acquitted. Meanwhile, Fullarton—who, a spendthrift as well as a humanitarian, had squandered the treasury surplus accumulated under Picton's hard-headed management—fell into disfavor and died. Back in Port of Spain, Vallot's jail, with its torture chambers, its tiny, stinking cells, its *cachots brûlants* (windowless hotboxes), was pulled down by Picton's friends. No plan of it remains. Vallot disappeared; Begorrat remained a prominent planter into the 1830's; Picton's destiny took him into the peninsular campaign with Wellington, storming and sacking Badajoz, and on to Waterloo and a valorous death and a memorial statue at Carmarthen and the immortal good name enshrined, if you look him up, in the *Encyclopaedia Britannica*.

The Loss of El Dorado concludes with a summary of Trinidad's next hundred and fifty years, as a "ghost province" now of the British Empire, and touches on Mr. Naipaul's childhood in Port of

Spain, when it seemed "a place at the rim of the world." Then, in the 1940's, "Picton was the name of a street; no one knew more. History was a fairy tale about Columbus. . . . History was also a fairy tale not so much about slavery as about its abolition." These two impressions, of history as layers of fantasy and of Trinidad as a place on the rim of the world, animate Naipaul's zealous and intricate work of research and lurk behind his curious thesis that the New World is hopelessly "simple" and unreal. Himself a resident of England for twenty years, Naipaul voices this thesis, or suspicion, through the exiled revolutionary Miranda. "After the years in Europe, the books, pictures, and study, after the talk of liberty and constitutions, the colonial world remained, still knowing only about blood and money, cacao and tobacco, the management of Negroes and shops. . . . Miranda was applying the concepts of Europe as words alone, accurate but misleading, to a simpler world: the Negro-worked plantations of Venezuela, the low wooden houses of Port of Spain, the muddy shore, the rough Spanish shops, the one printery." The reader puzzles over this "deeper colonial deprivation, the sense of the missing real world." Is it that Europe has no muddy shores? Is greater length of history the token of superiority? Another exile, the Venezuelan lawyer Level de Goda, in Spain, is excited "to be close for the first time to the real world and real events, to be in a country that could support classical illusion." Illusion or allusion? Naipaul's indictment is slow to form. "It wasn't only that the wines, the manners and the graces, the books and the art and the ideas of a living culture came from outside. The simple society bred simple people" —"too simple for lasting causes," so simple that their revolutions are "second-hand," "with energy but without principles," "the imperfectly constituted society decaying into minute egoisms." And what is the cause of this decay, which turned the Spaniards feckless, which made Frenchmen into monsters of cruelty, which sapped British liveliness and idealism? Slavery. "In the slave society . . . this liveliness began to be perverted and then to fade, and the English saw their preëminence, more simply, as a type of racial magic." Inhumane laws are enacted by people "who have ceased to assess themselves by the standards of the metropolis and now measure their eminence only by their distance, economic and racial, from their Negroes."

> This was what stalled and perverted every stated metropolitan principle, French, Spanish, English, of revolution, intellectual advance, law, social drive, justice and freedom: race, the taint of slavery: it helped to make the colonial society simple.

If for "colonial" we substitute "southern," the situation, and the truth of the charge, become recognizable. There is no denying the evidence Naipaul has resurrected concerning the cruelty and folly enacted in the provinces of El Dorado, where slaves poisoned each other to destroy the master's wealth and ate dirt to destroy themselves. Naipaul's sense of an evil unreality presiding over the New World makes it possible for him to sympathize on all sides, to bring into rounded life his great variety of doomed actors. "Fantasy," with "simple," is a recurrent word: there was the fantasy of a city of gold, and the fantasy of the underground slave life of voodoo and midnight courts, and the fantasy of bookish revolutionaries like Miranda, and the fantasy of the British that they could manipulate South American revolutions to serve their economic ends. But in viewing an entire hemisphere as a corrupted dream, Naipaul dissolves what realities there were. *The Loss of El Dorado* rests upon an unexamined assumption, of metropolitan superiority. In this it is like Naipaul's last, fine but cold novel, *The Mimic Men*, which presented the men of the West Indies as poor imitations of Europeans. Yet were the conquistadors more fanatic and quixotic than the captains of the Thirty Years' War? Were the English planters more rapacious and callous than the mill-owners of Lancashire? Were the South American revolutionaries more deluded or ineffectual than the French prototypes, who slew each other and prepared the way for Napoleon? Was the cruelty of slavery not an extension of the cruelty already present on the African continent? Does not the collapse of "metropolitan" values amid "simpler" conditions demonstrate their own frailty and unreality? For the fallacy of the primitive paradise, it seems to me, Mr. Naipaul wants to exchange that of the metropolitan paradise. This desire gives *The Loss of El Dorado* its bleak and caustic tone, yet also its persuasive sadness and the power of poetry.

Sons of Slaves

THE SULTANS, by Noel Barber. 304 pp. Simon & Schuster, 1973.

THE SULTAN: *The Life of Abdul Hamid II*, by Joan Haslip. 309 pp. Holt, Rinehart & Winston, 1973.

It is a pity that Noel Barber, in writing *The Sultans*, could not muster more of the prose-empurpling zest of an Edgar Saltus, who found the follies and atrocities of the Caesars and of the Czars so perversely enchanting; for Mr. Barber tells the supreme saga of decadent misrule in an efficient journalistic manner that in the end seems rather overwhelmed and wan, and he leaves us with no moral beyond the implication that all Turks are crazy. Perhaps it would take a Beelzebub drunk on blood to sing with appropriate inspiration the annals of the royal descendants of Othman and the Magnificent Suleiman. Mr. Barber is a reasonable modern man, who, with the cumulative numbingness of the *Guinness Book of World Records*, sets down the odd facts as one more madman, imbecile, sot, and terror-stricken impotent succeeds another on the throne of the Shadow of God on Earth. Selim II (who reigned as Sultan from 1566 to 1574) laid siege to Cyprus—a siege in which thirty thousand Christians were massacred in Nicosia alone—to ensure himself a steady supply of Cyprian wine. Mahomet III (r. 1595–1603) had his nineteen brothers strangled upon his accession to the throne. Osman II (r. 1618–1622) practiced archery upon live targets, and used his own page boys when the supply of prisoners of war gave out. It amused Murad IV (r. 1623–1640) to pick off his hapless subjects with an arquebus from a corner of the Seraglio wall, "exercising the royal prerogative of taking ten innocent lives a day"; a sultan of action, he executed twenty-five thousand suspected malefactors in one year, beheaded his chief musician for playing a Persian air, and sank a boatload of women that drifted within range of his palace cannon. Ibrahim (r. 1640–1648), perhaps the maddest of the lot (though the 19th-century Abdul Aziz is an impressive contender), adorned his beard with diamonds and raped the daughter of the Mufti and drowned his entire harem on the suspicion that one concubine was conducting a romance. Not all the excesses were of cruelty: Ahmed III (r. 1703–1730) admired tulips (from the Turkish *tulbend*, meaning "turban") to such an extent that he was deposed for the extravagance of his moonlit tulip fêtes; Osman III (r. 1754–1757) in his obsession with food prowled Istanbul by night to sample the city's eating houses. Abdul Mejid (r. 1839–1861) built a palace, Dolmabache, that incorporated fourteen tons of gold leaf, the biggest mirrors in the world, and a bed of solid silver for himself; when one of his daughters married, he spent forty million francs on her trousseau and the wedding breakfast, which lasted one week. Abdul Aziz, his brother and successor, expanded the harem to nine hundred women, fed three hundred dinner guests most evenings, bought locomotives from Britain though there were no tracks to run them on, sometimes refused to sign any documents written in black ink, played soldiers with real soldiers, and bestowed upon cocks and chickens the Ottoman Empire's highest decorations for gallantry.

One does not need to be Dr. Spock to be reminded, by such behavior, of insanely indulged children begging for someone to set "limits." The sultans fascinate, indeed, as examples of how far human appetite will go when no obstacle to its satisfaction is posed. They are a spectacle to comfort the average deprived man. Several of them, early given the run of a harem, developed impotence; a surprising number, in a teetotalling culture, drank themselves to death. Over *half* of the sultans after 1600 had to be deposed! Mr. Barber, though his energetic scholarship displays itself in pages of colorful details, does not seize the opportunity to analyze the peculiarities of Ottoman kingship that shaped so preponderantly ineffective a dynasty. Rather, he offers the dark suggestion that the "unbroken line of weaklings" after Suleiman were not Othmans at all but sprang from a coupling between Suleiman's empress Roxelana and an unknown lover. Yet the background of Barber's perhaps too sensational and anecdotal chronicle of the sultanate contains more sociological reasons for its uncorrected debilitation. The Sultan was not only the administrator of a terrestrial empire but a holy man, the Caliph of Islam, and as such (though the claim to the caliphate was shadowy and emphasized chiefly in the latter centuries of the sultans) he enjoyed among the Muslim masses a religious prestige impervious to mortal shenanigans. Though the sultans' extravagance and the corruption they fostered sorely burdened the empire, the need for *a* sultan was never questioned, and except in cases of blatant imbecility the rules of succession were followed. A second insulating factor was these rules of succession, whereby not the son but the eldest male in the family inherited the throne; the welter of intrigue this invited was combatted, initially, by the extraordinary sanction of fratricide that Ottoman law offered to the newly enthroned—"the right to execute their brothers, in order to ensure the peace of the world"—and then, in a humane modification that proved surpassingly disastrous to the health of the sultanate, by the institution of the *Kafes*, the Cage, a two-storied building, within the Seraglio, set aside by Ahmed I in 1603 for the perpetual confinement of the heirs to the throne. High walls surrounded it; the ground floor was windowless; here, with no company but that of deaf-mutes and sterilized concubines, the sultans' brothers and sons awaited either the silken bowstring of assassination or the call to supreme power. Mustafa I, the first alumnus of the Cage, emerged demented; Ibrahim, who had spent twenty-two of his first twenty-four years there, proved a monster of debauchery; and Suleiman II, who logged the record of forty-five years in the Cage, had, when at last he was proclaimed Sultan, "all but lost the power of speech." Has any other nation ever so devalued human personality as to immure its future rulers in total isolation from the workings of the world? The Ottoman Empire gave an extraordinary centrality to the institution of slavery. The Sultan was the only free Turk in the government; the rest were all his personal slaves, often converted Christians from the European realms of the empire. The Janissaries, his personal troops, were impressed Christian boys; an Albanian father and son, the Kuprilis, served as highly effective grand viziers for some of the Cage-crazed sultans; two of the most powerful of the sultanas who dominated events from the harem were the Russian Roxelana and Aimée Dubucq de Rivery, a convent girl captured by Barbary pirates. (The melodramatic annals of the Seraglio contain few incidents as tender* as the summons of Mahmud II, Aimée's son, for

---

* Or as indubitably fictitious, several correspondents have assured me.

a Catholic priest to absolve his dying mother in her native faith.)
Every sultan was the son of a slave; and the dehumanizing designs
of slavery are felt everywhere, from the rigor of the pageantry to
such animate constructs as the black eunuch and the deaf-mute
assassin—his eardrums broken, his tongue slit, and his life consecrated to the use of the bowstring, as that of the concubine was
consecrated to a call from the imperial bed which often never
came. In his world of slaves the Sultan found little resistance to his
fantasies and little helpful advice. Of Abdul Hamid II, the last of
the absolute monarchs and one of the few with some gift for government, Mr. Barber says, "As his terror bore increasing signs of
madness, he chose the most incredible characters to guide him. His
advisers included a slave he had bought in the market, a circus
clown whose act he admired, the son of one of his cooks, a Punch
and Judy performer, and a bootblack." Everything, in short, but
a graduate of Whittier High School.

Yet one wonders if even a continuous line of philosopher-kings
or elected charismatics could have kept the Ottoman Empire from
shrinking. Its reduction, in any case, was less rapid than that of the
British Empire, and, unlike that of Rome, left the heartland un-
conquered. Even after generations and generations of being "sick,"
Turkey proved capable of the heroics of Plevna. The reader, grateful for so much that Mr. Barber has unearthed from the archives
of this curious despotism, regrets that he did not choose to meditate upon his basic subject—that of decadence. Do extravagance
and obtuseness in high circles significantly affect the human tides
that Tolstoy saw mysteriously sweeping back and forth across the
surface of the globe? Or do the expansion and contraction of empires have to do simply with the technology of warfare: the Ot-
tomans organized the first standing army in Europe and developed
an artillery that, in the words of Gibbon, "surpassed whatever had
yet appeared in the world." To what extent does this kind of military vitality reflect spiritual vigor or efficacious political institutions? The Ottoman bureaucracy of slaves, a model of efficiency
in the short run, proved cumbersome and unresponsive in the long.
But what possible administrative magic could have enabled the
Caliph of Islam to rule forever over the Christian peoples of the
Balkans as Christian Europe waxed mighty? The wonder is that

the Turkish "yoke" lasted so long. One would like to know in what ways Turkish rule impinged upon the subject peoples—if present-day America is taken as an empire, would the analogy be with Puerto Rico or South Vietnam?—and, for that matter, what the sultans *did* all day, aside from playing pranks on their harem and holding hieratically formal audiences, throughout which the audient's arms were pinned by two stout pashas as a safeguard against assassination.

Joan Haslip, in *The Sultan*, gives a portrait of Abdul Hamid II considerably more sympathetic than that of Mr. Barber, who makes the last of the all-powerful sultans a maze-loving paranoid surrounded by "incredible characters" and the drab tatters of an outlandish panoply. Miss Haslip sees him as an agile and prescient statesman, able, for the more than three decades of his reign, to play the European powers off against each other and safeguard Turkey's survival without the entangling alliances that, once he fell, drew the Young Turks into the First World War. A runty younger brother placed on the throne by his sibling's insanity, Abdul Hamid had some experience of cosmopolitan Europe, more knowledge of history than any sultan before him, a flair for mathematics and carpentry, an engaging fondness for the tales of Sherlock Holmes. He had in his youth enjoyed a bourgeois liaison with a woman not of the harem, a Belgian shopkeeper called Flora Cordier, and even in his reactionary old age his conservatism had the rationale of a Pan-Islamic vision, a sound instinct to salvage the empire's Muslim East and to let the European fragments go. Abdul Hamid had the self-knowledge to exclaim, in discourse with an English businessman, "What can you expect of us, the children of slaves brought up by eunuchs?" But his story, so respectfully told by Miss Haslip, who even takes the Sultan's side against the massacred Armenians, is a dreary one, of a devious holding action against a desperate need for reform. It is, furthermore, mere history, full of problematical conferences and détentes and peoples' uprisings, and tells us little more than the morning's newspaper. Whereas Mr. Barber's less solid survey, with its idiots turned sultan and its convent girls turned into complacent concubines and its claustrophobic sense of an entire empire being crushed into a few terror-filled tiled halls, has the enigmatic depth of a dream, a dream that could tell us some truth about our natures, could we but fathom the symbols.

Coffee-Table Books for High Coffee Tables

Erotic Art of the East, by Philip Rawson. Introduction by Alex Comfort. 380 pp. G. P. Putnam's Sons, 1968.

Primitive Erotic Art, edited by Philip Rawson. 310 pp. G. P. Putnam's Sons, 1973.

Erotic Art of the West, by Robert Melville. With a Short History of Erotic Art by Simon Wilson. 318 pp. G. P. Putnam's Sons, 1973.

Here we have a new genre: the coffee-table book that should be kept out of the reach of the children. Higher coffee tables would seem to be the answer; but the Japanese are using all our tall lumber to make bowling alleys with. So the alternative is to raise a generation for whom there is no pudendum, and that can call a vulva a ——. That generation is here, leaning on my coffee table, and when it takes over I fear G. P. Putnam's Sons will go begging for buyers as avid as I to wallow in the formerly forbidden delights (1,001 pages, more or less) of their so-called World History of Erotic Art.

These three compendia have texts that, though beside the selling point, in decency should be reviewed. The oldest publication, dating back to staid old 1968, is *Erotic Art of the East*. Dr. Alex Comfort, well known to loving couples as the master chef stirring the stew of *The Joy of Sex*, was announced as general editor and contributed an introduction regretting the "Victorian *terror sexualis*" and our present lack of "a technology of the emotions." Philip Rawson then, in his long chapter on Indian erotic art, described an elaborate technology based on the notion that semen is a divine substance which prolonged intercourse without orgasm will force up the spinal column into the head, producing enlightenment. By way of technical illustration, there were many tinted depictions of a rubbery prince squatting *en face* with his smiling, netherly exposed lady, his lingam thrust into her yoni as patiently as the little Dutch boy's finger in the dike. The Chinese, a later chapter told us, took this Tantric principle—copulation without male consummation—a Confucian step further by making their supreme sex symbol the ancient sage; his longevity and spiritual well-being bore witness to a lifetime of absorbing concubines' beneficial *yin* without surrendering any considerable portion of his precious *yang*. The Chinese, incidently, considered jade congealed dragon semen. Whatever the cosmological delusions behind them, the Asian doctrines of sexual conduct did place value, Rawson argued, on the gratification of the female. And it is true, the women in these representations look much less alarmed than those in Western erotica. This volume was rounded out by David James's game plea for the skimpy amorous art of iconophobic, homosexual Islam, and by Richard Lane's fussy monograph on *shunga*—Japanese "spring pictures," pictures of sexual activity traditionally part of the printmaster's production and often given as wedding presents. The shyest bride, after studying the monstrously exaggerated genitals that *shunga* shows, could only be relieved at the sight of her husband's.

Five years later, Dr. Comfort has vanished as general editor and two new volumes sumptuously appear. *Primitive Erotic Art*, edited by Rawson and written by a variety of hands, suffers from the disparity of material included under "primitive" and from what I take to be some undue haste in the assembling. Rawson's opening essay, on early sexual art, is excellent, once he has given the Christian missionaries and Western sexual neuroses their compulsory lumps. He takes art to be at the very beginning erotic—a descent, via sinuous caves, into the womb of Mother Earth, there to stimulate her, with rites that included drawings, to continue her generation of the wildlife that fed a hunting society. Primitive magic, Rawson feels, should be understood less as a mechanistic effort to cause a result than an effort of identification and possession through analogy and symbol; rite and its attendant art "exalt the sense of life, and elaborate a mystery-cult to conserve and renew it." The feminine sex of the earth was the first metaphor; the first works of art appear to be vulva-like cups gouged on the underside of a tomb slab. The maze, as visual pattern or narrative theme, betokens the mystery of the female innards. Until the rise of agricultural society, generic energy was identified as female; with seed-sowing came phallic art. Rawson, as he pursues analogies through prehistory, seems sometimes too agile to be true: "It is not at all difficult to associate these objects both with the feathered phalli painted in the Palaeolithic caves and with the bunched besoms which the medieval witches were supposed to straddle and ride to the Sabbat; supposed examples of witch-besoms even have handles carved as penises. The bunch attached to the end must be a graphic image for the seminal jet, a plastic analogue to the colored water sprayed about at the Indian Holi procession and the rice or confetti thrown at modern Western weddings." Well, maybe so; but a cigar, as Freud said, can be just a cigar.

By comparison, the following essays on Celtic, Indian, African, and Pacific art seem plodding and bereft of a thesis. Tom Harrison's account of Borneo and New Guinea has the strength of testimony from the field, mixing art objects with anecdotes and with artifacts like the all-too-vividly-depicted penis bar. Cottie Burland on sub-Saharan Africa, on the other hand, seems rattled by the richness of his vast topic, grateful for all signs of "restraint" from the frequently "violent" artists, and prone to take refuge in the undefined concept of "naturalness" and "close to nature." Very bothersomely, the plates, many of them beautiful, are not well related to the texts. Though the two other books in the series usefully key the plates to the discussion by means of numbers in the broad margin, this device is not employed here; nor are the plates included in the index. There are almost as many pictures without explanation as there are descriptions without illustration. The tribal name "Colima" identifies eight of the American pottery pieces, including one on the cover, yet the word doesn't occur in the index or, that I can find, in the text. An editorial disservice has been done to both the scholarly authors and the compilers of the photographs: they should have been introduced to each other.

Erotic Art of the West, however, is a singular production. Robert Melville, art editor of the *New Statesman*, has not so much written a history of erotic art in the West as he has threaded an essay on eroticism through a personal anthology of works of art.

Medieval to modern illustrations range unchronologically under chapter heads like "The Toilet," "Violence and Violation," and "Treatment of the Parts"; sensitive and lively explications of visual images mingle with startlingly physical speculations—"few men could honestly claim that they have not at some time or another desired to urinate inside the beloved." Melville has an engaging way of concerning himself with the physical comfort of the figures in Renaissance tableaux, nude on their sometimes awkwardly placed pillows. He rarely says too much, though his eye sees worlds, and his sense of flaws is as keen as his warmth of response—Renoir's later nudes became "a kind of slow-breathing earthenware," the uneasy perspective in Vermeer's *At the Procuress's* betrays that the "real psychological situation is between the woman in the yellow bodice and the painter." His discourse on the ways and parts of love touches on a number of works that, by the standards of the Asian book, are not erotic at all; indeed, one of the fascinations for the reader, if he looks at the pictures first, is to discover how the author will work each one of them in. To be sure, Melville's fine fancy can become merely tricksome—William Copley's women "come forth in their bras and suspender belts as the issue of a drop of sperm that fell on to an advertisement in a woman's magazine" —and even for a personal anthology, the choice of reproductions seem unbalanced. There are seven Hans Bellmers but not one George Grosz; seven Dalis but none of Arp's or Moore's suggestive biomorphs; no Bonnard, though there is a section devoted to "The Bath"; no Courbet, though his nudes are described as revolutionary and (figuratively) seminal; no obscene or priapic Gothic gargoyles or miserichords, though many exist; and no modern pornography, though Victorian, 18th-century, and Renaissance examples are given. A British bias shows, I think, in the generous sampling of post-war English painters (plus Jim Dine, who lives in London) and the almost total ignoring of American Pop Art, which reeks of sex as heavily as Art Nouveau. The entire New York Pop scene, indeed, is represented only by one rather bland Marisol—better, for this book, her slyly ithyphallic "Guy" or the Coke-bottle fellatio of "Amor."

Yet Melville has made a book to please himself, that begins and ends in air (with a quote from Henry James that means as near nothing as grammatical English can) and that by its very blitheness somewhat refutes the imputations of Western anti-sexuality made by the exponents of primitive and Asian art. Broadly, one might say that the purpose of primitive erotic art is to participate (in the processes of vitality; an art whose phallic emblems double as initiatory dildoes), that of Asian erotic art is to show (as marriage manual, as religious illustration), and that of Western civilization seems to be to divulge, to confess, to expose. The resonances of a shared mythology are replaced by those of private psychology; from Bosch and Botticelli on, personal meanings subvert and super-charge overt symbolism. The atmosphere of Western erotic art is relatively "anxious," to use Alex Comfort's word; the very surface of many paintings feels tangled and restless. Whatever the lovers are portrayed together or one is the rendered model and the other the unseen artist, a dimension of individual psychological invasion has been added to sexual possession. The faces, even in ecstasy, are not masks. Melville's book, at least to this Westerner, never is monotonous in the way the other two are. A variety of blind men have touched the sexual elephant standing in our midst; here are their impressions. If a spirit of anthropological dispassion is to be applied consistently, the repressions that Christianity and then in-dustrialism asked of the West need be no more deplored than the genital mutilations common in primitive societies or the cruel rigidity of Oriental social structures. Nowhere is love free, any more than men are free, even in a wilderness. The beautiful whores of the Hindu temple "heaven-bands" smile out at us from a his-torical remission that ended; Moslem Puritans came and mutilated them. Now we stand in a moment when again sex seems worth studying and celebrating. More, it now appears our last uncon-taminated act, the sinuous passageway down into the womb where worship is possible, in a unifying darkness of instinctive purpose. In this sexiest of times, as a tug of reaction begins to be felt, our set of three volumes offers us a comradely perspective, as wide as the world and deep as history, into the erotic images with which other men have sought "to exalt the sense of life." "Exaltation," indeed, in the sense of lifting high into visibility, describes the crudest lavatory graffito as well as the noblest nude.

*

And what of these pictures themselves? Having passed my eyes over so many images of copulation, flirtation, erection, and excitation, I feel as if, like the weary headmaster surveying his June ocean of unruly eternal youth, I should bestow a few prizes. *Best Phallus:* Aubrey Beardsley. *Best Vulva:* Hokusai (*shunga* tradition generally leaves the lovers clothed; the heads show and, at an often unlikely remove, the cloth parts to reveal genitalia like hairy actors on a puppet-stage). *Erotica with Least Hang-ups:* Mochica (Peru) pottery vessels (produced, surely, in a joking spirit, as are the obscene Cherokee pipes "smoker" jokes). *Nicest Couple:* a very dearly drawn Chinese pair, from a 19th-century album, he with a dark but honest penis, she with a bib and bound feet, both with tiny, utterly kindly smiles. *Most Repulsive Couple:* four-armed goddess with Shiva in two aspects, 20th-century Bengal painting. *Most Disturbing Artist:* Hans Bellmer, who combines pornographic fury with linear facility; can erotic art have any further to go? *Best Venus:* Lucas Cranach. *Masterwork Most Missed:* Popeye, Olive Oyl, and Wimpy fellating and gamahuching one another, in comic book circulating in southeastern Pennsylvania in the late 1940's.

Before the Sky Collapses

XINGU: THE INDIANS, THEIR MYTHS, by Orlando Villas Boas and Claudio Villas Boas, translated from the Portuguese by Susana Hertelendy Rudge. 270 pp. Farrar, Straus & Giroux, 1974.

Xingu: The Indians, Their Myths is certainly one of the best books of 1974 whose title begins with "X." The volume shows love, from the publisher's handsome two-color printing job to the lifetimes of service the authors have devoted to the Brazilian Indians. Since 1946, the Boas brothers (a third brother, Leonardo, died in 1961) have dwelt with small intermission among the dozen or so tribes that live in villages along the Rio Xingu and its tributaries, in virtual isolation from the modern civilization that dominates and threatens them. This book, edited from the brothers' journals by

Kenneth S. Brecher, an American anthropologist who himself spent two years among the Xinguanos, consists in the main of thirty-one tales, or "myths," transcribed from oral narrations in, evidently, the rough Portuguese of bilingual Indians. The Boases state, in their introduction, "There were no pressures of time; instead, our interest was to transmit with the greatest possible accuracy everything heard and understood over . . . twenty-five years of daily, hourly, and minute-by-minute communal living with the Indians." The stories are shared, with some exceptions, among the tribes, and they are prefaced by a brief but affecting description of the region's geography and fauna and climate and history. Affecting, that is, in its sense of achieved intimacy with the alien, of modern men willfully dissolving their calendars and chronometers in the joyous cycles of the natural year:

> In April the rains taper off and the waters recede. . . . The clouds turn white and vaporous and are propelled by cold gusts of wind coming from the south and the southeast. It is the beginning of "summer."
>
> At this time of the year, it is common to see birds flying across the skies, beautiful formations of jabiru storks, flocks of white herons, and pairs of colhereiros in search of lagoons and *igapós*.
>
> As the waters recede from the shores, gulls, *bacuraus de coleira branca*, ducks, and marrecãos fly in. The *tracajas* [fresh-water turtles] and small alligators, who at flood time had clung to floating tree trunks, search for sandy shores to enjoy the heat of the sun.

There are worlds sequestered from our world; there is a history remote from our history:

> As a result of violent attacks unleashed on them by a nation called Aussumadí, who invaded their lands, the Trumái decided to move. Under the leadership of two great chieftains, Auaturí and Jaquanarí, they headed for "where the sun sets." After trekking through extensive forests, they arrived at the banks of a river that they said was the Kuluene (the Xingu, in our nomenclature).

Amid our human multitudes, how much such history has been hidden and lost! Even within the microcosm of the Xingu, there are mysteries, problematical events just beyond the reach of memory, and tribes that are "hostile" or "asocial"; they have the vividness of the half-seen:

In temperament, the Txikāo are nervous and restless, reacting to any novel stimulus or situation that crops up. This trait, very pronounced in them, may be a natural result of the isolation in which they live.

Isolation within isolation. More exotic still are the reports of the Minatá-Karaiá. In a bygone time, a legend among the Kamaiurá tribe runs, some of their men, travelling, heard a whistling sound:

> Curious to know what it was, they walked in the direction the sound was coming from. After a while, they reached the village, which belonged to the Minatá-Karaiá. The village was full of people, and the men had a hole in the top of their heads that produced the whistle the Kamaiurá had heard from far away. The Minatá-Karaiá had another peculiarity: from underneath their armpits bunches of *minatás* [coconuts] grew, and they were constantly snatching the fruits off, breaking them against their heads, and eating them.

What the Boas brothers in their introduction call "the human mind's natural penchant for the marvellous" does become, as the white introducers yield to the Indian tellers of the thirty-one tales, wearing. These myths make stiff reading. Some of the fault, perhaps, belongs to the translator. There seems an unnecessary plethora of italicized un-English terms; in the passages already quoted, why not simply say "turtles" and "coconuts" instead of "*tracajas* [fresh-water turtles]" and "*minatás* [coconuts]"? Is there *no* sufficiently accurate English equivalent of *jakuí, püa, itóto, irracuitáp, imurã, tucunaré-aruiáp, moinrucú*, etc., etc.? A conscientious, if not ideal, reader of this volume would be turning to the glossary several times for every page. An ideal reader would know Portuguese and the relevant Indian languages and would have already read the Boas journals in the original. While an excessive verbal pedantry constantly pricks the eye, footnotes are rigorously excluded, where a clarifying note on ritual, or animal habits, or Xingu customs would often be helpful. And though the original was probably not a masterpiece of style, does the English have to be quite so flat, colorless, and arhythmic? "The Jurana had everything when the waters began to grow with the rains." Was there no more concrete way of putting that? "She had plunged into a murky part of the woods, and finding the ladder by way of a shortcut, she climbed up and was gone." Is "by way of a shortcut" really the thought? For me, it imposes upon the murky part of the wood a suddenly urban pedestrian, saving valuable seconds on the way to an appointment on an upper floor.

But the mind meets resistance in the texture of these tales mostly, I think, because they are indeed primitive, and not only is the milieu an alien one but the habits of narration are different. The laconic closeness of event, no doubt relieved in oral rendition by pause and gesture, tests the attention of a modern reader. One can skim a paragraph by Henry James, get the general picture, and either go back for the furniture and nuance or get on with the story. Skim a paragraph of these myths, and one is lost:

> When the boys fell, the tapir went around stepping on them and burying them with his foot. The tapir, after killing and burying the boys, went a long way away. After a while the boys in the ground began to be born, some in the form of little turtles, others as real people. The one up in the tree said to the others down below, "How are you doing down there?"

A relatively transparent passage. But this reviewer's mind—after trying to imagine how to bury boys with a tapir's foot, where "a long way away" is, why the dead boys so easily begin to resurrect, and why some only make it "in the form of little turtles"—is too boggled to recall that one boy, the paragraph before, had managed, despite the kicking of the wicked tapir's foot, to stay up in the genipap tree, whence he calls down his cheery and—considering the circumstances—rather bland greeting. The story continues (in case you've been gripped) with the boys following their murderer by interrogating successively warmer piles of excrement and killing him when he is asleep; then, "seeing that they had come a long way, the boys decided to climb up to the sky," where they casually turn into stars.

A modern story, however fabulous, proceeds subject to the discipline of some reality-derived premises; these Brazilian Indian narratives seem closer to the flow of dreams, wherein nothing is questioned. The sheer authority of the narrator is justification enough for any turn of event. His own decisiveness is echoed in the decisiveness of his characters: the boys decide to climb the sky; and, in one of the more vivid openings, "There once was an old man who wanted to get married, but no woman wanted to marry him. He was very ugly. Saddened by this, he decided to die."

As the distinctions between animals and men, the living and the dead, earth and sky are vaguely felt, so is the opposition between the inner will and the outer world. Things happen easily; in "The Origin of the Twins Sun and Moon," an old jaguar, "very angry, peeled a piece off her fingernail and threw it at her daughter-in-law, cutting her head off." Beheaded by a fingernail, the daughter-in-law thrashes, is referred to as now "dead," now "dying," has vitality enough to give birth to twin boys, the Sun (Rit) and the Moon (Une), and, pages later, after the sons have grown and avenged her by killing their wicked grandmother, still seems to be alive, and talking. A Western reader might expect from the title (imposed, I suspect, by the anthropologists) a coherent if fanciful account of cosmic origins, but this story takes place in an already created cosmos, wherein the growth of the twin Sun and Moon is measured in moons. The twins figure in many of the stories, yet with hardly a trace of celestial grandeur; they are often victimized, sometimes impotent, and rarely luminary. The elemental connection between the Sun and daylight is curiously grasped; in one myth, day is stolen by Sun from a village of vultures. Another story is reminiscent of the Greek myth of Phaëthon. The Sun has been slain (by a bunch of coconuts!), and his widow, seeing the world lost in the ensuing darkness, persuades her three sons to don their father's headdress of feathers. Two of them find the headdress too hot, and come down from the sky; the third manages to wear it across the firmament, but runs. When he learns to walk, he becomes the Sun, and his mother weeps, knowing he can never return home. The weeping mother is also the motif of the Xingu equivalent of the Adam myth, so brief that it can be quoted entire:

> In the beginning there was only Mavutsinim. No one lived with him. He had no wife. He had no son, nor did he have any relatives. He was all alone.
> One day he turned a shell into a woman, and he married her. When his son was born, he asked his wife, "Is it a man or a woman?"
> "It is a man "
> "I'll take him with me."
> When he left, the boy's mother cried and went back to her village, the lagoon, where she turned into a shell again.
> "We are the grandchildren of Mavutsinim's son," say the Indians.

The Judaic differentiation of man and God has not yet occurred; Mavutsinim is both. Metamorphosis, in this slippery Amazon world, is no miracle but a mere matter of wishing. The heroes, animal and human, are not agonists, struggling to allocate eternally the one life that is theirs, but spirits, with something of the spirit world's playful elasticity. The lack of final moral consequence encourages a kind of teeming nastiness absent from Biblical legends. "Kanaratê and Karanavarê" is an Abel-and-Cain story in which Abel keeps "messing around" with his brother's wives and Cain keeps botching the attempt at murder by such tortuous methods as scarification and starvation, but Abel at last slays *him*, and inherits his wives. The moral: "Now it will always be this way. Husband will be jealous of wife and brother will fight with brother." A kind act is as rare in these tales as a logical progression. If any moral principle emerges, it is that sexual relations with women interfere with a warrior's hardness. Though there are glimmers of humor, of earthy wisdom, of a quickening sympathy with animal life, this is a low-ceilinged world, murky and mean; the myths seem drained of religion, perhaps by an unacknowledged awareness on the part of the Xinguanos that they are, as a culture if not as a population, doomed. Though presented as if timelessly isolated, they were visited by a German ethnologist as long ago as 1887 and have ever since been subject to infiltration by white adventurers, predators, missionaries, and saintly anthropologists. *Xingu*, as a presentation of a cultural situation, is deficient just where Lévi-Strauss's *Tristes Tropiques*, describing not dissimilar primitive societies in the Mato Grosso, is rich: in the sense of cultural interplay. Humanity, from Lévi-Strauss's ironical self-portrait to the half-caste adventurers living on the margins of Indian territory to the forlorn Indians themselves, presents itself as a giant weave nowhere totally broken. In one of the book's many beautifully melancholy passages, Lévi-Strauss, emerging onto the Amazon and the outposts of white civilization, witnessed (or thought he witnessed) a tribe, the Tupi-Kawahibs, in the process of liquidating itself, in November of 1938. There, on the banks of the upper Machado, as the departing anthropologist hastened "to reconstruct from its last fragments a culture which had fascinated Europe," the Tupi-Kawahibs prepared also to depart, and to sink the remnants of their tribe into a stronger one. At this juncture, one night, the chief, Taperahi, startled Lévi-Strauss by rising from the hammock of apathy and singing a song, a many-voiced dramatization that, in the summary, sounds like a lot of the stories collected in *Xingu*—the farcical adventurers of a *japim* bird amid talking jaguars, tapirs, lizards, and spirits. In the myth that concludes *Xingu*, the Godlike Sinaa (who becomes "young again each time he took a bath, pulling his skin off over his head like a sack") shows us the forked stick that supports the sky and says, "The day our people die out entirely, I will pull this down, and the sky will collapse, and all people will disappear."

The forked stick in this case is the so-called Xingu National Park, set up, at the urging of the Boas brothers, by the Brazilian government in 1961 and now gnawed at, if not yet knocked aside, by the trans-Amazon highway. Of course, honor is due the effort of human preservation—by legislation as long as the needs of the powerful allow it, and by museums and literature afterward. One regrets of this book that the fragments were not given a context to enhance their value. Much that seems incongruous or unintelligible must allude to circumstantial details that could have been specified. Parallels with other myths and fables, especially those of other American Indians, might have highlighted the seldom memorable flux of incident. How many primitive peoples, for instance, have, like the Xinguanos, coined myths to explain the invention of the anus and the origins of toothache? Beneath the muddy surface of these tales, the deeper significances swim unfished-for, while on the surface dance wonderfully spindly and clear-eyed drawings of animals and artifacts by Wacupiá, a Waura tribesman who had never before put pen to paper. Including them as illustrations was a happy editorial stroke; they bring one Xinguano as close to us as Picasso and Klee, and brighten an otherwise rather tristful volume.

A New Meliorism

THE LIVES OF A CELL: *Notes of a Biology Watcher*, by Lewis Thomas.
153 pp. Viking, 1974.

Who dares now doubt that empirical science is the only legally
licensed hunter of truth and the one legitimate dispenser of information about reality? Yet who but the scientists themselves can
comprehend what science is saying? So a class of essayists has
grown up—they are almost the only surviving specimens of that
delicate breed—that seeks to acquaint us with the astonishing facts
revealed by research and to place them in a perspective that we
might call philosophical, did not the word itself embarrass us.
Loren Eiseley, Desmond Morris, Annie Dillard, Joseph Wood
Krutch, H. G. Wells—each of these, with his own special tone
and own field of specialized knowledge, makes "sense" of the surreal scientific facts that loom beyond our lives like Oz, a benevolent
kingdom ever receding into strangeness, but one that now and then
deigns to send us, in whimsical emission, a new immunity, or
photographs of other planets. Dr. Lewis Thomas, whose essays
for *The New England Journal of Medicine* have been collected as
The Lives of a Cell: Notes of a Biology Watcher, is by profession a
pathologist, by position the president of the Memorial Sloan-Ket-
tering Cancer Center in New York City, and by avocation a lively,
thoughtful writer. His field of expert knowledge, and of meditation, is the microcosm within the cell, but he also draws thoughts
from entomology and etymology, and believes that the best thing
about the human race so far is Johann Sebastian Bach. Writing for
his fellow physicians and researchers, Dr. Thomas does not trouble
to spare them hard words like "haptene," "eukaryotic," and "myxotricha." In several essays he deals candidly with the practice of
medicine. ("The great secret, known to internists and learned
early in marriage by internists' wives, but still hidden from the
general public, is that most things get better by themselves.") In
other essays, he twits the anthropologist C. M. Turnbull's dire report on the Ik, ruminates about computers, dotes with a hobbyist's

fervor on the intricacies of word derivations, and pays tribute to the Woods Hole Marine Biological Laboratory. But the collection as a whole is by no means random; it has a voice—awed yet optimistic, with little of Loren Eiseley's melancholy sense of inhuman vastness—and a theme. The theme is, in a word, symbiosis.

The first essay states, and several others remark upon, the fact that has impressed Dr. Thomas most:

> At the interior of our cells, driving them, providing the oxidative energy that sends us out for the improvement of each shining day, are the mitochondria, and in a strict sense they are not ours. They turn out to be little creatures, the colonial posterity of migrant prokaryocytes, probably primitive bacteria that swam into ancestral precursors of our eukaryotic cells and stayed there. Ever since, they have maintained themselves and their ways, replicating in their own fashion, privately, with their own DNA and RNA quite different from ours. They are as much symbionts as the rhizobial bacteria in the roots of beans.

Similarly, chloroplasts in plants are "independent and self-replicating lodgers"; the flagellae that propel myxotricha turn out to be fully formed spirochetes that have tidily attached themselves; the enzyme-producing colonies in the digestive tracts of many animals illustrate "meticulously symmetrical symbiosis"; giant clams possess small lenses in their tissue that focus sunlight for the engulfed, symbiotic algae. The moral seems plain: "There is a tendency for living things to join up, establish linkages, live inside each other, return to earlier arrangements, get along, whenever possible. This is the way of the world." Most diseases result from overreaction on the part of the body's defenders, "a biologic misinterpretation of borders." Apparently malevolent microörganisms "turn out on close examination to be rather more like bystanders." "Pathogenicity is not the rule. . . . There is nothing to be gained, in an evolutionary sense, by the capacity to cause illness or death." What a benevolent world the microscope reveals! "Most bacteria are totally preoccupied with browsing," just like cows. Subtle and harmonious arrangements abound: insects, harboring beneficent bacteria in their tissues, coöperate to build cathedral-like anthills and beehives; apparent adversaries among living things are "usually [in] a standoff relation, with one party issuing signals, warnings,

flagging the other off"; animals and human beings are interconnected by codes of sound and odors and "chemotactic" "vibes";
the very atmosphere of our Earth, the sky, is "the grandest product
of collaboration in all of nature." Benevolent coöperation reigns
from top to bottom of at least this terrestrial sphere; "nature red
in tooth and claw" has been transfigured by the "something intrinsically good-natured about all symbiotic relations." Small
wonder that Dr. Thomas' perky, compact essays usually end on
the upbeat—even his pages on death, which bid us take comfort
"in the recognition of synchrony, in the information that we all go
down together, in the best of company."

The marvels of symbiotic interconnection intoxicate this scientist and lead him into flights of what must be fantasy: "Any word
you speak this afternoon will radiate out in all directions, around
town before tomorrow, out and around the world before Tuesday,
accelerating to the speed of light, modulating as it goes, shaping
new and unexpected messages, emerging at the end as an enormously funny Hungarian joke, a fluctuation in the money market,
a poem, or simply a long pause in someone's conversation in Bra-
zil." Is this meant literally? The image of the joke returns later:
"Maybe the thoughts we generate today and flick around from
mind to mind, like the jokes that turn up simultaneously at dinner
parties in Hong Kong and Boston . . . are the primitive precursors
of more complicated, polymerized structures that will come later,
analogous to the prokaryotic cells that drifted through shallow
pools in the early days of biological evolution. Later, when the
time is right, there may be fusion and symbiosis among the bits."
Such identity between molecules and ideas seems more mystical
than demonstrable. Dr. Thomas has the mystic's urge toward total
unity. He views the Earth as a single cell in its membrane of
atmosphere. He quotes approvingly the 14th-century hermitess
Julian of Norwich, who saw "all that is made" in "a little thing, the
quantity of an hazelnut." He rejoices, in good mystic fashion, in
the dissolution of the Self: "The whole dear notion of one's own
Self—marvellous old free-willed, free-enterprising, autonomous,
independent, isolated island of a Self—is a myth." Not that he
professes any use for old-fashioned supernaturalistic religion. Yet
his doctrine of universal symbiosis soars with an evangelical exalta-

tion, and it is interesting that even his careful prose lapses into the grammar of teleology:

> There is an underlying force that drives together the several creatures comprising myxotricha, and then drives the assemblage into union with the termite.

> [Dying] is, after all, the most ancient and fundamental of biologic functions, with its mechanisms worked out with the same attention to detail, the same provision for the advantage of the organism . . . that we have long since become accustomed to finding in all the crucial acts of living.

> To assure themselves the longest possible run, [mitochondria] got themselves inside all the rest of us.

> A framework for meaning is somehow built into our minds at birth.

Whence the underlying force? Why the attentive "provision for the advantage of the organism"? What do mindless mitochondria care about the "longest possible run"? How the "somehow"? Not that Dr. Thomas is obliged to solve all biological riddles, or that the teleological fallacy (as, say, Jacques Monod would view it) can be easily erased from language attempting to describe intricate phenomena. But Dr. Thomas' celebration of symbiotic relationships does seem tinged by the antique notion of Providence, rechristened "luck": "There may have been elements of luck in the emergence of chloroplasts." "It is another illustration of our fantastic luck that oxygen filters out the very bands of ultraviolet light that are most devastating for nucleic acids and proteins." Without exactly stating that this is the best of all possible worlds, Dr. Thomas approaches a kind of biochemical Leibnizism. His willingness to see possibility where others see only doom is, like McLuhan's, tonic and welcome. Yet his announcement that the adversary system is obsolete in nature feels premature. Every day, my well-fed cat brings as tribute to my back porch the mauled body of a field mouse or baby rabbit; one wonders how complacently the little corpses submitted to their part in our triune symbiosis. One does not have to live very close to nature to cringe at all the carnage and waste it contains. That our cells harbor useful aliens, that ants perform miracles of coöperation, that we are all more sensitive and permeable than we know—this is sheer observed fact, and provocative as such. On the other hand, Dr. Thomas' shimmering vision of a "fusion around the earth" that will spring from "more crowding, more unrestrained and obsessive communication" seems less a prognosis than a hope defiant of much we *can* observe about our increasingly crowded, irritable, depleted, de-institutionalized, and cannibalistic world.

Alive and Free from Employment

MY DAYS, by R. K. Narayan. 186 pp. Viking, 1974.

The autobiography of a writer of fiction is generally superfluous, since he has already, in rearrangement and disguise, written out the material of his life many times. A novel like *The Man-Eater of Malgudi*, though its hero, Nataraj, and its author, Narayan, are not to be confused, tells us more about the India that R. K. Narayan inhabits, and more explicitly animates his opinion of what he sees, than his recent brief memoir, *My Days*. Not that Mr. Narayan's mischievous modesty does not lend an agreeable tone to this account of his rather uneventful life. Nor are his delightful gifts of caricature entirely inhibited by factuality. In *My Days*, as in his novels, one meets men so absorbed in self-interest that they become grotesque and emblematic: the young Narayan, seeking employment, grooms himself smartly to meet a prospective employer, who comes onto his veranda "bare-bodied and glisten[ing] with an oil-coating, as he prepared himself for a massage; he blinked several times to make me out, as oil had dripped over his eyes and blurred his vision. . . . All my best efforts at grooming were wasted, for I must have looked to him like a photograph taken with a shivering hand." The man barks a rebuff of the boy, and then paces "like a greasy bear in its cage." This sense of imprisonment within character, of each person energetically if ruinously fulfilling his dharma—his vocation, a Christian might say —reached its peak in English fiction with Dickens, and perhaps requires a religious basis. In the liberal view, character is significantly malleable, whereas the traditional character-creators fatalistically look into men for a fixed posture, an irrevocable passion. Narayan tells us that another uncle served as "an inescapable model for me—his approach to other human beings, his aggressive talk wherever he went, his dash and recklessness . . . his abandon to alcohol in every form all through the day. (I portrayed him as Kailas, in *The Bachelor of Arts*, and he provided all the substance whenever I had to portray a drunken character.)" Few writers since Dickens can match the effect of colorful teeming that Narayan's fictional city of Malgudi conveys; its population is as sharply chiselled as a temple frieze, and as endless, with always, one feels, more characters around the corner.

Yet the creator's life, as described in *My Days*, begins in loneliness. A little boy, living with his grandmother and uncle, has only pets for company, and the pets all die. He goes to school, and hates it. "On the first day I wept in fear. The sight of my classmates shook my nerves." He cannot shape clay, and his slate is always smudged. Throughout his schooling, though he toughens into an athletic child of the streets, he remains difficult, intractable, uninspired. "I was opposed to the system of being prescribed a set of books by an anonymous soulless body of textbook-prescribers, and of being stamped good or bad as a result of such studies. . . . I liked to be free to read what I pleased and not be examined at all." Taking his university entrance examinations, he flunks English —his best subject. And in the idle year this gives him, he begins to discover his own dharma—the vocation of a writer.

An aspect of this vocation, one feels after reading Mr. Narayan's fascinating middle chapters, is to have no other. His interviews for employment in business are humorous disasters; his enrollment as a teacher in the school where his father had been headmaster, a plausible route to respectability, is sabotaged by Narayan himself with the manic pugnacity of one of his own characters. His chapter describing the regimented foolishness of schoolteaching and his repeated escape from it approaches vehemence; the chapters following drop in emotional temperature, and trace a slow climb to success, contentment already achieved.

> That settled it. After the final and irrevocable stand I took [not to be a teacher], I felt lighter and happier. I did not encourage anyone to comment on my deed or involve myself in any discussion. I

sensed that I was respected for it. At least there was an appreciation of the fact that I knew my mind. I went through my day in a businesslike manner, with a serious face. Soon after my morning coffee and bath I took my umbrella and started out for a walk. I needed the umbrella to protect my head from the sun. Sometimes I carried a pen and pad and sat down under the shade of a tree at the foot of Chamundi Hill and wrote. Some days I took out a cycle and rode ten miles along the Karapur Forest Road, sat on a wayside culvert, and wrote or brooded over life and literature, watching some peasant ploughing his field, with a canal flowing glitteringly in the sun. My needs were nil, I did not have plans, there was a delight in being just alive and free from employment.

It speaks well, I think, of the Indian society of the early Thirties that it allowed, after due resistance, this prospectless young man's rebellion against gainful employment; a contemporaneous American family might have driven such a child to France, or into bohemia—altogether out, in any case, of the home environment that has continuously nurtured Narayan's creativity. Madras, where he was raised, and Mysore, where he came to live, spontaneously fostered a fictional city: "On a certain day in September, selected by my grandmother for its auspiciousness, I bought an exercise book and wrote the first line of a novel; as I sat in a room nibbling my pen and wondering what to write, Malgudi with its little railway station swam into view, all ready-made. . . ." This novel, under the title of *Swami and Friends*, was finally published in England.

The literary London of Shaw and Wells, Conan Doyle and Wodehouse, the *Strand* and the *Mercury* had been brought, via magazines subscribed to by his father's school, into the center of Narayan's boyhood, and colonial India abounded in English-language journalism, though of a threadbare sort. (This reviewer once had the opportunity to ask Mr. Narayan if present, nationalist India, which has discouraged the teaching of English, would produce any more masters of the language like himself; his answer was affable but not affirmative.) In his first year of free-lance writing, Narayan earned nine rupees and twelve annas (about a dollar and a quarter); the second year, a short story sold for eighteen rupees; in the third, a children's tale brought thirty. He labored as the Mysore correspondent for the Madras *Justice;*

Graham Greene became his champion in England, and found a fresh publisher for each of his earlier novels, which were critical successes merely. The author married, and his beloved wife's sudden death from typhoid, and his own slow recovery from sorrow via psychic communication with her, form the only significantly adverse incident in his gradual progress from journalistic piecework to international distinction, movie deals, and—crown of crowns—a travel grant from the Rockefeller Foundation. In prosperity and fame, his imagination seems to work as fluently as when Malgudi with its railway station swam into view: "During my travels in America, the idea [of *The Guide*] crystallized in my mind. I stopped in Berkeley for three months, took a hotel room, and wrote my novel."

Narayan's few revelations about his practice of writing heighten the value of this memoir. His desire to write in English was born of an early infatuation with English novels, beginning with Scott and Dickens ("I . . . loved his London and the queer personalities therein") and going on to the romanticism of Rider Haggard and Marie Corelli and Mrs. Henry Wood ("I looked for books that would leave me crushed at the end"). When he turned from mystical poems to his first novel, he let the incidents invent themselves: "Each day as I sat down to write, I had no notion of what would be coming. All that I could be certain of was the central character." The tale-teller, that is, is nearer the tale-hearer, in his openness to surprise, than college instructors of plot mechanics may know. "The pure delight of watching a novel grow can never be duplicated by any other experience." But Narayan's fertility would be tedious without his control and economy; he goes on to describe how his days of pure delight were followed by nights of "corrections, revisions, and tightening up of sentences" so that a "real, final version could emerge . . . between the original lines and then again in what developed in the jumble of rewritten lines." His one confessed doctrinal resolve, as he set out, was "to see if other subjects than love . . . could be written about. I wished to attack the tyranny of Love and see if Life could offer other values than the inevitable Man-Woman relationship to a writer." The predominantly masculine interplay of his novels develops, one feels, from street life, from the skein of casual and passing conver-

sation that he alludes to lovingly more than once. His days of journalistic news-gathering no doubt reinforced his habit of sociable
curiosity, but the impulse perhaps dates back to the time when, an
only child in his grandmother's house, he found it "exciting, one
day, to be asked to go with my uncle to the street of shops." His
days as a writer customarily began with a walk:

> All morning I wandered. At every turn I found a character fit to
> go into a story. While walking, ideas were conceived and developed,
> or sometimes lost through the interludes on the way. One could not
> traverse the main artery of Mysore, Sayyaji Rao Road, without
> stopping every few steps to talk to a friend. Mysore is not only
> reminiscent of an old Greek city in its physical features, but the
> habits of its citizens are also very Hellenic. Vital issues, including
> philosophical and political analyses, were examined and settled by
> people (at least in those days) on the promenades of Mysore.

Narayan is one of a vanishing breed—the writer as citizen. His
citizenship extends to calling up municipal officials about inade-
quate street lighting, to "dashing off virulent letters to newspapers
about corruption and inefficiency." Such protests do not feel, as
with so much American social consciousness, forced—a covert bid
for power and self-justification. "If I have to worry, it's about
things outside me, mostly not concerning me." What a wealth of
material becomes accessible to a writer who can so simply proclaim a sense of community! We have writers willing to be mayor
but not many excited to be citizens. We have writers as confessors,
shackled to their personal lives, and writers as researchers, hanging
their sheets of information from a bloodless story line. But of
writers immersed in their material, and enabled to draw tales from
a community of neighbors, Faulkner was our last great example.
An instinctive, respectful identification with the people of one's
locale comes hard now, in the menacing cities or disposable suburbs, yet without it a genuine belief in the significance of humanity, in humane significances, comes not at all.

APPENDIX

One Big Interview

The interviewers are as follows:

SAMUELS: Charles Thomas Samuels, who taped our conversations for several days in August 1968 on Martha's Vineyard, and permitted me to revise the transcript for publication in the *Paris Review* the following winter as "The Art of Fiction XLIII."

RHODE: Eric Rhode, whose radio dialogue with me for the BBC Third Programme was published in *The Listener* on June 19, 1969.

GADO: Frank Gado, professor of English at Union, Schenectady, New York; for simplicity's sake I have identified with his name not only his own questions but a few from his students, whose taped session with me in the winter of 1971 was printed as a special issue of *The Idol*, that spring.

BUCKINGHAM: Hugh Buckingham, a poet and critic then teaching at Harvard, who came and talked to me about *Bech: A Book;* the transcribed interview appeared in the Sunday *Herald-Traveler* (Boston) Books Guide supplement for January 19, 1971. His machine failed to record our first take; the second lacked much of the sparkle of the irrecoverable first.

SRAGOW: Michael Sragow, an undergraduate reporter for the Harvard *Crimson*, where this interview appeared on February 2, 1972, having been taped in Cambridge the preceding December.

OGLE: Jane Ogle, of *Harper's Bazaar*, whose written questions about *Buchanan Dying* were answered by me, in exceptionally lavish detail, on December 18, 1972, on the typewriter, and were never published.

HOWARD: Jane Howard, who spent three days in Ipswich with the Updikes in September 1966, and whose sprightly and courteous account, under the somewhat discouraging title "Can a Nice Novelist Finish First?" appeared in the November 4, 1966, issue of *Life*.

ONE BIG INTERVIEW

SAMUELS: *You've treated your early years fictionally and have discussed them in interviews, but you haven't said much about your time at Harvard. I wonder what effect you think it had.*

My time at Harvard, once I got by the compression bends of the freshman year, was idyllic enough, and as they say successful; but I felt toward those years, while they were happening, the resentment a caterpillar must feel while his somatic cells are shifting all around to make him a butterfly. I remember the glow of the Fogg Museum windows, and my wife-to-be pushing her singing bicycle through the snowy Yard, and the smell of wet old magazines that arose from the cellar of the Lampoon and hit your nostrils when you entered the narthex, and numerous grateful revelations in classrooms—all of it haunted, though, by knowledge of the many others who had passed this way and felt the venerable glory of it all more warmly than I, and written sufficiently about it. All that I seem able to preserve of the Harvard experience is in one short story, "The Christian Roommates." There was another, "Homage to Paul Klee," that has been printed in *The Liberal Context* but not in a book. Foxy Whitman, in *Couples*, remembers some of the things I do. Like me, she feels obscurely hoodwinked, pacified, by the process of becoming nice. I distrust, perhaps, hallowed, very O.K. places. Harvard has enough panegyrists without me.

SAMUELS: *After graduating from Harvard you served as a* New Yorker *staff writer for two years. What sort of work did you do?*

: 493 :

I was a "Talk of the Town" writer, which means that I both did the legwork and the finished product. An exalted position! It was playful work that opened the city to me. I was the man who went to boating or electronic exhibits in the Coliseum and tried to make poems of the objects and overheard conversations.

SAMUELS: *How do you feel about being associated with that magazine?*

Very happy. From the age of twelve when my aunt gave us a subscription for Christmas, *The New Yorker* has seemed to me the best of possible magazines, and their acceptance of a poem and a story by me in June of 1954 remains the ecstatic breakthrough of my literary life. Their editorial care, and their gratitude for a piece of work they like, are incomparable. And I love the format—the signature at the end, everybody the same size, and the battered title type, evocative of the Twenties and Persia and the future all at once.

SAMUELS: *You seem to shun literary society. Why?*

I don't, do I? Here I am, talking to you. In leaving New York in 1957, I did leave without regret the literary demimonde of agents and would-be's and with-it non-participants; this world seemed unnutritious and interfering. Hemingway described literary New York as a bottle full of tapeworms trying to feed on each other. When I write, I aim in my mind not toward New York but toward a vague spot a little to the east of Kansas. I think of the books on library shelves, without their jackets, years old, and a countryish teen-aged boy finding them, and having them speak to him. The reviews, the stacks in Brentano's, are just hurdles to get over, to place the books on that shelf. Anyway, in 1957, I was full of a Pennsylvania thing I wanted to say, and Ipswich gave me the space in which to say it, and in which to live modestly, raise my children, and have friends on the basis of what I did in person rather than what I did in print.

RHODE: *I don't see any affiliation in your work to the French idea of experiment, or indeed to the kinds of experiment that go on in the States. It seems to me that you are much closer to the English novel: there is a very strong sense of the domestic in your work— of the world as it is.* [A pause.]

I'm just trying to think of the word "domestic." I suppose this is true. It may be less a matter of conscious choice than of the fact that I seem to be a domestic creature. My first novel, *The Poorhouse Fair*, was, at least in my mind, something of a *nouvelle vague* book, particularly in the ending: that is, I tried to create a pattern of tension and then, instead of resolving it, dissolved it. It ended with a kind of brainless fair: people come to a fair and you hear their voices and it all dissolves. In my mind it was a somewhat experimental book, and my publishers then, Harper, seemed to think it was, because the ending puzzled them so much that I took it away from them and went to Knopf, where I've been happy ever since. In each of the books there has been, in my mind at least, a different experiment, an adventure: in *Rabbit, Run* the present tense may seem a mild adventure. It's more and more used now, but at that time it wasn't.

RHODE: *Coming back to* The Poorhouse Fair, *the most striking thing there, I think, is the fact that you have so clearly kept yourself out of the book, that you have created these very old men and women. This is an act entirely of the imagination, or so it feels. In fact Mary McCarthy said that she finds it a rather spooky accomplishment—like those boy actors who play old men—that you have created these characters so credibly. How far was it based on actuality?*

Not very. There was indeed a poorhouse a couple of blocks from where I grew up, but I very rarely went into it, and there was a fair that must have impressed me as a child. I had written prior to this, while living in New York City, a six-hundred-page novel, called *Home* and more or less about myself and my family up to the age of sixteen or so. It had been a good exercise to write it and I later used some of the material in short stories, but it really felt like a very heavy bundle of yellow paper, and I realized that this was not going to be my first novel—it had too many of the traits of a first novel. I did not publish it, but I thought it was time for me to write a novel. I was—what?—twenty-five, twenty-six. Getting to be an old man, as writers go in America. They were tearing the poorhouse down in Shillington, and I went over and looked at the shell. My grandfather, who is somewhat like John Hook in that book, was recently dead, and so the idea of some kind of memorial gesture, embodying what seems to have been on my part a very strong sense of national decay, crystallized in this novel. I wrote it in three months and then rewrote it in three months. It was my first real venture into what you might call novelistic space and it was very exciting. I haven't read it since the last set of proofs, but I'd like to think that there was some love, and hence some life and blood, in these old people.

SAMUELS: *But if I'm not mistaken, you once expressed a desire to write for the films and I think* Rabbit, Run, *in particular, is quite a cinematic novel. Do you have any such plans now?*

Rabbit, Run was subtitled originally "A Movie." The present tense was in part meant to be an equivalent of the cinematic mode of narration. The opening bit of the boys playing basketball was visualized to be taking place under the titles and credits. This doesn't mean, though, that I really wanted to write for the movies. It meant I wanted to make a movie. I could come closer by writing it in my own book than by attempting to get through to Hollywood.

GADO: *How do you react to the idea of a film being made of one of your books?*

I had the eerie experience the other day of sitting in an empty theatre looking at a movie made from *Rabbit, Run*. The picture fails in a number of ways, but one of the ways was in trying to be faithful to the book. They'd been faithful to it in a literal-minded way, but by not being so to the underlying spirit, they produced an enigmatic version of what is very clear in the book.

And yet certain things, like the furniture in the people's apartments, had been done with a richness that I had never even approached. I couldn't have imagined all these things they found to put in those sets: these identifying kinds of calendars, the style of furniture, all just for a few seconds on the screen. How incomparably more solid and entertaining the physical environment became, and yet, curiously, the inner story of the book became thin and even nonsensical.

Funnily enough, when they made a movie out of this book, they didn't see that it was written as a film in my mind. They didn't put the titles over the opening with the kids playing basketball. Instead they made a little box out of it and surrounded it with the titles. The big hands, the ball bouncing on the ground—it would have been a natural thing for an overlay. Which goes to show. . . .

GADO: *Haven't I read that someone is making a movie from* Couples?

I doubt if he'll ever do anything with it. An enterprising fellow called Wolper, who made a good thing of various television documentaries, got hold of *Couples*. He had quite ambitious plans for it. In writing to me, he kept using the word "important" all the time. "Most important book," and then, "Make an important movie."

At one point, I intended to say to him, "Would you like me to come out to Hollywood and write the movie for you?" I can see it as a film, and I know I could do it. I understand the book; I understand that it is a romantic book, a book written by a boy who went to a lot of movies. It has a happy ending. It's about a guy meeting a girl and the guy getting the girl. But I know that they don't see it that way. You know, they were talking about it as satire! Satire—this elegiac story. It's a loving portrait of life in America. No, I don't think I will write the screenplay, even if they were to ask me out there. They'd just break my heart.

One of the advantages of the kind of writing I do is that you are your own boss. You shoot your own stock, choose all the scenes, cast all the characters. You're your own everything really—and the product, then, is yours. If it plays, great—and if it doesn't, there are no alibis.

SAMUELS: *Why do you write so much about what most people take to be your own adolescence and family? Numerous critics, for example, have pointed to similarities between* Of the Farm, The Centaur, *and stories like* "My Grandmother's Thimble." *"Flight," for example, seems an earlier version of* Of the Farm.

I suppose there's no avoiding it—my adolescence seemed interesting to me. In a sense my mother and father, considerable actors both, were dramatizing my youth as I was having it, so that I arrived as an adult with some burden of material already half-formed. There is, true, a submerged thread connecting certain of the fictions, and I guess the submerged thread is the autobiography. That is, in *Of the Farm*, although the last name is not the name of the people in *The Centaur*, the geography is not appreciably changed, and the man in each case is called George. *Of the Farm* was in part a look at the world of *The Centaur* after the centaur had indeed died. By the way, I must repeat that I didn't mean Caldwell to die in *The Centaur;* he dies in the sense of living, of going back to work, of being a shelter for his son. But by the time Joey Robinson is thirty-five his father is dead. Also, there's the curious touch of the Running Horse River in *Rabbit, Run* which returns in the Alton of *The Centaur*. And somehow that Running Horse bridges both the books, connects them. But apart from the somewhat teasing little connections, there is in these three novels and the short stories of *Pigeon Feathers* a central image of flight or escape or loss, the way we flee from the past, a sense of guilt which I tried to express in the story, the triptych with the long title, "The Blessed Man of Boston, My Grandmother's Thimble, and Fanning Island," wherein the narrator becomes a Polynesian pushing off into a void. The sense that in time as well as space we leave people as if by volition and thereby incur guilt and thereby owe them, the dead, the forsaken, at least the homage of rendering them. The trauma or message that I acquired in Olinger had to do with suppressed pain, with the amount of sacrifice, I suppose, that middle-class life demands, and by that I guess I mean civilized life. The father, whatever his name, is sacrificing freedom of motion, and the mother is sacrificing in a way—oh, sexual richness, I guess; they're all stuck, and when I think back over these stories (and you know, they *are* dear to me and if I had to give anybody one book of me it would be the Vintage *Olinger Stories*) I think especially of that moment in "Flight" when the boy, chafing to escape, fresh from his encounter with Molly Bingaman and a bit more of a man but not enough quite, finds the mother lying there buried in her own peculiar messages from far away, the New Orleans jazz, and then the grandfather's voice comes tumbling down the stairs singing "There is a happy land, far, far away." This is the way it was, is. There has never been anything in my life quite as compressed, simultaneously as communicative to me of my own power and worth and of the irremediable grief in just living, in just going on.

RHODE: *I wonder, in the case of* The Centaur, *why you related the immediate experience of the schoolmaster to myth.*

It seemed to me that there was something mythical about the events. It's an experiment very unlike that of *Ulysses,* where the myth lurks beneath the surface of the natural events. In a way, the natural events in my book are meant to be a kind of mask for the myth. The genesis of it was reading in an old book of my wife's this footnote to the Hercules legend. It is part of the comedy of Chiron's plight that he is living in a town full of gods, and he's not quite a god himself, hence this failure of communication all the time. In fact, my father, who came from New Jersey, *did* have this feeling about Pennsylvania, that he wasn't quite clued in about what was going on. Secondly, there is a way in which to a child everything is myth-size: people are enormous and ominous and have great backlogs of mysterious information and of a life lived that you lack. I don't think that without the myth you'd have a book. It seemed to me to fit a kind of experience that I'd had: my father's immersion in the world of Christian morality, in trying to do the right thing and constantly sacrificing himself, always going off to church meetings, and yet complaining about it all the time. There was an ambivalence that seemed to make him very centaur-like. I think that initially art was tied in with theology and has to do with an ideal world: the artist is in some way a middleman between the ideal world and this, even though our sense of the ideal—and I'm speaking really of our gut sense, regardless of what we think we believe—is at present fairly dim. It may not always be so. And I find I can not imagine being a writer without wanting somehow to play, to make these patterns, to insert these secrets into my books, and to spin out this music that has its formal side.

RHODE: *Do you improvise or do you plot things out very carefully beforehand?*

I really begin with some kind of solid, coherent image, some notion of the shape of the book and even of its texture. *The Poorhouse Fair* was meant to have a sort of Y shape. *Rabbit, Run* was a kind of zig-zag. *The Centaur* was sort of a sandwich. I can't begin until I know the beginning and have some sense of what's going to happen between. There are some hinges, but really a novel, even quite a bulky one—you think of Henry James's eight hundred pages—has only a few hinges. I don't make an outline or anything. I figure that I can hold the events in my head and then hope that things will happen which will surprise me, that the characters will take on life and talk. I keep a kind of loose rein on the book. I would not begin a book, I would not advise people to begin a book, without knowing where it's going.

RHODE: *This image of the book that you have in mind is in fact a rather geometric image. It's not, say, a visual image, an image of events in the book which you're leading up to.*

It's sort of an abstract sensation, but of course you have to have a lot of other things to begin a book. You have to have at least some of the people and have to be in some ways stirred by the central people. The main motive force behind *The Centaur* would be some wish to make a record of my father. For fifteen years I'd watched a normal, good-doing Protestant man suffering in a kind of comic but real way. I think it left me rather angry. There is a lot of anger in my books, really. Their secret ingredient.

SAMUELS: *If I'm right in regarding* [The Centaur] *as formally uncharacteristic, I wonder why you prefer it to your other novels?*

Well, it seems in memory my gayest and truest book; I pick it up, and read a few pages, in which Caldwell is insisting on flattering a moth-eaten bum, who is really the god Dionysus, and I began laughing. . . . The mythology answers to my sensation that the people we meet are *guises*, do conceal something mythic, perhaps prototypes or longings in our minds. We love some women more than others by predetermination, it seems to me.

SAMUELS: *Why haven't you done more work in this mode?*

But I *have* worked elsewhere in a mythic mode. Apart from my short story about Tristan and Iseult, there is the St. Stephen story underlying *The Poorhouse Fair*, and Peter Rabbit under *Rabbit, Run*. Sometimes it is semi-conscious; for example, only lately do I see that Brewer, the city of brick painted the color of flowerpots, is the flowerpot that Mr. McGregor slips over Peter Rabbit. And in *Couples*, Piet is not only Hanema/anima/Life, he is Lot, the man with two virgin daughters, who flees Sodom, and leaves his wife behind.

SAMUELS: *Let's turn from myth to history. You have indicated a desire to write about President Buchanan. Yet, so far as I can see, American history is normally absent from your work.*

Not so; quite the contrary. In each of my novels, a precise year is given and a President reigns; *The Centaur* is distinctly a Truman book, and *Rabbit, Run* an Eisenhower one. *Couples* could have taken place only under Kennedy; the social currents it traces are as specific to those years as flowers in a meadow are to their moment of summer. Even *The Poorhouse Fair* has a President, President Lowenstein, and if one is not named in *Of the Farm* it may be because that book, in an odd way, also takes place in the future, though a future only a year or so in advance of the writing—a future now in the past. Hook, Caldwell, the Applesmiths, all talk about history, and the quotidian is littered with newspaper headlines, striking the consciousness of the characters obliquely and subliminally but firmly enough: Piet's first step at seducing Foxy is clearly in part motivated by the death of the Kennedy infant. And the atmosphere of fright permeating *The Centaur* is to an indicated extent early Cold-War nerves. My fiction about the daily doings of ordinary people has more history in it than history books, just as there is more breathing history in archaeology than in a list of declared wars and changes of government.

SAMUELS: *What about violence? Many critics complain that this is absent from your work—reprehensibly, because it is so present in the world. Why is there so little in your pages?*

There has been so little in my life. I have fought in no wars, and engaged in few fistfights. I do not think a man pacifist in his life should pretend to violence in fiction; I feel a tenderness toward my characters that forbids making violent use of them. In general, the North American continent in this century has been a place where catastrophe has held off, and likewise the lives I have witnessed have staved off real death. All my novels end with a false death, partial death. If, as may be, the holocausts at the rim of possibility do soon visit us, I am confident my capacities for expression can rise, if I live, to the occasion. In the meantime let's all of us with some access to a printing press not abuse our privilege with fashionable fantasies.

RHODE: *You are religious yourself?*

I'd say, yes, I try to be. I think I do tend to see the world as layered, and as there being something up there; certainly in *Couples* it would seem to be God who in a certain sense destroys that inoffensive Congregationalist church. My books are all meant to be moral debates with the reader, and if they seem pointless—I'm speaking hopefully—it's because the reader has not been engaged in the debate. The question is usually, "What is a good man?" or "What is goodness?" and in all the books an issue is examined. Take Harry Angstrom in *Rabbit, Run:* there is a case to be made for running away from your wife. In the late Fifties beatniks were preaching transcontinental travelling as the answer to man's disquiet. And I was just trying to say: "Yes, there is certainly that, but then there are all these other people who seem to get hurt." That qualification is meant to frame a moral dilemma.

RHODE: *You see the institution of marriage, the institution of the Church, as something that carries you back to the past, which I think again is very important in your books. For instance, in* The Poorhouse Fair *the one moment that I felt that you emerged as a person was close to the end when you say something about how we go backwards, how we become our father's opinions, and eventually our grandfather's.*

True enough, there is this interest in the past, but in a way the past is all we have. The present is very thin, it's less than a second wide, and the future doesn't exist. I think that *Of the Farm*, say, is about moral readjustment, and the readjustment is of course in terms of harsh deeds done in the past; the mother and boy need, in a way, to excuse each other, or somehow to give a blessing. It's a little hard for me to see my work from the outside, as it were, but I do notice a recurrence of the concept of a blessing, of approval, or forgiveness. The basic problem may be simply one of encouragement, because of the failure of nerve, the lassitude and despair, the sense that we've gone to the end of the corridor and found it blank. So the characters beneath the surface are exhorting each other to action. In *Couples* Piet is quite a modern man in that he really can't act for himself because he's overwhelmed by the moral implications of any act—leaving his wife, staying with her. While the women in that book are less sensitive perhaps to this oppressive quality, of cosmic blackness, and it is the women who do almost all of the acting. I don't want to say that being passive, being inactive, being paralyzed, is wrong in an era when so much action is crass and murderous. I do feel that in the generations that I've had a glimpse of—I can see my grandfather at one end, and I can see my boys coming up—there has been a perceptible loss of the sense of righteousness. But many evils are done in the name of righteousness, so perhaps one doesn't want it back. Nevertheless, I suspect that the vitality of women now, the way many of us lean on them, is not an eternal phenomenon but a historical one, and fairly recent.

SAMUELS: *In an interview you gave* Life *you expressed some regret at the "yes, but" attitude critics have taken toward it.* Did the common complaint that you had ducked large subjects lead to the writing of* Couples?

No, I meant my *work* says "yes, but." Yes, in *Rabbit, Run*, to our urgent inner whispers, but—the social fabric collapses disastrously. Yes, in *The Centaur*, to self-sacrifice and duty, but—what of a man's private agony and dwindling? No, in *The Poorhouse Fair*, to social homogenization and loss of faith, but—listen to the voices, the joy of persistent existence. No, in *Couples*, to a religious community founded on physical and psychical interpenetration, but—what else shall we do, as God destroys our churches? I cannot greatly care what critics say of my work; if it is good, it will come to the surface in a generation or two and float, and if not, it will sink, having in the meantime provided me with a living, the opportunities of leisure, and a craftsman's intimate satisfactions. I wrote *Couples* because the rhythm of my life and my *oeuvre* demanded it, not to placate hallucinatory critical voices.

---

* What I had said to Jane Howard, as quoted, was: "There's a 'yes-but' quality about my writing that evades entirely pleasing anybody. It seems to me that critics get increasingly querulous and impatient for madder music and stronger wine, when what we need is a greater respect for reality, its secrecy, its music. Too many people are studying maps and not enough are visiting places."

SAMUELS: *What do you mean by attributing the setting up of religious communities in* Couples *to God's destruction of our churches?*

I guess the noun "God" appears in two totally different senses, the God in the first instance being the one worshipped within this nice white church, the more or less watered-down Puritan God; and then God in the second sense means ultimate power. I've never really understood theologies which would absolve God of earthquakes and typhoons, of children starving. A god who is not God the Creator is not very real to me, so that, yes, it certainly *is* God who throws the lightning bolt and this God is above the nice god, above the god we can worship and empathize with. I guess I'm saying there's a fierce God above the kind God and he's the one Piet believes in. At any rate, when the church is burned, Piet is relieved of morality, and can choose Foxy—or can accept the choice made for him by Foxy and Angela operating in unison— can move out of the paralysis of guilt into what after all is a kind of freedom. He divorces the supernatural to marry the natural. I wanted the loss of Angela to be felt as a real loss—Angela is nicer than Foxy—nevertheless it is Foxy that he most deeply wants, it is Foxy who in some obscure way was turned on the lathe for him. So that the book does have a happy ending. There's also a way, though, I should say (speaking of "yes, but") in which, with the destruction of the church, with the removal of his guilt, he becomes insignificant. He becomes merely a name in the last paragraph: he becomes a satisfied person and in a sense dies. In other words, a person who has what he wants, a satisfied person, a content person, ceases to be a person. Unfallen Adam is an ape. Yes, I guess I do feel that. I feel that to be a person is to be in a situation of tension, is to be in a dialectical situation. A truly adjusted person is not a person at all—just an animal with clothes on. So that it's a happy ending, with this "but" at the end.

SAMUELS: *I was impressed by the contrast between the presentation of oral-genital contacts in* Couples *and its single appearance in* Rabbit, Run.

Well, *Couples*, in part, is about the change in sexual deportment that has occurred since the publication of *Rabbit, Run*, which came out late in '59; shortly thereafter we had *Lady Chatterley* and the first Henry Miller books, and now you can't walk into a grocery store without seeing pornography on the rack. Remember Piet lying in Freddy's bed admiring Freddy's collection of Grove Press books? In *Rabbit, Run* what is demanded, in *Couples* is freely given. What else? It's a way of eating, eating the apple, of knowing. It's nostalgic for them, for Piet of Annabelle Vojt and for Foxy of the Jew. In de Rougement's book on Tristan and Iseult he speaks of the sterility of the lovers, and Piet and Foxy are sterile vis-à-vis each other. Lastly, I was struck, talking to a biochemist friend of mine, how he emphasized not only the chemical composition of enzymes but their structure; it matters, among my humans, not only what they're made of, but exactly how they attach to each other. So much for oral-genital contacts.

RHODE: *We're talking about* Couples *as a book about sex. It's something quite different, isn't it? What astonishes me is that these descriptions are written with extraordinary delicacy and tact. You must have found them very hard to write.*

They were no harder than landscapes and a little more interesting. It's wonderful the way people in bed talk, the sense of voices and the sense of warmth, so that as a writer you become kind of warm also. The book is, of course, not about sex as such: It's about sex as the emergent religion, as the only thing left.

BUCKINGHAM: *I believe that one of the chapters of* Bech *originally appeared as a short story.*

Several did.

BUCKINGHAM: *Does that mean the book was conceived piecemeal?*

It was indeed conceived piecemeal. When I returned from the Soviet Union and Eastern Europe in '64 I had a number of impressions that only a writer could have collected. So, in trying to utilize some of them I invented Henry Bech, just to serve as a vehicle for my own impressions in a story entitled "The Bulgarian Poetess."

Distrusting writers as heroes, I made Bech as unlike myself as I could. Instead of being married with four children, he's a bachelor; instead of being a Gentile, he's a Jew—of course, a Jewish writer is almost as inevitable as an Italian gangster. I made him somewhat older than myself and gave him, sketchily, a career; the book

Travel Light was his initial success—probably I had most in mind Jack Kerouac's *On the Road.*

O.K., so there Henry Bech sat in this story, which *The New Yorker* took and published; and to my surprise the story had a degree of success. Friends said they liked it, and it got the first O. Henry Award of that year. So, never wanting to let a good thing go unflogged, I wrote another story, about Rumania this time, and made a third attempt, a story about Russia. I wrote a long journal, Henry Bech's Russian Journal, which didn't work out, though I salvaged parts of it for an appendix in the book. The little story "Rich in Russia" was done later—the bigger the country, the smaller the story, somehow.

Then out of quite a different set of memories or impressions I wrote "Bech Takes Pot Luck," which is an American story and takes place on an island a touch like Martha's Vineyard. (Is this boring you? How to build a coffin, nail by nail.) At this point I began to think that they might be a book. I wrote the London story and it was quite important that it work out—by working out I mean that *The New Yorker* take it. It did. And then I wrote two more, one to wind the book up and the other to sort of make a bridge—that is, "Bech Panics" takes us from the Bech of the Vineyard story to the somewhat older and rather hallucinating writer of London. And that's how you cook up a book.

BUCKINGHAM: *When did you do the fake bibliographies and things? They're great fun.*

They were kind of fun. Of course, the preface is very short, even though it took Bech eight days to write it.

BUCKINGHAM: *And you?*

It took me a day.

GADO: *At the end of* Bech, *you supplied the reader with bibliographical appendices. I tried to make some sense of them but couldn't. Is there a key? Or was it just the vestigial gagster in you wanting to play games with the magazines, critics, and writers?*

It was meant two ways: first, as a light-hearted attempt to give Bech a concrete bibliographical existence as a writer; second, as a means of reëstablishing a distance between Bech and myself. He's nine years older than I, and partly for that reason, his career is quite different from mine. In this respect, the bibliography was intended to be a specimen history of an American literary career of the period. He began as a kind of war correspondent, a soldier who wrote stories with gung-ho titles for magazines like *Liberty* and *Collier's*. He was intellectualized in New York in the post-war period. And now he has fallen into silence. There are careers like this. Salinger? Irwin Shaw?

To be candid, the bibliography was also a matter of working off various grudges, a way of purging my system. I've never been warmly treated by the *Commentary* crowd—insofar as it is a crowd—and so I made Bech its darling.

And then, I don't know, it just seemed to help make it a book.

BUCKINGHAM: *You say* Bech *was written piecemeal, not on firmly drawn lines like* Couples?

Mm hmm.

BUCKINGHAM: *And yet at the end I find the final chapter just as serious, as poetic, just as heavyweight.*

I'm always at the same weight; I mean, I may be groggier some days than others, but I tend to be equally serious about everything. Of course, *Bech* is a serious book. I never thought of it as satirical, really; it was never really a concern of mine to poke fun at the Jewish writer, or the New York-Jewish literary establishment in this country. I hope I always gave Bech my full sympathy, my full empathy.

BUCKINGHAM: *What drove him toward the literary life, that gallery of immortals?*

In the London story he has this hope that one more woman, one more leap up the falls, will bring him safe into that high, calm pool of immortality where Proust and Hawthorne and Catullus float, glassy-eyed and belly-up. (I love that sentence.) He wants to be lifted out of flux, the way that literary immortals are. Also, Bech is one of the last "moderns." He believes in Eliot and Valéry and Joyce and Rilke and those others who were convinced of the sacred importance of the written word. They believed themselves custodians of the language and therefore of the values of their society.

I think we're all attracted toward excellence of this sort, wishing to associate this very mixed deteriorating bag of our physical and egotistical selves with something fine, and Bech was drawn to

literature out of that, and for a while found it, perhaps, but his
success has thrown him into a very baffling world of the wrong
kind of praise, or being used by younger people as in the London
story, or being asked to join dead people, as in the last story, or of
women constantly trying to lure him out of his monkhood. . . .
It's all rather sad. Think of Mailer. He began as a war novelist, a
novelist in the Steinbeck sense; and so he arrives and finds the
party is breaking up. The novel couldn't be for his generation
what it was for the generation of Hemingway and Fitzgerald.
We're not going to get anybody like Hemingway for a while,
who so intensely and instinctively cared about language. When
he died there was nobody around who cared so much, cared so
much he killed himself because he couldn't do it as finely as he
thought it should be done. Instead you get showmen and professors. Bech becomes a showman against his will. A display piece.
A toy.

SRAGOW: [Rabbit Redux] *has been hailed for its portrait of "Middle
America." Did the necessity to get that close to a man who is
inarticulate and guided by mass culture to as great a degree as
Rabbit require a . . . leap?*

Intellectually, I'm not essentially advanced over Harry Angstrom. I went to Harvard, it's true, and wasn't much good at
basketball; other than that we're rather similar. I quite understand
both his anger and passivity, and feeling of the whole Vietnam
involvement as a puzzle, that something strange has gone wrong;
but it's no great leap of the imagination to do *that*.

There may be something also in the novelist's trade which shades
you towards conservatism. Things exist because they evolved to
that condition; they cannot be lightly or easily altered. It is my
general sense of human institutions that they are outcroppings of
human nature, that human nature is slow to change, that in general
when you destroy one set of institutions you get something worse.

SRAGOW: *You've written that "an easy humanism" pervades the
land. Given the fact that you deal on a very personal basis with
human stress, how do your distinguish your . . .*

Difficult humanism? I feel that, as a writer, I put into practice a set of democratic assumptions. Just as in a democracy anybody can be president, so anyone can be a character in a novel, at least in one by me. Every human being who is more than a moron is the locus of certain violent tensions that come with having a brain. In fact there is an easy humanism that insists that man is an animal which feeds and sleeps and defecates and makes love and isn't that nice and natural and let's all have more of that. But this is omitting intrinsic stresses in the human condition—you foresee things, for example, you foresee your own death. You have really been locked out of the animal paradise of unthinking natural reflex.

You are born into one political contract or another, whose terms, though they sit very lightly at first, eventually, in the form of the draft, or taxes, begin to make very heavy demands on you. The general social contract—living with other people, driving cars on highways—all this is difficult, it's painful. It's a kind of agony really—the agony vents itself in ulcers internally, rage externally. . . . In short, all of our institutions—of marriage, the family, your driver's license—everything is kind of precarious, and maintained at a cost of tension.

SRAGOW: *Easy humanism, then, lies in the belief that these individual problems can be ignored for the sake of larger panaceas.*

Or taking humanity as some kind of moral index, saying that to be human is to be good and our problems all arise from not being human enough. I think I take a rather darker view. We must of necessity lose our humanity all the time.

When asked about what my philosophy was I tried to write it down in *Midpoint* in handy couplets and discovered that of all my books it is the least read, and it was hardly reviewed at all. I concluded that nobody really cared what my philosophy was. That's all right. The novelist is of interest only for what he does through empathy and image-producing, image-arranging; the more consciously a theorist he is the more apt he is to become impotent or cranky or both. Like Harry, I try to remain open. Revolt, rebellion, violence, disgust are themselves there for a reason, they too are organically evolved out of a distinct reality, and must be considered respectfully. I try to love both the redneck and the flower child, the anarchist bomb-thrower. People are basically very anarchistic. Harry's search for infinite freedom—that's anarchy too. He loves destruction. Who doesn't?

SRAGOW: *At the end of* Rabbit Redux, *Rabbit talks of going back to a farm. Are you thinking of bringing him back again?*

I left the book open, I even dangled a few threads that could be picked up. Janice talks about how he never should have had that awful indoor job. I already have a title—*Rural Rabbit*. That's going to be their next stage. I couldn't write that book now. Maybe in 1979 enough will have happened to both him and me that I can, but if it doesn't, that's all right. Maybe I should stop while I'm ahead—at least as far as *The Times Book Review* goes.

These two complement each other well enough. Anybody who really cared could get some interesting formal things out of the two books together. Certainly Janice bringing Stavros back to life is some kind of counterweight to the baby's death in the first book. She too had to make a passage—go through something to return. All that's there, I'm not sure that a third book could do it again. It would have to be a different kind of a book—a short book, a pastoral book, an eclogue.

[*The interview with Sragow transpired before I broke my leg in December of 1971, as the handsome full-length photograph in the* Harvard *Crimson attests. After my release from the hospital, Lee Wohlfert of* Women's Wear Daily *gouged from me the following drug-dazed utterances:*] "Like Harry, I'm hog fat, reactionary, passive. I'm a plugger. Even the way Rabbit sits in front of his Linotype machine day after day reminded me of myself, of the way I sit in front of the typewriter. . . . I decided to write it a while back when I couldn't get started on another book I was trying to write and the Sixties pressed heavily upon me. And I got sick of people talking about Rabbit, sick of them asking me what happened to him. So I decided to revisit my old friend. . . . [I appeared surprised that among the critics] no one's given serious consideration to the idea that Skeeter, the angry black, might *be* Jesus. He *says* he is. I think probably he might be. And if that's so, then people *ought* to be very nice to him."

*

OGLE: *You describe* Buchanan Dying *as a final homage to Pennsylvania, whose "mild, misty doughy middleness, between dangerous norths and souths," remains "your first taste of life, the authentic taste." Do you think of Buchanan as a typical Pennsylvanian?*

Well, yes, indeed I do, insofar as this large area, transected by the Alleghenies and ranging from Philadelphia to Pittsburgh, would admit of having a state character. In his fondness for good living and his distrust of radical solutions, in a certain comfortable fudging talkativeness, he seems familiar to me. Buchanan must have also seemed to his contemporaries representative, for he never lost a state election, and his Presidential victory hinged on his carrying the Keystone State. He could have been governor, also, but that his advisers, John Slidell foremost, felt that the governorship would have forced upon him a stand vis-à-vis slavery that would have marred the perfect ambiguity that did, in the end, win him the Presidency. My own muddled, middly sense of the metaphysical essence of Pennsylvania-ness has been often expressed in my fiction, and indeed is evoked one more time in my Afterword. I have often wanted to write about Wallace Stevens and John O'Hara, as Pennsylvania artists; their work, in some ways so different, shares a splendid leafiness, no? You may say that Thaddeus Stevens, the super-radical Representative, was a fellow-Lancastrian and nodding acquaintance of Buchanan's; my answer would be that Stevens came from Vermont, and was a New Englander at core. The only other President with claim to be a Pennsylvanian was, of course, Dwight Eisenhower, another lover of the middle way and the opportune evasion. Pennsylvanians tend to take the fascinating form of clouds. If the Middle Atlantic states have a psycho-history, it is that Puritanism skipped over them on its way west.

OGLE: *In recent years, there has been a lot of controversy about Presidential powers and how they are used. Are there any similarities or dissimilarities between Buchanan's Presidency and Nixon's that strike you?*

Both men were on surest ground in foreign affairs, both were surrounded by subordinates who committed dubious acts, neither projected much moral authority or personal charisma. The Covode

Investigation of 1860 bears some resemblance to the Watergate inquiry of today; and the shadow of impeachment hung over Buchanan also, as the letters of the youthful Henry Adams jubilantly confirm—though why Adams would have wanted John C. Breckinridge in the Presidential chair instead, I can't imagine. But for me the parallels run out there: Nixon is decried for riding roughshod (and blindly) over the Constitution; the main criticism of Buchanan was that he took the Constitution too seriously, and too circumspectly argued the exact limits of his powers and of such legalities as slaveholders' property rights and the federal government's right of coercion. He was too much the lawyer and conciliator, Nixon is too much the loner. Buchanan's White House was the most socially brilliant and active it had been since the days of Madison; contrast that with today's Kremlin on Pennsylvania Avenue. Most crucially, Buchanan's crisis, whatever he made of it, was a mighty and genuine one, it was the divergence between North and South that had been growing upon the nation since 1820; whereas this Watergate mess is thoroughly petty, comic opera with some sinister bass notes. It is a crisis strikingly devoid of tragic inevitability. A more worthy analogy to Buchanan's travail would be Johnson's Vietnam. But the correct spirit of historical inquiry and dramatization, surely, is one that seeks out, not facile analogies or contrasts, but what was unique to this moment, this predicament, this set of decisions, this man. My play is not about the Presidency but about a man who was President for four of his seventy-seven years. In attempting to understand him sympathetically, to a degree I attempted sympathetic understanding of every President, including the present beleaguered specimen.

OGLE: *Buchanan seems to have gotten a raw deal from at least some historians. Would you say that Lincoln has been correspondingly overrated?*

Not overrated, but deified. The accident of his assassination, and the happy chance of his literary genius, ennobles him beyond appraisal, at least in the popular impression. We are taught that he freed the slaves, without being reminded that the Emancipation Proclamation was a military maneuver, or that the slaveholding states on the Union side were exempted. And we are invited to invest the cause of the "Union" with the mysticism of war propaganda, without inspecting the legal case for secession, or weighing how much cosmic virtue resides in the determination to keep a big country big. In the crucial four months between Lincoln's election and his inauguration, while Buchanan desperately sought to prevent war, Lincoln himself said nothing, either in the way of reassurance to the border states or by way of warning to the seceding states. Demagoguery and fear went their way unchallenged, and while the Lincoln administration, once in office, heaped blame upon its predecessor, it initially pursued identical policies. But my purpose, insofar as it is historical, is not to bury the immortal Lincoln, but to revive the forgotten Buchanan.

OGLE: *Do you think the Civil War might have been avoided if Buchanan had followed a different course in 1860 and early in 1861?*

Allan Nevins, by no means pro-Buchanan, in his history of this period says that a show of force or punitive threat against South Carolina would have precipitated civil war, rather than cow the Palmetto State as Jackson did in 1833. Earlier in 1860, Buchanan possibly might have exerted his leverage as titular head of the Democratic Party to urge a single nominee (Douglas?) upon the Charlestown Convention. But, even if this unlikely work of compromise were achieved, an analysis of the voting in that fall's election suggests that Lincoln would have won even had his opposition been one united party instead of three splinters. And would another Democratic President have succeeded, more than Pierce and Buchanan, in reconciling irreconcilables, in solving the unsolvable question of fugitive slaves and making sense of the nonsensical question of the territories? It's hard to imagine how. Would the North, growing in power and population, have indefinitely accepted a Washington controlled by Southerners and doughfaces? My point (which I make in the play, and giving it a human context I cannot give here in these answers) is that time was on the side of the North, and that by buying time Buchanan did all that the Union could ask.

OGLE: *Some passages in the play suggest that Buchanan, despite charges of rakery, might be called* The Virgin President. *Was he?*

In my play I say he was. I would bow to contrary evidence if there were any. The availability of sex in the 19th century is a mysterious variable. Since no rumors of his rakery ever developed substance, his enemies developed the opposite line, that of impotence, of an androgynous fussiness. He was surely not a rake; he was a gallant, very fond of female company in the ballroom and parlor.

OGLE: *Buchanan is a great quoter of La Rochefoucauld's maxims in the original French. Is this historically correct or are you just very fond of La Rochefoucauld yourself?*

Buchanan learned French for his mission to the court of St. Petersburg as American ambassador (1832–1833), and he kept up a reading acquaintance with French the rest of his life. In a letter to Harriet from London, on January 25th, 1856, as strong indications of his nomination as President were coming to him, he wrote, ". . . I feel quite indifferent. There is profound wisdom in a remark of Rochefoucauld with which I met the other day:—'*Les choses que nous desirons n'arrivent pas, ou, si elles arrivent, ce n'est, ni dans le temps, ni de la manière que nous auraient fait le plus de plaisir.*' "

Strange to say, in the edition of *Maximes* out of which I supplied other aphorisms to put into the mouth of Buchanan's stage persona, I was not able to locate this particular saying. If any reader of *Harper's Bazaar* can help me here, I would be grateful.

[Stranger to say, the readers of *Harper's Bazaar* never saw any of these painstakingly composed answers. However, Ms. Ogle herself supplied the correct source of the quotation—La Bruyère (1645–1696). I feel adequately recompensed.]

SAMUELS: *I wonder why, with few exceptions, you only write light verse.*

I began with light verse, a kind of cartooning in print, and except for one stretch of a few years, in which I wrote most of the serious poems in *Telephone Poles*, I feel uncertain away from rhyme, to which something comic adheres. Bergson's mechanical encrusted upon the organic. But the light verse poems putting into rhyme and jaunty metrics some scientific discovery have a serious point—the universe science discloses to us is farcically unrelated to what our primitive senses report—and I have, when such poems go well, a pleasure and satisfaction not lower than in any other form of literary activity. Indeed my old poems give me more re-reading pleasure than anything I have written. Especially the little ones—"Nutcracker," with the word "nut" in boldface, seems to me as good as George Herbert's angel-wings.

GADO: *Who are your contemporaries in terms of fiction?*

It's in Salinger that I first heard, as a college student in the early Fifties, the tone that spoke to my condition. I had a writing teacher, Kenneth Kempton, who read aloud to us some of Salinger's stories as they appeared in *The New Yorker*. They seemed to me to say something about the energies of people and the ways they encounter each other that I did not find in the short stories of Hemingway or John O'Hara or Dorothy Parker or any of that "wised-up" style of short-story writing. Salinger's stories were not wised up. They were very open to tender invasions. Also they possessed a refreshing formlessness which, of course, he came to push to an extreme, as real artists tend to do. However, in those early short stories there's a marvellous tension between rather random, "soft" little events which pulls the whole story together into the final image of, say, a dead Easter chick in a wastebasket.

GADO: *Are there others you regard as contemporaries?*

Some, about my age, are not very well known: Harold Brodkey, a writer who is a little more than a year older than I, is a contemporary. His writing seems to go deeper into certain kinds of emotional interplay than the things written by older writers. Were I to try to make all this into an essay, I'm sure that I could find more ways in which writers now in their thirties and forties resemble each other.

Kerouac I would also claim as a contemporary. Clearly, he is not a man of Salinger's intelligence, but there is something benign, sentimentally benign, in his work. He attempted to grab it all; somehow, to grab it all. I like him.

GADO: *That's strange. Kerouac and Updike! I couldn't propose two writers who I thought were more unalike in their approach to literary art. Kerouac, with his binges at the typewriter, dumping the words down onto a continuous roll of teletype paper and leaving the cutting of it into pages to a more sombre moment. . . . That's not the picture I had of you at work at all.*

No, I don't agree. I don't use teletype paper, but there isn't an awful lot of revision when I'm writing—things either grind to a halt or they keep on moving. I think he was right. Kerouac was right in emphasizing a certain flow, a certain ease. Wasn't he saying, after all, what the surrealists said? That if you do it very fast without thinking, something will get in that wouldn't ordinarily. I think one tends to spoil not only the thing at hand, but the whole art form, by taking too much thought, by trying to assert too much control.

SAMUELS: *What is it that you think gets into sloppy writing that eludes more careful prose?*

It comes down to, What is language? Up to now, until this age of mass literacy, language has been something spoken. In utterance there's a minimum of slowness. In trying to treat words as chisel strokes you run the risk of losing the quality of utterance, the rhythm of utterance, the happiness. A phrase out of Mark Twain— he describes a raft hitting a bridge and says that it "went all to smash and scatteration like a box of matches struck by lightning." The beauty of "scatteration" could only have occurred to a talkative man, a man who had been brought up among people who were talking and who loved to talk himself. I'm aware myself of a certain dryness of this reservoir, this backlog of spoken talk. A Rumanian once said to me that Americans are always telling stories. I'm not sure this is as true as it once was. Where we once used to spin yarns, now we sit in front of the TV and receive pictures. I'm not sure the younger generation even knows how to gossip. But, as for a writer, if he has something to tell, he should perhaps type it almost as fast as he could talk it. We must look to the organic world, not the inorganic world, for models; and just as the organic world has periods of repose and periods of great speed and exercise, so I think the writer's process should be organically varied. But there's a kind of tautness that you should feel within yourself no matter how slow or fast you're spinning out the reel.

SAMUELS: *I'd like to ask a bit about your work habits if I may. What sort of schedule do you follow?*

I write every weekday morning. I try to vary what I am doing, and my verse, or poetry, is a help here. Embarked on a long project, I try to stay with it even on dull days. For every novel, however, that I have published, there has been one unfinished or scrapped. Some short stories—I think offhand of "Lifeguard," "The Taste of Metal," "My Grandmother's Thimble"—are fragments salvaged and reshaped. Most came right the first time—rode on their own melting, as Frost said of his poems. If there is no melting, if the story keeps sticking, better stop and look around. In the execution there has to be a "happiness" that can't be willed or foreordained. It has to sing, click, something. I try instantly to set in motion a certain forward tilt of suspense or curiosity, and at the end of the story or novel to rectify the tilt, to complete the motion.

SAMUELS: *As a technician, how unconventional would you say you were?*

As unconventional as I need to be. An absolute freedom exists on the blank page, so let's use it. I have from the start been wary of the fake, the automatic. I tried not to subdue my sense of life as many-layered and ambiguous, while keeping in mind some sense of transaction, of a bargain struck, between me and the ideal reader. Domestic fierceness within the middle class, sex and death as riddles for the thinking animal, social existence as sacrifice, unexpected pleasures and rewards, corruption as a kind of evolution—these are some of the themes. My work is meditation, not pontification.

SAMUELS: *Are you bothered by having to write for a living?*

No, I always wanted to draw or write for a living. Teaching, the customary alternative, seemed truly depleting and confusing. I have been able to support myself by and large with the more respectable forms—poetry, short stories, novels—but what journalism I have done has been useful. I would write ads for deodorants or labels for catsup bottles if I had to. The miracle of turning inklings into thoughts and thoughts into words and words into metal and print and ink never palls for me; the technical aspects of bookmaking, from type font to binding glue, all interest me. The distinction between a thing well done and a thing done ill obtains everywhere—in all circles of Paradise and Inferno.

SAMUELS: *In "The Sea's Green Sameness" you deny that characterization and psychology are primary goals of fiction. What do you think is more important?*

I wrote "The Sea's Green Sameness" years ago and meant, I believe, that narratives should not be *primarily* packages for psychological insights, though they can contain them, like raisins in buns. But the substance is the dough, which feeds the storytelling appetite, the appetite for motion, for suspense, for resolution. The author's deepest pride, as I have experienced it, is not in his incidental wisdom but in his ability to keep an organized mass of images moving forward, to feel life engendering itself under his hands. But no doubt fiction is also a mode of spying; we read it as we look in windows or listen to gossip, to learn what other people *do.* Insights of all kinds are welcome; but no wisdom will substitute for an instinct for action and pattern, and a perhaps savage wish to hold, through your voice, another soul in thrall.

SAYINGS

(taken mostly from Jane Howard's article in Life)

There is a great deal to be said about almost anything. Everything can be as interesting as every other thing. An old milk carton is worth a rose; a trolley car has as much right to be there, in terms of aesthetics, as a tree.

*

Everything is infinitely fine and any opinion is coarser than reality.

*

I've never much enjoyed going to plays. The unreality of painted people standing on a platform saying things they've said to each other for months is more than I can overlook.

*

The idea of a hero is aristocratic. You cared about Oedipus and Hamlet because they were noble and you were a groundling. Now either nobody is a hero or everyone is. I vote for everyone.

*

[My characters] go back to work; that's the real way that people die.

*

We do survive every moment, after all, except the last one.

*

A man has to build his life outward from a job he can do. Once he finds one he's got eight hours of the day licked, and if he sleeps eight more, he's two-thirds golden.

*

My own sense of childhood doesn't come from being a father, it comes from having been a child. We're all so curiously alone. But it's important to keep making signals through the glass.

*

I've touched a kind of bottom, when I've felt that existence itself was an affront to be forgiven.

*

You can't be satirical at the expense of fictional characters, because they're your creatures. You must only love them.

*

My life is, in a sense, trash; my life is only that of which the residue is my writing.

*

HOWARD: *If you could be an animal, which would you be?*
A turtle. Turtles live quite long and can retreat immediately, and live very close to the grass, the smell of which I've always liked. I also like the sound of the rain on the roof, which a turtle must get quite a lot of.

Index

A Note About the Author

JOHN UPDIKE was born in 1932 in Shillington, Pennslyvania, which he has described as "a square mile of middleclass homes physically distinguished by a bend in the central avenue that compels some side streets to deviate from the grid pattern." His father was a high-school mathematics teacher and his mother a writer. He graduated *summa cum laude* from Harvard in 1954, and spent a year in England on the Knox Fellowship, at the Ruskin School of Drawing and Fine Art in Oxford. From 1955 to 1957 he was a member of the staff of *The New Yorker*, to which he has contributed short stories, poems, humor, and, since 1960, book reviews. His own books include seven novels, five short-story collections, three volumes of poetry, a play, and a previous miscellany, *Assorted Prose*. In 1964 his novel *The Centaur* won the National Book Award for Fiction, and that same year he was elected to the National Institute of Arts and Letters. His short stories have won eight O. Henry Awards, including a first prize in 1966; in 1971 he received the Signet Society Medal for Achievement in the Arts. Updike has lectured in the Soviet Union, Africa, Australia, Korea, and Venezuela. The father of two sons and two daughters, he has lived since 1957 in Massachusetts.

A Note on the Type

The text of this book was set on the Linotype in Janson, a recutting made directly from type cast from matrices long thought to have been made by the Dutchman Anton Janson, who was a practicing type founder in Leipzig during the years 1668–1687. However, it has been conclusively demonstrated that these types are actually the work of Nicholas Kis (1650–1702), a Hungarian, who most probably learned his trade from the master Dutch type founder Dirk Voskens. The type is an excellent example of the influential and sturdy Dutch types that prevailed in England up to the time William Caslon developed his own incomparable designs from them.